EDITORS R. TOLTEKA CUAUHTIN • MIGUEL ZAVALA

RETHINKING ETHNIC STUDIES

A RETHINKING SCHOOLS PUBLICATION

Rethinking Ethnic Studies
Edited by R. Tolteka Cuauhtin, Miguel Zavala, Christine Sleeter, and Wayne Au

A Rethinking Schools Publication

Rethinking Schools, Ltd., is a nonprofit publisher and advocacy organization dedicated to sustaining and strengthening public education through social justice teaching and education activism. Our magazine, books, and other resources promote equity and racial justice in the classroom.

To request additional copies of this book or a catalog of other publications, or to subscribe to *Rethinking Schools* magazine, contact:
Rethinking Schools
6737 W. Washington St. Suite 3249
Milwaukee, WI 53214
800-669-4192
rethinkingschools.org

Follow @RethinkSchools

© 2019 Rethinking Schools, Ltd.
First edition
First printing

Cover and Book Design: Nancy Zucker
Cover Illustration: Ricardo Levins Morales
Production and indexing: Kjerstin Johnson
Proofreading: Lawrence Sanfilippo, Bridget Carrick

ISBN: 978-0-942961-02-7

Rethinking Ethnic Studies
Library of Congress Control Number: 2018958756

ARTISTS

Contents

PART 2: INDIGENEITY AND ROOTS

PART 3: COLONIZATION AND DEHUMANIZATION

PART 4: HEGEMONY AND NORMALIZATION

PART 5: REGENERATION AND TRANSFORMATION

About the Editors

Miguel Zavala is associate professor and teacher educator at the College of Educational Studies at Chapman University. His research interests center on decolonizing and Freirean pedagogies, critical literacies, and their intersection in social movements. His most recent work involves working with teachers, youth, and parents using Ethnic Studies and participatory action research as resources for apprenticeship into community organizing. He is a board member of the Paulo Freire Democratic Project (PFDP) and co-president of the California Chapter of the National Association for Multicultural Education (CA-NAME). His forthcoming book is titled *Raza Struggle and the Movement for Ethnic Studies*.

R. Tolteka Cuauhtin is an interdisciplinary educator, artist, and organizer. He helped open Social Justice Humanitas Academy high school in Los Angeles Unified School District (LAUSD), teaching, developing curriculum, and serving in leadership roles there from 2011 to 2018. He is on Ethnic Studies Now Coalition's Coordinating Committee as its liaison to the California Department of Education, and also on California Teachers Association/ Stanford's Instructional Leadership Corps, Pukúu Cultural Community Services' board of directors, and LAUSD's Ethnic Studies Teacher Leadership Team and Task Force. He has represented as a keynote speaker, presenter, or emcee/poet/performer, from housing projects and community events to ivory tower universities and continental Indigenous gatherings, and his xdisciplinary work has been noted and shared in several publications and media outlets. Tolteka enjoys writing, theorizing, teaching, learning, rhyming, and participating in community empowerment for past, present, and future generations.

Christine E. Sleeter is professor emerita in the College of Professional Studies at California State University Monterey Bay, where she was a founding faculty member. She began her teaching career as a learning disabilities teacher in Seattle while it was undergoing desegregation. She is past president of the National Association for Multicultural Education and past vice president of the American Educational Research Association. Her research focuses on anti-racist Multicultural Education, Ethnic Studies, and teacher education. She has published more than 150 articles and 21 books (such as *Un-Standardizing Curriculum*) and two novels that feature teachers as main characters (*White Bread* and *The Inheritance*).

A former public high school teacher, **Wayne Au** is a professor in the School of Educational Studies at the University of Washington Bothell, and he is a longtime editor for the social justice teaching magazine *Rethinking Schools*. His work focuses on both academic and public scholarship about high-stakes testing, charter schools, teaching for social justice, and anti-racist education. Recently, Au has been working in the Seattle area to support Black Lives Matter and Ethnic Studies in Seattle Schools. His recent books include *Teaching for Black Lives* (co-edited with Dyan Watson and Jesse Hagopian, Rethinking Schools, 2018), *A Marxist Education* (Haymarket, 2018), and *Reclaiming the Multicultural Roots of U.S. Curriculum* (co-authored with Anthony Brown and Dolores Calderón, TC Press, 2016). He was awarded the UWB Distinguished Teaching Award in 2015, and he was given the William H. Watkins Award for scholar activism from the Society of Professors of Education in 2017.

Introduction

At a Seattle School Board meeting, students, teachers, and parents held signs reading "Teach Us Real History," "Decolonize Seattle Public Schools," and "Ethnic Studies Is the Truth." In Portland, Oregon, students yelled, "Fists up, everyone!" and cheered as the Portland Public School Board passed a resolution in support of Ethnic Studies. Students descended on the California State Capitol in Sacramento to testify about how Ethnic Studies taught them about their histories and cultures and encouraged them to perform well in schools. In Providence, Rhode Island, student activists rallied for Ethnic Studies outside the Providence School Department, with one speaker proclaiming, "I deserve an education that makes me feel powerful." In Texas, as the State Board of Education was considering the adoption of Ethnic Studies, student and community activists rallied with signs reading "We Are MAS [Mexican American Studies] Students, Hear Us Roar!"

On the heels of the banning of Ethnic Studies in Arizona in 2011 and atop a wave of California school districts making Ethnic Studies a graduation requirement, a movement has been unleashed in the United States. It is a powerful movement for K–12 Ethnic Studies that has sprung from students, teachers, and community activists seeking to transform curriculum and teaching into tools for social justice in public schools.

The Tucson Unified School District in Arizona is a touchpoint for K–12 Ethnic Studies. Although not the first to offer high school Ethnic Studies classes, Tucson Unified was the first to do so at a districtwide level with its Mexican American Studies program. Tucson's Ethnic Studies program had a powerful impact on students that was documented by several studies: In Tucson's schools, Mexican American Studies reversed the low-achievement/high–push out levels and general intellectual stagnation for Latinx/Chicanx students typically produced by the Eurocentric, standards-based curriculum and test-driven teaching of the past three decades.

In short, Latinx/Chicanx students who had seemed apathetic came alive through Ethnic Studies classes.

Teachers across the nation who had been teaching Ethnic Studies in their own classrooms already knew of its positive effects. Many teachers knew their textbooks fell far short of including Ethnic Studies knowledge. Many teachers viewed their purpose as not simply to raise students' test scores but rather to equip students with the knowledge and experiences they would be able to use to improve conditions in their communities and their lives. These teachers knew from their own teaching that when students of color see their experiences, realities, histories, and intellectual frameworks represented in the classroom, they wake up and dive in.

In response to the progressive politics of the Ethnic Studies program, right-wing conservatives in Arizona viciously attacked the program and eventually banned Ethnic Studies in Arizona's K–12 schools through state law HB 2281 in 2010. This law essentially outlawed Ethnic Studies for several years. The uproar it caused had a tremendous effect around the country, however, inadvertently launching what has become a national movement.

In a short period of time, the Ethnic Studies movement has spread like wildfire. Numerous school districts across California now require Ethnic Studies, and the state of California is in the beginning stages of developing model Ethnic Studies and Native American curricula. Oregon has a statewide requirement to develop and offer Ethnic Studies K–12, and in Kansas there are efforts to introduce statewide legislation. Indiana high schools will soon be required to offer Ethnic and Racial Studies as an elective course. States with large Indigenous populations—like Montana, Washington, and Alaska—have standards for including Indigenous knowledge in the curriculum. Seattle is in the process of implementing Ethnic Studies across the district; students in Providence, Rhode Island, have successfully lobbied for an Ethnic Studies pilot; and Albuquerque, New Mexico, is launching Ethnic Studies courses in all of its high schools. There are also individual Ethnic Studies courses popping up in individual schools around the country.

An Ethnic Studies Framework

The growing movement to bring Ethnic Studies into K–12 schools raises many important questions for teachers. What does Ethnic Studies mean and how should it be taught? Does Ethnic Studies mean teaching separate units about the cultures and histories of different ethnic groups? Does it have to be a separate class? Can one Ethnic Studies curriculum be developed, packaged, sold, and taught everywhere? Can anyone teach Ethnic Studies? If not, what kind of training and knowledge do Ethnic Studies teachers need? Is Ethnic Studies just for social studies or is it a way of envisioning and teaching the entire curriculum? Is Ethnic Studies the same as multicultural education or something else entirely? These are the kinds of questions we address in the pages of *Rethinking Ethnic Studies*.

Rethinking Ethnic Studies is organized around a holistic Ethnic Studies Framework that was initially proposed by co-editor and high school Ethnic Studies teacher R. Tolteka Cuauhtin. The framework connects directly with a review by co-editor Christine Sleeter on themes that run across the literature in African American, Latino, Asian American, and Native American Studies. Principles within this framework have been articulated by co-editor Miguel Zavala's conceptualization of a rehumanizing and decolonizing pedagogy for Ethnic Studies, as well as co-editor Wayne Au's ongoing work in anti-racist teaching and education for social justice.

The framework is based on four basic premises:

1. All human beings have holistic, ancestral, precolonial roots upon our planet.

2. For many students of color, colonization, enslavement, and forced diaspora attempted to eliminate and replace their ancestral legacies with a Eurocentric, colonial model of themselves.

3. This Eurocentric, colonial model has been normalized for all students, translating to a superficial historical literacy and decontextualized relationship to history today and negatively impacting academic identity for students of color in particular.

4. In order for colonized students to initiate a process of regeneration, revitalization, restoration, and decolonization, they must honestly study this historical process as an act of empowerment and social justice.

Language and Ethnic Studies

We also need to address how language is used in this volume. Our language very often fails us. This book is written in English—a linguistic vestige of settler colonialism and white supremacy in the United States. It is the language of the "victors," and it was used to carry out attempted cultural genocide. Our use of English carries this legacy with it. We recognize that when we use English to communicate, we are fundamentally bound by the politics of racism, patriarchy, sexism, capitalism, and colonization buried within the English language. Indeed, even when communicating in Spanish (which three of us also do), we are also using a Eurocentric language of colonization. Because Ethnic Studies is so strongly centered on anti-racism, cultural revitalization, and decolonization, it has always (and rightfully) struggled with the inherent contradiction of our use of the language of the colonization: Fundamentally we are trying to use what historically has been a tool for domination as a tool for resistance and liberation.

The word "ethnic" in Ethnic Studies symbolizes this contradiction perfectly. Although we currently use "ethnic" to refer to culture or a cultural group, the origin of the term is imbued with politics and power: Originally it meant "heathen" or "pagan"—both terms used to refer to non-Christian groups. More specifically, "ethnic" comes through the Latin and Greek *ethnikos* (heathen) to *ethnos* (nation), connoting a non-Christian (and, we might argue, non-Western) "other." The politics of this should not be lost on us considering that "ethnic" is most often used to refer to non-white groups.

That said, Ethnic Studies is both about the critique of unequal power and the reclamation of power by marginalized and oppressed communities. In this way, the term "Ethnic Studies" itself is an example of one such reclamation. We've taken the word "ethnic" back, flipped the old meaning on its head, and are using it to build a movement that focuses on anti-racist and decolonizing curriculum and teaching. A term of oppression has been transformed into a term of potential liberation.

The chapters in *Rethinking Ethnic Studies* embody the overall struggle between Ethnic Studies and the English language in two ways. The first has to do with terminology. The English language categories for talking about race, culture, and gender are rigid, constrictive, and built on legacies of racism, patriarchy, sexism, and white supremacy. They are too inflexible to really describe our realities, especially if we want to name ourselves in ways that move beyond gender binaries and challenge the politics of race. In response to the confines of English, Ethnic Studies has pushed on the spellings and pronunciations of many commonly used racial and cultural categories and the gendered nature of the English language.

For instance, here in the pages of *Rethinking Ethnic Studies*, you will find a range of terms being used to identify the Indigenous and colonized peoples of the Americas (even the Italian roots of the term "America" communicate the political legacies of naming; Abya Yala, Turtle Island, and Ixachilan are three Indigenous names for the continent). While no *Rethinking Ethnic Studies* authors use the term "Hispanic" (which problematically means "of Spanish origin"), authors use "Latinx" or "Latin@" or "Latina/o" for peoples commonly referred to as Latin American. We see the limits in this terminology as well, given that the root of all these terms is "Latin"—thus based in a language of colonization, since Latinxs can actually be of any precolonial continental ancestry, which the term obscures. For these reasons, several authors also use "Chicana/o" or "Chicanx" or "Xicanx" to challenge gender binaries and to move closer to more Indigenous words, spellings, and identities.

Authors in this volume also try to challenge the gendered nature of several terms, including "history." So you will see the term "herstory" used as a gendered counterpart, or even "hxrstory" (still pronounced *herstory*) as another step beyond the gender binary. Out of respect for the variety of terms and the politics and power of naming, we as editors of *Rethinking Ethnic Studies* have chosen to follow the lead of our contributors in how they've named many of these categories. This means that terms may shift from chapter to chapter.

In addition to new terminology, the second way the chapters here embody the struggle between Ethnic Studies and the English language is through the use of more academic and intellectual language. Ethnic Studies rests on the foundational understanding that education has been used for colonization and white supremacy, and as part of these processes, knowledge has either been kept from communities of color or offered up in safer, tamer forms that keep us from struggling for liberation.

So there is a tradition in Ethnic Studies of recognizing that those in power do not want us to know particular hxrstories, theories, politics, cultures, and forms of resistance; do not want us to be "smart"; do not want us to be intellectuals capable of thinking deeply about our existence. In response, Ethnic Studies has developed its own tradition of using academic and intellectual language as a point of resistance—a way to say, in the face of racism and white supremacy, "Yes, we are smart, and we have a right to understand the world in complex ways too." As such, while *Rethinking Ethnic Studies* is not an academic text, it respects students and teachers enough to recognize that we can learn important and powerful concepts that can help us understand ourselves and the world.

Organization of the Book

Although *Rethinking Ethnic Studies* is not based on all the dimensions in the comprehensive Ethnic Studies Framework (see p. 65 for a more detailed discussion of the framework), elaborations of central elements are present throughout the volume.

Chapters in Part 1, "Framing Ethnic Studies," offer holistic conceptualizations of Ethnic Studies that connect curriculum, pedagogy, students, and community. Prior to the chapter that elaborates on the Ethnic Studies Framework that organizes *Rethinking Ethnic Studies*, chapters explain what Ethnic Studies is and is not, the centrality of students' lives and student activism to Ethnic Studies, why Ethnic Studies matters for everyone, and what it means to teach Ethnic Studies. The four subsequent sections of the book are expressions of the four "macroscales" or "macrothemes" in the Ethnic Studies Framework.

Part 2 develops "Indigeneity and Roots"—the recognition of the sovereignty of the Indigenous nations on whose land teaching is taking place, as well as the identities, ancestral roots, and intergenerational legacies of students in the classroom. Chapters describe various strategies used by teachers from elementary through high school levels to help students explore their family backgrounds, in some cases opening up space to consider painful experiences of family members, such as having fled a war, having been enslaved, or having been forced to forget their ancestral family languages and stories. Chapters illustrate tapping into ancestral knowledge students may have learned at home or community members may hold and be willing to share.

Part 3 delves into "Colonization and Dehumanization"—the historic processes through which peoples of color have been robbed of land, labor, dignity, and autonomy. If students are to heal from the historic traumas of colonization and racism and learn to work for justice, they need to be able to understand oppressive relationships in historical terms. Chapters in this section take on issues such as genocide, segregation, institutional racism, and white supremacy, with some drawing connections to oppressive systems such as capitalism.

Part 4 unmasks "Hegemony and Normalization"—the processes through which oppressive relations have come to be seen as normal or natural. Some chapters in this section critique and move beyond textbooks; others engage students in activities such as simulation and role play that are designed to prompt students to question "realities" they had previously taken for granted.

Part 5 addresses "Regeneration and Transformation"—the potential of working toward rehumanization and social justice activism. Chapters show multiple processes and concepts teachers have used to help students claim powerful identities of themselves as historically and culturally located people who are intellectually as well as politically capable of making a difference. Through combinations of hxstorical study, community study, role plays, and humanizing experiences in the classroom, young people learn to take on pressing issues in their own communities such as militarization of schooling and police violence.

The last section, Part 6, looks at the work of "Organizing for and Sustaining Ethnic Studies." Here, authors from diverse parts of the country—ranging from San Francisco to Providence, from Chicago to Austin, from Sacramento to Portland—reflect upon their efforts alongside students and communities to advocate for and build Ethnic Studies programs. We envision this last section as an extension of the fourth macroscale, Transformational Resistance, and as an opportunity for organizers working for Ethnic Studies to learn from counterparts who have engaged in that work themselves.

Limitations of *Rethinking Ethnic Studies*

We recognize that there is a tension here: Our teaching is often contradictory in that we take part in designing lessons and developing units that are linear and exist within the standardization of public schools, yet we are also interested in being creative, engaging, and responsive, if not also liberating, in our teaching. Our hope is that our vision and orienting frameworks embrace a particular kind of "visionary pragmatism," in the words of Patricia Hill-Collins, in which we keep our hearts in and our eyes on Ethnic Studies as a movement while also respecting the planning and carrying out of instruction that teachers must do within their specific contexts, institutions, and communities.

We also see contradictions in the pull for Ethnic Studies needing to be defined by and solely grounded in the politics and needs of local communities. As a published collection, *Rethinking Ethnic Studies* partly contributes to the institutionalization of Ethnic Studies itself, because it becomes a kind of Ethnic Studies textbook. This raises important arguments about whether or not there even should be Ethnic Studies textbooks or Ethnic Studies standards—especially given that peoples' lives and stories can never be standardized or fully encapsulated in textbooks. In addition, we recognize that blindly committing to local politics does not always work in the interest of justice. For instance, we might argue that white supremacists are also engaged in place-based politics and practices.

Further, we know that Ethnic Studies textbooks and standards *are happening already*, with districts like Los Angeles Unified Schools recently ordering over 23,000 Ethnic Studies textbooks and states like Oregon and Indiana creating Ethnic Studies standards. Our hope is that *Rethinking Ethnic Studies* can play a role in this process by being a book where the voices of those directly involved in the K–12 Ethnic Studies movement are able to shape the movement itself, as opposed to allowing outsiders, textbook companies, politicians, or administrators to take control.

Rethinking Ethnic Studies reflects and attempts to navigate these tensions and contradictions. We hope that the chapters collected here can help facilitate Ethnic Studies theory and practice for teachers both within and outside of our classrooms while also solidifying how we understand Ethnic Studies without succumbing to the oppressive rigidity of standards or formal textbooks.

As teachers, professors, scholar-activists, and community educators, we are also cognizant of the limitations in creating such a volume as *Rethinking Ethnic Studies*. We do not pretend that *Rethinking Ethnic Studies* represents all groups and communities. Even in regard to the macroscales, we would like to include more connections and go in-depth with more groups and communities. We recognize that this work as a whole is not as intersectional as it could be. By "intersectional" we mean a deliberate attempt to reflect upon what bell hooks terms the interlocking nature of race with class, gender, sexuality, and religion, among other axes of difference and power. Given these limitations, in the spirit of Ethnic Studies, we collected the works for *Rethink-*

ing Ethnic Studies with the express intent that readers/practitioners/teachers would use the chapters, resources, and teaching ideas as tools to be adapted, reinterpreted, and remade for use in local contexts and communities.

Even so, we also recognize the potential limits created by our identities as editors and the identities of the authors collected in *Rethinking Ethnic Studies*. Who we are greatly influences the kind of book we have created—e.g., how our own positionalities intersect with institutions to inform and shape this volume and the emergent vision of Ethnic Studies. However, rather than see these identities purely as a problem, we believe that they are also a resource for articulating, envisioning, and dreaming what is possible within and across the movement for Ethnic Studies nationwide.

Finally, we understand that the current movement for Ethnic Studies at this historical moment is neither random nor coincidental. The rise of white supremacy and white nationalism in the United States in recent years, matched by the sharpest economic inequalities this country has witnessed in a century, sends a clear message to communities of color and justice-oriented white people: We are all locked in an increasingly violent struggle over the racial identity of this country, and Ethnic Studies is one concrete and powerful way that teachers, students, schools, and parents can find their own power and take a stand for justice. As such, we hope this volume pushes readers to think more deeply about race, ethnicity, identity construction, and activism. ✳

FAVIANNA RODRIGUEZ

FRAMING ETHNIC STUDIES

The Movement for Ethnic Studies
A Timeline

BY MIGUEL ZAVALA, R. TOLTEKA CUAUHTIN, WAYNE AU, AND CHRISTINE SLEETER

This timeline outlines the development of key policies and programs integral Ethnic Studies in the United States. Its focus is on the movement for Ethnic Studies within public schools nationwide rather than Ethnic Studies in higher education. The timeline is not meant to be exhaustive.

1867

Howard University is charted by the U.S. Congress, one of the first historic Black colleges in the nation.

1887

Kamehameha Schools open in Hawai'i, serving native Hawaiian children.

1915

The Association for the Study of African American Life and History (ASALH), founded by Carter G. Woodson, seeds the foundation for African American studies.

1920s

Japanese language schools in California, which are aimed at language and cultural maintenance, are framed as "anti-American."

1926

Carter G. Woodson establishes Negro History Week, which later became Black History Month in 1969.

1951

The American Studies Association is founded.

1964

Mississippi Freedom Schools are established by the Student Nonviolent Coordinating Committee (SNCC); the schools center on civic participation and political education of African American children and youth.

1966

The Navajo Curriculum Center is founded in Rough Rock, Arizona.

1968

The Third World Liberation Front (TWLF) is founded. The struggle to institutionalize Ethnic Studies at San Francisco State and University of California, Berkeley, is spearheaded by Asian American, African American, Chicano, and Native American students.

The Mexican American Studies program is instituted at California State University, Los Angeles.

1969

"El Plan de Santa Barbara: A Chicano Plan for Higher Education" is drafted, which includes a blueprint for Chicano Studies programs and organizations at colleges across the nation.

The first Ethnic Studies College at San Francisco State is institutionalized, comprising American Indian Studies, Asian American Studies, Africana Studies, and Latino/a Studies.

Chicano Studies and Pan African Studies programs are established at California State University, Northridge.

The Institute of American Cultures (IAC) is founded at UCLA, establishing Ethnic Studies research centers.

1970

The Native American Materials Development Center (NAMDC) creates a K–6 culturally relevant curriculum for Navajo schools.

1972

The National Association for Chicana and Chicano Studies (NACCS) is founded.

The National Association for Ethnic Studies is founded.

The Inter-Ethnic Studies Association in Detroit develops *Ethnic Studies Projects: Training Teacher Trainers*.

The American Indian Curriculum Development Program in North Dakota is established.

1973

Centro de Estudios Puertorriqueños at Hunter College in New York City is founded.

1975

James Banks' *Teaching Strategies for Ethnic Studies* is published.

1979

Association for Asian American Studies is founded.

The Ethnic Studies Department at Bowling Green University in Ohio is founded.

1982

Institute for Puerto Rican Policy Analysis and Advocacy is founded.

1986

Escuela Aztlan, a grassroots school with culturally relevant social activism, is founded by Unión del Barrio in San Diego.

1987

The Center for Studies of Ethnicity and Race in America is founded at the University of Colorado, Boulder.

1991

HB 2859 in Illinois passes, mandating that Black history be integral to the curriculum in Illinois public schools.

1992

The National Association of African American Studies is founded.

1993

The Berkeley Unified School District becomes the first district nationwide to make Ethnic Studies both a 9th-grade course and graduation requirement.

1995

The Alaska Rural Systemic Initiative becomes a vehicle for rooting curricular, pedagogical, and other types of projects in Alaska Native knowledge systems.

1998

The Mexican American/Raza Studies (MARS) program is founded in Tucson, Arizona.

The Betty Shabazz International Charter School, a free Afrocentric school, is founded in Chicago.

2001

Pin@y Educational Partnerships (PEP) is founded to address culturally relevant curriculum, teacher preparation, and institutionalization of Filipina/o curriculum in local San Francisco schools.

Asian American/Asian Research Institute (AAARI) is established by the City University of New York, serving as a hub for research on policies impacting Asian Americans.

Academia Semillas del Pueblo, a language revitalization academy, is founded as part of the Los Angeles Unified School District

2005

Some Philadelphia high schools add an African American Studies graduation requirement.

2007

The San Francisco Unified School District develops a pilot 9th-grade Ethnic Studies course.

Kailua High School in Hawai'i establishes Ethnic Studies as a required 9th-grade course.

2010

HB 2281 is passed, banning Tucson Unified School District's Mexican American/Raza Studies; with 48 course offerings, MARS is the largest Ethnic Studies program for any school district nationwide.

Institute for Teachers of Color Committed to Racial Justice (ITOC) is formed.

2013

Chicago Public Schools moves to mandate a comprehensive Black history curriculum.

Academia Cuauhtli (Eagle Academy) is formed, offering a Mexican American history curriculum rooted in Indigenous principles, serving public school 4th graders in Austin, Texas.

Xicanx Institute for Teaching and Organizing (XITO) is founded in Tucson by Anita Fernández, Sean Arce, Norma "Mictlani" Gonzalez, Jose Gonzalez, and Curtis Acosta.

2014

The Ethnic Studies movement in California is ignited when El Rancho Unified (Pico Rivera, California) passes a high school graduation requirement.

The Ethnic Studies Now Coalition (ESNC) is formed in California.

Two major districts in California—Los Angeles Unified School District and San Francisco Unified School District—adopt Ethnic Studies as a graduation requirement.

2015

Chicago Public Schools introduce districtwide Latinx and Latin American Studies curriculum.

Sacramento City Unified School District, Coachella Valley Unified School District, and Oakland Unified School District make Ethnic Studies a graduation requirement.

2016

AB 2016, sponsored by Luis Alejo, requires the development of a California statewide model Ethnic Studies curriculum by 2020.

Ethnic Studies elective courses are implemented throughout Austin school districts.

Ethnic Studies pilot courses are created in Providence, Rhode Island.

In the San Diego Unified School District, the board votes to fully fund the implementation of Ethnic Studies K–12 throughout the district.

"White" Washing American Education: The New Culture Wars in Ethnic Studies, edited by Denise M. Sandoval, Anthony J. Ratcliff, Tracy Lachica Buenavista, and James R. Marín, is published.

2017

Judge A. Wallace Tashima rules HB 2281 unconstitutional on the grounds that banning of Mexican American Studies was motivated by racial animus.

Ethnic Studies curriculum becomes integral to social studies curriculum in Portland, Oregon.

Oregon HB 2845 passes, requiring Ethnic Studies integration in K–12 social studies statewide.

Seattle Public Schools passes resolution to begin districtwide integration of Ethnic Studies courses.

California passes Native American studies model curriculum (AB 738).

The Board of Bridgeport Public Schools in Bridgeport, Connecticut, moves to add a graduation requirement that students pass either an African American, Latinx, or Race Studies class.

Indiana Senate Enrolled Act 337 is passed, requiring all Indiana high schools to offer Ethnic Studies as an elective, and for state standards to be developed to guide the course in communities throughout the state. ✳

Multicultural Education or Ethnic Studies?

BY CHRISTINE SLEETER, JONI BOYD ACUFF, COURTNEY BENTLEY, SANDRA GUZMAN FOSTER, PEGGY MORRISON, AND VERA STENHOUSE

"Multicultural Education is more on the surface; Ethnic Studies goes deeper."

"Ethnic Studies is for one group; Multicultural Education is for everyone."

"They're the same thing."

"They're very different from each other."

We often hear statements like these when asked about the relation between Multicultural Education and Ethnic Studies. At the same time, we also encounter conceptualizations of Multicultural Education and Ethnic Studies that seem to overlap. Consider the following definitions. Which refers to Ethnic Studies and which to Multicultural Education?

1. A "form of education or teaching that incorporates the histories, texts, values, beliefs, and perspectives of people from different cultural backgrounds." (The Glossary of Education Reform)

2. "The interdisciplinary study of race and ethnicity, as understood through the perspectives of major underrepresented racial groups in the United States." (The Northern Arizona University website)

3. "The interdisciplinary study of difference—chiefly race, ethnicity, and nation, but also sexuality, gender, and other such markings—and power, as expressed by the state, by civil society, and by individuals." (Wikipedia)

We will argue that it is important to recognize the overlapping complementarity of Multicultural Education and Ethnic Studies. And ultimately, we will argue that rather than one being seen as better than the other, what matters is how practices found in both impact kids.

History of Ethnic Studies and Multicultural Education

In the United States, both Ethnic Studies and Multicultural Education have roots in the writings of African American scholars such as W. E. B. Du Bois, Carter G. Woodson, and Anna Julia Cooper, who analyzed the impact of racism (and sexism, in the case of Cooper) on African Americans' lives and consciousness. In his book *Multicultural Education, Transformative Knowledge, and Action*, James A. Banks explained that over a period of about 90 years, African American writers produced a continuous body of scholarship that African Americans read and used but whites generally ignored. The Institute of the Black World, founded by Vincent Harding and Stephen Henderson in Atlanta in 1969, for example, drew on Black intellectual resources within historically Black colleges and universities in the Atlanta area and came to serve as an activist Black Studies think tank.

The *Brown v. Board of Education* Supreme Court decision in 1954 and the Civil Rights Act of 1968, which led to the desegregation of schools and other institutions, opened floodgates of suppressed hopes and expectations. African Americans, followed by Mexican Americans, Puerto Ricans, American Indians, and Asian Americans, sought to redefine how race works, what it means to be American, what it means to be a member of a group that experiences oppression on the basis of race or ethnicity, and how schools and universities address these questions. In 1968, the Third World Liberation Front coalition, formed on the campuses of San Francisco University and the University of California, Berkeley, demanded inclusion, access, democracy, and autonomy for students and faculty of color. This Ethnic Studies movement quickly spread across California and then to university campuses across the rest of the United States.

The Ethnic Studies movement on university campuses supported what became the Multicultural Education movement in elementary and secondary schools. African American parents and educators confronted massive white resistance to school desegregation and additional forms of racism, such as white-dominant curricula and white educators' perception of Black children as culturally deprived and/or mentally retarded. In response, during the 1970s and early 1980s, textbook publishers addressed the most glaring omissions and stereotypes, adding more people of color, especially African Americans.

As students from multiple communities of color experienced personal and institutional racism in school, multiple racial and ethnic groups began to work collectively to restructure education more holistically. Writing in the *Phi Delta Kappan* in 1983, Geneva Gay explained that this became the multiethnic education movement, which other marginalized groups (particularly women, people with disabilities, and LGBTQI communities) subsequently joined. This broader reform umbrella became the Multicultural Education movement.

In the United States, Multicultural Education and Ethnic Studies have been largely complementary, but this has not been the case in many other countries. In Canada, for example, Ethnic Studies was established with the formation of the Canadian Ethnic Studies Association/Société Canadienne d'Études Ethniques in 1971, the same year Canada adopted its national Multicultural Policy, designed to complement the 1969 Official Languages Act that placed multiculturalism within an English-French bilingual framework. This framing elevated the significance of English and French while marginalizing other immigrant groups and Indigenous nations and denying the significance of race and racism. Carl James argued that it constructed Multicultural Education as a way for white educators to "manage" the "problems" brought about by ethnic minority

students. Aboriginal Canadians saw the policy as ignoring them entirely, particularly their efforts to control their own education. Canadians of color saw it as ignoring racism. In response, communities with significant Black populations began to celebrate Black history, and African Canadian scholars began to distinguish between multicultural and anti-racist education, which grew from community activism. By the 1990s, Carl James, George Sefa Dei, and others had articulated an anti-racist framework that focused on dynamics of power rather than cultural symbols and that supported African Canadian parents' advocacy for African-centered, rather than multicultural, education.

Ethnic Studies in K–12 Schools

Until recently, a major difference between Ethnic Studies and Multicultural Education was that the former was found mainly at the higher education level, while the latter was found mainly at the K–12 level (with the exception of Multicultural Education coursework in professional programs such as teacher education and counseling). That is no longer the case, as Ethnic Studies has become an active movement to transform K–12 schooling in many school districts.

Ethnic Studies at the K–12 level initially took the form of African-centered schools founded mainly in the 1970s. In these schools, curriculum is constructed around experiences, accomplishments, and perspectives of peoples of African descent, and relationships between students and teachers are built intentionally on respect. Examples of schools that are still in operation include Marcus Garvey School in Los Angeles, Nation House in Washington, D.C., and Betty Shabazz International Charter Schools/Barbara A. Sizemore/DuSable Leadership Academy in Chicago.

In addition, beginning in the 1970s, many high schools offered electives in African American history and literature, and textbooks for them began to appear. However, when schools were pressed to align their curricula with state standards in the 1990s, many of these electives disappeared and the textbooks went out of print.

The best-known contemporary Ethnic Studies program at the K–12 level was the Tucson Unified School District's Mexican American Studies program, in existence from 1998 until the state enacted legislation banning it in 2010. The best-known part of that program—the Social Justice Education Project, described by Julio Cammarota and Augustine Romero elsewhere in this volume (see "Creating We Schools," p. 48)—connected Ethnic Studies with Multicultural Education and critical pedagogy. While Arizona State Bill 1108 shut down the program, it did not completely close down Ethnic Studies in Tucson. The district had been under court order to desegregate, which placed it under the auspices of the U.S. Office of Civil Rights. Under the new Unitary Status Plan, the Office for Culturally Relevant Pedagogy and Instruction was established. New courses are being written and taught, some from Mexican American viewpoints and others from African American viewpoints.

The Tucson experience ignited and strengthened movements for Ethnic Studies in other parts of the United States. For example, in California, the Ethnic Studies Now Coalition, which has helped coordinate efforts to establish Ethnic Studies in school districts across the state, maintains information on the status of requirements, programs, and courses being established around the state. Ethnic Studies Now has been instrumental in more than a dozen school districts in California adopting an Ethnic Studies graduation requirement and the state passing a law authorizing the development of a model Ethnic Studies curriculum. The Pin@y Education Partnerships program (PEP), started in San Francisco in 2001, has been instrumental in institutionalizing Ethnic Studies in the San Francisco Unified School District and a strong advocate for full implementation of Ethnic Studies throughout the state and the nation. In 2016, Center X at UCLA published a special issue of its online journal, *XChange*, highlighting K–12 Ethnic Studies praxis in California.

Ethnic Studies is also growing rapidly elsewhere. For example, in Texas, Tony Diaz, who established the organization Librotraficante (book trafficker), has been one of the leaders pushing for state support for K–12 Ethnic Studies courses. In Portland, Oregon, all high schools will begin offering Ethnic Studies classes by 2018, an act prompted by the organizing of students of color. In New Mexico, Albuquerque Public Schools will have Ethnic Studies courses in all of its high schools by August 2017; and active movements for Ethnic Studies are underway from Seattle to Providence, Rhode Island. (For more on Ethnic Studies organizing, see Part 6.)

One can also find charter schools that are designed around the culture(s) of communities they serve. For example, the Anahuacalmecac autonomous charter school in Los Angeles and the Native American Community Academy in Albuquerque are founded upon Native cultural knowledge of the tribes in the regions they serve.

Multicultural Education in K–12 Schools

While one can identify many teachers who work actively with Multicultural Education in their classrooms, it is much more difficult to identify schools that not only have a set of Multicultural Education policies but also work to put the principles of Multicultural Education into practice. This is probably because Multicultural Education entails holistic school reform that, while consistent with Ethnic Studies, goes beyond the curriculum and pedagogy that is usually the focus of Ethnic Studies. James Banks' five dimensions of Multicultural Education illustrate this complexity (from the eighth edition of *Multicultural Education: Issues and Perspectives*): 1) *content integration*: "the infusion of ethnic and cultural content into the subject area" or discipline; 2) *knowledge construction process*: the extent to which teachers help students to analyze how "implicit cultural assumptions, frames of reference, perspectives, and biases within a discipline influence the ways in which knowledge is constructed within it"; 3) *equity pedagogy*: how "teachers modify their teaching in ways that will facilitate the academic achievement of students from diverse racial, cultural, gender, and social class groups"; 4) *prejudice reduction*: "lessons and activities teachers use to help students develop positive attitudes toward different racial, ethnic, and cultural groups"; and 5) *empowering school culture and social structure*: fair and equitable practices of grouping students, as well as school climate that impacts student learning.

Some Ethnic Studies curricula, however, embody critical Multicultural Education by attending to multiple racial/ethnic perspectives and intersections between racism and other forms of oppression. For example, the San Francisco Unified School District Ethnic Studies curriculum is organized around manifestations of humanization and dehumanization, hegemony and counter-hegemony, oppression and social movements, and youth participatory action research. These themes cut across experiences and perspectives of diverse, historically oppressed communities within the San Francisco area; the curriculum rests within a pedagogy that aims toward high academic achievement and student empowerment.

Research on the Impact of Ethnic Studies and Multicultural Education

In an effort to defend Ethnic Studies teachers, the National Education Association commissioned Christine Sleeter to review research on the academic and social impact of Ethnic Studies on students; the review was published in 2011. Essentially, as Sleeter wrote, Ethnic Studies counters the traditional Eurocentric curriculum that, as research finds, leads many students of color to disengage from academic learning. She located studies reporting data on the impact of 16 Ethnic Studies projects on students of color, which were mainly at the middle and high school level. The kinds of outcomes that were studied were engagement in the classroom, academic achievement (mainly on state tests), and sense of personal empowerment. Out of the 16 projects, 15 reported a positive impact on students of color. In varied curriculum areas (language arts, social studies, mathematics, and science), Ethnic Studies benefited students in observable ways: They became more academically engaged, did better on achievement tests, graduated at higher rates in some cases, and developed a sense of self-efficacy and personal empowerment. Since that time, the rigorous statistical studies reported in the *American Educational Research Journal* by Nolan Cabrera, Jeffrey Milem, Ozan Jaquette, and Ronald Marx in 2014, and then by Thomas Dee and Emily Penner in 2017, have found the achievement of secondary-level students of color to excel markedly when taking Ethnic Studies courses.

There has not been a comparable research review on the academic impact of Multicultural Education on students, probably because it is com-

plicated to put into practice—unless one considers programs such as San Francisco's Ethnic Studies that arguably melds Ethnic Studies with Multicultural Education. However, there are studies showing the impact of Ethnic Studies and Multicultural Education on students' attitudes about racially and ethni-

Ethnic Studies benefited students in observable ways: They became more academically engaged, did better on achievement tests, graduated at higher rates in some cases, and developed a sense of self-efficacy and personal empowerment.

cally diverse groups. According to Sleeter's review, many research studies (especially at the higher education level) find that diversity coursework generally has a positive impact on the racial attitudes of diverse student groups that include white students. With respect to the K–12 level, Ogo Okoye-Johnson conducted a meta-analysis of 30 studies, published in the *Journal of Black Studies*. Comparing the impact of a multicultural curriculum or program with that of the traditional curriculum on students' racial attitudes, she found a multicultural curriculum to produce a large effect size. Further, when the multicultural curriculum is part of the school's regular programming rather than extracurricular, it has a much more powerful positive impact on students' racial attitudes.

Beyond Either-Or to Classroom Practice

More useful than the question of whether Multicultural Education or Ethnic Studies is "better" is the question of what practices impact most positively on students. Let us look at this question with reference to the National Association for Multicultural Education's five student outcomes in relationship to Multicultural Education and Ethnic Studies.

1. Positive academic identities. This outcome focuses on classroom practices that link students' social identities (ethnic identity, gender identity, language identity, etc.) with an identity as a strong academic learner. Ethnic Studies programs that specifically work to disrupt negative images that students of color have internalized about themselves can do this well; Tucson's Mexican American Studies program did this very well. At the same time, students bring multiple identities into the classroom. For example, a class of Mexican American students likely contains a small number of students who are wrestling with their sexual orientation, a struggle that will likely affect their academic work. Students may have internalized gendered identities about who is good in what. Thus, it is incumbent on teachers to get to know their students' multiple identities, consider negative or limiting ideas from the larger society they may have internalized, and work to build strong senses of complex selves that connect who students are with their full capabilities to learn relevant academic material.

2. Positive social identities. This outcome attends to students being knowledgeable and affirming of their own multiple identities based on race/ethnicity, social class, language, religion, gender, and so forth. This outcome goes hand in hand with positive academic identities, in that both focus on how students understand and value themselves. Whether coming from a perspective of Ethnic Studies, gender studies, disability studies, or any other identity, the teacher needs to help students unpack their multiple identities and explore how they intersect. It is likely that the language of Multicultural Education directs teachers to multiplicity more readily than the language of Ethnic Studies, but we also know Ethnic Studies teachers who do this well and teachers who see themselves as multicultural educators but do not do so well.

3. Respectful engagement with diverse people. Unlike the two outcomes above, this one focuses on how students understand and engage with others. A Multicultural Education that intentionally helps students learn about, develop empathy with, and communicate with people who differ from themselves across multiple lines of difference can address this outcome well. An example would be a teacher who helps build allies to LGBTQI students in a classroom where the majority of students are cisgender and heterosexual. At the same time, multicultural educators sometimes make the mistake of starting out by focusing on appreciating the "other" when the students do not love or appreciate themselves. All of us need to develop a positive sense of self before we can really engage positively with others.

4. Social justice consciousness. Under this outcome, students identify and analyze varied forms of institutional discrimination and colonization and their impacts on themselves and others. This outcome entails shifting from understanding social inequalities in terms of stereotypes about what groups are "like" or presumed characteristics of people to focusing on the workings of unjust systems of power. While students generally understand systemic oppression more readily when it's applied to injustices they experience for themselves, they can use that foundation to develop their understanding of how multiple forms of discrimination and oppression are linked and to examine ways in which students may (perhaps inadvertently) act as perpetrators of discrimination. This outcome is fundamental to both Multicultural Education and Ethnic Studies.

5. Social justice action. This outcome calls on students to learn to work collaboratively with others to make changes that support equity and social justice. Like development of social justice consciousness, learning to take action is fundamental to both Ethnic Studies and Multicultural Education. For many young people, learning to address real social justice problems in their schools and communities using tools of education is both academically and personally empowering and links education with a significant purpose. ✳

An earlier version of this chapter appears on the website of the National Association for Multicultural Education, at nameorg.org/learn/ethnic_studies_or_multicultura.php.

Ethnic Studies
10 Common Misconceptions

BY MIGUEL ZAVALA, NICK HENNING, AND TRICIA GALLAGHER-GEURTSEN
California Chapter of the National Association for Multicultural Education

In our engagement with teachers, scholars, school officials, and other groups, we receive an array of responses to Ethnic Studies. Responses vary, but the following expressions capture their essence. Some quotes are taken directly from what individuals have said, and others are reframed to represent a general perspective.

The purpose of naming these as misconceptions and challenging them is to generate dialogue on the public interpretation of Ethnic Studies practices. We find this dialogue to be essential to the development and expansion of the field.

1. "We already do Ethnic Studies; we have culturally responsive teaching."

One underlying assumption in this statement is that Ethnic Studies and culturally responsive teaching are synonymous. Or, more striking, that Ethnic Studies is a subfield of culturally responsive teaching. Culturally responsive teaching is a powerful pedagogical framework informed by distinct epistemological traditions.

Another problem with this expression lies in the emphasis on "already": The presumption is that Ethnic Studies is already taking place in classrooms (and perhaps we don't need to name practices, programs, etc. as "Ethnic Studies").

While Ethnic Studies is a contested and emergent field, we define it broadly as a movement for curricular and pedagogical projects that reclaim marginalized voices and histories and create spaces of healing, two processes tied to social action that challenge and transform oppressive systems and cultures of domination.

2. "Ethnic Studies is simply a version of social studies/history."

The underlying assumption here is the idea that the field of social studies/history, as a normative practice, already includes Ethnic Studies. Therefore, according to this view, Ethnic Studies is reduced to a particular kind of revisionist history, marked by the inclusion of marginalized voices/perspectives. Yet this view does not interrogate dominant conceptions of history, historicality, and subjectivity.

The message communicated here is that Ethnic Studies should not be regarded as its own field. We believe Ethnic Studies intersects with social studies/history but is transdisciplinary.

3. "Ethnic Studies is focused only on race."

This is an interesting generalization because it's true that Ethnic Studies takes as a major precept the analysis of race/racialization/racism. Some may argue that Ethnic Studies does not include an analysis of class, gender, and sexuality. Perhaps the mistake in this view is that conceptualizations of, for example, "class struggle" and "capitalism" are separate from "racial supremacy" and "coloniality." Rather than think of social class as a superior lens, Ethnic Studies is equipped with conceptual tools that can account for the intersection of race and class (and others axes of difference), what Frantz Fanon termed a "compound standpoint."

Moreover, this statement negates the fact that Ethnic Studies, since its inception in 1968 in California, always included a particular intersectional analysis that looked at race and gender along with other axes of power and difference.

4. "Ethnic Studies teaches students to hate whites. Worse, it teaches them to hate other groups of people."

This expression encapsulates the propaganda that enabled the dismantling of the Mexican American/Raza Studies program in Arizona. Rather than undertake a critical historical analysis of white supremacy as a process of naming one's pain and reality, people may be led to think that such analyses only lead to resentment and feelings of hate toward the dominant group. While we do not promote hate, such strong feelings are part of students' sense-making and development.

The statement is most grotesque when expressed as "Teaching about group X is teaching to be separate and to hate Y." For example, "Teaching about Mexican Americans is teaching to be separate and to hate Central Americans." Often, this expression represents an anti–Ethnic Studies stance; its alternative, then, is not to teach about particular groups but to teach about individuals and generic "human beings."

5. "Ethnic Studies is a remediation program for at-risk youth."

While the scholarship highlighting positive outcomes for students enrolled in Ethnic Studies programs is growing, advocates can sometimes frame it as if Ethnic Studies' main purpose is to increase graduation rates, GPAs, or college-going practices.

But Ethnic Studies is more than a remediation program in high schools—it is an emerging field and its pedagogical praxis is aimed at broader goals, such as reclaiming students' cultural identities and generating community movements.

6. "If adopted as a graduation requirement, students may not want Ethnic Studies."

School officials and leaders have articulated this. It tends to be an argument against institutionalizing Ethnic Studies graduation requirements in high schools.

One problem with this position is that it suggests that what students are already forced to take (as part of the normative and institutionalized curriculum) is what students want and need.

7. "Ethnic Studies courses are successful because of teacher efficacy rather than the curriculum."

This is a tricky statement, as it provides an alternative explanation for why Ethnic Studies programs have been quite successful. The statement fails to understand what Ethnic Studies classrooms look like and how they can be transformative spaces while minimizing the value and significance of the curriculum itself. While many Ethnic Studies teachers may also be phenomenal educators, students seeing themselves in the curriculum deeply impacts their engagement and learning.

8. "Ethnic Studies is most effective at the high school and college level."

We don't know if this is true or not. Current scholarship documents effective practices at the high school level. Nevertheless, to argue that Ethnic Studies is "most" effective at the secondary level presumes that (a) adolescent students are more cognitively prepared for such courses and (b) that children may not grasp complex concepts or will have trouble engaging with issues of race.

9. "College professors of Ethnic Studies are most qualified to teach Ethnic Studies courses."

Some districts, in meeting their graduation requirements, have sought partnerships with universities. While faculty in Ethnic Studies programs may be some of the most qualified in terms of knowledge and research pertaining to Ethnic Studies, Ethnic Studies faculty and teacher educators both play a critical role in the development of Ethnic Studies curriculum. Ethnic Studies is not simply about informing or knowing—it is complex and involves the creation of meaningful learning contexts.

Moreover, the strategy to hire Ethnic Studies professors at universities bypasses the importance of preparing teachers and the vital role teacher educators play in their development. It's almost as if teachers at the high school level are regarded as ill-equipped (because they are not "experts" of Ethnic Studies) and so university faculty place themselves on the front lines of teaching Ethnic Studies courses at the high school level.

10. "Ethnic Studies classes might engage students, but I don't see how they address real learning."

This statement conveys the misconception that Ethnic Studies lacks rigor. Many who are unfamiliar with Ethnic Studies (or who don't see value in teaching that grapples with difficult questions about race) promote a caricature of Ethnic Studies classrooms as easy and engaging because students watch films, listen to hip-hop music, and seldom engage in "real learning."

This caricature is patently false. The classrooms we have observed and curriculum we have analyzed demonstrate a high level of both engagement and rigor. Literacy practices happen throughout these courses. Reading and writing are central to learning content. In some instances, students engage in action research projects that are academically demanding. ✳

What Is Ethnic Studies Pedagogy?

BY ALLYSON TINTIANGCO-CUBALES, RITA KOHLI, JOCYL SACRAMENTO, NICK HENNING, RUCHI AGARWAL-RANGNATH, AND CHRISTINE SLEETER

On February 23, 2010, the San Francisco Unified School District's (SFUSD) Board of Education unanimously adopted a resolution to support Ethnic Studies in their schools. San Francisco's institutionalization of Ethnic Studies was the result of K–12 educators, university faculty, community organizations, students, and families joining together to fight for an education that could potentially address gaps in educational achievement, opportunity, equity, and justice. Although these groups believe Ethnic Studies holds great promise, challenges in its implementation became clear in its early stages.

As a select group of SFUSD high schools began to place Ethnic Studies on their master schedules, a committee of teachers was charged with developing the 9th-grade Ethnic Studies curriculum. Since SFUSD, following the California state curriculum framework, housed Ethnic Studies courses in social sciences/history departments, the only requirement to teach them was a social science credential. This resulted in an eligible pool of teachers with drastically varying levels of Ethnic Studies content knowledge and teaching experience. Teachers with an Ethnic Studies background, either by having taken Ethnic Studies courses, engaged in Ethnic Studies professional development, or participated in extensive work in communities of color, felt Ethnic Studies involves teaching students how to understand their experiences with race and racism through a critical lens. Teachers who lacked that background and experience were initially resistant to reflecting on their racial identity and responding to the needs of students of color to critique race and racism.

Much of the tension centered on not just what to teach but also how to teach Ethnic Studies. Can anyone with Ethnic Studies content knowledge teach it well? Conversely, can any good teacher of other subjects take up Ethnic Studies content and teach it well? What is the relationship between Ethnic Studies content and pedagogy?

We decided to examine what effective Ethnic Studies K–12 pedagogy looks like in the classroom by reviewing the research on K–12 teachers of Ethnic Studies. We then connected what *those* teachers were doing with other bodies of related research. While there aren't a lot of studies of Ethnic Studies teachers, we were able to locate six.

Four studies examined exemplary teachers of Ethnic Studies:

- Steffany Baptiste's 2010 dissertation analyzed how three teachers implemented New Jersey's Amistad legislation.
- Roderick Daus-Magbual's 2010 dissertation examined teachers in San Francisco's Pin@y Educational Partnerships program.
- Jerry Lipka and colleagues, writing in *Anthropology of Education Quarterly*, studied teachers in the Math in a Cultural Context program in Alaska.
- Lucille Watahomigie and Teresa McCarty described teachers working with a Hualapai curriculum at Peach Springs School in Arizona in the *Peabody Journal of Education*.

Two studies revealed a mixture of good and poor Ethnic Studies teaching:

- Diane Pollard and Cheryl Ajirotutu's 2001 chapter in *Educating Our Black Children* analyzed two Afrocentric schools in Milwaukee, one of which demonstrated exemplary teaching and the other generally poor teaching.

- Felicia Sanders' 2009 dissertation examined Ethnic Studies teaching in Philadelphia that ranged widely in quality.

We sought key differences between effective and ineffective Ethnic Studies teachers, differences that shed light on K–12 Ethnic Studies pedagogy. Here is what we found.

Purpose of Ethnic Studies: Toward Decolonization and the Elimination of Racism

Strong Ethnic Studies teachers sense the purpose of Ethnic Studies goes beyond teaching untold or undertold histories: It also helps students critique structures of racism and its personal and social impact, as well as challenge oppressive conditions. Effective Ethnic Studies teachers are grounded in this purpose and engage in coursework and/or professional development of Ethnic Studies content knowledge and intellectual frameworks.

Ethnic Studies' purpose is to respond to students by developing their critical understanding of the world and their place in it, and ultimately prepare them to use academic tools to transform their world for the better. This purpose guides its pedagogy. Early Ethnic Studies activists were inspired by Frantz Fanon's classic *Wretched of the Earth*, first published in 1963. His analysis of decolonization includes both the physical act of freeing a territory from external control of a colonizer and freeing the consciousness of the colonized from the alienation caused by colonization. Decolonization as a liberatory process is central to Ethnic Studies pedagogy because it allows for a systematic critique of the traumatic history of colonialism on Native and Third World peoples and, subsequently, healing from colonial trauma, which includes having learned to see oneself as academically incapable. Decolonization, however, should not be mistaken as only an academic exercise; the aim of decolonization is to move toward self-determination, the claiming of an intellectual identity, and active participation in the transformation of material conditions.

Ethnic Studies pedagogy, as an anti-racist project, encourages both teachers and students to critique racial oppression at the institutional, interpersonal, and internalized levels while also showing how each level influences the other. Scholars in education have borrowed from—and built Ethnic Studies to support—a racial analysis of school inequities. One such framework is critical race theory, a theory from legal studies now used within other fields like education to center racism as the cause of racial disparities in schooling. As Ethnic Studies courses enter K–12 school contexts, critical race theory offers concrete tools for framing pedagogies of race, such as counter-storytelling—narratives of people of color that challenge dominant narratives that center those with institutional and social power. Counter-storytelling has been used in education for students of color, their families, and their communities to rewrite and reclaim their educational experiences.

An anticolonial education that promotes a critical consciousness and teaches students to challenge racial oppression has a markedly positive academic impact on the lives of students of color. One of the best-documented examples is the Social Justice Education Project (SJEP) in Tucson, Arizona, which intentionally linked development of an academic identity with Chicana/o studies (see "Creating We Schools," p. 48). Evaluations of the project over several years—the best known being Nolan Cabrera, Jeffrey Milem, Ozan Jaquette, and Ronald Marx's 2014 evaluation—have been strongly positive. Cabrera and his colleagues found that students enrolled in SJEP courses graduated and went on to college at a much higher rate than other students in the same schools and tested higher on the state's tests for reading, writing, and math. Similarly, based on an evaluation of the 9th-grade SFUSD Ethnic Studies program mentioned earlier, in 2017, Thomas Dee and Emily Penner reported that participating students earned higher GPAs and more credits toward graduation and had better school attendance than peers who did not participate.

Critical Reflection on Teachers' Own Identities

Strong Ethnic Studies teachers continuously reflect on their own cultural and racial identities, their relationships with diverse ethnic communities, and the impact of dominant Eurocentric perspectives on their own views and senses of self. As a result, effective Ethnic Studies teachers learn to take action individually and collectively toward social justice and self-decolonization. Both whites and people of color need to engage in this process of critical self-reflection, but because they occupy different positions in a racial hierarchy, the issues they must work on are significantly different.

Because teachers of color often personally connect to the historical and current racialized realities represented in Ethnic Studies curriculum, they may be more likely than their white counterparts to connect to its content and to students of color. Teachers of color generally bring a greater degree of multicultural knowledge, support for Ethnic Studies, commitment to social justice, and commitment to provide students of color with challenging curricula than do white teachers. However, teachers of color often have experienced racism in their own K–12 education, which parallels what students of color face today. Many times, teachers of color have internalized that racism and must go through an intensive process to unlearn and heal from their experiences.

White teachers who have learned to teach Ethnic Studies effectively serve as models for white people coming to understand racism, culture, and ethnicity, and learning to locate their experiences and identities within a racially inclusive paradigm. For white teachers especially, issues of identity involve unpacking the impact of benefiting from racism, as well as learning to recognize themselves as cultural beings. Critical autobiography, critical storytelling, and critical life history can help white teachers examine connections between their individual lives and identities and broader social and political contexts. Rather than assuming that whites have no experience with race and racism, these activities assist white teachers in analyzing experiences they do have that contribute to their identity, beliefs, and position within the racial hierarchy. Regardless of whether teachers are white or of color, their effectiveness is directly connected to their ability to be *responsive* to the histories, experiences, and communities of the students in their classrooms.

Culturally Responsive Pedagogy

Strong Ethnic Studies teachers use culturally responsive pedagogy. They know how to connect students' questions and lives with Ethnic Studies content, are able to lead students through a process of identity exploration and transformation in relationship to Ethnic Studies, and believe in their students academically.

Ethnic Studies pedagogy that is culturally responsive puts students' lives, culture, and funds of knowledge at the center of the curriculum. For example, in an ethnographic study of a high school Filipino Heritage Studies class reported in *Pedagogies: An International Journal*, Korina Jocson describes *kuwento* as a culturally responsive pedagogical tool. Kuwento, a story or an approach to telling/sharing stories, is linked to Filipino cultural traditions of passing down history, lived experiences, and values. The teacher's use of kuwento engaged students in sharing lived experiences and learning about their peers within a larger sociohistorical context. This process affirmed students' cultural identity and knowledge and enabled them to make critical connections between their history, familial relationships, and community.

Ethnic Studies pedagogy that is culturally responsive explores and supports students' critical consciousness. Many students who are newly exposed to Ethnic Studies have to unlearn dominant Eurocentric perspectives they have been taught throughout their whole academic and social lives. As Patrick Camangian argues in *Research in the Teaching of English*, marginalized youths of color must go through a process of recovering themselves and their identities. This process helps students to value their own cultural knowledge. It also helps them to develop a critical lens to question and understand their realities in the context of relations of power in society.

Culturally responsive Ethnic Studies pedagogy means investing in students' academic success by creating caring environments where student knowledge and skills serve as the primary point of departure. Students identify teachers caring as crucial. For instance, Tyrone Howard reported interviews with African American elementary students within urban school contexts in an article titled "Telling Their

Side of the Story" in *The Urban Review*. Students said that teachers' willingness to care and bond with them created optimal learning environments. Teachers expressed caring through nurturing behaviors, the expression of high expectations, and respect for students. Students mentioned the teachers' abilities to structure the classroom in a way that valued the students' homes and communities and specifically created a homelike atmosphere or feeling.

Because learning to reframe stereotypical images and how we understand power relations is challenging in an Ethnic Studies classroom, it is fundamental that students feel safe and cared for. Culturally responsive teachers ensure an environment that values students as whole beings, encouraging success within and beyond the scope of their classrooms.

Community Responsive Pedagogy

Strong Ethnic Studies teachers interact with local communities of color on an ongoing basis: They are community responsive. They recognize the importance of building relationships with their students and students' parents and wider communities on a regular basis. The teachers build curriculum around those relationships as they prepare young people for leadership in addressing issues in their schools and communities. Many Ethnic Studies teachers use Jeff Duncan-Andrade and Ernest Morrell's elaboration of Paulo Freire's cyclical praxis model: 1) identify a problem; 2) analyze a problem; 3) create a plan of action to address the problem; 4) implement the plan of action; and 5) reflect on the plan of action. In *The Art of Critical Pedagogy*, Duncan-Andrade and Morrell explain how this model connects theory, practice, and reflection to address social issues and provide opportunities for students to apply what they learn in Ethnic Studies to their broader communities. Key components include developing critical consciousness, developing agency through direct community experience, and growing transformative leaders.

Ethnic Studies pedagogy develops students' critical consciousness by connecting classroom learning with their home and community life and helping students learn to analyze and act on community needs. To do this, many Ethnic Studies teachers use Youth Participatory Action Research (YPAR)

to engage youth as critical action researchers in the context of social justice activities informed by students' lived experiences. For example, Antwi Akom developed a model of YPAR in a high school Africana Studies class, which he called Black Emancipatory Action Research (BEAR), to focus on the implications of "racing research and researching race." His framework, elaborated in *Ethnography and Education*, develops students' critical consciousness through questioning objectivity and reexamining the researched-researcher relationship, while emphasizing principles such as self-determination, social justice, equity, healing, and love. With its commitment to community capacity building, local knowledge, asset-based research, community-generated information, and action as part of the inquiry process, BEAR represents a possibility for youth to use their research to develop liberatory action plans toward the elimination of racism. By learning self-advocacy through YPAR, critically conscious students have the opportunity to see themselves as knowledgeable, intellectual, capable, and empowered.

Ethnic Studies pedagogy develops students' identity and agency by engaging them directly in action that responds to their research on their community. For example, in the Social Justice Education Project in Tucson's Mexican American Studies program, students developed critical consciousness and agency through YPAR community-based research that directly addressed social injustices in their lives, schools, and communities. Julio Cammarota and Augustine Romero describe in *Educational Policy* how students' research-based findings, produced in conjunction with their intellectual development, led Tucson schools to make changes such as replacing missing urinals in the boys' bathrooms, repairing falling tiles in the gym ceiling, repairing water fountains, updating books in the library, and ensuring classroom safety.

Through community responsiveness, Ethnic Studies grows leaders who aim to transform their communities. For example, Pin@y Educational Partnerships (PEP) created an Ethnic Studies pipeline that promotes the development of students' "critical leadership" praxis, which focuses on practicing leadership skills that directly address equity and social justice (see "Barangay Pedagogy," p. 96).

Critical leadership builds on one's relationship to oneself and one's relationships to one's neighborhood and racial/ethnic, cultural, and global communities, according to Roderick Daus-Magbual and Allyson Tintiangco-Cubales in their chapter in the book *"White" Washing American Education.*

It is not enough to adopt an Ethnic Studies curriculum without attending to pedagogy. Ethnic Studies pedagogy must be rigorous, culturally and community responsive, and reflective to be effective in living its promise of decolonization and challenging racism.

PEP addresses the need to train leaders who focus on improving social conditions for themselves and their community. PEP began in 2001 to serve the academic and personal needs of Filipina/o American youth through a mentorship program between college and high school students. Expanding to elective courses at the high school and middle school levels, an after-school program at the elementary school level, and various courses at the community college level, PEP's pedagogy became rooted in a "partnership triangle" between the public schools, university, and community. PEP's critical leaders have a foot in each of these three spaces. PEP utilized Ethnic Studies as a vehicle to confront educational inequities while also growing their own leaders. PEP was part of a coalition that came together with SFUSD Ethnic Studies teachers and students to develop a successful campaign to establish Ethnic Studies in San Francisco high schools. Students and youth involved in this mobilization gained lessons in agency and self-determination from an Ethnic Studies community-responsive pedagogy that shaped the organization of the campaign and encouraged students' engagement in shaping their own educational futures.

Ethnic Studies Responsiveness

Ethnic Studies pedagogy is directly connected to the purpose, context, and content of what is being taught where the goal of community responsiveness is central. In the pursuit of this, teachers do not compromise academic rigor but rather heighten it through applied critical consciousness, direct and reflective action, and the growing of transformative leaders. Ethnic Studies pedagogy that is culturally responsive allows students to see themselves, their families, their communities, and their histories in the curriculum and practices of the classroom, as multiple sources of knowledge and cultural experiences are validated and celebrated. Ethnic Studies that is community responsive builds upon students' cultures and seeks to provide opportunities for students to create culture and communities among themselves and also use their education to respond to needs in their communities outside of classrooms. Community-responsive methods along with a culturally responsive curriculum support the goals of Ethnic Studies to align education with the historical experiences and current needs of communities of color. Through YPAR and the development of student agency and leadership, Ethnic Studies students become critical-action researchers and intellectuals who use what they are learning in the classroom to serve their communities. To engage in the complex Ethnic Studies pedagogy outlined above, teachers must have more than content knowledge. To embody a sense of purpose and a culturally and community-responsive pedagogy, they must be reflective and be able to critically interrogate their own identities and experiences.

Conclusion

Tintiangco-Cubales, Peter N. Kiang, and Samuel Museus defined pedagogy in the *AAPI Nexus* as:

a philosophy of education informed by positionalities, ideologies, and standpoints (of both teacher and learner). It takes into account the critical relationships between the PURPOSE of education, the CONTEXT of education, the

CONTENT of what is being taught, and the METHODS of how it is taught. It also includes (the IDENTITY of) who is being taught, who is teaching, their relationship to each other, and their relationship to structure and power.

It is not enough to adopt an Ethnic Studies curriculum without attending to pedagogy. Ethnic Studies pedagogy must be rigorous, culturally and community responsive, and reflective to be effective in living its promise of decolonization and challenging racism. Ethnic Studies pedagogy, defined by its purpose, context, content, methods, and the identity of both students and teachers, includes 1) engagement with the purpose of Ethnic Studies, which is to address racism by critiquing, resisting, and transforming systems of oppression on institutional, interpersonal, and internal levels; 2) knowledge about personal, cultural, and community contexts that impact students' epistemologies and positionalities while creating strong relationships with families and community organizations in local areas; 3) development of rigorous curriculum that is responsive to student's cultural, historical, and contemporary experiences; 4) practices and methods that are responsive to the community's needs and problems; and 5) self-reflection on teacher identity and making explicit how identity impacts power relations in the classroom and in the community.

Strong Ethnic Studies teachers are responsive to their students and what they bring with them to the classroom whether that be their histories, experiences, or the cultures of their families and communities. It is the responsibility of the teacher to learn how to develop a pedagogy that speaks to the students' lived realities. Ultimately, Ethnic Studies needs to be developed and implemented in localized ways to provide all students, especially students of color who have been historically marginalized, with a meaningful, relevant, rigorous, and responsive curriculum and pedagogy where multiple perspectives are respected, affirmed, and honored. ✳

Ethnic Studies Pedagogy as CxRxPx

BY R. TOLTEKA CUAUHTIN

First, a persistence of faulty and simplistic conceptions of what culturally responsive pedagogy is must be directly confronted and replaced with more complex and accurate views.
—Christine Sleeter, from "An Agenda to Strengthen Culturally Responsive Pedagogy" (2011)

Ethnic Studies is often associated with *culturally relevant* and/or *culturally responsive pedagogy* (CRP), terms first widely popularized about 20 years ago by Gloria Ladson-Billings (1995) and Geneva Gay (2000). Some teachers wonder what the differences are between Ethnic Studies and CRP, and too often, the schools of thought are conflated or considered one and the same, which can unintentionally be detrimental to Ethnic Studies programs.

While surface levels of culture have their place in CRP, educators sometimes stop at that level, thinking the work of being culturally relevant and responsive with their students is complete. CRP itself has been found wanting, and critics have pointed out that it needs to be further grounded in Ladson-Billings's original criteria and go deeper with culture. In her book *Culturally Responsive Teaching and the Brain*, Zaretta Hammond elaborates on the neurological explanation of why and how CRP works when practiced in a deep and meaningful way in classroom instruction and provides a visual to represent this depth (as shown on opposite page).

Given the potential shortcomings of how CRP is often used today and in the spirit of making connections with Ethnic Studies, scholars have integrated additional terms including *community responsive pedagogy* and *historically responsive pedagogy*. There have also been formal proposals to respectfully and lovingly revise the terminology, stance, and practice of CRP itself: Django Paris, later in collaboration with H. Samy Alim, offered *culturally sustaining pedagogy* (CSP) from his 2012 article of the same name to emphasize the necessity of sustaining the dynamic cultural and linguistic discourses students come to the classroom with. In Paris' initial proposal, Ethnic Studies—specifically Tucson's Mexican American Studies program—was noted as a robust form of CSP. Ladson-Billings supported this proposal in her article "Culturally Relevant Pedagogy 2.0: a.k.a. the Remix," which focused on hip-hop and community spoken-word events as relevant, dynamic expressions of youth culture that can be leveraged and sustained in educational contexts. Teresa McCarty and Tiffany Lee felt it was necessary to add a further revision to CSP for many Indigenous youth, proposing the term *critical culturally revitalizing and sustaining pedagogy* (CCRSP), since colonialism and acts of genocide, ethnocide, and linguicide have put many of today's Native youth in situations where they are missing parts of their dynamic ancestral Indigeneity as human beings. Pedagogy that simply maintains a status quo of coloniality—what these students enter the classrooms with—is not enough; what was forcibly lost, stolen, erased, and replaced must also be revitalized. *Decolonial pedagogies, pedagogies of love, healing pedagogies, pedagogies of authentic care, humanizing pedagogies,* and more have also been used in association with Ethnic Studies. Still, we are increasingly seeing Ethnic Studies equated with CRP. Does it suffice for Ethnic Studies pedagogy to be simply referred to as a form of CRP?

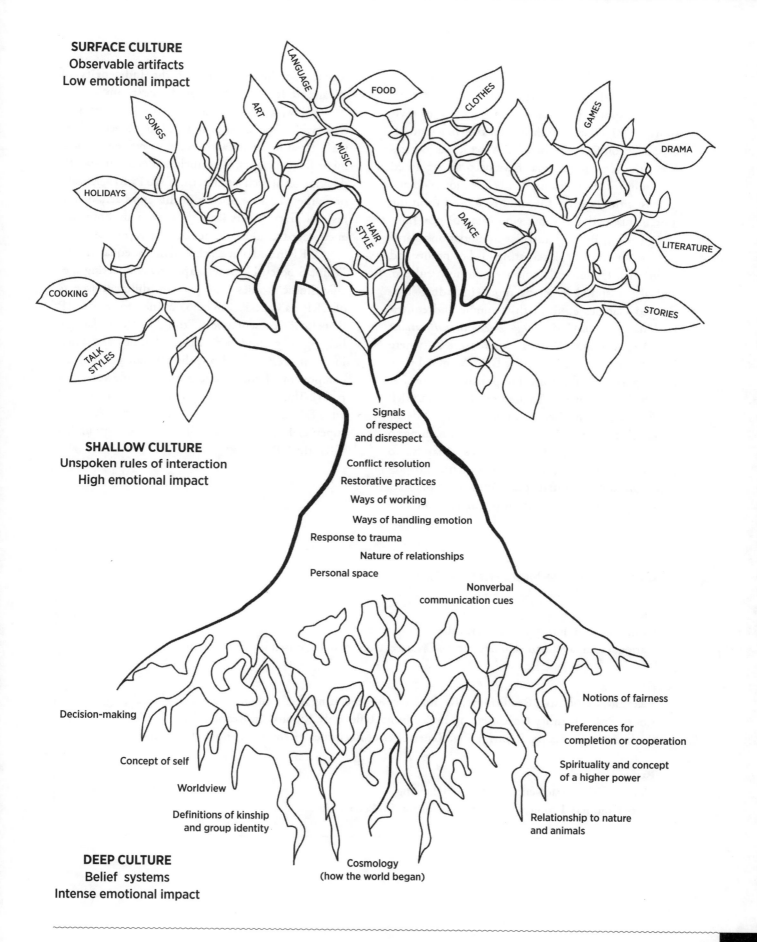

SURFACE CULTURE
Observable artifacts
Low emotional impact

SONGS

LANGUAGE

ART

FOOD

MUSIC

CLOTHES

GAMES

DRAMA

HOLIDAYS

HAIR STYLE

DANCE

LITERATURE

COOKING

STORIES

TALK STYLES

SHALLOW CULTURE
Unspoken rules of interaction
High emotional impact

Signals
of respect
and disrespect

Conflict resolution

Restorative practices

Ways of working

Ways of handling emotion

Response to trauma

Nature of relationships

Personal space

Nonverbal
communication cues

Decision-making

Notions of fairness

Concept of self

Preferences for
completion or cooperation

Worldview

Spirituality and concept
of a higher power

Definitions of kinship
and group identity

Relationship to nature
and animals

DEEP CULTURE
Belief systems
Intense emotional impact

Cosmology
(how the world began)

Are they the same or are they different? Must we still work to clarify this further?

In response to these questions, I offer my revision to CRP relative to Ethnic Studies in a semi-algebraic form: CxRxPx, or CRP-X, which as its basis keeps the same letters that have become ingrained with multitudes of teachers and education scholars. This is with gratitude for and inspiration from the aforementioned and those who came before, honoring Ladson-Billing's and Gay's foundations, Paris' request for revision (integrating his key points and additions), Hammond's emphasis on deep culture, and also inspired by many more, including Tintiangco-Cubales et al. in this volume and contributions in *"White" Washing American Education: The New Culture Wars in Ethnic Studies*, where both Sean Arce and Roderick Daus-Magbual note the importance of historical responsiveness. In that same volume, I first elaborated on the "R" in CRP as educationally medicinal, student centered, decolonial, and organic: Rx, with its role in helping to heal identity through Ethnic Studies. Adaptive to diverse student needs, it is a sort of organic anti-prescription to neocolonial education and emphasizes McCarty and Lee's contribution in relation to a regeneration/revitalization of the Indigeneity of Xicanx students in my 9th-grade classroom.

Below, a table summarizes the key points of these various pedagogies and building blocks of the CxRxPx as a concise and accessible reference document for educators. Also included is a semi-poetic description of each letter in the CxRxPx to help elaborate the relevance of each in this approach. Scholars and practitioners (and those who are both) are encouraged to add, edit, or clarify it as you see fit.

CRP in and of itself should not be equated with Ethnic Studies. However, explicitly connecting specific Ethnic Studies concepts with different aspects of CRP via CxRxPx can help outline a form of CRP that also is representative of Ethnic Studies Pedagogy, helping to ground both Ethnic Studies and CRP in the process. This also is the referent pedagogical component of the Ethnic Studies Framework (see p. 65). Thus, the next time you hear CRP associated with Ethnic Studies, it may be helpful to ask, is it a superficial, hxrstorically shallow CRP, or a grounded CRP, the CRP-X? ✳

Ethnic Studies Pedagogy as CxRxPx

Cx:
Cultural, Community-Based, Critical,
Caring, Compassionate, Collaborative, Creative, Contextual, Conscious, Competent;

Rx:
Relevant, Responsive, Reaffirming, Revitalizing, Regenerating, Remembering, Restoring, Realizing, Roots, Racial Identity Development, Reflectively, Reflexively, Rigorously, Resistantly, Reclaiming, Remixing, Reimagining, Repertoires of Reciprocal, Rehumanizing, Relationships;

Px:
Pluraliterate, Pluradiscursive, Power-Balancing,
Post+Colonia!, People, Planet, Praxis, Purposeful Pedagogies.

Ethnic Studies Pedagogy (ESP) as CRP-X

When Ethnic Studies is simply conflated as a form of CRP, refer to the CxRxPx/CRP-X for deeper understandings about what that means.

Cx:

Cultural: ancestry, home, everyday funds of knowledge of students (as holistic, linguistic beings) matter.

Community-Based: students' community and holistic community cultural wealth are assets.

Critical: students challenge systems of power and oppression, social inequities, historical amnesia.

Caring: teachers authentically care and commit to students, helping them to authentically care and be

Compassionate: with empathy in action rather than mere sympathy, solidarity rather than charity.

Collaborative: collective decision-making, working together for these goals with intentionality and soul.

Creative: dynamic, multidimensional, outside of the box, thinking, interpreting, working expressively.

Contextual: storify; gamify; socialize it; the settings matter, affecting the energy, connectively;

Conscious: conscientization, growing a counterhegemonic critical consciousness as leaders, necessarily.

Competent: the ability and actualization of putting this all into praxis (reflection + action) skillfully.

Rx:

Relevant: related to students as holistic human beings, with deep roots, dynamic presents, and futures.

Responsive: responsive to who students are, where they're at, and what they have to work with daily.

Reaffirming: sustaining, validating, appreciating, and celebratory to who students are as human beings.

Revitalizing: when more than sustaining is needed; life, livelihood, liveliness, vitality is awakened by

Regenerating: currents of energy and ancestral memory of "stolen generations" courageously.

Remembering: students are temporal-spatial, intergenerational hxrstorically responsive beings.

Revealing: cultural genocide in the ancestral legacies of many Students of Color, demasking hegemony.

Restoring: helping to heal and make whole again, restorative justice, humanizing;

Realizing: real eyes realize real lies. Realizing colonialism's effects and our holistic greatness. Realizing

Roots: the ancestral plane, its active presence and futurity. Ancestry, Indigeneity, Diasporic Indigeneity.

Racial Identity Development: understanding the pervasive social construction of race and our place in it.

Reflexively: in realms of social justice, neutrality is an illusion; the side that teachers are on may be evident,

Reflectively: as students and teachers, learning through feeling, thinking, dreaming about our experiences,

Rigorously: with high expectations of ourselves as intellectuals, with critical compassion and dignity,

Resistantly: transformatively, critical of oppression and motivated by social justice, knowledge + action.

Reclaiming: People of Color stories, narratives, legacies, knowledges, names, identities, and exponentially more.

Remixing: ever evolving and adaptive yet rooted and grounded with third-space synergies, and

Reimagining: how things can be, a world where many worlds fit, we are the change, representing

Repertoires: of practice, humanizing and growing these repertoires with dexterity, through

Reciprocal: completing the circle of community, transformationally, with self-determination,

Rehumanizing: preparation, instruction, facilitation, assessment; the glue between it all are the respectful

Relationships: holistically liberating through . . .

Px:

Pluraliterate: empowering students to read the words and the read the world, the universe is a text set;

Pluradiscursive: expressive in multiple discourses as creative scholar warriors and holistic human beings;

Power-Balancing: challenging asymmetrical power relations, transforming legacies of colonization;

Post+Colonia!: recognizing coloniality never ended, keeping posted on it, decolonizing knowledge daily;

People: that's us; who we are as human beings, honoring, respecting each other's dignity, humanity, and

Planet: relational with all ecology, from the place we are based, locally to globally, and beyond;

Praxis: in reflection and action;

Purposeful: we know why we're here, continuing to grow and learn every day, teach each other; Ethnic Studies

Pedagogies: involve much more that what is usually associated with mainstream CRP. ESP as CxRxPx!

A Few Important Building Blocks of ESP/CxRxPx

Gloria Ladson-Billings' Three Features of Culturally Relevant Pedagogy
1. Academic success/student learning
2. Critical consciousness
3. Cultural competence

Geneva Gay's Six Dimensions of Culturally Responsive Teaching
1. Social and academic empowerment
2. Multidimensionality
3. Cultural validation
4. Social, emotional, and political comprehensiveness
5. School and societal transformation
6. Emancipation/liberation from oppressive educational practices and ideologies

Christine Sleeter's Three Areas of Concern in an Agenda to Strengthen Culturally Responsive Pedagogy
1. A persistence of faulty and simplistic conceptions of what culturally responsive pedagogy is must be directly confronted and replaced with more complex and accurate views.
2. The research base that connects culturally responsive pedagogy with student learning must be strengthened.
3. The political backlash from work that empowers minoritized communities must be anticipated and addressed.

Django Paris and Samy Alim's Sustenance in Culturally Sustaining Pedagogy
1. A focus on the plural and evolving nature of youth identity and cultural practices
2. A commitment to embracing youth culture's counterhegemonic potential while maintaining a clear-eyed critique of the ways in which youth culture can also reproduce systemic inequalities

Teresa McCarty and Tiffany Lee's Revitalization in Critical Culturally Sustaining/Revitalizing Pedagogy and Indigenous Education Sovereignty
1. Attends directly to asymmetrical power relations and the goal of transforming legacies of colonization, involving a knowingness of the colonizer, as well as a struggle for self-determination
2. Recognizes the need to reclaim and revitalize what has been disrupted and displaced by colonization (focusing on language education policy and practice)
3. Recognizes the need for community-based accountability, with the "Four R's": respect, reciprocity, responsibility, and the importance of community relationships

Tintiangco-Cubales et al.'s Community Responsive Pedagogy
1. Developing critical consciousness
2. Developing agency through direct community experience
3. Growing transformative leaders

Daus-Magbual's Historically Responsive Pedagogy
1. Critical hermeneutics (the study of interpretation)
2. Critical pedagogy
3. Community Cultural Wealth
4. Culturally Relevant Pedagogy

A Few Important Building Blocks of ESP / CxRxPx (continued)

The Ethnic Studies Framework's Double Helix and CRP-X

1. **Holistic Humanization**, respecting students as holistic beings: intellectual, emotional, physical, spiritual, relational; terrestrial, cosmic, spatial; intergenerational, temporal, hxrstorical; intersectional; multidimensional; community cultural wealth based; ecological; beings with identities and (counter) stories to share.

2. **Critical Consciousness**, standing against dehumanization; identifying origins of knowledge; critiquing the "master narrative" and claims of objectivity/neutrality (including "color-blindness") and highlighting marginalized worldviews; addressing cultural-hxrstorical, sociopolitical, economic, and moral levels of analysis; naming and confronting systems of intersectional power, privilege, and oppression; interrogating ideological, institutional, interpersonal, and internalized levels of privilege and oppression; understanding geo-hxrstorical literacy and causality; cultivating critical hope and self-determination; nurturing critical solidarities for past, present, and future generations.

3. Interwoven through 1 and 2, recognizing relationships to the four macrothemes of a) Dynamic Indigeneity, Diasporic Indigeneity, Ancestry, and Roots; b) Coloniality, Dehumanization, and Genocide; c) Hegemony and Normalization; d) Regeneration, Rehumanization, Decoloniality, Transformational Resistance, Social and Ecological Justice.

4. Interwoven through 1, 2, and 3: Student Responsive; Academically Responsive; Community Responsive; Globally Responsive

All together and more = ESP as CxRxPx

C: Culturally, community-based, critical, caring, compassionate, creative, contextual, conscious, competent;

R: Relevant, responsive, reaffirming, revitalizing, regenerating, remembering, revealing, restoring, realizing, roots, and racial identity development; reflectively, reflexively, rigorously, resistantly, reclaiming, remixing, reimagining, repertoires, reciprocal, rehumanizing, relationships;

P: Pluraliterate, pluradiscursive, power-balancing, post+colonia!, people, planet, praxis, pedagogies.

Counter-Storytelling and Decolonial Pedagogy

The Xicanx Institute for Teaching and Organizing

BY ANITA E. FERNÁNDEZ

> *They tried to bury us.*
> *They didn't know we were seeds.*
> —Mexican proverb

After seven years of students, teachers, and activists battling for Mexican American Studies (MAS) in Tucson, Arizona, the trial arguing whether the anti–Ethnic Studies law, HB 2281 (now ARS 15-112), and the actions of the state of Arizona violated the Equal Protection and First Amendment rights of the Tucson Unified School District's Mexican American students took place during the sweltering summer of 2017. Much like the 9th Circuit Court of Appeals hearing held two and a half years earlier, this formal marker in the timeline of the movement highlighted the trauma inflicted on both my colleagues and our community, as well as the resilience and pure *fuerza* of our people. I watched and listened in the courtroom as Chicanx scholar after scholar skillfully educated the court on the pedagogy, philosophy, history, research, and methods of the highly acclaimed Tucson MAS program. I also watched and listened as the state's attorneys and their witnesses, in particular the two former Arizona superintendents of instruction, John Huppenthal and Tom Horne, belittled and degraded the program and Mexican Americans in general. At one point, Huppenthal's infamous blog post, "MAS=KKK in a Different Color," was brought up in testimony. Huppenthal did not apologize for the comment and went on to elaborate on his war with MAS:

> Plaintiff Attorney: But in fact, Mr. Huppenthal, you said your war with MAS was a battle that never ends, right? Right?

> Huppenthal: It's eternal. It goes back to the plains of the Serengeti, you know, when we were evolving as a human race, the battle between the forces of collectivism and individualism. It defines us as a human race.

The state of Arizona's "eternal war" with MAS finally had its day in court. After the trial, as we debriefed the experience of testifying and witnessing testimony, everyone expressed the physical and emotional toll this experience had taken, a repetition of what had transpired so many times before and during this movement. There was a visceral feeling of being dehumanized by having to even testify that Mexican American history and culture are appropriate to teach in public schools. As I write this chapter with an emphasis on counter-stories as a methodology for teaching Ethnic Studies, I'm struck by the fact that we are, in essence, a counter-story. If a counter-story is technically an alternative or opposing narrative or explanation, the MAS program is a counter-story, and the urban education institute we developed after the dismantling of the program, the Xicanx Institute for Teaching and Organizing (XITO), is also a counter-story.

XITO Carrying on the Legacy of MAS

Our collective, made up of four of the MAS teachers and myself, made a conscious decision to carry on the work they had developed and that had been researched and proven to be highly successful with youth of color and countered the statistics nationally seen in public education. While our collective could not continue the work in Arizona (where the state had banned the program), we created professional development training that focused on supporting teachers and organizers to become critically conscious, culturally responsive and rehumanizing, and community-responsive practitioners across the country. We define those terms as such:

Critically conscious: Critically conscious teachers and organizers aim to understand the necessary links among pedagogical practice, power relations, and the lived experiences of teachers, parents, administrators, organizers, and the community. Critical is an essential element in the process of developing analyses of social injustices in our world and building toward the transformation of such practices with emphasis on human dignity and equality.

Culturally responsive and rehumanizing: In public schools, curriculum plays as important of a role as pedagogy. Multicultural and culturally responsive education and curriculum that embraces themes of social justice, youth empowerment, and emancipation from the social reproductive aspects of education that lead to disengagement and failure can be pivotal in students acquiring a sense of self. For generations, the Eurocentric curriculum of American public schools fostered a sense of alienation and inadequacy for students of color that was often reflected in low achievement, disengagement, and abandonment of their scholastic career before graduation. Critically responsive education that is oriented around a framework of social action and transformation can be used as a corrective to low academic results and reverse the trend for students to drop out or feel pushed out of the public school system.

Community responsive: Community responsiveness is a sociopolitical-cultural framework that encourages the local community to implement their vision of social justice. Community responsiveness is critical to ensuring that the individuals most impacted by specific policies, systems, and structures are the ones organizing and determining the response for the larger community.

We quickly discovered that while Arizona would not support these practices, other states were asking for more training in the area of Ethnic Stud-

ies. XITO is a grassroots, urban education consulting collective developed to carry on the legacy of Tucson's Mexican American Studies program after it was banned in 2012. This decolonial project, consciously built as a direct form of resistance and liberation, offers professional development to schools across the country in the rehumanizing Ethnic Studies pedagogy that was researched and proven to flip the "achievement gap" in Tucson Unified School District. XITO is a counter-story to mainstream professional development, counter to the deficit ideologies held by many educators and administrators, and counter to assumptions of what constitutes "legitimate" knowledge and learning. As a decolonial project, XITO seeks to create new structures rather than reforming old ones, starting with integrating decolonial pedagogies into the K–12 classroom.

One specific methodology we use when training teachers in rehumanizing and Ethnic Studies pedagogy, and also in our own high school classrooms, is the use of counter-stories or counter-narratives. Counter-storytelling stems from critical race theory (CRT) and offers students exposure to stories of the lived experiences of minoritized people rather than the pervasive master narrative. Counter-storytelling is one way to "read the world" (Freire, 1970) through telling stories that require a critical consciousness and critique of stories that are seen as "truth" and historically accurate. At all grade levels, counter-storytelling allows students to see themselves, their histories, their ancestry, and their identity as an integral part of the historical narrative.

Decolonial Pedagogies in the High School Classroom

Decolonial pedagogies, and specifically counter-storytelling, recognize oppression in its multiple forms and then takes action in the classroom to interrupt the cycles of oppression. How do we do this as high school teachers? One example is using a powerful visual or auditory prompt for students to analyze while considering the question "How is the past alive in the present?" My high school students, whom I had the privilege of teaching while also teaching at the undergraduate level, considered this question in connection with three powerful images.

The first task my students engaged in was to

dialogue about the connections between several images: The first is a Theodor de Bry engraving depicting Indigenous people being attacked by dogs in the 1500s at the hands of Spanish conquistadores; we then contrast this image with a photograph by Tomas Alejo from the 2017 Standing Rock protests where Indigenous people were attacked by dogs from a private security firm. In both instances, my students noticed, a similar strategy (attack dogs) is being unleashed for the same purpose, which was and still is the accumulation of land and resources. The third image—a 1963 photograph of Birmingham, Alabama, police using attack dogs on Black youth protesting for civil rights—demonstrates the same strategy being used by the same system (law enforcement) on another group of oppressed people to prevent their rights from being expressed and discriminatory laws from being questioned and overturned. Students connected this specific strategy to the question "How is the past alive in the present?" with critical, analytical observations. After much discussion, students reframed the question to "How is colonization still alive in the present?" Students also focused on the concept of dehumanization, as we had previously brainstormed examples of humanizing versus dehumanizing practices both current and in the past. They commented on how this is obviously a dehumanizing practice and that the repetition of the same practice being inflicted on the same group of people hundreds of years later must also have an impact on a group's consciousness.

After students recognize this painful cycle of oppression, part of working to interrupt that cycle is the awareness that it still presently exists. Presenting counter-stories to the mainstream history texts we are assigned allows students to begin the process of disrupting the status quo narrative they are traditionally taught. Interrupting the cycle of oppression also takes place by developing a humanizing approach to teaching and learning that centers the curriculum on the lives of our students and offers them the tools to begin to dismantle systems created to oppress specific groups and communities. Part of this dismantling process is unpacking examples of cultural resilience to highlight the counter-story of specific groups' strengths, which is critical in an Ethnic Studies curriculum.

An extension of this lesson led to readings on the effects of colonization, specifically the concept of a colonized mind. Students were introduced to Frantz Fanon's conception of a colonized mind, and from that we used the definition used in our XITO workshops: "A colonized mind is a form of conceptual incarceration that is a by-product of deculturalization." We unpacked "conceptual incarceration" and how we individually, and as a collective, suffer from conceptual incarceration. With Fanon's definition in mind, students brainstormed examples of a colonized mind-set and then how to begin the process of decolonizing our minds. My colleague Jose Gonzalez presents this framework beautifully using Paulo Freire's levels of consciousness and asking students to identify specific readings or videos and naming which level of consciousness (naive, magical, or critical) is being demonstrated (see "Teaching Freire's Levels of Consciousness," p. 275). These types of exercises allow students to begin to name how and why we think the way we do with the end goal of developing a critical consciousness with which to view the world and to move ourselves and our communities toward liberation.

Another powerful counter-story prompt I've used with my students and with practicing teachers is the music video for "Strawberry Fields Forever" by La Santa Cecilia (available on YouTube). In this animated film, a counter-story to the Beatles' "Strawberry Fields Forever" is told through the eyes of a migrant farmworker who picks strawberries. The video begins with the end product, a strawberry on a cake, and works backward to unpack how that strawberry arrived in the grocery store and into someone's home. Throughout the video, La Santa Cecilia's rendition of "Strawberry Fields Forever" mixes Cumbia and Norteño influences with a familiar beat led with the accordion. Along with the animated story, the music itself counters the traditional version of this song.

For this prompt, I ask students to look for visual images that tell a counter-story, and practicing teachers are encouraged to think of a unit or guiding question this video could help to kick off. Students immediately comment on the structure of the story, end to beginning, as a form of counter-storytelling, as well as the conditions under which farmworkers produce the delicious produce we consume often without consideration of the work, exposure to pesticides, labor conditions, etc. that went into this product. This story is not usually told and it provides a lens into one very familiar to many of our students whose families themselves are migrant farmworkers.

Teachers have come up with a number of uses for this video as a kickoff for a unit, from a kindergarten teacher developing a unit titled "Where Does

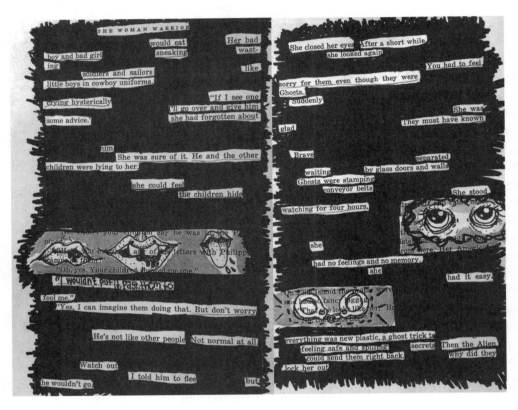

My Food Come From?" to an Ethnic Studies high school teacher focusing on the farmworker movement and the current impact of immigration policies on U.S. production of food. Using counter-stories in an Ethnic Studies classroom allows students to not only hear and experience stories that reflect students' lives, but can also provide students an opportunity to document their own experiences. In addition, these topics open up opportunities for action projects, participatory action research, and student activism. One strategy I've applied in the high school classroom to encourage students to "talk back" to a text so they can document their own analyses or perspectives is using blackout poetry. Using this process specifically

to encourage a counter-narrative to a text allows students to read closely and then focus on specific words or phrases that capture a narrative or theme they'd like to highlight or retell. Blackout poetry, or the literal "blacking out" of text on a page to allow for other text to emerge, can also be used as an introduction to counter-stories in general or the topic of counter-storytelling and CRT. In one instance, my student chose to black out a page from Amy Tan's *Woman Warrior*, creating not only a counter-narrative but also counter images, integrating illustration into the blackout prose.

Imagery and art always seem to capture students' interests and attention, leading me to a final example of counter-story practices developed by my colleagues in Los Angeles, the Xicanx Pop-Up Book Movement (XPUB). XPUB is an allegory for the banning of books in Tucson Unified School District, as well as the burning of the Mayan codices in the 1500s. XPUB's tagline—"You can ban Chicano books, but they'll still POP UP!"—is a literal and figurative statement as their movement developed a curriculum for creating pop-up books that tell counter-narratives to traditional literature and history texts. In this curriculum, students research and analyze specific movements or novels not usually covered in mainstream curriculum and then develop an artistic rendition that "pops up" with a pop-up book. Topics might include the Black Panther Movement, the Chicano Moratorium, Standing Rock, Black and Brown Unity, *The House on Mango Street*, Dolores Huerta and the farmworker's movement, or thematic pop-up books on oppression, resilience, developing consciousness, or a colonial mind-set. These counter-stories give students an opportunity to use a variety of skills, including research techniques, critical analysis, writing strategies, art integration, and finally presentation skills, when they share their final products.

La Voluntad

All of these strategies for integrating counter-stories into Ethnic Studies classes support the tenets of an Ethnic Studies curriculum to develop critical literacies and skills that let youth of color articulate, address, and act upon issues facing their communities so as to improve the conditions of their communities (Arce, 2017). The action component to these processes is crucial for students to engage with their communities in a positive and productive manner that encourages a focus on cultural resilience. In the former MAS program, and now in XITO, the Mexican element of *Huitzilopochtli* encompasses this will to act—*la voluntad*. In our work through XITO, we refer to these practices as decolonial barrio pedagogies, which counter deficit ideologies and encourage rehumanizing, anticolonial practices.

By framing XITO's work with a decolonial lens, our collective seeks to highlight the need for educational praxis to be rooted in local struggles that connect to national and global histories. In our case, the battle for Mexican American Studies locally in Tucson has had a national impact on the creation and implementation of Ethnic Studies programs around the country. As we awaited the verdict on the trial deciding whether the Arizona anti–Ethnic Studies bill was written with racial animus, our students' and teachers' First Amendment rights to teach and learn about our *cultura* were literally on trial. Our decolonial framework seeks to name the world and the sociopolitical, economic, and racial policies and processes that have impacted our movement as a way to engage in praxis to begin to rethink our educational systems and dismantle these practices that dehumanize our youth and communities.

Counter-storytelling is one decolonial method of reframing and rewriting history to authentically represent our students. Counter-storytelling is also a praxis of critical consciousness that supports students to read their world and critique, analyze, and change the social conditions under which they live. This process of retelling and disrupting the status quo often becomes so threatening to the stakeholders

of white supremacy that we hope the lessons we've learned in Tucson can support Ethnic Studies educators across the country when they come under attack. Our decolonial barrio pedagogies and frameworks have worked in our community and we encourage teachers to build off of our work to develop their own decolonial frames and pedagogies.

The experience of being in court and witnessing the trial for Mexican American Studies highlighted for me that we are rewriting histories, even in the most dehumanizing spaces, by redefining whose knowledge is legitimate and who are the holders of that knowledge. Each witness who testified for the plaintiff's side was Raza, and while the state grilled each witness and tried incessantly to delegitimize every one of them, our ancestors spoke through them with *confianza*, challenging dominant narratives and reclaiming our positions in the historical narrative.

On Tuesday, August 22, 2017, Judge Tashima issued his ruling on the Mexican American Studies case, finding that "The court is convinced that decisions regarding the MAS program were motivated by a desire to advance a political agenda by capitalizing on race-based fears" (*González v. Douglas*). This landmark civil rights case sets national legal precedence and will support future Ethnic Studies programs as well as First Amendment rights in education. This is a major step in the process of decolonizing educational spaces and dismantling colonial structures and policies in our public schools. ✳

REFERENCES

Arce, Sean. 2017. "Chicano and Latino Studies Should Be Mandatory in Schools." In Rodolfo F. Acuña (Ed.), *U.S. Latino Issues, 2nd Edition*. (86–89). Praeger.

Freire, Paulo. 1970. *Pedagogy of the Oppressed*. Herder & Herder.

González v. Douglas, 2017. United States District Court of Arizona.

The Matrix of Social Identity and Intersectional Power

A Classroom Resource

BY R. TOLTEKA CUAUHTIN

The Matrix of Social Identity and Intersectional Power visual and accompanying chart, which I originally based upon the Flower of Identity and Filter of Oppression published in Rethinking Schools' *Open Minds to Equality*, breaks down eight levels of social identity across 29 intersections. When developing it and collaborating with my colleague and talented graphic designer Steven Acevedo, we imagined this tool not only serving a purpose in Ethnic Studies classes at our school but also envisioned it assisting and facilitating pedagogy on these topics for teachers, professors, and students in many more classrooms at high school and university levels. A summary of the tool, accompanying guiding questions, and student handouts are provided here.

Ethnic Studies programs work to understand and analyze intersectional identity, relationships, and dynamics of power in order to resist oppression and help actively change the world for the better. While the curricular time needed to go in-depth into this matrix of social identity could easily go beyond a unit, semester, or even a school year, it may also be summarily introduced and referenced when directly applicable throughout a course or program and subsequently used as a foundational reference tool/framework for these higher levels of theory.

Following are a few guiding questions I developed to help educators and students better understand the matrix. The first eight questions are intended to explain the visual and how to read it. The questions relate to all interlocking intersections, but you can also zoom in on specific intersections of focus—for example, race, gender expression, nationality/"citizenship," survivor status, age, or even spe-cies. Question number 9 is the first question to really address personal positionality/reflexivity, which is a core purpose of this tool and can be the focus of autoethnographic assignments—some of the most transformational projects students may engage in to better understand their relationships to identity, space-time, society, and power.

1. What are the multiplicities and intersections of social identities we have as human beings?

2. Who are the Dominant/Hegemonic/Privileged Identities at each intersection?

3. What are the forms of discrimination present at each intersection?

4. Who are the Oppressed/Marginalized/Nonprivileged Identities at each intersection?

5. What are the Definitive Marginalizations at each intersection?

6. What are the Internalized Oppressions at each intersection?

7. What are the Transformational Resistances, Critical Hopes, and Elements of Social Justice at each intersection?

8. What are Hegemonic, Societal, and Institutional Structures, Systems, Oppressions, and Effects at each intersection?

9. What are your positionalities, your intersectional standpoints? In what ways are you privileged and oppressed? What are you doing about it?

10. Are there certain intersections that affect dynamics of power on a larger and/or stronger scale in society? How can we ask and respond to this question and not allow the injustices of "oppression Olympics," "horizontal oppression," and "suboppression/subhegemony" to manifest themselves in the process?

11. Considering this matrix, how does it all relate to each other? What can we do now to transformationally resist injustice in our communities, nationally, and throughout the world for past, present, and future generations?

12. Do you see anything missing here? What is fixed and what is fluid? What would you like to edit/change in your version of the Matrix of Social Identity and Intersectional Power?

13. How can you put this tool into praxis in the classroom?

So, how does this even work and what does it help us explain?

The Breakdown of the Matrix of Social Identity and Intersectional Power

0. The center star is the matrix's subtitle, "Who Are We?" It is not numbered.

1. The first ring contains a multiplicity of identities we carry as human beings. Many identity charts or identity wheels stop here, on a somewhat superficial plane, noting different social identities but rendering any analysis of related dynamics of power invisible. This tool expands upon this basic approach on several necessary levels.

2. The second ring represents the privileged group at each intersection of identity.

3. The third ring (both concentric circles, considered 3a and 3b) represents forms of discrimination and

oppression that relate to each intersection—there is some overlap.

4. The fourth ring represents the oppressed, marginalized, nondominant target groups at each intersection.

5. The fifth ring represents "the definitive marginalized" (while always being cautious of the "oppression Olympics"). This ring notes the focal identities marginalized at each intersection, with group members who cannot "pass" as the dominant identity and whose characteristics correspond to often having to deal with the oppression in a more concentrated way than those who do not correspond to that identity as "definitively."

Many identity charts or identity wheels stop here, on a somewhat superficial plane, noting different social identities but rendering any analysis of related dynamics of power invisible.

6. The sixth ring represents the internalized levels of these oppressions, which relate to self-hatred and zoom in to the "definitive marginalized" of the group. For instance, internalized racism within a people of color group with darker skin colors being the target may be referred to as colorism. Also, the internalized forms of oppression cause oppressed peoples to want to conform to the dominant, hegemonic, oppressor group (the second ring), thus oppressing each other and causing suboppression/horizontal oppression/hegemony in the process. There is repetition here because certain internalizations (e.g., self-hate) are present across intersections.

7. The seventh ring represents the intersectional transformational resistances of how oppressed groups are critical of the oppression and motivated by social

justice. This ring is important for solidarities, or how oppressed peoples unite with each other across intersections and how privileged peoples from oppressor groups unite in solidarity with oppressed peoples to actively and transformationally resist hegemony and oppression. Certain general elements of resistance (e.g., love and dignity) also apply across intersections.

8. The eighth ring is on the outside because it works to

After the basics of the tool are understood, the matrix provides a helpful companion when students are doing autoethnographic projects, social analysis assignments, or applying their understandings in other creative endeavors.

house the matrix with its structure, regardless of the changes and strides for justice made. It works to absorb these moves toward justice in ways that it can "flip" or appropriate while continuing to maintain its hegemonic, societal, and institutional structures, systems, oppressions, and its effects at various levels.

This theoretical and curricular tool responds to several parts of the Ethnic Studies Framework (see p. 65), including respecting students as holistic human beings as well as developing critical consciousness and addressing intersectionality, dynamics of power, privilege, oppression, and solidarity.

As a teacher in the classroom, I've had students use colored pencils to shade in whichever intersectional social identity and its dynamics of power are addressed in class. At times, we also read and annotate a handout that explains how the tool works (usually just a one-page handout version of nos. 0 through 8 as listed in the breakdown found above and on p. 39). For students to demonstrate their understanding in

an engaging way, after modeling an example myself, I've had students in small groups come up with basic questions for other groups, who then have a timed countdown to show their answers on mini-whiteboards when time is called. The student group who came up with the question then chooses a group to share and explain their answers to the whole class. An example of a student-created question for this group activity might be: "For the social identity element of education level, who are the marginalized group?" Questions may also increase in difficulty, such as "What are the institutional hegemonic structures at the intersection of race, gender, and class?"

In a different activity, when an intersection is addressed, students may complete the corresponding cells on the accompanying chart ("My Intersectional and Multiple Identities and Their Relationships to Power") by shading or circling their standpoint/location at that particular intersection, which can help them on their paths of understanding this theory in a very personal way. It is important to note that at certain intersections, students may have hybrid/mixed identities, be in the "borderlands," in-between identities, or even "pass" as a dominant identity though they themselves may actually identify as a marginalized identity at that intersection; those who can "pass" carry more privilege in that sense than those who cannot. After the basics of the tool are understood, the matrix provides a helpful companion when students are doing autoethnographic projects, social-analysis assignments, or applying their understandings in other creative endeavors.

When students are familiarized with a deeper understanding of social identity and intersectional dynamics of power with a tool such as this, a variety of pedagogical approaches can be fruitful in relation to it for further shared inquiries, dialogues, discussions, reflections, creations, and actions.

A blank version of the matrix of intersectional social identity can be used for those who prefer a pedagogy where students fill in the text themselves or who wish to adapt the resource further for their own needs. When a simpler version of the matrix is necessary, and especially for younger grade levels, I highly recommend the Flower of Identity and Filter of Oppression from Rethinking Schools' *Open Minds to Equality*.

Included here are two poems by Vanessa Villaseñor, an 11th grader at Social Justice Humanitas Academy who wrote them in 2015. Inspired by her study of the matrix of social identity, she wrote the first, simply titled "Intersectionality," which was later presented on PBS; at California State University, Northridge; and at the Central Library in downtown Los Angeles. It started in our Poetic Justice class; I offered students an assignment where the goal was to distribute teacher leadership among students, who would teach each other Ethnic Studies vocabulary through poetry and then create and perform a poem for each vocabulary term.

As students were working with different Ethnic Studies concepts and academic language, I offered scaffolds and helpful tools as necessary—both general guidance and more particular assistance that focused on scaffolding certain terms. When it came to Vanessa and her focal term *intersectionality*, I reflected and thought of how useful this curricular tool may be for it. I explained how the matrix of social identity works, what the different layers represent, gave her space to ask any clarifying questions (even through the process of drafting of her poem), and emphasized she could utilize whatever parts of it that were helpful to her process. Connecting this resource with content we had previously experienced in class, her prior knowledge, and events that were happening at the time (and continue to in different ways), she created her poem "Intersectionality," included below. Immersed in spoken word and inspired after reading bell hooks' "Understanding Patriarchy," Vanessa penned a second poem, also presented here. She zooms in on that intersection through her poetic expression in "A Poetic Letter to Patriarchy." Vanessa's poems are found here on p. 43.

Vanessa went from a quiet student to being proud of her voice and story when encouraged to write and share her poetry in relation to our course and her own life as part of her path of healing. She shared with me how this theoretical tool helped her better understand intersectionality and articulated that understanding and language into praxis. For further poetry and reflection, I would encourage her to go deeper into how the intersections relate to each other and perhaps in response to her concluding line, ask the questions "Is the blame all on the patriarchy, or do white supremacist, capitalist, hetero-sexist, xenophobic, ableist, ageist anthropocentrism also have a lot to do with it, and what are our roles in the complicity of all of it? How do we best move forward?" And of course, she may respond, "Yeah, but this poem is about gender justice and that's about combating gender injustice, which we do have patriarchy to blame for, so we move forward by stopping the patriarchy and toxic masculinity that goes along with it!" Good point.

Vanessa's work is one example of how the matrix of social identity and intersectional dynamics of power can be tapped into to help generate creative and analytical student work for purposes of inter-sectional social justice, in Ethnic Studies courses and beyond.

Lastly, gratitude and respect are due to the mandalas, tonalmachiotls, and tzolkins worldwide which provide inspiration for the design of this curricular and pedagogical tool. ✳

The Matrix of Social Identity & Intersectional Power

Who am I?
Who are you?
Who are we?
Who decides?

Hybridities,
Borderlands, &
"Passing"
May Apply

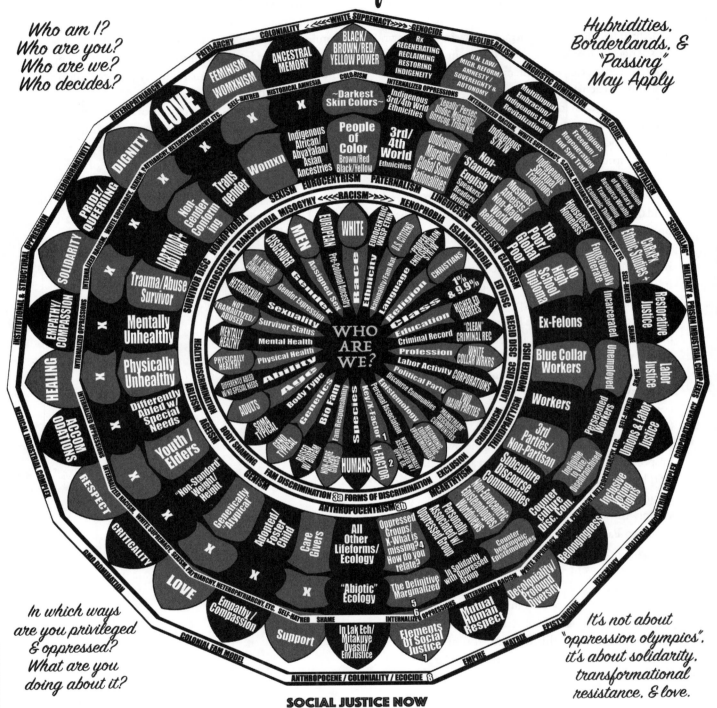

In which ways
are you privileged
& oppressed?
What are you
doing about it?

It's not about
"oppression olympics",
it's about solidarity,
transformational
resistance, & love.

SOCIAL JUSTICE NOW

Key: 1. Social Identities   2. Dominant/Hegemonic/Privileged Identities   3a/3b: Forms of Discrimination/Oppression
4. Oppressed/Marginalized/Non-Privileged Identities   5. "Definitive Marginalizations"   6. Internalized Oppressions
7. Transformational Resistances, Healing, Critical Hopes, & Elements of Social Justice
8. Hegemonic Societal & Institutional Structures, Systems, Oppressions, & Effects

Theory/framing by R. Tolteka Cuauhtin. Graphic design by Steven Krieg Acevedo. Inspired by Rethinking Schools' Open Minds to Equality + Rx.
With gratitude and respect to mandalas, tonalmachiotls, and tzolkins worldwide. **Printable version: b.link/drive48**

INTERSECTIONALITY
by Vanessa Villaseñor

Intersectionality
that goes from
ethnicity
Ability
Age
Race
Gender
Sexuality
And we can go on
and on and on and on
For we are all different
but those differences can either make our lives great
or make us wish we had a different fate
Intersectionality
you see when you grow up you have to face reality
people will treat you different by the way you express yourself and who you are
and that is
Intersectionality
White
straight
cis male
will never understand the loneliness and isolation from society
because he is not a black transgender woman getting beaten to death inside a dark alley
Intersectionality
because sadly we live in a world where we have to create awareness that's #BLACKLIVESMATTER
and it's even worse because white people have to audacity to response after
coming back with #ALLLIVESMATTER
and won't accept the police brutality
Intersectionality
Men can go out and be as free as they want and become each other's wingman
but i can't do that without being called a slut just because i am a womxn.
You see i can't walk alone at night
without being afraid that i won't be alright
Womxn are being raped and they are the ones still getting blamed
"what were you wearing?" "why were you alone?"
"it's your fault for walking alone to get home."
Intersectionality
because the action of one minority speaks for everybody
Islamophobia is sadly a thing
because people saw in the news a bombing in the buildings
we still have yet to recover from 9/11
because we still have hate crimes towards Muslims from all the aggression
Don't you understand all the oppression?
We are all different from

social class
language
religion
education
i.d by association
and let's not forget nationality
and that is
Intersectionality.

A POETIC LETTER TO PATRIARCHY
by Vanessa Villaseñor

Patriarchy
a system of society or government in which the father or eldest male is head of the family and descent is traced through the male line.
Patriarchy
a system of society or government in which men hold the power and womxn are largely excluded from it.
Patriarchy
a society or community organized on patriarchal lines.
It's amazing how society was able to maintain between these lines from time to time
When you are born a girl society gives you a set of rules you must follow
Or else who's gonna bother
You have to learn from a young age how to clean and cook
That way in the distant future a man will look
You have to dress all nice and pretty
And when you are old enough you'll have your makeup ready
And maybe you'll find a man and start going steady
Because apparently that's all we are here for
The attention of men is our goal
And that is what i was taught growing up as a girl
But that's not all
there is so much more
You see within these rules are more rules
Not only must you look pretty you also have to act like a lady
Which means
No burping
No spitting
You make sure you do your own cleaning
Don't speak your mind about things and throw a fit
Because that just makes you look like a total bitch
Don't question the power of men
Because they are the ones who are dominant
Now let's go a little deeper
Because it's time to get a little personal
You see when i was a little girl

I didn't like dressing up in "girl" clothes
And because of that my mom would get upset
But she picked out my "cute perky pink outfits" anyways
Now in school it was a different story
All the girls hated me because i didn't like barbies and ponies
And all the boys hated me because it was out of the ordinary
Then as i grew older
And went through puberty
There was a large amount of pressure on me
By society
On how to get the "Perfect" body
But since i didn't fit the criteria
And since i was taught from a young age that my goal is to get a man to look my way
It put me in a bad mental state
Now i'm going left and right
Trying to find anything to help me turn out alright
And it took up everything in me
To the point where i just gave up
And since then my life went downhill
But i won't get into detail
But it's ok because of certain people
I got the help that i needed
And no my confidence isn't back up there
But it's enough to give me a breath of fresh air
And made me realize the truth
That what society has done to me isn't cool, not a bit
And i know i'm not the only one who goes through this
And i blame Patriarchy for all of it.

My Intersectional and Multiple Identities and Their Relationships to Power
Who am I as an intersectional human being?

To the extent possible and that applies to you: 1. Highlight, shade, or circle the group(s) that signify your own identity (e.g., whether you are privileged or oppressed) in that element of identity.
2. Take it further by highlighting/shading additional columns if you think they apply to you (for instance, which forms of resistance do you participate in?).
3. Use for hxrstorical or contemporary figures beyond yourself. 4. Use as a quick reference for the Matrix of Social Identity. Fluid/blank/editable chart can be found at goo.gl/1y4Yib.

Social Identity	Privileged / Hegemonic Group(s)	Form of Discrimination / Oppression	Oppressed / Marginalized Groups	Internalized Oppressions	Forms of Resistance	Institutional / Structural Oppressions
1. Precolonial Continental Ancestry	European ancestries	Eurocentrism	American Indian; African; Asian; Oceanic Ancestries	Internalized Eurocentrism; historical amnesia	Ancestral memory	Coloniality's hegemonic matrix
2. Race	White	Racism	People of Color: "Black, Red, Brown, Yellow"	Colorism; internalized racism	People of Color Power; anti-racism	White supremacy
3. Ethnicity	European WASP ethnicities	Ethnocentrism; paternalism	Third/Fourth World ethnicities	Internalized Eurocentrism; historical amnesia	Regenerating, reclaiming, and restoring roots	Genocide; ethnocide; culturcide
4a. Nationality / "Citizenship"	U.S. / "First World" citizens	Chauvinism	Undocumented migrants; Global South nationalities	Internalized chauvinism as less than the dominant	U.N. law; migration reform; asylum; amnesty; sovereignty	Neoliberalism; neocolonialism
4b. Familial National Origin	"First World" / U.S. / Western European	Xenophobia	Undocumented migrants; Global South nationalities	Internalized xenophobia; assimilation above all	Connectedness to family's national cultural origins	Neoliberalism; Eurocentrism
5. Language	"Proper" English speakers, readers, writers	Linguicism	"Nonstandard" English speakers, readers, writers	Internalized linguicism; self-hatred	Multilingual embracing; Indigenous language revitalization	Linguicide; linguistic domination
6. Religion	Christians	Creedism; Islamophobia; anti-Semitism	Muslims; Jews; non-major world religions; atheists; Indigenous spiritual traditions	Internalized creedism or specific religious oppression	Religious freedom; regenerating Indigenous spiritual traditions	Theocide
7. Class	The richest 1 percent; the 9.9 percent, the global 1 percent	Classism	Socioeconomically disadvantaged; poor; global poor; houseless, homeless	Internalized classism	Redistribution of wealth; shift in economic thinking	Capitalism; neoliberalism
8. Assigned Sex	Men	Toxic masculinity +	Womyn; intersexual people	Internalized patriarchy	Womanism; feminism	Patriarchy
9. Gender	Cisgender (males in particular)	Sexism + transphobia	Transgender people; (in particular womxn)	Internalized patriarchy	Gender justice; inclusion; love; integrity	Heteropatriarchy; cisnormativity
10. Gender Expression	Male/female gender-conforming	Misogyny + heteronormativity	Gender-nonconforming	Internalized patriarchy	Dignity	Heteropatriarchy; cisnormativity
11. Sexuality	Heterosexual	Heterosexim; homophobia	LGBTQIAP+	Internalized homophobia; self-hatred	Pride; queering;	Heteronormativity
12. Survivor Status	Not traumatized or abused	Survivor discrimination	Trauma / abuse survivor	Internalized guilt and unworthiness	Solidarity; trust; self-worth	Culture of silence

13. Mental Health	Mentally healthy	Health discrimination	Mentally unhealthy	Shame	Empathy; compassion	Medical industrial complex
14. Physical Health	Physically healthy	Health discrimination	Physically unhealthy	Self-hatred	Healing	Medical industrial complex
15. Ability	Able-bodied; differently abled without special needs	Ableism	Disabled; differently abled with special needs	Internalized ableism	Accommodations; modifications	Medical and institutional industrial complexes
16. Age	Adults	Ageism	Youth; elders	Internalized ageism	Mutual human respect	Generational isolation
17. Body Type	Body "typical"	Body shaming	"Atypical" weight, height	Self-hatred	Acceptance; self-love	Eurocentric beauty standard
18. Genetics	Genotypical	Genism	Genetically "atypical"	Shame	Humane genetic literacy	Neo-eugenics
19. Bio Family	Raised with both bio parents	Fam. discrimination	Single parent; adopted; foster children	"Non-real" family member	Empathy; compassion; love	Colonial family models
20. Family Responsibility	Non-Caregivers	Family discrimination	Caregivers	Guilt for caretaking	Support	Colonial family models
21. Species	Human beings; homo sapien sapiens	Anthropocentrism	All other lifeforms/ecology; abiotic ecology	NA	Environmental justice; In Lak Ech; Mitakuye Oyasin	Anthropocene; coloniality; ecocide
22. Personal Association	Not personally associated with oppressed groups	McCarthyism	Personally associated with oppressed groups	Self-traitor	Mutual human respect; solidarity	Empire
23. Epistemology	Hegemonic Eurocentric epistemologies	Exclusion	Non-Eurocentric epistemologies and worldviews	Internalized hegemonic Eurocentric thinking	Decoloniality; profound diversity	Epistemicide
24. Discourse Communities	"Mainstream" discourse communities	Mainstream as the only stream	Subculture discourse communities	Internalized "normality"	Belongingness	Hegemony
25. Political Party	Two major parties	Third partyism	Third parties; nonpartisan; ineligible; disenfranchised	Disengagement; "My vote doesn't matter"	SJ-based third-party wins; inclusive voting rights	Political industrial complex
26. Labor Activity	Corporations	Labor discrimination	Workers	Internalized classism	Unionization	Corporatocracy
27. Profession	Owners; white-collar workers	Worker discrimination	Blue-collar workers; unemployed	Internalized classism	Labor justice	Corporatocracy
28. Criminal Record	"Clean" criminal record	Recidivist discrimination	Criminal record; ex-felons; incarcerated	Internalized recidivist mind-set	Restorative justice	Prison industrial complex; school-to-prison pipeline
29. Education	Higher-education degrees	Education discrimination	No high school diploma; illiterate in "Western" sense	Internalized deficit thinking	CxRxPx; Ethnic Studies; healing the education debt	"Schooling"; the education debt; education industrial complex

There is considerable overlap, fluidity, interchangeability between several of the cells in the matrix, represented by having dotted rather than solid lines. Chart by R. Tolteka Cuauhtin.

Creating We Schools:
Lessons Learned from Critically Compassionate Intellectualism and the Social Justice Education Project

BY AUGUSTINE ROMERO AND JULIO CAMMAROTA

We gon' speak for ourselves
Knowhatimsayin? Cuz see the schools ain't teachin'
    us nothin'
They ain't teachin' us nothin' but how to be slaves
    and hard workers
For white people to build up they shit
Make they businesses successful while it's exploitin' us
Knowhatimsayin? And they ain't teachin' us
    nothin' related to
Solvin' our own problems, knowhatimsayin?
Ain't teachin' us how to get crack out the ghetto
They ain't teachin' us how to stop the police from
    murdering us
And brutalizing us, they ain't teachin' us how to
    get our rent paid
Knowhatimsayin? They ain't teachin' our families
    how to interact
Better with each other, knowhatimsayin? They
    just teachin' us
How to build they shit up, knowhatimsayin?
    That's why my n----s
Got a problem with this shit, that's why n----s be
    droppin' out that
Shit cuz it don't relate, you go to school the fuckin'
    police
Searchin' you, you walkin' in your shit like this a
    military compound
Knowhatimsayin? So school don't even relate to us
Until we have some shit where we control, fuck
    the school system
    —from "They Schools" by Dead Prez

The key lesson from the Dead Prez song "They Schools" is that we want to be a "We School" or "Our School." In We School, we love our students, we love our parents, and we love our community. In We School, we know They Schools: what they teach, how they teach, and how they historically and presently have been nonresponsive, exploitative, and abhorrent for the majority of our students. It is from this position that we recognize the insidious nature of They Schools. The historical and present-day intent of They Schools is not to intellectualize our students but rather to domesticate our students—domesticate as a matter of controlling our students for the benefit of the They School group. The goal of We Schools therefore was to bring about the critical consciousness of our students so that they could take action to better themselves, their schools, and their communities.

Teorías de la revolución educativa (revolutionary theories of education) was the focus of one of our (the authors) initial meetings. During this meeting, we discussed the topic of remediation/domestication of schooling that has been forced upon historically underserved students, especially those with great needs. We knew that the They School approach had served its purpose by marginalizing, othering, domesticating, subordinating, etc. our students, their parents, and their *antepasados* (ancestors). We realized that we needed to counter the They School approach with what we are calling We School, which focused on primarily Latinx students' intellectual needs and sociopolitical development by validating their experiences and capacities to co-construct knowledge.

The Social Justice Education Project (SJEP) was the We School we created with our students as part of the broader Mexican American and Raza Studies (MARS) program in Tucson Unified School District (TUSD). The SJEP centered on the development of a strong sense of identity, purpose, and hope as well as critical Ethnic Studies content, youth-led qualitative research, and action plans to rectify social problems in education. Our first cohort began in 2002 and consisted of approximately 17 high school students of color who were predominately Latinx with some Native American and African American youth. The overarching goal of the SJEP was to develop the critical consciousness of youth of color. We believed if we were successful at helping our students achieve critical consciousness, then other traditional benchmarks of academic achievements would be more attainable.

The issue of critical consciousness versus domesticated minds is one of the main reasons why the state of Arizona and its oppressive leadership felt it was necessary to eradicate the SJEP and the rest of the MARS courses. To be clear, the state and its They School leaders recognized that our students were becoming intellectuals who were developing a strong critical consciousness; and as a matter of being intellectualized and critically conscious, our students could not be domesticated. The SJEP's mission of critical racial literacy and our focus on the students' current experiences of social oppression—in particular the racism of power maintenance and how They Schools reproduce racial disparities—was the thorn that the state and its They School leaders could not live with. They realized that our students resisted domestication and would not serve their interests. Furthermore, the students/barrio intellectuals in our classes developed their voices and were unafraid to speak out against the oppression of the racial state. The state of Arizona, ultimately, was afraid of empowered, intellectualized, and engaged young people (primarily of color) challenging the oppressive system and They Schools.

We School meant that students would invest more of themselves into their education by guiding us (facilitators) to an approach that would meet their intellectual needs. This approach, critically compassionate intellectualism (CCI), emerged from our interactions with students and how they informed us about what was necessary for developing their own critical consciousness. Both the notions of intellectualism and critical consciousness were deepened by helping our students tri-dimensionalize their reality—an intellectual practice of creating a nexus between past, present, and future so that the merger of these different temporal realities leads to anti-oppression projects. We know the most relevant moment is the social moment, the present day—and what exists in the present day is the student and the attendant social context. How are we responsive to the needs of our students?

Critically Compassionate Intellectualism

The educational approach that we implemented in the SJEP was an amalgamation of different learning and teaching theories, and we were not sure how they all would come together or how effective they might be. We tried different approaches and came up with the CCI model through consistent feedback from our students about what was and was not effective.

Since Paulo Freire influenced much of our thinking about learning and teaching, we thought the foundation of the model should be based in *critical literacy*. Our objective for implementing critical literacy was to provide students with the opportunity to engage in the co-construction of knowledge, in which we (facilitators) were working together with them to share in the process of learning. Critical literacy refers to Freire's method for reading/learning words as a process to better understand the world in which one is situated. The process is what Freire calls "praxis"—critical reflection and action. The objective of praxis is to help those engaged in critical literacy see past ideological obfuscation and capture the root causes of oppression. Co-constructing knowledge is central to critical literacy and thus praxis, as nonoppressive relationships are necessary to challenge the domination that holds people in a subordinate/domesticated reality. Facilitators and students were both involved with teaching and learning so that dynamics in the classroom shifted to a more democratic structure. The initial move toward a democratic construction of knowledge was to have all of us (facilitators and students) read and study *Pedagogy of the Oppressed*. The intention here was to familiarize everyone with the ways that oppression limits intellectual potential and the role of domesticating education by perpetuating this oppression.

The problem-posing method was presented as an alternative to the domesticating standard of banking education. The facilitators gathered the students and had them restructure the learning environment into a circle format, where everyone, including the facilitators, was seated in a circle. Then we problem-posed the reading by asking the students if anything that they had read connected with their experiences. The response: blank stares and silence. This reaction from the students was not all that surprising given that most, if not all, had spent many years "learning" in a domesticated environment where it was never expected for them to share or express their ideas. For the most part, their colonized minds only allowed them to think of school as a place where they just absorb information and become indoctrinated to the They School belief of how we (the historically underserved) should exist in this world without responding to or questioning this indoctrination. We realized there needed to be significant unlearning of this colonization/domestication.

Moreover, a student told us after the silent circle/class that one reason for the lack of participation was that the students did not trust us. And why would they? They had seen a variety of different models come down the pike. Why would our version be any different? So we reflected on this feedback and realized we needed another layer for CCI. We (facilitators) had read the work of Nel Noddings and were particularly drawn to her assertion that authentic caring was vital for meeting the needs of the students and strengthening the relationship between students and facilitators. One thing we know from Lev Vygotsky is that strong social relationships within particular learning communities are key to a child's intellectual development. The assimilation model so often deployed for students of color negates the importance of their cultural values/practices for facilitating healthy, positive relationships. Our relationships with our students emerge from and through core cultural values/practices such as *confianza* (trust), *respeto* (respect), and *cariño* (caring). Without the cultural dimension, learning will be strained from a disconnection between teacher and student.

Critical literacy lacks the cultural dimension at least as it pertains to communities of color. Therefore, the additional layer of authentic caring would be articulated through a Latinx perspective that fosters a more humanistic, as opposed to instrumental, approach to learning. Although learning to promote intellectualism was a key focus, we decided to broaden our reach to include the students' full human experiences of hopes, dreams, feelings, emotions, fears, concerns, and joys. To highlight the students' humanity, we asked students to create "I Am" poems that express their experiences and identities at a deeper level. The facilitators also created and performed "I Am" poems to the entire class as a way to build confianza and demonstrate cariño. Standing up there reciting our poems made us appear vulnerable, multidimensional, and thus more human by sharing experiences that in many ways were similar to what some of the students were expressing. Although facilitators and students recognized generational differences, there were some experiential commonalities that brought us together. One commonality that immediately stood out is race/racism.

Another layer was therefore needed to construct a more solid and complete CCI model. This last layer, *social justice*, would indicate the focus of authentic caring by recognizing and understanding the students' social experiences. In particular, we would not only care about the general human experience but also focus our caring on the injustices young people encounter on a daily basis. We also would ensure they had the tools to identify and address these injustices. It was not enough to "know" but also to take action to overcome oppressive realities. This action would lead to bettering their circumstances, which in turn would affect their intellectual development. Once students accomplish some degree of social change, they realize they have the intellectualism and intelligence to make change happen. This realization is empowering! Knowing how to effect change leads to a heightened sense of students' self-transformational capacities and their abilities to impact social transformation and the lives of their *vecinos* (neighbors). At this point, the students achieve critical consciousness by understanding how root causes foster injustices that impact lived experiences. As we mentioned earlier, awareness is not enough, a critically conscious student looks to build from this awareness by taking action to challenge and thus transform oppressive realities of our world.

In summary, CCI is an amalgamation of different yet related theories of learning and teaching. We started with a critical literacy to engage both students and facilitators in the co-construction of knowledge. Co-constructing required a shift in dynamics between facilitators and students so that each takes up the roles of teacher and learner somewhat seamlessly. The shift would occur only if we (facilitators) placed the critical literacy in a context of authentic caring, in which we expressed genuine *compassion* for young people who encounter different and intersecting oppressions. To achieve a high level of intellectual praxis, students needed to participate in some form of social justice action. Their participation in social justice leads to a *critical consciousness* about the root causes of oppression and strategies to uproot them.

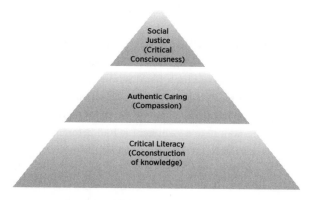

Critically Compassionate Intellectualism Model

The Social Justice Education Project

In the fall of 2002, after a significant amount of internal district battling, we implemented the SJEP in Tucson Unified schools. We hoped (and were correct) the SJEP pilot program would be the proving grounds for the development of an on-the-ground pedagogical and theoretical understanding of an educational paradigm that was effective for historically underserved Latinx students. This paradigm provided us with the educational, sociological, philosophical, and ideological trajectory and understanding that we would implement in order to facilitate the district mandate to alleviate the achievement gap for Latinx students.

The SJEP was housed within a MARS-sponsored social studies course at Cholla High School in Tucson, and with the support of Larry Lopez, we kicked off the program in August of 2002. Our approach to implementing the CCI model (co-construction, compassion, critical consciousness) was through a type of educational praxis—investigating a social problem at school and taking action to rectify this problem—called Youth Participatory Action Research (YPAR). It seemed as if YPAR was the best way for offering marginalized students the opportunity to experience and engage in praxis in their education. Since all the students in this first SJEP course were young people of color, we linked co-construction, compassion, and critical consciousness of CCI by establishing a critical race praxis in which they centered racism in their school-based inquiries.

By centering racism in the study of their educational experiences, we assumed the students would achieve two important goals. First, they would see how educational institutions, including their own school, are structured primarily by policies and practices embedded in racist ideologies. They could see how the education system intentionally marginalizes and ignores the needs and realities of historically underserved students. The notions of relevance and responsiveness are dedicated only to white students as a method of sociopolitical and economic control through the perpetuation of U.S. oppressive racial order. Second, recognizing the segregation in experiences, opportunities, expectations, and resources confirmed that "differences" in educational outcomes had little to do with intellectual deficiencies and more to do with the design and function of schools. In general, U.S. K–20 educational institutions have been constructed to enhance and perpetuate a tyrannical racial order. Most know that socialization into societal norms is a key purpose of schooling, yet few acknowledge that white oppression sits on top of the normative pyramid, so to speak, to reinforce the myth of minoritized students' racial inferiority. Once students realize the school's function is to preserve this myth, they stop blaming their failure on those things constructed and formalized by They Schoolers and shift their focus to socially constructed obstacles designed to make them feel and act inferior. This realization leads to accepting the fact that they are indeed intelligent and intellectuals.

Students acknowledging their intelligence and

intellect started to perform academically at a much higher level. Although there is some truth behind the importance of relevance, academic success emerged as a by-product of the students' engagement with critical race literacy. By reflecting on and then addressing racism in education, they could see the institutional mechanisms positioning them in

Many of our students developed the understanding that they can create all those things that have never been seen or realized. They come to understand that a dream can become reality in the blink of an eye or through a breath that delivers a single word.

the social hierarchy along with their potential to transform their own reality. Things were never quite the same after they analyzed racial tracking at their school and brought their analysis to teachers and administrators. The response to the students' recommendations was limited to infrastructural changes to the school, including the repair of bathroom toilets, fixing broken ceiling and floor tiles, and replenishing books in the library. Unfortunately, the long-term goal of disrupting racial tracks was never realized. Cholla and TUSD still track students into different "ability" levels. Nevertheless, the small changes and YPAR inquiry process were enough to empower SJEP students to see themselves differently—intelligent and possessing the potential to transform their own existence, community, and world around them.

SJEP Students and *The Matrix*: Understanding the True Context of Our World

Similar to what we have discussed above, the academic and personal transformation of SJEP students is fostered through CCI with the idea that they will become, as Antonio Gramsci termed it, organic intellectuals. In their arrival and in their pursuit of organic intellectualism, the tools and exercise of critical race praxis guided their self-transformational evolution.

In the second semester of the first year of the SJEP, one of our students, Tina Verdugo, came to us saying we were doing the "Matrix" with the class, referencing the 1999 film. The Matrix, or the analogy of a system generating a false reality, reveals the need to undertake a critical education that moves past lies to the truth about peoples' exploitation. In her explanation of the impact CCI had upon her, it is obvious that the academic identity and academic proficiency that was nurtured within Tina helped her in her development of her critical consciousness and her sense of organic intellectualism. Her organic intellectualism is evident by her desire to learn more and more as a means of advancing her community:

> The Project [CCI] helps us because we learned a new way of thinking. We took the pill [*laughs*]. Now we can't go back, but this is better because now we see the Matrix. They can't fool us. Sometimes it hurts more because we can see everything, well now we can fight it too. Before, we were fighting the wrong way. I love the project, it was great, and it helped me feel smarter and know that I could challenge the teachers, and the project gave the idea that I could help my community, and that is what I am going to do with my life.

The pill is a reference to *The Matrix* wherein Neo is asked to take a red or blue pill. If he takes the red pill, he will be able to see the world in its truest form; however, if he takes the blue, he will continue to see the world only as it has been constructed for him to see it. The facilitators found that this scene helped our students better understand the notion of a critical consciousness. Our students came to understand that if they took the pill of critical consciousness, they, like Neo taking the red pill, would be able to see the world in the most critical or truest form. However, if they did not take the pill of critical consciousness, they would remain in their naive or magical realties.

When the SJEP was created, the primary intent

was not to foster academic proficiency or an academic identity but rather to help students develop a critical consciousness, a sociocultural identity, a sense of purpose, and newfound sense of hope. Through this process, we would attempt to help the students develop a strong sense of organic intellectualism. We believed that through construction and reconstruction of consciousness and identity, our students would move themselves toward stronger academic identities and higher degrees of academic proficiency.

Very seldom, if ever, did we dialogue about doing better in this class, much less other classes. The same is true about the notion of academic identity; the dialogue regarding identity is that of the social, cultural, and historic self. In essence we discussed who the students are, where they come from, and what this means in the present-day context, as well as how this understanding could transform their lives and help them engage their epistemology today and transform the ontology they will carry into tomorrow. Equally important, many of our students developed the understanding that they can create all those things that have never been seen or realized. They come to understand that a dream can become reality in the blink of an eye or through a breath that delivers a single word. This evolution creates great happiness for us; in this evolution we are able to witness the blossoming of intellectualism and we are able to see and experience the fruit of what Edward Said refers to in *Representation of the Intellectual* as "a clerisy . . . since what they uphold are eternal standards of truth and justice that are precisely not of this world." We understand that in this state is the potential of untested feasibility or the truth or justice that may exist just beyond the walls of our consciousness.

They Schools to We Schools

Dead Prez's "They Schools" is a major resource for developing the CCI model. When people think about responsiveness, relevance, and equity in education, they need to give this narrative a deep and critical analysis. If we operate outside the needs and desires of our students as they exist in the social moment/the present/today, we are simply supplanting one form of hegemony for another. To be truly counter-hegemonic, our understandings, reflections, and actions must be based upon the needs and desires of our students as they are contextualized and revealed by them.

We School is the process by which we moved to educate, empower, and nurture the critical consciousness of our students. At the heart of We School is the notion of counter-domestication. What our students wanted and what We School calls for is an education that is real and both intellectualizing and action oriented, the true sense of praxis. We School brings to the center issues that are real, relevant, and in many cases even oppressive to our students. It is through this realization and process that students engage not only their educational but also their sociohistorical realities in the attempt to engage, understand, and overcome issues they face on a daily basis.

It is in the We School environment where students truly engage in an intellectual process, and it is in this environment where students engage in an educational experience that is real, relevant, and responsive to their needs. We School is devoted to a process that helps students question, name, engage, and in many cases overcome the issues that are most relevant in their lives.

In They Schools, they are offered a canon and pedagogy that at best ignores their realities and at worst holds their realities against them—their realities become the product by which they are labeled as inferior and our students are objectified as a means to exploitation. We School is the place wherein transformation can take place, a place where dreams are constructed. We School is the place where intellectualism and intellectuals are fostered. We School is the place where questions for answers are created, roots to the truth are explored, and hope is built. ✳

Six Reasons I Want My White Child to Take Ethnic Studies

BY JON GREENBERG

I'm very white, which makes me right at home as a public school teacher—a profession more than 80 percent white.

My wife is also white. So are our children. In fact, when one of our white friends (with whom I had never discussed race) met our first child, even she said, "Damn, that's one white baby."

And our children have been cashing in on their whiteness, romping around our white Seattle neighborhood—blending right in, oblivious to racial discrimination.

Because of these privileges, they will unlikely catch on anytime soon (at least not without conscientious parenting) that they are living during a movement for racial justice. And I don't mean the Black Lives Matter movement (at least not in this article).

No, I mean the movement to expand Ethnic Studies in our schools.

What is Ethnic Studies? Emerging out of the Civil Rights Movement and the concerns of students of color on college campuses throughout the United States, Ethnic Studies centers the curriculum—history, literature, perspectives—on people of color who have been historically marginalized and generally poorly represented in education.

In the recent student protests against racism on college campuses nationwide, Ethnic Studies is once again one of the top demands.

I know many white Americans also want racial justice, but the step that follows awareness always trips us up.

Even Macklemore, with two songs about white privilege, can't figure out a clear course. Should he march? Should he give his two cents? Should he rhyme "parka" with "parking lot"?

And activists agree that talking only gets us so far.

Well, here's a concrete step: Lobby your teachers, principals, school board members, and legislators to mandate Ethnic Studies!

These courses undeniably benefit students of color, who have been for too long poorly served by our public education system—benefits recently confirmed by Thomas Dee and Emily Penner of the Stanford Graduate School of Education. In fact, they were "shocked" by how effectively Ethnic Studies served struggling students in San Francisco, a district predominately composed of students of color.

Writing in a 2017 issue of the *American Educational Research Journal*, they said that "Attendance for those encouraged to enroll in the class increased by 21 percentage points" and that "GPA [increased] by 1.4 grade points and credits earned by 23."

These results are not breaking news.

In 2011, the dropout rate for Tucson Unified School District's now-terminated Mexican American Studies program, which served primarily Latinx students, was just 2.5 percent, while the national dropout rate for Latinx students soared at 56 percent. Even Hogwarts couldn't pull off that kind of magic.

The existing arguments for Ethnic Studies—making public education matter to students of color, drastically reducing racial disparities, and stemming the school-to-prison pipeline—should be enough to get everyone on board with Ethnic Studies, but I fear it will take even more to spur white Americans to action.

So here's more: It's in our own best interests as white Americans to take Ethnic Studies courses. Here are six reasons why:

1. Ethnic Studies ensures that white students learn more accurate American history.

Perhaps you've heard the proverb "Until the lions have their own historians, the history of the hunt will always glorify the hunter." Conventional history is undeniably biased in favor of white Americans, the one group that has consistently benefited from centuries of discrimination.

That's why slavery is too often sanitized, for example, through perpetuating the "happy slave" narrative in a children's book or mislabeling enslaved people as "workers" in a textbook.

That's why we too often call the invasion of Indigenous lands "Manifest Destiny" or "westward expansion." That's why we too often call the incarceration of 120,000 people of Japanese descent "internment."

That's why U.S. history textbooks rarely include "white" as a racial group in the index—unless otherwise noted, the entire book is about white people.

Ethnic Studies challenges this bias, and in the process, students—and teachers—benefit through the inclusion of voices that rarely make the curricular cut.

The reality is that we teachers teach who we are and teach what we know.

Consequently, in a profession so white, white teachers invariably teach curricula thoroughly bleached and warped by our whiteness. Ethnic Studies ensures that white teachers are not just replicating the whitewashed lessons we were taught.

It also ensures that both white teachers and students alike receive a counter-education to media's miseducation.

In short, Ethnic Studies decenters white as the dominant perspective of our education system—at least in one class. If white people are sincere about their desire for racial justice, they inevitably have to give up something. Wouldn't giving up the role of protagonist in one class, a role that too heavily relies on distorting history, in exchange for honest history constitute a fair trade?

Once white Americans overcome their fear of facing our history, they may even learn that this "loss" is ultimately a gain.

2. Ethnic Studies ensures that white students understand systems of oppression and privilege.

Ethnic Studies are color-conscious courses, ditching the "colorblindness" ideology that doesn't work as a solution to racism and keeps white Americans comfortably oblivious to the history and realities of racism.

And comfort is key here.

Too often, curricular choices are dictated by the comfort of white students, but when has comfort ever led to meaningful growth?

In sports, we don't keep our athletes comfortable. Even white athletes are expected to work up a sweat at practice. So why then, when it comes to discomfort, do white students get a pass in the classroom?

Ethnic Studies fairly distributes discomfort.

Regardless of the group at the center of an Ethnic Studies course, once race is on the classroom table, white students have to acknowledge that they too have a race. And once they do that, they have to figure out: Why the hell have I never had to think about my race?

This conundrum invariably leads to an exploration of whiteness and white privilege.

Inevitably, the reality expressed by Jose Lara, a Los Angeles–based educator championing the expansion of Ethnic Studies across California—clicks. Lara said: "White privilege is your history being part of the core curriculum and mine being taught as an elective."

While such realities are not easy to explore, more than 15 years of social justice teaching in primarily white classrooms have taught me that white youth overwhelmingly appreciate the learning, at least eventually.

It tends to be older white people who go apeshit about studies of race and racism. More on them later.

3. Ethnic Studies helps white students better understand inequality.

In recent years, integration has been, for the most part, a third rail, a political taboo. Schools today are more segregated than they were in 1968, a reality educator and writer Jonathan Kozol has dubbed the "shame of the nation."

And it truly is a shame. For one, integrated schools provide valuable lessons on inequality. According to author Carla Shedd, integration opens up students to "different experiences and perspectives so they can share with one another and think within and across whatever boundaries there are: race, class, gender. It gives them a fuller sense of how the world works."

Until we can get integration back onto our national agenda, Ethnic Studies, even in segregated schools, provides this valuable education on inequality.

And we desperately need it. When 62 people own as much wealth as the poorer half of all humanity—3.5 billion people—it's clear economic inequality is one of the most urgent issues of our time, correlated with a rates of life expectancy, literacy, infant mortality, incarceration, mental illness, and more.

Once students understand the fallacy of a level playing field, they can better understand the concept of fairness:

EQUALITY **EQUITY**

The burden of dismantling these unfair systems can't be placed on those most negatively impacted by these same systems. Fairness means white Americans too must join the fight.

JUSTICE

IMAGES COURTESY OF PAUL KUTTNER (CULTURALORGANIZING.ORG)

Education professor Katy Swalwell agrees. After a semester-long study of affluent, mostly white schools, she concludes, "We do need to focus on low-income students, but if educators don't also look at what's happening in these affluent schools, they become the golden standard and we ignore a huge piece of what's perpetuating the problem. Instead of solving the problem, we're putting a Band-Aid on the wound."

With more white Americans taking Ethnic Studies, we can gain the political power, not to mention the will, to actually treat the root causes of inequality, not just its symptoms.

4. Ethnic Studies helps white students flourish in a diverse world by countering institutionalized racism.

Racism takes many forms, including (but not limited to) cultural appropriation, implicit bias, microaggressions, and, of course, overtly racist acts.

Ethnic Studies helps white students improve on all of these fronts.

Cultural appropriation so often stems from a lack of historical context—one that history class is supposed to provide but, remember, we tend to learn it from the hunter's perspective. Ethnic Studies courses are far more likely to provide the context to understand the significance of Native headdresses or the racist origins of Blackface.

Ethnic Studies courses steeped in the experiences of those directly impacted by people's implicit biases also help white American students confront their own.

For example, if an African American studies class examined the implicit biases of drivers that led to a 32 percent longer wait at crosswalks for Black pedestrians compared to white pedestrians, white students with cars would be compelled to ask: "Do I do that? Am I part of the problem?"

Similarly, courses that regularly discuss the challenges that a particular racial group faces tune a white American's senses to the microaggressions that this group must endure.

One year, a classroom discussion on race that turned to the topic of touching the hair of Black and multiracial students quickly taught white students that you just don't do that, an uncomfortable lesson given how many of those white students had touched their friends' hair.

In the same way, discussing Asian American experiences has taught white Americans not to ask what too many of my Asian American students have been asked: Where are you from?

Such discussions no doubt require a safe classroom, but if these discussions aren't taking place, exactly how safe is the classroom? If students of color have to leave a part of their identities at the classroom door, then the teacher has created a "safe" environment only for some, not all.

And while some forms of racism, such as microaggressions, can be subtle and instigated by well-meaning white people, overt racism persists. Based on 6,500 interviews with students conducted by the U.S. Justice and Education departments and reported by Connor Adams Sheets in the *International Business Times*, researchers found that Asian American youth "are three times as likely to face web-based taunts and more than 20 percent more likely to face classroom bullying than many of their classmates."

Schools readily embrace anti-bullying programs, but anti-racist programs are far more likely to make an administrator sweat nervously.

However, based on studies like this one, anti-racist programs are anti-bullying programs, which means Ethnic Studies courses also serve as anti-bullying programs—if only we could make Ethnic Studies courses more available to white students.

In his CNN editorial arguing for mandatory Ethnic Studies, "One Class All Students Should Take," Albert Laguna writes, "Part of the reason why racist incidents persist—swastikas scrawled in feces, nooses hung from trees on campus, for instance—is because universities are failing to do what they do best: teach."

Unfortunately, until Ethnic Studies is mainstreamed in predominately white schools, white students will disproportionately instigate such torment, as they did recently at the University of Missouri and Western Washington University campuses.

5. Ethnic Studies strengthens white people.

Beyond the discriminatory behaviors listed above, a host of white-specific behaviors—all of which are connected to our insistence on white people's comfort—exacerbate and perpetuate institutionalized

racism: white fragility, white silence, white denial, and white entitlement, to name a few.

Professor Robin DiAngelo has spent much of her career researching these very white behaviors. She writes, "It became clear over time that white people have extremely low thresholds for enduring any discomfort associated with challenges to our racial worldviews."

Ethnic Studies works the muscles to raise these thresholds. After all, there's a reason why we so often bathe our children in foreign languages and music lessons at an early age: Children are amazingly adaptable and grow at seemingly superhuman rates.

Discussions of race with white people don't have to end in white tears, not if we start early—in fact, let's institutionalize discomfort so we no longer need documentaries like MTV's *White People* about how fragile we are.

As I mentioned earlier, it's the older white Americans who are debilitated by extremely low thresholds for discomfort, not the students.

It wasn't students in Virginia's Glen Allen High School who fought for the ban of a video that used the metaphor of a track race to illustrate that this country's history of racism gives white Americans a head start, a video shown at a Black History Month assembly. It was "outraged" white adults, claiming the video, created by the African American Policy Forum, was a "white guilt video" and "racially divisive."

Ravi K. Perry, president of the National Association for Ethnic Studies, defended the video, joined by the NAACP. Students did protest but for its return, not its banning.

And it certainly wasn't a youth-led movement that shut down the wildly successful Mexican American Studies program. It was a white guy, Tom Horne, former Arizona state superintendent of public instruction, who shows his record-low tolerance for other "racial worldviews" by calling racial identity "primitive" and "tribal."

If only in his youth he had taken the very course he helped ban!

6. Ethnic Studies embodies American values.

Despite our country's sordid and painful history—including genocide, colonization, and chattel slavery—we are now a country full of "beautiful colors," as states Ava DuVernay, director of *Selma* and *13th*.

And it's downright American to celebrate this diversity. We celebrate it through the expansive types of foods we savor and the cultural celebrations we attend throughout our schools and municipalities.

There's no reason why such celebrations should be left at the classroom door.

In fact, it's practically ironic that that white guy, Tom Horne, and his white successor, John Huppenthal (who was outed not so long ago as the author of anonymous racist blog posts), shut down Mexican American Studies because they deemed it anti-American.

Our diversity is quintessentially American, which makes Ethnic Studies quintessentially American.

If you remain unconvinced, let's turn to those who don't want Ethnic Studies. When I write publicly about teaching about race and racism, I am frequently trolled. Here's a taste of the characters of those who don't want such studies:

> "This guy is typically vapid anti-white Jew. And high school teacher."
> "Typical BS from the brainwashed liberals. Why not take a long walk after dark thru a black neighborhood."
> "Go fuck yourself libtard."
> "In America today whites as a group are the least racist with Blacks being the MOST racist."
> "Jon GRENN BERG BERG BERG. Stop antisemitism. Go be a jew and try not to lecture white people on racism. Otherwise, the OVEN is good and hot."

Is there a more compelling advertisement for Ethnic Studies? If racist and anti-Semitic people virulently fight against Ethnic Studies, shouldn't the rest of us fight even more passionately for them?

Instead of listening to trolls, I'd rather listen to those whose efforts have led to these recent headlines:

> "Teaching Tribal History Is Finally Required in Washington Public Schools"
> "Students Call for Ethnic Studies in Portland High Schools"
> "Oakland Schools Join Others in California in Requiring Ethnic Studies"
> "Yale President Responds: Ethnicity Studies to be Increased Following Two Weeks of Demands for Change"
> "Two Canadian Universities Make Indigenous Studies a Requirement"
> "After 20 Years in the Making, Faculty Submits Proposal for Asian American Studies Major"
> "Student Protests Result in Proposed Curricula Changes at D.C. Universities"
> "Students and Faculty Advocate Asian American Studies"
> "Students Launch Petition for Comprehensive Anti-Racism Program at Seattle Pacific University"

I'm borrowing a line of questioning by Tim Wise here, but when was the last time that masses of people of color were wrong about racism?

If Ethnic Studies are what people of color are fighting for, it's time for white America to do the same.

We are living during a movement for racial justice. Will you spend the movement enjoying the privilege to ignore it, or will you join it?

If my local public school begins offering Ethnic Studies—and they will if white America demands them—I'm confident my very white children, Zinn and Viola, will join it. ✳

Revisiting Notions of Social Action in Ethnic Studies Pedagogy
One Teacher's Critical Lessons from the Classroom

BY CATI V. DE LOS RÍOS

At 22 years old, I entered the secondary classroom seeking to unravel the seams of the miseducation of so many young people in this country. I hoped to innovate an Ethnic Studies curriculum that would work to restore and mobilize my students' histories, literatures, perspectives, and cultures to the center of the classroom. When I began my career, I had several assumptions about teaching Ethnic Studies in a high school context. I thought teaching Ethnic Studies was primarily about counter-narrating white supremacy and teaching the nuanced histories of Indigenous people and people of color in the United States. Borrowing in part from multicultural ideologies, I simply believed that the goal of teaching Ethnic and Chicanx Studies was to show how white supremacy has worked to dominate, silence, and erase our existence in the United States and throughout the world.

But in teaching from a counter-narrative approach, I later realized that I was borrowing from models of white supremacy; I found myself presenting "sanitized" and "exceptional" histories of people of color as if they ran parallel to the "greatness" of Western civilizations without nuances, complexities, and contradictions. In other words, I had presented our histories as static, rather than engaging Ethnic Studies as an ongoing, living and breathing critique of heteropatriarchy, misogyny, colonialism, structural racism, and racial capitalism.

I was teaching in my hometown of Pomona, California, a working-class immigrant community in East Los Angeles County, where most of my students were the children of immigrants or immigrants themselves from Mexico and Central America. During my first year of teaching Ethnic Studies, I realized that many of my students were *already* knowledgeable of their complex cultures and structural inequities—they are living, racialized subjects impacted daily by criminalization, carcerality, immigration, xenophobia, heteronormativity, sexism, classism, and racism. As a matter of fact, rather than me teaching them about systems of power, my students at Pomona High School taught me two powerful lessons: 1) the ways in which youth are racialized in 21st-century contexts and 2) the ways they resist and read their sociopolitical worlds through popular culture. I soon realized that my role as an Ethnic Studies teacher was instead to facilitate a space that allowed students to leverage their divergent entry points, positionalities, and points of view to name and critique structures of power that impacted their everyday lives and communities. While I might have taught my students terms like "hegemony" and "systemic oppression," they were already the living experts of those concepts and the racialization processes they bring forth.

Today, conversations around the teaching of Ethnic Studies at the secondary level often emphasize a counter-narration of dominant U.S. history as a form of healing from the cultural genocide that has been under way for centuries in our public school system. While our undermined and omitted histories are *certainly* central to Ethnic Studies—teaching said histories was among the main demands of the Third World Liberation Front of 1968—Ethnic Studies as a political project is much larger. Its pedagogy must continue to amplify the insurgent lessons from its original founding era of anti-racist, anti-imperialist social movements instantiated throughout the world. First identified as Third World Studies in the late 1960s, Ethnic Studies was indeed a social, political, and cultural intervention into the white and male supremacist university that worked to colonize and oppress knowledge systems and lives around the world. The essence of the founding of Third World Studies, however, permeated the public pedagogies occurring in the streets and in the everyday lives of those resisting imperialism globally, as well as the ways in which communities deftly organized to socially and politically align against this empire. This type of social action was especially alive in Southeast Asia, Africa, and Latin America. Ultimately, these insurgent lessons teach us that Ethnic Studies pedagogy must continue to transcend the confines of classroom walls and take learning into the streets and local community.

Ethnic Studies as Local Praxis and Community Partnerships: Las Posadas Project

Ethnic Studies pedagogy has always been tied to both anticolonial literacy development, a commitment to social and racial justice, and notions of activism and local praxis. In his article "Teaching for Social Change," published in 1999 in the *Loyola of Los Angeles Law Review*, Glenn Omatsu captured this action-oriented spirit and legacy in his five principles of teaching Ethnic Studies, which plants its pedagogy first and foremost in grassroots communities: 1) Learning must always be connected to social movements in the community, and students learn "best by doing," meaning getting involved in grassroots struggles for justice. 2) Knowledge of Ethnic Studies is too important to be kept within the bounds of classrooms. Once acquired, knowledge of Ethnic Studies must always be shared with others. 3) Learning is reciprocal and students and teachers learn from one another. Rather than bearers of knowledge, teachers of Ethnic Studies are primarily "organizers" of the learning process. 4) Knowledge of Ethnic Studies must always be used to change and transform systems of power within society. 5) Once "armed" with the teachings of Ethnic Studies, students can become agents of change when they join community social movements.

Ethnic Studies pedagogy thus 1) foregrounds the critical nexus between activism and emancipatory literacies; 2) reconnects our learning with the political world we inhabit; and 3) compels us all with the political and anticolonial work that we have the responsibility to continue. As Omatsu noted, fundamental to Ethnic Studies is a commitment to engaged learning through community partnerships. Rather than discussing contemporary issues of systemic injustice, Ethnic Studies pedagogy identifies the reservoirs of knowledge and resources beyond one's school campus and works in nonhierarchical and reciprocal ways with local grassroots communities, community-based cultural centers, and political organizations to work for social change on regional, national, and global levels.

As a teacher, my students and I regularly organized social justice Posadas, or candle light processions of peace, with day laborers from the Pomona Economic Opportunity Center, a local day labor center. These Posadas, which continue to exist today, advocate for the labor and human rights of undocumented immigrants in the greater Los Angeles and San Bernardino counties. Since 2008, hundreds of Pomona High School students, *jornaleros* (day laborers), parents, community members, teachers, and school leaders have walked in candle light processions every year in opposition to increasing xenophobic sentiments. In addition to being a collaborative endeavor, Las Posadas are also seen as a mobilizing strategy for communities to raise awareness around injustices and self-determine what is best for their communities. They are co-organized every winter season as a form of resistance to oppressive sentiments and hostile legislations toward immigrant communities—local campaigns uplifted through Las Posadas have included wage increases for undocumented laborers, a moratorium on the high number of checkpoints that racially profiled undocumented immigrants throughout Los Angeles and the Inland Empire, and pathways to citizenship and education for undocumented immigrant communities. Las Posadas are a type of civic partnership between the labor community and a public school district—two distinct enterprises that are rarely seen as collaborators. In this vein, Ethnic Studies pedagogy encourages us to re-envision teaching and learning from the ground up and points to the possibilities embedded in the rich tapestries of our communities.

The curricular unit that accompanies Las Posadas has shifted and changed every year, especially as it aims to respond to the current sociopolitical climate and the latest iterations of legislation targeting im/migrant communities. Traditionally, students first read excerpts of Francisco Jiménez's *The Circuit: Stories from the Life of a Migrant Child* and Helena María Viramontes' *Under the Feet of Jesus*. *The Circuit* is an autobiographical novel based on the author's journey as a young boy migrating from Mexico to the United States and living in migrant labor camps in California. Similarly, *Under the Feet of Jesus* features the story of a young girl and her migrant family's arduous struggle with working the fields in the summer months. These novels provide an important historical context for migrant labor and California agricultural history. Thereafter, for two weeks, students study the history of immigration as a global phenomenon, agricultural labor, and wage discrimination, and they hear firsthand *testimonios* from jornaleros in the Los Angeles and San Bernardino areas. Later, using some of the curriculum resources from Teaching Tolerance's *Viva la Causa* curriculum, high school students compare wages and labor conditions from the Delano Grape Strike in 1965 to various 21st-century agricultural strikes and conduct close readings of both federal and state legislations affecting immigrant families. Students then work in committees alongside jornaleros and parents to organize the community procession that stops and sings and chants at various local stores.

Furthermore, different local political issues are highlighted at Las Posadas every year. For example, many immigrants prior to and shortly after the passing of 2014 California Assembly Bill 60—which granted qualifying undocumented immigrants the right to a driver's license—were greatly affected by the frequent checkpoints throughout Southern California. Students and parents began to call for a moratorium on the practice of impounding vehicles in Los Angeles and San Bernardino counties, especially from undocumented immigrants awaiting state-issued driver's licenses. A student, Rudy, shared in an interview:

> It wasn't right . . . *Los retenes* [the checkpoints] were happening every week. We never knew if it was ICE (Immigration and Customs Enforcement) or a checkpoint that was there for the

"drunk drivers"—they kinda always happened together. Our parents' cars were being taken and they couldn't get to work anymore. Sometimes like for good and other times for up to 30 days and we'd have to get a lot of money to get [the car] out. Organizing Las Posadas *con los jornaleros* [with the day laborers] helped to bring awareness in the larger community about what was going on. Las Posadas help us to organize us against what they were doing to us. We just walked peacefully, you know? We sang and chanted together through downtown, all united in our fight. Las Posadas was a way for us to act as a big group. And every year is a new year with different attacks on immigrants, and we continue to do [Las Posadas] every year.

California AB 60, the Safe and Responsible Driver Act, enabled any eligible California resident to apply for a driver's license, regardless of immigration status. There was a critical period between passing the law and when the licenses began to be issued. During that four-month window, local and state governments faced pressure to order law enforcement agencies under their jurisdictions to stop impounding vehicles if drivers are unlicensed.

Las Posadas was one way that jornaleros, parents, students, and teachers worked collaboratively through an interconnected Ethnic Studies pedagogy, all taking up various forms of leadership—from peripheral to center—to address and amplify the injustices occurring in the community. The anti-immigrant sentiments that young people navigate on a daily basis have, to an extent, become commonplace. Through Las Posadas, though, students are able to position themselves as civic actors and imagine themselves as part of the solution by not only raising awareness but also through intergenerational organizing to collectively promote literacies of social awareness and action that disrupt racist and anti-immigrant sentiments.

Ethnic Studies as a Community-Responsive Methodology

Ethnic Studies as a community-responsive methodology is grounded in the notion that community members should collaborate in conducting research for social transformation, as depicted in Timothy P. Fong's 2008 book, *Ethnic Studies Research: Approaches and Perspectives*. Many Ethnic Studies teachers, including myself, have taken this up in their classrooms through participatory action research (PAR) models to engage communities in research and to address their most pressing needs. One of which includes Youth Participatory Action Research (YPAR), which works to unpack social, economic, and racial injustice in students' neighborhoods, schools, and communities. Over the years, students' YPAR projects have entailed rigorous work that included students reading from the social sciences,

Through Las Posadas, students are able to position themselves as civic actors and imagine themselves as part of the solution by not only raising awareness but also through intergenerational organizing to collectively promote literacies of social awareness and action that disrupt racist and anti-immigrant sentiments.

Ethnic Studies, and existing educational research. Students have engaged in various writing genres, including field notes, journals, persuasive essays, and designing protocols for and conducting semi-structured interviews.

For a number of years, I partnered with Pomona College Chicanx/Latinx Studies professor Dr. Gilda Ochoa to unite our two groups of students in critical praxis. Together, we sought ways to disrupt the long-standing racial and socioeconomic disparities between the primarily working-class and immigrant community in Pomona and the affluent college town of Claremont, California, where Pomona College is

located. Our yearly collaboration, which included her college students and my high school students—all enrolled in our respective Ethnic Studies courses at the time—resulted in yearly social justice *encuentros* (summits) and highlighted the ways in which young people learn in community and build expertise as critical pedagogues. Our engagement with YPAR through an Ethnic Studies pedagogy was situated within the processes of 1) developing youth's critical consciousness; 2) fostering agency; and 3) moving agency toward collective social action. Our students investigated divergent community issues like local racial segregation in their neighborhoods, lack of college access, anti-immigrant federal and state policies, excessive police force, and experiences with racism in their community—all of which provided implications for practice at their local schools. This yearly collaboration stressed the significance of centering community members in the problem-solving processes and the politics of positionality when working in their community. In addition, practicing YPAR centered forms of engaged writing, robust literacy skills (including close readings of complex texts), leadership development, and civic engagement.

Once I left the classroom for my PhD program, I continued to work with the Pomona High community and the subsequent Ethnic Studies teacher, Arturo Molina. One way Molina and I have collaborated on PAR methodology is through photovoice, a photo-elicitation method grounded in critical pedagogy and visual literacies. Engaging photovoice collectively as both a literacy pedagogy and research method has generated powerful pathways to bridge the social and political realities of students into their classroom writing instruction. With deep roots in the dialogical ethics of Paulo Freire, photovoice emerged as an approach to participatory research that cultivates humanization and an awareness of social conditions, as Caroline Wang and Mary Ann Burris discussed in their 1997 *Health Education & Behavior* article, "Photovoice: Concept, Methodology, and Use for Participatory Needs Assessment." This approach to research and writing seeks to embolden participants to take power and control over the research process through students' documentation of the social and political dimensions of their lives via photographs and accompanying written narratives for the purpose of social transformation. When coupled with a secondary Ethnic Studies course, photovoice can be a vibrant pedagogical practice and research methodology, as both seek to amplify critical dialogue, self-actualization, and sociopolitical change.

A participatory arts–based method, photovoice centers the lens of the student—a lens that has a racialized gaze of the world. Photovoice asks young people to take photographs of social issues in their community that matter to them and then respond to photographs through an accompanying narrative. This approach to literacy elicits multiple openings

for their description and explanation. As such, in our collaborative work, students have documented environmental racism, police repression, school/prison nexus, and heteropatriarchy, among other topics, through their photovoice projects. In this context, students' multimodal photovoice compositions within Ethnic Studies courses offer opportunities to expand our understandings of student literacy practices in more critical and diverse ways.

Miriam, a high school student, explored issues of extreme police force in her community and the ways in which her Chicanx Studies course allowed her to take up this topic through multiple modes. Miriam regarded notions of accountability as central to her high school Chicanx Studies course. Upon

analyzing the 2014 killing of Black teenager Michael Brown in Ferguson, Missouri, in class, Miriam began to see her life inextricably tied with Brown's, and she was inspired to use her photovoice project to raise awareness and take action. In her photovoice Google Doc journal she placed the picture below—a photo that she took of her protest sign that she made for her first #BlackLivesMatter march—and wrote the accompanying narrative:

> There was a peace march for the victims of police brutality that I participated in. It was a memorable experience because it was the first time I ever did something like this and was empowering because it was among friends. We were there voicing our displeasures and peacefully demanding change in our society. At the end of the peace march we held a vigil for the families of those lost to police violence in our community. This was an emotional moment for everyone because we were united and bonding over a struggle that our community has been facing for some time. Seeing how my classmates were involved and actually interested in the things we learned in Chicanx Studies and taking action on our own around those things outside of class made me believe that even young people like us can be encouraged to do something that matters and that can care about injustice in the community.

Her photograph captures an intentional close-up of her poster from the march, which poignantly notes that she will "probably need this [again] next year." In an interview with Miriam about why she selected this photo and participated in the march, she affirmed that she will likely continue to keep taking action around police brutality because as she stated, "It's not getting any better." Miriam's emerging practices of accountability toward community and the most marginalized in our society remain at the core spirit of Ethnic Studies pedagogy.

In the examples with Las Posadas and photovoice projects, the classroom-community connections rooted in culturally, politically, and community-responsive pedagogy provided students with important experiences that transcend their classrooms and classmates. They not only saw the course material come alive, but they became actors in creating new knowledge and spaces that unite groups often divided by geography, race, ethnicity, class, citizenship, and age.

Ethnic Studies as Literacies of Social Action

Ethnic Studies literacies and pedagogy center multimodal forms of reading, writing, and engaging sociopolitical worlds that lead to not only the self-actualization of both students and teachers but also toward acts of justice and solidarity outside of the classroom. The aforementioned research and pedagogical methods center youth as the primary thinkers and inno-

At the core of Ethnic Studies pedagogy is the aim to equip students with tools to better understand social inequities and the structural forces that shape their lives while also providing tangible strategies to socially transform their communities.

vators of solutions in their communities, especially around issues of race and racism. At the core of Ethnic Studies pedagogy is the aim to equip students with tools to better understand social inequities and the structural forces that shape their lives while also providing tangible strategies to socially transform their communities.

Ethnic Studies methodologies must continue to dynamically respond to both structural changes in the world and the forms of resistance people employ to simultaneously cope and challenge the oppression that accompany these global changes. The development of secondary Ethnic Studies methods and pedagogies can be seen as particularly distinct from the larger academic project of Ethnic Studies as racial and ethnic demographics in schools shift against the backdrop of emerging neoliberal policies and practices in education. Current secondary Ethnic

Studies teachers are concurrently honoring the original spirit of Ethnic Studies while also extending its conversation to practical approaches to translating anti-racist and anticolonial theories into practice in 21st-century schooling contexts. What has remained constant since 1968, however, has been the crucial role of students, families, and community organizers that have leveraged their lived experiences to build bridges of relevance from the classroom to the grassroots community.

Now as a university professor, I have shifted my teaching to primarily preparing future literacy and Ethnic Studies secondary teachers. I have gained a broader sense of the increasing stakes and challenges classroom teachers and students face. With growing efforts to bring Ethnic Studies into secondary classrooms and public schools more widely, the need to prepare and support Ethnic Studies teachers—especially in creating social action-oriented curricula—prevails as urgent as ever. ✳

The Ethnic Studies Framework

A Holistic Overview

SYNERGIZED BY R. TOLTEKA CUAUHTIN

In his 2016 keynote presentation at the Institute for Teachers of Color Committed to Racial Justice Conference, Wayne Au asked those in attendance a seemingly paradoxical question: "Can standards be used for liberation, and if so what would your dream standards be?" At the time, as Ethnic Studies Now Coalition's coordinator of curricular advocacy, I had been working on a holistic Ethnic Studies framework that could synergize and nest several other Ethnic Studies frameworks within it. As I worked on it, I was conscious of Christine Sleeter's 2004 *Rethinking Schools* article, "Standardizing Imperialism," about

JESUS BARRAZA

the role of Eurocentric standards in colonization and racism, and that it's often more transformational to "un-standardize" a curricular approach.

I wasn't sure if "standards" could actually be liberating because of their historical role in the oppression of students of color in American education, from the eugenics era when they first came of age to the corporate-backed high-stakes climate of today. However, I was left questioning, "Is it still oppressive if we're working to articulate a big-picture framework of Ethnic Studies as a form of liberation?" This is an important question to consider as we move into the next era of Ethnic Studies in K–16 education. The Ethnic Studies field and community need to play a central role in what happens in districts and classrooms, or we run the risk of it being defined for us by outsiders, district administrators, educational corporations, and politicians who are not critically grounded in Ethnic Studies. We've already seen Ethnic Studies diluted as it has moved into some districts, and we still have to justify basic elements of Ethnic Studies to teachers and administrators who do not have a background or understanding of the field. These on-the-ground realities have made it clear that there is a need for a framework that we can use within educational institutions that is still culturally and community relevant, responsive, and regenerating for this next era of the Ethnic Studies movement.

I first began creating the Ethnic Studies Framework (ES-FW) to help classroom teachers, schools, districts, and states support curricular thinking in the field and to offer Ethnic Studies advocates a common language and frame of reference when communicating among ourselves and with educational agencies about the tenets, curricular imperatives, and legacy

EDUCATION FOR LIBERATION

MELANIE CERVANTES

of Ethnic Studies. This robust framework is directly informed by and composed of key samples of Ethnic Studies academic literature, theory, course outlines, guiding principles, conferences, dialogues, and Ethnic Studies programs already in praxis, and it represents a synergy of the work of many individuals and groups. I credit all of you for making this possible.

There is a need for a framework that we can use within educational institutions that is still culturally and community relevant, responsive, and regenerating for this next era of the Ethnic Studies movement.

A core part of this ES-FW, which formally emerged during Los Angeles Unified School District curricular negotiations, is based around what I called "The Four Geohistorical Macroscales of Ethnic Studies," which could be broadly broken down into: 1) Indigeneity, Roots; 2) Coloniality, Geno-cide, Dehumanization; 3) Hegemony, Normalization; and 4) Regeneration, (Re)humanization, Social Justice and Decoloniality. These frames were further developed when I began dialogue with Christine Sleeter about concepts presented in her 1996 book *Multicultural Education as Social Activism* and later adapted for her 2011 National Education Association research review, "The Academic and Social Value of Ethnic Studies." During our collaboration, she recommended that I fold her six Ethnic Studies themes into the four macroscales framework in order to develop a rubric for implementation.

Importantly, these four consistent macrothemes of Ethnic Studies are not only geo-historical, but also intersectional, multidimensional, sociopolitical, economic, and more, as are the holistic human beings and communities who experience them. This "more" is where the need arose to make explicit what I call the "double helix" of Ethnic Studies: humanity (holistic humanization) and criticality (critical consciousness). Both are interwoven with and affected by the reflective study of each scale and are broken down further in the framework itself to 10 points each. Each scale/theme nests several more concepts and may go by many different names depending on their context, as long as they do not devoid the scale of its criticality (which would reveal the superficiality of the Ethnic Studies program upon that scale). This *Rethinking Ethnic Studies* version of the ES-FW is offered as a summary framing tool for Ethnic Studies curricular programming, writing, designing, evaluating, and advocacy work. Ethnic Studies onward. We are Ethnic Studies.

The Ethnic Studies Framework (ES-FW)

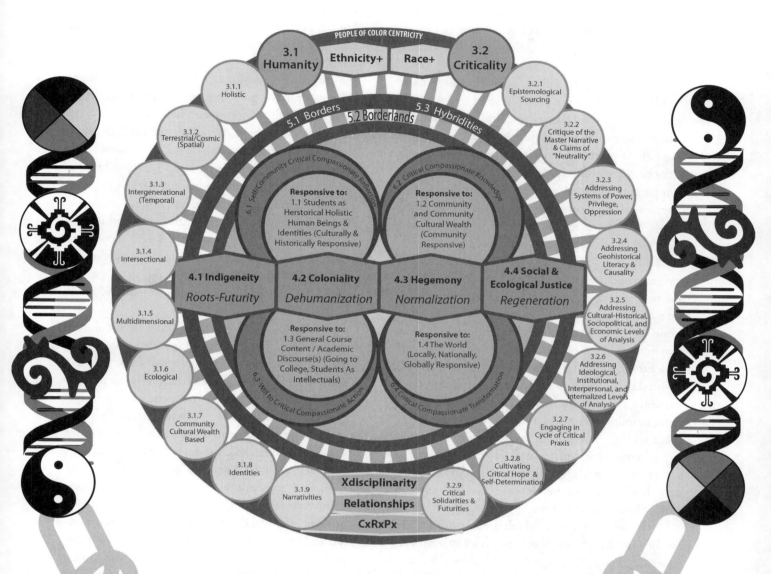

The Situation in American Education
Historical Cultural • Sociopolitical • Economic • Moral
Education Debt (Opportunity Gap) & Trauma

The Ethnic Studies Framework

Ethnic Studies (ES) is the xdisciplinary, loving, and critical praxis of holistic humanity as educational and racial justice. It is from communities of color and our intergenerational worldviews, memories, experiences, identities, narratives, and voices. It is the study of intersectional race, ethnicity, Indigeneity, coloniality, hegemony, and a dignified world where many worlds fit. Based on the principles and tenets of the field provided in this framework, Ethnic Studies curricular designs need to be responsive to: a) the students in the curricular program with considerations of the demographic imperative as well as of each student present; b) the community where the curricular program takes place; c) the academic discourses of Ethnic Studies respecting students as intellectuals; and d) our world—past, present, future.

The ES-FW does not prescribe Ethnic Studies curriculum; rather, it asks how Ethnic Studies curricular programs respond to core ideas within the field. Each group-specific program representing racialized groups of color responds to the framework on its own terms, specifics, and epistemological groundings. Ethnic Studies is **xdisciplinary**, in that it variously takes the forms of being interdisciplinary, multidisciplinary, transdisciplinary, undisciplinary, and intradisciplinary. As such, it can grow its original language to serve these needs with purposeful respellings of terms, including *history* as *herstory* and *women* as *womxn*, connecting with a **gender and sexuality** lens, along with a **socioeconomic class lens** at three of its primary intersections.

The four original fields that compose Ethnic Studies in the United States are Africana/African American/Pan-African Studies; American Indian/Native American/Indigenous Studies; Raza/Xicanx/Boricua/Latinx Studies; and Asian American Pacific Islander Studies. It is important when practicing Ethnic Studies, even within comparative Ethnic Studies courses, to not simply collapse each into a "group of the month" approach. A thematic/theoretically grounded and responsive approach is usually far more powerful. **Peoples of Color** have shared struggles as well as specific struggles to our racialized communities. **Critical solidarities** are foundational to Ethnic Studies.

Both within and beyond the realm of education, it is important to note that Ethnic Studies emerged as a **counter-narrative to the Eurocentric curricular and educational narrative**. What is often called the "achievement gap" is recontextualized by Ethnic Studies as the opportunity gap, and/or what Gloria Ladson-Billings frames as the **education debt**. This refers to what students of color in the United States are owed after centuries of educational **trauma**, dehumanization, and enforced sociopolitical, cultural-historical, economic, and moral constraints via the education system. As a discipline catalyzed by a righteous angst for justice and access to knowledge (rather than merely "closing a gap"), Ethnic Studies intentionally works toward helping **heal** this education debt. Students are asked to "achieve academic success" in a humanizing and critically conscious way, while demanding the education system reconsider what constitutes the parameters of academic success. The **hxrstory of the field of ES** is also a core part of this ES-FW. (See "The Movement for Ethnic Studies: A Timeline, p. 9.)

In Ethnic Studies, **"race"** is a (neo)colonial social construction. It is viewed as a "master category" based upon a Eurocentric biological fallacy that is central to inequitable power relations in society. As a social and historical construct, the idea of race is primarily filtered through physical traits (phenotype), including pigmentation (skin color) and other physical features; where people's ancestral origins are from (precolonial geographic ancestry); cultural traits; and sometimes economic class. Since race produces material impacts, it also produces racial consciousness and facilitates the process of racialization and racial projects, including both the oppositional projects of racism/colorism/anti-Blackness/anti-Indigeneity and anti-racism/**racial justice**. The People of Color Power movements that emerged in the 1960s (Black Power, Red Power, Brown Power, Yellow Power) are key examples of how race has also been embraced and leveraged in the resistance against racism; they are the movements that Ethnic Studies rose from. In the United States today, races very broadly break down as people of color (POC) and white people.

"Ethnicity" refers to many of the associated dimensions of identity that define who we are culturally. These include personal, familial, communal, and societal experiences in local, regional, continental, and global contexts: Indigeneities, migrations, diasporas, colonialities, ancestries, kinships, homelands, nationalities, peoplehoods, spiritual/religious traditions, and linguistic heritages. Specific ethnicities may carry a name that can be based on any of those above categories or their combinations. For instance, someone who identifies as Black Yoruba African American Baptist is simultaneously signaling racialized color, regional and diasporic Indigeneity, precolonial continental geographic ancestry, colonial nationality, and practicing religious denomination. Ethnicity is vast in the different dimensions of heritage and identity it may refer to and may combine to form panethnicities or meta-ethnicities, which include many ethnicities within them. An example is "Latinxs," a term signaling legacies of colonial territory and colonial linguistic heritage, but whose members may be of any race and of multitudes of precolonial ethnic groups. All races are themselves panethnicities in a sense, since many ethnicities compose each race.

Ethnic Studies also recognizes **borders**, **borderlands**, **mixtures**, **hybridities**, *nepantlas*, **double consciousness**, and **reconfigured articulations**, even within and beyond the various names and categories associated with our identities. Most people do not fit neatly into boxes, and identity is complex, including the intersections among race, ethnicity, humanity, criticality, and the four macroscales as related to holistic human beings and communities.

The Four Macroscales/Macrothemes of Ethnic Studies

INDIGENEITY AND ACTIVE ROOTS: PAST, PRESENT, FUTURITY

Ethnic Studies recognizes and respects the sovereignty and autonomy of the Indigenous peoples/first nations of the land where the courses are being taught, their multimillennial and generative Indigenous legacies today, and their futures as dynamic and holistic human beings and communities. K–12 school boards have passed Ethnic Studies resolutions on the lands of the Tohono O'odham in Tucson Unified; Cahuilla in Coachella Unified; Tongva and Tataviam in El Rancho Unified, Los Angeles Unified, and Montebello Unified; Ohlone in San Francisco Unified and Oakland Unified; Miwok in Sacramento Unified; Chinook in Portland Public Schools; and Duwamish in Seattle Public Schools. Recognizing the original peoples of the land/community is imperative to all Ethnic Studies programs; Indigenous peoples are holistic, dynamic, and complex sovereign nations and must not be lost in the panethnic/pantribal racialized group of American Indians.

A helpful framing of Indigeneity in its holistic form is from the United Nations Permanent Forum on Indigenous Issues, which in part declares:

> Considering the diversity of indigenous peoples, an official definition of "Indigenous" has not been adopted. . . . Instead, it has developed an understanding of this term based on the following:
> - Self-identification as Indigenous peoples at the individual level and accepted by the community as their member.
> - Historical continuity with precolonial and/or pre-settler societies.
> - Strong link to territories and surrounding natural resources.
> - Distinct social, economic, or political systems.
> - Distinct language, culture, and beliefs. [...]
> - Resolve to maintain and reproduce their ancestral environments and systems as distinctive peoples and communities.

Indigeneity, in its holistic form, has been severely impacted for many Indigenous peoples due to coloniality, dehumanization, and genocide (the next scale).

Ethnic Studies programs also work to recognize the precolonial roots, worldviews, cosmovisions, perspectives, and discourses of the ancestral and intergenerational legacies of all students as holistic human beings (wherever upon our planet those roots are from) for the demographic imperative the curricular program serves and for each student, as much as possible. For instance, the eight ancient culture hearths of the world are all located outside of Europe and were catalyzed by people of color populations several millennia ago. The holistic hxrstorical legacies of African Americans do not begin with transatlantic enslavement, and the legacies of those considered

Latinxs of color do not begin with Spanish and Portuguese colonization; their roots go much deeper, epochally deeper.

Ethnic Studies facilitates a space, curriculum, and pedagogy where students collaborate on this search into their roots, their critical family herstories as geo-hxrstorically situated human beings and encourages inquiry as to how those stories have become lost, hidden, or suppressed. In this sense, students in Ethnic Studies reflect and work to access mirrors of their holistic, ancestral, and intergenerational legacies of Indigeneity, diasporic indigeneity, and/or precolonial ancestry, as manifested herstorically, today, and while at school.

COLONIALITY, DEHUMANIZATION, AND GENOCIDE

Ethnic Studies is about honesty and courage, including the courage to honestly learn about our relationship to history, as painful as it may be at times. Coloniality, as used here, includes all of the *explicit* traits and interrelations of colonialism—neocolonialism, settler colonialism, internal colonialism, and double (or triple or exponential) colonialisms—upon holistic human beings and communities that render them no longer whole.

Colonialism is a totalizing practice of dehumanization, domination, oppression, and theft that involves the subjugation of one people to another; this includes the process of European settlement and/or socioeconomic and political control and traumatization over much of the rest of the world. The global era of coloniality began on the Eurocentric Gregorian calendar date of October 12, 1492, when Cristobal Colon/Christopher Columbus and his men invaded and landed upon the island of Ayiti (colonially named Hispaniola, and then named Dominican Republic and Haiti), an island of Abya Yala (colonially named Las Americas [or North America and South America]). Columbus claimed Indigenous Taíno land for Spain, Europe, and the Roman Catholic Church, and soon after, for purposes of accumulating power and wealth, forcing peoples indigenous to West Alkebulan/Africa into intercontinental, diasporic chattel enslavement, natal alienation, gratuitous violence, and dishonor. The European nation states of England (later United Kingdom/Great Britain), France, Ger-

many, Belgium, Netherlands, and Italy all engaged in intercontinental colonialism. The United States of America was founded as a settler colonial state 284 years after Columbus' invasion, despite hundreds of Indigenous nations already present, before the colonies of Great Britain declared their sovereign independence from their imperial homeland. This national independence, however, was predicated on a particular Eurocentric, white supremacist (racist, anti-Black, anti-Indigenous), capitalist (classist), patriarchal (sexist and misogynistic), heteropatriarchal (homophobic), and anthropocentric paradigm brought from Europe. In Ethnic Studies, it is imperative that students understand the historic roots and present-day manifestations of colonialism and dehumanization in order to begin to help heal and reconcile this deeply damaging historical legacy.

A 10-part model of coloniality includes: 1) settlers grabbing the land and imposing borders; 2) hatching hierarchies; 3) dividing and conquering; 4) bringing chattel—i.e., slaves in chains as property; 5) erasing, displacing, and replacing Indigenous peoples, cultures, and memories; 6) mining/growing for Europe; 7) developing for Europe/whiteness; 8) converting local cooperative economics to (neo)colonial economic consumption; 9) privatizing, exploiting, and destroying the land and ecology; and 10) legislating this coloniality to make it "legal" and institutionalized. To different extents, these mechanisms and the effects from them still continue today in the United States and beyond. The excess wealth that Europeans, followed by Euro-Americans, generated from these processes became the basis for the capitalist economy. This understanding of coloniality reframes the United States from "a nation of immigrants" to "a nation of settler colonialists," given the country's historic lack of recognition and respect for the Indigeneity of the original peoples of the land and those forced into diaspora as chattel slaves.

Neocolonial policies often displace communities and convert them into migrants today, as has been the case in Mexico and throughout "Latin America." Some earlier migrants to the United States, like the Chinese, fled war and poverty created by European colonization elsewhere, thus their role as a settler-colonialist force is distinct from that of many whites. Even for certain European groups, while settlers themselves, becoming "white" in the United States has often meant taking steps to shed their familial European ethnicity for that of a more assimilated Anglo-American one.

Colonialism also depends upon the imposition of an oppressor's system and worldview over other groups; this dehumanization, deindigenization, and detribalization has and can lead to genocide of Indigenous peoples. Ethnic Studies emphasizes that race is a colonial construction, only invented over the past few hundred years; understanding the relationship of the social construction of race to continental Indigeneities, migrations, voluntary and forced diasporas, social life and social death, and to ourselves as human beings, herstorically and today, is key.

The processes suffered under colonialism for millions of Peoples of Color, relate to genocide, per the United Nations definition:

> Any of the following acts committed with intent to destroy, in whole or in part, a national, ethnical, racial, or religious group, as such:
> a) killing members of the group;
> b) causing serious bodily or mental harm to members of the group;
> c) deliberately inflicting on the group conditions of life calculated to bring about its physical destruction in whole or in part;
> d) imposing measures intended to prevent births within the group; [and]
> e) forcibly transferring children of the group to another group.

Coloniality indicates that colonialism continues today, intertwined with white supremacy, capitalism, patriarchy, heteropatriarchy, and other traumatic dynamics of power, imposing its model of the world on others and teaching people of color to hate ourselves in the process. As such, in U.S. Ethnic Studies, the term "postcolonial" may today more accurately represent keeping each other posted (or up to date) on the status of coloniality, rather than signify that it has ended.

HEGEMONY AND NORMALIZATION

Hegemony refers to making explicit and intersectional power relationships based on colonization implicit, institutionalized, and "normal," erasing memory of these geo-hxrstorical processes that produced and maintain oppressive relations. The 11th pillar of coloniality is to create and maintain hegemony and manufacture consent so coloniality can appear to be over when a colonial country's independence is achieved. Through socialization, domes-

Hegemony normalizes the erasure of Indigenous peoples of the land where a course is taught, sometimes relegating them solely to the past, sometimes invisibilizing them completely so that they appear to have never existed.

tication, and "zombification" under hegemony, the dominant beliefs of an oppressor (hegemon) become normal and implicit in a society, manipulating and submerging oppressed peoples, causing memory loss of their Indigenous and ancestral beliefs as holistic human beings and communities, concretizing dehumanization, and in certain cases, completing intergenerational cultural genocide and making it appear normal. Corporate-backed mass media—in service of consumerism, corporatocracies, neoliberal capitalistic economic structures, propaganda, and saturation of consumer consciousness—is one of hegemony's most powerful weapons of normalization.

Five dimensions of hegemony include: a) material asymmetry in favor of one social group (or country, depending on the foregrounded xdiscipline of focus), i.e., the hegemon, who has b) enough military power to systematically defeat any potential contester in the system; c) controls the access to raw materials, natural resources, capital, and markets; d) has competitive advantages in the production of "value-added" goods; and e) generates an accepted ideology reflecting this neocolonial status quo.

Ethnic Studies works to reveal hegemony in all its forms, including cultural-hxrstorical, sociopolitical, military, economic, and moral. This involves revealing the implicit, normalized, internalized, microaggressive, and large-scale cultural hegemony of coloniality, and the horizontal oppression it often causes (i.e., oppressed groups dehumanizing other oppressed groups). Hegemony normalizes the erasure of Indigenous peoples of the land where a course is taught, sometimes relegating them solely to the past, sometimes invisibilizing them completely so that they appear to have never existed. By recovering, attending to, and creating counter-narratives from subordinate social positions at various intersections (race, gender, sexuality, class, etc.), Ethnic Studies engages students in demasking hegemony's (neo)colonial gaze, and creating narratives that question and repudiate oppressive relationships while encouraging them to embrace themselves and their communities as fully human.

DECOLONIALITY, REGENERATION, AND TRANSFORMATIONAL RESISTANCE

Ethnic Studies works toward a respect and regeneration of holistic humanity, Indigeneity, cultural memory, ancestral roots, and sustenance today. Further, it rejects colonialism and hegemony and nurtures critical understandings and analyses of intersectional oppression. This scale, holistically and critically, is an awakening and growing of the consciousness of the three other scales with decolonization of the mind being a core purpose.

Decolonization is not a metaphor. It is multidimensional and works to bring about the repatriation of sovereign Indigenous land and life where Ethnic Studies programs are located. The relationship between sovereignties and autonomies—and the understandings and implications of each for interrelated peoples of color communities—is an ongoing dialogue in the field as each group has its own stories to share and grow.

Ethnic Studies offers oppositional stories and counter-narratives that name, speak to, resist, and transform the hegemonic Eurocentric neocolonial condition. Ethnic Studies and this liberatory scale signify an inward gaze and for many, the transition from being lost to becoming woke as a living part of hxrstory. This scale signifies working to help ourselves, our communities, and our world transform into a world in which many worlds fit—one based on belonging, solidarity, love, empathy, honor, mutual respect, dignity, intellectualism, intercommunalism, reciprocity, and humanizing work. Transformational resistance is critical of oppression and motivated by social justice, including multiple intersectional forms of social and ecological justice.

Ethnic Studies goes far beyond a superficial "heroes and holidays" approach, while recognizing and learning from specific organizations/groups and individuals involved in movements of social justice throughout hxrstory. It recognizes that in dynamics of power, the breakdown is not so simple as a binary of the oppressors (or hegemons) and the oppressed, in that there are also intersectional considerations where individuals and groups may be oppressed and privileged simultaneously (for instance, oppressed as POC and privileged as males). Further, there are members of marginalized groups who unconsciously (hegemonically) or voluntarily help the oppressors oppress (considered sub-hegemons or sub-oppressors in Freirean theory), and members of dominant groups who recognize their own privilege and actively work to combat inequities of power, as allies in solidarity. These dimensions are also reflected in group-specific explanations of dynamics of power, including the dichotomies between "masters and slaves," or "settlers and indigenes." Leading the struggle against oppression are members of marginalized groups who are in transformational resistance—it is important students know about these figures, organizations, and movements as testaments to the possibility of positive and systematic changes.

Ethnic Studies helps youth move beyond the toxic impacts of (geo)historical amnesia, dehumanization, self-hatred, deficit thinking, anti-Blackness, anti-Indigeneity, and ongoing processes of hegemonic coloniality and move toward self-love, healing, empowerment, and critical reflection about their identities and futures as *holistic human beings and communities*. In Ethnic Studies, youth are intentionally respected as reflective intellectuals who engage with their own lived experiences, as well as with theory and frameworks of the field, while coming to see themselves as active agents in their own communities and producers of knowledge and authors of their own lives. Students use academic and cultural tools to create and to transform environments in which they live; they use their knowledge, wisdom, and understanding to participate in the work for social and ecological justice and liberation.

* * *

Holistically and critically, the four scales flow into one another; they are not hermetically sealed boxes and each may be simultaneously present in any given context, even in hybrid forms. In a sense, hegemony is a dimension of coloniality, and in necessary response, social justice and decoloniality are dimensions of Indigeneity today. Further, though their inceptions may have been chronological initially, they are not to be read as only linear or chronological; they have each been present hxrstorically to different extents, and each are present today in dialogue, debate, and action, within themselves and with each other in an epistemological and pragmatic struggle for the future. It is imperative that study of these scales relate back to holistic human beings and communities, and be approached with a critical consciousness; here, these two imperatives are presented as the double helix of Ethnic Studies.

The Double Helix of Ethnic Studies

The double helix of Humanity and Criticality spiral through Ethnic Studies and are interwoven through its life in the classroom and beyond. As an integral part of the ES-FW, the double helix signifies "holistic humanity and critical consciousness" in a manner that is general enough for xdisciplinary programs at both K–12 and higher education levels to respond to. ES courses may be taught through the lenses of several different xdisciplines (the disciplines that are intertwined with the discipline of Ethnic Studies in praxis) and by teachers who have their secondary school teaching credentials in diverse areas, including history-social sciences, language arts, visual and performing arts, sciences, technology, engineering, and mathematics, ideally with Ethnic Studies teaching certifications also in place.

While all Ethnic Studies programs and courses should be responsive to each of the 20 points upon the double helix and their interrelation to the four macroscales/macrothemes, different parts of the double helix are organically emphasized depending on the specific programs and courses. For instance, an Ethnic Studies geography course may xdisciplinarily co-foreground the point about students being terrestrial/spatial/cosmic beings, and an Ethnic Studies environmental justice course might co-foreground the point of students being ecological beings, while still connecting to the four macroscales and tenets of the double helix. Regardless of the xdisciplines of focus, deepening students geo-hxrstorical literacies so they better understand who they are and where they come from is central to Ethnic Studies; reading

Without compromising the tenets and principles of Ethnic Studies, part of the power of ES is in its xdisciplinarity and ability to connect to multiple disciplines, including the discipline of students' lived experiences, discourses, and home knowledge within its curricular programming.

the word and the world is imperative across all xdisciplines of ES. Further, the four hxrstorically racialized disciplines of ES (American Indian Studies, Africana Studies, Asian American Pacific Islander Studies, Latinx/Xicanx Studies, and newer group specific studies) respond to this double helix in their own disciplinary ways. Having a common big-picture ES framework should not detract from this; instead it serves to strengthen the field as a whole.

Without compromising the tenets and principles of Ethnic Studies, part of the power of ES is in its xdisciplinarity and ability to connect to multiple disciplines, including the discipline of students' lived experiences, discourses, and home knowledge within its curricular programming.

The following chart more fully breaks down what is meant by the double helix of humanity and criticality in the ES-FW, with each strand interwo-

We Are the Double Helix of Ethnic Studies:
Humanity & Criticality

HUMANITY: HOLISTIC HUMAN BEINGS

Who are we as holistic human beings and communities?

1. We humanize, with healing compassion, belongingness, dignity, life, love, unity, reciprocity, interdependence, collectivism, solidarity, mutual respect.
2. We are *holistic*: physical, intellectual, emotional, spiritual, relational beings.
3. We are *terrestrial/spatial/cosmic* (related to land, cosmos, and space-time).
4. We are *intergenerational/herstorical/temporal* (related to time-space).
5. We are *intersectional* and related to power; as such, our full holisticality (or wholeness) considers our race, ethnicity, class, gender, sexuality, ability, age, and more.
6. We are *multidimensional*, multidiscursive, complex, creative and dynamic.
7. We are *ecological* (interrelated to the ecology/environment/nature).
8. We are *cultural*, at both surface levels and deeper levels, and we have community cultural wealth.
9. We each, all, have *identities and names*.
10. We each, all, have important *narratives, stories, voices* to share.

CRITICALITY: CRITICAL CONSCIOUSNESS

As critically conscious holistic human beings, how do we understand ourselves and our world in relation to the four macroscales and help to bring about transformational change for the better?

1. We bear witness to and stand against negativity, oppression, and dehumanization.
2. We identify the sources, epistemologies, explicit and implicit biases, insider and outsider perspectives, herstoriographies and herstoricities of narratives, contextualizing and corroborating them as necessary.
3. We critique the "master narrative," claims of neutrality and complete objectivity, essentialism, reductionism, "color-blindness," and "meritocracy," and we highlight narratives emerging from herstorically marginalized and invisibilized standpoints, epistemologies, perspectives, and worldviews.
4. We address xdisciplinary, cultural-herstorical, sociopolitical, economic, and moral levels of analysis.
5. We name and confront systems and problems of power, privilege, and oppression at multiple intersections of social identity.
6. We interrogate ideological, institutional, interpersonal, and internalized levels of privilege and oppression.
7. We deepen geo-hxrstorical literacies and an understanding of causality.
8. We engage in reflection, cycles of critical praxis, and transformational resistance, and we are action oriented in working toward solutions to the problems we name.
9. We cultivate critical hope, creation, and self-determination.
10. We nurture critical solidarities for past, present, and future generations.

We study how holistic human beings and communities—including ourselves, our ancestral legacies, and our futures—relate to the four macroscales of Ethnic Studies: Indigeneity, Coloniality, Hegemony, and Decoloniality. The macroscales themselves directly interact with this double helix of Humanity and Criticality. As such, the elements present within this chart are imperative to consider in a complex understanding of each of the four macroscales and their interactions with each other.

ven with and affected by each macroscale.

The Ethnic Studies Framework offers a big-picture conceptual and curricular tool to help describe and understand the holistic, herstorical, cultural, sociopolitical, economic, moral, intersectional, and critical dimensions of the field across historically marginalized and racialized groups.

In summary, with necessary gratitude, recognition, and respect for the sovereignty, autonomy, and survivance of the Indigenous peoples and roots of the land where any Ethnic Studies program is located, the premise of the four macroscales/themes is that: a) all human beings have holistic ancestral precolonial roots to somewhere(s) upon our planet; b) for the holistic ancestral legacies of many students of color, colonization and/or forced diaspora attempted to dehumanize, eliminate memory of, and replace these roots with a *totalizing* Eurocentric colonial model of themselves; c) hegemony normalizes this process and geohistorical amnesia, translating to a superficial historical literacy and decontextualized relationship to history today, negatively impacting human and academic identity; d) honest acknowledgement and study of this hxrstorical process is necessary, as a cause of Indigenous and human hxrstorical empowerment, solidarity, transformational resistance, regeneration, revitalization, restoration, critical educational expectations, humanization, liberation, social and ecological justice, for *holistic human beings and communities*.

Ethnic Studies Pedagogy

Ethnic Studies teachers are reflective, reflexive, and transparent about their standpoints in regards to social justice rather than claiming neutrality in these regards and are dynamic and resourceful in K–16 classrooms. Ethnic Studies pedagogy (ESP), being based in relationships and oriented toward the critical, cultural, and academic success of students of color, is often considered a form of, or associated with, Culturally Relevant and Responsive Pedagogy (CRP). However, this is with a serious caveat that needs further grounding/clarification. In service of this purpose, please see the CxRxPx chapter in this volume (p. 26) for an elaboration, of how this Ethnic Studies Framework understands pedagogy in relation to it.

In Sum

As holistic human beings and communities with critical Ethnic Studies consciousness:

Who are we, where are we from, what are our stories, where are we going, what will our relationships to each other be? Who decides?

How are we related to the core concepts present in this Ethnic Studies framework, and how can we help transform ourselves, our critical understandings, our communities, and our world for the better, with Ethnic Studies curriculum and praxis? ✳

A NOTE ON REFERENCES

This framework utilizes an element of style of many state content standards and frameworks, where specifics are most often not cited explicitly. With that approach, key terms, phrases, and even excerpts and certain frame elaborations are integrated and synergized. To directly honor and recognize more of the work explicitly integrated here, an annotated version with notes and references is available at goo.gl/G17B7h. It is a continuously working document, and as such is an open document for more connections and contributions any Ethnic Studies community members may like to make—it is better to grow it and annotate it with the hearts, minds, and spirits of many. Ethnic Studies onward.

The Four Macroscales of Ethnic Studies Graphic Organizer

This diagram may be utilized as a handout graphic organizer tool for analysis. For instance, in praxis, after experiencing a (multimodal) text, students may first annotate what they notice in a text (without interpretation and analysis) in their notebooks, and as a subsequent step, they may interpret/sort/transfer their notes through an ES analytical lens to this macroscales graphic organizer. Classroom dialogue may follow in response to the question "What goes where and why?"; application of the concepts and the graphic organizer notes may then assist with further student creations.

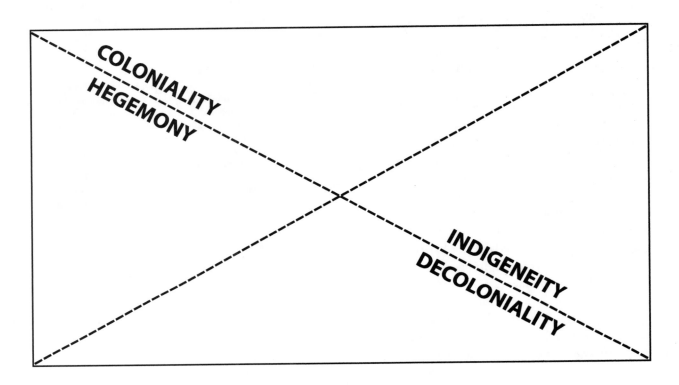

Four Macroscales of Ethnic Studies: Associated Words Handout

When this framework was first conceptualized, there was a handout that went along with it, describing each scale/ theme and listing a few associated words/concepts with each. The evolution of that is included here, with detailed associated words and concepts for each of the four scales. This may serve as an elaboration in the framing of each scale for teachers and/or may be annotated/highlighted by students as they learn different terms/concepts in the course and supplemented with vocabulary/concept teaching praxis of student/teacher choice.

1. Indigeneity and Roots

We are holistic human beings and communities: a) intellectual, emotional, physical, spiritual, relational; b) terrestrial, cosmic, spatial; c) intergenerational, temporal, hxrstorical; d) intersectional; e) multidimensional; f) community cultural wealth based; g) ecological; h) with identities; and i) (counter) stories to share.

Indigeneity: Respect due, gratitude to the holistic Indigenous peoples and communities of the land where any course is taking place, as the original, autochthonous, sovereign and autonomous first nations present since time immemorial, and still upon that land today, more than 500 years after colonization, and into the future.

Diasporic Indigeneity: Respect due to holistic colonized peoples who are in diaspora upon the land where a course is taking place. In the cases of multitudes of People of Color, macroscales two and three displaced their families from their precolonial ancestral homelands as "normal." If/when they connect to their Indigenous roots, their Indigenous peoplehood and legacies of that homeland, that is called Diasporic Indigeneity.

In different contexts, Indigeneity is considered at tribal/national; local; regional; linguistic; "statewide"; "federal"; continental; hemispheric; international levels, and sometimes, beyond. The local-regional tribe/nation scale is imperative here, for dishonoring that even when connecting to a diasporic indigeneity, then becomes settler colonialism instead, the second macroscale, designed to erase and replace this first macroscale.

Indigeneity considers the sovereignties and autonomies of human nations and of Ecological relatives, for past, present, future generations.

Indigeneity and Diasporic Indigeneity signify dynamic, complex, holistic:

1. Peoples who believe they are ancestrally related and identify themselves, based on oral and/or written histories, as descendants of the original inhabitants of their ancestral homelands;
2. Peoples who may, but not necessarily, have their own informal and/or formal political, economic, and social institutions, which tend to be community based and reflect their distinct ceremonial cycles, kinship networks, and continuously evolving cultural traditions;
3. Peoples who speak (or once spoke) an indigenous language, often different from the dominant society's language, even where the Indigenous language is not "spoken," distinct dialects and/or uniquely Indigenous expressions may persist as a form of Indigenous identity;
4. Peoples who distinguish themselves from the dominant society and/or other cultural groups while maintaining a close relationship with their ancestral homelands/sacred sites, which may be threatened by ongoing military, economic, or political encroachment or may be places where indigenous peoples have been previously displaced and expelled creating a diaspora, while seeking to enhance their cultural, political, and economic sovereignty and autonomy.

Precolonial Ancestry and Roots

Indigeneity is not the same thing as ancestry, and though we're all indigenous to our mother planet, we're not all Indigenous to the local land/nations/continents we're upon. We all have precolonial ancestry and roots, though we may not know to what people and where. Many people have ancestors who are Indigenous, colonized, Diasporic Indigenous, and who were/are settler colonizers themselves (also with precolonial roots). People have various moral imperatives of identity; some identify with certain ancestral roots and groups over others, for many reasons—some reasons of their own deciding, some of the group's deciding, and some decided by macroscales two and three—in historical amnesia. We are all historically situated, a part of this process and struggle, and related to these four macroscales to different extents, whether we actively realize it or not. Indigeneity and Roots, live on, in solidarity with macroscale four, confronting scales two and three, hxrstorically, now, and into the future.

2. Coloniality, Dehumanization, and Genocide

~~We~~ *are colonial.*

Explicit and Totalizing

Dehumanization • Colonization • Settler colonialism • Neocolonialism • Internal colonialism • Double/triple colonialism • Imperialism • Chattel enslavement • Oppression • All intersectional forms of explicit oppressive power and privilege • Establishing systems of colonial hierarchy/knowledge/culture • Deculturalization • Deindigenization • Detribalization • Divide and conquer • Multidimensional violence • Genocide • Forced migration • Forced diaspora • Enslavement • Social construction of race and racism • White supremacy • Anti-Blackness • Anti-Indigeneity • Patriarchy and misogyny • Heteropatriarchy and Heterosexism • Capitalism and classism • Neoliberalism • White property rights • Explict toxic masculinity • Exclusion • Containment • Control • Dispossession • Displacement • Carcerality • Subtractive schooling • Education debt • Traumas • Pain • Explicit macroaggressions • Continued colonial occupation • Neoliberal globalization • Legislative oppression • Explicit erasure and replacement of holistic Indigeneity and humanity with a (neo)colonial model of itself • Victimization • Societal bullying • Imposed power imbalance • Imposed lack of rights • Discrimination • Disempowerment • Imposed low self-worth • Imposed lack of respect, alienation, being kept down, isolation • Explicitly imposed internalized oppression and inferiority complexes • Restrictions/barriers to freedoms of behavior and speech • Stop being yourself • Forced assimilation • Imposed abuse/misuse of power • Explicitly forbidding original Indigenous worldviews and knowledge • Explicit colonial futurity for ~~holistic~~ totalized, dehumanized beings.

3. Hegemony and Normalization

~~We~~ *are colonial hegemonic.*

Implicit and Totalizing

Normalized domination and internalized forms of everything explicitly noted in macroscale two (coloniality), disguised as being for the good of society • Hxrstorical amnesia, cultural-hxstorical vacuum, invisibilization • Stereotypes, self-hatred, shame, deficit thinking • Complicity and collusion • Ahistoricity • Submersion • "Neutrality" and "objectivity" • Zombification • Naive and magical consciousness • False consciousness • Superficiality • Concision • "Color-blindness" • "Meritocracy" • "Heroes and Holidays as Ethnic Studies" • White-supremacist capitalist heteropatriarchal normativity • White privilege • White fragility, white silence, white denial, white anxiety, and white entitlement • Standardizing imperialism (and coloniality) • Microaggressions subtly housed in the macroaggressions • Scapegoats • Horizontal oppression • Sub-oppression • Hidden curricula of coloniality • Imposter syndrome • Faux civility • False democracy • Hokey hope • Appropriation • Surface integration of social justice demands in order to dilute and weaken them • Implicit/hegemonic (neo)colonial futurity • Complicit participation in furthering it all as normalized neocolonial hegemonic beings in the empire and "Matrix."

4. Decoloniality, Regeneration, and Social Justice

We are holistic human beings and communities: a) intellectual, emotional, physical, spiritual, relational; b) terrestrial, cosmic, spatial; c) intergenerational, temporal, hxrstorical; d) intersectional; e) multidimensional; f) community cultural wealth based; g) ecological; h) with identities; and i) (counter) stories to share.

Regeneration of Indigeneity and Roots • Love • Humanization • Healing • Equity • Decolonization • Post+Colonial! • Belongingness • Solidarity • Critical/compassionate/creative consciousness • Cultural memory • Empowerment • Remembrance • Recognition • Reclamation • Reimagination • Restoration • Resurgence • Revitalization • Reconciliation • Self-determination • Sovereignty • Agency • Critical hope • Creation • Transformational resistance to hegemonic/oppressive/colonial systems of power • Counter-narrativity • Counterhegemony • Countergenocide • Protest movements and revolutions • Community cultural wealth • Community organizing • Civil rights • Intercommunalism • People of Color Power • Positive image of self and community • Anti-racism • Anti-sexism • Anti-heterosexism • Anti-ableism • Anti-Ageism • Anti–white supremacy • Anti–settler colonialism • Anti-patriarchy • Anti-heteropatriarchy • Anti-heteronormativity • Anti-xenophobia • Anti-oppression in all its forms • Pro-love • Honesty • Interrupting implicit bias • Empathy • Solidarity • Reciprocity • Peace • Dignity • Rematriation • Liberation • Freedom • Regeneration of Indigenous epistemic and cultural futurity • Self and community care • Queering • Conscious hip-hop and creative art forms • Critical race theorizing • Multiple subjectivities • One dignified world where many worlds fit • Dreaming • Transformation in reflection (study, theory) and action • Cycles of critical praxis • Critical solidarities and futurities • CxRxPx • Ethnic Studies for all! •_____!

Critical Consciousness: Standing against dehumanization; identifying origins of knowledge; critiquing the "master narrative" and claims of objectivity/neutrality (including "color-blindness") and highlighting marginalized worldviews; addressing cultural-hxrstorical, sociopolitical, economic levels of analysis; naming and confronting systems of intersectional power, privilege, and oppression; interrogating ideological, institutional, interpersonal, and internalized levels of privilege and oppression; understanding geo-hxrstorical literacy and causality; cultivating critical hope and self-determination; nurturing critical solidarities for past, present, and future generations.

INDIGENEITY AND ROOTS

Collective Healing
Release the Tears, Confront and Bypass the Fear

BY ROSE BORUNDA

Tears Withheld

Several years ago my father, out of the blue, told me, "Back in Mexico, the Spaniards would force Indians to work. If an Indian refused to do a job, he would be whipped to death right then and there. Another Indian would be brought in to finish the job."

I was surprised to hear this from him because up until that point, he had not expressed any affinity with our Indigenous roots. If anything, he leaned toward disassociation. His occasional references to his nation of birth, Guanajuato, Mexico, generally focused on the poverty he experienced as a child; and when it came to our lineage, he would proudly state about his mother, "Your Mama Lupe was full-blooded Spaniard!"

This statement would perplex me. I have travelled to Spain, and it was quite apparent that my Mama Lupe would not have passed as a Spaniard. Not even close. My grandparents' features and deep-brown skin conveyed what was most certainly, and predominantly, Indigenous ancestry. Of course, being of and claiming one's Indigenous heritage are two separate matters because most of us would not know, for certain, how we would personally respond to the threat and fear of violence. Conquest and colonization has left in its wake a spectrum of responses, including adherence with the colonizer—the one holding the whip—leading to psychological, physical, and emotional distancing from the abused Indian.

There is, however, a cost for this disassociation. When we fail to identify with and/or acknowledge those who have suffered, we reject our full human nature. Such a departure from our full sense of humanity requires that we withhold our tears. At a physical level, prolactin—a hormone associated with stress and sorrow that is emitted in our tears—remains in our system. When we relieve this and other related hormones through our tears, we are left in a better state of being that enables us to reverse our emotions. In order to reach this "Reset," we must first acknowledge the suffering and pain. Then and only then, after releasing the burdensome tears, are we able to respond to the needs of others with greater psychological, physiological, and emotional clarity. We are in a better position to restore our collective humanity.

Confronting Horizontal and Vertical Violence

Though not California Indian, I have joined a committed group of California Indian cultural experts, educators, and advocates who are pursuing the vision of integrating California Indian–vetted perspective in our K–12 curriculum. Vertical violence, we must note, is conducted through acts in a hierarchical structure in which people who have more power and privilege oppress those who have less power or authority within the structure. Without a collective or constructive response to vertical violence, those on the receiving end can, at times, direct their sense of anger or helplessness in the form of destructive behavior—horizontal violence—toward their peers. For those who are willing to look upon the face of this issue, it is a difficult topic to challenge. Considerable time has passed since a person could, with impunity, murder an Indian and even commit, as was evident in California, genocide. Yet the reverberations of the violence from the past are now coupled with a repackaged violence in the present.

Placing oneself in the crosshairs of vertical and

horizontal violence has a cost. For those who choose to stand with, acknowledge, and embrace the aforementioned indignant Indian, there is an inner fortitude required to confront, at a personal and at a societal level, the forces unleashed today from a different sort of colonizer's whip.

For example, my mother's lineage is mostly European. As a child, I recall how her fairer-skinned sister would openly laugh at me when I would run back inside the house after playing outside. The reason for her ridicule was that my skin turns shades darker with a touch of the sun. Her sister's derision compelled my humiliated mother to discourage me from playing outdoors, but rather than comply, I simply spent more time outside.

When she saw me preparing to run outside and play she would yell, "Put on a hat! It will keep the sun off of you." I pretended not to hear her.

When I got to junior high, I selected and often made my own clothes, frequently choosing deep purples and bold golds, black moccasins, and beaded jewelry. I cheered on the Indians in the old Western movies; of course the Indians never won, but I didn't care. I embraced the dispossessed. Their narrative resonated with me, and when old enough to learn about my own Indigenous roots, I actively searched (our) story because (his)story left me feeling like a planet out of orbit. In that estranged place, I embraced rather than denied the reality of the "whipped Indians" who, in the region of the Americas from where my father came, were subjected to the encomienda system, a predecessor to the California missions. My personal experience of horizontal violence bolstered my ability to recognize the vertical violence embedded in our social system, remnants of our history.

For example, conquering Spaniards created two systems of vertical violence—the encomiendas in Latin America and the California missions—for the purpose of expanding and fortifying Spanish rule in the Americas. In doing so, Original Nations were exposed to subjugating forces that included weapons, disease, rape, and other means of torture with the intention of eliminating Indigenous culture, spirituality, and language. All things Spanish and European—including culture, language, and religion—were heralded as superior. The "whip" that fell across the Americas may look different today, but it still stings nonetheless.

In the face of overt and subliminal hostility to Indigeneity, there has been an array of responses to the subversive messages of "European superiority." Personally, I have taken my cues from the indignant Indian, armed with nothing more than a desire to retain my dignity rather than risk shame for acts of denial. Though lacking the cultural attributes and practices of my distant ancestors, I nonetheless compensated with a doctorate degree, a weapon that when put to good use can be more dangerous than a whip. Fortified with Freirian theory, I have chosen to not look away and disassociate from acts of oppression that exist today. My question now, however, is whether you—the reader of this rendering, whether Indigenous or not—are willing to acknowledge, stand firm, and confront the vertical violence that persists in our midst, or will you look away in fear and disassociation? The path I have chosen in addressing the societal violence may perhaps provide a blueprint to bolster your decision to choose the former rather than the latter.

Tears in the Path Forward

My first step toward confronting vertical violence in the present entailed presenting at the California Indian Conference (CIC) in October of 2013. It was sponsored at my home campus, California State University, Sacramento (CSUS), where I serve as a professor. This was the 28th annual gathering, with locations alternating every other year between northern and southern regions of our state. I co-presented at this conference at the invitation of Dr. Crystal Martinez-Alire, an enrolled member of the Ione Band of Miwok Indians. Our presentation, "Honoring California's First Nations as First Stewards of the Land; Healing by Setting the Historical Record Straight," was inspired by our understanding that truth about California Indians should be taught in our schools. My growing sensibility to this topic, as it relates to California Indians, was enhanced by having moved less than a year before to the region where Martinez-Alire's tribal community has lived for thousands of years. As a descendent of refugees from the encomienda system, I am a steward in the region and have grown to appreciate the depth of Miwok landmarks and history.

I attended a presentation at this conference in which a panel of speakers was addressing the topic of the California missions. While discussing the topic, one of the presenters unexpectedly shed tears. For the first time, I heard from this presenter and the other panelists about what transpired at the California missions ... from the perspective of a California Indian. They spoke honestly and openly about the suffering inflicted on California Indians at the missions and how the intrusion of the mission system changed the way of life for Original Nations in California.

Furthermore, they called out the fact that children across the state are taught a romanticized version of the California missions in which the colonizers are heralded. In doing so, the California Indian voice and experience are muted, obfuscated, suppressed, and quite simply absent. (Mis)education becomes the weapon to marginalize, as even California Indian children are expected to memorialize the structures and missions that embody the attempted annihilation of their culture, their people. This is what vertical violence looks like today. It is a disturbing picture and, more so, a symbolically violent practice. Inadvertently, our children—in California and across the United States—are taught via omission that the lives, the voice, and the experiences of California Indians do not matter. Without being told, children learn "Don't cry for the Indian." Unintentionally, the same (mis)education fosters children's disassociation from their own sense of compassion and ability to be fully human. The presenter at the conference had not lost his own humanity, despite being routinely subjected to vertical violence in our classrooms year after year.

As I sat in the audience watching the presenter's tears fall, I thought of my colleagues, Drs. Mimi Coughlin, Maggie Beddow, Mae Chaplin, and Tom Owens who teach social science methods courses in our college of education. I know their hearts, and in the spirit of "calling it out," I concluded that we could do something about this issue. The tears inspired me to ask:

What would it take to not only stop the practice of expecting children in our schools to physically replicate and glamorize the missions but to also teach the "truth" about what transpired at them?

The following fall, at the 29th annual CIC held at California State University, San Bernardino, I had the opportunity to see Gregg Castro's presentation. Castro is a writer and activist who focuses on issues regarding cultural preservation, protection, education, and traditional practices for over two decades. He actively protects the heritage of his late mother's Rumsien Ohlone homeland, the Monterey Bay area; on his father's side he is a founding member of the Salinan Nation Tribal Council, having served as Tribal Chair, and co-founded their nonprofit organization, Salinan T'rowt'raahl. He is an advisor with the California Indian Storytelling Association and a long-standing member of the Society for California Archaeology, serving as their Native American Programs Committee co-chair.

When it was time for Castro to present, he stood up from his seat, crossed over to the far-right side of the stage, and leaving several feet of space between himself and the wall to our right, gestured with his hand at the small distance between himself and the wall. He then said, "This is the history of California as is told to children, which began just a mere several hundred years ago."

Those of us in the audience regarded the small distance between him and the wall. We could easily picture how it represented the time period from approximately the late 1700s to present day, a mere 300 years or so. Then Castro turned toward the opposite wall and gestured from himself to the far wall, which was a considerably farther expanse. He then said, "This is the history of California from a California Indian perspective. Our timeline extends way beyond a mere several hundred years."

I was stumped. The expanse of time that Gregg indicated was vast, and I knew nothing about it. I would venture to say that most people don't, yet here I was once again presenting "Culturally Responsive Curriculum in the K–12 Public Education System" at a CIC with Martinez-Alire and my research assistant, Samantha Britto-Jacoby. Yet Castro was pointing out an immeasurable collective lack of knowledge perpetuated by historical devaluation and disregard of California Indians. The apparent price from this lesson means that the vertical violence inherent in our (mis)education fosters our collective ignorance.

We approached Castro after his presentation to discuss the larger issue and from this discussion, a second question emerged:

How do we facilitate the implementation of California Indian knowledge, wisdom, and perspective into our K–12 public education system?

Castro suggested that the following year we hold a California Indian Curriculum Summit under the umbrella of the following year's 30th annual CIC that would be sponsored at UC Berkeley. The tears had been shed, the issue acknowledged, and it was time to move forward. We were ready to "Reset."

Collectively Moving Forward

With a growing group of visionaries who we now call the California Indian History Curriculum Coalition (CIHCC), we have embarked upon a journey to identify and create California Indian–vetted curriculum while also promoting the adoption of this curriculum by sponsoring California Indian Curriculum Summits (CICS). The efforts, supported by the Doctorate in Educational Leadership program of CSUS and hosted several times by California Indian Conferences, have prompted two major movements. First, we have identified the elements of vertical violence and sponsored a resolution entitled "Repeal, Replace, and Reframe the Mission Project." This effort heightens awareness about a symbol of vertical violence and calls for its replacement.

It is not that we ask that the missions of California not be taught in our classrooms; it is, however, the content taught that is now under examination. Further catapulted by the California State Board of Education's recently adopted History–Social Science Framework that promotes a broader and more inclusive view of education, there are specific questions contained in the framework that address the questions that have been previously posed:

- What was life like for Native Californians before other settlers arrived?
- How were people's lives affected by missions?
- How did the region change because of the mission system?

Second, replacement units are being created by California Indian content experts so that educators can learn how to present the topic with inclusion of California Indian voices. This content includes multiple perspectives and experiences for the classroom so that children will have the opportunity to examine history from a more critical and expansive lens.

In this "Reset" being undertaken in California, the efforts to create curriculum and write publications that are accessible to teachers are vital. The Ethnic Studies Now coalition in our state has produced the book *Our Stories in Our Voices* (Kendall Hunt Publishing Company, 2017) by professors Dale Allender and Gregory Yee Mark. This textbook has been adopted by local school districts for use in 9th-grade Ethnic Studies courses. I co-authored the opening chapter with Martinez-Alire, and it was a privilege to secure the following quote from Richard Johnson, Tribal Chair of Nevada City Rancheria: "The most important thing that people need to know about the Nisenan people is that we are still here. The other thing that needs to be known is that we need to correct the history books. The history books have it wrong."

It is healing for me to put Johnson's words to print, because seeing the truth in print heals. All of us have agency in our positions, and how we use our voice and capacity can initiate healing, harmony, and restoration of fractured intergroup relationships. Furthermore, being able to restore my own humanity not only provides opportunity for my own growth in this cross-cultural alliance, but it also leaves me grounded and restored with each lesson learned. And with this, the coalition expands, includes, and fearlessly moves forward. In doing so, we restore our sense of humanity with one another and subsequently collectively heal. For the reader, consider the nature of confronting vertical violence as we have and whether this is something you can do where you are. To this end, I leave you with the following steps.

Restore

A groundswell means growth, expansion, and a movement that extends beyond the individual. I think back to the individual Indians who stood up to their oppressors even knowing it would result in their death. What would they think of this groundswell? Our efforts have resulted in creating an accessible website that contains the California Indian–vetted curriculum that we are encouraging educators across the state to draw from.

Our website (csus.edu/coe/cic) includes the previously discussed Resolution to Repeal, Replace, and Reframe the Mission Project and contains other relevant resources. We are in the beginning stages and recognize that there are other states who are further ahead. Yet as we look to the future in our own realm, we have secured the commitment of forward-thinking educators like Dr. Stephanie Biagetti, chair of credentials department at CSUS who, along with the social science professors in her department, has requested that all future teachers in their teacher-education pipeline be trained in the curriculum created and offered by California Indians.

One article on our website, "Long-term Relationship Building and Inclusion in Curriculum Development," was inspired by two CIHCC founders, Gregg Castro and Beverly Ortiz. For the purpose of using this opportunity to inspire you, I will include a few recommendations from this article. Perhaps, if you haven't already, you may consider joining the effort of restoring our full humanity wherever you may be. First we begin by reaching out to the Original Nations in your region. Who are the Original Nations in your region? There may be more than one. Do these Original Nations have a local tribal office? Do they have curriculum that they are willing to share?

Are there families attending your school from these Original Nations? Are there elders from the community who can provide guidance and direction? There may be multiple cultural groups. There may be one. Invite them to participate with you in collaboration on this journey.

In your classroom, your conferences, and your region, openly recognize and honor the Original Nation. For example, on our Sacramento campus, when my colleagues co-chair the annual Multicultural Conference, they recognize the Original Nation, the Miwok, and when possible, have an elder from the Miwok community open the event.

If you are adopting curriculum or resources for use in your classroom, always acknowledge the source of information that you are using, i.e., "The following story is from [*name tribe*] given to us by [*name person*]."

In identifying resources, recognize that Original Nations have persevered despite culturecide,

so it cannot be assumed that people from any community know all their stories, cultural practices, etc. For example, I am Purépecha and speak English and Spanish (two overlays of conquest and colonization) but do not know a single Purépecha word.

You may identify resources that are already published. Is the data from a primary source or has it been appropriated? For this purpose, ascertain that information (i.e., stories) are what Original Nations have offered. For example, there is original Native American art and then there is "Native American inspired." There is nothing wrong with the latter; however to truly recognize and honor, go to the source.

Finally, identify and extract symbolically violent terms and practices when and where you can. Consider the language and practices that promote the "master narrative." When these practices/words are given life in our reality, they promote the narrative of dominance and, subsequently, imply and condone subjugation. As previously discussed, in California we are looking to replace the "Mission Project" in our educational system. It doesn't mean that we don't want the missions to be discussed, but we want them to be discussed in full context of what transpired. Additionally, certain terms and phrases—such as "the natives are getting restless," "circle the wagons," "New/Old World," "discovery of America," "primitive people," "civilized," etc.—continue to riddle our vernacular. Considering the paradigm from which these words emanated requires mindfulness in our communication; although we may struggle to extract that which is violent, we then replace it with harmony and restore our connection with one another.

To this end, the effort to acknowledge and not turn away from what has transpired in the Americas is not easy. There are multiple overlays of horizontal and vertical violence to contend with and the road to a better vision of our relationships with one another is wrought with misunderstanding, distrust, and opposition. As educators and agents of change, we can do nothing if we are immobilized by fear or by indifference. I chose to step forward with those in our visionary coalition and hope to leave the world better than how I found it for the generations that come. May we share this vision and work toward restoration of our personal humanity through collective healing. ✳

The Kids 'n Room 36
Cognates, Culture, and the Ecosystem

BY JAIME CUELLO

Early in the year I asked, "How many of you know about the Mexica?" The students in my 5th-grade science class responded, "What's a Mexica?"

I immediately changed the name "Mexica" to "Aztec" and repeated the question. "How many of you know about the Aztecs?" The response now was "Indians." It was obvious to me that the children really didn't have any understanding of their culture. From their responses, I could tell that they weren't being taught about their *cultura*, a culture that appears to be hidden from them since their initial baptism in kindergarten all the way up to 5th grade.

I proceeded to ask them about Aztlan, Tenochtitlan, and the symbolism of the eagle perched on the cactus. Of course by now, you can predict their responses. Giselle, an inquisitive child, asked, "What is Tenochtitlan?"

The lack of personal knowledge of their Chicano culture has become clearly obvious to me. This has been my observation over the past 23 years teaching 4th and 5th graders in rural Califas (California), in classrooms where the population is 90 percent or more Latino. I prefer the terms *Mexican American*, or better yet *Chicano*, but I often use the generic term *Latino* because it is more clearly understandable to many.

As a bilingual, bicultural 5th-grade science teacher of the Kids 'n Room 36, I have learned over the past decades that English language learners of Mexican descent lack basic academic knowledge in science as well as in their ancestral heritage.

In order to help create an appreciation, respect, and understanding for scientific thinking, and to teach them the curriculum in a manner relevant to their cultures, I made two connections. First I incorporated cognates to make the lessons connect beyond simple basic knowledge to mastery. Second, I connected the learning to their Native American culture in hopes that in next year, or even five years from now, they will still carry this science knowledge and vocabulary with them.

In a lesson on the ecosystem and food chains, I thought long and hard about adding cognates to create a more equitable playing field for my English language learners. I know that it would be easier on me as a teacher to teach everything in English. I grew up on it, the state tests are written in English, every other teacher in Califas is going to teach it in English, so why not me too? I contemplated the thought of adding the cognates. I knew that the research said to use them in helping English language learners. I knew that it would help increase understanding and take my students from basic knowledge and facts to an at-grade level.

So rather than take the easier route, I created a list of science cognates. After all, I have a responsibility to teach to a higher level of science understanding and not be merely satisfied to just encourage a passion for science for the Kids 'n Room 36.

I listed cognates like:
- producers/*productores*
- consumer/*consumidor*
- energy/*energía*
- ecosystem/*ecosistema*

I took my 5th graders' culture as well as their primary language, Spanish, into consideration. It's important to show them to embrace the language of their parents and grandparents and help them with their understanding of the science curriculum.

Beyond Cognates to Indigeneity

After using the translated cognates as a basic tool for understanding scientific concepts, I moved beyond just language to their cultural identity. I wanted to focus on their relationship to their ancestors and their Native American heritage as well. Though my students are not Chumash themselves, I needed them to understand that when connecting to their own Indigenous roots, it is important to honor the local Indigenous peoples as well.

To help my children better understand the local Indigenous Chumash tribe, we read *Island of the Blue Dolphins* and *Rainbow Bridge*. Both books talk about the Chumash relationships with animals and mother nature. They provide us with insights about Chumash understandings of the food chains, food webs, and ecosystem. We go outside the classroom and burn sage inside an abalone shell in the same manner as the Chumash. This is part of a traditional Native American Chumash ceremony to say good morning to Father Sun, Mother Earth, and the Four Winds. We begin by creating a large circle in the middle of our playground area. I stand in the center with my sage, abalone shell, and a match or lighter to ignite and burn the sage. We all face east toward the sun and say, "Good morning, Father Sun," then we look down at the earth and say, "Good morning, Mother Earth." We then face north and say, "Good morning, winds of the north," then face east and say, "Good morning, winds of the east." All four cardinal directions are faced and we repeat our good morning. Then I bring in guest speakers like Akima Castaneda (a local Chumash elder and Hollywood actor who passed to the spirit world recently) to talk to the children about the Chumash culture, language, art, and lifestyles. This includes conversations about diet, music, respect for Mother Nature, and the freedom enjoyed before the arrival of the Spanish and colonialism.

Finally, children experience the simulation of making acorn mush, a traditional Chumash food staple. Children are assigned to bring in a *molcajete* (originally from the Nahuatl *molcaxitl*, or mortar and pestal) from home to create this simulation. My students always show up to school with at least three to six molcajetes. We use peanuts instead of acorns. We crack them and crush them in our molcajetes to create a dry powder, which will serve for us as acorn mush.

This hands-on simulation serves to recreate an experience similar to that of the Chumash, but it also helps make a personal connection between them and the Chumash culture: Many of their mothers might use the same tool at home, which helps to bridge the similarities between themselves and the local Indigenous tribe. It is up to us as teachers to dig deep like rock hounds into our curriculum to find those hidden gems and make connections between our areas of study and our brown students' Native American roots.

This year, science and Mexica/Aztec language would be that bridge to connect child to curriculum. Over many years of trial and error, I found a hot spot in the science curriculum. It is by nature a study that lends itself to cognates, since the Chumash, Mexica, Mayans, and Incas (to name a few) were and are inquiry-based learners of the sciences of nature, chemistry, life, and astronomy.

With the knowledge that many of my Chicano children are direct descendants of the Mexica and Mayans, I also connect to their parents, my own upbringing, and the internet to find scientific words in Spanish that have Nahuatl origins. This process required researching Nahuatl words that could be used in the teaching of the science curriculum. I talked to people in the community, including students' families, and asked them to recall words they grew up hearing from their parents and grandparents, and then I committed to researching those words. This led to a homework assignment where children had to go home and ask their parents for Spanish translations of the following words: *grass, corn, grasshopper, raccoon,* and *owl.*

I created a science anchor paper and handout from scratch because I couldn't find any ready-made resources. I drew the pictures and created my first-ever ecosystem/food chain with both Spanish and English cognates, as well as a handout of Spanish words of Nahuatl origin.

My multilingual, illustrated food chain began with the title/*titulo* "Ecosystem/Ecosistema" and a picture of the Sun/*Sol* and the words "energy/energía" inside the drawing. Along the left-hand side going from bottom to the top, I wrote *Energy is being transferred/transferido* and at the bottom "Producers/Productores." I then created the food chain intentionally using Spanish words with Nahuatl origins. This part took the longest in my lesson planning; it would produce the biggest understanding of the science curriculum.

Above the word "Producers/Productores," I drew grass and corn. I also added *zacate* and *elote*, as the Spanish words for grass and corn with Nahuatl origin. My students were surprised by this. They expected to see cognates, but instead they saw the ancestral roots of their home cultura. Next are the "Consumers/Consumidores": the grasshopper/*chapulín*, raccoon/*mapache*, squirrel/*techalote*, and then at the top, "Predators/Depredadores." At the top of my handout are owl/*tecolote* and coyote.

Many kids raised their hands to eagerly tell me, "Mr. Cuello, my mom uses the words *elote* and *chapulín*."

Henry came over to talk one-on-one with me. He said, "Mr. Cuello, these words sound funny to me."

"What do you mean Henry?"

"Yeah, they don't sound like Spanish to me." He pauses and says, "They just don't sound right to me."

"But Henry, they are Spanish words."

"No, they just don't sound right."

"Well what do you think they are, Henry?"

"I think they're Native American words!" he says and tilts his head, staring into my face for a reaction to confirm his theory.

"Yes, Henry, they are Mexica words."

"I knew it, I knew it. They just didn't sound like Spanish words to me."

"Don't tell anyone yet, Henry. I'm going to tell the class later, but congrats, because you are the only one who has figured it out."

Henry immediately rushed back to his seat with the biggest smile imaginable. His joy was contagious, and it made me smile. Children at his group gathered around him and asked, "What is so funny?"

"Tell us, Henry, tell us!"

Henry, true to his word, only smiled and said nothing.

We discussed last night's homework of asking our parents about the Spanish translations. "My mom uses the same Spanish words that you wrote on the chart," Gracie said, "All of my family, even my uncles use the same words—*chapulín*, *mapache*, and *tecolote*."

Children were even engaged in conversations at home with immediate and extended family; Giselle came back and said, "My mother uses most of the Mexica words, but she has a different word for *tecolote*." It was wonderful to hear that she spoke with her mother about the Nahuatl words and awesome that she discovered that her mother had a different word for *tecolote*. After all, just because we are of Mexican or Native American descent doesn't mean that we all have to be exactly alike, a lesson she learned and taught to the rest of the class, including myself.

I then proceeded to inform them that this was a special food chain because the words on the chart were Spanish, but their origins are Mexica. At this moment in time children began to whisper, "My family uses these words." I asked them to share how many of their families use these words at home. Two-thirds of the class shot up their hands with pride and exclaimed, "We do," and "Me too."

I explained that if their families use these Mexica words at home, then they are practicing the Nahuatl language of the Mexica. And since they are using many words of the Nahuatl language at home, they are probably descendants of the Nahuatl-speaking peoples, the most well-known of which are the Mexica. Again, shouts are heard from the east to west side of the classroom. "I'm a Mexica. I'm a Mexica."

Next I encouraged the children to pair share with their partners about what their families said at home. They then began to write an information essay about the ecosystem and the food chain, with one condition: Everyone had to use their Mexica Nahuatl words when describing the food chain. This meant that the repetition of *zacate*, *elote*, *chapulín*, *mapache*, and *tecolote* would be written to help not only ensure the science of a food chain but also respect the language of their ancestors in the process.

The children began to write a flash draft. Unlike other writing assignments, this time the children wrote without me having to ask twice. It was obvious that when the Kids 'n Room 36 were communicating about their personal and ancestral connection to the science curriculum, they did better work. This sense of being a part of science encouraged them to write more about the subject matter.

The Kids 'n Room 36 are now armed with the science curriculum, cognates, and a consciousness and recognition of the words of their ancestors. The knowledge from the ancient ones is really not so ancient because they—we—are still here through us. ✳

"My Family's Not from Africa —We Come from North Carolina!"
Teaching Slavery in Context

BY WAAHIDA TOLBERT-MBATHA

As a student, I always dreaded when we came to "my" section in the history book: the section on the transatlantic slave trade. I remember wondering, "If I sink down far enough in my seat, can I become invisible?" As far as the textbook was concerned, and perhaps my teachers as well, my history as a Black person began in West Africa with my ancestors being abducted and sold into slavery, herded onto ships, and piled on top of one another in shackles as we set sail for the "New World." My teachers would present this section almost as news anchors, emotionless and neutral as they recounted the horrors experienced by people, my people: "Once they arrived to the New World, they had no rights, they were considered three-fifths human, they were forced to work without pay, and their children were taken away from them and sold to the highest bidder, until one day Abraham Lincoln decided that slavery was wrong and set the slaves free. Class, make sure that you take solid notes, you will be expected to know this information for the unit test."

I remember sitting there, feeling powerless, humiliated, and victimized by a teacher presenting such a sordid part of human history in a matter-of-fact manner, with no attempt to humanize the topic of slavery or engage me with information about the many acts of resistance and rebellion that led to the emancipation of the enslaved. Nor was I invited into a discussion about who we were before slavery or how something so horrific ever came to be in the first place.

Now I teach history myself. I will never forget the blank stares that gazed back at me one day from my 7th-grade geography class at a public school in Washington, D.C. As we were wrapping up our unit on Latin America, I said to the class: "So, everyone in the United States, with the exception of Native Americans, has roots in other parts of the world. For example, many Latin Americans in Washington have ancestral roots in El Salvador, many African Americans can trace all or part of our ancestry back to West Africa, while white Americans can trace their ancestry to various countries in Europe."

"My family's not from Africa," sparked Ra'Sean. "We come from North Carolina!"

"I see what you mean, Ra'Sean. I was born in Kentucky and my grandparents were born in Tupelo, Mississippi. But if I trace my roots back far enough, I can trace them to West Africa and perhaps even to a specific country."

The class erupted in mumbling and discontent. Marcus shook his head the hardest as I unloaded information that he was just not prepared to take in.

"Well, if we came from West Africa, how did we get here?" demanded Keona.

I had unintentionally opened up a can of worms. I couldn't believe this was new information for my middle school students. And that, as African Americans, they couldn't deal with the fact that their ancestors were from Africa. Clearly they had been inundated with the same racist media images that I was exposed to, images that showed Africa and its people as helpless and hungry.

As I paused to take in my unwelcome discovery, Karla chimed in: "My mother told me we used to be kings and queens until we were taken from Africa and brought here as slaves."

I rolled down my world map to show students the route of the transatlantic slave trade. "Karla's right. Then, over hundreds of years, European slave traders captured millions of people in West Africa, including many of our ancestors. They transported them, against their will, across the Atlantic Ocean to the New World and sold them into slavery."

I breathed a sigh of a relief as I glanced at the clock and noticed that it was time for students to transition to their next class. They quickly packed their belongings and I was left to grapple with this new information.

Teaching the History of Slavery Differently

I shared my shock and frustration with Jeff, my friend and co-planner, and discussed with him my desire to divert from the scope and sequence to teach students a bit about Africa and the transatlantic slave trade. But I wanted to do it very differently from my experience as a student. I wanted to center on the many acts of resistance to colonial conquest, in Africa and

More often than not, slavery is the only time African history is considered, leaving many Black students no choice but to feel like their only place in history is that of a victim.

in the diaspora, up until the present. I knew that it was important to start with an overview of Africa as a continent, as a place with a rich history prior to slavery and colonialism. This piece was especially critical because, more often than not, slavery is the only time African history is considered, leaving many Black students no choice but to feel like their only place in history is that of a victim.

I knew that most of my students viewed Africa as a homogeneous place and, moreover, a place that they wanted no connection to. I wanted to be sure that I presented this unit in a way that empowered students and made them proud of their ancestry, as opposed to leaving them feeling the shame and humiliation that I once felt. I wanted to show them

the beauty and diverse realities of Africa in order to shift their perceptions, but I also wanted to give an honest representation of some of the struggles.

That Sunday evening, I drew a blank outline of Africa on a large poster board, wrote "Africa" in large black letters at the top, and divided it into three sections: What do you know or think you know? What do you want/need to know? What have you learned?

As students walked into the classroom on Monday, the warm-up exercise on the board said: *On the blank Post-it notes on your desk, record what you know about Africa and what you think you know.*

Students struggled to write anything. As I circulated around the classroom, I thought aloud: "Perhaps you know the names of a few countries in Africa, or maybe you know a language that people speak in a particular country. Perhaps you know fruits and vegetables that grow in some parts of Africa or a bit about the history of some countries."

I asked students to share with a neighbor and then called on a few partnerships to report back: Africa is hot, many people speak French, people wear colorful clothes, Africa is dirty, people are starving, Africa has kings and queens, and people live with elephants and lions.

I bit my tongue, wanting desperately to correct student responses. A few student volunteers collected the Post-it notes and placed them on the first section of the wall chart. As we progress through the unit, I told the class that we would go back and check our assumptions for accuracy.

Then I explained: "We are going on a cross-continent tour to a few specific countries in Africa, but before we go, we need to prepare. If you were preparing for a tour of countries in Africa, what would you want to know before heading there?"

Students jotted down responses on their Post-it notes: What languages do people speak? How do they dress? What money do they use? What is the history? Religion? Weather? Is it safe?

Then I introduced one of my favorite picture books: *Africa Is Not a Country* by Margy Burns, a collection of 25 short stories about children in various countries in Africa. It portrays families on the continent with integrity, highlighting the beauty of Africa and loving relationships, as opposed to the glaring poverty and doom that is all too familiar to most students.

I started with the story about Thomas, who lives in Lesotho, a small country in southern Africa. The Lesotho story provides readers with a glimpse into a day in Thomas's life as he navigates the cold winter weather in rural Lesotho in July. Lesotho is one of the few places in Africa where you can actually find snow. Thomas and his father snuggle up with blankets to remain warm in the frigid weather as they travel by horse to do errands and visit friends and family. After we read the story, I asked students to jot down new learning and questions and then share with a neighbor:

"I can't believe it snows in Africa. I thought it was hot all year round."

"Does everyone in Lesotho travel by horse?"

After a few partners shared new information and questions with the class, we explored a second short story about two siblings, Arim and Efrem, who live in a colorful row house on a bustling street in urban Eritrea. This story focuses on the importance to their family of religion and respecting elders.

Students as Researchers

For day two of our cross-continental tour, I arranged desks in groups of four. Each group had a sign that included the name of a country, its flag, and the students assigned to that group. The countries I selected were South Africa, Eritrea, Ivory Coast, and Algeria. On the whiteboard in the front of the classroom was the country that I would focus on: Ghana. I chose countries to represent the various regions and diversity of Africa. I also had to be intentional about selecting countries for which information was readily accessible online and in the public library.

After students had a few moments to find their seats and share anything they knew about "their" country, I made an announcement: "Students, for this unit you will become resident experts on your assigned country. You will learn a ton of information that you will eventually develop into a brief research paper on a specific topic. But first you need to gather general information about your country. I have the country Ghana and I will become the resident expert on that country. I selected Ghana because it is one of the countries that many African Americans trace their ancestry back to, so Ghanaian history is very much a part of our collective history. When I was a

student at Berea College, I had the opportunity to travel to Ghana. So I know quite a bit about Ghana, but I still want to learn more."

I gathered the class's attention for the day's strategy lesson: "We are researchers and I want to demonstrate strategies that researchers use to collect information. We will collect important information and organize it using this research tracking sheet. The tracking sheet is divided into four sections: Land and Climate, People and Culture, History, and Economy. These are the four categories that we are going to focus on this week. Right now, information is important if it helps us understand our country better and fits into one of the categories on your tracking sheet. We are going to record important information on a Post-it note and then determine which category it fits into best.

"Last night, as I was browsing through my research bin for information on Ghana, I came across a helpful article about the history of ancient Ghana. Listen carefully as I read an excerpt from the passage and notice how I think aloud about the steps I just identified.

> Despite its name, the old Empire of Ghana is not geographically, ethnically, or in any other way related to modern Ghana. It lies about 400 miles northwest of modern Ghana. Ancient Ghana encompassed what is now modern northern Senegal and southern Mauritania.

"Hmm, I had no idea that modern-day Ghana is not related to the old Empire of Ghana. This is important information to note, so on my Post-it I'm going to write: *Ancient Ghana is not related to modern Ghana; modern Ghana is actually 400 miles away from the old Empire of Ghana.* What category does this fit in? I think history makes the most sense, so I will place this information under the history category. I want to make sure I can find this article again if I need it, so I have to cite my source. I am going to include the title of the article, the author's name, the name of the website, and the page number. To help you remember what you need to do, there is an enlarged version of my Post-it on the board."

After walking through another example, I asked my students to share the steps with a neighbor and then to share any new information that they learned about Ghana:

"I can't believe that Ghana had gold mines. I always thought of Africa as being poor."

"They traded slaves for salt and copper."

A few student volunteers recorded our new knowledge on our wall chart. Then the students were ready to delve into research on their own.

I had loaded small plastic bins located in each "country" with several short books and articles on their assigned country to choose from. (The selection included readings that provided an overview of pre-, colonial, and postcolonial history.) I asked my students to skim the text looking for information that fell into each of the four categories. As students dug into their reading materials, I circulated around the classroom, checking in with students to ensure that they were on the right track. Students continued with their research on these four categories for the next week. Each day I modeled strategies for capturing important information based on my research of Ghana. We continued to fill our Africa wall chart with new information about the countries that we were exploring.

The following week, I wanted students to begin working on specific topics about their countries. I revisited the public library and checked online for more resources. I tried to find two to four topics and two to four texts that explored those topics for each country's bin. My plan was to model researching a specific topic by looking at the history of the transatlantic slave trade as it related to Ghana.

A Focus on Resistance

By the end of the first week of mini-lessons, I had briefly explored the ancient Empire of Ghana and arrived at the 15th century, when the first European slave traders appeared. I wanted to provide students with an overview, but I did not want the trading of human cargo to be the only focus, as it had been in my own middle school experience. Instead, I wanted to focus on the acts of resistance and rebellion that ultimately brought the institution of slavery to shambles. I looked for texts that highlighted slave rebellions, were written from the perspective of the enslaved, and those that detailed everyday acts of resistance that led to the emancipation of

Black people in the United States.

I began the week's lessons: "Last week I was impressed with how focused you were doing background research on your countries. Now it is time to focus on a specific topic or person. Your research bins have new texts in them. Today you will decide on a topic to explore. For example, in the South African bin, you will find books and articles on Nelson Mandela, Oliver Tambo, Robben Island, and the Soweto Uprisings of 1976.

"I'm going to walk you through the process of selecting a topic for your research. I've created a new research tracking sheet. At the top of the sheet there is space for your country's name and the topic that you have chosen to explore. Underneath the topic, you will find two columns: Facts About My Topic and My Reactions/Opinions on My Topic. Watch me model the steps for conducting round two of your research. First, I need to browse through my research bin to see what interests me."

I began to look through the books and articles in my Ghana bin: "This is a short biography written about Ghana's first president after independence, Kwame Nkrumah. I could choose to focus my research on him and his contributions. Here is an article about the Ashanti Kingdom. Hmm, here is one that discusses everyday acts of resistance by enslaved people. I want to focus on this. At the top of my new research tracking sheet I am going to record my topic: *Antislavery Resistance and Rebellion*. Next, I am going to thumb through my research bin to find more books and texts on the same topic."

I looked through the bin and thought aloud with students as I pulled out the relevant texts and placed them in the tray holder on the whiteboard for students to view. There were narratives written from the perspective of the enslaved, picture books about resistance, and encyclopedia articles on the history of slavery. We reviewed the process of identifying important information, recording it on a Post-it note, and then writing our opinion or reaction next to the information.

Over the next few days, I modeled the research process by exploring the history and impact of slavery. We discussed ways that Africans resisted slavery from the beginning until it was abolished. I raised the issue of mental slavery. I recorded facts along with my reactions/opinions: "According to my research, African men, women, and children were seen as goods to be bought and sold, just like silver or gold. Many people actually jumped into the Atlantic Ocean as they were being carried to the New World. This is really tough for me to believe—that human beings were treated like merchandise and that so many white people went along with it. Didn't they think this was wrong?"

After each lesson, students shared with a partner or talked with members of their group and with the class as a whole. I wanted to be sure they had time and felt safe processing their thoughts and feelings about the history of slavery and the history of Africa. Many students were sympathetic to the plight of the enslaved, some were less so:

"I can't believe that the slaves let the master talk to them like that."

"I bet that it must have been really scary to be a slave."

"If I would've lived during slavery days, I wouldn't have taken that!"

In one lesson, I read a picture book about an individual story of resistance: *Henry's Freedom Box: A True Story of the Underground Railroad* by Ellen Levine tells the true story of a man who courageously shipped himself to the North. Henry was born into slavery. Once he was grown, his family was sold away from him. As I shared Henry's bittersweet story of loss, triumph, and rebirth, I sensed that students' perceptions were beginning to shift from the distance and disdain they previously held—their perception that enslaved Black people had been docile bystanders, forever victims.

Shame into Pride

Once students had amassed enough information on their research projects, I did specific lessons on turning their findings into cohesive essays.

We culminated our unit with a closing celebration and invited others to come and share our newfound knowledge. Our resident experts on South Africa beamed with pride as they shared their research with classmates and the teachers who came through during their planning periods. They spoke with passion about the Soweto Uprisings of 1976. They had immersed themselves in research about this revolutionary event in human history and learned the power of uniting around a cause.

"Students were so angry that they were forced to learn Afrikaans, the language of the oppressor, that they organized a student protest," Marcus said.

Other members of his group explained that 20,000 students had participated, and some of them were murdered during what began as a peaceful protest. They described how learning about Soweto shifted their perception from South Africans as victims to South Africans as victors, willing and able to rebel against oppression. I glanced at Marcus as he brought his presentation to a close. He was one of the students who at first could not fathom why he would want to have any association with Africa. Now he spoke with pride about the power of the human spirit and the bravery of the youth of Soweto.

We went back to our Africa chart and added our new knowledge. I asked students to reflect on the new information that they had learned. What seemed most significant?

It was no longer necessary for me to ask probing questions or give examples of what one might write. Students quickly filled up their Post-it notes: Africa is diverse, the climate is different in different regions, many people resisted slavery, enslaved people used to sneak and learn to read, enslaved people escaped to the North, young people in Soweto died for the right to learn their own language, Lesotho is located inside of South Africa, Nelson Mandela was in prison for 27 years because he fought against apartheid, there was a genocide in Darfur, and—most moving for me—enslaved Africans were brave. ✳

Reprinted from *Rethinking Schools*, Fall 2012 (vol. 27, no. 1).

Barangay Pedagogy
Teaching as a Collective Act

BY ARLENE SUDARIA DAUS-MAGBUAL, RODERICK DAUS-MAGBUAL, RAJU DESAI,
AND ALLYSON TINTIANGCO-CUBALES

In the spirit of *barangay* pedagogy, we wrote this article as a collective act. Our purpose was to give readers a sense of what it's like to become a teacher with Pin@y Educational Partnerships (PEP). As four former teachers in PEP who also have held or currently hold a leadership position in PEP, we have 16 years of stories, some of our own and some that were shared with us over our many years of involvement. As we sat down to begin the process of writing this essay, we spent hours doing talkstory, reminiscing about the good, the bad, and the funny along with the pain, love, and growth that was shared in the space. We wanted to provide a format where our readers could understand what it feels like to become part of the PEP community. Piecing together our 16 years of collective stories, research, observations, interviews, and interactions, we co-created a composite character that represents first-year teachers who enter into the PEP space with a set of expectations colored by their own personal educational experiences. We use "I" to represent the voice of the composite character, but in reality, it is not only meant to be one singular voice but rather the character of the collective "we." Throughout the essay, we weave in themes indigenous to Filipinas/os to demonstrate ways in which this character develops and transforms. Come along—hop onto our *balangay* (boat) as we journey together into a PEP teacher's life.

* * *

In April I was on Facebook and I saw this message at the top of a post:

Looking for an opportunity to try out teaching? The Pin@y Educational Partnerships (PEP) are looking for teachers for the 2017–2018 school year!

When I read this, I imagined myself standing in front of a class of students and imparting the knowledge I learned from my favorite Asian American Studies course focused on Filipina/o Americans. I fantasized standing at the head of the room with my fist up and my students nodding their heads, praising me for being their favorite teacher because I looked just like them and every single thing I said transformed their lives. I thought to myself, "I'm going to be the best teacher in the world because I am hella #woke." I knew PEP was for me.

I wrote my cover letter, updated my résumé, and asked two of my professors to be my references. Every minute I worked on my application, I felt like I was on my way to serving youth and becoming a teacher. I turned in my application an hour before the deadline. A few days later, I received a call from a PEP director to come in for an interview. After scheduling a time, I received an email explaining how to prepare for the big day. I had to create a five-minute lesson plan on a topic regarding Filipina/o American history and I had to teach that lesson plan during the interview. When I looked up the address of the interview location, Google Maps showed me a condo. *A condo? That's strange. Am I interviewing at someone's house? Wait, is that my old professor's home?*

Then I clicked on the link to their website (pepsf.org) in the email and memorized their vision, mission, and goals. I Googled and Facebooked the staff, and I even called my friends about their experiences in PEP. On their website, I read:

Pin@y Educational Partnerships (PEP) is an award-winning educational leadership pipeline and critical space for the development of Filipina/o American curriculum and research. PEP is dually located in the academy and in the community. PEP partners with SFSU's Asian American Studies Department in the College of Ethnic Studies, Skyline College's Kababayan Program, the University of San Francisco's (USF) Yuchengco Philippine Studies, the Filipino American Development Foundation (FADF) and its affiliates, and with San Francisco public schools. PEP's teaching pipeline connects SFSU and surrounding Bay Area upper-division undergraduates and graduate students who have an interest in pursuing careers in the field of education with community college, high school, middle school, and elementary school students who are primarily from low-income backgrounds. One of the main objectives for the PEP program is to reach out to students who are underperforming their potential and provide them with the support and opportunities necessary to achieve their goals.

I was juiced. I wanted so badly to teach at one of the high schools and gain the experience necessary to become a teacher in the future. I also heard they help students like me get into graduate school and credential programs, so that would definitely look great on my résumé. A friend then reminded me that PEP teachers do not get paid. *What? All this work and no pay? I guess I will just see what they are all about.*

On my interview day, I wore my best outfit with my favorite pair of shoes and printed out copies of my lesson plan on Kapwa and an extra copy of my résumé, just in case. I walked up the stairs and rang the doorbell. A little girl poked her head out of the door and told me they were still interviewing someone and that I should sit on the bench and wait. *Another person?* Thoughts raced through my mind; confidence shifted to nervousness. *Wait, there are more people who want to teach for free? Are they only hiring one person?* Minutes later, I sat in front of

seven strangers, one of them a small child at least 9 years old and another about 13. The two children stared at me at the end of a long dinner table. During introductions, I learned that they were students from PEP. My former professor was cooking in the kitchen and asked if I would like some *ube* waffles and coffee. *Am I allowed to eat? Is this a test?* This did not feel like a normal job interview; it felt like a big Filipino party and I was the new person everyone was sizing up.

The interview began with the first question, "Why do you want to be a PEP teacher?" As I felt my heart palpitate, I thought about moments during my first Ethnic Studies course. I recollected how the mystery of my own identity began to unravel as pieces of the unknown materialized into understanding. I felt validated in sharing stories of my family's immigration from the Philippines to the United States and the struggle to economically survive in a new country. My favorite project in the class gave me the opportunity to teach young people about Filipina/o American experiences. I was able to gather my emotions and said, "I want to become a PEP teacher because Ethnic Studies gave me the key to unlock the questions I had about myself and the opportunity to transform the world." I saw the faces around the table nodding and I knew—*I got this.*

After responding to questions about my teaching philosophy, leadership, working in groups, and my strengths and weaknesses, it was time for my teaching demonstration. I had a super critical and Indigenous lesson planned out on the concept of Kapwa, *I am you and you are me.* I had every step written out and had a PowerPoint presentation ready. I was just about to stand up to show I was ready to teach, then a curveball was pitched my way. The designated interviewer asked me to pick a teacher from around the table to co-teach my lesson with. *Wait? Teach with whom? I thought I was teaching alone.* I was dumbfounded. *But I wrote this lesson and why do I need to co-teach? I got this.* The interviewer went on to talk about how they do not teach alone in PEP and this part of the interview was learning how to work with each other to teach as a team, as a barangay. Although I had dreams of myself at the head of the classroom, single-handedly changing the lives of each of my students, I realized that being a teacher in PEP was different than being a teacher anywhere else; it meant I would not be teaching alone. This was my introduction to barangay pedagogy.

I learned that barangay pedagogy applies Emily Lawsin's "Bayanihan Spirit" in the classroom through the development of barangay building. The term *barangay* refers to the smallest political units in the Philippines; in essence, villages and/or communities. Through the creation and establishment of barangays in the classroom, PEP students work together to complete projects and tackle global, local, and personal problems. PEP aims to provide ways for students to transform the classroom into a community where they serve each other. The main pillars of PEP's barangay pedagogy are:

Purpose: *Katarungan* (justice) and *kalayaan* (freedom)

Teaching Ethnic Studies with a collective of teachers made me realize justice and freedom could not be achieved without creating community. Working in a teaching team taught me how patience, communication, struggle, and developing group harmony embody freedom. This struggle to work in a team was part of a larger picture. Working together uncovered Filipino Indigenous qualities of *katarungan* (justice) and *kalayaan* (freedom). If we can work through different perspectives in creating a unified curriculum, syllabus, and specific lesson plans, this type of work in the classroom can represent the possibility of what our community can become. Working in a teaching barangay characterized the struggles of solidarity with the larger purpose of freedom and justice in mind.

I learned putting together lesson plans was more than just delivering content. It was a responsibility, a sense of duty, and it was action. The more I read about the history of Filipina/o Americans, the more I felt a historical connection and accountability to the struggles of my ancestors. By developing our pedagogy, our curriculum, units, and lesson plans emerged out of understanding a critical narrative of our people. I realized teaching our history was more than just understanding dates and facts; the history served a purpose to uncover the vestiges of colonial trauma, resistance, and hope. Our learning and teaching of Filipina/o American history allowed my teaching team to respond and understand con-

temporary social issues. We connected the critical relationship to the past, our identities, and our historical duty to address oppression. Uncovering our narratives of what it means to be Filipina/o American placed me on a journey toward personal freedom and being accountable to my community. It placed the realities of what my family and community have endured within a sociohistorical context and the political motivation to change the world.

The process of freedom is one of struggle, challenges, and understanding. The planning of units and lessons with my barangay was achieved through intense critical dialogue. I learned how to battle through my own individual insecurities in taking feedback on lesson plans from my peers, becoming OK with not know everything about a topic and learning with my barangay how to improve in the classroom. With our different depths of understanding Filipina/o American history, we were challenged to unify our voices and come to an agreement on how to create and deliver our lesson plans. We wrestled through moments of silence and confusion; katarungan was at the heart of every breakthrough. Our belief and practice of justice allowed our barangay to find hope through our strengths, weaknesses, talents, personalities, and egos to reach an accord. By communicating through an emotional and constructive dialogue, sometimes we clashed as our views and experiences led us to intense emotions and arguments that got to a fever pitch. Despite the challenges it took to navigate through the barangay building process, the catharsis that brought our group to understanding was achieved through our practices of humanization and seeing the hope in one another. Building inclusion, legitimizing each other's perspectives, and embodying practices of freedom were at the core of achieving inclusion and community in PEP.

Empathy: *Pakikiramdam* (shared feelings) and *kagandahang-loob* (shared humanity)

From the first interactions with my new PEP family, I felt *pakikiramdam* (shared feelings) and *kagandahang-loob* (shared humanity) with this new group of people. I remembered my first PEP teacher event: TIBAK training (short for the Tagalog term *aktibista*, or "activist"). TIBAK training introduced the foundation of PEP by building the pedagogical groundwork for the upcoming school year. I walked into classroom 121 at the San Francisco State University library, which was packed with over 50 PEP teachers. The space felt like a family reunion: folks giving each other hugs, high fives, and kisses on the cheek, and sharing smiles and stories. *Why was everyone so joyful?* I awkwardly tiptoed to my seat as I scanned the room to find familiar faces. Was this going to be worth it? I originally planned a trip to New York this week, but in order to join PEP, I had to commit to attend trainings, weekly Wednesday night meetings during the school year, barangay meetings, fundraising events, and two weekend-long retreats in August and December. I brought everything I needed for the training: my class schedule, a copy of Paulo Freire's *Pedagogy of the Oppressed* that I was supposed to read prior to TIBAK, my trusty water bottle, and some snacks. Some of the teachers I recognized from previous classes, and I saw my professor with two other PEP directors. I sat down next to someone I recognized, then said my hellos and waved at some folks who had interviewed me. When 4 p.m. hit, we started with introductions and a community energizer that involved a 10-round barangay dance battle. They really wanted us to get to know each other fast!

After we sat down and took a breath, one of the PEP directors shared her *talam buhay* (life story). I noticed on the training-week agenda that each director would share their talam buhay on each day of training. She started off by telling us, "If we are to start a relationship with each other, we need to be honest and truthful. Whatever is shared in this sacred space, we keep it sacred." I nodded my head in full confidence and noticed a collective agreement of gestures that ranged from "Yes!" to deep breaths of assurance. She followed up by asking, "When you first met me, what was your first impression of me?" I thought this was a trick question. *If I told her what I honestly thought about her, would I get fired?* But some teachers raised their hands and said "intimidating," "unapproachable," "confident," "caring." She smiled at the last one and said no one had ever said that about her in response to that question. She said, "We often assume we know someone based on what they look like, whether it is your students or your fellow teachers, but when you get to know their narrative, we will

connect through our pakikiramdam, shared feelings."

She shared where her ancestors came from in the Philippines, what her parents did for a living, who her siblings and cousins were. She was open about the struggles of being poor and losing everything, family expectations, navigating spaces as a Pinay who looked too intimidating and confident for her own good. I never had a teacher be so open and raw about who she is and how she got to where she is now. There were times during her presentation when

The term "barangay" refers to the smallest political units in the Philippines; in essence, villages and/or communities.

I thought she was telling my story. I felt her words resonate in my body, my heart started to race, and tears formed in my eyes. I looked around the room hoping no one would see me get so emotional, but I saw others being emotional too. I felt connected with her as if we met in another lifetime. I saw my cousin in her, my grandmother, and my best friend.

At the end of her talam buhay, I felt a sense of comfort. I could not imagine having to do this in front of strangers as she has for her last 14 years in PEP and in all the classrooms she has taught. I saw some teachers get up and give her a hug. She asked if her presentation was OK and they said, "Every year I hear your talam buhay, you do something different each time. You had different stories, but I also think it is because throughout the past few years, I have gotten to know you more and I feel so connected with you since we know each other's stories." This is where I learned about kagandahang-loob, a shared humanity.

At the end of TIBAK training, I learned about our three directors through their personal narratives; PEP coordinators taught chapters of *Pedagogy of the Oppressed*; Filipina/o American scholar and historian Dawn Mabalon taught us about primary resources; and one of our directors introduced the overwhelming process of creating a lesson plan. At the end of TIBAK, they revealed our teaching barangays. I was placed at the high school where I would co-teach with two other people. Our homework assignment for the summer was to create a five-minute presentation of our own talam buhays to share with fellow

It was difficult to bring the realities of our lives to the classroom, but we were able to build from our trust with each other. We found that creating a space of hope was necessary to serve our students' needs and to address issues in our communities.

teachers and our future students. When I got home that night, I started crafting my presentation: collecting pictures, videos, and formulating stories. It was harder than I thought. This journey unveiled memories of the past that I kept silent, but it helped me identify why I felt oppressed and my motivation to teach Ethnic Studies. After reflecting on what I learned about *Pedagogy of the Oppressed*, I started to think about my family and how we fit within Filipina/o American history. It started to feel painful. I closed my laptop and thought that this might be the hardest story I tell. I guess it was true what they said in TIBAK: "To teach Ethnic Studies with a community, you have to start with yourself in relation with the other."

Praxis: *Pakikipagkapwa* (shared identity, struggle, survival) and *pakikibaka* (collective action)
Developing my purpose in PEP and growing my capacity to be empathetic was only the beginning to truly understanding the cultural wealth of barangay pedagogy. As the school year went on, I developed strong bonds with the other PEP teachers and students. I began to see our interconnectedness through our shared experiences. This was how I started to understand *pakikipagkapwa*, or shared identity, struggle, and survival. Enriquez (2004) describes pakikipagkapwa as "humanness at its highest level," where you see yourself in the other—I am you and you are me."

In the spring semester, we spent weeks working on our Youth Participatory Action Research Project (YPAR). It was a stressful time and I was not always sure where our students would go with the project. As part of YPAR, students researched problems important to them and their communities. Then they chose research methods to provide primary and secondary data to devise an action plan that addressed the problem. Teachers and students had to all trust one another and believe we were going to get through this project. The students chose the topic of violence but were apprehensive to examine the impacts of violence in their lives.

One day when it seemed like we were not getting anywhere, I decided to share a personal story about violence I experienced as a child. It was a struggle for me to be vulnerable in the classroom, and this was a story I did not share with many people, but I decided to share it because of my trust in this community and space. I teared up in the middle of my story and my voice trembled. I was able to finish after encouragement from some of the students. The next day, a student opened up and shared a similar story. A few days later, another student shared her experiences. Suddenly, this was no longer something about the larger community but something that impacted all of us on a more personal level. We spent the beginning of YPAR having profound discussions and examining the impact of violence in our lives. It was difficult to bring the realities of our lives to the classroom, but we were able to build from our trust with each other. We found that creating a space of hope was necessary to serve our students' needs and to address issues in our communities. We could not just talk about the deficits in our communities without also acknowledging our community wealth. This experience showed me the importance of being vulnerable with my students. If I ask my students to confront an issue like violence in their lives, I must do the same. It was necessary for us to find hope in our struggles and places to heal while in pain, but the lesson learned was to do it together as a community.

At the end of the year, all PEP sites came together to present their YPAR projects in a creative way through a story called "The PEProx." Every site embodied a creature that addressed the YPAR problem and plan of action. Our class decided to be the Balbaloots, bearlike creatures that were fighting to heal their community. The thought of speaking and performing in front of our friends, family, and PEP community was terrifying. Some students, and even teachers like myself, felt like we were too cool to be acting in some school play. When the community show started, I initially felt like a fool and became self-conscious. As the show progressed and other PEP sites performed their YPARs with pride and love, my perspective changed. When we put on our bear ears and danced to Clyde Carson's "Slow Down," I let my inhibitions go. It was no longer about me, but about us... all of us. It was about being vulnerable and laughing with my fellow teachers and students, sharing our stories to a larger audience, and advocating for real change. It felt like I was at a party having fun with my family, but these folks were different. We were able to talk about things that I could not talk about with my family. This was a space where the traumas of colonialism and capitalism were not ignored or normalized but called out and directly addressed so that we could heal together.

Conclusion

During our last class of the spring semester, we facilitated a "classroom check out" where everyone went around and shared something they learned from our PEP class. Many of the students shared how they did not have high expectations of the year, that it would be another easy A, a classroom with rows and columns, or a boring lecture about the same old history. I never thought the last day of a class could make me so emotional. I saw the transformation of our students throughout the school year. The PEP students expressed that they learned how to build community through their barangays, apply what we learned in the classroom to our communities, see themselves in history, and see how change begins with them. Not only did our students transform, but I did as well.

This experience changed my life. I am not going to lie, my first year in PEP was challenging, and at one point I did not know if I was going to come back. The commitment to the PEP space, my fellow teachers, students, and the community was a lot on top of being a full-time undergraduate student working a retail job. It was not easy to collaborate with 50 other PEP teachers and to serve 250 students a week during an entire school year. After struggling to get through weekly meetings, lesson plans, teaching, and projects, I barely had time to do homework or engage in self-care. In our last PEP meeting of the year, PEP teachers concluded a three-hour roundtable sharing stories, tears, achievements, and future plans. It was 10 p.m. on a Wednesday night and all the emotions built up to a fever pitch of energy that led to a harmonious crescendo of "Isang bagsak!" "Dalawang bagsak!" "Tatlong bagsak!"—a ritual and response to counter the oppressive structures that surround us and the dominant narrative that threatens to erase us, a reclamation of our Indigenous roots and being. The road to decolonization is not something that is done alone, nor is it a destination to be reached; rather it is a journey of becoming one with the self and in relation with another. PEP has become a community, a support system, and a family that sustains and nourishes me to become a community-engaged teacher, scholar, and leader. ✳

RESOURCES

Enriquez, Virgilio G. 2004. *From Colonial to Liberation Psychology: The Philippine Experience.* De La Salle University Press.

Tintiangco-Cubales, Allyson, Arlene Daus-Magbual, Maharaj Desai, Aldrich Sabac, and Maynard Von Torres. 2016. "Into Our Hoods: Where Critical Performance Pedagogy Births Resistance." *International Journal of Qualitative Studies in Education* 29.10:1308–25.

Tintiangco-Cubales, Allyson, Roderick Daus-Magbual, and Arelene Daus-Magbual. 2010. "Pin@y Educational Partnerships: A Counter-Pipeline to Create Critical Educators." (Allyson Tintiangco-Cubales, Peter Nien-chu Kiang, and Samuel Museus, Eds.) *AAPI Nexus Asian Americans & Pacific Islanders Policy, Practice and Community* 8.1:76–100.

Do I Need to Mail in My Spit?
The Importance of a Teacher's Roots in Teaching Ethnic Studies

BY DOMINIQUE A. WILLIAMS

"I can't do this. I don't even know my dad."
—Amerie

In my 9th-grade Ethnic Studies class, I ask students to explore their own roots and ancestry in our unit on Indigeneity. "It's OK if you don't wanna call your dad and ask a bunch of questions. Just focus on your mom's side," I announced when one student expressed that she did not want to do this assignment. I understood. I did not meet my dad until I was 18 years old.

"I know you don't know," I said as I sat on my stool next to Amerie's desk (student names have been changed). "That's the point of the assignment: to research your family history beyond what you already know." In the Indigeneity unit I ask my students to explore their own roots as we learn about local Indigenous nations, including the Miwok, Maidu, and Wintu. Where I teach in Sacramento, California, I feel energized and excited when my students return to class telling me what they learned about their families. On that day, I had just passed out a questionnaire to activate prior knowledge about their family. The questionnaire was a step toward getting them to write about their upbringing and culture as it related to their family history.

Here was the problem: I was asking my students to engage in an activity, reflect, and be vulnerable in ways that I myself had not done until my early 20s, let alone as a high school freshman. Because of this, I began to doubt my ability to teach the Ethnic Studies class despite having a bachelor's degree in African American Studies and experience organizing with Ethnic Studies Now–Sacramento. I had this nagging question: "Do I need to mail in my spit?" I had watched enough cable TV to have my curiosity piqued by Ancestry.com's many deals and specials. "Am I delaying finding out some things that I ought to know about myself?" I wondered. "Can I really teach Ethnic Studies if I don't know my roots?"

I think these are legitimate questions for any person who experienced removal from their land, culture, and language. As a Black woman teaching Ethnic Studies to youth, exploring my own identity and subjectivity is integral to my ability to teach a subject centered on identity, humanity, ancestry, indigeneity, and a host of other areas that often merit critical introspection.

The discussions we have on identity and family are rich in my Ethnic Studies classes. Period by period, in my multiracial and multiethnic classrooms, I look at my students and have hope that they will be able to ask their mothers, fathers, aunts, uncles, older siblings, cousins, and grandparents to share family knowledge and oral histories with them. This feeling remains but, at that moment with Amerie, I found myself not having the same hope and optimism for my African American students. When the class started in spring, I was aware that several of my students had relationships with only one of their parents and that one of them had been adopted. I was also aware of how some of my African American students, like my younger self, had internalized anti-Black/anti-African ideas and desired to distance themselves from being Black or African.

Some of this lack of hope came from the insecurities I had about my own lineage and ancestry. It was one (undesirable) thing to only be able to trace one side of the family; it was another to trace that lineage back to the South where Black people were once enslaved. I recalled questioning my mom about our family history. I had gathered that we were from Texas, but I wanted to know more. I wanted to know if we were mixed. I was in middle school when my mom told me that we have Native American ancestry. I remember her saying, "At my great-grandma's funeral, this man with long hair came and spoke about her. He looked Indian," she said. Then she continued, "I have no idea who he was, but he was from Beaumont [Texas]." Despite this tidbit of information from my mother, I decided to self-identify as Black. Other students at school would ask me if I was mixed (usually as a reference to my complexion or hair), but I was uncomfortable with my beauty being associated with how Black or not I am. Before ever hearing the term colorism, I knew that being seen as mixed upheld beauty standards that were based in anti-Blackness, such as having "long" or "good" hair rather than short and coarse.

What Are You Mixed With?

We were standing in the hallway near my classroom when my colleague asked "What are you mixed with?" For the second time, I told him, "I'm Black." Annoyingly he responded, "That's it?" At that point I hesitated. I had never had any "proof" of my Native American ancestry and I was still grappling with some paternal family history.

Around this time, a friend had written a Facebook status about how she, despite hearing that she was Native American her entire life, had hardly a trace of Native American ancestry. Even if she were a detribalized Black Indigenous person, was she supposed to show up to the places her ancestors lived and hope to be accepted by a tribe there? Is that something I would do? With skepticism about whether what my mother said was true and my desire to not look foolish, I grew up identifying as solely Black. And I wanted to be extra Black. Maybe it was a 1990s thing, but as a lighter-skinned Black girl with "long" hair, I knew I had better choose a story and stick to it. I knew that some people felt like mixed girls weren't as Black, and not being able to prove I was mixed was grounds for being teased.

My freshman year of college, when I met my father and his side of the family, I learned about our German ancestry. Although my mother had told

me about my paternal grandparents here and there, I knew little about them—let alone that they were mixed race. When I met my father's family for the first time, I sat with my Aunt Sheila and wrote out a family tree that began with my grandparents and their nine children. I learned my grandmother's maiden name and of our roots in Arkansas. I realized that having a family tree of just one generation before me was significant in understanding and documenting a history to pass on to my children.

Nonetheless, since I had spent my life raised by my Black mother in California, I had no sense of urgency to claim the German heritage of my Arkansas-born father or an alleged Native American heritage from what is now Texas. The question from my colleague made me uncomfortable—not just because my ethnicity was none of their business, but because at that moment I became very aware that I had been denying this German identity. I wanted to distance myself from whiteness, and I did not want to be another Black girl "mixed with Indian" as the reason for my complexion, eye color, or facial features. I was secure in my carefully curated Black aesthetic and I wanted to be seen as simply Black—an acknowledgement of diasporic Blackness, culture, and my political status rather than a validation of European standards of beauty, colonialism, and the legacy of African slavery in America.

Understanding What It Means to Be Black

From that day in middle school to this day, I have considered what it means to be Black. By college my understanding of Blackness grew more complicated. I learned, through conversations and meeting people, that being Black was not just a matter of being African American, but a multiethnic, multilingual, international amalgamation. In the African American Resource Center where Black students hung out at my university, we talked about issues like colorism, homophobia, our names, police brutality, and what it meant to be Black or African or West Indian. Regardless of our nationality or ethnicity, we had racialized Black-skinned experiences in common, but we also had unique diaspora-specific experiences and values. Time would tell that African American students who, like me, grew up (and whose parents grew up) in the United States were generally unaware and unconcerned with issues of Black people abroad and had our own ways of internalizing white supremacy. Meanwhile, Black immigrant students or children of immigrants—whether from Africa or the West Indies—seemed removed from or oblivious to the complexities of the African American experience.

I recall a moment during a Black History Month dialogue on cultural appropriation when a friend aired out his internalized ideas about Black students and education. My friend raised his hand and asked, "Well, aren't we appropriating white culture by attending a university?" In hindsight, I hope my mouth was not agape. My heart was racing. "Did he just say what I think he just said?" I looked across the room to another friend and then coordinator of the African American Resource Center. I firmly said, "No, we are not!" and explained the little I knew about universities in Timbuktu.

I thought about that interaction for days. At the time, I was working in an after-school program in Compton and I had been with many students from kindergarten to 8th grade throughout the district. I wondered, "Could it be that Black children really, actually think that education is for white people?" I thought about my own family and how so few of us were honor roll students or college ready when we graduated high school. I thought about how a "good" education was related to tracking and Eurocentric curriculum. I further thought, "What was the point of me and other Black people attending universities and learning research methods, specializations, and skills if we left with no sense of self? Why did we bother to have an African American Resource Center if we did not think of ourselves as Africans?" I wondered, "Why bother with all this head knowledge about Black people, subject ourselves to the experiences of a large, primarily white institution, and incur student-loan debt if the return on our investment would be taxed with not being good enough for the rest of our lives?"

Indigeneity Envy

In my early 20s, I found myself envious of friends who, when they finally had the money to do so, traveled to the homeland of their parents and saw it with their own eyes. It seemed they could find a state, city, or someplace outside the United States to call home.

In college, one friend went as far as studying abroad in a Japanese town where her parents met. Another friend had flown with their mother to Mexico and learned of where she was raised. In both cases, my U.S.-born friends were not only able to leave home and find their motherland, they had the language to speak when they arrived.

I brought up the issue of exploring family history with one of my colleagues, a *Mexicana* and fellow Ethnic Studies teacher. "It feels hard for me to ask my students to explore their family history," I said. "Several of them have told me that they don't have a relationship with, or speak to, their father or their father's side of the family." I told her that while I knew that reality all too well, one of the most important things I had done after I met my dad's side of the family was to draw out my family tree and that I wanted my students to do a variation of this for themselves.

I continued, "Honestly, the whole indigeneity thing is complicated because of the slave trade. It's not like me or my Black students can *really* find out exactly where our families are from." The words lingered in the air. I was on the verge rambling into a stream of consciousness when I brought up a conversation that I stumbled across on Twitter. The conversation was framed in several think pieces essentially asking "Do African Americans appropriate African culture?" I had read Nigerians criticize Black Americans who adorned themselves in adinkra and African textiles such as Ankara and dashikis, and even kente cloth, saying, "Y'all know we don't dress like this every day, right?"

I considered those comments and looked inwardly. On the one hand, I am an African American woman who incorporates that aesthetic into my style as a young professional, and I see myself as an enthusiastic patron of Black-owned businesses. In college I had internalized the values of Kwanzaa, a holiday known for Black affirmation in the United States. I considered dressing myself in African styles an extension of *ujamaa*, or cooperative economics. *Ujamaa* is one of the seven *nguzo saba*, a Kiswahili word meaning "the seven principles." When I became a teacher, I encouraged my students to join the Black Student Union, which I have been an adviser of. Although I was not teaching Ethnic Studies when I first became a BSU adviser, I was at a school with a few hundred Black students, so in my day-to-day look I started incorporating West African adinkra symbols and Ankara wax cloth with my usually otherwise Ann Taylor and Banana Republic outfits. My students complimented me often. They would ask me how I moisturize my Afro and where I bought my dashikis.

On the other hand, I wondered, are continental Africans really calling into question our Africanness like there was no slave trade? And mocking our taking up space in the world in bright, bold patterns while they willingly (or not) assimilate into American, British, or other colonialism? Surely my carefully coordinated Ankara pieces were meaningful purchases, not only for my own sense of pride that I hoped would transfer to my students, but also because I had bought them from Black women across the diaspora—Senegalese, Ghanaian, and African American by way of Oakland.

As I was lost in my thoughts, my colleague pondered and interjected. "It's not like Mexicans are all Aztecs and Mayan," she said. I was pretty confused as to where she was going with this. I nodded, silently asking for her to tell me more. "These are identities we have adopted to unify and empower ourselves. There are many Chicanxs who claim those heritages, but as with all colonized people, they have mixed blood. Look at me." She framed her white face in her white hands, pointing out her very light skin. "Both my parents are Mexican. I was raised Mexican."

My mind was blown. I understood what she was saying, so my mind struggled with the fact that since college I had spent years envious of my Latinx/Chicanx friends who had such pride in their culture and heritage. As a newer teacher, I was impressed by the Latinx teachers whose classrooms were decorated with serapes, *papel picado*, posters of Frida Kahlo, and Día de los Muertos imagery. They inspired me to bring West African aesthetic and imagery into my classroom, yet here I was both questioning my authenticity as an Ethnic Studies teacher and whether I ought to be wearing wax cloths as casual wear.

What Do I Need to Know About Myself to Teach Ethnic Studies?

So, did I need to know myself, specifically my ancestry, in order to teach Ethnic Studies? It was a good

question at face value, but I had placed too much value on "knowing myself" as a matter of DNA and ancestry. Mailing in my spit would not help me establish a sense of belonging to a people or a culture. Knowing my ancestry would not help me deliver the content better or improve how I teach kids to read, write, and resist. My goal as an Ethnic Studies teacher is to shift the space to being anti-oppressive and to challenge colonial and imperial norms. That meant that I had to complicate notions of heritage and family for myself and my students.

The family history assignment overlapped with the timing of our school's open house. The mother of Chandra, the student who was adopted, approached me to tell me about the conversations she had had with Chandra. Chandra's adoptive family had known

Mailing in my spit would not help me establish a sense of belonging to a people or a culture. Knowing my ancestry would not help me deliver the content better or improve how I teach kids to read, write, and resist.

her birth family at one point, but they were hardly in touch. Even though Chandra's mother could provide some of her birth family's history, Chandra ultimately decided to write her family history around her adopted family. Chandra had revealed to me that family history is beyond DNA and biology.

A friend and colleague, Dr. Stacey Ault, further helped me interrogate the ways to engage notions of family and family history in ways that de-center the nuclear family. She questioned how foster youth who may not have access to their immediate families, unlike Chandra, might engage this assignment. The next semester when I passed out the questionnaire to my students, I deemphasized the notion of a family tree and emphasized the importance of their own narrative and storytelling.

From Amerie and Chandra's class I was left with questions: How do I teach resistance when understanding my own heritage is an act of resistance I haven't yet done? How do I truly lead students to self-empowerment without that empowerment for myself? How do I challenge narratives about people of color, low-income earners, and women without challenging my own narrative in the same ways? How much of my identity has been based on stories I've

My objective for the life journey project is trifold: I want to intimately introduce myself to my students, learn about them beyond the surface, and teach self-reflection.

been told about myself rather than stories I've uncovered through oral histories and my lived experience?

For Christmas I got a DNA test kit that I still have not used. I have resolved that the kind of knowledge about myself that I've sought is not a matter of DNA. Instead, I do believe that as an Ethnic Studies teacher I need to constantly seek knowledge of myself. We all do—in whichever ways are meaningful to us. The reality is that many of us teachers do not live in the circumstances we were born into, and because of this, we are at risk of upholding values around the nuclear family, white supremacy, and even competition. After all, we attended universities, work in a profession in which most practitioners are white, and have normalized Eurocentric curriculum as well as tracking practices such as AP and Honors. To counter that, I believe that when I make conscious efforts to validate and honor my community, my family, the people who look like me, and my ancestors, I am not only making an effort to know my (collective) self better; I also have more affirming values on which to stand.

This has absolutely impacted my teaching. As I present my "life journey" project to my students

(another assignment), I reflect on the very experiences that made me who I am and take inventory on what has grown and forged me. Equipped with knowledge of myself, self-compassion, and self-love, I am comfortable with and even certain that my own knowledge, vulnerability, and compassion are necessary to transform my classroom into a healing space. My objective for the life journey project is trifold: I want to intimately introduce myself to my students, learn about them beyond the surface, and teach self-reflection. The first time I assigned this project, I shortened my storytelling and even skipped the parts of my story that made me uncomfortable because I was embarrassed. I learned that skipping the parts that make me cry did not serve anyone. In the periods where I shared deeply, my students also shared deeply and we had greater connections. I cannot imagine this being possible without me doing the work of self-reflection beforehand.

I remember a colleague being excited about the positive research results of community circles as laid out by the International Institute of Restorative Practices, but she admitted that while she loved the idea of student check-ins and grappling with touchy issues that affected teens, she was nervous and, at times, unwilling to open up to students. I had felt that way too, but now I think scaffolding my students through self-reflection is important groundwork for what R. Tolteka Cuauhtin lays out as the double helix: humanity and criticality (see "The Ethnic Studies Framework," p. 65). The sharing of stories is an effort to address the humanity of my students in order to help process our experiences, and the content, critically.

Beyond DNA, who I am has been passed down to me from generation to generation in my family, in our subtle traditions, in our African American Vernacular English and, however masked in dominant culture, with hundreds of nuances. My awareness and living in these dynamics are essentially my identity, and I have since come to terms with being part of a diasporic indigeneity that is my being African in America. ✳

Our Oral History Narrative Project

BY AIMEE RIECHEL

*"This interview made me happy because now I am
more proud of my dad. I learned that he works
towards providing a better life and education for the
family. This project makes me feel proud of my Mexican heritage because it's part of who I am."*
—Arron Nevarez, October 8, 2009

These are the words of Arron Nevarez, a student in my Ethnic Studies class at San Francisco's Mission High School, where I have
been teaching since 2008. Arron wrote the above
in response to the Oral History Narrative Project
I teach in my Ethnic Studies class, which has been
transformational for not just my students but for me
as a teacher too.

The Oral History Narrative Project asks students to interview a family member and write an
oral history narrative of their identity in terms of
race, ethnicity, culture, and/or nationality. The
assignment allows students to explore the power
of ancestral legacies and the humanizing nature of
retelling family narratives. Sometimes students cannot complete an interview with a family member,
but the assignment still allows for a lasting connection to be built as a result of the intimate relationship created between interviewer and interviewee. I
have seen dramatic changes in student performances
and ideas of self as outcomes of this project. This
project allows students to develop as serious writers
and to express pride and love in their own ancestors.
Furthermore, the project embodies the visionary
goals of an Ethnic Studies course: academic engagement, student achievement, self-determination, and
transformation for the betterment of the individual
and the community.

Armani

As an incoming 9th-grade student, Armani went out
of her way to make sure everyone understood that
she was a tough kid; she wasn't going to let anyone
mess with her. I remember one of the first days of
class, a boy who knew her from a previous school
made a comment under his breath. Before I could
say anything—or figure out what had been said—she
was quick to defend herself, assuming the comment
had been made about her. She yelled and cursed at
him, to the point where I had to ask her to step outside and regroup herself. I talked with Armani to see
what she had been reacting to. She admitted that she
didn't really know what he had said but thought she
heard him say her name. The boy apologized but said
he hadn't said anything about her; both Armani and
I accepted that. After this miscommunication, the
two were fine in class, but Armani's defensive reactions became a pattern in her other classes and she
was constantly receiving referrals or getting kicked
out for her behavior.

Armani had a strong family connection to our
school: A fellow history teacher knew her family
well—she had actually housed them soon after they
emigrated from Eritrea—and Armani's sister was
a star student two years her senior. It seemed like
Armani's tough exterior was her way of creating her
own unique identity at school. However, this façade
was soon to change.

Armani had a hard outer shell, but it was clear
that it did not reflect the essence of who she really
was. Throughout the fall semester there were many
moments in class when she expressed deep care for
her work, excitement about the content, and empathy for her peers. However, these moments would

usually be followed by an intentionally oppositional reaction, as if she was trying to hide her genuine feelings. As the semester progressed, Armani and her true personality began to emerge. Her work began to improve and her exterior began to soften. She was most successful in Ethnic Studies, especially compared to her other courses, because she was engaged with the material and received sufficient support from myself and my co-teacher, Elena Hillard.

When I passed out the oral history assignment and it came time for students to choose a family member to interview, Armani could not decide on an interviewee. This surprised me because most students could choose quickly and were excited about their prospects. I suggested interviewing her mom, whom I knew she lived with. She responded angrily by saying, "I don't want to talk to her." And then she stormed out of class.

Before I began teaching, I thought that pedagogy only included methodology. Teaching Ethnic Studies taught me that pedagogy includes the purpose of education as well as the identity of who is being taught, who is teaching, their relationship to each other, and their relationship to structure and power.

I asked a colleague who was close to Armani for insight, and she explained that there were growing tensions within the family. Because Armani was not as successful in school as her siblings, she was receiving a lot of pressure from her mom and they were in constant conflict. She also informed me that Armani's mother was the only parent she had access to. Her father was still in Eritrea, leaving her mother to raise four children alone. However, my colleague told me

she would talk to both Armani and her mother to see if it would be possible to conduct the interview in order to complete the final project.

Even though my colleague had promised she would talk to the family, I was still nervous that Armani would not have her interview done in time. I remember being extremely anxious since she was the only student who had not yet completed the interview, which is essential to completing the final narrative. However, by the time of our next class, Armani had successfully conducted a long, in-depth interview. What was even more exciting for me was that she presented it with pride and accomplishment.

Over the course of five weeks, I saw Armani change both personally and intellectually through the process of writing. She worked carefully and meticulously with love for her mother's story and for the pride she had in her own development as a writer. Her transcription was impressive; not only did she translate her mom's story into English, but her interview had turned out to be longer than most and she worked hard to capture every word her mom said. During the narrative process she was constantly asking for help, and she revised multiple times in order to get everything aligned with my standards as well as her own. Her final product far exceeded the expectations of the assignment and beautifully captured her mother's life and demonstrated her improvement as an academic.

I learned a lot from teaching and reflecting on my experience with Armani. My pedagogy began to develop as I continued to improve on my ability to guide students through the rigorous process of the oral history narrative. Before I began teaching, I thought that pedagogy only included methodology, or how you teach. However, teaching Ethnic Studies taught me that pedagogy also includes the purpose of education as well as the identity of who is being taught, who is teaching, their relationship to each other, and their relationship to structure and power.

While one purpose of the Oral History Narrative Project is to allow students to have an opportunity to discover who they are through the interview process of a family member, another equally important purpose is to help them become better writers and thinkers through a demanding, multidraft writing process. The methods used throughout the process allow for a variety of differentiation and scaffolding, which the project demands in order for all students to be successful. Armani taught me that when asking students to reflect on sometimes sensitive elements of their identity I needed to be conscious of my own identity and the power I hold as teacher. I learned that I needed to be incredibly flexible when it came to allowing students to navigate their sometimes-complicated relationships with their family. Every student's relationship to their family is different from mine and from each other's. I became increasingly open to the needs that students had to complete the assignment and was able to make my assignment fluid enough to accommodate individual situations in order for each student to access the assignment and demonstrate their learning. These are just some things that I have learned through the eight years of teaching this project.

Why the Oral History Narrative Project?

I first taught the Oral History Narrative Project in 2008. The curriculum was adapted from a similar project taught by former San Francisco Unified School District (SFUSD) teacher, Lisa Moorehouse. Since the 2008-09 school year, the project has been a central assignment of the district curriculum created by the Ethnic Studies Curriculum Collective, a core of 10 SFUSD teachers—including myself—and San Francisco State University faculty support.

On December 10, 2014, the San Francisco Board of Education voted unanimously to provide every high school student with the opportunity to enroll in an Ethnic Studies class by the school year 2015-16. After years of implementation and reflection, the Oral History Narrative Project now fits within a course framework created by the Ethnic Studies Curriculum Collective that draws from Ethnic Studies curricula used in other districts and university programs across the country.

Currently, the Oral History Narrative is the central project for our unit where students learn the key concepts of humanization and dehumanization: The Oral History Narrative is developed as a humanizing counter-narrative in opposition to the dehumanization caused by white supremacy and other systems of oppression. The unit emphasizes that humanization can foster social justice and liberation and that counter-narration can be a humanizing process that asserts the agency of marginalized people and validates identity. The Oral History Narrative Project is used to teach students that the telling and retelling of their family stories can be an act of counter-narrative, and that their own lives and experiences can be important texts to study and can be vital to making transformative, positive change in their community.

It is especially important for students at our school to see their stories validated. Ninety percent of the student population in our school are students of color, close to 50 percent identify as Latino, and many have newly emigrated to the country. These are students who do not traditionally see themselves in textbooks, whose ancestral history is rarely honored. The Oral History Narrative Project is important because it allows all students—especially historically marginalized students—to see that their ancestors count, that their history is rich and worth recording and treasuring.

The Project Outline

I get excited when I start preparing to teach the Oral History Narrative; it has become my favorite project to teach and one of the most memorable for my students. While it is a laborious and sometimes stressful process, it is usually well worth the struggle for all involved.

The unit takes five to six weeks. I start the first week revisiting the concepts of race, ethnicity, nationality, and culture—concepts students learn in the previous unit that they will use to explore the identity of their interviewee. Students are then presented with the concepts of humanization and dehumanization. They investigate how these concepts have impacted them throughout their education, analyzing whether their educational experience has been humanizing, dehumanizing, or both. Finally, students are introduced to oral history as a form of storytelling that can humanize marginalized people and validate identity.

After I frontload key concepts, I present students with the Oral History Narrative assignment and a few student examples. I make sure that the student examples offer a variety of stylistic approaches and demonstrate a clear story of how the interviewee was impacted by race, ethnicity, nationality, and/or culture. Once students have a clear idea of the assignment and final product, they are asked to choose three interviewees; just in case their first choice interviewee falls through, they are guaranteed to have at least two backups.

Two things I have found to be incredibly important to the success of this project are my ability to be transparent on the deadlines of each individual step and to effectively plan class time so that students can complete the majority of those steps in class.

Once students have decided on an interviewee, they have one week to write 20 questions for their interview. Before simply writing 20 questions, I take students through a series of lessons teaching them how to write good questions and how to conduct an effective interview. We start by identifying open- and close-ended questions. Students then take turns interviewing each other and play a few games where they act out bad interview scenarios. I always plan to have someone come into class whom I can interview in front of the students. This person is an individual who works at the school, oftentimes a security guard or secretary. During the demonstration, students are given a copy of my questions and are asked to follow along, noting which questions I asked, which ones I skipped, and if I added anything. These questions are available when students are writing their own in case they need examples. On the day the questions are due, students work in assigned groups of three or four to write and type their final 20 questions. I find this to be incredibly helpful because if students get stuck in writing, they have peers to help. Finally, I collect the questions to review and comment on. I return these by the next class period with any suggestions for improvement before they conduct the interview.

After students complete their interview, they have one week to create their transcript. The first step is to transcribe their interview, which can be a very tedious and difficult assignment. However, I make sure to always tell my students that once this step is complete, the rest is easy and much more creative! After students complete their transcription—"ums," coughs, and all—they work in assigned groups to highlight the best stories from the interview, adding follow-up questions where needed.

Once the transcript is complete, I tell the students that the hard work is done! For the remaining two to three weeks, students work carefully to craft their transcript into a third-person narrative. Their job is to focus on the parts of the interview that capture a story about their interviewee's experiences with race, ethnicity, nationality, and/or culture. While the narrative must highlight the life of their interviewee, the author's voice and style should also come through; this is no easy task. As the teacher, it is my job to help guide students to the point where they feel proud that they have honored their interviewee with integrity and clarity. Most students will turn in at least two drafts, while others will revise three or four times before we are all satisfied.

A Rigorous Writing Program as Social Justice

The Oral History Narrative project has become the heart of my 9th-grade Ethnic Studies writing program; I assign other writing assignments, but this is the most intensive and intentional. Therefore, this project has taught me the most about how to be a good teacher of writing. I believe that developing a rigorous writing program is essential for any teacher who professes to teach for social justice. All students must be given equal opportunity to become successful writers and to see themselves as academics. In order for this to happen, they must have access to engaging assignments and supportive, rigorous environments.

There are many students who teach us unforgettable lessons and cause us to reflect and ultimately improve our craft; Armani was only one of these students. She taught me the importance of flexibility when teaching a successful writing project—or any project for that matter—and highlighted the need to create assignments that were not too rigid in their expectations. For example, years ago I had to ask myself what the real purpose of this assignment was. Of course, I think it is important for students to connect with their family and document their legacy. However, I also understand that sometimes family relationships are complicated, and in order for students to complete such a significant assignment—

which assesses their understanding of key course concepts—sometimes I need to be open to alternative modes of completion and mastery.

It is important to acknowledge that some students may have difficulty completing the assignment and to prepare individual game plans for them. While my strategy was successful with Armani, the same has not worked with other students. Usually I can identify the students who are resistant to the assignment right away. I don't push them to talk with a family member if they insist they don't want to. Instead, I have school staff or other community members in mind for them to connect with. For example, last year I had a student, Noelle, who really wanted to interview her mom. Noelle said she wanted to know more about her Pinay side. Unfortunately, she was never able to connect with her mom since she lives with her dad, who is African American. As a result of this complication, Noelle refused to complete the assignment. "Just give me an F," she said. I had anticipated this response, so I contacted Katherine, a popular Filipina security guard, and asked if she would be open to Noelle interviewing her. Katherine was more than willing to be interviewed. When I told Noelle, she was surprised to find out that Katherine was Pinay and was excited to learn more about her story.

Not only did the connection between Katherine and Noelle lead to a successful narrative, it also led to Noelle creating a supportive relationship with an adult in the building at a time when she needed one. Furthermore, it allowed Noelle to learn more about Filipino culture and what it means to be Filipina; even though this information didn't come from a family member, it was important to Noelle's understanding of self and made her interested in finding out more about her cultural background.

What I learned when I was interviewing Katherine was more about her beliefs. And we have similar beliefs in our Filipino culture, which I thought was interesting. I also grew closer to her during this process of the interview. I definitely have a different perspective on her because I learned new things and I got used to talking to her. And I still want to know more about the Filipino community.

After numerous situations like that of Armani and Noelle, I realized that the Oral History Narrative Project would be most successful if I employed a communal approach by intentionally including community and family members. This meant that if students did not complete the interview on time, I would make calls to the homes of those students and inform parents of the assignment and due dates. If I did not speak the home language of the students, I would ask someone to make calls for me. While these

This project can't just be treated like a normal writing assignment. It is imperative that students have the opportunity to reflect on their experiences with the process and that they are given the space to share their work with the community.

calls were nonpunitive, they did give me a chance to touch base with family about student performance. These calls usually meant that most students completed the interview without falling significantly behind. For those students like Noelle, who still did not have an interview after family contact, I made connections within the building. Sometimes I couldn't connect students with someone who shared a similar cultural or racial background. In these cases, I had conversations with these students about whom they would like to interview. Usually this person was a favorite teacher or someone who the student simply wanted to know more about. For example, a few years ago, I had a student who wanted to learn more about a co-worker who was very active during the Civil Rights Movement.

Before conducting this interview, I only knew a few things about Robert Roth like he was Jewish. After doing this interview with Mr. Roth and the oral history project I learned a lot more about the Civil Rights Movement and activism. And doing this really opened my eyes to the world and the people. And that there is a lot of interesting and helpful things you can learn about and gain when you talk to people that are very mature and have a lot of experience about something you might be very interested in. And after this interview I see Mr. Roth as a fourth role model in my life, because he has taught me a lot about values and the world just in one whole day.

Despite the fact that this student didn't learn more about his own family history, he learned more about something he found interesting and relevant to his life; in the process he became a better writer and was proud of his final product. Furthermore, he developed an important relationship with an adult in the building whom he admired.

One thing that must be said about this project is that it is incredibly hard to teach alone. As any of us who teach multidraft writing projects know, it is extremely difficult to effectively comment and edit every student paper. Well before the project begins, I make sure I have additional adults prepared to help in the editing process. I have been very lucky to have had the support of an outside organization, 826 Valencia, which is dedicated to supporting students with their writing skills by offering access to well-trained tutors. While the level of support that 826 Valencia can offer is not always available every year for every class, I have also used the help of other teachers and community members who volunteer their time. These volunteers help with everything from the question development to the final editing and are essential to the success of all students. For example, fellow Ethnic Studies teacher Cat Reyes and I will go into each other's classes and help individual students through the process. What this communal approach means is that for the last three years we have both had a 100 percent project-completion rate and have been successful with students at all levels.

Once students are done with their project, we celebrate. This project can't just be treated like a normal writing assignment. It is imperative that students have the opportunity to reflect on their experiences with the process and that they are given the space to share their work with the community. This means that I always have a plan for community sharing. I have students choose a piece to read and bring in a picture of their interviewee. I often invite interviewees to come in and participate with the community reading. This final step in the Oral History Narrative Project reinforces the fact that the telling and retelling of their family stories can be an act of counter-narration and that these texts can be vital to making transformative, positive change in their own lives and community. For example, in reflecting on her work, Armani had the following to say about her experience with the Oral History Narrative Project:

> I think that I've learned a lot from my mom . . . I felt that I was being rude and disrespectful to my mom, but I didn't know I was acting differently. When I interviewed my mom I said why aren't I listening to her, she's the one who raised me. She brought me here so I can get my education, finish college, and get a job. She cares about me more than anyone in the world. I felt ashamed for how disrespectful I have been, but I am not going to act like that anymore. I am going to show my mom that I have changed. I feel happy that I interviewed my mom. At first I wasn't that excited, but when I started interviewing my mom I was very interested to hear her story and she was also happy to tell it to me.

As I enter into this project with students, I am always reminded of Armani and the opportunity that the Oral History Narrative Project has to empower and transform. It is also with this reminder that I stay committed to the rigorous teaching I must adhere to in order for all students to realize their full potential. ✻

REFERENCES

Tintiangco-Cubales, Allyson, et al. 2010. "Praxis and Power in the Intersections of Education." *AAPI Nexus: Policy, Practice and Community* 8.1: v–xviii.

Rethinking Islamophobia
A Muslim Educator and Curriculum Developer Questions Whether Religious Literacy Is an Effective Antidote to Combat Bigotries Rooted in American History

BY ALISON KYSIA

The increasing violence against Muslims, Sikhs, South Asians, and others targeted as Muslim suggests we, as Americans, are becoming less tolerant and need educational interventions that move beyond post-9/11 teaching strategies that emphasize our peacefulness or oversimplify our histories, beliefs, and rituals in ways that often lead to further stereotyping. Although I support religious literacy—increasing our knowledge of religious texts, beliefs, and rituals—as a common good and believe increasing religious literacy in schools challenges stereotypes, my experience teaching Islam makes me question whether it is an effective antidote to Islamophobia.

Hate crimes against Muslims increased 67 percent from 2014 to 2015 and were also up a frightening 91 percent in the first half of 2017 compared to the first half of 2016, according to the FBI and the Council on American-Islamic Relations. And in a recent survey conducted by the Institute for Social Policy and Understanding (ISPU), 42 percent of Muslims reported bullying of their school-aged children, and even more disturbingly, 25 percent of those cases involved a teacher.

In reviewing current pedagogies around Islam, I haven't seen many lessons that address the historical connections between Islamophobia and anti-Black and anti-immigrant racism, yet through my own study of U.S. history, those connections are clear and relevant. Instead, the teaching strategies and content I see reproduced most often in textbooks, teacher workshops, online teaching lessons, and even in graduate lectures are what I call the "Five Pillars of Islam" teaching approach, which represents Islam as a religion that can be summed up in a memorizable list of beliefs and rituals. This approach reduces Muslims to a set of stereotypes that reinforce media caricatures of Islam as foreign and unidimensional and Muslims as automatons who blindly follow an inflexible faith. It also does not allow students to make critical connections between Islamophobia and racism.

There is a set script with certain narrative threads that the Five Pillars of Islam teaching approach follows and it comes with a number of profound weaknesses. The story often contains references to violence without providing examples or any real context, making it easy for readers to assume Islam is a foreign religion from a foreign land that is inherently violent. For example, under the heading "The Homeland of Islam," *Ways of the World*, a popular high school and college world history textbook published by Bedford/St. Martin's, explains that "The central region of the Arabian Peninsula had long been inhabited by nomadic Arabs. ... These peoples lived in fiercely independent clans and tribes, which often engaged in bitter blood feuds with one another." After describing Muhammad's 22-year prophecy from 610–632 CE, which is collected in the Quran, the textbook says, "The message of the Quran challenged not only the ancient polytheism of the Arab religion and the social injustices of Mecca but also the entire tribal and clan structure of Arab society, which was so prone to war, feuding, and violence."

How are students supposed to make sense out of these statements? Free from examples and context, readers can assume that there is something fundamentally violent about the place and people, reinforcing the terrorist stereotype. Nor are these descriptions ever followed by an explanation of the differences between Muslims and Arabs, mimicking the way they are often confused as identical (the majority of Arabs are Muslim; the majority of Muslims are not Arabs).

The *Ways of the World* textbook then launches into a description of this new religion: the Five Pillars of Islam. A quick Google search for "teaching lessons on Islam" or "teaching lessons on Muslims" illustrates the dominance of the Five Pillar teaching approach. For example, a PBS lesson states that "students explore and understand the basic beliefs of Islam as well as the Five Pillars that guide Muslims in their daily life: belief, worship, fasting, almsgiving, and pilgrimage. They will view segments from *Religion & Ethics NewsWeekly* and information from internet sources to look closely at each pillar. Then, as a culminating activity in groups, students will create posters about the Five Pillars for classroom display."

In this lesson, "Muslims" are represented as all one people and Islam is a fixed set of beliefs dating to 7th-century Arabia. It is instructive to think about what the lesson does not teach. It doesn't teach us the names of diverse identities that fall under the category of Muslim (Ithna'ashari, Ahmadiyya, Ismaili, or Druze, to name a few). It doesn't talk about the Muslims who don't follow all Five Pillars or add a few more to the list. It doesn't talk about the mind-boggling diversity of rituals and beliefs and texts that have been in continuous flux for 1,500 years across the entire world. Suspiciously, the Five Pillar script sounds a lot like the sanitized Saudi-sponsored version of Islam that is as popular in academic institutions as it is in the halls of government and missionary venues.

These simplistic descriptions have consequences. While describing the legal system that formed in the "Islamic empire" after the death of Muhammad in 632 CE, *Ways of the World* claims "No distinction between religious law and civil law, so important in the Christian world, existed within the realm of Islam. One law, known as the sharia, regulated every aspect of life." This is incorrect. There was never a singular Islamic empire but rather multiple centers of power ruled by different leaders. Rulers used a variety of legal codes other than the sharia, like in the Ottoman Empire for example, where they included a secular code known as Kanun. There were no polities that exclusively used sharia in their legal systems. This kind of misinformation reinforces popular beliefs that sharia is an all-or-nothing total-

itarian ideology that is intent on overthrowing the U.S. government—and it can lead to absurd and racist public policy. According to the Southern Poverty Law Center, 120 anti-sharia law bills have been introduced in 42 states since 2010 and 15 of those bills have been enacted. One of the chief architects of such legislation, David Yerushalmi, noted the functional purpose of the laws "was heuristic—to get people asking this question, 'What is sharia?'"

Even when I search for lessons on Islamophobia, I either get Five Pillar results or the lessons take the conversation out of the United States. For example, in a *Teaching Tolerance* article called "In a Time of Islamophobia, Teach with Complexity," the introductory paragraph says, "When teaching about the Middle East and North Africa (MENA), U.S. teachers are often confronted with a dearth of accurate and nuanced material about the history, politics, and people of the region." The authors suggest lessons about the MENA, which is great if you are teaching about the region. If the goal is to challenge Islamophobia, these lessons won't be as effective because they communicate that Islam, Muslims, and Islamophobia are from somewhere else rather than from the United States and that Islamophobia is not also rooted in U.S. history. Rather, I am looking for teaching resources that make Islamophobia personal by connecting it to shared American histories before taking the story global.

Disappointingly, some curricula on Islamophobia include discussion of violent extremism, a choice that keeps terrorism central to any discussion of Muslims. In an article from *Teaching Tolerance* called "Expelling Islamophobia," the authors suggest "integrating Islam" more fully into the curriculum. One teacher explains that "We look at Islam from three different perspectives: history, violent extremism, and Islamophobia. ... The history of Islam acts as the introduction ... helping students get a handle on vocabulary and context. The course then pivots to violent extremism—who and where such groups are, their motivations, and how they compare to extremists in other major religions, including Christianity." The coupling of Muslims and extremism is troubling because it is a consequence of Islamophobia and fuels further pairing. We must talk about terrorism more, not less, but we need to do it in a way that acknowledges multiple relationships between Islamophobia and terrorism, like U.S. military interventions (it has been 27 years since the first Gulf War), drone warfare, and financial imperialism. And we also need to contextualize any terrorism committed by Muslims with the fact that among the more than 1,600 extremist groups in the United States. being tracked by the SPLC, the majority are white supremacists and anti-government militias. Regardless, these lessons still don't give students the opportunity to make connections between Islamophobia and racism, nor do they reinforce the fact that Muslims have been part of U.S. history since colonization.

I have seen how common it is to walk away from these Five Pillar recitations thinking that Islam can be summed up in a set of bullet points easily regurgitated on a test. Yet Muslims are complicated people who have rich and varied relationships with their religious identity. The caricatures we see in the media become all that more believable when we are taught that 1,500-year-old traditions can be summed up in neat, formulaic ways. I'm not suggesting these caricatures are used intentionally on the part of educators; quite the opposite, I sympathize with these educators. I taught this way myself in my early years in a community college because the Five Pillar teaching strategy is how I was taught about Islam academically.

Through my teaching experience, I began to ask myself: Will learning about rituals I practice (or don't) with different levels of dedication over my life span effectively help students make connections between dehumanization and violence? Maybe we should begin our inquiry into Muslims and Islam and Islamophobia in the place where we live rather than in some other place. How does that choice shift our perception about what Islamophobia is and where it comes from? If Islamophobia is a process of dehumanization, who else has been demonized this way in U.S. history? Is there something we could learn from connecting those experiences that will aid our fight against Islamophobia?

After coming to the conclusion that religious literacy does not produce the outcomes I want to achieve in fighting Islamophobia, I decided to write a lesson I could share with other educators who want to teach about Muslims and Islam but don't want to teach from a religious studies perspective. I work in a variety of educational settings, so I wanted the lesson to be effective in middle and high school classrooms and in activist or nonprofit professional development workshops. I wanted to share some of the stories I read in academic texts like *Black Crescent: The Experience and Legacy of African Muslims in the Americas* by Michael Gomez, *African Muslims in Antebellum America* by Allan Austin, *Servants of Allah: African Muslims Enslaved in the Americas* by Sylviane Diouf, *Islam in Black America* by Edward Curtis IV, *A History of Islam in America* by Kambiz GhaneaBassiri, *Inside the Gender Jihad* by Amina Wadud, and others that have enriched my thinking about the stories we use to teach about Muslims, Islam, and Islamophobia. In addition to narrative-changing content, I wanted to use a teaching strategy that reflects an active inclusivity rather than a passive authoritarianism between

Muslims are complicated people who have rich and varied relationships with their religious identity. The caricatures we see in the media become all the more believable when we are taught that 1,500-year-old traditions can be summed up in neat, formulaic ways.

teacher and students. I wanted everyone to be part of the conversation. I wanted a lesson that would give all of us, Muslims and non-Muslims alike, the opportunity to think differently about our shared history as Americans. I wanted the lesson to blur the lines between who "us" and "them" are, since this is one of the steps of dehumanization we want to interrupt.

Taking all these goals into consideration, I developed a Black Muslim meet-and-greet teaching activity. The lesson empowers participants to fight Islamophobia by raising up voices we rarely hear in the media when we talk about Islam and Muslims—Black Muslims. The personalities included in the lesson are all

Black, which not only teaches us about Islam in America but also advances themes in Black history.

Why Black Muslims and not all Muslims? I envisioned this lesson as the first in a series that helps students see Islamophobia as a consequence of racism. American racism is an ideology originating in white supremacy and in the need to steal land, resources, and labor. Islamophobia, like racism, is used to justify American imperialism or the stealing of land, resources, and labor in Muslim-majority countries. I want students to make connections between the abuse of power at home and abroad. There are a lot of heavy topics to cover if we want to empower students to make these connections that must include lessons in both U.S. and global history. I wanted this first lesson to introduce students to a new way of learning about Islam and Muslims that raises awareness of stories most Americans have not heard, setting the stage for deeper inquiry.

I wrote half-page biographies of 25 Black Muslims who lived in the United States from colonization to the present. When identifying the characters who would populate my lesson, I soon discovered that there were too many examples to choose from. In order to remedy this, I defined three time periods—colonization to the Civil War, Reconstruction to 1970s, and 1970s to the present—and then tried to balance out the names according to each time period. The earliest time period contained, predictably, almost exclusively male biographies. For this reason, I overrepresented women in the 1970s–present period, allowing me to also highlight the accomplishments of contemporary women. I chose to tell the story of Betty Shabazz rather than her husband, Malcolm X/Malik el-Shabazz, as I did for Clara and Elijah Muhammad. (Elijah led the Nation of Islam from 1934 to 1975.) These women were fierce activists and educators in their own right but their stories are almost always told in relation to their husbands. I mined a variety of sources—academic texts, documentaries, and interviews—for the major events in their lives and then wrote about those experiences in a conversational first-person voice.

I reached out to a friend, Neha Singhal, who teaches social studies at John F. Kennedy High School in Silver Spring, Maryland, which serves the suburban communities within short commuting distance to Washington, D.C. The school is racially, ethnically, and financially diverse and provided a welcoming setting for piloting the lesson among 25 juniors and seniors.

I introduced myself to the class and asked, "Do you know any Black Muslims?" One of the students, Fatima, said, "I am a Black Muslim. I was born here but my parents emigrated from Senegal." Nino said there was a Muslim woman in the 2016 Summer Olympics, but no one could give me her name. Derrick offered Elijah Muhammad and told me he started the Nation of Islam. I corrected him that technically, Fard Muhammad started the Nation, but Elijah was the leader for many years. They couldn't list any other names. I explained to them, "I want to remedy this problem. Black Muslims have been in the United States for 400 years. Why can't we name more of them?"

I gave each student a half-sheet biography of one Black Muslim and asked them to take two minutes to read the descriptions quietly. I also told them that the names can be difficult for some students to pronounce and they should ask me if they needed help. While they read, I circulated around the room and said the name of the character for each student. I asked them to think quietly about which pieces of information were most important to share with someone who has never heard of their character. This was more challenging than I thought it would be for them. Later, I changed the instructions for the lesson, asking students to flip over their half-sheet biography and create this list in five bullet points. The content in this activity is unfamiliar to most students, so they need an extra minute to absorb the story, summarize the main ideas, and ask for clarification.

I then explained to the class, "In a minute, you will all get out of your chairs and meet and greet one another. How do you do that? You introduce yourself just like you would at a party, but instead of introducing the real you, you will introduce yourself as your Black Muslim character." Neha and I stood in the front of the room and briefly role-played for them. "Hello, who are you?" I asked. Neha answered, "I am Aisha al-Adawiya. I was born in 1944 and grew up in the Black church but I converted to Islam after reading the Quran in the early 1960s. I am the founder and president of Women in Islam, Inc., an organization of Muslim women that focuses on human rights and social justice. I represent Muslim women at the United Nations. I make sure the stories of Muslims are included in Black history through my work at the Schomburg Center for Research in Black Culture at the New York Public Library." I explained that I would then introduce myself to Neha, and we could follow up with additional questions, particularly those listed on the worksheet.

I gave students the worksheet and explained, "These are questions to help guide your conversations and collect information we can use later in our discussion." I asked individual students to read them out loud: Find one person who was enslaved. Where were they from? Where did they end up? How did they resist? Find one person who experienced discrimination based on their race or religion. Describe their experience. Find two women. Describe some of their achievements. Find two people who worked for justice. Explain how they do/did that.

Some of the students got up and immediately launched into introductions. "Hi, I am Carolyn Walker-Diallo . . . " "I am Mahommah Gardo Baquaqua . . ." "Were you discriminated against because of your race or religion?" Others needed to be coaxed to get up. Sure, it was one of the last days of school before summer break. But as Neha noted in our post-activity feedback session, some students find it intimidating and uncomfortable when asked to take more responsibility for teaching one another, making it hard to get some of them to take their attention off the teacher. As the lesson progressed, we could see the students becoming more comfortable with the format and it made clear to Neha and me the way that inclusive pedagogies can help students more actively engage in their learning.

The students continued to meet one another for about 25 minutes. After we finished, I asked them to take a seat. I gave them each a handout and said, "At the top of the paper, please list three things you learned about Muslims from this activity."

After giving them one minute, I asked them to share their answers with the group. Melanie said, "I was shocked to find out that Muslims were enslaved in the U.S. I never heard that before." Joon quickly added, "I like learning about the successes of Muslim women, so many of them are scholars." I asked her,

"What do you hear about Muslim women in the media?" She looked up in the air inquisitively and said, "I don't really hear about them." I said, "OK, what comes to your mind when you think of a Muslim woman?" Another student, Carrie, yelled out, "They are oppressed." Joon added, "Yeah, I see that, but the women I learned about today, they are a strong group of people." Other students found it surprising that so many Black Muslims were from West Africa. When I asked why that is important, Nicole said, "We never hear anything about Black people before slavery. They were kidnapped and then end up picking cotton in the South." Mika said, "I didn't know Mos Def was Muslim, he changed his name to Yasiin Bey and his music uses Islamic principles." I asked, "What kind of Islamic principles are reflected in hip-hop?" She had to look at her biography again but then answered, "like being worried about poor people and people who have to deal with discrimination."

On the same handout, there is a list of questions for students to discuss in small groups. Because we got started a little late, we decided to keep the group whole for the entire discussion, but given the full class period, I would have let the students discuss the questions in small groups before we debriefed together, since this will maximize student participation.

I asked the class to give me a few examples of the first Muslims to come to the United States. Fatima offered, "Ayuba Suleiman Diallo was born in West Africa; he was enslaved and ended up in Maryland, on an island off the Chesapeake Bay. He eventually made it back to Africa." I quickly followed, "Where in Africa? It is a continent, not a country." She scanned her paper and replied, "Gambia."

Lydia relayed the story of Margaret Bilali, whom we know about because her granddaughter, Katie Brown, was interviewed by the Works Progress Administration (WPA). The WPA, the largest New Deal agency during the Great Depression, employed millions of Americans for public works projects, including the construction of buildings and roads, but they also supported art, music, and theater projects. Fortunately, they chose to collect oral histories of enslaved people and their descendants. It is from these interviews that we get Margaret's story. "Margaret's dad was enslaved on Sapelo Island off the coast of Georgia. She remembers seeing her dad and his wife praying on the bead and kneeling on a mat to pray," Lydia explained. "What does that mean—praying on the bead and kneeling on mat? Why would they do that?" I asked. One of the Muslim students explained that some Muslims use a string of beads to pray, called a tasbih or *misbaha*, that is similar to a rosary, *japa mala*, or other prayer beads. Muslims often use a small carpet or mat when praying because they fully prostrate by putting their forehead, knees, and hands on the floor. The prayer mat ensures you are praying on something clean. What's nice about this lesson is that it makes the connection between Muslims and Black history, and within those biographies, the stories can include religious literacy lessons without religion being the central focus.

We also talked about the ways Muslims fight injustice. Neha offered, "Kenneth Gamble fought injustice. He is the guy in Philadelphia who was a musician and then started a nonprofit to help fix houses in the South Philly community and then sell them to people who are from those neighborhoods. With gentrification taking over entire neighborhoods right now, this is important work." Sandra offered the story of Clara Muhammad, who started her own schools so they could teach their kids about their religion. "Her husband, Elijah, was put in jail because he wouldn't fight in WWII," she added. Marcus said, "Keith Ellison is a Muslim in the U.S. House of Representatives." I asked, "How does he fight injustice?" Marcus replied, "Being there is important so that when people have questions about Muslims, he can answer them." Lydia, who played Keith in the activity, added, "He also worked on police brutality issues before he came to Washington." As we were waiting for the bell to ring, a couple students pulled out their cell phones and started looking up photos of the Muslim characters they learned about. For example, once they saw a picture of Ibtihaj Muhammad, the Olympic fencer, they made the connection between the face and the story about her shared in the meet-and-greet. After seeing how effective it was at grabbing their attention and making them continue talking about the lesson, I decided to add a PowerPoint presentation with as many open-source pictures of the characters as possible that teachers can use after the discussion.

After working with Neha and her students, I decided to add some questions to emphasize the fact that many of the characters in the activity are still alive. It is important that students be asked to connect the past to the present. In the worksheet, I included the prompt, "Find at least one person who has been active during your lifetime. Describe some of their experiences." In the discussion, I added, "Who would you want to meet or research more? Why?" This last question gives the student a chance to make the story more personal and the character more relatable by thinking about whom they admire and why.

In June 2017, a Somali American Muslim woman living outside of Columbus, Ohio, Rahma Warsame, was beaten unconscious and sustained facial fractures and the loss of teeth by a white man who screamed, "You will be shipped back to Africa" before he attacked her. As educators committed to pedagogies of equity and inclusion, we have to help students make connections between race, religion, and the racialization of Muslims.

Our students are bombarded with violent images of Black men and women being killed by the police, immigrants being forcibly removed from their communities, and increasing hate crimes against Muslims. We cannot allow our students to think these are discrete events. The Movement for Black Lives platform reads, "We believe in elevating the experiences and leadership of the most marginalized Black people, including but not limited to those who are women, queer, trans, femmes, gender nonconforming, Muslim, formerly and currently incarcerated, cash poor and working class, disabled, undocumented, and immigrant." Lessons like the Black Muslim meet-and-greet help students build vocabularies that increase their ability to talk about racism in ways that capture these intersections of oppression. We have to give them new ways of understanding racism if we want them to create solutions in the present and future that humanize all of us. ✳

RESOURCES

Kysia, Alison. "Black Muslims in the United States: An Introductory Activity." *Teaching for Change*. teachingforchange.org/black-muslims.

Reprinted from *Rethinking Schools*, Winter 2017 (vol. 32, no. 2).

Hmong Club
Empowering Us

BY PANG HLUB XIONG

"When is Hmong Club going to start?" is one of the first questions I am often asked during open house night at my elementary school in the Twin Cities in Minnesota, which is now 26 percent Asian students—most of whom are Hmong. Over the years, our Hmong Club has grown to be a life center for our Hmong students. A survey I conducted found that 81 percent of the participants felt like they belonged at Hmong Club. In contrast, only 61 percent of these students felt like they belonged at school.

Hmong Club helps students belong and understand themselves more deeply so they can proudly go out into the world and connect with and teach others. As 9-year-old Darla reminisced on her four years of Hmong Club: "At Hmong Club we learned about our culture. Hmong Club is important because it's a part of me—I was born Hmong. During the day, we only learn about reading, writing, and math. At Hmong Club, we talked about Hmong games, Hmong food, and Hmong things."

I wish I would have had Hmong Club when I was a child growing up in Wisconsin. I had a great support system, such as my teachers. However, I knew that I led a very different life at home—which I had to keep secret from school because no one understood. Even as an adult today, I still struggle with identity issues.

For the better part of my life, my identity was clouded as I navigated and juggled the taboos and struggles of being bicultural in America. Growing up, I was often confused—about who I was and about who we are as a people—and Hmong Club plays a role in giving our Hmong students more clarity about their identity.

Hmong Club is now an important part of our community, and in many ways, the story of Hmong Club begins with my own story.

My Truths: Survival

I am Hmong, and it took me some 20-plus years to realize I am actually Hmong American. My life began in America, where I was born and raised. Yet my story began years earlier, in the countryside of Laos—a place I have never set foot on. Hmong people are a minority group from the mountains of Laos who were recruited by the CIA to assist Americans in the highly unpopular Vietnam War.

After Laos fell into the hands of the Viet Cong, my family was forced to flee. With a rifle in one hand and a child in the other, my father led the way for my mother, my three young siblings, and several relatives on a dangerous journey through the jungles of Laos. Freezing nights, starvation, and unknown dangers were daily battles they faced. Fear motivated them through exhaustion. Survival was the only goal because tomorrows were never promised for anyone.

The raging Mekong River was the last obstacle before reaching safety in Thailand. Not only was the Mekong River lined with soldiers ready to shoot, there were also stories that dragons and unknown beasts lived there. No one knew how to swim—we are mountain people with little water experience. Hope and a little bamboo raft carried my family as they dared across the river in the dark of the night, in search of refuge in Thailand. At last, they reached their final destination of the barbwire fences of Ban Vinai Refugee Camp in Thailand. This became their new reality, with food dropped from the skies and long lines that only afforded them small rations.

Becoming Bicultural

These are the truths I grew up with. These stories alone show how different I am from the average middle-class student growing up in the safety of America. Undoubtedly, the warriors that my parents and grandparents were forced to become affected my upbringing. I am a strong believer that one's past greatly defines who they are and who they become. Understanding their struggles has greatly helped me contextualize my life and led me to be an educator.

I was born and raised in Wisconsin. I grew up in a time when the public school systems were just learning about Hmong people. I remember the sense of urgency around having to learn English and the stigma of being an ESL student. It was important to learn the rules of school and the ways to be at school because the life I knew was *wrong*. Learning the rules of America were not priorities for my parents because their experiences taught them that survival took precedence.

At the time, I did not know I was bicultural. I was Hmong and had to learn how to navigate through a school system that did not operate by the same set of rules I knew. Being bicultural meant that I was misunderstood again and again because of the way I looked, the things I said, the foods I ate, the beliefs I valued, the choices I made, and the life I lived. Out of embarrassment of my culture and convenience for others, I learned the lies to tell in order to gain approving nods from classmates and teachers. Pizza is far from being my favorite food, but it was a convenient answer to give.

It was respectful to speak Hmong at home, which meant speaking English was not encouraged. I had an extensive Hmong vocabulary. However, the majority of these words were not relevant to my education. Never once did I need to use the word "glutinous" in my American life.

Because all they have ever known is the fight to survive, my parents each worked multiple jobs to provide for the family. This meant that my sisters and I were responsible for the domestic housework—this was our contribution. We cooked dinner for 10 people every night, made sure the house was clean, and took care of our younger siblings. This was just the way our world worked. We had limited free time. Aside from our health and safety, our education was my parents' top priority. It was expected that we balance all of our home responsibilities with school. Therefore, we were not allowed to participate in extracurricular activities and we were not allowed to socialize with friends.

All of my experiences led me to where I am today. I entered the education field because I noticed that Hmong students were still battling the same struggles that I had 20 years earlier. Many Hmong students still seemed disconnected from school. Becoming a teacher was my chance to directly impact students and help them define who they are and who they want to be. Sharing my narrative has empowered many students to deepen their understanding of their own stories and reciprocate their stories and experiences. Understanding ourselves will allow us to better understand each other.

Hmong Club

After my first year of teaching kindergarten in Wisconsin, I was lured to the Twin Cities with the hopes of joining the progressive Hmong community. The Twin Cities is home to the largest Hmong population per capita in America. I wanted to be inspired and further discover myself.

I got a job teaching kindergarten. The school of 500 students was approximately one-third white, one-third African American, and one-third Asian American, which was predominately Hmong. Staff of color consisted of a young Lebanese woman and myself. Each August, my team and I sat down to look at students' scores and profiles to create our class lists. Secretly, or maybe not so secretly, I took as many Hmong students as I could. They would have a great teacher regardless of whom they got, but I desperately wanted to be able to validate and empower as many Hmong students as I possibly could. I wanted Hmong students to have the chance to experience having a teacher who reflected them. I was the only Hmong teacher and likely the only adult who would know what students were talking about when they said they had to *ua neeb* over the weekend.

Putting all the Hmong students in one class was neither realistic nor best practice. This is where Hmong Club came in. Hmong Club became the space for me to validate Hmong students who were not in my class. Because I was so personally connected to the historical context of Hmong people and history, I understood the implications of things said and not said: why students (especially girls) were not allowed to participate in extracurricular programs, why parents were not able to make it to open house, and the different expectations between boys and girls. Hmong Club was my chance to change students' mind-set about being bicultural and bilingual. Lingering questions surrounding my own bicultural identity, along with my childhood experiences, paved the way for my vision for Hmong Club. I wanted students to have an opportunity to explore their identity, know who Hmong people are, and be proud of their heritage.

We had over 60 students during my first year, ranging from prekindergarten to 5th grade. During the 75 minutes that we met, students proudly shared stories and cultural information with others. I immediately noticed the stark difference it made with the Hmong students. They appeared to walk the halls in school with greater confidence—they seemed happier. These traditionally quiet, respectful, and obedient kids suddenly needed reminders to be quiet and to display self-control in the hallways as they enthusiastically waved to me and mustered up any relevant Hmong words they knew ("*Nyob zoo*, Ms. Xiong!"). My mere existence and confidence embracing my cultural heritage transferred as if through osmosis. I was a reflection of who they are.

Hmong Club was a space for Hmong students only—a concept that not everyone agreed with. A couple staff members questioned my motives and many non-Hmong students begged to join. However, I was intentional about limiting Hmong Club to those from a Hmong background because I did not want non-Hmong students to feel the all-too-familiar feelings of isolation. I wanted students to be able to enjoy a conversation about *qaub* without being interrupted to teach and explain it to someone else, and most importantly without judgment. Imagine having to explain what pizza is every time you talk about it, only to be met with disgusted responses. (Quab is papaya salad: a common Hmong dish made of shredded raw papaya mixed in a mortar with many ingredients including fish sauce, shrimp paste, crab paste, tamarind paste, chili peppers, garlic, tomatoes, and more.) I wanted a space where we can be Hmong without having to explain ourselves to anyone.

The activities we did at Hmong Club varied each year. Many of the students were second-generation, with many far removed from their heritage and no longer speaking Hmong. The first year of Hmong Club was simply an introduction to Hmong culture and language. Other years, we explored areas of interest such as science, art, and atypical careers.

As students gained more confidence and interest, we dove deeper into Hmong history. Although many Hmong people's stories begin with the same humble beginnings, I wanted the students to learn from the true experts—their families. Students had the opportunity to study their personal family histories, which parents and grandparents were thrilled about. Students were grounded in basic Hmong history from the pre–Vietnam War to post-war era. From there, students were tasked to interview their

> **Hmong Club was my chance to change students' mind-set about being bicultural and bilingual. I wanted students to have an opportunity to explore their identity, know who Hmong people are, and be proud of their heritage.**

own families for their own stories. We brainstormed questions as a group and students were allowed to choose what they wanted to focus on. Some students chose to focus on their life, beginning from their birth in America. Many chose to focus on stories beginning with their parents' and/or grandparents' lives in Laos.

The final project resulted in students individually creating a traditional Hmong story cloth art project depicting their own family story. Many were able to trace their family history back to Laos and their family's journeys seeking refuge in Thailand and onward to America.

Six-year-old Melody described her family harvesting rice in Laos: "This is my grandpa and my grandma. They are teaching my mom how to get rice. When the rice grows taller and taller, you cut them and then my grandma flips the rice to clean it."

The round woven bamboo tray is a recognizable household item for many Hmong students. Yet Hmong children are rarely able to describe the purpose or process of separating rice grains from the husk. In fact, it was not until my adult years that I

Imagine having to explain what pizza is every time you talk about it, only to be met with disgusted responses. I wanted a space where we can be Hmong without having to explain ourselves to anyone.

learned the words "winnowing basket." Rice is not only a staple of Hmong diet, but rice seasons were also the standard measurement for time. Birth dates don't exist for Hmong elders because the rural countryside of Laos only had the rice seasons to mark the passing of time. Ages were all estimates according to the number of times they planted and harvested rice. But in Minnesota, most of us buy rice from grocery stores, so many of us who were born in America did not have the personal experiences or language to articulate the experiences that were a daily part of our parents' livelihoods in Laos.

Hmong Club helped bridge generations and gave students the vocabulary to discuss Hmong practices with mainstream America. I couldn't help but chuckle a little as I read the rest of Melody's family history:

> There is a path where the bombs came. My mom almost got killed because she was trying to get the baby chick. Then my grandma and grandpa found a house on an island. They had to swim across the river that had dolphins in it. There were fish in it and there were seahorses in it. There were also sharks that eat people.

The Hmong language is extremely underdeveloped with certain topics, such as colors and fish types. My parents referenced all things with fins that swam in water simply as "fish." I never knew that dolphins existed in Southeast Asia and quickly assumed that Melody was innocently wrong. A quick Google search confirmed that Melody was indeed correct. Irawaddy dolphins are common in the Mekong River. Melody's parents were old enough to remember Laos and proficient enough in English to give Melody a more accurate version than my parents did.

The older generation was limited with their English proficiency and we were limited with our Hmong proficiency and experiences. Thus, many details were literally lost in translation, leaving much room for misunderstandings. As another example, the English language has a different name for every hue and tone of blue. My mom interchangeably uses blue to describe anything ranging from gray to green. My mom often talks about my sister's blue dog in Laos; like many other stories she tells me, I am left to my own imagination to figure out what the blue dog actually looked like. Similarly, Hmong Club served as a mediator to clarify questions and misconceptions.

Other students, such as 8-year-old Sue, learned about the pervasive gender inequalities that run deep in Hmong culture. Sue wrote:

> My grandma lived in Laos when she was little. Her family go gardening together. They have a house to rest called a gardening house. My grandma she had to garden everyday so she didn't go to school. Her brother had to go to school while my grandma worked so hard on gardening. She lived in Laos till the war came and she had to leave with my dad and uncle.

Families who were able to afford an education had to prioritize who would get educated. Traditionally, very few girls and women had the opportunity to attend school. This directly contradicts the current Hmong statistics in America, where more Hmong women are choosing higher education than Hmong men. Understanding the oppression that Hmong women have traditionally faced in a patriarchal society helps us understand the current disparities. Hmong women today are hungry to receive the education we were traditionally excluded from.

Students' personal interviews ranged from everyday life to the poverty and struggles their families faced. Some students were more interested in the war.

Nine-year-old ChaLee shared the struggles his mom endured: "My mom had to move to Thailand because it was dangerous in Laos. Viet Cong soldiers were coming. There was a bomb. They had to cross the Mekong River. She didn't know how to swim—only my dad did. So my dad had to carry my mom across the Mekong River. When they got there, they took an airplane to America."

Although these interviews were brief, students' curiosities were definitely sparked to engage in future conversations. Students learned about their personal histories, which will likely not be included in their school curricula. Growing up, the textbooks I read in school and the history lessons we learned did not tell the stories of my father and uncles getting recruited as young boys to fight in the Vietnam War. Nowhere did we learn about the refugee camps that my older siblings lived in. For Americans, the Vietnam War was known as the highly unpopular and most contentious war. For Hmong people, the Vietnam War was known as *teb chaws tawg*—when the country shattered.

During this family history project, students learned important Hmong history words such as "Mekong River" and "Ban Vinai Refugee Camp." These became their stories and truths as well. It was my honor to guide students through their learning and validate their truths in a school setting. It is my hope that they will continue to learn and tell their stories.

I proudly wore pieces of my Hmong clothes to school, despite being laughed at by my own family members. However, I was humbled when my students started wearing pieces of their Hmong clothes to school as well. Not only were they proud of their heritage, they were also able to share their culture with students and staff. My reflection of the students, along with my ability to validate some of their previously unknown and misunderstood experiences, helped build their confidence and strengthen their sense of self and belonging as they walked the school halls.

During a fire drill, students debated whether the bright object in the sky was the sun or moon. A Hmong student shyly announced that your ears would get cut if you point at the moon. As non-Hmong students began to laugh, other Hmong students quickly jumped in to defend this girl. This began a conversation on respecting different beliefs even if you disagree. The students continue to make me proud in ways I didn't expect.

The response to Hmong Club was overwhelmingly positive. Parents were eager to connect their children to their cultural roots. Furthermore, parents appreciated their child's identity being validated by a person of authority in a school setting. Transportation was not available, but parents found Hmong Club important enough to transport their children weekly. This also gave me an opportunity to connect closely and consistently with families. In turn, many

My reflection of the students, along with my ability to validate some of their previously unknown and misunderstood experiences, helped build their confidence and strengthen their sense of self and belonging as they walked the school halls.

of these same Hmong families became more involved with school events as their needs and voices were heard more.

The students' excitement was my fuel. In hindsight and all honesty, I think I needed Hmong Club just as much as the students did, if not more. I was new to Minnesota and had a longing to speak Hmong and discuss Hmong-related politics and events. I wanted recommendations on where to find the best Hmong foods. My co-workers were of no help to me for these things. However, the kids had many resources and recommendations to share with me. Hmong Club was about having fun and discovering ourselves as Hmong people. We were able to just be Hmong, without judgment.

Furthering Ethnic Studies

Hmong Club is definitely not the first of its kind. Clubs and organizations have long existed to support students across the country. However, Ethnic Studies is finally getting the national attention it has long deserved and we must keep the momentum going. Despite the many responsibilities being added to educators' plates, schools need to prioritize and find resources to sustain Ethnic Studies programs. Hmong Club was a passion project and I received little to no financial support. For years, I volunteered my time and purchased supplies from my own pocket—because that's what we do as teachers. I never knew I could ask for financial compensation and no one ever offered me anything. Hmong Club was great, but we have the potential to be much better with financial support. Sustaining strong ethnic programs requires financial support. Schools that truly value Ethnic Studies programs such as Hmong Club must also provide adequate resources for those passionate enough to take on the work.

One of the most important lessons I learned is that I need allies: allies for moral support, allies for financial support, and allies for manpower. Part of my success was because of the trusting administrators I had. They gave me complete freedom to do what I wanted because they trusted me and believed in my vision. My principals also valued diversity and continuously found ways to diversify the staff. I am proud to say that I am now one of six Hmong teachers in my school. I no longer have the need to put all of the Hmong students in my classroom. The staff diversity has increased exponentially, meaning that more truths, different perspectives, and different narratives will be heard more often.

Especially with the extremely polarizing state of the world today, it is more important than ever to give students a platform to safely discuss issues that matter to them. Students need to know that talking about race and ethnicity is not taboo. We have the opportunity to raise the quality of education for our students and should take advantage of it. It has been clear to me that students want to discuss race and ethnicity, especially because these differences are so physically visible and identifiable. Students as young as preschool already notice racial differences and are able to hold intelligent conversations about them. Everyone's interest in discussing race and ethnicity will vary, but we must provide interested students with the space to discuss. This is important because race and ethnicity have been at the center of many current events and political debates, and it is crucial that we learn to discuss these matters. Nurturing students to appreciate their identities will allow them to go out into the world and also learn how to appreciate others' differences. We must empower our students to all be brave enough to celebrate their truths. ✳

Critical Family History

BY CHRISTINE SLEETER

Several years ago, while visiting a middle school English language arts classroom, I witnessed a white teacher struggle to prompt a discussion of ethnic roots with her students—about one-third each African American, Mexican American, and white.

After explaining that the story they were about to read was set in Puerto Rico, she asked, "Who would like to tell us about your nationality?"

Having been born in the United States, the students simply could have replied that they were American. But the term "nationality" so often serves as a misnomer for ethnic roots that everyone in the room appeared to understand it that way.

Several white students volunteered European national origins. "Scotland," said one. Another yelled out, "France!"

The Black students, however, sensing the question opened up the minefields of slavery and negative images of Africa, shouted out countries they obviously did not come from. "China!" said one student. "India," said another.

Flustered, the teacher moved quickly to the story itself. She had a good idea—we all have ethnic roots. But she didn't know how to work constructively with it and didn't realize she didn't know until students sabotaged what for many of them could have become a painful experience. The teacher hadn't considered how often understandings of family roots are entwined with the dominant, triumphalist, national narrative. She wasn't not prepared to dig into ethnic histories and family roots in a way that would question that narrative.

Roots and National Narratives

Everyone has roots, and our roots inform much about how we see the world. But most of us do not know our roots very well. In my university classes, I had noticed students bringing stories from their family experiences to discussions of various historical events—stories that often bumped up against each other. For example, a white fifth-generation Californian and a Filipino-American second-generation Californian got into an argument about California agriculture, their very different vantage points rooted in conflicting family histories. I got to wondering whether the family histories themselves may be a venue for deeper learning.

In his 1998 book, *A Larger Memory: A History of Our Diversity, with Voices*, Ron Takaki wrote:

> I often found myself stirred by the ways people responded to circumstances not of their choosing. Always, I was reminded that people are history: their experiences, feelings, adjustments, imaginings, hopes, uncertainties, dreams, fears, regrets, tragedies, and triumphs compose our past. Everywhere, I found their stories bursting in the telling.

With reference to his students, he said, "Our parents and grandparents, I have been telling them, are worth of scholarly attention: They have been actors in history, making choices as they left their homelands and settled in America."

From time to time, I tried engaging my university students in family history projects to make their own roots more visible. But I realized that simply tracing family trees or writing family stories didn't produce the critical reflection I sought. While some students had no knowledge at all about (and sometimes no interest in) their family histories, most constructed portraits that echoed a recurring national narrative: immigrant ancestors who worked hard and confronted challenges, attaining eventual success they passed on to their offspring. The portraits by students of color generally framed racism as a huge barrier their forebears confronted, but the white students never mentioned it.

In fact, my white students' narratives reminded me of Matthew F. Jacobson's analysis of the European American ethnic revival movement of the 1970s–90s in his book *Roots Too: White Ethnic Revival in Post–Civil Rights America*. Following the Civil Rights Movement and rapid diversification of the U.S. population, descendants of eastern and southern European immigrants were drawn to the language of ethnic identity and collective rights. In an effort to reclaim identity, tracing ancestors to European homelands became quite popular. But these "up by the bootstraps" narratives denied that descendants of more recent European immigrants benefit from racism with the argument that post–Civil War immigrants had not owned slaves nor taken land from Indians. Further, they ignored forms of racial discrimination that *did* benefit them, such as in housing and hiring.

I began to wonder how, as a teacher, I could prompt all of my students, especially my white students, to use an examination of their families' pasts to critically analyze how our families experienced, enacted, confronted, or in other ways were implicated in social relationships based on racism, colonization, capitalism, and patriarchy.

Genesis of Critical Family History

As I pondered how to push my students, I realized that I wasn't even sure of my family history. So over the winter holidays one year, I dove into Ancestry.com to see what I could find. I found much more than I had anticipated and became addicted. As I charted out an extended family tree, I began to use questions I normally ask about social justice issues, such as:

- What laws and other processes that benefit white people shaped opportunities for my ancestors?
- What kinds of relationships did my ancestors have with members of other groups around

them? How and why was most of my family history forgotten or suppressed?
- What happened to the diverse languages and cultures my ancestors brought?
- What role(s) did my ancestors play in the colonization of Indigenous peoples?
- What was my ancestors' location within the growing capitalist economy, and how did that location impact them?
- How did patriarchal systems and norms play out in my family's history?
- Did any of my ancestors work for equity and justice?

This work generated a research process I call Critical Family History, which involves locating ancestors within historical contexts shaped by membership in sociocultural groups and by conflict over power and resources. It includes genealogical research drawing on sources such as family stories and documents, vital statistics records, military records, digitized newspapers, and property records. Research into historical, social, and cultural contexts uses sources such as primary accounts written when the ancestors were alive, analysis of census data for demographic patterns in areas such as housing and jobs, and accounts written by contemporary historians.

For example, if you ask what other sociocultural groups were in the vicinity of an ancestral family and what the power relationships were among groups (a question white family historians rarely ask), you begin to situate your own family story within larger and sometimes conflicting conversations. A past involving homesteading, for instance, also involves taking up settler colonialism and dispossession of Indigenous peoples. What does it mean to both acknowledge hardships and challenges of one's ancestors *as well as* their participation in land theft?

With respect to my family, I made some startling discoveries and realizations. When I found out that an immigrant ancestor had become an anti-Chinese activist in San Francisco, I traced how her participation in the slave economy of the South had shaped her white supremacist racial identity and activism. When I discovered German American ancestors who had been actively bilingual and bicultural for about two generations, I realized the power of wartime xenophobic violence to erase culture, language, and memory. When I traced theft of Indigenous peoples' land to some money I inherited, I had to begin confronting what it means to descend from the colonizers.

Making my own ancestors "worthy of scholarly attention," as Takaki put it, did not give me comfortable stories. But the research did enable me to see myself within the jagged currents of race, ethnicity, and social class in U.S. history. I began to see how to engage students in family history through an Ethnic Studies lens.

"History Is No Longer an Abstraction I Can't Relate To"

I had an opportunity to teach Critical Family History to teachers a few years ago at the University of Colorado at Boulder. My 38 students and I began by considering who constitutes family and the limitations of conventional family trees. After I demonstrated how to access and use vital statistics records to trace ancestors, we considered the fact that our ancestors lived within wider cultural and social contexts than we normally think about. Students then selected one family unit or ancestor to research and to set within a larger context. I also gave them the option of researching the life of someone they are not related to at all. An international student, for example, dove into the life of Noam Chomsky, partly because he knew he would not be able to locate much online about his own family and because he was curious about how Chomsky's life had shaped his activism.

I have developed several research and reflection tools online that we used (available at christinesleeter.org/use-this-blog). Some of the tools guide genealogical research; others, contextual research. For example, the "Context Questions Framework" involves placing family data in a chart like the example below, which includes additional questions about historical and cultural contexts during specific decades in specific locations where ancestors lived.

"Hidden P Factors" asks questions about why ancestors immigrated and what happened on their arrival, looking at the following kinds of factors: *push factors* (why they left their homes), *pull factors* (why they went to a particular place), *punishing factors* (how they were punished or discriminated against once they arrived), and *privileging factors* (positive factors that helped them on arrival).

In the end, I found that the concept of Critical Family History made sense, not just to me, but to the teachers as well. "This is what engaged learning should be," one exclaimed as she described staying up late every night because she was so engrossed in the project.

"History is no longer an abstraction I can't relate to," another said.

I repeatedly heard that questions about the social or historical context helped the teachers delve

Context Questions Framework

DATE	SLEETER FAMILY	HISTORICAL CONTEXT	SOCIAL CONTEXT
1840–50	Wm H. arrived around 1846.	1840: U.S. Census, Macon County, Ill., pop: 531.	1840s: King Friedrich Wilhelm IV of Prussia cracked down on anything liberal, there was massive harvest failure in 1846–47. By 1848, several German states were in revolution.
	1846: married Catharine Farenhorst.	Dovring: Average farmland value in Ill. was $8 per acre in 1850	
	1849: bought 40 acres from U.S. govt.	German immigrants recruited into Illinois.	
		Although Illinois was not a slave state, some slaves were brought into Ill. seasonally during this decade.	

into why people in their pasts might have done what they did and that connecting history with their own families was immensely engaging.

Some of the white teachers followed my example of having probed how my ancestors benefited from racism and colonization. For instance, one traced an ancestor's homesteading experience, asking whose land homesteading policies enabled her ancestor to take and what happened to the Indian tribe that had been forced from that land. Another identified jobs her ancestors had access to that African Americans in the same city were barred from.

A handful of other white teachers, however, tried to avoid these questions. When I asked one teacher whether any American Indians or African Americans had been in the same county as his ancestors, he named an Indian tribe that was there at the same time but insisted that his ancestors had nothing to do with them. As I pressed him for how he knew that to be true, he finally acknowledged that he did not know and had assumed his ancestors had no impact on the local tribe.

"Then there's still a question you could research," I said.

He agreed that he could. Whether he ever did or not, I don't know, that conversation having happened on the last day of class. But I hope to have unsettled his assumption that racism and colonialism had nothing to do with his white ancestors' experiences.

Questions about the contexts of ancestors' lives helped some of the immigrant teachers in the class. Interviews with family members were the only source of information some were able to locate. For example, a teacher from Kenya interviewed her mother about her grandfather but could not find anything else online, and at first she wasn't sure whether she could complete this project. She told me she was surprised to learn from her mother that he had fought in a war during the 1940s but was not sure where else to look for information.

"World War II?" I asked.

"My mother didn't say," she replied.

"See what you can find out about Kenyans fighting in wars right around then," I suggested.

She went back online and ended up researching British recruitment of Kenyans to fight Italian-con-

trolled East Africa. As she read about experiences of Kenyans during that time period, bits of information she had about her grandfather jelled into a larger picture that made sense to her and gave her deeper insight into the man she knew when she was a child.

Family history is not a neutral subject. It is very personal, connected to the identities of students and people they are emotionally close to. The teachers experienced a range of emotional reactions, from surprise to learn that a name passed down orally was wrong, to pride in claiming a previously unrecognized identity, to shame or pain when learning about an ancestor's participation in taking Indigenous peoples' land or discovering alcoholism in the family. The best way I knew to prepare them for their own emotional experiences was to share some of my own.

Teaching Critical Family History

As Ethnic Studies is implemented in more classrooms, family history will likely become increasingly popular. What insights do I have for teaching Critical Family History? Start by considering why you want your students to engage with family history.

For example, do you want to link their family experiences with a concept in the curriculum? Several years ago, I spent time in a 5th-grade classroom where the teacher was teaching about immigration. About two-thirds of her students were from immigrant families, so she wanted to start with students' family stories. The first assignment was to interview someone in the family, preferably an older person, about the family's immigration experience or their experience moving, since not everyone had recently immigrated. Before students did their interviews, the class brainstormed interview questions, and she showed them how to take notes. When they brought their notes back to the classroom, she showed them how to write them up into a story. Students posted their write-ups, then read each other's. As the unit unfolded, their diverse family stories became an important part of it.

There are other possible purposes for family history in Ethnic Studies, such as:

- Do you want to delve into history in a way that is personalized? This is definitely worth doing, but it requires some familiarity with history told from multiple viewpoints. For example, how do Mexican Americans tell U.S. history? How do Japanese Americans tell U.S. history? Be prepared for multiple, even conflicting, viewpoints that can emerge from multiple family experiences.

- Are you developing a research and writing assignment with family history as the focus? If so, what options might you give students who prefer not to research their own family? Might they research the life of a community elder or local activist, for instance?

- Is your main purpose helping students get to know each other better? If so, you might invite everyone to bring a story or recipe from home and to find out as much as they can about its origin or significance in their own family.

- Have your students already done a family history project in a previous grade? If so, how might you build on, rather than duplicate, that earlier work?

Teachers can find many resources for doing family history with children. Five minutes in the children's section of many bookstores will give you options, which generally parallel adult guides for genealogy research in that they discuss family documents, interviewing family members, and tracing vital statistics records. The books for children do not necessarily take into account some important considerations, however.

First, garden-variety family history is not necessarily critical. Guides for children and youth rarely ask questions about the larger context of sociocultural relationships. You will have to plan that dimension yourself.

Second, most family history books for children are written as if everyone is of European descent and lives in a traditional two-parent home. Increasingly one can find helpful family tree templates that allow for all kinds of family structures, such as on FamilyTreeTemplates.net. Some of your students may be adopted; seek advice from parents, especially if children are young. Resources for racially and ethnically diverse classrooms are beginning to emerge; one good resource is ancestors-unknown.org.

Become sufficiently familiar with the backgrounds of your students so that you can anticipate what digging into family history might reveal, not for purposes of avoidance but rather to prepare yourself and the students for what might emerge. Parents, other family members, and community resources can be of great help if you seek them out proactively.

A Final Note: White People, Ethnic Studies, and Critical Family History

It is very easy for those of us who are white to sidestep the "critical" part of Critical Family History and focus on the family tree itself, as well as struggles and triumphs of our ancestors. After all, how can we develop a sense of pride and identity based on stories of stealing land, enslaving Africans and their descendants, and benefiting from all forms of racism?

Speaking for myself, as I've gotten to know my ancestors (and by now, I know a good deal about many of them), I have found a wide variety of people, some of whom I would probably admire and others, well, not so much. In terms of understanding myself better, I have some appreciation for roots of my interest in German literature and in sewing.

More importantly, I inherit a set of social circumstances I can make an impact on. My family and I do not exist outside the socially constructed United States and global racial structure, but rather within it. My ancestors helped to make the racial structure what it is, in fact. Given my inherited past, what future do I wish to work for? What will my grandchildren inherit, and what role will I have played in creating that world? Ultimately, these are the questions that ground both Ethnic Studies and Critical Family History. ✳

COLONIZATION AND DEHUMANIZATION

Burning Books and Destroying Peoples
How the World Became Divided Between "Rich" and "Poor" Countries

BY BOB PETERSON

Imagine going on a trip to a new place, one that you and your friends have never been to before. When you get there it seems strange: different types of plants and animals, and fruits that you've never tasted, but that are delicious. The people you meet appear friendly, but dress differently and speak a language you don't understand. In the middle of their large city, you find a building that holds thousands of books—proof that these people have a history of writing and education.

Needless to say, you can't read their books. So what do you do?

You burn all of their books, every single one that you can find.

Although this story might sound ridiculous, that is exactly what happened when the Spanish colonialists met the Mayan people in what is now Central America.

In 1562, Fray Diego de Landa ordered that all Mayan books be collected and burned. Landa wrote, "We found a large number of books and they contained nothing in which there was not to be seen superstition and lies of the devil, so we burned them all, which they [the Mayas] regretted to an amazing degree and which caused them much affliction." Not only the Mayas, but also the Totonac, Mixtec, and other Indians had books. They were all burned.

The mass book burnings deprived all of us of the Mayan people's written history and most of their written knowledge about mathematics and astronomy, two areas of science that they studied a great deal. Only three books remain, by mistake, and they are now in museums.

This is but one consequence of what colonialism meant for those who were colonized—the destruction of important parts of their cultures and the loss of their histories.

Portugal Attacks Africa

Colonialism is a system of control by a country over an area or people outside its borders. Modern colonialism started in the late 1400s, when those in power in a few European countries decided that they might become richer and more powerful by trading goods with people in other parts of the world. The rich people of Portugal, in an attempt to expand their country's trade with India and China, sent sailors on boats south along the Atlantic coast of Africa and then north into the Indian Ocean. The Portuguese traders found cities and peoples with a high level of education and culture. However, there was a problem: Although the people of east Africa and India had lots of items like spices, porcelain, and ivory that the Portuguese wanted, the Portuguese didn't have much that the Africans and Asians wanted besides metal pots and pans—and guns (which the Portuguese weren't eager to supply to others).

The Portuguese solved this problem on future voyages. They took well-armed ships and soldiers and forced the Africans and Asians to "trade" with them. A Portuguese ship would arrive on the east coast of Africa armed with cannons, guns, and soldiers. The soldiers would get off and circle the port city. The Africans who resisted the soldiers were murdered. The soldiers broke into houses and palaces, stealing all that was valuable. The Africans fled in panic, unable to resist the better-equipped European soldiers. The Portuguese filled their ships with gold, ivory, and other valuables. They then bombarded the cities with their cannons and burned them to the ground. In just a few years the splendid commercial cities along the coast were in ruins. The Portuguese also attacked Islamic merchant ships that had been trading between east Africa and Asia—bombarding the ships and taking the goods. The Portuguese eventually controlled almost all the ocean-based trading between Europe, Africa, and Asia. They set up trading enclaves and forts along the coast that acted as collection points for the gold, ivory, and slaves brought from the interior. This wealth flowed into Europe.

Spain Attacks the Americas

This was only the beginning. In the Americas, the Spanish became the main colonizers. They claimed lands that were inhabited by tens of millions of Native peoples and forced those people into virtual slavery. Spaniards took vast quantities of gold and silver from the Americas, which enriched small numbers of people in Europe. According to the Mexican Indigenous leader Cuauhtémoc, official receipts from Europe show that between 1503 and 1660, 185,000 kilos of gold and 16,000,000 kilos of silver were shipped from America. The Native people resisted and were almost wiped out by the superior weapons of the Europeans, as well as the diseases carried by the colonists. England, France, and Holland sent their own ships around the world in order to claim land and peoples as their own.

The Europeans wanted colonies for several reasons. They wanted raw materials from these places—not only gold and silver, but spices, cotton, cocoa, palm oil, timber, and rubber as well. They also wanted the Native peoples to work for them for hardly any pay at all, so that the products the Native people made could be taken by the Europeans. In the West Indies the main product was sugar; other areas produced tea, coffee, cocoa, timber, tobacco, and cotton.

Africans Stolen

The European colonizers had problems finding people to work their mines and plantations in the Americas. In part this was because so many Native peoples in the Americas died as a result of the initial arrival of the Europeans. Also, those who survived did not want to work as slaves. They resisted and oftentimes were able to escape because they knew the land better than the Europeans.

The European colonists tried to "solve" this problem by stealing millions of people from Africa. They brought them in chains, stacked in holds of ships like sacks of flour, without enough food or water. The 3,000-mile voyage across the Atlantic, which typically took five or six weeks, was grueling and deadly. Millions died in what became known as the Middle Passage.

Slavery devastated western Africa. Millions of people, particularly youths and young adults, were taken away or died resisting. Some Africans helped the European slave traders, increasing conflict between Africans themselves. Western Africa became so engulfed in the slave trade that little attention or resources were put toward improving farming or people's lives.

Haitian poet René Depestre described this in his poem "Black Ore," which reads in part:

> When all of a sudden the stream of Indian
>   sweat was dried up by the sun
> When the gold-fever drained out the final drop
>   of Indian blood in the marketplace
> And every last Indian vanished from around
>   the mines
> It was time to look to Africa's river of muscle
> For a changing of the guard of misery
>
> And so began the rush to that rich and limitless
> Storehouse of black flesh
> And so began the breathless dash
> To the noonday splendor of the black-skinned
>   body
> Then all the earth rang out with the clatter of
>   the picks
> Digging deep in the thick black ore.

Resistance to Oppression

The history of colonialism is full of stories of the horrible treatment of those who were colonized. It is also full of stories of resistance, when people fought back against the Europeans. For example, it took the Spaniards years of war to wipe out Native resistance in Peru, doing so only after suppressing a major revolt involving more than 100,000 people led by Tupac Amaru II in 1781–82. The Araucanian Indians of Chile weren't defeated until the late 1890s, after hundreds of years of battle. Native American armed resistance in what is now the United States continued up through the late 1890s with the Massacre of Wounded Knee. Colonialists met similar resistance throughout Asia and Africa.

But the results were more or less the same throughout the world. Resistance was crushed by the more militarily advanced European armies and navies. As a result, some Native peoples of Africa, Asia, and the Americas were completely wiped out. The wealth of those continents was sent back to Europe, which in turn made Europe all the more able to continue its domination of the world.

Types of Colonialism

Not all colonialism was the same. Some colonies were established by the migration of settlers from the colonizing country, as in the British colonies in North America, Australia, and New Zealand. Some colonies were founded by religious groups fleeing persecution, such as the Pilgrims who settled in what is now Massachusetts. Other colonies were organized by groups of merchants or businessmen, such as the British, Dutch, and French East India Companies.

In North America, most colonialism was of the settler variety, and the Europeans who moved to North America in the 13 colonies soon found themselves in disagreement with the "mother" country of England. The resulting American Revolution of 1776 led to a temporary decline in the power of England. In a very different kind of revolution, the slaves of Haiti, led by Toussaint L'Ouverture, rebelled and kicked out the French in 1804; the Mexicans, led by Miguel Hidalgo, and much of Latin America, led by Simón Bolívar, kicked out the Spaniards by 1825. Spain continued to hold Cuba and the Philippines until 1898, but otherwise retired from its role as a colonial power. England and other European nations, meanwhile, entered a new colonial era in the 19th century, looking to get rich off of other parts of the world.

Second Colonial Period

The riches produced by colonialism helped stimulate the Industrial Revolution of the 19th century. This tremendous increase in the use of machines greatly strengthened the military power of European countries, allowing them to extend their rule over areas of Asia and Africa. In parts of Asia and Africa where

before there had been only European commercial posts, European nations sent troops along with commercial agents, government officials, and Christian missionaries. The Europeans forced these areas to become markets for their industrial products and suppliers of raw materials.

By mid-century, the British controlled all of India, which was ruled by a British viceroy; the Dutch assumed similar control over Indonesia, then known as the Netherlands East Indies; and the French seized Indochina. The entire continent of Africa, except for Ethiopia and Liberia, was divided up among the European powers after the Berlin Conference in 1885. The British had almost all of eastern and southern Africa as well as large portions

The riches produced by colonialism helped stimulate the Industrial Revolution of the 19th century. This tremendous increase in the use of machines greatly strengthened the military power of European countries.

in the west; the French took over the areas north and south of the Sahara Desert; Germany took territories on the Atlantic coast and on the Indian Ocean; Portugal extended its coastal enclaves of Angola and Mozambique toward the interior; and Belgium obtained the Congo. One colonialist referred to the continent that was being so greedily sliced up as "this magnificent African cake." One young sea captain, later a famous author, Joseph Conrad, found a situation that he called "the vilest scramble for loot that ever disfigured the history of human conscience."

Historian W. E. B. Du Bois described the pillage of Central Africa by profiteers who supplied the world with ivory for billiard balls and piano keys this way:

Thousands of miles of fertile country were turned into wilderness and ruin. Hundreds of thousands of elephants were slain and thousands of human beings. It has been estimated that not more than one in five of the captives bearing ivory ever reached the ocean. Starved and weakened by disease and the strain of marching, they line the long paths with their dead.

Ivory was exported by the ton. As early as 1788, London was importing more than 100 tons of ivory a year. This continued for a century: 514 tons were imported in 1884. This meant the death of 75,000 elephants a year and, as Du Bois noted, thousands of people. Henry Morton Stanley wrote in 1891: "Every tusk, piece, and scrap . . . had been steeped and dyed in blood. Every pound weight has cost the life of a man, woman, or child, for every five pounds a hut has been burned, for every two tusks a whole village has been destroyed. . . . It is simply incredible that because ivory is required . . . populations, tribes, and nations should be utterly destroyed."

Forced Labor and Cash Crops

The European colonialists forced Africans to produce cash crops no matter how low the prices were. They did this mainly by taxing people. Africans could get money to pay taxes only if they grew the "cash" crops the Europeans wanted. In some cases colonial powers went to even greater extremes. According to Guyanese writer Walter Rodney, French officials banned the Mandaja people (now part of Congo-Brazzaville) from hunting, so they would engage solely in cotton cultivation.

British and French colonial governments would often use forced labor to get work done at no cost to the Europeans. They demanded that Africans "give" their labor to colonial officials for a certain number of days. According to Rodney, "a great deal of this forced labor went into the construction of roads, railways, and ports to provide the infrastructure for private capitalist investment and to facilitate the export of cash crops." He describes the impact of these policies on Africans:

Taking only one example from the British colony of Sierra Leone, one finds that the railway that started at the end of the 19th century required forced labor from thousands of peasants driven from their villages. The hard work and appalling conditions led to the death of a large number of those engaged in the work on the railway.

The French accomplished the same using different tactics. They forced Africans to join the French army and then used them as unpaid laborers. Rodney estimates that in one railroad project lasting 12 years, 25 percent of the workers died annually from starvation and disease—thousands of Africans.

Among the most barbaric of all the colonial powers were the Belgians under King Leopold II. According to historian Adam Hochschild, writing in *King Leopold's Ghost: A Story of Greed, Terror, and Heroism in Colonial Africa*, an estimated 5 million to 8 million people were killed in the Belgian colonialists' attempt to force the people of the Congo to supply rubber for Europe's needs.

Just as in earlier periods of colonialism, the European powers wanted the colonies only to provide raw materials, low-paid workers, and open markets so that European products could be bought. The English, for example, took fine cotton from India and Egypt but banned the Indians and Egyptians from processing the cotton into finished clothing. Instead, Indians and Egyptians had to buy imported (and more expensive) clothing made in England. Thus Indian artisans who made fine textiles were forced out of business, and India became poorer.

In this way the economies of many countries of Asia, Africa, and Latin America were stunted. Instead of "developing," they were actually "underdeveloped" by Europeans. Prohibited by European powers from continuing their own cultures based largely on farming, and also prohibited from developing manufacturing, the colonies came to depend heavily on a few crops or minerals, the prices of which went up and down in world markets. These policies led to African economies becoming "monocultures," relying on one agricultural crop or mineral for most of their foreign currency and trade. For example, the Gold Coast (present-day Ghana) grew mainly cocoa and Senegal and Gambia grew groundnuts (peanuts).

Resistance Continues

Africans and Asians continued to fight against European domination and were met with barbaric repression. In 1898, for example, British troops massacred 20,000 Sudanese at Omdurman, near Khartoum. The Boxer Rebellion in 1900 by the Chinese against European colonizers was another such example. The Chinese were particularly angered because the British were trying to get their people addicted to opium, a harmful drug, so that they could profit and control a vast part of Asia. The British successfully used military force against the Chinese so that opium could be unloaded in Chinese ports. This led to widespread opium addiction in parts of China.

The United States eventually became a colonial power itself. The U.S. military fought its own "colonial" wars early in the nation's history—dozens of wars with the Native peoples throughout the 1700s and 1800s. From 1846 through 1848, the United States fought a war with Mexico, which resulted in the U.S. seizure of one-third of Mexico. The United States annexed Hawai'i in 1898, and a short time later defeated Spain in a war, acquiring Puerto Rico, the Philippines, and Guam as colonies, and control over Cuba. The subsequent U.S. war against Filipino independence fighters was especially horrific. The United States had become a colonial power in its own right.

It wasn't until after World War II (1939–45) that the countries of Asia and Africa were able to force a weakened Europe into beginning to grant them independence. In some cases it came with huge struggles, such as that of the Indian people, led by Mahatma Gandhi and the Indian National Congress against the British, or that of the Vietnamese people, led by Ho Chi Minh and the Viet Minh against the French.

Even though almost all countries of Africa, Asia, and Latin America are now formally independent and have their own representatives at the United Nations, many of the economic and political relationships that were established during colonialism continue. Because of colonialism, many countries of the Global South still rely on one or two main crops. Most have never fully developed an industrial base. In addition, many of these countries owe lots of money to wealthy nations—that is, they are in debt and cannot afford to spend money on things their own people need.

When people in more wealthy nations think about helping other people who are hungry and in poverty, it's important to recognize how they got that way. The fact that Spanish colonialists, for example, took tons of gold and silver from the Americas is connected to today's widespread hunger in South America.

Walter Rodney explains this connection when he writes about a well-established European-based organization that sees itself helping people in the Global South. This organization "called upon the people of Europe to save starving African and Asian children from *kwashiorkor* [a deadly, protein-deficiency disease] and such ills . . . [but] never bothered their consciences by telling them that capitalism and colonialism created the starvation, suffering, and misery of the child in the first place." ✳

This article was previously published in *Rethinking Globalization: Teaching for Justice in an Unjust World* (Rethinking Schools, 2002).

Trial of the Genocide of Native Californians

A Role Play

BY AIMEE RIECHEL

INTERVIEW BY MIGUEL ZAVALA

Aimee Riechel teaches at Mission High School in San Francisco and has been an integral member in the development of Ethnic Studies in the district. Mission High School is composed of a diverse student population that includes immigrant youth from Latin America and African American students.

MIGUEL ZAVALA: Can you first provide some context about how you approach Ethnic Studies?

AIMEE RIECHEL: Teaching Ethnic Studies and workshops in San Francisco Unified [School District] have grounded me and allowed me to develop my pedagogical approach. I would say that it's to give students skills to become critical thinkers of the world around them, to give them opportunities to grow as learners and to see themselves as true intellectuals. And foremost to develop a sense of love in themselves, their histories, and their communities, thereby seeing hope in change they can take part in. Students can then change their society at whatever level that may be.

ZAVALA: How did you learn about the Genocide of Native Californians Role Play?

RIECHEL: It is based on *Rethinking Columbus: Rethinking the Next 500 Years*. It was developed in 2008 through a collective of teachers who have developed Ethnic Studies curriculum within San Francisco Unified. Working with Peter Hammer within the district in cooperation with Allyson Tintiangco-Cubales at the College of Ethnic Studies at San Francisco State, we came up with guiding questions and goals for the entire 9th-grade Ethnic Studies course. So the role play activity emerged as part of a larger unit on California Indians and the Spanish mission system.

ZAVALA: Sometimes learning activities are construed as isolated components, and I appreciate how you all designed it within a broader unit. Can you speak more about the California Indians unit?

RIECHEL: It was originally part of a larger unit on systems of oppression, with a focus on Spanish missions as an example of oppressive systems. We changed our approach to Ethnic Studies then, shifting from groups of people to broader conceptual themes. So the unit used to be called "Native Californians" but it changed to "Systems of Oppression." Within the district currently, the role play is not used anymore—but I use it within my modern world history curriculum and it fits within teaching about systems of oppression, specifically focusing on colonization, gender, class, and race. That is currently where it fits within modern world history, by looking at how colonization was perpetuated. The role play, as I teach it, gives students a local example of colonization by focusing on the ways the Spanish and then Americans colonized California. I want to add that teaching conceptually—about systems of oppression, for instance—gives students frameworks for understanding the world around them. These frameworks can therefore be taught in any course and are not bound to a particular historical period.

ZAVALA: How do you set up the role play?

RIECHEL: For me it's a culminating activity for teaching about the colonization of Native peoples, especially in areas where the Spanish missions expanded their empire. So in my world history class, I focus on southern Brazil then bring it back to California, which connects to them. Our high school is called Mission High School and so this history is important to students because it is so localized. We set it up within the context of what are the missions, what is missionization, what is colonization, and how do the missions work to colonize people? We look at the missions as a system of oppression and how they operated to physically and culturally destroy whole groups of people. In order to set it up as a culminating activity, students develop plenty of background information through their engagement with texts, film, primary sources—which enables them to dive into each of the roles. And the role play comes right before students are asked to do a final assessment in the form of a reflection on the material they have learned as part of the larger unit.

ZAVALA: It sounds like an enactment, where learning is embodied and comes to life. What challenges have you encountered in facilitating the role play?

RIECHEL: With any kind of role play activity that requires some form of acting, that pushes teachers and students to be out of their element; as teachers we fall into simplifications, asking students to read material and regurgitate information. Students don't have opportunities to learn from the experience—so whatever you are going to do, any kind of activity that is arts-based—especially an assessment that is experiential and less traditional—you have to ask yourself, "How am I letting students present what they have learned?" So how do we know students are really embodying these concepts? Are students expressing their knowledge through these particular modalities that I am asking them to perform? So I have them write things first, practice or rehearse, and reflect— so they go through an entire process. So before they engage in the trial in front of the whole class, they are learning about different points of view and how to debate. I give them feedback as they rehearse, which is a part of the ongoing reflection within the role play.

ZAVALA: It reminds me of the work with migrant farmworker youth where theater of the oppressed

is used. Yet this requires conceptual development, reading, but also practice, which takes place in what Boal terms "forum theater." I have a last question on recommendations for teachers. You have mentioned some, such as writing, reflecting, and rehearsing. What other recommendations do you have for someone who wants to reinvent the role play?

RIECHEL: I think it's important for teachers to see this as a localized example of what happened to Indigenous people. But this might not connect with students who live in another part of the country. So it's important to learn about the history of Indigenous people in their communities, what happened to them, and how to work on that level. Like any lesson, you can't just implement it, you have to contextualize it. How do you make something like this come alive for your particular students? ✳

Genocide of Native Californians Role Play

Lesson Plan

Length: Two days
Grade level(s): 9th, 10th, 11th
Subject area(s): World History, U.S. History, Ethnic Studies
Theme: Formation of the Colonial System and Early Resistance, 1849–70
Readings: United Nations Declaration of Human Rights, select texts on the Spanish colonization of California

DAY 1: PREPARING THE DEFENSE

I, the prosecutor from the International Court of Human Rights, am bringing charges against several groups involved in the colonization of California.

Your task is to defend, represent, or try to play the role of various figures involved in the Spanish colonization of California. Your group will be assigned a specific individual or group that you will defend against the charges before them.

Specific steps for Day 1:
1. Read the charges brought against you and your co-defendants. The following groups are charged:
   - The Spanish Empire
   - Bartolomé de las Casas
   - Juan Ginés de Sepúlveda
   - The Catholic Church/Junípero Serra
   - Spanish landowners
   - The Spanish army
   - Native Californians who resisted
   - Native Californians who willingly participated in the missions

2. You may not agree with the views or actions of this person/group, but it is your responsibility to try. Create a defense that deals with the following issues:
   - You can deny or accept the charges.
   - If they are not guilty, then who is and why?
   - If they are guilty, then how might this group/person justify their actions?
   - How would the person/group you are defending speak, if they could?
   - Did Indigenous Californians deserve to be seen as or treated like the Spanish treated other Spanish?
   - Are these charges fair? Should people with a modern conception of human rights be able to look back and judge those who did not have a modern conception of human rights?

3. Each member of the group needs to have a speaking part in the defense. No one should be silent.

Charge 1: You violated Articles 4, 15, 18, 20, and 23 of the United Nations Universal Declaration of Human Rights (UDHR) and are responsible for the cultural genocide of Native Californians. You, either directly or indirectly, contributed to the destruction of thousands of years of Indigenous traditions, history, religion, and way of life.

Charge 2: You violated Articles 3, 5, and 25 of the Universal Declaration of Human Rights and are responsible for the physical genocide of Native Californians. You, either directly or indirectly, participated in the physical destruction of Native Californian societies.

Use the sources of information that you have been given throughout this unit to help construct your defense.

DAY 2: DELIVERING THE VERDICT

You will also hear the defenses of other figures, and you will be responsible for delivering a verdict on their innocence or guilt based upon what you hear. You can find the accused guilty of one, some, or all of the charges.

You will use the Universal Declaration of Human Rights to justify the verdict that you deliver.

Genocide of Native Californians Role Play

Groups

THE SPANISH EMPIRE

You are not an individual, but a system. Your desire to expand your power and dominate others directly led to the destruction of Californian Native culture. Your desire to have colonies that enriched you allowed you to tolerate the erasing of the histories and traditions of many different people. It can be said that you expanded into the New World to compete with various other European nations, but you used your colonies to enrich yourselves at the expense of those who originally inhabited them. Without you there would be no motivation to explore, nor to establish missions from which Native culture was attacked. You believe that your culture was vastly superior to those cultures in California and believed that under your "guidance" these people could be brought into the "civilized" ways of European nations.

BARTOLOMÉ DE LAS CASAS

You are known as the defender of the Indians. You argued against Sepúlveda that Native Americans should not be forced into Christianity through conquest, but through good example. You believe that Native Americans, though sinful, are not beyond redemption and have the potential to become Christian. You are not opposed to colonization or the expansion of the Spanish Empire and think that it does not need to be as brutally done as it was in the past. You are accused of helping create the philosophical and theoretical justification for conquest and conversion that led to the destruction of Indigenous Californians in particular and Indigenous people in the Americas in general.

JUAN GINÉS DE SEPÚLVEDA

You believe that Native Americans are barbaric savages who should be conquered before they are converted to Christianity. You believe that they have committed crimes so severe as to barely make them human, chiefly that they practice cannibalism. You believe that they cannot be reasoned with and that they understand force more than the word of God. For you, there is little, if anything, worth saving in Native Americans and that if many die, then so be it. A principal belief in your life is that might makes right and that those who are mighty have power by the will of God. You are accused of helping create the philosophical justification for the enslavement and conquest of Native Americans.

THE CATHOLIC CHURCH/JUNÍPERO SERRA

Your organization is responsible for creating an environment that justified conquest and colonization. Your belief in the superiority of your own religion empowered people to feel justified in destroying, both physically and culturally, millions of Native Americans. Some members of your organization believed that Native Americans were not equally human to Catholic Christians and that their deaths were justified. Some argued Native Americans should be saved from eternal damnation by allowing them to have a choice, while still others said that they should be forced to convert. Members of your organization destroyed ancient relics and artifacts that they believed to be pagan/un-Christian. Some argued for the enslavement of Native peoples, while others against.

Junípero Serra was your most prominent representative in California. He was responsible for bringing the mission system to California. He oversaw the conversion, both forcibly and willingly, of hundreds if not thousands of Native Californians. It was under your protection and with your endorsement that he entered what would become California with the intent of converting and "civilizing" its people.

SPANISH LANDOWNERS

Your desire for land and riches drew you to the New World, where you took the land from its original inhabitants through trickery or deception. You claimed to be the rightful owners after encouraging the original inhabitants to trade for it, even though in their minds land belonged to everyone and could not be owned. You oftentimes exploited the Native Californians by not paying them for work, underpaying them, or forcing them to work for you directly. You drove many of them away from their ancestral hunting and gathering grounds, forcing them to look to the Spanish in order to not starve. You oftentimes supported the beliefs and arguments of Sepúlveda, who justified the taking of Native lands because they were not Christian. With you came deadly diseases that decimated the Native population as well.

THE SPANISH ARMY

You directly participated in the killing and conquering of Native Californians. It was you who, under the orders of the Spanish Empire and the Catholic Church, forcibly converted or killed thousands of Native Californians. You then defended the lands that were taken from Native Californians with force and brutally suppressed all resistance. Many of you raped Native women and stole from other Native people. You came to the New World seeking wealth and to spread the Spanish Empire's power. Without you, none of the destruction of the Indigenous population could have transpired.

NATIVE CALIFORNIANS WHO RESISTED

You are responsible for provoking a violent response from the Spanish and creating a justification for colonization. Had you accepted or tried to compromise with the Spanish, there might be a chance that your culture, lands, and heritage may have survived.

NATIVE CALIFORNIANS WHO WILLINGLY PARTICIPATED IN THE MISSIONS

To save your lives, you chose to do as the Spanish wished. In doing so, you made sure that your children, your children's children, and all of your descendants lost their culture. Your language, religion, and ways of life have been all but lost because you collaborated with your occupier.

Genocide of Native Californians Role Play

Defense Brief

Name _____ Defendant _____

Do you accept the charges? _____

Why/why not?

Justification 1 (evidence):

Justification 2 (evidence):

Justification 2 (evidence):

Did Native Californians deserve to be seen or treated like the Spanish treated other Spanish? Why/why not?

Are the charges fair? Why or why not?

- Be sure to use the language of the U.N.'s Universal Declaration of Human Rights.
- Be sure, if you are not guilty, that you implicate someone else.
- For help with your arguments, refer to your readings and your teacher.

Genocide of Native Californians Role Play

Who Is the Most Guilty? Why?

	CHARGE 1 Guilty of Cultural Genocide	Why?	CHARGE 2 Guilty of Physical Genocide	Why?
Spanish Empire				
De Las Casas				
Sepúlveda				
Junípero Serra/ Catholic Church				
Spanish Landowners				
Spanish Army				
Resisting California Indians				
Compliant California Indians				

Genocide of Native Californians Trial Voting Instructions

1. Distribute the ballots to the class.

2. Explain that students are limited to 12 total votes, and may only give 0–3 votes for each group.
   a. A 0 vote means that the group is not responsible at all.
   b. A 3 vote means the group is very responsible.
   c. A 1 or 2 represent limited guilt.

3. The left side is guilt over cultural genocide, and the right side is guilt over physical genocide.

4. When students have cast their votes, collect them.

5. Copy the below chart onto the board or butcher paper.

6. Have a student volunteer read the ballots to you as you write tally marks representing guilt.

7. At the end, add up the votes cast. The groups with the most tally marks are most guilty, and those with the least tally marks are least guilty.

8. Note: In criminal trials, unanimous verdicts are required. Make sure that students don't go away thinking that people are convicted of crimes by majority vote.

Trial Ballots

PHYSICAL GENOCIDE		CULTURAL GENOCIDE
	Spanish Empire	
	De Las Casas	
	Sepúlveda	
	Catholic Church/Junípero Serra	
	Spanish Landowners	
	Spanish Army	
	Resisting California Indians	
	Compliant California Indians	
	TOTAL	

- You have a total of 12 votes to cast for physical genocide and 12 votes for cultural genocide.
- You are limited to 0–3 votes per group. Zero votes means they are not responsible at all. Three votes means they are very responsible.
- Before turning it in, make sure your votes add up to 12 on each side.

The Advent of White Supremacy and Colonization/Dehumanization of African Americans

BY DEIRDRE HARRIS

At my high school, the African American Literature class is only one semester long. One particular class comprised 20 seniors—five Black girls, four Black boys, five Latinas, and six Latinos. I knew absolutely nothing about them, so we opened with introductions. We each gave our official "government" name, if the student felt comfortable, and/or a nickname, along with our pronouns (because I do not like to make assumptions, and pronoun examples are written on the board) and something about ourselves that no one would know by looking at us. One response included "People call me Tiny, 'cause I'm tiny. My pronoun is he/him/his, and no one knows that I play league football." Another response was "My name is Lizzie, and I like she/her/hers. No one knows that I don't have any brothers or sisters." (I have changed student names.) I went last, and I told them, "My nickname is Dei, my pronoun is she/her/hers, and no one knows that I have traveled to three different countries in Africa."

I was curious about why they signed up for this course and their level of knowledge regarding issues that would be brought up. Therefore, after introductions, we jumped into an Anticipation Guide, which allowed students to examine their initial understanding of white supremacy, colonization, and the dehumanization of Black people in general and of African Americans in particular. I introduced this five-statement guide as their first assignment for the semester and then passed it out:

1. The origin story of Christopher Columbus discovering the Americas is a myth.
2. The United States was destined to be the shape and the size that it is now.
3. Black people, literally, built this country with their own hands.
4. Slavery also occurred in other parts of the world between people of the same race.
5. The type of slavery that Africans endured also happened to people of other races.

"Which brave soul will read the first statement?" I asked. Tracy read it, and then I asked for any additional questions.

Ana asked, "What do you mean 'myth'? Like, it's not real?"

Instead of inserting my own ideas about the word "myth," I asked other students to explain their understanding of the word. Jocelyn's response was "Yeah, it's made up."

"So we take it that 'myth' could mean something that is made up?" Heads nod, so we continued. "Now, you don't have to agree with what the word 'myth' means. You only need to have an understanding of it for yourself, and when we have completed this Anticipation Guide, you will have a chance to discuss your responses. You will be given time to evaluate this statement and the other four statements after we first discuss what each one means. How are you going to do that? First, determine whether you agree or disagree with it, then you will explain your opinion on the lines provided below each statement."

As students wrote, I stressed, "There are no right or wrong answers at this point because we have just begun. These answers are based on your opinions." Upon the completion of this assignment, we created a tally. I asked for students who disagreed with a statement to raise their hands first. I wrote the tally on the board, then there was a show of hands for students who agreed with the statement. Afterward, we discussed why they disagreed or agreed. I told them, "You are welcome to read your written opinions from the guide or you can speak off the cuff. Also, you can respectfully respond to others' questions and comments without asking me."

For the first statement, two-thirds of the students disagreed that Columbus discovering the Americas is a myth. "That's what we learned in school," they said. I could tell by their demeanor that that was that, no questions asked. Kevin added, "We learn that in elementary school, but is it true?"

"Good question. This leads me to believe that you are open to questioning your education. So, of the third of you who agreed with this statement— that the Columbus 'discovery' is a myth—can any of you respond to your classmate's question? Is it true?"

"No, it can't be true because the Indians were already here, right?" Angel responded then looked at me for validation.

"Can someone speak to this?" I asked, continuing to throw their questions aimed toward me back to the class.

"Yeah, Indians, or Native Americans, were already living here, so they 'discovered' America," Jocelyn said.

"Raise your hand if you learned about the 13 colonies in Colonial America when you were in elementary school." All 20 students raised their hands. "You were most likely taught that they were brave because they dealt with the people who were already here, right? So do we agree that the Indigenous or Native people of this land 'discovered' it? Any other comments? No? One thing you will learn in this class is to examine how the information is framed. For instance, until people start to study these historical events outside of school, they tend to believe that colonization is a positive thing."

The discussions, as anyone can imagine, became lively and passionate; some students knew a lot about these topics, and others may not have given much thought to them prior to enrolling in the course. In any case, I immediately learned about students' prior knowledge, their comfort level with the subject matter, and their ability or hesitancy to share with their classmates. They learned from each other while I took all of this information in.

Occasionally, I entered the discussion to clarify a point that a student had raised or to answer a question. For example, no student could answer a classmate's question about the definition for the term "destined" in the second statement. For the most part though, they had the discourse under control. This discussion lasted two or three class periods, depending on how in-depth their opinions were and how many students shared out. I did not insist that all students share for this first assignment, because I was using it as a gauge to see their varying comfort levels regarding verbally engaging during discussions.

Upon the completion of the discussion, I let them know that we would be reading and writing about topics from each of these statements for the

We had to first critique the education that the majority of us had been taught in schools regarding this "discovery" myth, and we examined it from the standpoint of the roots of white supremacy and capitalism being intertwined from the beginning of the formation of the United States.

rest of the semester. I asked if there were any questions. As always, there were students who wanted to know what Christopher Columbus had to do with African American Literature and why there was more than one question about slavery.

This line of questioning was exciting because it pointed to the critical thinking aspect of the class. I in turn asked, "How can we begin to talk about African American Literature without discussing who benefits and who suffers from the belief that Columbus 'discovered' the Americas? Do we have to erase the Indigenous peoples of this land to accommodate the Eurocentric belief system that no one was here until Columbus arrived?"

This led us to the notions of Manifest Destiny, white supremacy, and, ultimately, the enslavement of Africans brought to this land. A great majority of African *American* literature is centered on how they survived, what it means to be human, what it means to be a citizen, what freedom is, and what we are willing to do for/with our freedom.

Therefore, we had to first critique the education that the majority of us had been taught in schools regarding this "discovery" myth, and we examined it from the standpoint of the roots of white supremacy and capitalism being intertwined from the beginning of the formation of the United States.

We see this from the millions of Indigenous people who were systematically killed off so that their land could be taken, leaving only a fraction of the population that is still here. We see this from the fact that the United States could not have developed

"Remember, African Americans, just like everyone else, are the answer to their ancestors' prayers. The enslaved Africans who suffered through so much did so for their descendants to be here today. It's up to us to determine how we will honor or dishonor the ancestors."

economically to become the financial power that it is today without enslaved African labor. Not enough Europeans were coming here, so abducted Africans provided the labor force that made the growth of the United States possible. We see this from the theft of more than half of Mexico by war. This allowed the United States to expand from the Atlantic to the Pacific Ocean, which opened up trade with Asia.

In class, we studied the writings from the Maafa, or Great Suffering, that refer to the Middle Passage, also known as the African Holocaust, where tens of millions of Africans were either killed in the march to the coast from the interior of the African continent (in which the continental United States can fit three and a half times), during their captivity in the dungeons on African shores, during the transatlantic passage to the Americas, during enslavement, during Jim Crow, or beyond.

We examined the etymology of the word "slave," and saw how it derived from the word for Slavs, who inhabited a large part of Eastern Europe, and how they were enslaved in Europe as early as the 9th century. We learned how slavery is an ancient practice. We examined how chattel slavery differed from all other forms of slavery—the manner in which people became enslaved, the length of servitude, the treatment while enslaved, and how they were viewed as nonhuman beings. In essence, they were property, not human.

We acknowledged that cultural beliefs come about as a function of survival. For instance, I told students that every culture created certain customs within their group in order to survive. This quest for survival is depicted in the novel *Kindred* by Octavia Butler and examined in the anthology *Crossing the Danger Water: Three Hundred Years of African-American Writing* edited by Deirdre Mullane and in the nonfiction book *Post Traumatic Slave Syndrome: America's Legacy of Enduring Injury and Healing* by Joy DeGruy. I introduced the titles of these texts as the books for the class.

I asked, "Does anyone know what those customs are that we need to survive as groups of people? For example, right now you are divided into groups of four. As a group, your goal is to 'survive' this class by passing it with the highest grade possible, correct? So think about what your group has to do to accomplish that goal. Each group will share at least one."

After working in their groups, each group responded with something that they had to do to reach their goal, such as communicate, distribute the work fairly, respect one another, show up, and actually do the work. As they shared out, I wrote each group's contribution on the left side of a T-chart on the board. We discussed what happens when someone does not do their job, how they can self-correct, and how to held each other accountable. If they found that they could not resolve it, however, they would come to me. Together, we addressed the situation. Upon finishing this discussion, we added rules/regulations and consequences.

I explained, "Cultural practices or customs based upon your ethnic group are not so different from the culture of the group work in classrooms. For instance, rules/regulations and consequences are like the law and order aspect of our U.S. culture. We also communicate via language in society, whether that language is Spanish, English, Russian, Korean, or American Sign Language. As ethnic groups, in addition to language, we must include food because we need to eat to survive. We must include housing, whether it's a teepee, hut, house, or cave. We must include medical practices to ensure survival of an illness, an injury, or giving birth. There are also child rearing and religious or spiritual practices."

At this point, students shared out what kinds of food they grew up eating and what kinds of medical practices and spiritual or religious beliefs that they have been taught.

On the other side of the T-chart, we added all of this information in a short list: law, medicine (we included food as medicine), science, politics, religion/spirituality, education (we included child rearing), and media (communication).

I told students, "These seven institutions, along with art, make up the basis of everyone's ethnic cultures." I explained how for Native Americans, Latinxs, and Africans, the highest value lies in relationship. "These groups of people recognized that we need each other to survive, first and foremost. Yet, for African Americans, who are descended from formerly enslaved Africans, we must ask, how did chattel slavery impact a people whose primary value system was relationship? Slavery destroyed families and all other forms of relationships. African American literature answers this question via literary depictions of how their relationships were destroyed and how they forged ahead to create a new life for themselves, carved out of their ancestors' desire for their unborn to have a better life."

Getting back to the T-chart, I inserted, "Now, imagine the default or the 'norm' for all of these cul-

tural practices being European-based, which is not kinship or relationship driven. What happens then?"

Lizzie astutely proclaimed, "A problem."

We all laughed, but we could not disagree. "The literature of African American people examines this 'problem,' and all the other problems that have risen out of white supremacy in this country. That is what we are talking about here," I added. "That's why this literature is so important to study and to know; it forces us to see the humanity of African Americans, a profoundly dehumanized people."

I paused to let it sink in, and then I added, "Don't get discouraged. Remember, African Americans, just like everyone else, are the answer to their ancestors' prayers. The enslaved Africans who suffered through so much did so for their descendants to be here today. It's up to us to determine how we will honor or dishonor the ancestors."

Through this process, the students determined that their cultural beliefs and practices were sometimes viewed as unacceptable or inadequate.

"Like when my mom got in trouble for speaking Spanish at school," said Tiny.

White supremacy has perpetuated itself as institutional racism at every level of society in the United States. Yet comments like this let me know that the students comprehend the concepts of this course because they were able to apply them to their own lives. Ultimately, together we sought to examine and dismantle our own colonized minds. ✳

Last Name, First Name: _____ Date: _____

Anticipation Guide

Directions: Read each statement, then circle either *agree* or *disagree*. Explain your response.

1. The origin story of Christopher Columbus discovering the Americas is a myth.
Circle: **Agree** or **Disagree**

Explain your opinion: _____
_____
_____

2. The United States was destined to be the shape and the size that it is now.
Circle: **Agree** or **Disagree**

Explain your opinion: _____
_____
_____

3. Black people, literally, built this country with their own hands.
Circle: **Agree** or **Disagree**

Explain your opinion: _____
_____
_____

4. Slavery also occurred in other parts of the world between people of the same race.
Circle: **Agree** or **Disagree**

Explain your opinion: _____
_____
_____

5. The type of slavery that Africans endured also happened to people of other races.
Circle: **Agree** or **Disagree**

Explain your opinion: _____
_____
_____

Challenging Colonialism
Ethnic Studies in Elementary Social Studies

BY CAROLINA VALDEZ

Why did European nations and American Indians compete in North America? Suppose that you found a place filled with valuable things. What if other people wanted those things? What if someone else already lived there? This is what happened when Europeans and American Indians began to compete for land and resources in North America.

—from *History-Social Science for California: Our Nation* (2006), p. 46

The above quote is one example of how U.S. colonialism is presented to elementary students within *History-Social Science for California: Our Nation*, the district-adopted social studies textbook. The lesson example above centers European competition for resources in the Americas, making Native Americans an afterthought in the final sentence of the reading. The students' textbook presented European arrival in the Americas as everything but economically motivated, with the initial unit titled "Age of Exploration." Each chapter failed to identify colonialism for what it truly is—the violent exploitation and dispossession of land, labor, and resources from Native Americans and Africans.

Thus, I set out to have my 5th-grade students critically examine settler colonialism within our California social studies curriculum and connect this dispossession to the foundation of the free market economy of present day. I taught the following social studies unit during the 2013-14 school year in South Central Los Angeles. My class was 75 percent Latinx (Mexican, Guatemalan, Salvadoran, and Honduran) and 25 percent Black (African American and Belizean).

The Slave Trade

The text presented a watered-down version of colonialism as exploration. So I focused on the page in the textbook that highlighted the Triangular Trade Route, and supplemented it with handouts from Chapter 2 of Howard Zinn and Rebecca Stefoff's *A Young People's History of the United States*. As a class, we examined the textbook image that highlighted colonial trade—enslaved Africans moving into the Americas and goods and resources moving out of the Americas to Europe. Students then read the handouts on slavery in the colonies in scaffolded pairs, which means pairing students at differing reading levels so they could support each other throughout the reading. The readings pinpointed U.S. slavery as unique from previous types of slavery in the role that race played in the dehumanization of slaves in the Americas.

I gave students the following prompt for their reflection journals: *Who benefited from the Triangular Trade Route? Did all people involved benefit? Explain your reasoning. Make sure to use key terms (exploitation, colonialism, etc.).*

Ana wrote:

In the Triangular Trade Route, the people who benefit were Europeans (Spain, France, and England), because they got everything from the Africans and Native Americans. Europeans often used slavery to supply the many people needed to work the land. You can tell [Native Americans] didn't benefit because of the disease that came with the Europeans, and they got enslaved and killed to find gold. If they didn't . . . they would chop their hands off. Europeans got everything when they didn't deserve it because they spread contamination.

Aaliyah wrote:

The 13 colonies benefited because they got enslaved Africans, sugar, molasses, tools, clothing, and other manufactured goods. England also benefited because they got timber, grains, tobacco, and rice. Native Americans didn't benefit because people were coming and giving them disease and exploiting them and they died. Africans also didn't benefit because people from other places exploited them.

Knowing the transformative power in being able to name the world, a large part of my teaching of counter-narratives included key vocabulary to challenge colonialism. I embedded social studies terms in our weekly language arts vocabulary activities, often adding terminology the curriculum failed to include, like *exploitation* and *colonization*. These vocabulary activities were not only engaging but they also helped students deepen their understanding of difficult concepts and terminology. Doing this helped ensure that students didn't regurgitate terms without fully understanding their meaning.

Native Genocide

After our thorough examination of slavery within the colonies, I returned to our earlier examination of Native American genocide that took place to secure Native land under colonialism. This time, the text presented a more honest depiction of the "conflict" between the Natives and settlers, albeit still using coded language such as *conflict* rather than *genocide*. The text mentioned massacres, such as Sand Creek and Wounded Knee, the Trail of Tears, and the deception used within treaties. I also showed a video clip on Wounded Knee and returned to *A Young People's History of the United States* (Chapter 7: "As Long as Grass Grows or Water Runs") to supplement the text because these resources offered more detailed descriptions.

Students read copies of Chapter 7 in pairs, completing text-dependent questions as they read, and synthesized the texts and video within tree maps,

which they then used to complete a writing task. In addition to synthesizing the information from multiple resources, students were asked to reflect and use the information to develop their opinion on the ethics of colonialism.

Maurus wrote:

In the Seminole War they fought back because they were tricked . . . it was right for the Seminoles to fight back because they got treated badly.

Eddie wrote:

I think it was bad to fight Indian against Indian because you're killing your own people. . . . It's like [Europeans] just don't want to stop growing. They told lies so Indians would fight Indians and [Europeans] just sat back and once the Indians were fighting they took over their land.

Candice wrote:

It was unethical because it's not fair or right to take land from Native Americans.

Colonial Economies

By now, students were rather familiar with the concepts of justice and exploitation, and found colonialism to be unethical. However, I wanted students to be able to connect present-day living conditions to European colonialism. So we took a critical literacy approach to their textbook lesson on the economic system in the colonies. The text introduced the concept of a free market economy and detailed several of the professions in the colonies, with the teacher's edition of the text offering a hands-on activity for students to learn more about the flow of funds within the colonial economy.

The activity involved organizing students into small groups, each representing a profession such as a carpenter, farmer, cooper, etc., and I was to play the king. I passed out squares of paper I had prepped the previous day, which represented money, in addition to the task cards that listed detailed directions for each group. I observed from the front of the room as students moved throughout the class to the various professions and exchanged monies for goods and services as detailed in their directions, with students also visiting me to pay the required taxes. It was evident that the intended goal of this activity was to illuminate the effect of Britain's high taxes, which left common folks making little profit, thus leading to the American Revolution. I had a different goal in mind.

At the end of the activity, I instructed each group to count their funds, and I recorded each amount on the board so we could examine and discuss them as a whole group.

"Who made the majority of money in this system?" I inquired.

"The king!" the students shouted in unison.

"And who else?" I probed. "Just the king?"

"The English merchant!" a few others answered.

At this point I stopped the conversation and put the lesson's journal prompt on the projector. "OK, pull out your reflection journals. I want you to look at our findings and answer the following questions: Who benefited from the English colonial economy? What groups were left out of the activity?"

Students pulled out the journals and began writing. As I walked around the room, a few students were confused by the prompt, but most were thoughtfully writing their responses. Once students laid their pencils on their desks, I pulled our red ball out of the back closet for a handing-off discussion

Colonial Economy
English King - $20
Famer - $3
Plantation owner - $3
Carpenter - $4
Store keeper - $2
cooper - $2
English Merchant - $12
Apothecary - $4
Miller - $3
Printer - $4
Shoemaker - $3

Left out
- Labor - slaves
- Land - Native Americans

Hierarchy
King
English Merchant
All other business
Slaves & Native Americans

Who benefited from the English colonial system? what group(s) were left of of the activity?

The person who benefited Was the English King And the English Merchant. The People that were left out of the activity was Slaves because they had to work a lot.

and tossed it to the first student speaker. One by one, students identified the English king as the beneficiary and began to name various professions they felt should have been included in the activity. They were stuck in the mind-set that European settlers were the only ones involved in the colonial economy—as the text had presented it—but with further probing questions, one student's light bulb lit. "They left the slaves out of the activity. They have the plantation owner but not the slaves that worked for them."

"Aha!" I shouted. "Slaves aren't included in the activity, but they provided the labor in the colonies! What else? Who else was missing from the activity?" Seeing the excitement in my eyes, several more light bulbs lit as hands raised.

"The Native Americans were left out of the activity!" shouted a student.

I returned to the board and drew a triangle, modeling the structure of hierarchy and labeled the three pieces. "Yes, the king benefited more than the colonists, but the basis for the whole economy is Native American land and resources and the slave labor used to work it. Our economy, the free market economy that is still used in the United States today, is built on top of slave labor and Native land." This was the critical point I wanted to stress—I was determined to help my students see that history is not just in the past but is the foundation for the conditions today. I wanted them to draw connections between the dispossession of land and labor with the founding of the colonies and the current conditions of poverty, violence, and police brutality in our community.

As the example below shows, students returned to their activity notes and reflection journals to add notes on hierarchy. Students added to their reflection journals, drawing on class discussion to add depth to their understanding of hierarchy within the colonial economy.

Closing Circle

On the last day of school, we conducted our final restorative justice circle to close out the year, with students sharing the most important thing they had learned that year. Most students reported learning to take their education seriously and not engage in "drama" with other students. Students passed the talking piece around the circle. Eventually it was Frankie's turn. Frankie was a small, sweet kid who wore glasses and didn't speak much in class. He paused for a moment to gather himself before he spoke; it was evident every time he talked in front of the class that he was pushing himself to do so. "I learned that if you take someone's land, they're going to get mad." Simple and concise, that 5th-grade analysis summed up an important takeaway from my social studies objective for the year. ✳

RESOURCES

White, William E. 2006. *History-Social Science for California: Our Nation.* Scott Foresman/Pearson Education.

Zinn, Howard and Rebecca Stefoff. 2009. *A Young People's History of the United States: Columbus to the War on Terror.* Seven Stories Press.

The Cherokee and Seminole Removal Role Play

BY BILL BIGELOW

In her book *A Century of Dishonor*, published in 1881, Helen Hunt Jackson wrote, "There will come a time in the remote future when, to the student of American history, [the Cherokee removal] will seem well-nigh incredible." The events leading up to the infamous Trail of Tears, when U.S. soldiers marched Cherokee Indians at bayonet point almost 1,000 miles from Georgia to Oklahoma, offer a window into the nature of U.S. expansion—in the early 19th century, but also throughout this country's history. The story of the Cherokees' uprooting may seem "well-nigh incredible" today, but it shares important characteristics with much of U.S. foreign policy: economic interests paramount, race as a key factor, legality flaunted, the use of violence to enforce U.S. will, a language of justification thick with democratic and humanitarian platitudes. The U.S. war with Mexico, the Spanish-American War, Vietnam, support of the Contras in Nicaragua, the Gulf War, and the invasion and occupation of Iraq come readily to mind. These are my conclusions; they needn't be my students'. Our task as teachers is not to tell young people what to think but to equip them to search for patterns throughout history, patterns that continue into our own time.

The Cherokee were not the only Indigenous people affected by the 1830 Indian Removal Act and the decade of dispossession that followed. The Seminoles, living in Florida, were another group targeted for resettlement. For years, they had lived side by side with people of African ancestry, most of whom were escaped slaves or descendants of escaped slaves. Indeed, the Seminoles and Africans living with each other were not two distinct peoples. Their inclusion in this role play allows students to explore further causes for Indian removal, to see ways in which slav-ery was an important consideration motivating the U.S. government's hoped-for final solution to the supposed "Indian problem." The role play encourages students to explore these dynamics from the inside. As they portray individuals in some of the groups that shaped these historical episodes, the aim is for them to see not only what happened, but also why it happened—and perhaps to wonder whether there were alternatives.

In previous years of teaching this role play, I did not include a "Missionaries and Northern Reformers" role. The omission of a sympathetic white role left students with the impression that all white people in the country were united in the quest to forcibly move Indian tribes and nations off their lands. In fact, white people as diverse as the abolitionist William Lloyd Garrison and the Tennessee frontiers-man-turned-congressman Davy Crockett opposed the Indian removal bill. The vote in the U.S. House of Representatives in favor of removal was 102 to 97—an underwhelming majority. Nonetheless, it's important that students recognize the racial and cultural biases of even those who considered themselves the Indians' friends and allies. As indicated in their role, missionaries described Cherokee families as "having risen to a level with the white people of the United States." Thus, as we seek to inform students of important currents of social reform in U.S. history, we need to do so with a critical eye.

Materials Needed

- Construction or other stiff paper for placards; crayons or markers.
- Copies of the role play roles—enough for every student to have a role.

Suggested Procedure

First, a suggestion on how to read these lesson procedures. Rather than reading all these in one, two, three order, it may be more clear if you review the student readings in the order they are mentioned in these instructions. This will help you imagine the role play more easily, and encounter it as students might.

1. Read with students the "Indian Removal Role Play: Problems to Consider" handout. Show them on a map how far it is from Georgia and Florida to Oklahoma. Tell them that each of them will be in a group representing one of five roles: Cherokee, the Andrew Jackson administration, plantation owners

Our task as teachers is not to tell young people what to think but to equip them to search for patterns throughout history, patterns that continue in our own time.

and farmers, missionaries and Northern reformers, and Black Seminoles. All of them are invited to a hearing to discuss the Indian Removal Act before Congress. They should consider the resolution, and in their presentations should be sure to respond to the three questions: whether they support the bill, what questions they have of other groups, and how they will react if the bill passes or fails. This last question encourages students to see that simply because Congress decides something does not necessarily mean people will passively accept that decision. [Note: The teacher plays the congressman (they were all men back then, of course) who runs the hearing, but an option is to select a few students to join you or to run the meeting on their own. This choice has the advantage of giving students a group of peers as an audience for their presentations. The disadvantage is that those who run the hearing have little to do during the session of negotiation between groups

and sometimes become targets for other students' ire if they manifest the slightest inconsistency in calling on people to speak.]

2. Have students count off into five groups. Students from each respective group cluster together in small circles throughout the classroom. They should begin by reading their assigned role. You can urge students into their characters by asking them to write "interior monologues" (the possible inner thoughts) about their concerns in 1830; they might invent a more detailed persona: a name, a place of birth, family, friends, etc. This is especially valuable for students in those groups that include people in somewhat different circumstances (plantation owner/farmers and missionaries/Northern reformers). Students in each group might read these to one another. You can interview a few individuals from different groups so others in the class can hear.

3. Distribute placards and markers to students and ask them to write their group name and display it so that everyone can see whom they represent.

4. In each group, students should discuss their ideas on the questions they will be addressing at the congressional hearing. Remind them that an important question to consider is what they will do if Congress decides against them. Will they resist? If so, how? If not, what might happen to them? When it seems that students have come to some tentative conclusions, ask them to choose half their group to be traveling negotiators. These people will meet with people in the other groups to share ideas, argue, and build alliances. Remind students that each of their roles includes different information, so this is an opportunity to teach each other. (To ensure maximum participation of students in the class, travelers may not meet with other travelers, but only with seated members of other groups. Travelers may travel together or separately.)

5. Begin the teaching/negotiating/alliance-building session. These discussions should last until students seem to be repeating themselves—perhaps 15 or 20 minutes, depending on the class. During this period, I circulate to different groups and occasionally butt in

to raise questions or point out contradictions. Don't skip this step; it may be the time students are most engaged in their roles.

6. Students should return to their groups to prepare the presentations they'll make at the congressional hearing. In my experience, if they write these out, they think more clearly and raise more provocative points. Encourage them to use the information in their role sheet (but not merely to copy it).

7. The class should form a large circle, students sitting with their respective groups. I structure the hearing by allowing one group to make its complete presentation. Then either I or the students running the hearing raise a few questions. After this, members of other groups may question or rebut points made by the presenting group. This process continues until we've heard from all the groups. The more cross-group dialogue that occurs, the more interesting and exciting the meeting.

8. As a follow-up writing assignment, you might ask students to stay in their roles and comment on the congressional hearing—whose remarks most angered or troubled them? At what points did they feel most satisfied with the deliberations? Or you could ask them to speculate on what happened in real life and why. Some discussion or writing questions include:

- What do you think actually happened to the Cherokee and the Seminole people?

- Might there have been tensions between the Cherokees and Seminoles? Why?

- Which group might have been in a better position to resist removal? Why?

- What reasons did some groups offer for why the Indians should be moved? What were their real motives?

- Why were the Seminoles such a threat to the Southern plantation owners? Do you remember some of the laws that were passed to keep Indians and Blacks divided in early America?

- In real life, a slim majority of U.S. representatives and senators voted to remove the Indians. What arguments might they have found most persuasive?

- Do you think that all those congressmen who voted against Indian removal did so because they cared about the Indians? Can you think of other reasons congressmen from Northern states wouldn't want the Southern states to expand onto Indian territory?

- Do you think the missionaries would have been as sympathetic toward the Seminoles as they were toward the Cherokees? Why or why not?

- What similarities do you see in the situations faced by the Cherokee and Seminole peoples and situations faced by any other groups in U.S. history? In our society today? In other parts of the world?

9. After discussion, you might assign students to do some research to see what actually happened to the Cherokee and the Seminole peoples. Pages 96 to 98 in Ronald Takaki's *A Different Mirror* provide a good short summary of what happened to the Cherokee along what came to be called the Trail of Tears. Chapter 4, "The Finest Looking People I Have Ever Seen," in William Loren Katz's *Black Indians: A Hidden Heritage*, is a valuable resource for learning more about how the Seminoles were affected by the events depicted in the role play. ✳

This article was previously published in *Beyond Heroes and Holidays* (Teaching for Change, 1998).

Cherokee and Seminole Removal Role Play

Indian Removal Role Play: Problems to Consider

The year is 1830. There is a bill before the United States Congress that would provide funds ($500,000) to move all Indians now living east of the Mississippi River to "Indian Territory" (Oklahoma) west of the Mississippi River. The Indians would be given permanent title to this land. The money would pay the Indians for any improvements made on the land in the east where they're now living. It would also cover the expenses of their transportation and for a year in their new homes in Indian Territory.

The U.S. Congress has decided to hold hearings on this bill and you are invited to give testimony and to question other individuals who will give testimony. The main question for discussion is:

Should all Indians living east of the Mississippi River be moved, by force if necessary, west of the Mississippi River to Indian Territory?

Questions for each group to consider in planning your presentation:

1. Do you support the Indian removal bill? Why or why not?

2. What questions do you have for members of the other groups that will be in attendance?

3. What will you do if Congress passes this bill? What will you do if Congress does not pass this bill?

Cherokee and Seminole Removal Role Play

Cherokee

Your people have lived for centuries in the area the whites call "Georgia." This is your land. At times you've had to fight to keep it.

You've had a hard time with whites. Ever since they began settling in Georgia, they have continued to push west, plowing the land, growing cotton and other crops. Long ago, as early as 1785, the Cherokee Nation won the right to their land by a treaty with the U.S. government. The United States recognized the Cherokee people as part of an independent country and not subject to the laws of the United States. After the U.S. Constitution was approved, the U.S. government signed another treaty with the Cherokee—in 1791, when George Washington was president. Article 7 of the Treaty of Hopewell said "The United States solemnly guaranty to the Cherokee nation all their lands not hereby ceded." In other words, the U.S. government agreed not to push the Cherokee out of the land where they were living.

But now the U.S. government is about to break its own treaty and steal your land. Many whites have already bribed and tricked some of your people out of their land. The whites say they need it to grow cotton and other crops, and miners have been trespassing in the foothills looking for (and finding) gold. These whites say you have no right to the land, that you're savages. Last year, in December 1829, the state of Georgia passed a law saying that you are under their control, and must obey their laws, their wishes. This new law forbids anyone with any Cherokee blood from testifying in court or protesting the plans to move you out of your land. But you didn't vote for this Georgia government, and besides, you have a treaty with the federal government that says you are citizens of an independent country. When the U.S. government made a treaty with you, that proved you are a nation.

The Cherokee are one of the five "civilized tribes." It was the whites themselves who taught you much of this "civilization." You have well-cultivated farms. By 1826, members of your Cherokee nation owned 22,000 cattle, 7,600 horses, 3,000 plows, 2,500 spinning wheels, 10 sawmills, and 18 schools. Like Southern whites, some of you also owned Black slaves. In 1821, Sequoya, a brilliant Cherokee Indian, invented an 85-character alphabet and now most Cherokee can read and write. It's said that more Cherokee people are literate than whites are in Georgia. You even have a newspaper, the *Cherokee Phoenix*. You've adopted a written constitution very similar to that of the United States. Many of your leaders attended white schools. Even by the white man's standards you're as "civilized" as they are, if not more so. But still they want to kick you off your land and move you to a place west of the Mississippi River—a place you've never even seen. You must continue to argue your case if you are to survive as a people.

Cherokee and Seminole Removal Role Play

Andrew Jackson Administration

You're the president of the United States. You must deal with a serious problem in the state of Georgia. This past December, in 1829, the state government said that all the land belonging to the Cherokee nation would from then on belong to Georgia. The Cherokee would have no title to their land and anyone with Cherokee blood wouldn't even have the right to testify in court. The Georgians want the Cherokee moved, by force if necessary, west of the Mississippi River. They support the Indian Removal Act, now before Congress. There is a place called "Oklahoma" set aside for all the Indians in the East, including the Cherokee. Personally, you agree that Georgia has a right to make whatever laws they want, but the Cherokee have treaties signed by the U.S. government guaranteeing them their land forever. Of course, you personally never signed any of those treaties.

You're getting a lot of pressure on this one. On the one hand, white missionaries and lots of Northerners say that Georgia is violating Cherokee rights. Cherokee supporters point out that the Indians have done everything they can to become like civilized white people: They invented an alphabet, started a newspaper, wrote a constitution, started farms, and even wear white people's clothes. Many church groups supported your election in 1828, and you want their support when you run for re-election in 1832. On the other hand, a lot of farmers and plantation owners would like to get on that good Cherokee land. Recently, gold was discovered on Cherokee territory, and gold seekers are already starting to sneak onto their land. Your main base of support was in the South, especially from poor and medium-sized farmers.

From your standpoint, you have to look after the welfare of the whole country. The main crop in the South is cotton—it is a crucial crop to the prosperity of the slave-owning South and to the new cloth factories of the North. Cotton, grown with slave labor, brings in tremendous profits to slave owners, and you're a slave owner yourself, so you understand their concerns. There is excellent land being taken up by the Cherokee, as well as some of the other Indian tribes in the region: the Creek, Choctaw, Chickasaw, and Seminole—though some of these have already moved west. This land could be used to grow cotton for the world. The exports of cotton to England and other countries are vital to the health of the economy. Cotton sent north is building up young industries and you can see there is great potential for manufacturing in the North.

The Seminole Indians who live in Florida represent a special problem. For years, they have taken in escaped slaves from Southern plantations. Sometimes, they've even raided plantations in order to free slaves. They are a threat to the whole plantation system in the South. A number of years ago, you ordered the U.S. military to attack the Seminoles in Florida and had their farms burned. The proposed Indian Removal Act would get rid of the Seminoles forever by moving them to Indian Territory. The escaped slaves living with them would then be taken away from them and sold.

Cherokee and Seminole Removal Role Play

Plantation Owners and Farmers

All I ask in this creation
Is a pretty little wife and a big plantation
Way up yonder in the Cherokee Nation.

That's part of a song people like you sing as you wait for the Cherokee to be kicked out of Georgia. Then you and your family can move in.

Some of you are poor white farmers. You live on the worst land in Georgia and other parts of the South. The big plantation owners with all their cotton and slaves take up the best land and leave you the scraps. You've heard that the Cherokee land in Georgia is some of the most fertile land in the country. Best yet, the government of Georgia is having a lottery so that even poor farmers like you will have an equal shot at getting good land. One of the reasons you voted for Andy Jackson for president is because you knew he was an Indian fighter who beat the Creek in a war and then took their land away from them. That's your kind of president. The Cherokee are farmers too. They grow corn, wheat, and cotton. If you're lucky, you'll be able to move onto land with the crops already planted and the farmhouse already built. Others of you aren't quite as poor; you have some land, and grow corn and raise hogs, but you too would like to move onto better land.

Some of you are white owners of big plantations who grow cotton on your land and own many slaves. You live in Georgia near the coast. The problem is that cotton exhausts the soil, so that after a number of years, your land is not as productive as it once was. You need new land with soil that hasn't been used to grow cotton for years and years. As of now, the Cherokee are living on the land that rightfully belongs to the state of Georgia. The Georgia Legislature recently voted to take over that land and divide it up so that whites like you could move onto it. That's a great law, but some people in Congress and around the country want to stop you from taking this territory from the Cherokee. What's the problem? There is a place set aside for the Cherokee and other Indians west of the Mississippi River. They belong with their own kind, right? Remember, the whole country—no, the whole world—depends on cotton. Your plantation and plantations like yours are what keep this country strong and productive.

But you have another big problem. In Florida, many escaped slaves live side by side with the Seminole Indians. Slaves throughout the South know about this haven for runaways. In fact, sometimes the Seminoles and escaped slaves raid plantations, burn them down, and free the slaves. You won't stand for this. The Seminole communities must be destroyed and the Indians shipped off to Indian Territory along with the Cherokee. As for the escaped slaves who live with them, they need to be recaptured and either returned to their rightful owners or put up for sale. There's also some good land in Florida that you might want to move onto once the Seminoles are gone.

Cherokee and Seminole Removal Role Play

Missionaries and Northern Reformers

Some of you are white Christian missionaries who live among the Cherokee people or once did. You are not plantation owners, gold prospectors, bankers, or military people. You are simply individuals who want to preach the word of God and do what's right. You are of many different Christian denominations. At great sacrifice, you moved away from the comfort of civilization to go live in much more difficult conditions.

You believe that the Cherokee people have made great progress advancing toward civilization. According to a resolution your missionary group recently passed, some Cherokee families have "risen to a level with the white people of the United States." Most Cherokee now wear clothes like white people and have given up their original Indian dress. Women wear decent gowns that cover their bodies from neck to feet. Before, the women had to do the hard work of tending the corn using hoes. Now, the men do the farming with plows. They are a much more industrious people and own more property and better houses than in the past. Slowly some are becoming Christians and—thankfully—are forgetting their old Indian superstitions. As your resolution points out, "Ancient traditions are fading from memory, and can scarcely be collected." When the whites came upon the Cherokee, the Indians were in a "purely savage state." But this is no longer the case. Many Indians and whites are beginning to intermix. This is good, as it brings Indians in closer contact with civilization.

You don't know a single Cherokee who wants to leave home and go west across the Mississippi River. As your resolution states, there is "an overwhelming torrent of national feeling in opposition to removal." And you ought to know: You live with these people. You are reluctant to take sides in political arguments, but you have to bear witness to what you see and hear.

Those of you who live in the North have read the writings of the missionaries who live among the Cherokee. They don't want to steal the Cherokee land, so they have no reason to lie. Senator Theodore Frelinghuysen from New Jersey has spoken eloquently about the Cherokee situation. He calls the Cherokee "the first lords of the soil." The senator puts himself in the Indians' position and asks, "If I use my land for hunting, may another take it because he needs it for agriculture?"

It's true that the richest Cherokee—about 10 percent—own some Black slaves. Some of you are abolitionists, who want all slavery to end, and don't approve of this. However, almost everyone who ever traveled in Cherokee territory agrees that the Cherokee do not treat their slaves as harshly as the whites treat theirs. Most slaves in Cherokee country have some rights, and individuals in families are almost never sold away from each other. But slavery is slavery, and some of you don't approve of any slavery.

Cherokee and Seminole Removal Role Play

Black Seminoles

You are Black and you are Indian, members of the Seminole people in Florida. You are descended from enslaved Africans who ran away from British plantations in Georgia more than 100 years ago and came to settle with Indians who left their lands farther north. This was before the United States was even a country. You are a free person. Some of the Black people who live in Seminole communities ran away from slavery in the last few years. Others were bought from white slave owners by Seminoles. These people are still called slaves, but are not treated as slaves. They can marry anyone, can't be sold away from their families, can travel where they want, have their own land, and carry guns. But every year they must pay part of their crops to other Seminoles as a kind of tax.

The Indian Removal Act of 1830 is now being considered by the U.S. Congress. It calls for all Indians east of the Mississippi River to be forced off their lands and moved to a place called "Indian Territory" west of the Mississippi River. Full-blooded Seminoles would be moved. But for you, a Black Seminole, they would make you a slave and sell you in one of the Southern slave markets. You would be forever separated from your community, your friends, your family. You will never allow this to happen.

The white plantation owners in Georgia and throughout the South are threatened by the Indians, free Blacks, and escaped slaves living peacefully side by side. They know that their slaves hear about these Seminole communities and want to run away to join them. The Seminole communities are a kind of symbol of freedom to enslaved Black people throughout the South. In the past, your people have attacked plantations, freed the slaves on those plantations, and brought them to Florida to live with you and become Seminoles. The whites also want to steal your land so they can grow their cotton with slave labor.

President Andrew Jackson is one of the biggest slaveholders in Tennessee. Some years ago, when he was a general in the army, he ordered his troops to attack your people and destroy your farms and homes. You know that in this debate about Indian removal he is not on your side.

He also wants to move the other Indian nations in the Southeast, especially the Cherokee. You don't have much to do with the Cherokee. You know that they own large numbers of Black slaves, though they say they treat them better than white plantation owners do. But if this law passes, they will try to move them too.

The United States government and the white plantation owners call the Seminoles "savages." But you have farms and raise horses, cattle, hogs, and chickens. And unlike white plantation owners, you know what freedom means. What is "civilized"? What is "savage"?

Sin Fronteras Boy
Students Create Collaborative Websites to Explore the Border

BY GRACE CORNELL GONZALES

Around one table, four 4th-grade girls chat quietly as they write on their laptops: Ruby interviews Alejandra about her experience crossing the U.S.-Mexico border as a 6-year-old. Meanwhile, Cindy turns notes from an interview with her uncle into a narrative about his immigration experience. Next to them, four boys work on the Sin Fronteras Boy website, a choose-your-own-adventure story about a boy who tries to cross the border and becomes a superhero after his mother is grabbed by *la migra* (immigration officials). I am working with the Indigenous Peoples group, helping Roberto understand a recent article about the U.S. government's attempted seizure of Lipan Apache land for the construction of the border wall, while Karolina looks for photographs of the Lipan Apache, Yaqui, Kickapoo, Yuma, and Tohono O'odham peoples, all tribes that are currently affected by U.S. border policy.

We are hard at work making wikis—simple websites that can be collectively written and edited. Wikis are easy to set up through hosting sites like pbwiki.com or editme.com, and are often free for educators. Once a wiki has been created, members can add content, create new pages, and make changes to the content. This allows students to write collaboratively, adding to and revising each other's work. (Teachers can also track students' individual contributions.) The three wikis created by the 11 English language learners in my reading group are very different from each other, ranging from the fantastical to the deeply personal. However, all explore our central question: How does the border affect our lives?

It is an important topic for these students, either immigrants themselves or the children of immigrants, living in a largely Latinx community in Oakland, California. The goal is for students to improve their writing and their English language skills through working together and for students to come together as a classroom community to support each other in exploring the sensitive and controversial topic of U.S.-Mexico border policy. I do my best to facilitate a collaborative writing experience by encouraging the group members to outline and research the websites together, read and discuss each other's contributions to the wikis, and revise each other's pages. As students collaboratively make their websites, they write and talk their way into not only a deeper understanding of the English language, but also of the world they live in. They begin, slowly but surely, to identify injustices and construct their own imaginative visions of a more just world.

How Does the Border Affect Our Lives?

During the first several days of the project, we read three picture books about immigration and the U.S.-Mexico border: *Super Cilantro Girl* by Juan Felipe Herrera; *Friends from the Other Side* by Gloria Anzaldúa; and *From North to South* by René Colato Laínez. Students used Post-it notes in the books to record questions and connections, which were often to their own families and their own life experiences. Then I asked the students to walk around the room and write responses on chart paper beneath three key questions:

- What is the border?
- Why does the border exist?
- How does the border affect our lives?

Afterward, I read some of the students' responses aloud and conducted a whole group discussion centered on these three questions. It was quickly apparent that my students knew that the border was an imaginary line or a fence between countries, but they could not articulate why it existed. Its effects, however, were clear from the comments scrawled on the chart paper: "It hurts us because our families are in other countries." "It affects us because if we don't have money or a home we can't go to the United States and have a better life." "It affects your life because you risk yourself and you go to jail and don't have any money when you get out of jail and you go back to your country."

We next pulled out the computers and got familiar with how wikis work. We looked at examples of wikis created by students as well as large wikis like wikipedia.org and wikihow.com. I showed the students how to edit an existing page and how to create and name a new page through wikispaces.com. That was all the introduction needed. They soon figured out for themselves how to change the look of a page, add pictures, and comment on each other's writing. At this time we also talked about important rules for internet safety and appropriate behavior. They picked pseudonyms to use on their websites to protect their privacy (which I use in this article as well).

Once we had the basics down, I initiated a whole group brainstorm on chart paper of topics for border-themed websites. I asked students to talk to each other about what they would like to learn about the border and then suggested some topics that lend themselves easily to a wiki format: encyclopedias, choose-your-own-adventure stories, and book reviews. Then I opened the floor and let students brainstorm. They suggested a dictionary of words related to the border, a website that chronicled the history of the border, a collection of interviews, and a website about borders around the world, to name a few. I steered them away from ideas that would not work well as collaborative writing projects (a large map of the border, for example) by explaining why these topics might not be ideal and suggesting ways of folding them into other topics (a history of the border website could include maps). At the end of the brainstorm, we starred four or five topics that seemed the most promising.

Next, I asked the students to form small groups around the ideas that most interested them. I trusted them to do this organically by getting out of their seats, talking to each other, and choosing groupmates and a topic at the same time. One group immediately latched on to the idea of a choose-your-own-adventure, creating their hero, Sin Fronteras (without borders) Boy, modeled on Super Cilantro Girl. Another group decided to create oral histories by interviewing family members and writing their immigration stories as narratives. The final group wanted to write about how the border affected the Mayans and Aztecs. Not wanting to guide with too heavy a hand, I let them research and find out for themselves that the Mayans and Aztecs lived far away from the U.S.-Mexico border. With the help of a guest teacher with ties to the Native groups of the Southwest, they turned their research to the current Indigenous peoples who are affected by the border today.

Sin Fronteras Boy:
Real Writers in the Real World

The Sin Fronteras Boy website was by far the simplest of the projects. It involved little research for the participants beyond reading some choose-your-own-adventure books to get a feel for the format. Then the boys let their imaginations run wild, creating powerful villains, exciting battle scenes, vivid illustrations,

Once a wiki has been created, members can add content, created new pages, and make changes to the content. This allows students to write collaboratively, adding to and revising each other's work.

and both good and bad endings for the story. It was a meaningful experience for these children, a few of whom were somewhat reluctant writers, to truly get to write creatively and elicit the help of their friends.

Perhaps most significant was the realization that they were writing for real audiences and creating a story that other people would get to read and enjoy. This is part of the beauty of wikis as an instructional tool: They give students the sense that they are doing real writing in a real-world space and for an authentic audience.

As time went by, the students' participation in the authentic task of creating websites began to change their concepts of themselves. Jimmy, a student in the Sin Fronteras Boy group, exclaimed on several occasions, "We're comic writers!" Another student, Nina, wrote in her autobiography, "I feel like an author because I am writing like one." For an

It was quickly apparent that my students knew that the border was an imaginary line or a fence between countries, but they could not articulate why it existed. Its effects, however, were clear.

English language learner reading and writing two years below grade level, this was indeed a meaningful statement.

The students also talked about how their writing improved when they were crafting something that the whole world might see. Mario explained that, when writing for the world, he "put big words in it . . . so I can sound interesting." Nina remarked, "I add more things and . . . do my best grammar and punctuation and periods." Roberto explained: "That really changes how I write because then the pages would be longer. I would have writed more, lots more." When asked why he would write more if many people were going to read his writing, he responded simply, "Because they inspire me."

Oral Histories: Family Connections

From the beginning, the oral histories group was driven to tell their families' stories about crossing the border. They made lists of people to interview, drafted questions, interviewed one to four people each, and then turned those interviews into vivid narratives of participants' often difficult experiences

crossing the border. In this way, the girls' parents, aunts, uncles, cousins, and siblings became involved in the project. Alejandra spent hours talking to her dad about the details of his experience crossing the border. Her final narrative described how her father had almost died when he was left behind in the desert by his *coyote*, and painfully recounted the nights alone in the United States when he had gotten drunk and cried out of loneliness for his wife and children back in Mexico. As Alejandra interviewed her father, mother, and brother and was interviewed herself, she kept telling me that this was the first time she was remembering her experience crossing the border as a 6-year-old. Cindy also felt a sense of rediscovering her family history: "Although they live with me, I've gotten to know more about the persons' lives that I interview."

After their first round of interviews, the group designed a second set of interview questions to ask family members what they thought should be done to "change the current border situation." To their surprise, not all of their family members advocated getting rid of the border, saying that "countries need to have borders" and "not just anyone should be able to cross." However, those interviewed also stated that their own lives would be better if the border didn't exist and they could cross freely between the United States and Mexico to find work and see their families. This left the group pondering what sort of border policy could be fair, safe, and humane.

The girls in the oral histories group decided on their own to make their website completely bilingual. They found the work of writing in Spanish challenging, constantly exclaiming how much they had already forgotten. But there was also a sense that they were rescuing their Spanish language skills, reteaching themselves and each other, often with the at-home help of their parents. In turn, it was deeply meaningful for them that their families could read their websites.

Indigenous People and the Border: Asking Hard Questions

The Indigenous peoples group did by far the most research. Their topic—the current struggles of Native American groups on both sides of the U.S.-Mexico border—was a complex one. In order to scaffold their research, I spent a good deal of time finding and printing relevant websites and news articles. Sometimes the reading level of these articles was so complex that I needed to summarize them or highlight the key points. We read the articles together, discussed them, and sometimes used graphic organizers to analyze the information.

Through this process, I watched the students in the group grapple with unfamiliar ideas and contradictory information. They struggled to understand the complex relationships among the Native American tribes, the U.S. government, and the Mexican government. They drew parallels between the ways that the border separates them from family members and the way the border has cut several Native American tribes in half. They asked poignant questions: "How come Yaqui people in the United States can cross into Mexico whenever they want, but the Mexican Yaqui often cannot get visas to come to the United States?" "Why does the U.S. government think it can just take people's land away from them to build a big border wall?" "Why is the United States building a border wall anyway?" The answers to some of these questions led them to difficult realizations of ways that the United States discriminates against some and privileges others. Throughout the course of the project, they worked to wrap their minds around the struggles and perspectives of groups of people whose experience with the border is both similar to and profoundly different from the experiences of members of their own communities.

Developing a Sense of Social Justice

The most challenging aspect of the unit was the tension between cataloging social injustices—writing narratives of undocumented immigrants, reading articles about Native Americans whose lands or resources had been confiscated due to the U.S. government's border policies—and analyzing these injustices as situations that could, and should, be changed. When I talked with my students about these issues, I sometimes had the sense that they saw their reality as fixed. Although they could recognize injustice, they didn't immediately assume that they could do anything about it.

Not wanting to push my own views onto them, I chose to counter this by asking questions—con-

stantly. When they told me stories about the border or recounted what they had learned about the political issues involved, I asked them if they thought the situations they described were fair. When they explained to me the way things worked, I wondered aloud if there was anything anyone could do about that.

Sometimes there were sudden sparks of passion, moments of "That's not fair!" or "Isn't that racist?" or "Maybe we could write a letter!" These were fleeting but recurring. As the project continued, students began to construct, through repeated discussion with me and with each other, a sense that things didn't have to be the way they were: People shouldn't have to risk their lives walking through the desert to support their families. Native American tribes shouldn't lose their land or natural resources because of failed border policy. People should be free to live the lives they choose.

For example, in early April, Nina's autobiography page focused on her excitement about using a laptop and writing a web page. By mid-April, the page included a reference to her "messaging President Obama" and "trying my best to convince the president to let Mexican people come to the United States." Her May revision, completed with my help and the help of other students, showed a more distinct sense of history:

> Long ago, California was part of Mexico. Now California is part of the United States of America and Mexican people try to cross the border. However, sometimes they can't come because the government won't give the Mexican people the papers that they need to cross the border legally. . . . It's not fair because these people may need to see their families in the United States and they want to have a better life and a better job.

Her final draft ended with a rallying cry: "Yes we can change the government and the president's mind!"

Writing Development

Although a deeper understanding of social issues was a priority for me in this project, measurable academic growth in writing was the other primary goal. To measure students' developments in English language writing, I had them complete 40-minute pre- and post-writing assessments. I was amazed at the improvements. Over time, students wrote longer pieces with more complex sentences. All but one student's rubric score for the traits of quality writing went up between the pre- and post-assessment.

These improvements to students' individual writing are reflected in the successive drafts on the wiki as well. This is a first draft of the home page of the Sin Fronteras Boy website:

> Here is a little summary about the book At the Biggining, SINFRONTERASBOY is a normal boy.He becomes a SUPERHERO. THERE IS A BORDER CALLED MR.BORDER.Why does SINFRONTERAS became a superhero.? He his going to save his mother.He is going to save his father. He lives in Mexicali,Mexico. This a choose your own adventure.You can choose your own first,second,and end.There are a.b.and c. Some of them are funny.We even have alittle bit of rap if you read begening of the story fast.

After many revisions, expansions, and edits, done by all four members of the groups, and several conferences with me, the final version looked like this:

> This is a choose your own adventure story created by four fourth grade boys studying the border and how it affects people's lives. You can select your own beginning, middle, and end. On each page, you can pick between a, b, and c.
>
> Here is a little summary of the story. At the beginning, SINFRONTERAS BOY is a normal boy who lives in Mexicali, Mexico. Unexpectedly, he becomes a SUPERHERO. There is a big, bad, mean border called Mr. Border who doesn't let people pass to the other side. Sinfronteras Boy is going to save his mother from la migra (immigration police) and fight against Mr. Border in order to make a world in which people can be free.
>
> Some of the pages are funny and some are sad. YOU can always come and read! Everywhere, anytime!! We think this story is great for everybody! We are writing this story so they

can take the border away and people can be free and come into the United States if they want to have a better life. Some people do not know how the border affects the lives of people who do not have papers. Those people cannot cross it to support their children. This is a story that you will read, and it will knock your socks off!!! Not even an author has written a story like this one! This story is the one!!!

This final draft shows many improvements from the initial paragraph: It is full of exuberant voice, organized in a logical way, and highlights the main ideas of the website. Such distinct improvements in students' writing over the course of the unit illustrate the great things that happen when children are allowed to write for authentic purposes and real-world audiences, work collaboratively, exercise choice, write about topics that are relevant to them, and engage in inquiry around genuinely complex social questions.

Lessons Learned

One of the most important lessons that I took away from this experience, and one that I hope to share with other educators, is the feasibility of engaging students in authentic writing about culturally and socially relevant subject matter through the use of the internet. Wikis are a particularly promising technology because of the ways in which they facilitate collaboration while allowing teachers to monitor individual student contributions. However, collaboration must be encouraged strategically and specifically. I was lucky to try this project with a group of students whom I had already worked with for most of the year and who already had some training in collaborative work. As anyone who has ever tried to set up cooperative learning situations knows, a great deal of community building is necessary before students will work productively and noncompetitively with each other. Even in the case of this project, near the end of the school year—when deadlines loomed and I was no longer as focused on the teaching concepts of collective authorship and collaboration—students' deeply rooted assumptions of individualism and competition began to reassert themselves. It was a reminder for me of the important role that teachers play in establishing the type of community in which students can act as both co-teachers and co-learners.

I was also lucky to be able to work with a small group of students in a setting in which I could devote myself entirely to literacy instruction. However, I have also worked as a classroom teacher, and I believe that group projects like this could be incorporated into a classroom setting. Even in a school with no laptop cart, where students have access to just a handful of classroom computers, this type of project is feasible: Groups could take turns using the computers during the writing block. They could work during computer lab time if available or even at home or after school. The beauty of wikis is that participants can write asynchronously—they can collaborate over time and distance by editing each other's work, sending messages, and posting discussion threads, all without needing to be in the same place at the same time.

However, the most important lesson that I learned from this project was that students, when allowed to inquire into topics that are deeply relevant to them, can become powerfully engaged in projects that force them to question their worlds and their conceptions of what is fair. Teachers play a fundamental role in this process. They do this by asking the right questions at the right times, and also by creating classroom environments in which students are encouraged to tackle difficult subject matter and are allowed to work as a community to construct their own ideas about the ways in which our society is unjust and their own alternative visions of the future.

Although my students' nascent sense of themselves as social agents has not yet blossomed into definite action, I think certain seeds were planted. I continue to be moved by my students' dreams and visions of a world that is free and borderless, dreams that they shared on their websites. And I hope that they will continue to develop an enduring concept of themselves as wiki writers, real-world authors and researchers, and potential social activists with the power to make concrete changes in their worlds. ✳

Reprinted from *Rethinking Schools*, Spring 2012 (vol. 26, no. 3).

The Color Line

BY BILL BIGELOW

This lesson was written to accompany Howard Zinn's A People's History of the United States *and was first published by the Zinn Education Project (zinnedproject.org).*

Colonial laws prohibiting Blacks and whites from marrying one another suggest that some Blacks and whites *did* marry. Laws imposing penalties on white indentured servants and enslaved Blacks who ran away together likewise suggest that whites and Blacks did run away together. Laws making it a crime for Indians and Blacks to meet together in groups of four or more indicate that, at some point, these gatherings must have occurred. As Benjamin Franklin is said to have remarked in the 1787 Constitutional Convention, "One doesn't make laws to prevent the sheep from planning insurrection," because this has never occurred, nor will it occur.

The social elites of early America sought to manufacture racial divisions. Men of property and privilege were in the minority; they needed mechanisms to divide people who, in concert, might threaten the status quo. Individuals' different skin colors were not sufficient to keep these people apart if they came to see their interests in common. Which is not to say that racism was merely a ruling class plot, but as Howard Zinn points out in Chapters 2 and 3 of *A People's History of the United States*, and as students see in this lesson, some people did indeed set out consciously to promote divisions based on race.

Because today's racial divisions run so deep and can seem so normal, providing students a historical framework can be enlightening. We need to ask, "What are the origins of racial conflict?" and "Who benefits from these deep antagonisms?" A critical perspective on race and racism is as important as anything students will take away from a U.S. history course. This is just one early lesson in our quest to construct that critical perspective.

Suggested Procedure

I'd suggest doing this activity before students read Zinn's Chapters 2 or 3. With students, review the reading "Colonial Laws: Divide and Conquer" (see p. 175). How they work with the problems posed in the reading is a matter of teacher preference. Students could come up with some tentative ideas on their own and then work in pairs or small groups to assemble a more complete list. Or they might from the very beginning work in small groups.

However they approach the "Colonial Laws" problems, ask students to compare their answers with the information contained in Chapters 2 and 3. Here are some actual laws and policies initiated to respond to the problems described in the student reading. Not all of these are included in Chapters 2 and 3.

For valuable insights on the first question, see William Loren Katz's *Black Indians: A Hidden Heritage* (Atheneum, 2012), Chapter 8: "Their Mixing Is to Be Prevented." Most high school students can easily read this chapter. It is highly recommended.

Where indicated, students can find this information in either Chapter 2 or 3 in *A People's History of the United States*.

1. Predict the measures that were taken to keep Indians and Blacks from uniting or that may have even made them feel hostile toward one another.

- As one white Carolinian put it, we need a policy "to make Indians & Negros a checque upon each other lest by their Vastly Superior Numbers we should be crushed by one or the other." Laws were passed to prohibit free Blacks from traveling in Indian country. Treaties with Indian tribes required the return of fugitive slaves. [Chapter 3]

- A 1683 New York law made it a crime for "Negro or Indian slaves" to meet anywhere together in groups of four or more or to be armed "with guns, Swords, Clubs, Staves, or Any Other kind of weapon." A 1690 Connecticut law forbade Indians and Blacks from walking beyond the town limits without a pass. Connecticut, Rhode Island, and Massachusetts all had a 9 p.m. curfew for Blacks and Indians. A 1773 New York law was passed "to prevent Negro and Indian slaves from appearing in the streets after eight at night without a lantern with a lighted candle in it."

- Whites often hired local Indians to hunt down escaped African slaves. In 1676, Maryland offered rewards to Indians for capturing enslaved Blacks who had run away. In 1740, South Carolina offered Indians £100 for each slave runaway captured alive and £50 for "every scalp of a grown negro slave." In 1729, South Carolina hired Catawba Indians to recapture or kill enslaved Blacks who had rebelled in Stono, South Carolina. [Chapter 3]

- In 1725, South Carolina outlawed bringing any enslaved Blacks to the frontier. As a British colonel said, "The slaves . . . talk good English as well as the Cherokee language and . . . too often tell falsities to the Indians which they are apt to believe."

- Whites sold a large number of Indians as slaves to traders in the West Indies. In a single year, more than 10,000 Indian slaves were shipped in chains to the West Indies from the port of Charleston, South Carolina.

- The British encouraged the so-called Five Civilized Tribes—the Cherokee, Creek, Chickasaw, Choctaw, and Seminole—to enslave Africans, as the whites were doing. Ultimately, slaves made up between 10 and 20 percent of all five groups but the Seminoles. The Cherokee adopted a "slave code" to prevent Blacks from learning to read and write and provided that if a slave ran off, other tribe members were obligated to catch the runaway. Slavery contributed to inequality within each Indian nation. Only a relatively small elite of 12 percent of the Cherokees owned slaves.

2. Predict laws or policies adopted to discourage white indentured servants and Black slaves from running away together.

- A 1661 Virginia law provided that "in case any English servant shall run away in company of any Negroes" the servant would have to suffer extra years of servitude to the master of the escaped slave. [Chapter 2]

3a. Predict how poor whites and white indentured servants were taught to believe that they were superior to and didn't have anything in common with Blacks.

- All whites were encouraged to believe that they were superior to Blacks and all-white legislatures passed laws that underscored white superiority. For example, a 1723 Maryland law provided for cutting off the ears of any Black person who struck a white person. [Chapter 2]

- A Virginia colonial law sentenced whites to 25 lashes for stealing a pig, but increased it to 39 lashes if the person were Black or Indian.

- Poor whites were enlisted to hunt down runaway slaves and were put on slave patrols. [Chapter 3]

- A 1705 Virginia law required that when a white servant's period of indenture was over, a master must provide men with 10 bushels of corn, 30 shillings, and a gun; and women with 15 bushels of corn and 40 shillings. The freed servants were also to be given 50 acres of land. [Chapter 2]

- After Bacon's Rebellion in 1676, amnesty was given to whites but not to Blacks. [Chapter 3]

- White lawmakers gave white servants numerous advantages not given to enslaved Blacks, including the right to testify against their masters in court if they were not treated properly.

3b. Predict how Blacks and whites were kept separate, so that whites would not even imagine getting together with Blacks.

- A 1691 Virginia law provided that "any white man or woman being free who shall intermarry with a negro, mulatoo, or Indian man or woman bond or free" shall be banished. [Chapter 2]

- Virginia, Massachusetts, Maryland, Delaware, Pennsylvania, the Carolinas, and Georgia all passed laws prohibiting interracial marriage. [Chapter 3]

- In Southern colonies, according to historian Joseph P. Cullen, if a white female indentured servant had a child by a Black man she would be punished by public whipping and her period of indenture would be doubled.

4. Predict the measures adopted to ensure that on every plantation there were enough white overseers in relation to enslaved Blacks. How might white owners have found more white indentured servants to help supervise Blacks?

- In 1698, South Carolina passed a "deficiency law" that required every plantation owner to have at least one white servant for every six male enslaved Black adults. [Chapter 3]

- As Howard Zinn points out in Chapter 3, servants were acquired from Great Britain, and later from Ireland and Germany, by "lures, promises, . . . lies, by kidnapping . . ." Kidnappers would sell servants to the highest bidder in the American colonies.

- In 1717, the British parliament made transportation to the American colonies a legal punishment for committing certain crimes. Tens of thousands of convicts were sent to Maryland, Virginia, and other colonies. [Chapter 3] ✳

Colonial Laws: Divide and Conquer

Christmas day, 1522: On a sugar plantation owned by Christopher Columbus's son, Diego, enslaved Africans united with enslaved Taíno Indians in the first recorded Black/Indian rebellion in the Americas. They killed their white overseers and ran away. In Great Britain's North American colonies, Black and Indian slaves *and* white indentured servants often ran away together.

Throughout the history of early America, white ruling elites worried about what Blacks and Indians might do if they got together. The people with property were also concerned about uprisings of white indentured servants, poor whites, and enslaved Blacks, as occurred in 17th-century Virginia in Bacon's Rebellion. Conditions were different in different colonies, but everywhere people who had some wealth wanted to make sure that no one took it away from them.

Below are a number of specific problems that colonial legislatures faced. **Try to predict the laws they passed to deal with these problems and protect their privileged position.** Some laws may deal with more than one problem, and some problems required several laws. Sometimes legislatures passed no specific laws, but white leaders promoted general policies. **For each problem, except #4, come up with at least three laws or policies—some require more than others.**

The Problems

1. At times, Indians would attack white settlers on the frontier, kill them, and take their slaves. In parts of North America, enslaved Black people and Indians greatly outnumbered whites. If Blacks and Indians united, they could crush the white rulers. **Predict the measures that were taken to keep Indians and Blacks from uniting, or that may have even made them to feel hostile toward one another.**

2. Some white indentured servants, along with enslaved Blacks, escaped from their masters. **Predict laws or policies adopted to discourage white indentured servants and enslaved Blacks from running away together.**

3. Black slaves, indentured servants, and even some poor but free whites organized together to threaten rebellion.

   a. **Predict how poor whites and white indentured servants were taught to believe that they were superior to and didn't have anything in common with Blacks.**

   b. **Predict how Blacks and whites were kept separate, so that whites would not even imagine getting together with Blacks.**

4. In some areas, there were not enough whites to supervise enslaved Blacks. This made rebellion more likely. In some colonies, there were not many poor whites or indentured white servants in relation to the number of enslaved Blacks. **Predict the measures adopted to ensure that on every plantation there were enough white overseers in relation to Black slaves. How might white owners have found more white indentured servants to help supervise Blacks?**

...around us. We, as huma...
...e in and form part of...
...ment. We are affected by...
...ront, but we also affect...
...and changing it.

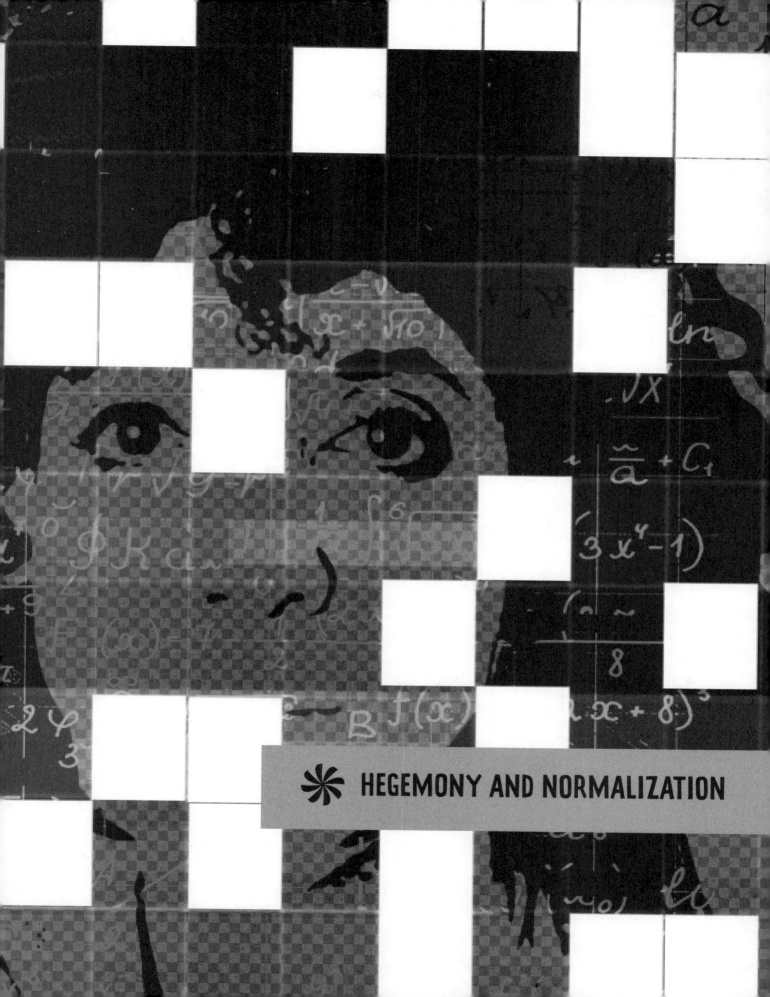

HEGEMONY AND NORMALIZATION

Connecting the Dots

BY STEPHEN LEEPER

Day 1

On Monday morning students noisily zigzagged through the hallways. As my first-period students approached the door, I stopped them and told them to line up.

"Jane! Matt! Cara!" I started calling off names to come to the front of the line. When they arrived at the door, I placed a star sticker on their hand and motioned for them to enter. They walked in with puzzled looks on their faces, especially when they read the board: *If you received a star, sit only at one of two tables near the front of the room.*

Once I finished calling names, I had the remainder of the students come in one by one. As they entered, I placed a dot sticker on their hands. They filled in the seats in the back of the room according to the seating chart on the board. Students started mumbling and whispering among themselves trying to figure out what the stickers meant. I quieted the class down and explained the new classroom rules:

Star rights and responsibilities:
- Get snacks on Wednesdays and unlimited water breaks
- Leave class first when the bell rings
- Have exclusive use of MacBooks

Dot rights and responsibilities:
- May not talk to or work with Stars during class
- Must leave class after Stars
- Must pick up any trash Stars leave behind after bell rings

I justified the new rules by saying: 1) I had done research on improving learning outcomes and found that organizing the class this way would promote academic growth; 2) this would help ensure that the classroom remained clean; and 3) the short supply of MacBooks due to testing required rationing. After a few moments of teeth sucking, groans, and more confused glances, students proceeded with the Do Now: Make a list of five words that come to mind when they think about the Declaration of Independence and the U.S. Constitution.

After students completed the Do Now, I had them turn and talk, then we had a whole class discussion. I called on Stars first to share out their responses. If only Dots raised their hands, I waited until a Star raised their hand and called on them to speak first. Students picked up on it right away and grumbled but didn't resist it. The same pattern of confusion, mild outrage, and resignation existed in every class the first day.

The lesson was focused on introducing the topic of the last unit (and the final project) of the year: social movements. I framed the project by explaining that social movements represented democratic collective action, many of which use the language and promises of the Constitution and Declaration of Independence—liberty, equality, fairness, and other related concepts students came up with for the Do Now. These movements, I explained, were a response to the failure of the country in honoring its ideals laid out in the founding documents that we'd studied this year. Students then completed a Give One, Get One activity with the rubric for the final essay on social movements. In giving instructions for the assignment, I reminded students that Stars and Dots could not work in pairs. I walked around the class to make sure students were following the instructions.

None of the Stars attempted to work with Dots. In one class, a Dot tried to work with a Star until I came over and restated the rules. The lesson ended with me introducing several possible contemporary and historical social movements they could choose from for their project.

In one class, a Dot raised her hand and asked if she could work on her project with her friend, who was a Star. When I told her no, because she was a Dot, she said, "But why? I don't understand why—"

"I already explained why at the beginning of class," I said, cutting her off. I ended class handing out a topic sign-up sheet in which students had to select the social movement they wanted to research.

At lunch, students typically come by to eat in class or just to say hello. One of the Stars came in and said, "Some are taking this too far. Outside of class people are coming up to me in the hallways saying, 'I can't talk to you because you're a Star.'"

Day 2

I stood at the door like I had the day before. Some Dots, forgetting the new classroom system, tried to enter without lining up first and receiving a sticker. I stopped them and told them to get in line. "This again?" some of the Dots responded. One Latino Dot said, "I feel like we're lining up to be deported." Most of the Stars came to the front without me asking and entered the class. I had to call a few reluctant Stars to come to the front and enter first. After everyone was seated, they began the Do Now: How do ordinary people change systems of injustice and unfair laws in a society?

A few minutes into class, one of my African American students, who was absent the day before, arrived late. The students lifted their eyes from their notebooks and waited to see where he would be seated. When I put a star on his hand and sat him up front, someone whispered loudly, "How did *he* get made a Star?" A low murmur began rising from the mass of Dots.

"Why do I hear talking? Do Nows are silent and independent. I find it interesting that the noise is coming only from the Dot tables."

"Oh my God, did you hear what he just said?" one of the Dots whispered.

"That's racist!" another one muttered.

The classes in the afternoon showed even more resistance. When it was time for the whole class share-out of the Do Now, no one raised their hand. I called on a Star to answer and she responded, "I don't know." Then I called on a Dot to answer, and she too responded, "I don't know." Smirks began to emerge on the faces of the students.

"Oh, I see what's going on here," I responded. "You're staging a little disobedience. OK, I'll tell you what. The first Dot that responds to the question I'll make a Star. And the next Star that refuses to answer I'll make a Dot." Students gasped and whispered to one another. I called on a Dot to answer.

"Don't do it!" another Dot whispered loudly.

"Ben, answer the question please."

"I . . . uh . . . I don't know." The Dots made a collective sigh of relief. I called on another student, a Star this time, to answer. I reminded her that if she refused to answer she'd be made a Dot.

"Mr. Leeper, I have a question for you. Do you believe in segregation?"

"Why on earth would I believe in that when my ancestors fought to end that horrible treatment?"

"Do you really believe that?"

"Yes, I do. Where is this coming from?"

"Then why are you doing this?"

"Doing what? You need to be specific."

"Separating us like this. It's not right."

"OK, listen to me," I came from behind my podium and stood in front of her, "all of you." I shifted my glare to the whole class. "I am the teacher, not you. You didn't go to grad school to get credentials to teach. I did. The principal, assistant principals, and your parents all trust me to make decisions in the classroom that I think are best for students. If they all trust me, you need to do the same." I paused, scanned the faces in the room, then settled my eyes back on the Star who challenged me. "Now answer the Do Now question."

The student's lip began to quiver and her eyes began to water. "I'm going to answer the question but then I'm going to move and sit with the Dots after," she started, her voice cracking.

"Ordinary people can make a change by standing up and fighting back!" She struggled to get it out, but when she did she burst into tears. Another Star that was sitting next to her rubbed her back to comfort her. I paused before giving commentary on the student's response: "Throughout American history, as we learned this year, regular people have stood up and fought back, just as this Star has said. The Native Americans fought against European colonialism. The patriots fought against unjust British rule in the colonies. Social movements are built by people who are willing to take a risk and fight back."

I walked over and whispered to the student that she could take a moment outside if she needed to collect herself. She left, and the student who comforted her left too. A chilling silence overtook the room as students looked on with incredulity and embarrassment. The irony of what I was saying juxtaposed with what I was doing wasn't lost on anyone. Here I was, extolling the virtues of those who stood up and fought back against injustice while actively shutting down dissent among students. But at this point, they didn't know what to do. I stepped outside to speak with the Star and asked her friend to go back inside.

"Are you OK? What's the matter?" Without facing me, she responded, still choked up with tears.

"It's just really hard," she sobbed a bit and then continued, "to see my friends not have the privilege that I have." I told her how impressed I was that she stood up to me in class. I told her that, though I understood how she feels, this is the way the class was going to be run. Then I told her that she could come back into class when she felt ready.

The lesson objective on this day was for students to analyze the group concepts related to social movements. Each table had an envelope with individual words on strips of paper. The words were: *disobedience, protest, action, injustice, rights, crime, goal, change,* and *government.* Students were asked to sort the words into groups in whatever way that made sense to them. Then they had to create labels for each grouping of words. Students at the Star tables received sticky notes to use as labels. Students at the Dot tables received an index card they had to cut into strips to manually create labels for their words. After students had finished, I projected each group's sortings on the board via Apple TV using an iPad. I chose a Star table to go first then took volunteers.

Two recurring categories across all classes among Dots and Stars were "good" and "bad." The words that commonly appeared in the "bad" category were *dis-*

obedience, crime, and *injustice.* I asked the Dot groups about why they chose to put *disobedience* in the "bad" category. The common explanation was that you get in trouble when you disobey and therefore it's a bad thing. Every time, I would follow up with a question: "What if you're disobeying something you think is unfair. Is it still bad?" They thought about it, said it could be good or bad, and some switched *disobedience* to the "neutral" category (if they had one). One group even created a "neutral" category on the spot and moved the word there. To wrap up, I introduced a definition of *social movement,* which contained several of the words from the sort.

The irony of what I was saying juxtaposed with what I was doing wasn't lost on anyone. Here I was, extolling the virtues of those who stood up and fought back against injustice while actively shutting down dissent among students.

Students then had to input the word in a visual dictionary template. Here, they had to write the meaning of the concept, think up synonyms, draw a picture that represented the concept, and rate their comprehension from one to four. Stars received a visual-dictionary graphic organizer while the Dots had to trace the template in their notebooks by hand. Dots groaned as they opened their notebooks to trace the template from the board. As I walked around the room, I noticed some of the Stars were not using the handout provided to them. When I asked why, they responded, "Because if the Dots don't get handouts, then I don't want one." In one class, a couple of Stars gave Dots their handouts to use when I had my back turned. The definition they wrote down was: *A group of people that come together and take collective **action** to achieve a common **goal** of social and political **change**.* Several students drew a picture of a Dot uprising in their entry.

Day 3

Midweek was the boiling point for almost every class. Students lined up without me having to tell them in first period and the class began without a hitch. As the class progressed, though, some Dots began talking out of turn.

When I passed by one, he turned to me and said, "We're going to boycott." When I asked who, he replied, "The Dots."

"You will boycott nothing; turn around and get back to work."

The Do Now on this day was asking students to respond to a quote by Kate Nash, professor of sociology at the University of London, which said, "Social

"Who organized this little civil disobedience?" They all looked at each other until the Star who had been the spokesperson turned to me and yelled out, "All of us!"

movements challenge the criteria of citizenship that define some individuals as 'Others' and as belonging to a group that [is] unworthy of equal rights." The two questions students were asked to answer were 1) What are some of the "others" that we've studied this year, and 2) what actions did these groups take to change the criteria for citizenship in this country?

During whole class share-out, students mentioned the otherization of colonists, enslaved Africans, and Native Americans. Then one of the students blurted out, "Dots!" Another student agreed, saying, "Yeah, Dots!" I responded by asking them to elaborate. One of them went on to explain that the Dots did not have the same rights as Stars and how it was unfair. I followed up by asking that if it were true, what action were they taking to change it? Dumbfounded, the student became silent, and I moved on to reviewing the lesson objective for the day: Students will be able to name and explain the four stages of a social movement.

Just as we were about to start, the fire alarm went off. When we arrived outside, I had students line up in the spot designated for us. I called for all the Stars to stand in the front of the line and Dots in the back. As the Stars made their way to the front of the line, the Dots created a gap to delineate Dots from Stars. They began taunting the Stars, asking them why they listen to me and accusing them of thinking they're better than the Dots. When administration gave the all clear to enter the building, I led the class back. The Stars walked close to me while the Dots hung back and marched, chanting "Dot lives matter, Dot lives matter!"

One of the Stars turned to me and said, "They're saying that because they're against us."

"Why do you think that?" I asked.

"Because they think we don't like them and that we're better than them."

"Do you?"

"No, we don't think that at all."

Second period became the first class to successfully rebel. Just like first period, they lined up without having to be asked, except that 90 percent of them refused to enter—including several Stars. I tried to cause some Dots to break rank by promising to make any who entered a Star. None took the bait. When that didn't work, I resorted to threats of punishment, e.g., referrals and calls home. I even called security to my room to take down names and to try to scare them into entering the class. One Star, who had previously been sympathetic to the Dots' cause by refusing to accept certain privileges as a show of solidarity, was now trying to persuade them to come inside, saying, "Just stop you guys. Come on. It's not worth it!" A couple folded but the rest remained steadfast. I then negotiated with the rebels, asking them what their demands were.

"For things to go back to the way they were before!" one of the Stars blurted out.

"Be specific. What do you mean by that?"

"No Dots and Stars."

"So you want me to remove the labels Dots and Stars? OK."

"No, not just remove the labels. No one gets special privileges or is prevented from working together. We all get treated equally. Everyone must clean up after themselves. Everyone can leave when the bell rings."

"That all?"

"Yes."

"Who organized this little civil disobedience?" They all looked at each other until the Star who had been the spokesperson turned to me and yelled out, "All of us!" After class, one student came up to me and said, "I'm sorry for disobeying you, Mr. Leeper, but I had to do what was right."

Their impact on the other classes was like that of Toussaint L'Ouverture and the Haitian Revolution on the enslaved in North America. They'd heard about what happened and followed suit, hoping to achieve a similar outcome. The last two classes of the day staged an identical protest, refusing to enter. This time, I called the counselor and the assistant principal to the room. In addition to referrals and calls home, they were threatened with the loss of 8th-grade privileges—including promotion. This spooked the overwhelming majority of the protestors until only about seven students remained. When I asked why they were willing to sacrifice so much to change the rules, several of them replied, "Because it's the right thing to do" or "I believe in standing up for what I believe in—no matter the cost." One of them followed up this sentiment saying, "You taught us well, Mr. Leeper." Like second period, the last class of the day also successfully abolished the unfair class system.

Sixth period, however, was a special case. During the negotiations, the spokesperson for the protestors said they wanted the labels of Dots and Stars gone and no special privileges. However, they did not specify that they wanted the segregation rule abolished. Therefore, I maintained the segregated seating arrangement. Realizing they had been deceived, they grumbled and threw up their hands. Some of the former Stars got up and sat at tables of former Dots to show their dissatisfaction with the rule.

All the student protesting that day happened roughly within the first 15 minutes of class. Once all the students were inside, I had them do another Give One, Get One activity. This time, the handout was a partially completed chart with the four stages of a social movement: emergence, coalescence, bureaucratization, and decline. In two of the classes, all students could work together to complete the activity. In the other two classes, seg-regation remained and the Dots were not allowed to partner with Stars. Once they finished filling out their chart, I reviewed the definition and an example of each stage with the class. I explained that emergence was the stage characterized by widespread discontent about an injustice, coalescence is when people come together to develop goals and strategies to address the injustice, bureaucratization is when the people formalize roles and train their constituents, and decline is when the movement ends. Students then took notes on the five reasons for the decline of a movement in their notebooks: 1) repression, 2) co-optation, 3) success, 4) failure, and 5) establishment in the mainstream. For homework, I asked students to draw a comic illustrating the four stages of a social movement.

Day 4

First period was the only class that had not staged at least a partially successful revolt. Several students came marching down the hall toward my class with Star stickers all over their faces chanting "Dot lives matter!" and holding up protest signs. Emboldened by the success of the other classes and perhaps feeling history was on their side, they stood resolutely outside when the bell rang and refused to enter. Just as I had done with the classes before, I called security and the assistant principal and threatened them with referrals and loss of privileges. All the students folded and entered the class except the two holding the signs.

As the students entered the class, I commended them for making the right choice. The assistant principal yelled at the two remaining protestors to get inside. They hung their heads and marched in. As they entered I confiscated their signs. The Do Now on the board read: *Students have the power to lead in social movements and change systems that are unfair. Agree or disagree?* After students wrote and talked at their tables we had a share-out. I called on a Dot to answer and she replied, "No, students don't." When I asked why, she said, "Because we weren't able to." I then introduced the essential question: "What role can students play in social movements?" and the lesson objective: *Students will be able to identify the stages of a social movement in the Moton High School walkout case study.*[1]

Originally, Dots were going to read a handout about the Moton High School walkout while Stars would watch a video about it on the MacBooks. Instead, I told the class that I would allow both Dots and Stars to use them so that they wouldn't think I was being unfair and insensitive to their concerns. Students watched the video and filled out a chart detailing the social movement stages that students went through to change the conditions at their school. We concluded by going over the chart together and making corrections as we went along. The exit ticket had two questions on it: 1) Based on what you've learned about the Moton High School walkout, what role can students play in social movements? 2) Would you have been part of the Moton High School walkout if you were there? Why or why not?

Day 5

I officially ended the simulation with a community circle debrief. The conversations were audio recorded to capture as much of their reflections as possible. The debrief was completed in three parts: independent written reflection, partner share, and community circle share. The written reflection questions were:

> Which of the following feelings best reflects how you felt being a Star or Dot and why?
> I felt powerful because . . .
> I felt angry because . . .
> I felt hopeless because . . .
> I felt happy because . . .
> I felt afraid because . . .

> Which of the five Ethnic Studies principles (Community, Love & Respect, Hope, Unity & Solidarity, and Critical Consciousness, per San Francisco Unified School District) did you practice or see practiced during the simulation? Explain.

> What did you learn about social movements and about yourself through this simulation?

The tenor of first period's debrief was markedly different from the other classes. This was partly due to how demoralizing their failure was and how divided the Stars and Dots were. Though they knew the simulation was over, Stars still sat next to each other in the community circle. They expressed feeling unfairly singled out and blamed by Dots. Dots expressed a sense of hopelessness and anger directed at both Stars and me—but more so toward me. One Star reflected that the reason they had failed was because they weren't able to successfully move through the stages of a social movement like the Moton High School students had. One of the Dots said the reason they failed was because of fear. She went on to express that one of the most powerful learnings for her was that if you're going to fight to change something you think is unfair, you must understand the risks and be willing to accept the consequences.

In another class, a student asked why I had done it and how I felt about it. I let another student answer the first question. She explained that creating unjust conditions in the class created the opportunity for students to put social movement theory into practice. To the second question, I shared how I wrestled with the moral implications of the simulation and that I came close to ending it. Students in multiple classes said they were glad I didn't.

Afterword

Implementing a simulation like this should not be done at the beginning of a school year. It is critical for the teacher to adequately assess the depth and quality of the relationship they have with their students and that students have with one another before trying any variation of this simulation. This is a subjective assessment—meaning it's something you must determine for yourself. No one knows your students in your class better than you. Having said that, there are some indicators you can use to help you make a good judgment about whether students are ready for an activity like this:

1. You've had discussions about controversial topics related to oppression and injustice throughout the course of the school year.
2. You have developed a strong classroom culture in which students feel safe to express their thoughts and ideas.

3. You have strong classroom management and have had very few instances of interpersonal conflicts throughout the school year.
4. Your students respect you, trust you, and feel safe with you.

The first time I attempted this simulation was during my third year as a teacher, which was my second year teaching Ethnic Studies. I only did the simulation with my one 8th-grade class for just two and a half days. I would have never tried this as a first-year teacher and I would not have done it with my 6th- or 7th-grade students. Since it went well that first year, I decided to attempt it again this past school year. This time, students had a much more visceral reaction to the experience. One important reason for this, I believed, was the difference in the political climate of our country. This is an important factor to take into consideration when deciding whether to attempt it.

Good teaching requires skill. Transformative teaching requires skill and risk. This is the premise from which I operate as an Ethnic Studies educator when deciding on what to teach and how. The question of ethics for me, thus, is a matter of three major considerations: First, does the educational benefit outweigh the potential stress this lesson will induce? Second, will this lesson move the class out of our comfort zone into our learning zone or will it push us into the panic zone? Third, are there students in the class who I know have a history of traumatic experiences that would be severely triggered by this lesson? These factors determine the extent to which I modify the lesson to accommodate students or whether I teach it at all. When I made the decision to do this simulation, I weighed these considerations. Halfway through the simulation, I reassessed to make sure my judgment was still sound and whether I should adjust or end it. I consulted with colleagues, friends, and family and decided to continue. I would advise all attempting this simulation to follow a similar process, because ultimately students' emotional and physical well-being is our top priority. The safety of our students cannot be sacrificed for the sake of a "good lesson."

One of the challenges I've had as a middle school Ethnic Studies teacher is making dense and inaccessible concepts real for students. So much of the literature, research, and materials produced in this field are written for academia. I wanted my students to understand hegemony and normalization and knew that no vocabulary lesson could adequately facilitate this. It had to be done experientially. When Stars from one class began to propose the invention of new rules to buttress their ruling-class position, this was an example of cultural hegemony. When many students, only after a couple days, began to accept the new social order in the classroom and continue with "business as usual," this was the beginning of the process of normalization. Being able to map concepts such as these onto experiences makes the learning more concrete and meaningful, which was the major goal of the lesson. ✳

ENDNOTE

[1] Student strike organized by 11th grader Barbara Johns that drew the attention of Thurgood Marshall and became part of the class action lawsuit known as *Brown v. The Board of Education*.

History Textbooks—"Theirs" and "Ours"
A Rebellion or a War of Independence?

BY JOHN DEROSE

Was it the "Philippine-American War" or the "War of Philippine Independence?" Was Emilio Aguinaldo a "rebel leader" or the "president" who led the Filipinos in the war against the United States?

For the past 12 years, I have tried to help my 11th-grade students view U.S. history critically from multiple perspectives. Most of my students are white, suburban high school juniors, but my classes also include some African American students who come from a wide range of socioeconomic backgrounds and generally come to our school from the city. While I use primary sources and other historians' interpretations, I continually search for sources that go beyond the mostly benign representations of U.S. actions overseas, which have dominated textbooks for generations. This is not just academic; how students regard U.S. conduct in the past influences how they view the exercise of U.S. power today. Therefore, when I read Dana Lindaman and Kyle Ward's *History Lessons: How Textbooks from Around the World Portray U.S. History*, I was excited to find textbook passages from countries that could help my students recognize that their texts are not impartial.

History Lessons contains passages translated into English from textbooks around the world that describe many major historical events. The passages that have proved the most valuable are ones that directly challenge the accounts found in my students' textbooks and provide them with a different way of seeing the same event. While every account is not totally at odds with their own textbook, passages like the Filipino version of the Philippine-American War, the Cuban version of the Cuban Missile Crisis, and the Vietnamese account of the Vietnam War—

the Vietnamese call it the American War—have been invaluable in allowing my students to examine opposing historical perspectives.

Recently, I asked students to compare an account from their U.S. history textbook on the Philippine-American War with a Filipino textbook passage from *History Lessons* about the same event—called the War of Philippine Independence in the Filipino book. In order to help students unravel the perspectives presented in both nations' textbook accounts, I first taught lessons that offered students a range of viewpoints on this event.

First, students watched the video *Savage Acts: Wars, Fairs, and Empire 1898–1904*. This documentary depicts U.S. racism to help explain the expansionist policies to "civilize" the Philippines at the turn of the century. For instance, the video describes how 1,200 Filipinos were brought to the 1904 St. Louis World's Fair and placed on exhibit. One American observer said that she saw "the wild barbaric Igorots who eat dogs and are so vicious that they are fenced in. They thirst for blood and are the lowest type of civilization I saw." With the prevalence of these racist attitudes, it is not surprising to hear U.S. Colonel Frederick Funston say that the Filipinos "are as a rule an illiterate, semi-savage people who are waging war not against tyranny but against Anglo-Saxon order and decency."

Savage Acts points out that after Filipinos expelled the Spanish, they established their own independent government. But instead of recognizing Filipino independence, the United States annexed the Philippines and sent troops to crush any resistance. The video examines these events from multiple points of view, ranging from antiwar activists like

Mark Twain to supporters of imperialism like President William McKinley and describes the camps where U.S. soldiers tortured Filipinos.

After the video, I gave students eight primary source documents representing an array of perspectives on U.S. annexation. These included speech and article excerpts from McKinley, William Jennings Bryan, Senator Albert Beveridge, labor leader Samuel Gompers, the "Colored Citizens of Boston," Filipino leader Emilio Aguinaldo, a Filipina activist named Clemencia Lopez, and a Filipino newspaper. I divided the class into eight groups and assigned each group one of the packet's eight documents. Students wrote summaries and their own assessment of the strengths and limits of the document's perspective. Then, one student from each group represented the perspective from their group's assigned document in a panel discussion. (I borrowed this lesson idea from the website of the American Social History Project/Center for Media and Learning, the organization that created the *Savage Acts* video. The website includes all the documents.)

The eight students on the panel, representing the points of view in the documents, faced the rest of the class. I asked the student audience, representing McKinley, Aguinaldo, et al., to comment on or challenge other positions. It didn't take long before "Clemencia Lopez" and the "Colored Citizens of Boston" confronted "President McKinley" and demanded that he justify how the United States could claim to spread "democracy" to the Philippines when U.S. women did not have the right to vote and our government sat idly while African Americans were lynched. "Emilio Aguinaldo" also argued against "Sen. Beveridge's" viewpoint that Filipinos were incapable of self-government, suggesting that Filipinos deserved a chance to rule themselves. "Aguinaldo" also pointed out that Filipinos had already governed themselves in a republic prior to the U.S. takeover.

After this debate, students read and discussed excerpts from letters by American soldiers who fought against the Filipinos (also adapted from the American Social History Project/Center for Media and Learning's website—ashp.cuny.edu). The soldiers' letters included extensive comments ranging from soldiers' descriptions of Filipinos as savages and

expressions of satisfaction over killing them to statements of opposition to the U.S. action in the Philippines and condemning of the brutalities against Filipinos. For instance, Ellis Davis, a soldier from Kansas, wrote, "They [Filipinos] will never surrender until their whole race is exterminated. They are fighting for a good cause, and the Americans should be the last of all nations to transgress upon such rights. Their independence is dearer to them than life, as ours was in years gone by, and is today." Students saw that the term "American soldiers" included a wide range of individuals with sometimes conflicting points of view.

Offering students multiple perspectives on the U.S. involvement in the Philippines helped prepare them to compare the Filipino textbook account of the war to their textbook's description of this same

I continually search for sources that go beyond the mostly benign representations of U.S. actions overseas, which have dominated textbooks for generations. This is not just academic; how students regard U.S. conduct in the past influences how they view the exercise of U.S. power today.

event. My high school offers an Advanced Placement U.S. history course and a "regular" U.S. history course. I taught this lesson four different times in one day in a regular U.S. history course with a great deal of diversity in terms of students' academic success.

In *History Lessons*, students read about the Philippine-American War from a Filipino textbook, and from their own textbook, McDougal Littell's *The Americans: Reconstruction to the 21st Century*. After they finished reading both accounts, I asked students to list similarities and differences between the two passages. I then asked them to use their knowledge from our previous activities to describe significant perspectives or information that may have been left out of each textbook passage and to explain if they felt either of the textbooks offered a more adequate retelling of this event. Finally, I asked them to explain how reading both textbook passages will affect how they read historical accounts in the future.

Students observed some similarities. One student said that both U.S. and Filipino textbooks indicate "Filipino citizens suffered" under U.S. occupation with American soldiers burning villages. Another pointed out "both texts mention [Emilio] Aguinaldo as a Filipino leader." And one student explained that both textbooks mention that Filipinos used "guerrilla tactics" when fighting U.S. soldiers.

At the same time, students observed differences. For example, one student thought that the Filipino

A number of students said that their textbook seemed limited in its portrayal of the brutality that American soldiers influcted on Filipinos.

textbook "glorifies Filipino [military] victories that the American text doesn't even mention." Another student said that the Filipino textbook referred to the Filipino leader as "President Aguinaldo" whereas their textbook described him as a "rebel leader." According to one student, our textbook claimed that "the Filipinos started the war, but the Filipino version says that the Americans started the war." Finally, a few students noticed that the Filipino textbook defined the event as "the War of Philippine Independence" and their textbook referred to it as "the Philippine-American War."

When we focused on missing information or slanted perspectives from the Filipino textbook, a number of students observed that the Filipino textbook offered an overly simplistic view of both Filipinos and Americans. One student wrote, "The Filipino textbook wants Americans to be seen as

heartless devils." She supported her claim by pointing out a quote from the Filipino textbook that describes a town called Balangiga as "a peaceful little port off the southern tip of Samar" and highlighted an incident described in the Filipino text where American soldiers massacred villagers. Students recalled that in the letters we read, some American soldiers expressed disgust with the brutal treatment of Filipinos.

Students were equally critical when we discussed missing aspects from their own textbook. In particular, a number of students said that their textbook seemed limited in its portrayal of the brutality that American soldiers inflicted on Filipinos. For example, a student noted that *Savage Acts* briefly described a torture treatment where U.S. soldiers forced water down a person's throat, but their textbook did not mention torture. While the U.S. textbook acknowledged that villages were burned and many Filipinos died of disease and malnutrition due to American soldiers' actions, the Filipino textbook and some of the soldiers' letters seemed to highlight how vicious and racist some American soldiers were. Finally, a number of students pointed out that their textbook, contrary to material in the Filipino textbook, never mentions that a U.S. soldier fired the first shot without provocation to begin the war.

I asked whether either textbook provided a more authentic retelling of the event. Many students commented that both textbook accounts were equally limited and authentic in their presentations. However, I wanted students to analyze the limitations in greater depth, and I challenged them to consider the war's portrayal by highlighting particular words, phrases, and omissions from each textbook. Suddenly students' comments became more precise and less neutral.

For example, I asked students which title—"president" or "rebel leader"—was more adequate in representing Emilio Aguinaldo. One student remembered from *Savage Acts* and our panel discussion role play that Filipinos had already begun to set up a republic prior to U.S. annexation. He argued that "president" was more accurate, and a number of students nodded in agreement. Similarly, some students contended that since the Filipinos had the desire (as expressed by each "Emilio Aguinaldo" in our panel discussion) to become independent from both Spain and the United

States, the phrase "War of Philippine Independence" was a more accurate title for the conflict.

A few students also commented that contrary to their own textbook, the Filipino textbook did a much better job of describing the way the war began by not only explaining that Americans initiated the military conflict but also even citing the name of the American soldier who fired the first shot. One student wrote, "Our textbook justifies our invasion by calling the actions of the Filipinos 'a rebellion.'"

Students acknowledged that their textbook connected the hypocrisy of the United States fighting a war to spread democracy while maintaining racial segregation at home. Students representing the Colored Citizens of Boston pointed out that some African Americans refused to support the war since they were victims of racist violence in their own country, and this was acknowledged in their own textbook account. The students' textbook even went as far as *Savage Acts* in pointing out that some African American soldiers formed alliances with Filipinos and a few even deserted to the Filipino side.

Finally, I asked if these activities would affect how they would read their U.S. history textbook in the future. One student noted that she would "realize that not every perspective is being presented." Another student added that it was crucial to consider multiple points of view about events to avoid blindly accepting the version of events passed on either in textbooks or the news media as if these were complete and unbiased.

Every history teacher has an obligation to offer students diverse perspectives about our nation's historical role in world affairs, including those that criticize U.S. policies. Our classrooms should be democratic spaces that help students think about history and current events beyond the tidy textbook narratives. How students view the past will shape how they view the present. Especially in times of war and occupation, students need to seek a fuller story than what is offered by mainstream media or official government sources. Without practice detecting limited perspectives in historical accounts, students will not be prepared to exercise the critical thought necessary to participate in a democracy. ✳

RESOURCES

American Social History Project. "Creating an Empire: U.S. Expansion at the Turn of the Twentieth Century." Accessed July 7, 2018. herb.ashp.cuny.edu/exhibits/show/creating-an-empire

American Social History Project. "Savage Acts: Wars, Fairs, and Empire 1898–1904." Accessed July 7, 2018. ashp.cuny.edu/savage-acts-wars-fairs-and-empire-1898-1904

Reprinted from *Rethinking Schools*, Fall 2007 (vol. 22, no. 1).

Learning About the Unfairgrounds

BY KATIE BAYDO-REED

The Puyallup Fair, 35 miles south of Seattle, ranks as one of the 10 largest fairs in the world. When I was growing up, every September my mom, dad, brother, sister, and I drove the 20 minutes from our house to the fairgrounds to spend the day. We kids looked forward to cotton candy and bumper car rides. Mom and Dad held our hands as we ooh-ed and ah-ed over 200-pound pumpkins. There were magic shows, animals to pet, cows to milk, and the world-famous Earthquake Burger.

When I was growing up, local school districts released children early on the second or third Wednesday of the school year with free tickets to attend the Puyallup Fair. Even today, districts distribute free admission tickets to schoolchildren. For people who grow up in this area, the fair is a tradition.

I'm sure I was not more than 2 years old the first time I attended the fair. Still, it was another 10 years before I learned some of the fairgrounds' history. In middle school, I was close friends with a girl whose father was Japanese American. In 1988, she told me that her grandmother would receive several thousand dollars from the government as part of an apology for detaining her and her family at the Puyallup fairgrounds during World War II. I couldn't believe that she had the story straight and convinced myself that she must have misunderstood her father. It was impossible that my fairgrounds, those hallowed grounds of tradition, had been used for something unjust. It was not until college that I realized that she was right. During World War II, the land on which the fairgrounds stood was dubbed the Puyallup Assembly Center, or, as some referred to it in an attempt to mask the nature of the place, Camp Harmony.

Executive Order 9066

Following the bombing of Pearl Harbor on December 7, 1941, U.S. officials issued a series of proclamations that violated the civil and human rights of the vast majority of Japanese Americans in the United States—ostensibly to protect the nation from further Japanese aggression. The proclamations culminated in Executive Order 9066, which gave the secretary of war the power to "prescribe military areas" wherever he deemed necessary for the security of the nation. This order provided license to incarcerate more than 120,000 Japanese Americans in internment camps (as well as several thousand Italian Americans and German Americans). Most of the people held in the camps were taken from the West Coast, where the feds believed "the enemy within" might be able to alert the Japanese military of U.S. vulnerabilities via a shortwave radio or, ludicrously, perhaps send a signal with a lit cigarette in a window.

Camp Harmony was one of 18 civilian assembly centers—temporary holding areas for the Japanese Americans who were rounded up for incarceration. More than 7,000 people were held at Camp Harmony. Most were from the Seattle area, but some were brought from as far away as Alaska. It did not take long for the new residents to realize they were living in stalls that had previously housed livestock.

Once the government completed construction of the more permanent war relocation centers (commonly referred to as "internment camps"), authorities boarded those being held in the assembly centers onto buses and trains and shipped them to the internment camps. In all, 10 War Relocation Centers were built between March and October of 1942, located as far west as Tule Lake, California, and as far east as Desha County, Arkansas. Many people were held until 1945, three years after the first camps opened.

Civil Rights in the Northwest

When the day came in early September for me to distribute Puyallup Fair tickets to my 4th-grade class, I asked if any of them knew the history of the fairgrounds beyond its use as a place to display large vegetables. No one raised a hand. I took this as an opportunity to investigate with my class some of the local roots of a national injustice.

There is something mythological about the Civil Rights Movement. Over the years I've discovered that most children in my classes think that civil rights struggles were fought long ago in faraway places. Here in the Northwest, the movement is often revered as a unique time in our nation's history when brave souls spoke truth to power in distant places like Montgomery, Birmingham, and Selma. However, teaching about civil rights struggles as only occurring Someplace Else disempowers students. I wanted my 4th graders to understand that injustice has played a role in the shaping of our community and that the responses of people being treated unfairly do not always look the same. I wanted them to see that sometimes activism against injustice can be as quiet as refusing to answer a question. My hope was that the class would understand that it was unfair to assume that Japanese Americans as a group were a threat to the safety of the country based on an attack by a foreign nation. Further, I wanted them to see that blanket incarceration was a violation of human rights.

We began by reading several children's books (see p. 196). These all provided an accessible way for the children to see how fundamentally unfair it was for thousands of people to be persecuted based solely on their ancestry. We discussed how the families' civil rights were violated. We also looked at how the voices of those incarcerated were hopeful and resistant.

To provide the class with a deeper understanding of the issues, I wanted to include a longer work of literature. I found the book *Thin Wood Walls* by local author David Patneaude. I read the novel and found it to be a valuable look at the many ways incarceration affected people in the Northwest. The protagonist is Joe Hanada, an 11-year-old boy living in Auburn, Washington, during World War II. The FBI takes his father prisoner and holds him, away from his family, for two years. Eventually the government sends the remaining Hanada family—Joe, his mother Michi, his paternal grandmother, and his older brother Mike—to the Tule Lake internment camp. While the novel focuses on Joe's experiences, Patneaude does an excellent job of showing how, even within the Japanese American community, people reacted differently to government actions.

A Tea Party to Introduce a Challenging Novel

The book has a recommended reading level of ages 12 and up, and my class included 9- and 10-year-olds. To help them better understand the nuanced differences in how the characters reacted to Executive Order 9066, I held a "tea party." A tea party takes a novel or historical event and assigns each student a literary or historical character. Students circulate in the classroom and initiate conversations, introducing themselves (in role) and asking questions of other characters.

I picked out 21 characters from the novel and wrote up "persona cards." Here are a few examples:

JOE HANADA: I am 11 years old and live in Auburn, Washington, in the early 1940s. My parents are Japanese. I was born in the United States, so I am a U.S. citizen. I enjoy playing basketball, baseball, and marbles. My best friend is Ray O'Brien—an Irish American boy who is in my class at school. I love to write and hope to be an author when I get older. I am nisei (second-generation Japanese in America). When Japan bombed Pearl Harbor, the government arrested my father and moved my family to two different camps. I keep a journal to write about my feelings.

MICHI HANADA: I am the mother of Joe, 11, and Mike, 16. I was born in Japan but came to the United States 20 years ago with my husband. While by law I cannot become a citizen, my children are citizens because they were born on U.S. soil. I have worked hard to make sure that my household is beautiful and to provide what my family needs. I do everything I can to keep my spirits up and fill the shoes of my husband, who has been arrested by the FBI. The government has still not charged him with any crime. I do not know when he will return to our family.

DAVID OMATSU: They call me a No-No Boy. Let me tell you why: The government gave a questionnaire to all of the Japanese Americans at the camp. Question 27 asked if we would agree to fight for the United States in the war. I said no—how could I be in the Army when my whole family is jailed in this camp? Question 28 asked if we would "forswear any form of allegiance to Japan." I answered no because I was born in the United States—I'm an American! But anyone who answered no to both questions is called a No-No and sent to a special prison camp.

MR. LANGLEY: I live on the same block as the Hanada family. I am not surprised to hear that Japan has attacked the United States. I knew they were a no-good country. I think all the Japanese should be rounded up and sent back to Japan. My son Harold goes to school with one of the Hanada boys and I told him to stay away from that traitor's family. I don't want my own son to catch any of that disloyalty.

SERGEANT SANDY: I joined the Army because I knew it would help my future. I have a wife and I'm excited to begin building a family. I have been stationed as a guard at the Tule Lake Relocation Camp in Northern California. I'm sad because I think that the government has made a bad decision to lock up so many innocent people. However, I have my orders and I will not disobey. I try to get to know as many of the families at the center as I can.

I handed out the persona cards and gave the children a worksheet to guide their interactions during the tea party. Then I had them write, from their characters' standpoints, answers to the following questions: "How do you feel about the war with Japan?" and "What is your opinion about how Japanese Americans were treated by the U.S. government? Why do you feel that way?"

Once the children finished writing, we began the tea party. I asked the students to find other individuals who could help them answer the questions on their worksheets. For example: "Find someone who feels the same way you do about the Japanese

American experience during World War II. Who is this person? What do you agree about? Why do you think this person feels similarly to you?" "Find someone who feels differently than you do. Who is this person? How is this person's opinion different than yours? Why do you think you feel differently?"

Following the tea party, I asked students to reflect in writing about what they had learned.

As I circulated throughout the activity, I overheard snippets of conversations and wrote down key phrases. I was pleasantly surprised that several children seemed able to internalize aspects of their characters:

Shawna (as Michi Hanada): "This is sad because they took my husband away."

Henry (as Mrs. O'Brien, a family friend): "I am sad and sorry about what happened to the Hanada family. I wish there was something I could do to help, but I can't think of anything to help them."

Kim (as David Omatsu): "I am angry because I was treated like dirt, just because I am Japanese American."

Karen: (as Sergeant Sandy): "I think what we are doing to the Japanese Americans is wrong, but I am doing what is right for my future by staying in the Army."

The tea party was invaluable in introducing the children to some of the complexities of the period. It helped equip most students to comprehend *Thin Wood Walls* as I read it aloud to them. The variety of roles in the book allowed the children to realize that there were many, many ways people reacted to what was happening. Some of the Japanese Americans, despite being forced to leave their homes and livelihoods, felt it was their duty to do as their government asked. Some felt their rights were being violated, but did not know how they could resist alone. Others felt that the best way to prove loyalty was to enlist and fight in the war for the United States. Still others openly resisted the policies of incarceration and discrimination.

Throughout our reading, the children engaged in a series of activities and reflections. As I read, they sketched scenes I described, "drawing along" to increase comprehension. Joe Hanada saw himself as a writer and kept a journal, so I had the children write from the perspective of various characters in the book. I tried to provide enough concrete information to make these types of activities accessible to all children. Several children in the class spoke English as a second or third language and needed more support than I initially provided in terms of vocabulary and context.

Over the next few weeks, I incorporated aspects of what we were learning into as many lessons as possible. For example, we used data from the incarceration camps to do plot and line graphs in math. I obtained the numbers of people held in the various camps and wrote the names of the camps on the x-axis of a graph and the numbers up the y-axis. The children then worked to construct tables and graphs that showed population distribution in the camps throughout the western United States. This activity opened up opportunities to discuss big numbers and led to a deeper understanding of place value. Here was a direct connection for my students between important mathematical concepts and a chapter in U.S. history.

A Mock Trial

During the Japanese American incarceration, there were three attempts to find Executive Order 9066 unconstitutional. I chose two of the cases to conduct mock trials in my class: the cases of Gordon Hirabayashi, whose story is told in the documentary *A Personal Matter*, and Fred Korematsu. Hirabayashi and Korematsu were convicted in federal court of violating curfew and refusing to relocate in 1942 and 1943, respectively. Both men were retried over 40 years later: Hirabayashi's conviction was overturned; Korematsu's case was vacated and his name cleared.

The children wanted to find the men not guilty, and they conducted their court based on their beliefs of what was right and wrong. It took a lot of coaching to get them to see the cases from the perspectives of government agents, lawyers, and the Supreme Court of the early 1940s. The class ultimately found both men not guilty, and defended their judgments based on the Constitution. They were stunned to find that the U.S. government had been so negligent in its dispensing of justice more than 60 years earlier. I told them that it wasn't until the passing of the Civil Liberties Act of 1988 that the government admitted that "racial prejudice, wartime hysteria, and failure of

political leadership" fueled the mass incarceration of innocent people during World War II.

The unit culminated with a trip to the Wing Luke Asian Museum in Seattle. I prefaced this trip by sharing stories about Wing Luke, who fought for equal housing rights in Seattle from the 1950s until his death in 1965. Although Luke's name is not as well known as that of Martin Luther King Jr. or Rosa Parks, the work he did to combat anti-Asian discrimination was groundbreaking. Prior to his activism, Asian Americans were confined to living mostly in Seattle's Beacon Hill neighborhood, much as African Americans were restricted to the Central District.

Luke ran for and was elected to the Seattle City Council in 1962 and was instrumental in passing the 1963 Open Housing Ordinance, which established punitive provisions for racial discrimination in the selling or leasing of real estate. A special exhibit at the museum about World War II helped my students build on what they had learned and broadened their understanding of the impact of racism on the community.

Ultimately, this curriculum taught several valuable lessons. The first lesson was that, even though the signs of past discrimination are not obvious when we walk down the street, the history of our region holds evidence of injustice. The second lesson was a deeper understanding of human rights and the need that we all have to be treated with respect and justice. Students who had never experienced racial discrimination themselves learned that it exists even in their own backyards. Finally, students learned that there are many ways people react to and resist injustice: sometimes overtly by challenging laws in court, sometimes quietly by refusing to comply, sometimes by an act of kindness or empathy.

The notion that our nation's struggles for civil rights took place only in the South was replaced with the knowledge that people here in the Northwest, too, have been active in creating the world we live in today. I hope that students in my class learned that even though we say we are "the land of the free and the home of the brave," the U.S. government has acted against its people. We must demand justice when it is being violated; otherwise, we may find ourselves in the same place we were 60-plus years ago. ✳

RESOURCES

A Personal Matter: Gordon Hirabayashi vs. the United States. Dir. John
    De Graaf. 1992. Center for Asian American Media. DVD.

Bigelow, Bill. 2008. "The U.S.-Mexico War Tea Party," *A People's History
    for the Classroom*. Rethinking Schools.

Densho: The Japanese American Legacy Project. densho.org

Patneaude, David. 2004. *Thin Wood Walls*. Houghton Mifflin.

This Was Minidoka. Dir. Jack Yamaguchi. 1989. Independently
    produced and distributed. VHS.

Reprinted from *Rethinking Schools*, Spring 2010 (vol. 24, no. 3).

Children's Books About Japanese Americans During World War II

Baseball Saved Us by Ken Mochizuki
This is the story of a Japanese American family that is interned and ends up building a baseball diamond in the camp. Ultimately, it is the story of how, even when forced to live within the confines of an internment camp, people find ways to retain their spirits and create community.

Flowers from Mariko by Rick Noguchi and Deneen Jenks
This book illustrates the difficulties that many families experienced after being held in the camps. Often, homes had been sold, businesses ruined, and possessions lost. In this story, the child, Mariko, helps her family build upon a dream that might easily have died after three years of internment.

The Bracelet by Yoshiko Uchida
The author of *Journey to Topaz* writes here of a friendship strong enough to withstand the trauma of being forced to leave one's home and live in an internment camp. This book demonstrates that there were allies and friends both inside and outside of the camps who expressed solidarity through acts of kindness.

When Justice Failed: The Fred Korematsu Story by Steven A. Chin
Fred Korematsu was rejected for military service in 1941 because of his Japanese ancestry and then fired from his job in the shipyards for the same reason. He refused the order to evacuate from his home and go to an internment camp. This short biography recounts his life and his struggle against unfair treatment. Appropriate for upper elementary grades.

Weedflower by Cynthia Kadohata
I recommend this novel even more than *Thin Wood Walls* (it was published after I first taught this unit). It is the story of Sumiko, a 12-year-old girl of Japanese ancestry who is being raised by her grandparents and whose family is incarcerated at Poston—which is adjacent to a Native American reservation—following the issuance of Executive Order 9066. This novel provides an excellent look at the intersections of identity and oppression between and among characters.

Whose Community Is This?
The Mathematics of Neighborhood Displacement

BY ERIC "RICO" GUTSTEIN

The equation went up on the board as my 12th-grade "math for social justice" class silently and soberly stared at it.

$$150{,}000 - 291{,}000 = 92{,}000$$

I talked as I wrote: "You've paid $291,000 on a $150,000 mortgage, and you still owe $92,000. Check that math out. That's good math, let's look at that math: $150,000 minus $291,000 equals $92,000." I paused for 20 seconds as students looked and mumbled to themselves and neighbors. "Think about that. Hey! You started with 150, you paid 291, and you still owe $92,000. What's going on here?"

Antoine: "They're taking your money."

Daphne: "The bank is taking advantage of you."

Rico: "This is legal—this is how banks lend money and make money." I paused and repeated it slowly. "This is legal—this is how banks lend money and make money."

I asked students, "What are some questions you could ask here?" Renee said, "Why is it legal?" Daphne asked why more people didn't look into it so they wouldn't end up in that situation.

So went a typical day in this class, one in which everything we did focused on learning and using mathematics to study students' social reality. I wanted students to understand the root causes of oppression in their lives—*read the world*—to prepare them to be able to change it—*write the world*—as they see fit.

Our Setting

We were in the Social Justice High School ("Sojo") in Chicago's Lawndale community. Sojo was born through a multiyear battle in the 1990s for a new high school in Little Village (South Lawndale)—a densely populated, largely Mexican-immigrant community with one overcrowded high school. A victorious 19-day hunger strike by neighborhood activists in 2001 forced the district to build the new school. In 2005, Sojo and three other small high schools opened on one campus. Although the building is in South Lawndale, 30 percent of the students are Black, from the bordering community of North Lawndale, and the other 70 percent are Latinx. Almost all students are low-income (approximately 97 percent) as Lawndale, a spiritually and culturally rich community with deep reservoirs of resilience, is also economically battered. Sojo is a quality neighborhood public school—not a charter, alternative, or selective-enrollment school; any student in Lawndale can attend any of the four schools. I was part of Sojo's design team and worked there from 2005 to 2011. I taught this class in the 2008–09 school year.

Studying Neighborhood Displacement

Displacement was part of students' realities—gentrification in North Lawndale, deportation in Little Village, and foreclosures in both. I started the unit by telling the story (with family permission) of Carmen, a student in class. Her grandmother paid off her North Lawndale mortgage years before but, because of rising property taxes and a leaking roof, took out a subprime (adjustable) home equity loan. When the rate set upwards, she lost the house. The families of two other students in class were struggling to stay in their houses, and boarded-up homes were all around. As students discussed their lives and observations, then analyzed local house prices (see graph above), their questions emerged: Will we be able to

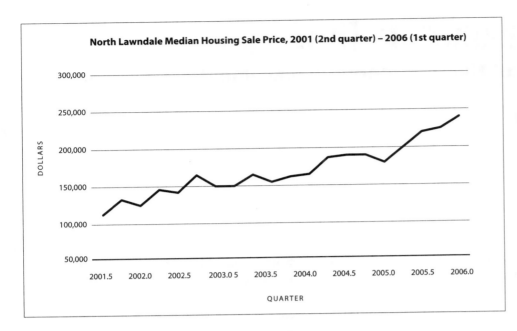

North Lawndale Median Housing Sale Price, 2001 (2nd quarter) – 2006 (1st quarter)

cost) mortgages worked, the relationship of interest to principal, concepts like negative amortization, and more. I wanted students to begin to appreciate how banking works as part of a larger capitalist economic system and its relationship to their lives and experiences.

I started by teaching students to use a DDS to model an interest-bearing savings account and gave them an assignment to put their knowledge to use. The next day, we began by reviewing the homework: Create the DDS and find the balance after one year on a $500 deposit at 3 percent annual interest.

Marisol wrote on the board:

$a_0 = 500.00$

$a_n + 1 = a_n + .0025 \times a_n$

Using our overhead graphing calculator, she showed the results after one month, then up to 12, and said, "So, overall in a year, you're gonna be left with $515.21."

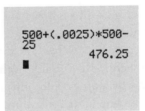

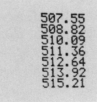

stay here? From where and how does gentrification arise? What is the original purpose or plan? Why our neighborhoods? Where are families supposed to go?

To study displacement, students initially learned what a *discrete dynamical system* (DDS) was. A DDS is complex, and even simple ones can behave chaotically. A DDS has at least one baseline and one recursive equation, and one can use them to produce a mortgage or credit card schedule. (More complicated DDSs have multiple sets of equations, with which students learned to model HIV/AIDS transmission in Lawndale later that year.) For example, the monthly payment on a $150,000, 30-year, fixed-rate mortgage at 6 percent annually is $899.33. Its DDS is:

$a_0 = 150,000.00$
[a_n represents balance due at start of month n]

$a_n + 1 = a_n + .005a_n - 899.33$
[what you owe at the start of a month is what you owed the previous month, plus the interest on what you owed, minus your monthly payment]

My plan, specifically about mortgages as part of the larger unit, was for students to unpack them and see how much more than the actual cost of a house one actually pays over the years. In addition, I wanted students to understand how subprime (high-

After some back and forth, with her clarifying, we moved on. The next problem was:

Assume you have this $500 deposit that pays 3 percent per year, but you withdraw $25 a month. Create the DDS—when will you run out of money?

Vanessa tackled this: "OK, I did the same as Marisol, but I subtracted the $25 because you also withdraw 25 a month." She showed us that we'd run out of money in 20 months:

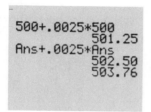

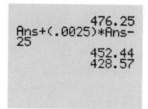

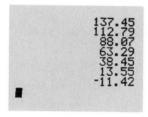

These preparations took us to the reality of students' communities, in which foreclosures had tripled over three years. Students examined the graph on Lawndale foreclosures and discussed how mathematics reflected what they were seeing and experiencing.

Why were foreclosures rising so dramatically? Our next step was to find how much a median-income family in both North and South Lawndale could afford for housing without "hardship," using the U.S. Department of Housing and Urban Development's guideline of 30 percent of monthly income going toward housing. Minerva said that a median-income South Lawndale family—earning

$32,317 a year—could afford $807.92 monthly. She explained: "I divide their annual income by 12 to get how much they earn per month and multiply that by .3 to get 30 percent."

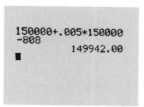

So far, the mathematics hadn't challenged students much. But my next question did:

If a median-income family in your community (either North or South Lawndale) takes out a 30-year, fixed-rate $150,000 mortgage at 6 percent interest:
1) Create a DDS with a_0 being $150,000 and 6 percent interest annually.
2) Determine whether they can afford the mortgage "without hardship." If yes, how large a mortgage can they afford? If no, explain why not.

As we worked as a whole class, the students' initial attempt was:

$$a_0 = 150,000$$
$$a_n + 1 = a_n + .06a_n$$

This equation was wrong on two counts. I helped students through their first misconception: No payment was subtracted. Then Antoine said that the .06 was annual and should be .005 (monthly). Daphne, Ann, and Vanessa then discussed the meaning of each term in the equation. I stayed out of it until I pushed Vanessa to explain every symbol that Ann had entered into the overhead calculator:

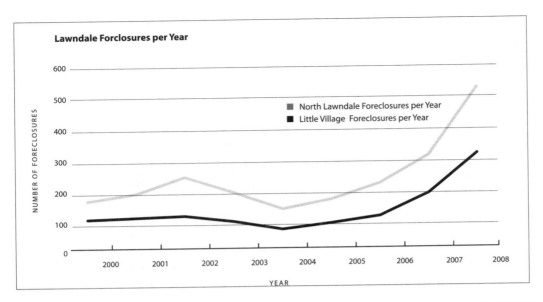

Lawndale Forclosures per Year

NUMBER OF FORECLOSURES

■ North Lawndale Foreclosures per Year
■ Little Village Foreclosures per Year

YEAR

Rico: "Yes, we're trying to see, can they afford this mortgage? How many payments are there altogether?"

Calvin: "360."

I had Ann press the calculator button 360 times as she counted aloud while we watched the balance shrink on the projector. After 360 presses, the board showed:

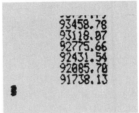

After 30 years, the family still owed almost $92,000. I asked what was the total paid after 30 years and, on the overhead calculator, multiplied 360 by $808, roughly $291,000. That prompted the dialogue and equation that starts this article:

$$150,000 - 291,000 = 92,000$$

The lesson here: No median-income South or North Lawndale family could afford this mortgage without hardship. And, as we discovered when we examined neighborhood prices, many houses were this much or more—especially new condos. A student brought in an advertisement for a new North Lawndale condo for $285,000, not including the $10,000 gated parking space.

Over the next few days, I had students answer two related questions:

- What income is needed to afford a mortgage of $150,000—a 30-year, fixed-rate, 6 percent annual interest mortgage?
- What mortgage amount, with the same terms, can a median-income North Lawndale/Little Village family afford?

Vanessa: ". . . your monthly payment, and then $149,942 is how much you owe."

Rico: "When?"

Vanessa: "After you give . . . your first payment."

Rico: "Exactly. That $149,942 is what you owe after your first payment. OK, how much less than your initial payment is what you owe now?"

Antoine: "$58."

Rico: "$58. How much did you pay? $808. Out of the first payment of $808, $750 goes to interest to the bank. Only $58 reduces your loan balance. Understand how capitalism works, how banking works. Almost 15 times as much money goes to the interest as goes to the principal—the money you owe. That is profit for the bank. Yes, they have to pay their employees, but there is still a huge profit. That's how they make money."

I was trying to interweave students' realities, mathematics, and a broader political and economic analysis, but I didn't belabor the point and returned to the math, knowing that students would shortly uncover the "strange equation" that begins this article.

Ann then taught the other students how to set up the equation in the calculator so that each time she pressed ENTER, the calculator would show the next month's balance.

I interrupted to refocus us: "So what is the problem? What is the question?"

Daphne: "Are we trying to see how long before they pay it off?"

Rico: "Not only are we try—"

Carleton: "Can they afford it!"

By graphing the DDS on their calculators and adjusting their numbers, students uncovered that a $150,000 mortgage would require roughly a $36,000 income and that median-income families in Little Village and North Lawndale could afford mortgages of $134,750 and $84,500, respectively—not $150,000.

Although students saw and lived with displacement, understanding how and why it worked involved examining complex global processes of finance capitalism. The two Lawndales experienced displacement in ways both similar and different, due to real estate development, the economic crash, (un)authorized immigration status, geography, housing stock, deindustrialization, and proximity to public transportation and highways.

As the unit continued, I told students about a plan to build a massive gentrification complex in Little Village. Antoine was very interested, and at my suggestion, we investigated after school. Through internet research, we uncovered that a transnational capital investment fund was trolling the globe for investors to profit from displacing him from his community. Antoine was livid and presented his findings to the class, including a four-minute promotional video for the proposed development.

Students also delved into the math of subprime mortgages to better understand how banks profited from them. They were fascinated by this topic. I had students create a scenario, including some negative amortization, for each of three types of subprime mortgages: adjustable-rate, pay-option, and balloon mortgages (respectively, a mortgage whose interest rate changes or "adjusts" periodically; one in which the buyer has the "option" to decide how much to pay per month within limits, often accumulating negative amortization; and one in which the whole balance becomes due and "balloons" at the end of a relatively short period, e.g., seven years). They were to turn in, for each:

1. The mortgage terms as they changed—i.e., interest rate, amount borrowed, monthly payment, and number of months.
2. A table showing how much the borrower paid at different time periods, at what interest rate.
3. What the borrower paid over the loan term, itemizing principal, interest, and refinancing costs, if a balloon.
4. A comparison of the total amount from #3 with the cost of a 30-year, fixed-rate, 6 percent per year mortgage.

Immigration and Deportation

In the second part of the unit—immigration and deportation—students investigated the complicated role of the U.S. government and NAFTA in displacing Mexican farmers from their land to the *maquiladoras* along the U.S.-Mexico border, and eventually to South Lawndale—where displacement for unauthorized migrants does not just mean out of the neighborhood, but out of the country itself. We studied the table showing the concentration of USDA corn subsidies to agribusiness and examined the graph showing that, after NAFTA, the price paid to Mexican corn growers dropped while the cost of tortillas soared (further impoverishing rural Mexicans and increasing migration). Students investigated and created graphs showing how corn subsidies to U.S. agribusiness were highly concentrated in huge conglomerates (e.g., the top 1 percent of com-

Concentration of USDA Corn Subsidies to Agribusiness

Pct. of recipient	Pct. of Payments	Number of Recipients	Total Payments 1995–2006	Payment per Recipient
Top 1%	19%	15,729	$10,726,604,754	$681,964
Top 2%	30%	31,458	$17,053,420,149	$542,101
Top 3%	39%	47,187	$21,870,918,998	$463,495
Top 4%	46%	62,916	$25,767,405,826	$409,553
Top 5%	52%	78,645	$29,022,040,929	$369,026
Top 17%	84%	267,395	$46,941,027,794	$175,549
Top 18%	85%	283,124	$47,629,179,204	$168,227
Top 19%	86%	298,853	$48,258,099,906	$161,478
Top 20%	87%	314,582	$48,834,286,526	$155,235
Remaining 80% of recips.	13%	1,258,332	$7,336,588,731	$5,830

Corn and Tortilla Prices in the Mexican Market

Although we didn't have time for a full run-through and students were anxious the first night, they presented what they had learned and received much positive feedback.

For example, the students who presented on immigration showed the following slide:

NAFTA's Impacts on Mexico
- Corn subsidies to large U.S. corn growers
- Cheaper to produce U.S. corn
- Cheaper to import U.S. corn than grow in Mexico
- Mexican government stops corn price supports
- Mexican government stops tortilla price controls
- Immigration increases to the United States

The theme that both Lawndales have more commonalities than differences surfaced strongly at the forums, as their presentation's final slide captures:

Why Should We Care?
- Both communities face the same problems but different situations.
- There are many lies and stereotypes about both Mexicans and African Americans:
  –"Mexicans steal the jobs of U.S. citizens."
  –"African Americans are lazy."
- Don't let them pit us against each other!

panies receiving the largest subsidies collected—on average, 117 times more than firms in the bottom 80 percent). We considered how these subsidies undercut Mexican farmers who could not compete with cheaper, imported U.S. corn, and how this contributed to displacement from the Mexican countryside.

Students also analyzed data on Mexican migration to the United States in relation to NAFTA policies. We looked at the concentration of Mexicans in various U.S. occupations, examined the volume and rate of change of immigration over time, and used linear and quadratic regression to analyze and predict future immigration trends. We studied, graphed, and analyzed the loss of manufacturing jobs in Lawndale over time and discussed this in relation to demographic changes, NAFTA's rise, and capital's drive to maximize profit by leaving areas with well-paid union jobs to reduce costs. These explorations helped students understand the complex and multiple ways that people in both Lawndales experience similar and different ways of being displaced.

Taking It to the Community

As a way to "write the world," students held two public forums to share what they learned with family, friends, and community. The public presentations (which they titled "Our People, Our Issues: Math as Our Weapon") were at the end of the year, one in each neighborhood. Students created an 81-slide presentation, with my minimal feedback and editing.

In written reflections, students said they felt good that they had informed their families and communities, applauded their own and classmates' collective presentations, and critiqued themselves for insufficient preparation, nervousness, and reading too much from their PowerPoint. To a person, students thought it was worthwhile and important to teach their people. From my point of view, providing students the opportunity to "take it to the community" and share what they learned is an important component of teaching for social justice and lets students develop competencies that they will need as future agents of change.

Reflections

Developing and teaching a curriculum that supported learning about these interlocking sociopolitical processes *and* college preparatory mathematics challenged me, despite my experience with critical math. My academic goal was for students to learn serious math—precalculus, algebra, discrete mathematics, quantitative reasoning, and statistical analysis—to better understand neighborhood displacement and to appreciate math's usefulness in doing so. It's nonnegotiable that students learn math to have full opportunities for education, life, and individual/community survival. Social justice mathematics demands this as part of supporting marginalized communities' self-determination, and educators cannot shortchange students' mathematical learning or life chances.

My sociopolitical goal was, as much as possible, to have students understand the causes, mechanisms, and roots of displacement in each neighborhood. I wanted them to see that both Lawndales have the same larger context—a global, racialized political and financial system that plays out in particular and sometimes contradictory ways—and, thus, whatever differences students saw between their own and others' communities were far outweighed by commonalities.

Did all my students achieve this? I cannot definitively say. Not all students learned the same amount, based on my assessments of their mathematics learning and sociopolitical understandings. In hindsight, creating and teaching an interdisciplinary curriculum through which students could unwind the interconnections of neighborhood displacement was more complicated than I had anticipated for both students and me. Nonetheless, students said they learned a lot. In a reflection, Mónica, a Latina and lifelong South Lawndale resident, wrote:

> Some connections that I see between these two parts of the unit are that in both communities, people are being forced out of their homes. Of course, it's different situations, but similar causes. African Americans are being forced out of their homes because they can't pay for their homes. The taxes go up so much that they can't afford to keep living in those communities, so they are forced to look for another place to live. For Mexican people, the problem is that they don't have jobs in Mexico because corn isn't being sold, because it's cheaper to import subsidized U.S. corn than to grow their own. That forces Mexicans to leave their family and homes to come to the U.S. to look for a job. . . . Also, the house mortgages don't only affect one community, but both. They are sometimes the target of bad loans that only make banks richer! I want the people in my community to know that we are really similar in these situations. That there is more that makes us similar, less that makes us different. If we want to fight the bigger people out there, the best way is to unite. Fighting each other is not going to take us anywhere. I think this is something very important our community should know.

Renee's comments were particularly powerful in linking the unit to her reality as a Latina:

> The unit made many relations between Black and Brown communities. There are so many misconceptions about Black people as well as Brown. Both communities think bad about each other. In the Black community, they might say that Mexican people don't belong in this country because we're illegal aliens. As well, there are Mexican people who say that all Black people have a Link card and spend all their money on clothes, etc. What people don't understand is that we both have the same struggles. They might seem different because of the color of our skin but deep down inside, our parents struggle to get by with sicknesses, drug addictions, or unemployment. People are dealing with foreclosures and then become homeless. . . . When we did the 30 percent of the median household income for both communities, we figured that we can't afford the houses that we are living in. Our family members kill themselves in factories trying to make ends meet. This unit taught us that we have the same struggle. People always ask what similarities do we all have, and this unit tells us why we are the same.

As for how mathematics helped them, Carleton explained what he learned, critiqued the system, and wrote about helping others:

> Learning the dynamical system helped me really understand how and why people were losing their homes. It showed how small of an amount of income the average Black/Brown family was making and, since it was a small amount, how hard it was to pay off the mortgage loans. Not only was it hard but the banks were really stealing money from these people because they would end up paying a double amount of money than they took out because of this thief called Interest. . . . These were also the most important things that I learned because they helped me understand what I know now. It helped me to be able to predict whether or not a family would be able to pay off their loan with certain types of mortgages, and this is very important in being able to read the world so we can be able to share with the world.

And Renee used what she learned to analyze her own particular circumstances:

> It's crazy how banks give you this loan with a monthly payment that eventually people don't really get out of debt. There are people who don't know this and believe in their capitalist country. People need to know what happens—why they get into debt, especially that what the banks do is legal with our government. People such as my sister lose their homes because they don't read the papers they are signing when they get a loan for a mortgage. People need to know the difference between the different loans that are out there. The only question that I have after this unit is can what the banks do be made illegal?
>
> The most helpful part of this unit was the dynamical systems. As soon as I really learned how to work with the dynamical systems, I came home and grabbed my credit card bill and the mortgage and plugged them into the calculator. Paying the minimum balance on my credit card wasn't enough. I would have to pay double my minimum balance to get out of it in less time. Obviously, what my mother is paying isn't

enough to finish paying the house in 30 years. The worst part about this is that what she pays isn't 30 percent of her income—it's more.

Despite these and other students' claims of understanding DDSs and finding them useful to read the world, learning the math, with conceptual understanding, was not easy. Almost all my students had attended under-resourced neighborhood schools that, despite many teachers' efforts, insufficiently prepared most for advanced mathematics. Some students in class had solid mathematical backgrounds, some quite shaky ones, and others in between. However, I believe two factors contributed to students' persistence. First, students were overall engaged in the year's topics, which they chose to study and which were personally meaningful—the 2008 presidential election, displacement, HIV/AIDS, criminalization of youth/people of color, and sexism. Second, math provided a way to understand their lives and answer their questions, including: Whose community is this?

Conclusion

It was important that students came to understand, as Renee said, that they had the same struggle, in a context of divide and conquer. Racism has long impacted Lawndale, and racial division between African Americans and Latinxs is one of its many effects—in Sojo's first years, Black students were sometimes unwelcome in Little Village and even attacked after school. The displacement unit supported Black-Brown unity (as people here call it) by having students analyze the sociopolitical conditions of their lives—through mathematics—and realize that they have common enemies *and* a common struggle. As Mónica wrote, the best way is to unite to "fight the bigger people out there" and not each other. Though not all students experienced or knew much about each other's neighborhoods, I am confident that all students left class with a deeper understanding of their commonalities. To reemphasize: This unit was based on interconnected mathematical and political analyses. In my view, this provides a basis for multiracial solidarity, which we will need in order to read and write the world—with and without mathematics. ✻

Reprinted from *Rethinking Schools*, Spring 2013 (vol. 27, no. 3).

Reclaiming Hidden History
High School Students Face Opposition When They Create a Slavery Walking Tour in Manhattan

BY MICHAEL PEZONE AND ALAN SINGER

A group of more than 60 high school students chanted, "Time to tell the truth, our local history; New York was a land of slavery!" and "Resist, resist, resist! Time to be free! Resist, resist, resist! No more slavery!" as they marched around New York City's financial district. At each of 11 stops they hung up posters detailing New York City's complicity with slavery and stories of heroic resistance, and they handed out hundreds of fliers to tourists, workers, and students on school trips.

According to Shiyanne Moore, a senior at Law, Government, and Community Service Magnet High School in Cambria Heights, Queens, and a trip organizer, "I learned the truth about our city's past from this project. I also learned the more noise you make, the more things can change. Permanent historical markers about slavery could inspire people to fight for change. I am proud that I was involved in helping to create the African American Slavery Trail."

Shouting was especially spirited at the downtown offices of Citibank, because one of the bank's founders helped finance the illegal transatlantic slave trade from 1830 to 1860. Kerry-Ann Rowe, another high school senior, told assembled students, "New York City's role in the African slave trade has been erased from history. This trip gives us a chance to write it back in."

Evidently the students had an impact. A reporter from *Newsday*, one of New York's major daily newspapers, accompanied them on the walk and wrote a feature story on the project that included photographs of their posters.

They also had an impact in other ways. The director of public safety for the Downtown Alliance, a nonprofit group that advocates for businesses in the New York financial district, sent one of the tour guides an email that read "It is not legal to place these posters on traffic poles, light poles, or pedestrian poles. We, the Alliance, are removing the posters and have them at the office of public safety located at 104 Washington Street, NYC."

When the class met to evaluate the trip, students engaged in a provocative discussion about the ways in which corporate interests dominate public spaces. They wanted to know "How can the voices of the 'little people' be heard?"

The students were outraged by the actions of the Downtown Alliance. "Who gave the Downtown Alliance the authority to touch our signs?" asked Jennifer Caroccio. "We put back some of the pieces of history that the people in power would rather stay hidden." The students believed the Downtown Alliance violated their freedom of speech by taking down the posters.

The class decided to contact the reporter from *Newsday* and see if she could help them make their grievances public. The following Friday, *Newsday* ran another feature story, this time focusing on civil liberties issues. The story was picked up by a local ABC television affiliate that sent a crew to the school to interview students. The television news story brought the history of slavery in New York to a much broader audience. The broadcast journalist also went to a number of the Lower Manhattan sites visited by the students.

But the story did not end there.

The *New York Post*, a right-wing tabloid, published an editorial denouncing the high school students for illegally hanging up "homemade signs" on public property: lampposts. It sarcastically suggested that the name of their school be changed to the "High School for Ignorance and Law-Breaking."

Once again students met, and with the help of their teachers, they drafted a response. Although the *Post* refused to publish their letter, they disseminated it widely on the internet. Students explained that the "field trip was not designed or intended as an act of civil disobedience" and apologized "if any city ordinance was violated." However, they did not "believe anyone should be faulted for making an incorrect assumption about the law concerning the hanging of temporary posters. Any resident or visitor to the city sees posters hanging all over. Last election cycle, [New York City] Mayor Michael Bloomberg

> ## "Who gave the Downtown Alliance the authority to touch our sign? We put back some of the pieces of history that the people in power would rather stay hidden."

had campaign posters hanging all around the city. We believe the law is used selectively as a device to censor unwanted messages."

They explained that they are "committed to working within the law to get permanent historical markers erected commemorating the history of slavery in downtown Manhattan," and planned "to meet, and hopefully to work with, the Downtown Alliance and any other interested parties in a productive manner."

The bulk of their letter focused on the "hostility and name-calling" in the editorial that they found "counterproductive" and insulting. "It was inappropriate for the *New York Post* to mock the students and the school. The students at Law, Government, and Community Service Magnet High School are African American, Caribbean, and Hispanic. We question whether your editorial would have had a similar mocking tone if the students were from a suburban school."

They also accused the newspaper of irresponsible journalism, saying the editorial mischaracterized a statement by one of the students.

In the following weeks, a committee met with the Downtown Alliance to secure its cooperation in a campaign for permanent historical markers. Students plan to resume their campaign for permanent historical markers in the 2006–07 school year. On May 25, students are planning another walking tour of the slavery sites. Teams of students from Law, Government, and Community Service Magnet School plan to station themselves at the historical sites in Lower Manhattan. Some students will hold up posters and act as tour guides, and others will escort middle and high school classes from other schools as they visit the sites. They are planning to hold the tour in May because in May 1741 Africans accused of plotting a slave rebellion in Lower Manhattan were publicly executed.

New York and Slavery

The project developed out of discussions of the conflict over slavery in the early years of the settlement of the British North American colonies in Michael Pezone's 12th-grade Advanced Placement government class at Law, Government, and Community Service Magnet High. Students were especially knowledgeable about the history of enslavement in New York City and its merchants' involvement in the transatlantic slave trade because many had taken Pezone's African American history elective course where they helped field-test lessons from the New York State Council for the Social Studies' curriculum guide *New York and Slavery: Complicity and Resistance*.

The students were able to plan one field trip and decided they wanted to take a walking tour of slavery-related sites in Lower Manhattan. The difficulty was that other than the colonial-era African Burial Ground, which was uncovered during excavations for a federal office building in 1991, these sites, and slavery in New York in general, have been erased from historical memory. There is not even a historical marker at the South Street Seaport in the financial district of Manhattan where enslaved Africans were traded in the 17th and 18th centuries and where illegal slaving expeditions were planned and financed until the time of the American Civil War.

New York City has scores of museums listed on a popular website for tourists (ny.com). They celebrate art, science, culture, and history, including the histories of numerous ethnic groups. But there is not one museum or permanent exhibit on slavery in New York City. There is plenty of material and a high demand for this type of museum. The New-York Historical Society has sponsored two special shows on the history of slavery in New York City that have drawn thousands of visitors, including tens of thousands of secondary school students.

Students met with Hofstra University's Alan Singer, editor of the curriculum guide, and many realized that the problem was largely political rather than historical or educational. Students decided on a bit of guerrilla theater that would combine the study of history with political action. Students mapped out the walking tour and designed poster-sized placards including information about the "Slave Market" on Wall Street, the bank that financed the slave trade, the meetinghouse where "blackbirders" (slave traders) planned their voyages, and Black insurrections in 1712 and 1741.

The students wrote a press release, invited local politicians and students from other schools to join them, and then visited the sites and posted their own historical markers. Two local council members expressed interest and have remained in contact with the teachers, although they were unable to attend. However, 20 students from a high school in another part of the city whose teacher had received an invitation via email joined the Law, Government, and Community Service students. Two other classes that were visiting Lower Manhattan on field trips also joined the group for part of the tour.

The students expressed amazement at what they learned during the project. In her evaluation, Naadira Nemley wrote, "It is hard to believe that Citibank comes from a bank that helped to finance the slave trade or that Wall Street was once a slave market. I am African American and I never knew about this history. Learning about the African Free School in 1787 really helps me to appreciate the opportunity I have to learn in school. Taking part in this political action made me feel like a young activist. Now that they have taken down our posters, I understand that I took part in one of the steps to change New York."

Celeste Rimple wrote, "I never realized how many locations and businesses were directly connected to slavery and the slave trade. It is disappointing that there are no permanent markers in the downtown area. It is disrespectful to the people who were enslaved and the people who fought against slavery. My topic was the Amistad Committee. They worked hard to end slavery but their office was destroyed by a pro-slavery mob right here in New York City."

In their class letter to the *Post*, students expressed a new understanding of both education and social struggle. They wrote, "We are proud to have engaged in an activity that has helped to educate many New Yorkers about a crucial part of the city's history. We believe that students should be actively engaged as citizens, and we are happy to say that our teachers and our school encourage us to do so." ✳

Reprinted from *Rethinking Schools*, Winter 2006/2007 (vol. 21, no. 2).

Teaching a Native Feminist Read

BY ANGIE MORRILL WITH K. WAYNE YANG

Her face drained, her body went stiff,
and she stared at me as if I had risen,
an Indigenous skeleton clad in decrepit rags,
from beneath the clay bricks of the courtyard.
—Deborah Miranda, from "Lying to Children
About the California Missions and the Indians"

Native writer, poet, and professor Deborah Miranda describes visiting Mission Dolores in San Francisco where some of her ancestors once lived (and died). By chance, she meets a young girl and her mother in the process of shooting a video for the girl's 4th-grade California mission project. Each year, half a million 4th graders and their parents build a model Spanish mission. Half a million mini-monuments to genocide. But this particular student had chosen to do an informative video on her assigned mission. "Guess what?" Miranda reveals to the enthusiastic videographers, "I'm a member of the Ohlone/Costanoan-Esselen Nation myself! Some of my ancestors *lived* in this mission." The result is a bit of cognitive dissonance for the 4th grader, who had been taught that California Indians were missionized out of existence.

Having me suddenly appear in the middle of her video project must have been a lot like turning the corner to find the (dead) person you were talking about suddenly in your face, talking back.

Miranda's story, "Lying to Children About the California Missions and the Indians," which appeared in a 2015 issue of *Indian Country Today* and was later was reprinted by *The Huffington Post* and the Zinn Education Project, helps us think through the stakes and state of curriculum about and not by Native people: curriculum that teaches Indigenous disappearance. Schools train students to see the world as non-Indigenous and to never see modern Native peoples. You may have experienced this already. As Native parents who volunteer in their children's classrooms, as Native educators who generously share stories in classrooms that are predominantly not Native, as Native professionals who show up for Indigenous Peoples Day, students will ask you where your headdress, your moccasins, your quiver are. They cannot see you unless you are encased in costume and surrounded by archaeological artifacts. Even history lessons that critique European, American, Canadian, and Mexican nations' perpetrations of Indigenous genocide nonetheless teach disappearance because genocide is such a totalizing narrative. We are taught that Indigenous people are few and far removed, especially from urban areas where people of color live, despite the fact that all urban land is Indigenous land and despite how most Indigenous people live in urban areas outside of their traditional homelands. When we only teach histories of genocide, we can accidentally reify genocide as the future.

Even Ethnic Studies can teach a curriculum of disappearance when it only equates Indigeneity with ancestry, with everybody's precolonial roots. When Native people become only our precolonial predecessors, this comes dangerously close to saying all Indigenous people are dead and all colonized people are Indigenous. Furthermore, Ethnic Studies has a tendency to group Indigenous peoples as another racialized ethnic group instead of as sovereign nations. This teaches students to assume that being Indigenous is connected to phenotype ("looking

Indian") or genotype ("having Indian blood"). However, Indigenous peoples are complex politically, culturally, phenotypically, and yes, genetically.

Back to Miranda's story—how can it be that a student cannot see a Native woman before her? Because students are trained to look for "real Indians," they are unable to see real ndns at all. I use "ndn" here because I am also writing to Native readers. Hi, Native reader! The use of it for this article does not mean non-Native readers should use it to address Native or non-Native people in any context at any time. I am trying to be specific to my own location, and ndn is the most appropriate word for a particular North American Indian 21st-century experience. Not all Indigenous people are ndn. Kānaka Maoli, Taíno, and Purépecha, for example, are Native but not ndn. When I read ndn everywhere, I am talking about my own ndn recognition of your experiences—that we are related. The intent is to show-not-tell how ndn Native feminists recognize Indigeneity outside of the logics of federal tribal recognition.

A Native feminist read resists disappearance through ways of recognizing Native people beyond the usual lenses of costumes, culture, ancestors. In skateboards and vintage cars, wizards and lightsabers, bad jobs and bad boys, Black girls and white-appearing girls, Native feminists read Indigeneity everywhere all the time. In my article "Time Traveling Dogs (and Other Native Feminist Ways to Defy Dislocations)" (*Cultural Studies* <—> *Critical Methodologies*, vol. 17, issue 1), I describe it this way:

> A Native feminist reading practice . . . is a methodology that attends to the transhistorical feminist labor of bearing an Indigenous future into existence out of a genocidal present. It is a methodology that involves reading against disappearance; it involves reading futures yet in store for Native lives.

Native feminists read the future. It is a decolonized future, an Indigenous future. We welcome you to join us.

Think of this as a starting primer on Native feminisms. In this short space, we introduce lots of teachable film and television story lines—*The Outsiders, Game of Thrones, Queen Sugar, One Day at a Time*—

in hopes that one or more of these may find their way into your classroom. We spend some time with the film *Lilo & Stitch* and provide some step-by-step ways of using this movie to teach about settler colonialism and Native feminisms.

We write this as two friends who are lucky to collaborate in writing, teaching, and art. Angie is a Native mother, educator, filmmaker, Klamath tribal member, Modoc and Cherokee descendent, and current director of Indian Education for Portland Public Schools. Wayne is a father, sometime math and science teacher, Asian settler "of color," school founder, and current professor of Ethnic Studies at the University of California, San Diego. Yet at times we write in the first-person singular in this essay—the "I." In these moments, we hope you hear a Native feminist voice, Angie's voice in particular.

It's a Postapocalyptic Situation: Reading Settler Colonialism

> *"Hello, Cobra Bubbles?*
> *Aliens are attacking my house!"*
> —Lilo from *Lilo & Stitch*

I am inspired by and feel kinship with writers and educators like Cutcha Risling Baldy, who teaches her students to read the zombie apocalypse in *The Walking Dead* as settler colonialism. She says that for Native peoples, colonization was *the apocalypse*, and waking up every day is *the postapocalypse*. It is a reality of never knowing who is going to pop up and try to kill you, kill your children in your own neighborhood. It is the reality of postapocalypse stress disorder. It is the reality of confronting profound moral and ethical dilemmas that "normal" Americans only see on TV—imagining what you have to do to survive, wondering whether the apocalypse is ever gonna end. This read of *The Walking Dead* is a Native feminist read of an AMC TV series. It is also a read of reality.

Settler colonialism is when an empire comes to your lands to not only exploit your people and extract natural resources, not only to dominate and oppress your nation, but also to send settlers to occupy your home, to replace you, to make your home their home. Settler colonialism is when external colonialism and internal colonialism converge on the same place, when the center of empire is built on top of the colony. Settlers claim to be the new "native," a lie that in order to appear true requires the death of all Native peoples. Natives somehow survive, but you see how this is a postapocalyptic reality.

One obvious way to teach about settler colonialism is to use films by and about Native people. *Rhymes for Young Ghouls* is one of my favorites, featuring Aila, a Mi'kmaq youth who exacts her revenge against an abusive Indian agent after her father is jailed and she is thrown into a boarding school.

However, we want our students to observe neighborhoods, communities, and cities that are ostensibly not Indigenous and still be able to read modern Native experience, complexity, and life

> ## Survivance implies a life beyond survival, beyond bare life, a set of creative strategies beyond simply not-dying, beyond victimry. At the heart of it are stories—stories that we tell, and also stories that we are making, stories that time travel from the past into the future.

everywhere. Thus, we also encourage you to watch television and film not about Indigenous peoples and to read Indigenous peoples' situations in there anyway. From an ndn Native feminist perspective, I read super ndn stories everywhere—that is, narratives seemingly not about ndns that are oh-so ndn.

For me, *The Outsiders* is one such super ndn love story. Sodapop, Ponyboy, and Darry are orphans—their parents died in a car accident. They live in Oklahoma, which is Indian Country—another clue. Darry is a gifted athlete who works hard to keep his family together. They are outsiders on their own land, struggling to survive, and their clique, the Greasers,

are a kind of warrior band of brothers. After being attacked on their own land, they have to run away. Their bonds are tested and they hold up.

Many school districts have classroom book sets of *The Outsiders*, plus school libraries often keep the 1983 film adaptation of S. E. Hinton's 1967 novel. Teaching *The Outsiders* as a super ndn story would not require a radical change in curriculum, just a radical re-reading. We think that the book could be taught in parallel to the American Indian Movement, to the creation of the reservation system, to ongoing encroachments on Native land. For advanced high school and college students, the film could be paired/queered with Craig Womack's *Drowning in Fire*.

Super ndn stories are not just about desecrations. They are about decolonial love. We quote Leanne Simpson quoting Junot Díaz: "Is it possible to love one's broken-by-the-coloniality-of-power self in another broken-by-the-coloniality-of-power person?" Teenage love in the time of the postapocalypse feels like decolonial love.

We Are Nations: Reading Sovereignty

> *"A dragon is not a slave."*
> —Daenerys Targaryen from *Game of Thrones*

Game of Thrones has a Native feminist story line. Daenerys Targaryen is the super white queen. The Dothraki are a plains people with a horse culture, complete with bows and arrows, often referred to as "savages." They appear like the Indians that our students have been taught to see. Some might say that Daenerys is the white savior coming to rule over the Indigenous Dothraki. Maybe Ethnic Studies scholars might say this.

But my Native feminist read also sees in Daenerys an Indigenous sovereign nation, sovereign always, sovereign forever. Sovereignty is like the Silvan Elves in *Lord of the Rings*: kinda badass, kinda scary, occasionally kind, and super sovereign from the nations of men. We understand plant and animal relatives to be sovereign nations. They do not belong to us. They might not even like us. They might fight us. They might sometimes help us. In his book *Drowning in Fire*, Womack describes an underwater nation of monsters, the Tie-snakes, "something white man has never saw or caught." Dragons are like that. A sovereign people with whom you might have a treaty.

High school teachers might compare this to the ways tribal nations resist the Marshall Trilogy and Western legal constructions, the way a people decide outside of colonial issues of blood quantum and federal recognition who belongs to them. The Dothraki choose Daenerys. They choose who belongs to them. This is not about phenotype or genotype. Indigenous nations exist outside of the racial recognition that settler governments have set aside for them. We recognize ourselves. Like Daenerys says, "Do not touch me. I am Daenerys Stormborn of the House Targaryen. The First of Her Name, the Unburnt, Queen of Meereen, Queen of the Andals and the Rhoynar and the First Men, Khaleesi of the Great Grass Sea, Breaker of Chains, and Mother of Dragons."

Daenerys as a representation of Indigenous sovereignty is a Native feminist reading because it reads complexity in descent, in politics, and in belonging. Indigenous peoples are politically complicated. We are not just warriors, not just resistance fighters. We are also dragons. We are nations.

One Day at a Time: Reading Survivance in Black and Latinx Television

> *Don't you worry none, we'll just take it as it comes. One day at a time.*
> —from the theme song of *One Day at a Time*

Survivance is word that was sung into existence by Anishinaabe writer Gerald Vizenor in 1994. It looks like the word *survival*, as well as *resistance, vivacity*. Life. Vizenor deliberately never defines it, because you are supposed to just get it and play with it. Survivance is not quite English. It's dragonese—because everyone knows that dragons tell great stories, riddles, and jokes. Survivance implies a life beyond survival, beyond bare life, a set of creative strategies beyond simply not-dying, beyond victimry. At the heart of it are stories—stories that we tell, and also stories that we are making, stories that time travel from the past into the future. Let us call these survivance stories. A Native feminist read reads survivance stories everywhere.

If you are a Black feminist, you might get this part better than we can explain it. Black feminisms and Native feminisms are connected.

Queen Sugar is a Black show for Black audiences, but it is super ndn to me. Ava DuVernay, who helped create the show and who directs the first two episodes, lingers with so much affection on the actors who portray the Bordelon family. The pilot episode deals with the death of the family patriarch. He suffers a stroke and his grandson, Blue, is brought to his hospital room by his son, Ralph Angel. Ralph Angel helps to arrange his father's arm over his young son. This moment reminded me of my son and my late mother's hospital room interactions, where familial love is bare, and I think, decolonial.

In the second episode, the family prepares for the funeral. The eldest daughter, Charley, is well-off, college educated, and in a troubled high-profile marriage to a basketball star. She returns from Los Angeles to Louisiana, but her siblings resent her attempts to help. Charley hires caterers for the funeral. Her sister, Nova, lets her know what's up, saying the difficult things that you can only say at home:

> How long you been gone, huh? You ain't been gone that long. How come you don't remember how it is done?

Nova then reminds her:

> We don't honor our father by having strangers serve those who are grieving. We serve comfort food to those that need comfort and we do it with our own hands! That's how a family does a repast.

Nova telling Charley that she forgot where she came from feels super ndn. There is that fear of becoming white, of losing who you are out there away from family. Your family won't let you forget how to act. Even though she is younger, Nova speaks to the ancestors and honors them in the appropriate ways. I don't know if this Black family is Native or not, but I recognize the things that they do that are like the things we do. And in this way I read Native presence and survivance through this family story. Because they want to keep the 800 acres their father left them, they have to confront painful truths. They were enslaved and then made to sharecrop on the land. The land they are trying so hard to hold on to has been paid for in blood, paid for too many times through white families (and their former owners) murdering their relatives. This story about a Black family resonates with themes of violence, murder, and dispossession in my family history. Our familial connections are not analogies. Black and Indigenous connections are historical and material—land and labor made white wealth possible.

I also see Native presence in Latinx stories. In 2017, Netflix produced a reboot of the once-popular CBS series *One Day at a Time*. The original debuted in 1975, featuring Ann Romano, a white single mother with two teenage daughters. I was a kid living with a single mother and two sisters, and I did not have to perform a Native feminist reading to see similarities between the television family and my own. Ann Romano was a feminist mother raising feminist daughters. She was struggling and she was not ashamed.

The reboot kept the song, the single mom, and the two kids. But this time the family is Cuban-American. The mother is army vet Penelope Alvarez, who supports the family as a nurse and suffers from PTSD.

Although the family is not Native, they are not not-Native. Cuba is home for the Taíno and Ciboney. I refuse to accept colonial narratives of their erasure any more than my own. Still, this is a Latinx family and the whole season is leading up to the contested *quinceañera* of Elena.

Elena has a close friend, Carmen, who wears dark goth or punk makeup and speaks in a don't-care deadpan. In the episode "Strays," the girls are sitting very close together on the couch sharing a Snuggie. The grandmother expresses some concern about their relationship, floating the idea to Penelope that her daughter Elena is "queer." Carmen's parents have been deported and she is supposed to go to Texas to stay with her brother and finish school, but she hangs on to what she knows and her friendship with Elena. When Penelope finds out Carmen has been secretly staying with them, leaving the house in the evening then sneaking back into Elena's room through the fire escape, she is kind but arrangements are made for Carmen to do what her parents want, to go to Texas with her brother.

It is never defined whether the girls are lovers or not, but their friendship and Carmen's punk style remind me of two famous teenage lovers, Maggie and Hopey, from Los Bros Hernandez's groundbreaking graphic novels *Love and Rockets*, which connects urban Chicanx punks with Indigenous Mexican villagers with science fiction futures. Maggie Chascarillo is Mexican American via Texas, and Hopey Glass is white and Colombian. Since their creation in 1981, they have become queer punk Chicana icons. In their connection, and in the one between Carmen and Elena, there is lifesaving survivance. It is a super ndn love story.

Carmen is my queer ndn woman, a survivor. She shows up, and I see her. I do not want to erase anyone by claiming your queer Latinx Carmen as mine. But if I waited for an ndn woman to show up on my television, I would still be waiting.

The relationship between two young queer Chicanas brings futurity to the narrative. Young brown women will find each other, will help one another survive. Maggie and Hopey live in a present that is also a sci-fi sort of future. Later in the TV series, Elena and Carmen are seen talking on their computers. I think of those picture phones we were promised long ago when we still used landlines. The postapocalypse is still a future.

Lilo & Stitch: A Native Feminist Unit

Lilo & Stitch is about a Kānaka Maoli misfit girl, Lilo; and Nani, her sister who raises her; and Stitch, a criminal extraterrestrial who ultimately befriends her. It directly engages many themes that support a Native feminist read. It is a useful film in being flexible in age appropriateness. Disney rates it G. Molly Swain and Chelsea Vowel, Native women podcasters of *Métis in Space*, rate it "good enough to recommend for my *kookum* [grandma]." They also say the movie could well be called "Nani has a really stressful week." Nani is Lilo's big sister and legal guardian. She loses her job, fends off aliens, and keeps her sister from becoming a ward of the state all in the same week. Molly and Chelsea's read is a super Native feminist way to see the realities of the welfare state, underemployment, navigating white society, orphaning, and non-normative motherhood in a Disney movie.

As a film about Kānaka Maoli sisters, Indigeneity is front and center. Below are some possible guiding questions to enhance a Native feminist read of *Lilo & Stitch* and to organize a unit for your class. If you're a teacher, the guiding questions are probably all you need for your alchemy of lessons, assignments, and pedagogy. But if you need help exploring these questions, listen to Molly and Chelsea's Season 3, Episode 6 podcast of *Métis in Space*.

Reel and "real Indians" are not real.
What are examples of stories about Indigenous people?

As a pre-assessment discussion, you might ask your students for examples of stories about Native youth, children, or families. Perhaps some of your Indigenous students will have stories from their own families or communities. Perhaps a student may recount a tale they heard from a Native storyteller. Someone might identify a film representing modern Indigenous peoples, like *Whale Rider* or even *Frozen River*. More than likely, many students will mention Pocahontas or some other settler narrative about an Indigenous historical character. Maybe none of them will mention a survivance story.

This is a good time to demythologize "reel" and "real" Indians.

Hollywood and dime novel Westerns helped to create "reel Indians": celluloid fantasies of woo-able Indian princesses, murderable savages, emulatable horseback warriors, and adoptable noble sidekicks. Professional and amateur anthropologists in the shape of photographers, documentarians, and travel writers have helped to create "real Indians": persistent representations of "authentic" Indigenous peoples engaged in traditional handicrafts, living in the bush, wearing full regalia, unsmiling, fading into a sepia-toned past. These reel/real hegemonic representations have been extensively critiqued and disrupted by many Native cultural producers.

Cinematic representations of Native peoples—whether flattering like "Iron Eyes Cody" and "Pocahontas" or not flattering like every John Wayne movie—train students not to see us. Textbooks that focus on anthropological descriptions of "real Indians" or "authentic" Native Americans train students not to see us. You might ask your students, if we take away the cinematic and the anthropological—the reel and the "real"—what makes for an Indigenous story?

Enter Lilo and Nani. Do they fit into these categories of reel Indian or "real Indian"? If not, then what themes make theirs an Indigenous story?

By the way, Lilo has an interesting hobby of taking photos of tourists. How does her hobby compare to anthropological photos of Indigenous peoples by the famous Edward Curtis?

Settler colonialism is postapocalyptic.
What was Lilo and Nani's apocalypse?

Lilo's name echoes that of Queen Liliuokalani, the last reigning monarch of Hawai'i. Hawai'i is unceded Indigenous land, illegally annexed by the United States in 1898. Queen Liliuokalani fought the white-settler, corporate interests that were taking over Hawai'i, fighting to reverse the terms of the "Bayonet Constitution" forced upon the previous monarch in 1887. Corporate and missionary interests staged a coup d'état in 1893, seizing and imprisoning the queen. Even while imprisoned in her own home for two years, she smuggled out notes and songs. Perhaps the most famous of her songs is "Aloha Oe." Often interpreted as a love song, it is also read by many Native Hawaiians as a song remembering a sovereign Hawai'i. *Farewell to thee.* And a promise of a Kānaka Maoli future. *Until we meet again.*

"Aloha Oe" is sung a capella by the two sisters, Lilo and Nani—unusual for a Disney movie lush with soundtrack and music. It is a meditative moment, when Nani is about to tell Lilo that she is going to be given up to the state.

"No one is left behind," Lilo frequently says, "or forgotten." Lilo and Nani are orphans; their parents died in a car accident. The orphaning, the threat of family abduction by the state, and the right of the state to enter your home at will are Kānaka Maoli realities that feel super ndn too. "I remember everyone that leaves," Lilo says. Who else is Lilo remembering? What other loss is she recounting?

Settler colonialism is anti-Black.
Who is "Black" in Lilo & Stitch?

You might begin by asking your students, "What is Stitch's crime?" Stitch is "Experiment 626," the illegal genetic experiment of Dr. Jumba Jookiba. This alien is also alienated. Stitch has no birthright, no parents—manufactured into an existence already destined for violence. For college students, you might read Stitch through Orlando Patterson's writings about slavery and social death, where "natal alienation" is "the loss of ties of birth in both ascending and descending generations." Stitch is banished to a prison colony planet, but he escapes en route and crashes a stolen spaceship into Hawai'i. He is virtually indestructible with very destructive tendencies. He might bring destruction to Lilo and Nani, to Hawai'i, to Earth, to the United Galactic Federation. But he has committed no crime. He is the crime.

For advanced high school and college students, you might compare Stitch to the medieval legal concept of *homo sacer*—the sacred/cursed man who anyone can murder and it is not considered a crime. Homo sacer coincidentally was used as the legal justification for killing Indians without trial in the 1873 Modoc Wars and again used to justify torture of prisoners in Guantanamo in the infamous 2003 "torture memos." Homo sacer is also clearly in effect with the routine murder of Black people by police or by civilian vigilantes. Like homo sacer, like being Black in America, Stitch's is a crime of existence.

One defining feature of settler colonialism is the settler-native-slave triad. That is, settlers not only come to occupy a land by eradicating Native peoples, they also enslave other Indigenous people—making another class of people without human status or human rights—in order to work the land but never to settle on it. Thus colonized relationships are twisted into a triangle: "the settler" who owns property and has rights; "the native" who must be made extinct by genocide or by disappearance; and "the slave" who is not human and is subject to capture, torture, dislocation, dispossession, and death. We see how anti-Blackness in North America is part and parcel to settler colonialism: The killing, incarceration, and uprooting of Black people are part of the colonization of Indigenous land.

The criminalization of Stitch's very existence— your students might read this as anti-Blackness.

What about Mr. Cobra Bubbles? Wayne got a chance to ask Molly Swain from *Métis in Space* this very question. She said to think about the work that Blackness is called to do in white cinema. Black bodies are used to symbolize all kinds of things in the white cinematic imagination—magic, victimhood,

criminality, subservience to whiteness, sidekick to the white hero, urban hip, white anxiety about race, physical prowess, sexual prowess, swag. Images of big Black men are often used to represent threat. Here, Cobra Bubbles is many of these tropes wrapped into one contradictory package. He is Black cool. He is the shadow state, only with swag and a conscience like Nick Fury in *The Avengers* or Will Smith in *Men in Black*. He is threatening. He is poetic. But most of all, he is Black on demand for the Disney movie. Here, his Blackness is treated as the property of the Hollywood culture industries.

Blackness is often used to represent racial projects of the state. Toni Cade Bambara describes this as the "bribe contract" with the state, whereby Black people are expected to participate in the extermination of Indigenous peoples, of enemy Others in war, in exchange for a never-to-be-fulfilled promise of equal rights. We might remember the Black men who served as Rough Riders for Teddy Roosevelt in Cuba, in Panama, in the Philippines, or the Buffalo Soldiers who fought in the Indian wars, or Carter G. Woodson, author of *The Miseducation of the Negro* and the founder of Black History Month, who served as a supervisor for the U.S. Army colonial schools in the Philippines. Maybe this is not so different from being "a special classification" social worker in Hawai'i. Read this way, Cobra Bubbles got some double consciousness for sure.

Cobra Bubbles implies to Stitch that he will be temporarily left alone if he can just pretend to be "a model citizen." For high school and college students, you might discuss "model citizen" with respect to neoliberalism and the politics of respectability. Or with their own realities: What have they been promised in exchange for good grades and good behavior? Do they believe this promise will be kept?

Survivance stories show a complex and textured life. How is Nani and Lilo's story a survivance story?

> Lilo: We're a broken family, aren't we?
> Nani: No. . . . Maybe, a little. Maybe a lot.

Nani is struggling to be a parent to her younger sister. She is under surveillance, and if she cannot parent Lilo successfully, she will lose her to the state. Lilo is a lonely, awkward, and socially maladjusted kid.

But their "broken family" is more than just broken. Their lives are filled with humor, with loving moments, with awkwardly expressed desires. Lilo treats a doll for its brain infection, studies voodoo, languishes to Elvis, and collects photographs of tourists. Lilo and Nani are not waiting to be saved. They are living their lives one day at a time.

Indigenous relations are a decolonial love.
Who is hard to love in Lilo & Stitch?
Lilo has a "pet" who is not her property. Lilo talks to fish. Lilo talks to the girls who mock her and to the girl whom she socks in the face. Lilo is not her sister's property. Lilo treats herself as sovereign. She treats everyone else as sovereign too. Sovereignty is the basis for relation. Lilo sees relations in fish, in a criminal alien, in her sister, in photographs of ancestors.

Importantly, we can read *Lilo & Stitch* as a future for Indigenous and Black relations. Lilo treats Stitch as a relative. Therefore, Nani has to accept Stitch as her relative too. Can you read a decolonial love story between Native sisters, between Kānaka Maoli girl and criminal alien, between a living family and one that is no more?

Indigenous futurity
What is an Indigenous future?
Lilo & Stitch is a science fiction story. We are not only seeing aliens, we are seeing a kind of Western liberal future. In the United Galactic Federation, we can read liberal democracy, liberal notions of preserving species, and liberal notions of responsible and rational galactic citizens. Contrast this with earthly neoliberal notions of social workers, responsible parenting, having a job, being model citizens. This liberal democracy is backed by enormous firepower—almost absolute firepower. Contrast this with the modern military, prison, and policing industrial complexes. The United Galactic Federation represents one possible future for us: a neoliberal, settler future. It is the logical future of Western civilization.

By contrast, Nani, Lilo, and David (Nani's boyfriend) are forwarding a different Indigenous future, a Kānaka Maoli future. It is not a future based on wealth, on acquisition, on mastering white man's education. It is a future based on survivance and rela-

tion. This future has surfing holidays, breaks from the daily business of surviving the genocidal institutions of "benign" governments. In this future they recognize each other as family (we are not going to repeat that overused line about *ohana*, sorry). In this future, criminal alien and Kānaka Maoli are in relation, living free on Hawaiian waters and land.

* * *

Native feminisms are plural—*a* Native feminist read means that there are diverse Indigenous peoples with many other Native feminist reads. Mine is one that reads ndn stories—all but disappeared in our schools and media—and thus reads relation where others might not, recognizing, as Native feminists do, a story that could belong to our own families.

Many times a Native feminist read means recognizing Native experiences outside of where you might likely find them: in a show about a Cuban American family, about Black life, about kids trying to survive. A Native feminist read is not appropriative. It is a recognition. It is saying, "I see you."

I am a Native feminist and I see Indigenous people. Can you see me? Look for postapocalypse stress disorder, for complexity, for decolonial love, for survivance. You might find me. I am breathing smoke into your ear. I am teaching you to laugh. I am saving your ass. I am telling you a story. I am prophesying a decolonial world to come. I am teaching you the way to make it there.

Seeing genocide is not the hard part. Seeing modern Native people is the hard part. Seeing Native women is the harder part. And seeing what Native women see is the most important part—it is the Native feminist read. You may be Native, you may be non-Native. You may or may not feel ready to do this. You can and should teach your students a Native feminist read. We are asking you to teach nothing less than an Indigenist literacy. Teach your students to read against colonization, to read the Indigenous world that they inhabit. You got this. You got them. They will get this. ✳

Teaching John Bell's Four I's of Oppression

BY R. TOLTEKA CUAUHTIN

Oppression is complex and at times difficult to see, recognize, and name in its different manifestations. How can we even begin to break down these nuances in a way that is accessible to middle and high school students? Youth are very capable of these understandings, and undoubtedly many have already experienced oppression firsthand in their own lives, communities, and schools at a young age. Providing a framework and language for students is very helpful in moving from an experiential level of oppression to a conceptual level of analysis as a part of their empowerment. One such framework I've found useful in my teaching is John Bell's "Four I's of Oppression"—*ideological, institutional, interpersonal,* and *internalized*—which is also present in the Ethnic Studies Framework (p. 65). Bell was a co-founder of Youth Build USA, an organization that believes "the intelligence and positive energy of young people needs to be liberated and enlisted in solving the problems facing our society." On their website, they also share more about the educator/theorist/organizer:

> John Bell has 33 years of experience in the youth field as a teacher, counselor, community organizer, program developer, leadership trainer, director, and parent of three. He was a founding staff member of three youth organizations: Youth Action Program (in 1978) in East Harlem, the originator of YouthBuild; Children of War (in 1984), an international youth leadership organization; and YouthBuild USA (in 1988).

This framework has been used by more community organizations over the years, including the Grassroots Institute for Fundraising Training and the Western Justice Center (WJC). In particular, WJC has produced an excellent video, visually and thematically conceptualized and narrated by Eliana Pipes, that works as a multimodal pedagogical tool to help teach the four I's. (Find it on YouTube by searching for "Legos and the Four I's of Oppression.") Many others have used this framework as well within Ethnic Studies courses and beyond. Samantha Siegeler and Kaitlin Smith of Social Justice Humanitas Academy in the Los Angeles Unified School District have adapted Bell's text for classroom use, adding an annotation column to help teach the four I's of oppression framework. *

The Four I's of Oppression

Reprinted courtesy of John Bell

Ideological Oppression

First, any oppressive system has, at its core, the idea that one group is somehow better than another, and in some measure has the right to control the other group. This idea gets elaborated in many ways—more intelligent, harder working, stronger, more capable, more noble, more deserving, more advanced, chosen, normal, superior, and so on. The dominant group holds this idea about itself. And, of course, the opposite qualities are attributed to the other group—stupid, lazy, weak, incompetent, worthless, less deserving, backward, abnormal, inferior, and so on.

Institutional Oppression

Institutional oppression is when the idea that one group is better than another group (and that it has the right to control the other) gets embedded in the institutions of the society—the laws, the legal system and police practice, the education system and schools, hiring policies, public policies, housing development, media images, political power, etc. When a woman makes two-thirds of what a man makes in the same job, it is institutionalized sexism. When one out of every four African American young men is currently in jail, on parole, or on probation, it is institutionalized racism. When psychiatric institutions and associations "diagnose" transgender people as having a mental disorder, it is institutionalized gender oppression and transphobia. Institutional oppression does not have to be intentional. For example, if a policy unintentionally reinforces and creates new inequalities between privileged and nonprivileged groups, it is considered institutional oppression.

Interpersonal Oppression

Interpersonal oppression is the idea that one group is better than another and has the right to control the other, which gets structured into institutions and gives permission and reinforcement for individual

oppression: a concept that describes a relationship of dominance and subordination between categories of people in which one benefits from the systematic abuse, exploitation, and injustice directed toward the other.

It is important to me to resist the oppression of

_____

_____

_____

because _____

_____

_____

_____

_____ .

An example of ideological oppression is the belief in the idea that undocumented people are _____

_____

_____

_____

_____ .

This belief is harmful to the oppressed group because _____

_____

_____

_____

_____ .

Another example of ideological oppression is the belief that _____

_____

_____

_____

_____ .

members of the dominant group to personally disrespect or mistreat individuals in the oppressed group. Interpersonal racism is what racist white people do to people of color up close—the racist jokes, the stereotypes, the beatings and harassment, the threats, etc. Similarly, interpersonal sexism is what sexist men do to women—the sexual abuse and harassment, the violence directed at women, the belittling or ignoring of women's thinking, the sexist jokes, etc.

Most people in the dominant group have internalized the negative messages about other groups, and consider their attitudes toward the other group as normal.

No "reverse racism": Oppressive attitudes and behaviors are backed up by institutional oppression. This helps to clarify the confusion around what some claim to be "reverse racism." People of color can have prejudices against and anger toward white people or individual white people. They can act out those feelings in destructive and hurtful ways toward whites. But in almost every case, this acting out will be severely punished. The force of the police and the courts will come crashing down on those people of color. The individual prejudice of people of color, for example, is not backed up by the legal system and prevailing white institutions. The oppressed group, therefore, does not have the power to enforce its prejudices, unlike the dominant group. Understanding institutional power dynamics are at the core of understanding that "reverse racism," "reverse sexism," etc. are not genuine dynamics.

A simple definition of racism, as a system, is:

RACISM = PREJUDICE + POWER

For example, the racist beating of Rodney King was carried out by the institutional force of the police, and upheld by the court system. This would not have happened if King had been white and the officers Black.

Internalized Oppression

The fourth way oppression works is within the groups of people who suffer the most from the mistreatment. Oppressed people internalize the ideology of infe-

power dynamic: the formation and maintenance of hierarchical structures of control or influence.

When people study the power dynamics in my household, they notice that _____ _____ _____ _____ _____ .

_____

dominant group: a social group that controls the value system and rewards in a particular society

Because the dominant group dictates beauty standards, people believe that _____ _____ _____ _____ .

_____

oppressed group: a disadvantaged social group that has been stripped of power or privilege within a particular society and are often treated as outsiders.

Some examples of oppressed groups in the United States are _____ , _____ and _____ _____ .

_____

inferior: the state of being lower in status or value than another.

Everyone knows that _____ is an inferior snack to _____ because _____ _____ _____ .

riority, they see it reflected in the institutions, they experience disrespect interpersonally from members of the dominant group, and they eventually come to internalize the negative messages about themselves. If we have been told we are stupid, worthless, abnormal, and have been treated as if we were all our lives, then it is not surprising that we would come to believe it.

Oppression always begins from outside the oppressed group, but once the ideas are internalized, the damage is done. If people from the oppressed group feel bad about themselves and do not have the power to direct those feelings back toward the dominant group without consequences, then they often direct their anger at themselves and on the people in the same group. Thus, people in any target group have to struggle hard to keep from feeling heavy feelings of powerlessness or despair. They often tend to put themselves and others down. Acting out internalized oppression can range from passive powerlessness to violent aggression. It is important to understand that some of the internalized patterns of behavior originally developed to keep people alive—they had real survival value.

On the way to eliminating institutional oppression, each oppressed group has to undo the internalized beliefs, attitudes, and behaviors that come from the oppression in order to build unity among people in its group. A unified group can support its leaders; feel proud of its history, contributions, and potential; develop the strength to challenge patterns that hold the group back; and organize itself into an effective force for social change.

Internalized privilege: Likewise, people who benefit the most from these systems internalize privilege. Privileged people involuntarily accept stereotypes and false assumptions about oppressed groups made by dominant culture. Internalized privilege includes acceptance of a belief in the inferiority of the oppressed group as well as the superiority or normalcy of one's own privileged group. Internalized privilege creates an unearned sense of entitlement in members of the privileged group and can be expressed as a denial of the existence of oppression and as paternalism.

paternalism: a relationship in which the one in power justifies domination as being in the best interests of those being controlled.

The European colonizers had the paternalistic belief that they were helping the Indigenous peoples because_____

_____

_____ and _____

_____

_____.

_____

Questions to reflect on further in depth:

How can ideological oppression lead to institutional oppression?

How can institutional oppression, then lead to more interpersonal oppression, and how can all that lead to more internalized oppression?

The Four I's as an Interrelated System of Oppression in Coloniality's Hegemony

It should be clear that none of these four aspects of oppression can exist separately. As the diagram below suggests, each is completely mixed up with the others. It is crucial at see any oppression as a system. It should also be clear that trying to challenge (resist) oppression in any of the four aspects will affect the other three.

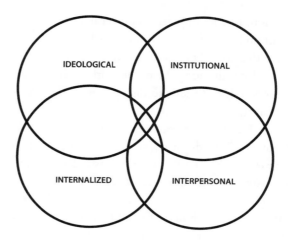

Ethnic Studies Educators as Enemies of the State and the Fugitive Space of Classrooms

BY TRACY LACHICA BUENAVISTA, DAVID STOVALL, EDWARD R. CURAMMENG, AND CAROLINA VALDEZ

Schooling is not an innocent project. Schools in their traditional sense are not sanctuary spaces for People of Color and never have been. However, for us, Ethnic Studies is a project that has sought to disrupt the white supremacist foundations of schooling in the United States. Ethnic Studies is the only academic discipline to be conceptualized for People of Color and by People of Color. Even though Ethnic Studies has been institutionalized, its intent to be critical remains—to encourage acts of subversion that challenge traditional notions of schooling. As Ethnic Studies educators we are explicit in our delineation between "schooling" and "education." For us, "schooling" is the state-sanctioned conventions of order and compliance that result in the intentional dehumanization and marginalization of students of color. Because schooling is rooted in a logic of white domination, "education" is understood as the process that allows people who are experiencing dehumanization to ask questions of their condition while working with others to change it. Education in this sense becomes an act of abolition and self-determination. It is a nonpartisan political act that is by definition linked to the claim to our humanity. In a system that would rather incarcerate certain populations before educating them, the work of the critical Ethnic Studies educator to disrupt the status quo is abundantly clear.

In framing our teaching as subversive, we as Ethnic Studies educators are often positioned as "enemies of the state" and our classrooms instantaneously become "fugitive spaces" in the literal and figurative sense, highlighting as many dangers as there are possibilities for education. Noted by scholars Stefano Harney and Fred Moten, fugitive space stems from the shared notion that oppressed peoples have always made a commitment to build spaces for our liberation beyond the rules and regulations thrust upon us by mainstream white society. Because we continue to struggle with various oppressions (e.g., racism, sexism, classism, ageism, audism, ableism, trans/homophobia, etc.), we are informed by scholars like Michael Dumas and do not make the bourgeois claim that "We've made it." Instead, we are not yet free; Dumas reminds us that to live in recognition of this reality also challenges us to make a collective decision to run as the initial act of resistance. It is "fugitive" because the decision to run is an intentional one, challenging us to find others along the way who are also willing to build capacity to create and protect our ability to educate. Instead of distancing ourselves from the realities of the current political moment, fugitivity demands that we run into the contradictions head-on, with a commitment to build something new.

Conditionally we also become "enemies of the state" in an abject refusal to teach history and culture on the terms and conditions of the colonizer. In making "a way out of no way," we as Ethnic Studies educators often find ourselves in trouble with systems not for nefarious reasons but due to a commitment to education over traditional, mainstream, white, Eurocentric, colonial "schooling." Given these realities, we are clear that it is never about "if" they come, but "when" they come. As Ethnic Studies educators, it is our duty and responsibility to be prepared when they do.

Lessons That Brought Us to Our Work

As forever students in Ethnic Studies, one lesson we consider particularly instructive comes from Filipino

American Studies curriculum, particularly lessons regarding the Philippine-American War of 1899–1902. Lessons on the conflict provide an example of intersectional Ethnic Studies, highlighting the inherent multiraciality of U.S. history and the potential of cross-racial solidarity. The war is an oft-obscured historical moment that defined U.S. coloniality through the unlawful ceding of a newly declared sovereign Philippines to the United States by Spain as a condition of the Treaty of Paris in December 1898. In this particular conflict, U.S. soldiers were sent to the Pacific to fight Philippine nationalists, or *insurrectos*. While few are aware of this history, even fewer know that the U.S. military in the Philippines included Black Buffalo Soldiers. These Buffalo Soldiers ranged from active participants in the colonization of the Philippines as a strategy to demonstrate patriotism and belonging in the United States to conscientious objectors. The latter group of resisters included David Fagen, who legendarily defected from the U.S. Army and fought against American imperialism alongside Filipinos. Despite their efforts, a more weaponized U.S. military would force a Philippine surrender.

Critical Ethnic Studies curriculum requires emphasizing how the Philippine-American War helps us to discuss the foundations of American schooling while historicizing the intended role of teachers. The Philippine-American War led to U.S. control of the Philippines and the establishment of a public schooling system. Concretized through state-sanctioned violence, schooling was considered a central tool in the colonization of the Philippines, or what Allyson Tintiangco-Cubales and co-author Edward Curammeng refer to as "an innovative maneuver in how war is waged." The first American teachers in the Philippines were U.S. soldiers, and then in 1901 the U.S. government began to recruit and deploy teachers to the Philippines via the USS Thomas. These teachers and those who were subsequently recruited to teach in the Philippines were known as the "Thomasites" and referred to as an "army of instruction." In total, there were approximately 1,000 Thomasites. Under the Thomasites project, teachers were federal employees charged with the development of a public education system that instituted English as the primary language of instruction in the Philippines. Although clearly a tool for colonization, even dom-inant narratives of the Thomasites obscure the fact that they were essentially a military intervention in the Philippines meant to erase the vestiges of Spanish colonization and replace it with an American version of a similar process. Continuing the theme of fugitive space, noted scholar of African American history Carter G. Woodson was a Thomasite. Upon observing the detrimental effects of colonization, he rejected U.S. imperialism and began his quest to create education for self-determination once he returned to the United States, highlighted in his seminal text *The Miseducation of the Negro*.

During his time in the Philippines, he observed how fellow Thomasites used and designed textbooks with lessons that were culturally damaging to young people in the Philippines. Below are two examples—in each iteration, students are indoctrinated into learning symbols of American patriotism.

Figure 1: Kirk, M. (1899). *The Baldwin Primer* (p. 14). New York: American Book Company. Retrieved from archive.org/details/baldwinprimer00scrigoog.

In figure 1, students are introduced to the flag; the red, white, and blue; and the American eagle—objects that have no relevance to Filipinos absent

Rita. O Mother, we are playing market.

Mother. What can you buy in your market?

Rita. I can buy flags, kites, and fans.

Mother. Can you buy a flag for Baby?

Rita. Yes, I can buy two flags for one centavo. Pedro is selling flags.

Mother. Take this centavo and buy two flags.

Rita. Is one flag for me, Mother?

Mother. Yes, one for you and one for Baby.

Rita. Thank you, Mother.

44

Figure 2: Fee, M. H., Purcell, M. A., Fillmore, P. H., & Ritchie, J. W. (1907). *The First Year Book* (p. 44). New York: World Book Company. Retrieved from archive.org/details/firstyearbook00ritcgoog.

colonialism. Figure 2 is a lesson considered to be more "culturally sensitive," as it includes Philippine references: images of a Filipino family and mention of the "centavo," Philippine currency. The family is "playing market" where the goal is to purchase a flag. From our perspective, figure 2 is actually more problematic in that it also introduces young people to consumerism or the idea that buying a flag is in and of itself an act of patriotism. Ultimately, both perpetuate a narrative that is focused on constructing notions of U.S. patriotism.

These lessons serve as a site to study the intersection of racism, militarism, and American imperialism; or rather, an intersectional, critical Ethnic Studies. For example, while the Philippine-American War is a unit typically included in Filipino American Studies curriculum, the role of Black American soldiers in the Philippines during this time creates the potential of comparative and intersectional analysis of racialized imperialism among Asians and Blacks in the United States and in diaspora. Moreover, the subsequent arrival of the Thomasites demonstrates how a critical Ethnic Studies necessarily draws on

lessons of sociohistorical events to understand contemporary phenomena. In particular, and in context of the original intent of the American schooling system, teachers have always been positioned as "agents of the state." And such intent remains emphasized in teacher education.

Agents vs. Enemies of the State

As agents of the state, teachers are responsible for carrying out the agenda of the state in local contexts. Their lessons are designed to promote abstract liberal ideas—equality for all, universalism, and a bootstraps work ethic—all of which are not realistic in a society characterized by racial and socioeconomic stratification. In doing so, teachers often emphasize the individual's role in determining their life chances and de-emphasize the direct role of the state in shaping one's living conditions and decision-making processes or the state's numerous attempts to destroy one's agency. Akin to teachers in Native American boarding schools, teachers in classrooms today often use violence and coercion to suppress dissent. This is why we see students with some of the most critical perspectives become subjected to punitive disciplinary school policies.

Continuing their responsibilities as agents of the state, teachers are expected to oversimplify complex histories. One example is the reductionist history of Dr. Martin Luther King, Jr. Teachers across the United States—both liberal and conservative—rely on superficial depictions of Dr. King to shape lessons on the Civil Rights/Black Freedom Movement and fictional narratives of American racial progress. From MLK Day to Black History Month, we commemorate him as a great American leader and construct a lie about his investment in the U.S. political project. Included in this fallacy is the complete removal of his rejection of the U.S. political project of citizenship and patriotism to a radical imaginary that shifted his attention to the racialized aspects of poverty and a stance against U.S. militarism in Vietnam. If teachers only operate as agents of the state, they are expected to teach Dr. King only as an exemplary citizen of the state.

Keeping in mind the perpetual expectation for teachers to operate as agents of the state, we invite readers to entertain the idea of how Ethnic Studies

Table 1. The Multiple Possibilities of Teachers

Agents of the State	Enemies of the State
Carry out the agenda of the state	Use education to subvert state agendas
Promote political liberalism	Critique abstract liberalism
Maintain the status quo	Challenge status quo
Suppress dissent	Organize or facilitate dissent

educators can fugitively position ourselves as "enemies of the state" due to our desire to create education that is transformative in nature. As enemies of the state, teachers of critical Ethnic Studies are in a position where we have made the conscious decision to engage in a practice that centers decolonizing practices while subverting white supremacist agendas. This process includes but is not limited to critiquing structural inequities that challenge dominant discourses that maintain hegemony and the status quo with the purpose of organizing for critical dissent and self-determination as a means to eliminate oppressive systems over time.

Taking in the previous discussion on Dr. King, we propose how a critical Ethnic Studies educator might reframe lessons on his significance to the Black Freedom Movement. For the entirety of his participation in the Black Freedom struggle, Dr. King was legally deemed an enemy of the state. For more than a decade, he was subjected to government surveillance, first under the FBI's Racial Matters Program and then under the domestic counterintelligence program COINTELPRO. While understanding this history provides a deeper understanding of Dr. King, there is more. The surveillance of Dr. King increased significantly after he delivered his "Beyond Vietnam" speech on April 4, 1967, an anti-war speech in which he outlined what he called the triplets of war: racism, militarism, and materialism—or in today's context, neoliberalism. In this sense, we are aligned with Arshad I. Ali and co-author Tracy L. Buenavista's argument in the anthology *Education at War: The Fight for Students of Color in America's Public Schools*, in which they state that Dr. King promoted what we can consider a critical Ethnic Studies perspective, one that outlines the need for us to understand white supremacy from an internationalist and intersectional perspective.

When one decides to go into teaching, a critical educator will always negotiate the tensions of meeting state standards and recognizing when such standards are not only problematic but harmful to young people. As critical Ethnic Studies educators, we must constantly revisit whether our practice upholds or subverts white supremacist state agendas. Unfortunately, to position oneself as a critical educator is a decision met with material consequences, as is demonstrated by the surveillance and eventual assassination of Dr. King, a year to the date after his "Beyond Vietnam" speech. In the same vein, enemies of the state are often targeted for forced or (en)forced disappearance.

Forced disappearance as defined by the United Nations is:

> [When] persons are arrested, detained, or abducted against their will or otherwise deprived of their liberty by officials of different branches or levels of Government, or by organized groups or private individuals acting on behalf of, or with the support, direct or indirect, consent or acquiescence of the Government, followed by a refusal to disclose the fate or whereabouts of the persons concerned or a refusal to acknowledge the deprivation of their liberty, which places such persons outside the protection of the law.

In short, disappearance is "enforced," one is deprived of their liberty, one's deprivation is state-sanctioned, and the state absolves itself from any responsibility of the disappearance and of the disappeared.

As people whose community members have been direct victims of (en)forced disappearance by both the Philippine and U.S. government, we do not use this example lightly. We apply the concept of (en)forced disappearance to understand the dire situation for critical educators of color, particularly those who engage in critical Ethnic Studies pedagogies. In other words, we need to be prepared to grapple with the question "How can we understand the lack of critical teachers of color as (en)forced disappear-

> **We have to uplift our communities' experiences and narratives while enhancing our ability to connect larger projects of U.S. imperialism and capitalism with domestic projects, such as the racialized policing of young people and the divestment of schools.**

ance?" From our perspective, we live in recognition of the fact that teachers of color have literally been disappeared. In the Philippines, the government has implicit and explicit directives to harm Indigenous schools they deem rebellious. In 2014 in Ayotzinapa, Mexico, 43 teacher education students were disappeared for opposition to state government. To this day the families of the disappeared are still trying to hold the government responsible for their murders.

Domestically, critical teachers of color with critical pedagogies are metaphorically disappeared: They experience state-supported marginalization, silencing, and/or pushout from schools. Critical Ethnic Studies educators are often deprived of their liberty through state-sanctioned practices that forcibly remove them from their classrooms. Subject to fabricated narratives surrounding the idea that Ethnic Studies is reflective of "a communist agenda intended to overthrow the government" or is "teaching students

to hate America," Ethnic Studies educators are criminalized before any facts are presented or reviewed. A prima facie example of the material effects of (en)forced disappearance is the dismantling of Mexican American Studies in Tucson, Arizona, resulting in the loss of employment for many veteran teachers.

(En)forced disappearance is a pressing issue in higher education in addition to K–12. The "Professor Watchlist" is affecting many Ethnic Studies faculty and/or critical pedagogues. A student-initiated surveillance project, the Professor Watchlist seeks to "expose and document college professors who discriminate against conservative students and advance leftist propaganda in the classroom." Faculty including but not limited to Ethnic Studies scholars Melina Abdullah, Rodolfo Acuña, David Palumbo-Liu, and education and critical race scholars Subini Annamma and Cheryl Matias have been targeted for their critical education perspectives.

Behind the watchlist is Turning Point, a conservative student organization with chapters across the United States. Many members of the organization are externally funded to attend college, enroll in Ethnic Studies classrooms, and display disruptive classroom behavior. Currently, faculty have developed classroom policies that prevent the recording of our lectures, while much of our course material has ended up on conservative blogs and news outlets and opened up faculty and their families to right-wing threats. Such is the context that currently shapes our work. For these reasons, we do not seek to frame the idea of harboring a critical Ethnic Studies perspective as one that comes without direct opposition and threat to our mental, physical, and spiritual health. Instead, our attempts to frame education from a critical perspective are taxing, reifying the idea that teaching from an Ethnic Studies perspective is difficult, and in many cases, hazardous. Nevertheless, these challenges affirm the dangerous relevance of Ethnic Studies, as we work to guide students to understand their material realities instead of engaging a cacophony of abstractions that have nothing to do with their lives.

Always Running: Love and Struggle in Perpetuity

In conclusion, we want to leave you with some ideas regarding how we can work against these literal and metaphorical attacks on Ethnic Studies educators and how we can move toward developing a PK–20 critical Ethnic Studies. First, we have to contend with the harmful foundations of schooling and begin or continue to collectively envision an education that is explicitly anti-racist, anti-colonial, and anti-capitalist. This requires an education that deconstructs the original intent of schooling, allowing for space to self-determine what learning looks like for ourselves and our students in our classrooms. To do this, we have to uplift our communities' experiences and narratives while enhancing our ability to connect larger projects of U.S. imperialism and capitalism with domestic projects, such as the racialized policing of young people and the divestment of schools. We need to entertain questions like "How can we help students to link global war projects with school pushout, the militarization of schools, and recruitment of young people of color who mostly join due to socioeconomic need?" Once we are able to connect the global with local, we must build what Dr. King referred to as a "Beloved Community," or one in which social, political, and economic equity is possible. In the context of education, a beloved community entails the ability for educators to better engage with our communities to protect ourselves and our students from being disappeared through schooling and work toward an education that is relevant to and humanizing of our communities. In other words, while some might interpret our call to be enemies of the state and foster classrooms as fugitive spaces as problematic, from our standpoint, all we are asking is how can we, as Ethnic Studies educators, understand such assertions as radical love in the context of white supremacy? ✳

RECOMMENDED READINGS

Constantino, Renato. 1970. "The Mis-Education of the Filipino." *Journal of Contemporary Asia*, 1.1:20–36.

Ignacio, Abe, Enrique de la Cruz, Jorge Emmanuel, and Helen Toribio. 2004. *The Forbidden Book: The Philippine-American War in Political Cartoons*. T'boli Publishing.

King, Martin Luther, Jr. 2015. *The Radical King* (Cornell West, ed.). Beacon Press.

Kramer, Paul A. 2006. *The Blood of Government: Race, Empire, the United States, and the Philippines*. University of North Carolina Press.

Robinson, Michael C. and Frank N. Schubert. 1975. "David Fagen: An Afro-American Rebel in the Philippines, 1899–1901." *Pacific Historical Review*, 44.1:66–83.

Tintiangco-Cubales, Allyson and Edward R. Curammeng. 2018. "Pedagogies of the Resistance: Filipina/o 'Gestures of Rebellion' Against the Inheritance of American Schooling." In *Education at War: The Fight for Students of Color in America's Public Schools* (Arshad I. Ali and Tracy L. Buenavista, eds.). Fordham University Press.

REGENERATION AND TRANSFORMATION

Reimagining and Rewriting Our Lives Through Ethnic Studies

BY ROXANA DUEÑAS, JORGE LÓPEZ, AND EDUARDO LÓPEZ

We teach at Theodore Roosevelt Senior High School, located in East Los Angeles in the Boyle Heights neighborhood. It is a predominantly Latinx community, and the school has historical significance as one of the sites where students walked out for educational equity during the Civil Rights Movement in an event known as the Chicano Blowouts.

We collectively created our 9th-grade Ethnic Studies curriculum with the goal to provide youth with a historical context from the perspective of those marginalized, silenced, and erased from traditional history courses, as well as the tools to critically analyze various issues that are relevant and important to our students. At the start of the school year, many of our students come in with negative perceptions of their Boyle Heights neighborhood and a limited belief in their potential and power to transform inequities. However, by the end of the year, our students are often changed. They begin to develop the tools to critically analyze their environment and view themselves as people who can make a difference, just like the students in the Chicano Blowouts decades earlier who protested, organized, and challenged a school system that was not meeting the needs of Chicana and Chicano students. For example, Michelle described a growing social awareness of oppressive conditions, questioned it, and reimagined her future with a desire to become an agent of change:

> In my Ethnic Studies class I learned about colorism, racism, police brutality, oppression, patriarchy, sexism. . . . I believe it's time for a change. I want to be known as the person who stood up for the people who couldn't stand up for themselves. I want to be known as the woman who stood up for justice. I want to be that woman in protests not afraid of speaking up. I want to inspire people to do the right thing, I want to be seen as a leader. I want to be the person you look up to. Someone who never stopped believing that there could be a change and keeps fighting for people's rights. We need to act now, we need to do it for our next generation.

Students like Michelle are engaged in critical dialogue, storytelling, and written reflections of issues, historical events, and culturally relevant topics. They begin to develop their critical consciousness and a deeper understanding of oppression and dehumanization. Through the written word, students learn to read the world as we apply the work of Paulo Freire's critical pedagogy. Grounding our teaching in Freire's humanizing pedagogy reminds us of the importance of developing relationships of dialogue and care while engaging students not only intellectually but also holistically—including their feelings, dreams, and hopes as a source of knowledge. Through dialogue, sharing lived experiences, and writing activities, students developed their critical literacy skills and relationships of care as a classroom community.

Another theoretical grounding that informs our practice is decolonizing pedagogy, as it speaks to our community of learners who descend from a people who historically experienced colonization and all that came with it: genocide, slavery, dispossession, deculturalization, and racism. We look at the work of various scholars to inform our learning on decolonization but particularly focus on the tenets outlined by Patricia Espiritu Halagao. In her article

"Liberating Filipino Americans Through Decolonizing Curriculum," Halagao states that curriculum and pedagogy were integral in moving through the stages of decolonization and that inspiring hope for change is at the center of a decolonizing curriculum. She asserts that a decolonizing curriculum (1) must require critical thinking of one's history and culture; (2) must be feelings-based with activities that promote empathy, love of self, and openly discussing emotions such as mourning, dreaming, confusion, or excitement; (3) must create an academic and social space; and (4) must have a social-action component.

When thinking what a decolonized life and community might look like, we ask students to use their imagination and reimagine their lives beyond the struggle and beyond unjust emotional and material conditions. We do this through various writing exercises that lead to a final book project.

Writing for the Book Project

Every year, our Ethnic Studies course concludes with a final writing project in collaboration with the nonprofit organization 826LA, whose mission is to support students with their creative and expository writing skills. They do this by providing in-school, one-on-one tutoring throughout the creative writing process. They also help us design, edit, and print the book for publication. Every student has the oppor-

Every year, the prompt changes but is always guided by the three major themes of the course: resistance, resilience, and reimagination.

tunity to publish a final writing piece in the book, which will ultimately be used as curriculum in the classroom the following year.

By this time in the school year, students have read various student narratives from previous books published by Ethnic Studies students. Students often ask throughout the year, "When are we going to start writing for the book?" There is a sense of growing anticipation on the part of students and a desire to have their story written and shared with the Ethnic Studies students who will follow. The written pieces become real and meaningful for students. Usually after reading from our youth-produced Ethnic Studies texts, students will comment things like "Wow, this was good" and "Can we read another one?"

Students usually have follow-up questions to student stories and letters, wondering how the student authors are doing now. This prompted us to begin inviting former Ethnic Studies students to read to our current Ethnic Studies classes. This process became powerful for several reasons. It brought the writing to life; it made it more personal when their Roosevelt High peers read to them. Also, the questions that surfaced for 9th-grade Ethnic Studies students prompted dialogue between current and former Ethnic Studies students. Former Ethnic Studies students would give students advice while building their resiliency when they shared stories of overcoming struggles or how they reimagined their own future. It was almost a glimpse of the possibilities of students' future selves.

As former Ethnic Studies students, now 12th graders, exchanged lived experiences with 9th graders, it was evident they spoke with agency, critical consciousness, and hope. They embodied identities as writers, scholars, and poets. The book project has become a powerful tool and foundational to our Ethnic Studies course.

Every year, the prompt changes but is always guided by the three major themes of the course: resistance, resilience, and reimagination.

Here are some examples of the writing prompts we have used over the last three years:

FUTURE SELF

Think of yourself years from now; how many years into the future is your choice. What do you want to tell yourself about the you of today and the important things in your life now? We are constantly changing, so what do you want to document about who you are now? What advice can you give yourself? What do you want to always remember? Make a list of the things you want to achieve, the dreams you have, the changes you want to make.

FUTURE ETHNIC STUDIES EDUCATOR

You are one of the first few classes of students to have the opportunity to take an Ethnic Studies class in high school, so you can be influential to help future Ethnic Studies teachers around the country. What do they need to know? Tell them what you learned and how it changed your views. What specifically changed in your life because of the things you learned in your Ethnic Studies class? Give many examples.

FAMILY MEMBER

Is there someone in your family who exemplifies resistance, resilience, or reimagination? Tell them what you think about their journey and how they influenced you. It is sometimes difficult to tell the people we are close to just how much they mean to us, so here is your chance to tell them! What do you admire about them? Tell stories of important memories and moments you have shared.

ANCESTORS

Think about the generations of people who came before you. Hundreds of years of people living, learning, struggling, surviving, migrating. And here you are, a product of all of their experiences, choices, and lives. Think about what happened in your past generations to create you and your life today. Think about what you want to create for your future or future generations.

We encourage students to write in a letter format to help establish an intimate, informal, reflective, and still informative tone. Students who choose not to write a letter are encouraged to come up with any other creative writing variation, so long as it incorporates one of the themes of the course. Students write letters, poems, or short narratives to express what they have learned in the class and how it connects to them. We use the letter-writing format because in our experience, it allows for students to be less restricted than other formats and surfaces students' authentic voices. Also, giving student options results in numerous stories to surface and collectively serve as counter-stories from some of the most marginalized communities of color. Freirean scholar Antonia Darder reminds us to move away from instrumentalized forms of learning and instead creatively engage students in activities that ignite their passions. We feel that through this book-writing process, as Darder reminds us, students can collectively envision a more utopian world and develop their social agency to be co-creators of their lives today as well as their future possibilities.

When students are given the menu of letter-writing options, some struggle to decide which to choose while others ask if they can write more than one. To better support students with the prompt-selection process, we read various completed samples from former Ethnic Studies students. Students are taken through several draft-writing and editing activities with the support of writing tutors from 826LA as well as handouts that guide students through a step-by-step thinking, reflecting, and writing process.

Student Letter Pieces

Here, Andrea chose to write to her ancestors, while creatively honoring them and describing them as a source of strength to the struggles she has faced in her life:

> To my Ancestors,
> I see you in the roots of where I stand
> Seeing over those under me, but looking up to those above me
> I feel your strength and courage inside of me, pushing me to fulfill my aspirations
>
> I think of your struggle
> The migration, depression, starvation, poverty, discrimination
> I think of how I'm blessed to be here, but I'm even prouder to say I come from indigenous ancestors.

Samantha also chose to write to her ancestors; in a letter filled with hope, she imagines herself beyond the hardships of the present:

> To my dearest ancestors,
> I hope I'm your wildest dream.
> You never would've imagined that despite all the pain and struggle, we'd come out on the

other side. I say we because without you there is no *me*. And with me I hope I've become everything you wished I could be. Because of you I know we're going to succeed. In the end I know I Am Your Wildest Dream. As crazy as it seems. So thank you for being everything you can be. In my heart, through my veins, it's going to forever be you and me.

With the deepest love,
Samantha

Reimagination as decolonization has been how we frame the process to have our students engage in thinking, dialogue, writing, and art so that they can envision what a liberated life in Boyle Heights can look and feel like. Practicing reimagination, as Andrea and Samantha do, has the potential to create a classroom space that can provide youth with a new vision on how to confront barriers and social toxins while connecting to their Indigeneity. It can guide youth with the realization that they have the power to change conditions of the world and inspire the will to pursue the reimagined world they hope to live in.

Oftentimes during student writing, traumatic experiences surface and need to be addressed. In one particular story, Alfredo mentions the trauma he dealt with from a young age:

I can relive the moment in my head, when I first saw a man die on my doorstep. I was about 10, pouring my late night bowl of cereal when I heard *pow* and immediately heard footsteps as my Pa (my dad) turned the doorknob, I stood quivering. He swung open our door, blood splattered, and then a man collapsed, he'd been shot in the back. My heart dropped as he fell to the floor and tears ran down my face. My biggest fear was leaving my home, my family, my comfort and one day it could be someone I care for collapsing at my doorstep.

For many students like Alfredo, these letters serve as a form of therapy where we collectively analyze the cause of violence and its emotional impact on community members while addressing students' well-being and healing in the process. Our classroom

community, especially at this time, becomes a space where traits such as love, hope, and resistance are seen as tools that can help solve problems. Also, these letters serve as reminders of how resilient students are and the importance of reimagining a better life for their community and themselves.

As such, Grecia embodies both reimagination and resiliency. In her letter to her future self, she writes:

Today I decided to write about you, the old me who I am still scared to talk about but able to talk about. Everything we've been through, the good and the bad, it is the reason I decided to write to you. Someone who got through it, the things people might not consider "hard" but the things that were difficult to us. Stay up, stay determined, and never give up!

Similarly, students like Nancy, who has experienced the silencing of undocumented family members and the oppression of patriarchy and sexism, used reimagination in her letter to her future self to embrace an identity of resistance:

Please enlighten me by saying the world has changed and I have helped. Tell me about all the protests I have been a part of, about all the marches I have marched in. . . . I am on my way to greater things and when I am done, I will say, "I am an activist. I am the cause of change. I am a fighter. I am a feminist. I am a leader. This is my revolution." Tell me about it soon.

By the following school year, Nancy was heavily involved in student organizing through Taking Action, a youth activist organization on campus.

Another student who also got involved in student activism was Liz, and she felt inclined to write a letter to future Ethnic Studies teachers. In her letter, she describes the power of seeing images and role models for communities of color:

Representation matters; we usually see people who look similar to us being constantly criminalized so when young people are put into a setting and seeing people that look like them doing great things makes us aware that we do not have positive role models and we are more than negative stereotypes. Some claim we're victimizing ourselves, but we're doing the opposite and learning what strong people we are. It's like, here are strong people that look like you and even though the system was built to tear you down, you will rise up. These people left a legacy for us and we're the future leaders, the students after us are as well, and so are you.

Jacqueline, who also dedicated her letter to future Ethnic Studies educators, sums up going through the course and realizing that student agency can be development:

> Overall, going through this journey helped me acknowledge the fact that anything is possible if you believe. Staring at two different views of the world. So, future Ethnic Studies educator, I am here to tell you to please teach them how life is in reality and how much their creativity can be used; how they can be helpful in their community and their imagination evolving in time. I hope you inspire future students to understand oppression and people showing resilience for their hard work. Speak the truth, don't put the lies in front of you.
>
> Yours Truly, Jacqueline

Conclusion

These letters clearly illustrate the critical hope/transformation our youth have experienced and/or undergone throughout the year. Our scholars identify and critique oppressive conditions and provide an analysis of hegemonic structures—always with a desire to move toward social justice in reimagining a future without these conditions. These pieces reflect what Elexia Reyes-McGovern says is essential in storytelling within an Ethnic Studies framework that moves people—in this case our youth scholars, from the margins to the center, highlighting the nuances and intersections in their lives. Throughout the academic year, our scholars are reminded that they are the centerpieces of our course and their written letters, narratives, and stories become the curriculum.

Through these narratives, our scholars construct knowledge and become youth intellectuals; their work, once published, is used the following year in our Ethnic Studies classrooms as required text. We are now on our fourth student-book project, and these stories have become a crucial part of the curriculum and validate their lives as a necessary component to our program. In doing this work, we constantly remind ourselves that this is a collective labor of love—we are committed to using a decolonial and humanizing curriculum framework to inform our practices and create transformative spaces for our students. We want them to develop as critical scholars and agents of change wherever they may go. Ultimately, the class we have created with our students is driven from a place of love—love for Boyle Heights, the Roosevelt High School community, the families who reside here, and most importantly, the love we have for our students. ✳

Advice to You, Letter Writer

Find ways to incorporate these throughout your letter.

HONESTY
You can say things in letters you often can't say in person or even in a text message. Imagine something lasting a very long time. Now imagine that letter changing another person's life, just like the letters of Malcolm X or Audre Lorde. This isn't a Snap that will disappear; this really matters. Letters are a space you get to create yourself, where you get to explore your own thoughts in a new way.

QUESTIONS
Big thinking requires big questions, so what do you need to ask? You can ask specific questions to people or you can ask grand questions as if you are speaking to society. In the book-length letter Ta-Nehisi Coates writes to his son, he asks, "Why was it normal for my father, like all the parents I knew, to reach for his belt?" Or like when a student in last year's book wrote to her cousin, she asked, "Did you know I've looked up to you like a role model my whole life?"

REFLECTION AND MEMORY
You can remember moments and write detailed stories of times that stood out to you. You can reflect on the past and make up dreams about the future. You can write poems or raps to include in the letter.

MAKE STATEMENTS OR COMMENTARY
When James Baldwin writes to Angela Davis, he is consoling her; he wants her to know she is not alone, but he is also commenting on the state of the world: "The American triumph—in which the American tragedy has always been implicit—was to make Black people despise themselves. When I was little I despised myself; I did not know any better." And the last line that is so powerful: "For if they take you in the morning, they will be coming for us that night." He is making strong claims; his opinions became words we quote often.

Regeneration/Transformation
Cultivating Self-Love Through Tezcatlipoca

BY MICTLANI GONZALEZ

Colonization's primary strategy is self-hate, therefore the most radical decolonizing concept that we can teach our Xican@ students is self-love; that is, to help our students learn to love their humanity.

In January 2012, the Arizona Department of Education threatened Tucson Unified School District with an imposed sanction of $14 million. This led to the termination of Tucson's renowned Mexican American/Raza Studies (MARS) Department, which implemented the only K–12 Xican@* Studies Program in the country. Mirroring Arizona's anti-Xican@ political climate, the Arizona Department of Education viewed the academic achievement of Xican@ students as a threat to their continued racist agenda. Accordingly, they moved to create legislation to eliminate MARS. In 2017 their racist agenda was exposed and a federal court found racial animus to be at the core of Arizona's legislation.

The Indigenous pedagogy of MARS advanced innovations in teaching and learning that have informed K–12 Ethnic Studies programs across the nation. By implementing this Indigenous, student-centered pedagogy and curriculum in a K–5 setting, I sought to transform my Xican@ students through the regeneration of stolen intellectual and cultural ancestral intergenerational wisdom.

My teaching was focused on countering colonization through a rehumanization process centered on self-love. The program made use of the *Nahui Ollin* (four movements) and what I have termed Culturally Humanizing Pedagogy (CHP) to yield unprecedented results in Xican@ students in the form of higher standardized test scores, graduation rates, and college matriculation rates. The most notable advance among students in MARS courses was the growth in human measures like hope, purpose, sense of identity, acquisition of an academic identity, and sense of responsibility—all of which contributed to academic success. The framework of the CHP, the Nahui Ollin, and specifically the concept of *Tezcatlipoca*, became "tools" to critically interrogate self-hate, a primary strategy of colonization.

Colonization in Education

Colonization permeates every segment of society. Colonization continues to be the mechanism that maintains a stratified and dehumanizing world order; specifically, minoritized, non-white students are assigned the bottom rung of our society.

Critical educators recognize education as a pillar of colonization for Xican@ students, as schools are so often a dehumanizing space that exerts educational racism. This racism is maintained through practices such as a Eurocentric curriculum that excludes the experiences of minoritized students, teacher deficit thinking about minoritized students, practices that contribute to the school-to-prison pipeline, and teacher behaviors informed by biased views of minoritized students, among others. To disrupt educational racism, the most radical decolonizing concept that we can teach our Xican@ youth (and all minoritized students) is self-love. Accordingly, because the CHP centers

---

* Xican@ is a person who is aware of and embraces their Indigenous history/roots; a Chicano is a person who identifies with their Mexican American history, post–Treaty of Guadalupe Hidalgo. Both monikers denote a strong sense of agency in engaging in the sociopolitical process demanding positive change. The @ at the end of Xican@ signifies the feminine and masculine in the Spanish language.

on cultural identity development, it cultivates student academic success through the development and growth of human measures connected to a strong sense of confidence. These human measures facilitate academic identity and achievement in students.

Culturally Humanizing Pedagogy and the Nahui Ollin: Toward a Humanizing Classroom

Internalized oppression or self-hate has been a key strategy in perpetuating colonization among Xican@s. CHP interrogates, exposes, and disrupts the colonization process by providing students a gateway toward rehumanization. One of the components of the CHP is the Nahui Ollin.

The Nahui Ollin is symbolic of the cyclical movement of nature with respect to the four directions. In the Nahuatl language, *Nahui* means four and *Ollin* means movement. The Nahui Ollin is a fundamental concept in Indigenous Mexica cosmology, a guide for everyday life and decisions. The objective is to strive toward a state of equilibrium with the self. The Nahui Ollin uses ancestral cultural concepts representing community, knowledge, education, willpower, transformation, and most importantly, self-introspection. The Nahui Ollin incorporates Aztec scientific concepts.

The four scientific energies that constitute the Nahui Ollin are *Tezcatlipoca, Xipe Totec, Huitzilopochtli*, and *Quetzalcoatl*.

Tezcatlipoca: Reflection/introspection/analysis/genetic memory/self-love. We must see with our heart and not our eyes. By not seeing with our eyes (metaphorically speaking), we avoid judgment. Seeing with our heart requires a heart and mind connection, i.e., reflection, thus critical thinking.

Xipe Totec: Transformation. This is a place of cohesion and order for our thoughts, whereby clarity is reached because of reflection (Tezcatlipoca). Through our reflection, we can begin to make sense of the chaos associated with a negative issue or event and thus find order. Finally, by giving order to our thoughts, a new, enlightened perspective is gained that must unequivocally, positively impact our actions.

Huitzilopochtli: Our will. Our actions must reflect our positive transformation. With new perspectives, we must act positively and move forward in a positive manner toward growth of self and the collective.

Quetzalcoatl: Stability. Acquired knowledge is gained through the wisdom of self-reflection and reconciliation, thus our consciousness serves to make us stable and balanced human beings. Wisdom is gained from the lessons we learn from our experiences. We must constantly draw on that precious knowledge to bring about beauty in our everyday lives.

I implement the Nahui Ollin in my classes as a culturally responsive approach that informs my teaching and ultimately supports the development of harmony and balance within my students' minds, bodies, spirits, and communities. The cycle of Nahui Ollin provides my students with a regeneration of intergenerational wisdom to draw on to produce positive and focused decision-making in their day-to-day interactions. Moreover, this cycle cultivates critical thinking and uses our intelligence the way our ancestors knew would facilitate our development as interconnected peoples. Accordingly, the Nahui Ollin teaches us to use our intelligence in a responsible manner as planetary citizens, thus giving us a purpose in life. The process of transformation begins by tapping into this ancestral knowledge.

By implementing the CHP, I provide students with a pathway for rehumanization through three essential components. The first is engaging students in developing a historical consciousness that exposes the pillars of colonization. Students focus on interrogating the Western canon of history that informs and reinforces the idea that minoritized groups are inferior to whites. For example, two of the main topics that I cover with my students (at the high school level) are machismo and feminism. Machismo is an ideology that has been associated with Xicano males as the owners of this patriarchal ideology. My students can always come up with a multitude of examples, from personal examples from men in their family to societal examples. Many of my Xicano male students have internalized machismo and can point out how it manifests itself specifically in their actions toward the women in their family.

We study the origins of machismo to discover that it is an ideology of patriarchy (a pillar of colonization), the system brought over by European colonizers. After identifying this ideology as one brought over by the colonizers, my students can recognize patriarchy, challenge it, and also develop a language to address its pathology.

The second component of CHP focuses on providing students multiple opportunities to engage in self-love and intergenerational wisdom as tools to combat colonization; as teachers, we must provide our students ample and varied educational activities that specifically address the notion of self-love. For example, I share with my students that our ancestors focused daily on learning about themselves. The ancestors believed that learning about themselves would help build a foundation for living a harmonious life. Providing my students opportunities for personal reflection on a daily basis allows them to continuously learn about themselves. Coupled with self-love, exposing students to "intergenerational wisdom" reconnects them to the wisdom of their ancestors. One topic we discuss to do this is studying what is typically known as the Aztec Sun Stone. The Tonalmachiotl (sun stone) is an account of thousands of years of research by various Mexican Indigenous people. Exposing students to their intellectual heritage in science and math counters the dehumanizing myth of Aztec human sacrifice that portrays their ancestors as a savage people. My Xican@ students negotiate their identity based on their intellectual heritage. Moreover, they begin the process of rehumanization.

Finally, the third component involves supporting students to navigate a colonized society through critical literacy development. As critical educators, we must assist students in acquiring the academic skill set that will support their academic interests. Typically, in our stratified system, minoritized students' dreams are often deferred and their life opportunities truncated. In ensuring that literacy development is centered on fostering critical literacies and skills, educators can equip Xican@ students with the capacity to articulate and act upon negative issues that limit their opportunities. It is not uncommon for minoritized students who have had a subtractive educational experience rife with low expectations

from teachers to disengage in a classroom. This can lead to a lack of classroom skills, which can limit their opportunities to move forward academically or pursue higher education. Too many of my students are skill deficient and find themselves ill-equipped to visualize themselves in higher education. To initiate this process, I expose my students to the characteristics of a scholar. I share with them that scholars are curious, prepared, responsible, and disciplined and

Providing my students opportunities for personal reflection on a daily basis allows them to continuously learn about themselves.

set high standards for themselves. I expect my students, from that point forward, to begin to embody those characteristics, and throughout the year I reinforce them, with the goal of my students becoming college ready. Instead of bolstering the self-fulfilling prophecy of being academically inferior, my Xican@ students tap into their intellectual heritage and begin to see themselves as scholars.

Tezcatlipoca: Toward Self-Love

I contend that teaching Tezcatlipoca (self-love through critical reflection) to minoritized students is an imperative to combat internalized oppression and colonization. We must work toward competency in the development of this literacy of self-love. Tezcatlipoca is just as important as teaching critical thinking because it helps us disrupt societally imposed notions of identity. Too often, Xican@ students' identity development is informed by stereotypical images that demonize them as gangsters, dropouts, apathetic, savage, undocumented immigrants, ugly, etc. Sadly, my K–5 Xican@ students internalize those stereotypes.

For example, when I asked Xican@ students in kindergarten and 1st grade to create self-portraits, the majority of the Xican@ students would draw themselves with yellow hair and blue eyes even though they all had brown hair and brown eyes. When I asked the students why they drew themselves in that manner, their typical response was "I am prettier with blond hair."

In addition, I recall an instance visiting a 5th-grade class where there was a boy who was reluctant to engage in class. When I asked him about this, his response was "Why do I need to work in here? I am going to go to jail just like my big brother." Being cognizant of these attacks on my Xican@ students' humanity, my thoughts were always centered on the following question: How do I address and provide redress to this internalized oppression?

We are hunters of knowledge, specifically as it relates to knowing and loving our humanity. I engage my students in researching themselves.

The methodology I utilize to engage students in Tezcatlipoca is counter-narrative through storytelling and poetry. A counter-narrative is a story that challenges the dominant, typically oppressive narrative about a group of people, and it is critical in assisting students in dismantling internalized self-hate. To provide the substance for counter-narratives, I encourage students to take inventory of their culture, family history, interests, passions, identities, and origins. In one lesson, I provide opportunities for students to reflect on the beauty of their skin color. I go about this by engaging students in an art project of mixing paint until they create a color that matches their skin color. Next, students will write about their skin color by associating it with something that is beautiful. For example, a student may write "My skin is brown; the color of life-sustaining soil." In this way, students are asked to create beautiful counter-narratives that challenge the dominant, racist portrayals of who they are as Xican@ people.

To facilitate this process, our classroom mantra is rooted in a quotation from professor Arturo Meza Gutierrez, a Tonalmachiotl scholar who states that "A true education starts with the knowledge of one's self." This is a constant reminder that we are hunters of knowledge, specifically as it relates to knowing and loving our humanity. I engage my students in researching themselves.

Setting the culture and climate of the room as a safe space for students is critical if I am to establish a place where my students are risk-takers as learners and have a sense of unconditional love in their day-to-day interactions. One way I do this is by ensuring that the materials I use reflect the cultures in the classroom. Furthermore, when identifying picture books, I also ensure that the protagonists in the stories students read reflect their cultures positively. Exposing students to the multitude of contributions made by minoritized people to society is a form of counter-narrative as well. I also work to create a classroom that centers students' voices and centers their experiences as a means of fostering culture and climate in my class. By creating the right conditions in the classroom, I am able to facilitate the development of self-love literacy with my Xican@ students. As my students develop their self-love, I am hopeful that they will navigate this colonizing society in a more humanizing manner.

My model of critical pedagogy is rooted in Indigenous ways of knowing that effectively interrogate educational racism and a system that upholds capitalistic inequality. It is vital that critical educators in the field of Ethnic Studies continue to use humanizing pedagogies that will reorient and strengthen our beautiful students in ways that will help them survive our dystopian world. Ethnic Studies is critical in this process because, as Frederick Douglass once said, "It is easier to build strong children than to repair broken men [sic]." ✳

Happening Yesterday, Happened Tomorrow
Teaching the Ongoing Murders of Black Men

BY RENÉE WATSON

Emmett Till.
Medgar Evers.
Henry Dumas.
Fred Hampton.
Mulugeta Seraw.
Amadou Diallo.
Sean Bell.
Oscar Grant.
Trayvon Martin.
Jordan Davis.
Eric Garner.
Michael Brown.

There is a history in our country of white men killing unarmed Black boys and men with little to no consequence. I taught the murders of Sean Bell and Amadou Diallo, using Willie Perdomo's "Forty-One Bullets Off-Broadway" as the model poem, to a class of 7th graders. But then there was Trayvon Martin, then Jordan Davis, then Michael Brown, and the list keeps growing.

After the murder of Trayvon Martin, I taught a version of "From Pain to Poetry." I wanted to use Perdomo's poem again—it is a strong example of how writers use facts and their imaginations to tell a story. I wanted to add a research component because my students needed to develop researching and note-taking skills and, just as important, I needed to show students that racial profiling and police brutality are not new.

Aracelis Girmay's poem "Night, for Henry Dumas" is a perfect pairing with "Forty-One Bullets Off-Broadway." We get the intense immersion into one man's story in Perdomo's poem, while Girmay plays with time and place, making us acknowledge that the list of Black men who have been unjustly killed is long and painful and ongoing. I wanted students to see both as approaches in their own work.

One of my objectives was to have students explore ways that poets use their work to respond to injustice. I also wanted them to create a collaborative performance by the end of the unit, so scaffolding in opportunities to work together was something I needed to think about. I decided to ask students to work in small groups for the entire unit and focus on a person who was killed as a result of racial profiling or police brutality.

"They Were Murdered"

When they came to class on the first day of the unit, there was a plastic bag with jigsaw puzzle pieces in the center of each table. Each group's puzzle, when put together, was a photo of one of five of the slain men: Henry Dumas, Oscar Grant, Amadou Diallo, Sean Bell, or Trayvon Martin. I made the puzzles by printing the photos on cardstock, turning them over to the blank side, drawing jigsaw pieces, and cutting them out. The pieces were big and easy to assemble, about 10 to 15 pieces for each photo.

The goal was to get the students to collaborate on creating something. "You have five minutes to work as a group to put the puzzle together," I told them as they began to pour the pieces out. I walked around the classroom, checking to make sure everyone in the groups was actively participating.

When each group finished, they received an index card with the name of their person written on it. I called out to the class, "Who has Henry Dumas?" The members of that group raised their hands. I taped his photo on the board and wrote his name underneath so that the whole class could see Dumas. I continued this, making a chart on the board with five columns. The last person we added to the board was Trayvon Martin.

I asked the class: "Do you recognize anyone on the board?"

All of the students knew who Trayvon Martin was.

There were a few students who felt they had seen Oscar Grant before. "There's a movie about him, right?" one student asked. *Fruitvale Station*, a movie

Seeing the faces of five Black men who had been murdered side by side, with facts about their lives written under their names, was sobering. Once all groups had shared, we had a class discussion. "What did you learn? What more do you want to know?"

that reconstructs the last 24 hours of Grant's life, had been released the same weekend as the Zimmerman verdict. (George Zimmerman, who killed Martin, was found not guilty by a jury in Sanford, Florida.)

I asked someone to give a very brief account of what they knew about Martin.

"He was shot by a neighborhood watch guy," a student answered.

"He was shot because he was wearing a hoodie," another student shouted.

I asked the class to hold off on adding more. "Based on what you know about Trayvon and Oscar, why do you think these other men are on the board?"

"Because they got shot, too?" James suggested.

"Yes. They were all murdered," I told the class. "Looking at these photos, what do you notice? What do they have in common?"

Lakeesha noticed that they were all Black.

"And they're all men," Sami added.

"And they probably didn't deserve to die," James blurted out.

I asked him, "What makes you say that?"

He considered what he knew about Martin and Grant. "They didn't even have weapons on them when they got shot. The others probably didn't, either."

"You all are being great critical thinkers. Let's find out more about these men—what happened to them, how their stories are similar, and where there are differences." I passed out an article to each of the five groups about the person whose photo they had. "Your group should take turns reading the article out loud. Underline important facts that stand out. If there are strong images in the article, underline those, too." I ask students to mark up their papers, whether it's an article or a poem. I think it's important for them to engage with their handouts, to write questions in the margins, to highlight phrases that grab them. "When you are finished reading the article, let me know."

Students were eager to learn what happened to the men in the photos. When the groups finished reading, I gave them a handout with three columns—Facts, Emotions, Images—and asked them to write at least four words under each heading. I explained that the images could be from their imaginations. "Even if the article doesn't mention blood-stained cement, that might be something that comes to your mind as you read the article. Think about the pictures your mind sees as you read the article and write them down." For the list of emotions, I told them they could write their own emotion or an emotion that they believe people in the article felt. "So, when I read about Henry Dumas, I felt shocked. I'm going to write 'shock' on my chart. I'm also going to write 'frustrated' because I think his family might have felt that way."

Students went back to their articles and searched for compelling facts, strong emotions, and vivid images. Shavon was in the group that read about Martin. Under Facts she wrote "acquitted" and "a voice can be heard screaming for help." Fania, who studied Diallo, listed "betrayal" and "resentment" under Emotions. Lakeesha, who focused on Bell, wrote "a wedding dress hanging on a hanger" and "a child standing at a casket" under Images.

After they filled out the charts, I asked for a representative from each group to share what they learned. "Give us at least three important facts," I said.

I wrote on the board under the picture of each person. "Make sure you copy this list in your notebook," I told the class. I wanted to keep them engaged, and I also needed them to have this information for the poems they would be writing.

Seeing the faces of five Black men who had been murdered side by side, with facts about their lives written under their names, was sobering. Once all groups had shared, we had a class discussion. "What did you learn? What more do you want to know?"

Sami wanted to know why this kept happening. Jason wanted to know why, in the cases of Diallo and Bell, there was such excessive force. "I mean, 41 bullets being shot is just not right!"

I asked students to share how they felt. I took the first risk and shared that I felt angry and sometimes hopeless. That I cried when I heard the verdict because I thought about my 17-year-old nephew and how it could have been him walking home with snacks from a corner store but never making it. Maria said she felt sad. Jeremiah shared that it made him afraid sometimes. Fania told the class: "It just makes me angry. It makes me so angry."

Poetry Holds Rage and Questions

It was important to me not to censor students but to welcome their emotions into the space. Just as I invited their boisterous laughter, their hurt was allowed here, too. Even if that meant tears. I believe young people need space to learn and practice positive ways of coping with and processing emotions. Art can provide a structured outlet for them to express how they feel.

I wanted them to know that poetry could hold their rage and their questions. The first poem we read was "Forty-One Bullets Off-Broadway." I played the audio poem and students read along. As I had asked them to mark up their articles, I asked them to do the same on the poem. "I'd like you to think about when Willie is using facts from the article and when he is using his own imagination."

Usually, as a ritual, we give snaps after a poem is shared in class, following the tradition of poetry cafés. But after listening to Perdomo's poem, students clapped.

Before discussing the poem, I asked them to number the stanzas. "I'd like us to talk like poets,

OK? So name the stanza you're referring to and, if you notice any literary devices that Willie is using here, we can talk about that, too." We noted when he used a fact from the case. "In the second stanza, he mentions the exact number of bullets," Maisha pointed out. Jeremiah read from stanza four:

> Before you could show your
> I.D. and say, "Officer—"
> Four regulation Glock clips went achoo
> and smoked you into spirit

He recognized that Diallo reaching for his wallet was factual and noted Perdomo's use of personification in making a gun sneeze. He also noticed that Perdomo used his imagination to describe the "bubble gum-stained mosaic" floor where Diallo's body fell.

The next poem we read was Girmay's "Night, for Henry Dumas." Just as we did when discussing "Forty-One Bullets Off-Broadway," we talked about where Girmay used facts and where she used her imagination. Students liked how she referenced Dumas' science fiction writing by saying he did not die by a spaceship. Most of them had underlined the

Just as I invited their boisterous laughter, their hurt was allowed here too. Even if that meant tears. I believe young people need space to learn and practice positive ways of coping with and processing emotions.

moment of the poet's imagination when she writes that Dumas died "in the subway station singing & thinking of a poem/what he's about to eat."

We talked about the different approaches each poet took. "Willie Perdomo focused on one incident and took us into Amadou Diallo's story," Lakeesha said. "Aracelis Girmay wrote about Henry but also talked about other Black men who have been murdered."

I asked the class: "What do you think the phrase 'happening yesterday, happened tomorrow' means?"

Maisha touched the puzzle at her table, moved the pieces even closer together. "I think she's saying that it happened in 1968 and in 2008 and in 2012—"

"And it's probably going to keep happening," James blurted out.

I asked him why he thought that.

"Well, there was Emmett Till," he said. James was in my class last year when we studied Marilyn Nelson's *A Wreath for Emmett Till* and watched excerpts of *Eyes on the Prize*. I was glad to see him making connections to previous lessons. "And in her poem, I think that's what she's saying. It happened way back in the day and it happens now and it will continue to happen everywhere."

"Where do you see that in the poem?" I asked.

"This part," Jason said. He read the lines to the class:

> under the ground & above the ground
> at Lenox & 125th in Harlem, Tennessee,
> Memphis, New York, Watts, Queens.
> 1157 Wheeler Avenue, San Quentin, above which
> sky swings down a giant rope, says
> Climb me into heaven, or follow me home

Lakeesha noted Girmay's list of Black martyrs. "There could be so many names added to that list," she said.

"How does this make you feel?" I asked the class.

"It makes me want to be careful."

"It makes me worry about my brother."

"I feel really angry because it isn't fair and it's not a coincidence that this keeps happening."

Then I asked: "Why do you think Aracelis Girmay and Willie Perdomo wrote these poems? Does it change anything? What's the point?"

"It makes people aware of what's going on."

"I think the point is to make people remember. If people don't write their stories, they could be forgotten."

"And it honors them."

Writing from Facts, Emotions, and Images

With that, it was time to write. "You can choose to write your poem like Willie did and focus on one person. Or you can include the stories or names of others, like Aracelis." I told them to be sure to use the brainstorming chart to help them with writing their poem. "Your poem should include at least three facts, three emotions, and three images from your chart." I also gave them options for point of view. "You can write in first, second, or third person. You can write a persona poem in the voice of one of the people involved in the story—for example, you can be Oscar Grant or maybe his daughter. You could even speak from the bullet's perspective or the ground."

I wrote line starters on the board, but most students didn't use them. They had a lot to say and already knew how they wanted to craft their poems. Since that day, I have taught this to racially diverse groups of students, as well as to professionals who work with young people, including teachers, counselors, and administrators at the college level; the words have spilled out of almost everyone.

I was deeply moved by the poetry my students wrote. For example:

Never Written by A. M.
for Henry Dumas

> 1968, underground,
> day or night,
> coming or going,
> under the eternal florescent
> flicker of subway lights
>
> the clamor of wheels,
> crackle of electric current
> maybe muffled the shooting
> sound that silenced.
>
> One cop's "mistake"
> two boys now to forever
> wait for their father's face.
>
> A mind full of memory and make-believe,
> stretched from sacred desert sands
> to sci-fi space and mythic lands,
> spilled out, running thick
> on worn concrete spans

as subway doors open and close
empty cars rattle ahead
blank pages blown behind
nothing but another man's
Black body laid down
in haste and waste.

For All of Them by L. V.

Who scrubs the blood-stained train track, tile,
lobby, car, sidewalk?
Who tears down the yellow tape?
Who sends the flowers and cards?
Who sings at the funeral?
Who watches the casket sink into the ground?
Who can get back to their normal life?
Who is holding their breath waiting for the
next time?
Who takes a stand?
Who demands justice?
Who knows justice may never come?
Who keeps fighting anyway?
Who fights by protest?
Who fights by teaching?
Who fights by writing a poem?
Who fights by keeping their names alive?

After students revised their poems, I encouraged them to take a small action. "The first brave thing you did was make yourself vulnerable enough to write this poem. Now what are you going to do with it?" I asked. "Remember the reasons you said it was important for poems like these to be written. How can you share your poem to get it out into the world?" We made a quick list that included posting the poem on Facebook, tweeting a line or phrase from the poem, recording the poem and posting the video, reading the poem to a teacher, parent, or friend.

Later in the semester, a few students shared their poems at our open mic, inviting parents and the community to witness the art their young people had created. Some students shared their poems through social media outlets. I encouraged them to not let this just be an assignment but something they took out of our classroom. I challenged them to pay attention to the news, to continue to use their pens and their voices to respond to what is happening in their world. ✳

Reprinted from *Rethinking Schools*, Winter 2014/2015 (vol. 29, no. 2).

We Have Community Cultural Wealth!
Scaffolding Tara Yosso's Theory for Classroom Praxis

BY R. TOLTEKA CUAUHTIN

Respecting students' funds of knowledge, third spaces, pedagogies of the home, cultural assets, and community cultural wealth (CCW) is critical to Ethnic Studies. In 2005, Tara Yosso introduced robust theorizing to help frame CCW in a way that serves as a counter-narrative to the prevalent, more Eurocentric forms of understanding culture. The prevalent forms are sadly primarily based around the dominant segment(s) of society, and they look at peoples of color as having cultural deficits, such as in French philosopher Pierre Bourdieu's cultural capital theory. Based in critical race theory, CCW flips that conception and asserts that people of color do possess great wealth: community cultural wealth.

Yosso's article, "Whose Culture Has Capital? A Critical Race Theory Discussion of Community Cultural Wealth," was originally presented in the scholarly journal *Race Ethnicity and Education*. The article quotes Gloria Anzaldúa in *Making Face, Making Soul/Haciendo Caras*, emphasizing why it is important for people of color to theorize in the first place:

> Theory, then, is a set of knowledges. Some of these knowledges have been kept from us— entry into some professions and academia denied us. Because we are not allowed to enter discourse, because we are often disqualified and excluded from it, because what passes for theory these days is forbidden territory for us, it is *vital* that we occupy theorizing space, that we not allow white men and women solely to occupy it. By bringing in our own approaches and methodologies, we transform that theorizing space. (Anzaldúa, 1990, p. xxv, emphasis in original)

In my high school Ethnic Studies courses, I integrate Tara Yosso's original six forms of CCW capital (aspirational, linguistic, familial, social, navigational, and resistant) and also include four additional capitals (political, ecological, ancestral, and discursive) to help expand students' consciousness of their own community cultural wealth. First, I share a classroom handout/reading that was initially adapted from Yosso's original text by my colleague Jael Reboh for our school's 9th-grade summer bridge program, which summarizes CCW and each form of capital she outlines, and which is expanded here to include the four additional capitals. Working with this handout as a scaffolded breakdown of each capital, with space for students to annotate their personal connections, helps facilitate the process considerably. We work through each form of capital as a class, stopping after each one to further scaffold any words as necessary, pair share or small-group share about ways that each capital may relate to their own lives, listen to various student-created examples aloud, and then ask them to annotate their own relation to the capital on their handout, before moving on to a reading, processing, and relating of the next capital. That is one approach; a variety of reading and annotation strategies may be utilized here.

To further help students understand CCW, I give them a diagram and chart (see p. 251). The diagram in part, with a bubble map for the six original capitals, was present in Yosso's original *Race Ethnicity and Education* article as an adaptation from a 1995 version from *Black Wealth/White Wealth* by Melvin Oliver and Thomas Shapiro. Here it is expanded in several ways: The four additional capitals are included, as well as visuals representing supporting theories that students at our school are also introduced to: a) The Indigenous Medicine Wheel (representing holistic human beings as physical, intellectual, emotional, spiritual, relational beings); b) Maslow's Hierarchy of Needs and the importance of self-actualization (including in ways that serve the community); c) having a growth mind-set (vs. having a fixed mind-set); and d) Gardner's Multiple Intelligences (students have intelligences that are verbal-linguistic, mathematical-logical, musical-rhythmic, visual-spatial, bodily-kinesthetic, naturalistic, intrapersonal, and interpersonal, which combine with the CCW capitals in students' articulations of their own community cultural wealth through their discourses, or discursive capital, which signifies their leveraging of CCW in real-life praxis, putting it into action).

I also use a CCW inquiry chart with guiding questions, which I designed to help students apply their community cultural wealth knowledge in creations, constructions, and articulations of their own (including their "CCW Interactive Notebook/Digital Portfolio Cover Pages and Accompanying Personal Narrative Poems") and to be used in combination with their annotated reading handout. Teachers may easily also create a blank graphic organizer (either as a handout or digital collaborative document—my preference when resources allow) that mirrors this inquiry chart, but with the spaces left blank so that students may have a structured space to further reflect on their personal and communal connections to the theory. Finally, I've included a student example of one of the accompanying poems to help illustrate how one student, with roots in Iran, makes sense of CCW in her own life and communities.

To elaborate further, two *Rethinking Ethnic Studies* editors weighed in on integrating Yosso's theories in class. Christine Sleeter shares, "It's important to understand that, while Yosso conceptualized community cultural wealth in relationship to communities of color who are marginalized by racism and routinely viewed from deficit perspectives, it can be applied to white students as well. First, by applying the guiding questions and examples to students' local communities, students can begin to identify ways in which they are cultural beings, shaped by the cultural resources around them. While the focus of this framework is on communities of color, the value of identifying community resources extends to all students. Second, many white communities (as well as many communities of color) are marginalized on the basis of social class. This framework can help to uncover the cultural resources students who live in impoverished communities bring to their learning."

And Miguel Zavala emphasizes that Yosso's theories should be used toward specific ends. "There is a key piece from Yosso regarding the purpose of CCW—not just that students (and communities) have these resources, but that they use them for particular ends. In the context of schooling, they can be said to use them to survive, navigate, and sometimes thrive/develop. So a key piece is not just about recognition but about nurturing CCW (or at least creating learning experiences that build from students' CCW) and then utilizing these resources toward defined goals. So, in the context of dominant communities, how might cultural resources be used and

> **"By applying the guiding questions and examples to students' local communities, students can begin to identify ways in which they are cultural beings, shaped by the cultural resources around them."**

toward what end? And what happens if some of the CCW of dominant students are values of competition, privilege (self-image), etc.?"

Delving into these questions takes much time and work, as nurturing community, fostering a sense of dignity, and helping students leverage their assets to transformationally resist is critical here—how can students of color be helped to feel empowered by embracing who they are and where they come from? As Ethnic Studies spreads to K–12 schools in counties across the country, how can white students also participate in this process while acknowledging it emerged as a People of Color–centric framework? Where to begin with actually teaching this theory and how to apply it? Many practitioners over the years have shared comments to the effects of "Community cultural wealth is great theory, but how do you make it accessible to our youth?" While these resources help teach CCW in the high school setting, the framework and its guiding questions may need to be adapted depending on who is in any given classroom. Importantly, what is provided here may be built upon with many different kinds of CCW lessons and activities and then connected throughout subsequent units; this is a starting point, with

Lastly, it should be noted that CCW is a part of the Ethnic Studies Framework (see p. 65), as both a key part of macroscale four, and explicitly included as point eight in the double helix of Ethnic Studies' holistic humanity strand, which flows through and helps bring scale four to life. We are CCW. ✳

Nurturing community, fostering a sense of dignity, and helping students leverage their assets to transformationally resist is critical here—how can students of color be helped to feel empowered by embracing who they are and where they come from?

a few ready-made resources provided for classroom use. In our grade-level team's classrooms, we take it much further. For instance, *How can we leverage our cultural wealth to resist hegemony's oppression and self-actualize as a community?* In response to questions such as these, 9th-grade students apply their understanding of the theory through shared inquiries aloud or interdisciplinary essays where they cite specific capitals related to their own lives and/or in relation to the multimodal texts they're interacting with. In their responses, students synthesize an understanding and application of CCW with other Ethnic Studies theories (including John Bell's Four I's of Opproesion) and general education theories (including Maslow's Hierarchy of Needs). The purpose being that we can do something about the oppression and education debt/opportunity gap. We have community cultural wealth, love, and critical consciousness. *Sí se puede!*

Community Cultural Wealth and Ethnic Studies

Directly adapted, scaffolded, and reprinted from key parts of the text "Whose Culture Has Capital? A Critical Race Theory Discussion of Community Cultural Wealth" by Tara Yosso in the scholarly journal *Race Ethnicity and Education*, Volume 8, 2005. tandfonline.com/doi/abs/10.1080/1361332052000341006

This class handout: a) updates the text's language with certain spellings and terms that are present in Ethnic Studies, for instance, adding the term "critical hope" to elaborate on a culture of possibility, or spelling *historical* and *histories* as *herstorical* or *hxrstories*; b) includes four additional capitals (political, ancestral, ecological, and discursive) beyond Yosso's original six; and c) adds a column for students to process and annotate the handout in a way that responds to their own lives and communities as theorists who value lived experiences and knowledge. Are we ready to get into Ethnic Studies theory?

A traditional view of cultural capital is narrowly defined by white, middle-class values, and is more limited than wealth—one's accumulated assets and resources. Critical race theory (CRT) expands this view. Centering the research lens on the experiences of People of Color in critical herstorical contexts reveals accumulated assets and resources in the hxrstories and lives of Communities of Color. Community cultural wealth (CCW) is an array of knowledge, skills, abilities, and contacts possessed and utilized by Communities of Color to survive and resist multiple forms of oppression. Indeed, a CRT lens can "see" that Communities of Color nurture cultural wealth through at least 10 forms of capital: aspirational, navigational, social, linguistic, familial, ancestral, resistant, political, ecological, and discursive capitals. These various forms of capital are not mutually exclusive or static, but rather are dynamic processes that build on one another as part of community cultural wealth.

1. Aspirational capital refers to the ability to maintain hopes and dreams for the future, even in the face of real and perceived barriers. This resiliency is evidenced in those who allow themselves and their children to dream of possibilities beyond their present circumstances, often without the objective means to attain those goals. For example, Xicanxs experience the lowest educational outcomes compared to every other group in the United States, but maintain consistently high aspirations for their children's future. These stories nurture a culture of possibility and what Jeff Duncan-Andrade calls critical hope, as they represent what Patricia Gandara calls "the creation of a history that would break the links between parents' current occupational status and their children's future academic attainment."

Provide an example (if possible, a personal example) of **aspirational capital:**

2. Linguistic capital includes the intellectual and social skills attained through communication experiences in more than one language and/or style. This aspect of cultural wealth learns from more than 45 years of research about the value of bilingual education and emphasizes the connections between racialized cultural history and language. Linguistic capital reflects the idea that Students of Color arrive at school with multiple language and communication skills. In addition, these children most often have been engaged participants in a storytelling tradition that may include listening to and recounting oral histories, parables, stories (*cuentos*) and proverbs (*dichos*). Linguistic capital also refers to the ability to communicate via visual art, music, or poetry. Just as students may utilize different vocal registers to whisper, whistle, or sing, they must often develop and draw on various language registers or styles to communicate with different audiences.

3. Familial capital refers to those cultural knowledges nurtured among *familia* (kin) that carry a sense of community history, memory, and cultural intuition. This form of cultural wealth engages a commitment to community well-being and expands the concept of family to include a more broad understanding of kinship. Acknowledging the racialized, classed, and heterosexualized inferences that comprise traditional understandings of "family," familial capital is nurtured by our "extended family," which may include immediate family (living or long passed on, which is then zoomed in further for ancestral capital) as well as aunts, uncles, grandparents, and friends who we might consider part of our *familia*. From these kinship ties, we learn the importance of maintaining a healthy connection to our community and its resources. Our kin also model lessons of caring, reciprocity, solidarity, coping, and providing, which inform our emotional, moral, educational, and occupational consciousness. This consciousness can be fostered within and between families, as well as through sports, school, religious gatherings, and other social community settings.

4. Social capital can be understood as networks of people and community resources. These peer and other social contacts can provide both instrumental and emotional support to navigate through society's institutions. For example, drawing on social contacts and community resources may help a student identify and attain a college scholarship. These networks may help a student in preparing the scholarship application itself, while also reassuring the student emotionally that she/he is not alone in the process of pursuing higher education. Scholars note that herstorically, People of Color have utilized their social capital to attain education, legal justice, employment, and healthcare. In turn, these Communities of Color gave the information and resources they gained through these institutions back to their social networks.

Provide an example (if possible, a personal example) of **linguistic capital:**

Provide an example (if possible, a personal example) of **familial capital:**

Provide an example (if possible, a personal example) of **social capital:**

5. Navigational capital refers to skills of maneuvering through social institutions. Hxrstorically, this infers the ability to maneuver through institutions not created with Communities of Color in mind. For example, Sylvia Alva notes how strategies to navigate through racially hostile university campuses draw on the concept of academic invulnerability, or students' ability to "sustain high levels of achievement, despite the presence of stressful events and conditions that place them at risk of doing poorly at school and, ultimately, dropping out of school." Resilience has been recognized as "a set of inner resources, social competencies, and cultural strategies that permit individuals to not only survive, recover, or even thrive after stressful events, but also to draw from the experience to enhance subsequent functioning." Indeed, People of Color draw on various social and psychological "critical navigational skills" to maneuver through structures of inequality permeated by racism. Navigational capital thus acknowledges individual agency within institutional constraints, but it also connects to social networks that facilitate community navigation through places and spaces including schools, the job market, and the healthcare and judicial systems.

Provide an example (if possible, a personal example) of **navigational capital**:

6. Resistant capital refers to those knowledges and skills fostered through oppositional behavior that challenges inequality. This form of cultural wealth is grounded in the legacy of resistance to subordination exhibited by Communities of Color. Furthermore, maintaining and passing on the multiple dimensions of community cultural wealth is also part of the knowledge base of resistant capital. In analyzing students' hxrstorical and contemporary efforts to transform unequal conditions in urban high schools, Daniel Solórzano and Dolores Delgado Bernal reveal that resistance may include different forms of oppositional behavior, such as self-defeating or conformist strategies that feed back into the system of subordination. However, *when informed by a critical consciousness, or recognition of the structural nature of oppression and the motivation to work toward social and racial justice, resistance takes on a transformative form. Transformative resistant capital includes cultural knowledge of the structures of racism and motivation to transform such oppressive structures* (see their diagram of the four resistances on p. 252).

Provide an example (if possible, a personal example) of **resistant capital**:

7. Political capital refers to how people and communities influence power and decision-makers, whether formally via electoral politics, elected officials, or representatives in institutions, as well as in nonformal expressions of democracy and community empowerment as related to sovereignty, autonomy, democracy, social justice, and politics in all its forms, i.e., when people and communities use their CCW to influence politics and power in cycles of critical praxis. This can be from using a combination of other capitals, e.g., resistant and navigational capitals.

Provide an example (if possible, a personal example) of **political capital**:

8. Ancestral capital refers to the dimension of cultural wealth that is often otherwise lost or hidden for colonized Peoples of Color's *deeper precolonial roots and community cultural wealth.* It is a deeper layer of familial capital. Ancestral capital within CCW represents the roots of one's ancestral legacy, one's ancestral funds of knowledge, and community cultural wealth in all its dimensions (familial, linguistic, aspirational, resistant, social, navigational, ecological, political, and discursive), especially before and through colonialism. For Peoples of Color, considering ancestral capital specifically relates to considering the relationship of one's ancestral legacy to the four macroscales of Ethnic Studies and not ignoring the indigeneity and roots scale, as is too often the case even in otherwise critical contexts.

Provide an example (if possible, a personal example) of **ancestral capital:**

9. Ecological capital connects to relational knowledge about nature, the environment, and all ecology and directly corresponds to the future of life upon our planet. Paul Ekins notes that ecological capital is based on: a) provision of resources—what gets made, *how*, for whom; b) absorption of waste—what gets disposed of, *how*; c) providing the basic context and conditions for which production is possible at all—including basic life-support functions of the environment/ecology; and d) amenity services—the aesthetic (beautiful) experience of nature. Ecological capital nurtures environmental relationships. A key example of leveraging ecological capital is found in the Principles of Environmental Justice, first proposed by delegates to the First National People of Color Environmental Leadership Summit held in Washington D.C. in October 1991 (available at ejnet.org/ej/principles.html).

Provide an example (if possible, a personal example) of **ecological capital:**

10. Discursive capital refers to the actual *doing* of community cultural wealth (not to be confused with discourse only as linguistic/speaking; it's multidimensional). Students may be CCW wealthy in certain ways, but if they don't put it into praxis, it never has a chance to actualize. In mainstream economics, "human capital" understands this as simply knowledge and skills (primarily of the dominant class). Here, discursive capital signifies People of Color knowledge and skills and CCW *put into praxis (reflection + action)*, or put into *Discourse* (considering James Paul Gee's Discourse as ways of being). This can be a range of understandings and actions, that a community is interested in and/or knows how to do, often sprouting from, *and beyond*, one of the other CCW capitals. Discursive capital is cultural capital in praxis.

Provide an example (if possible, a personal example) of **discursive capital:**

Diagrams for Teaching Community Cultural Wealth

DIAGRAM 1: COMMUNITY CULTURAL WEALTH

Based on Oliver and Shapiro (*Black Wealth/White Wealth*, 1995), the core of the bubble map (with the center bubble and Yosso's six capitals), was present in Yosso's foundational article, "Whose Culture Has Capital? A Critical Race Theory Discussion of Community Cultural Wealth," in *Race Ethnicity and Education*, Volume 8, 2005. tandfonline.com/doi/abs/10.1080/1361332052000341006

Bubbles for the additional four capitals were added as well as complementary and more mainstream education theory representations that students are taught at our school and that are leveraged in the discursive capital of their community cultural wealth. These include who they are as holistic human beings (represented here by an American Indian Medicine Wheel), their self-actualization (represented here by Maslow's Hierarchy of Needs), their fundamental needs (based on the work of Manfred Max-Neef), their growth mind-set (based on the work of Carol S. Dweck), and their multiple intelligences (based on the work of Howard Gardner); together, all of this and more are what students represent. Lastly, a title, our Social Justice Humanitas Academy school logo, quotes by Wade Nobles and James Paul Gee, and a summary statement were added to this half-page diagram handout that students receive to accompany their processing, understanding, and articulations of CCW.

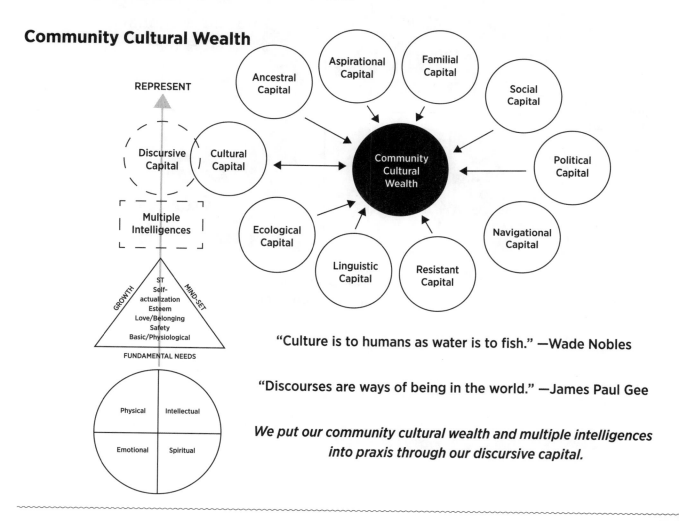

"Culture is to humans as water is to fish." —Wade Nobles

"Discourses are ways of being in the world." —James Paul Gee

We put our community cultural wealth and multiple intelligences into praxis through our discursive capital.

DIAGRAM 2: THE FOUR MODELS OF RESISTANCE BY DOLORES DELGADO BERNAL AND DANIEL SOLÓRZANO

This diagram shows the context of the criteria that characterize transformational resistant capital. This diagram itself was presented in Daniel Solórzano and Dolores Delgado Bernal's "Examining Transformational Resistance Through a Critical Race and LatCrit Theory Framework: Chicana and Chicano Students in an Urban Context" in *Urban Education* (2001) and reprinted with their permission. In the classroom, this diagram can be applied by students to hxrstorical and/or multimodal literary figures and movements as well as to themselves as human beings and communities in diverse classroom situations. For example: a) Which form(s) of resistance does this hxrstorical figure actualize? How do they meet the criteria for that resistance?; b) Which forms of resistance are you actualizing as a student and member of your community? How? Why?

The Four Models of Resistance

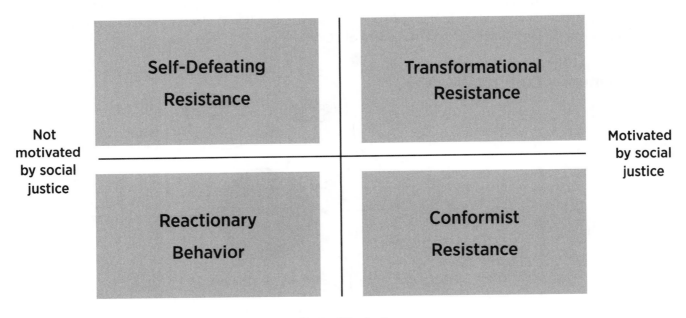

Ethnic Studies: My Community Cultural Wealth

NOTEBOOK COVER PAGE + PERSONAL NARRATIVE: GUIDING QUESTIONS

1. **Aspirational capital**

   Dreams, (critical) hopes, goals, aspirations; life, community, university, college major, career, visions, future. *What do you dream of and aspire to? Why?*

2. **Familial capital**

   a) Family nations/nationalities you're related to,
   b) Family cultural elements, c) Family work/*chamba*, d) Family pics
   How can you represent your family here?

3. **Ancestral capital**

   Precolonial ancestral focus (too often not considered in familial capital if not made explicit). *Where are your precolonial ancestors originally from, what are their knowledges, talents, and ways of being? How does their CCW relate to your CCW? How do the four macroscales of ES relate to your ancestral capital and CCW?*

4. **Linguistic capital**

   *What are your language(s), dialect(s), stories/narratives/*testimonios, *vocabularies/ lexicons, poetry, songs, multiple intelligence communications?*

5. **Navigational capital**

   Which social institutions (of power and of the people) do you know how to navigate and maneuver through (e.g., our school)? How do you navigate the four I's of oppression within institutions?

6. **Resistant capital**

   In what ways are you critical of oppression and motivated by social justice? What social and ecological causes do you care about and want to change for the better?

7. **Political capital**

   In what ways are you politically conscious, influencing decisions and power (yes, even with your navigational and resistant capitals)? Which grassroots or formal organizations do you connect to? Where on the political spectrum are you and which political parties do you (or do you not) connect to? Why?

8. **Social capital**

   Who do you know, connect to, network with, and informally or formally share resources with? How do you connect with the motto "lift as we climb," both as a climber and as a lifter?

9. **Ecological capital**

   How do you relate to nature, the environment, ecology, and interdependent species as beauty and as life support for the future of our planet? How do you think or care about what gets made for whom, how it's made, and how it's disposed of?

10a. **Discursive knowledges**

   Discursive capital knowledge: *What are your knowledge discourses, what do you know a lot about? Why/how?*

10b. **Discursive skills/being**

   Discursive capital skills: *What are your skills/discourses, what are you good at doing, what are your ways of being? Why/how?*

11. **Our community and world**

   For you, what represents the land/region in which you live, your community, and our world?

Community Cultural Wealth: Poetic Personal Narrative

This assignment is usually conducted toward the beginning of the school year and has an interactive notebook/digital portfolio cover page component to it as well, which is not included here. Teachers can view a model at goo.gl/bPrNSY.

COMMUNITY CULTURAL WEALTH—MY POETIC PERSONAL NARRATIVE
By Shaghayegh Lashgari

Shaghayegh: a flower that passionately burns with love for humanity
Lashgari: A group of people working in solidarity for a common cause
I am Shaghayegh Lashgari.

My roots run deep in deserts of Iran, my steps have pressed hard on soil of Turkey and my eyes glittering never loses the sight of the "American dream"
Upon realizing that I know too little, I have packed my inquiries and unpacked them in great companies
I unpacked my wonder of why I am titled "terrorist" and am a "refugee" in lecture halls of Yale
I unpacked questions of "who am I as an Iranian?" at Iranian Alliances Across Borders seminars
I unpacked my worries and began the journey of self-discovery
Along the way I shared cries, laughters, and worries with people
They have deepened my love for humanity and potentiality as I have learned how to work toward a common goal with them

Aspirational Capital
I am a philosopher, baptizing myself in every bit of knowledge I get my hands on
I am a Zoroastrianist, striving to always say good words, host good deeds, and entertain good thoughts
I am a humanitarian, crying for others' sorrow, seldom remaining at peace while others are not, and seldom stopping my effort to advocate for a world in which human rights are enjoyed by all instead of a lucky few
I aspire to be a lawyer, having the title to better advocate for human rights and humanity in a larger context and being able to establish systems that will sustain and empower humans long after my flesh turns into ash
Above all, I am a scholar, in juxtaposition to all the knowledge there is to learn, I know I know too little, I am inspired and excited for the vast amount of room there is for growth
I aspire to escape the many caves I am accustomed to, exploring the Truth or even confirming that there is no absolute truth
I aspire to learn to curl myself around the world like a friendly question mark, fighting my bones and mind that has been conditioned in this social construct that has taught me to be firm and judge, before it allowed me to learn to love

Familial Capital
I do not know how to accurately self-identify
I was born in Iran
I lived in Turkey and
Now I inhabit in the United States of America
But is it just to deny that I do not belong to every single other soil I come from after all their contributions to my being and knowledge? No . . .

Then, I identify as a human that is the product of human geographical evolution as I reap the customs and
   knowledge of my ancestors and ones around me that are not particularly from the same fabric as me
It takes a village to raise a child says my grandma
My village is the world, ones that came before me and after me, shaping this interconnected global community in
   which my values, being, aspirations, and perspective are formed

Ancestral Capital
I am Iranian: one who is given birth in soils of Persia but is of diverse ancestral background
The body I call mine, the words I speak, and the culture I practice are my true witness
The initial grass drove my ancestors to walk on two feet, the need for communication sparkled languages that
   have evolved into one I use to share my dreams and understand others (which resembles Latin, Arabic
   roots), and the way I sway in weddings and special occasions is originated from initial celebratory dances of
   my ancestors
Imperialism, colonialism, and dictatorship have distracted me and others of the influence of our ancestors to
   who we are
I credit who I am to a waste geography because I know that not always ones that deserve credit are given, I hope
   this will at least be a symbol of acknowledgement that nothing in the world is of one and all are product of
   one another (which together make one)—In Lak Ech

Linguistic Capital
Language to me is the window through which individuals are fortunate to explore universes
I have multiple windows
But three main ones are English, Turkish, and Farsi
I have seen storms, sunsets, sunrises, and flourishing gardens
I have been inspired and heartbroken
Most important of all I have been able to see the world from three perspectives, deepening and maturing my
   knowledge and stance in coordination with three different worlds

Political Capital
Politics is something I was taught to ignore as an Iranian girl
It was a concept that would bring perplexity
However, now I live in a world that it appears that politics is not the game of the old money
Rather, it is concept through which human rights and sovereignty of people is advocated for
The way in which Mohammad Zarif speaks of Iran sparkles hope within me
A hope for a flight back home to a country that stands for all people, nourishing all people's basic human rights
   and advocating for more opportunities to grow and elevate for all

Social Capital
You got a friend in me
Every human I have met have confirmed this conclusion
Some have taught me a lesson and others have taught me how to love
Some have taught me to stand on my feet and some have given me a body to lay back on

Navigational Capital
Organizations like Pars Equality, Iranian Alliances Across Borders, the mayor's youth council, Yale Young Global
   Scholars, and many more have become the members of my village
They are the ones that I tap into when I am startled by my lack of academic background

They are the ones I tap into when I aspire to advocate against all the hate I witness,
And navigate through it . . .

Ecological Capital
I am a village girl
Cows, sheep, and horses were my loyal companions far before I even knew the difference between humans and
   animals
Eating them was something I could not wrap my heart around after I began consciously pondering upon my
   actions
I have stopped ignoring my heart for the past 720 days, which is since I have stopped consuming animal flesh
I am my friend's keeper and nature's guardian
I am ecologically conscious and growing to be a better advocate

Resistant Capital
Resist!
Even if machines of ostracization and marginalization do not stop
Resist!
After all, at least by resisting the oppressor will realize that the oppressed is not fooled
Perhaps, like drops make an ocean the small acts of resistance will form a change
A change that will erase islamophobia and welcome all
To be able to resist in itself is a reward

Discursive Capital
Welcome,   , *hosgeldiniz*
Let calamiخوش آمدی:ome and strip me of my comfort, safety, and motherland
Take every little bit I have, but I will still love, learn, and advocate
The lessons I have learned, stories I have witnessed, and curiosity that drives me form a garden
A garden that faces all seasons, but regardless the harvest continues to nurture humanity, community with the
   fruits it bears

Standing with Standing Rock
A Role Play on the Dakota Access Pipeline

BY URSULA WOLFE-ROCCA

Like many teachers, I use my summers to fill gaps in my knowledge and curriculum. Last summer, I took a weeklong course with Colin Calloway on Native American history. He demanded two things of us: 1) that we not accept the inevitability of "what happened" and 2) that our historical analysis and curricula include Indian people as full participants in their own histories and in the history of the United States.

As Calloway writes, "American history without Indians is mythology—it never happened." When I reflected honestly on my own U.S. history and government curriculum, I decided that on No. 1, I was doing a passable job. But on No. 2, I was a failure. So, as I looked to the year ahead, I promised myself to hold true to Calloway's nonnegotiables for approaching Native history.

At the same time, my social media feeds began to blow up with references to a protest of Indigenous peoples in North Dakota. The more I read and learned about the Standing Rock resistance to the Dakota Access Pipeline (DAPL), the more obvious it became that this story must make its way into my curriculum. Here was a fascinating and important story—a story that literally cannot be told without recognizing Native peoples as full participants in their own, and U.S., history.

The resistance at Standing Rock began in April 2016 with the founding of the Sacred Stone Camp near the confluence of the Missouri and Cannonball rivers. The Standing Rock Sioux say they were not adequately consulted during the permitting process for the construction of the $3.8 billion, 1,172-mile pipeline that crosses unceded treaty lands and multiple waterways. This "black snake," as many in the movement refer to DAPL, would pump 450,000 barrels of crude oil per day under the Missouri River, just north of the Standing Rock Sioux Reservation. It threatens not just fresh water but also sacred sites. Writing in the *New York Times*, David Archambault II, tribal chairman of the Standing Rock Sioux, put the pipeline into historical context:

> It's a familiar story in Indian Country. This is the third time that the Sioux Nation's lands and resources have been taken without regard for tribal interests. The Sioux peoples signed treaties in 1851 and 1868. The government broke them before the ink was dry. When the Army Corps of Engineers dammed the Missouri River in 1958, it took our riverfront forests, fruit orchards, and most fertile farmland to create Lake Oahe. Now the Corps is taking our clean water and sacred places by approving this river crossing. Whether it's gold from the Black Hills or hydropower from the Missouri or oil pipelines that threaten our ancestral inheritance, the tribes have always paid the price for America's prosperity.

But if the expropriation of Sioux land is an old story, what may be a new story is the scope of Indigenous and non-Indigenous solidarity with the Standing Rock Sioux. More than 300 tribal nations have opposed the pipeline and pledged support to the tribe. Statements of solidarity have come from all corners of the globe. Social media lit up with #noDAPL campaigns that garnered millions of likes, clicks, signatures, and donations. By December, there were between 1,000 and 3,000 permanent camp residents. The number of Indigenous water protectors and allies on any one week averaged 6,000, swelling to as many as 10,000 on weekends. Soon there were camps within camps.

Aerial photos showed hundreds of tipis, tents, and vehicles arrayed under wide skies. Signs displayed now-familiar slogans like #noDAPL, *Mni Wiconi* ("Water is life" in Lakota), Protect Our Water, and Defend the Sacred, and less familiar ones like "I didn't go to Alcatraz. I didn't go to Wounded Knee. But before I die, I came to stand with the people." In camp, visitors reported an inspiring set of communal institutions. As journalist Xian Chiang-Waren wrote for *Grist*,

> Tidy donations tents are stocked with piles of warm clothing, blankets, women's sanitary items, baby food, and firewood. There's a daytime school for children to attend. When the state pulled water and port-a-potties from the camp, the tribe replaced them within an afternoon. Each day, hundreds of campers are fed for free.

Tribal leaders insisted on a simple but powerful mandate for the camps: peace and prayer. In a blog posted at the Greenpeace website, activist and organizer Peter Dakota Molof described his experience: "Every night we powwow—nations offering songs of thanks, resilience, and grief that we have to fight this pipeline at all. I wander back to my camp relatively early but the voices—the prayers—fill the night and begin early in the morning, greeting the sun as it rises."

Bringing Standing Rock to Our Classrooms

As the movement at Standing Rock gained steam throughout the summer and fall, I set my curricular sights on Thanksgiving. Unveiling lessons on Standing Rock in November would be a powerful symbolic rejection of the lies about Indian people promulgated in our national Thanksgiving myths, in favor of a real story about real Indians. When I was joined in this work by my colleague Andrew Duden and Rethinking Schools curriculum editor Bill Bigelow, we quickly agreed that the story lent itself to a role play and got to work.

Andrew and I both teach a sophomore-level U.S. history and government class at Lake Oswego High School in Lake Oswego, Oregon, an affluent suburb of Portland. After spending the first quarter of the year on an election project, we began the second quarter with an investigation and critique of our textbook's treatment of Columbus and Native peoples. For us, this was a natural place to insert a mini-unit on Standing Rock, even as our curriculum map indicated we should be in the midst of teaching about Colonial America and the American Revolution. Surely, we thought, students' grasp of the themes of early U.S. history could only be deepened by learning about a modern example involving the rights of Indigenous people.

Before launching the role play, we wanted to give students a visceral and visual sense of the resistance under way along the Missouri River. We thought immediately of Amy Goodman's wonderful coverage on *Democracy Now!*, specifically the horrifying footage of the use of dogs against water protectors by a private security firm. We also used "The Standing Rock Protests by the Numbers," a short documentary posted at the *Los Angeles Times*.

We asked students to jot down questions that emerged as they watched. Afterward, they shared out their questions and it didn't take long for them to name many of the fundamental issues at stake.

Greg asked, "Are the protestors angrier about the possibility of oil spills or that they're building on burial grounds?"

Kaia asked, "What guarantee does the pipeline company have against the breaking or leaking of the pipe?"

Lindsey asked, "Is this pipeline really needed? What is it for? Can they move it somewhere else?"

Serena asked, "Who owns the land the pipeline is being built through?"

Cassie wondered, "Does the government care about what could happen to the water of these tribes?"

The DAPL Role Play

Our first and most important goal was to create a context for students to confront the complex social reality of DAPL, which includes the history and contemporary status of Indigenous rights, the power of the fossil fuel industry, the support for pipeline infrastructure from segments of organized labor, and the extent to which our government is protecting—or failing to protect—the land, water, and air. The role play asks students to explore these complicated dynamics as active participants. (See "Resources" for role play materials.)

The setting of the role play is a meeting, called by the president of the United States, to hear input on whether the pipeline should be completed. Students, representing five different groups, try to convince him that the project should be abandoned or allowed to proceed. Two of the groups are in direct conflict:

- Members of the Standing Rock Sioux Tribe who are protesting the pipeline and are encamped along the Missouri River in North Dakota

- Energy Transfer Partners (ETP), the oil company building the pipeline

The other three groups provide additional context on the question of whether the pipeline should be built:

- Iowa farmers who have brought lawsuits and protested another section of the same pipeline

- Our Children's Trust, a national organization of youth activists who are suing the federal government over its insufficient action on climate change

- North America's Building Trades Unions (NABTU), a coalition of trade unions that supports the pipeline as a source of jobs

We assigned students to groups, handed out role sheets outlining each group's beliefs and interests, and gave students some time to assume their roles.

We wanted students to do some writing before launching into the role play. Here is the prompt for an interior monologue:

To get more deeply inside your role, write a first-person narrative or poem from the perspective of your group about the building of the Dakota Access Pipeline (DAPL). Draw on information from your role and your own imag-

ination to build a persona so you can explore the feelings and motivations behind your beliefs. Make sure to include your position on the DAPL and why you see things the way you do. Are you hopeful? Are you fearful? What are your goals for the future?

Then we gave students a chance to share their writing with each other to help them develop their positions, hone their arguments, and build confidence for speaking as representatives of their group.

Before the role play's main event, the meeting with the president, we asked students to travel around the room to meet with other groups. The goal was to learn new information (all the roles have different material) and to identify potential allies and opponents. In a class of 30, with groups of six, we asked three students to travel and three to stay "home" to meet with visitors from other groups. Students spent about five to seven minutes in each group and then rotated to a new group. As students met with each other, they filled out a note-taking sheet.

Surely, we thought, students' grasp of early U.S. history could only be deepened by learning about a modern example involving the rights of Indigenous people.

We reminded students to speak in the first person and stay in character. As the meetings progressed, so did the energy level. The more comfortable students grew with speaking as representatives of their group, the more passionate they became in defending their positions. Conversations between the Standing Rock Sioux and ETP became particularly heated. Manju grabbed the attention of the whole room when, playing a member of the Standing Rock Sioux, he banged his fist on the desk and loudly proclaimed to a representative of ETP, "But we were here first, and it is our water that will be polluted when—not if—that pipeline breaks!"

Once students had gathered information from the other groups, they met back at home base to begin work on their presentations to the president. We asked each group to write a short opening statement that introduced themselves and their position on DAPL. We encouraged them to include persuasive facts and find ways to go beyond their narrow interests to appeal to the president, who is, after all, supposed to represent all the people of the nation. Because the role play took place after the election but before inauguration, students were quick to ask which president they should be addressing—the outgoing Obama or the incoming Trump.

"Why?" we asked, playing naive. "Would that make a difference in terms of what you put in your presentation?"

"Of course!" they replied. Although students had simplistic notions of each man's interests (Obama pro-environment; Trump pro-business), their question—which president?—laid bare the fiction of our role play since, of course, presidents are never simply objective arbiters, giving equal time, consideration, and value to all interest groups.

As groups drafted their speeches, we walked

Students' question—which president?—laid bare the fiction of our role play since, of course, presidents are never simply objective arbiters, giving equal time, consideration, and value to all interest groups.

around, listening in, reminding students to consider the arguments of other groups, and encouraging them to anticipate counter-arguments and to plan rebuttals.

With speeches written and practiced, the whole class circled up for the meeting with the president, played by a teacher. We opened the meeting: "I have brought you here today to help me better understand the situation now unfolding on the Missouri River in North Dakota. Ultimately, I am trying to decide whether or not to move forward with this project. I'd love to hear your input."

We explained that students should carefully listen and take notes because they would have time after each speech to ask clarifying questions, state points of opposition or support, and provide additional, relevant information. If another group was mentioned in a speech they had an automatic right to reply. In addition, we often allowed other groups to chime in and offer a point. The result was a lot of heated conversation between and across groups.

Occasionally, as president, we interjected a follow-up question or tried to bait a group to make sure all dimensions of each group's position got sufficient air time.

The ETP group kicked off the discussion. As expected, they painted a picture of a nation seeking to break free from its dependence on foreign oil, emphasized the safety of their project, and touted the benefits of economic development. Before they were even done with their speech, the hands of the Sioux group were high in the air:

"So how are we supposed to benefit?"

"This is our land you are taking away."

"You can sit there and say the pipeline is safe, but it's not your water that's going to be polluted."

The members of Our Children's Trust also had grievances against ETP. Sarah was a particularly energized representative of this group. She found it outrageous that the company was ignoring the climate implications of the pipeline: "Oh. My. Gosh. Do you not understand that we are not going to survive if we do not take another route [other than fossil fuels]?"

Cassie, also of Our Children's Trust, undermined the safety arguments offered up by ETP: "Truck or pipeline, the oil is going to be burned. We're the next generation. We need to think about that. This is the common good."

When the debate moved to how quickly the economy might transition to renewable energy, Jacob, a member of the Standing Rock group, argued: "Wait a second. This is not just about climate change. This is about our land, which everyone seems to be ignoring."

Maria, also with the Sioux, added: "Our rights are being taken away. You're stealing our rights so you can benefit other people. That's what's happening here."

The Iowa farmers also made arguments about rights and land. They emphasized the flawed and unfair use of eminent domain to seize their land for the pipeline.

The building trades union retorted: "But if this pipeline is abandoned, what happens to our jobs?"

Again and again, students were forced to consider the way statistics and language can be distorted. For example, ETP asserted they had received permits for the project. A permit certainly sounds official, but the Standing Rock representatives were quick to explain that not all permits are alike. Manju pointed out that ETP had used a Nationwide 12 permit, usually reserved for much smaller projects, "like staircases and decks." When ETP argued that less than 1 percent of all oil spills from pipelines result in any environmental damage, even Owen, representing NABTU, a friend of the project, responded: "But isn't that statistic meaningless if we do not know how many oil spills happen overall? If there are 5,000 oils spills a year, that could be 50 spills that do damage the environment."

Getting Beyond the Roles

After almost a full hour of discussion—we have 90-minute classes—there were still hands in the air and passionate arguments, but we closed the meeting. We wanted time for students to reassume their own identities so they could write and reflect on what they had learned from the role play and their current thinking on the pipeline. We conceived of this as a way for students to transition out of their roles.

For some students, this transition can be difficult, but it was a necessary step to achieve our goal: for students to construct a deeper understanding of the issue, not one that had been provided for them.

Students' opinions varied considerably, although a majority opposed DAPL. Alexander reasoned the pipeline wasn't safe: "Though it seems impressive that 450,000 barrels of oil will be transported daily, this also means that one spill will result in an incredibly large amount of oil leaking into groundwater and rivers."

Kai focused on long-term climate effects: "I think the greenhouse gases in our planet are danger-

ous. If we do not act on the renewable energy alternatives sooner than later, we will eventually reach a point we cannot come back from."

Many students homed in on historical injustices to Native Americans. For example, Samantha wrote, "The Sioux have spiritual connections to the land that's being tampered with and it's really unfair after all the sacred land that's already been taken from them."

A number of students who supported the pipeline were compelled by the pipeline's purported economic benefits. Amy wrote, "I think the pipeline building should not stop because our society is dependent on oil and we will become more independent from getting our own oil our own way. . . . Oil prices will go down, the amount of oil will go up and get to consumers more quickly, which benefits our economy."

Even though we asked students to share their own ideas at this point, we realized that some students were repeating the information in their roles. Students who had played the NABTU, for example, were much more likely to write about the good, high-paying jobs associated with pipeline building, while students who played Iowa farmers were more likely to write about the pollution caused by oil spills and the unfairness of eminent domain. We realized how important it was not to conceive of this role play—and the follow-up writing—as a stand-alone unit. They are an entry point, not a destination.

History in the Making

When we were developing this Standing Rock lesson, we had no idea how things would unfold. But December 4, 2016, brought some good news for the Indigenous water protectors and their allies. The U.S. Army announced its decision not to grant an easement for ETP to cross under Lake Oahe. A detailed letter by Jo Ellen Darcy, assistant secretary of the Army, invoked treaty rights, called for a full environmental impact statement, admitted that outcomes of earlier environmental studies had been (improperly) withheld from the tribe, and initiated a robust exploration of alternatives. During the campaign, candidate Trump publicly stated his support of DAPL and, on his fifth day as president, issued an executive order to "expedite" the review and approval of the pipeline. His administration moved quickly to backtrack on the commitments the Army made on Dec. 4, 2016.

This reversal is just the latest instance of a promise made and broken. During the negotiations that would result in the 1744 Treaty of Lancaster between the colonial governments of Virginia and Maryland and the Haudenosaunee Confederacy, Onondaga leader Canasatego testified: "We are now straitened and sometimes in want of deer, and liable to many other inconveniencies, since the English came among us, and particularly from the pen-and-ink work that is going on at the table." The wonderful phrase "pen-and-ink work" referred to the treaty that was being written as Canasatego spoke. It captures the duplicity that characterizes the history of treaty-making between Indigenous peoples and European and U.S. invaders: government officers plying Indigenous negotiators with alcohol, providing documents in languages they could not read, or getting signatures from individuals who had no authorization from their tribe. The U.S. government has never stopped using bureaucratic and pseudo-legalistic tools to obscure the negative consequences of these treaties on the Indigenous people affected by them.

The situation in North Dakota has had its own "pen-and-ink work": ETP's insistence that it carried out a "thorough" environmental review; the U.S. Army Corps of Engineers' acceptance of the Nationwide 12 permit, which amounted to fast-tracking DAPL; and the refusal, by most media and the government, to take seriously the legal meaning of "unceded lands" in the history of U.S.-Sioux treaty-making.

Our job is to help students develop the skills and access the resources to cut through this "pen-and-ink work" so that they can fully participate in the national—and international—discussion of what should be done about DAPL. Although these lessons focus on a single pipeline during a particular historical moment, the issues raised are large, relevant, and timely: Indigenous rights, environmental racism and justice, and organizing and resisting.

So even as the Army Corps announcement initially brought much celebration, it will take vigilance on behalf of the Standing Rock Sioux Tribe, the water protectors, and their allies to hold the line. Their demands are clear and uncompromising: water is life, defend the sacred, and #noDAPL. Our teaching must be just as clear and uncompromising in its insistence that the voices of this movement take center stage—at least for a while—in our curriculum and classrooms. ✻

RESOURCES

Materials for the Dakota Access Pipeline Role Play available at the Zinn Education Project website: zinnedproject.org/materials/ Standing-with-Standing-rock-nodapl.

Archambault II, David. 2016. "Taking a Stand at Standing Rock." *The New York Times.* Aug. 24.

Calloway, Colin. 2012. *First Peoples: A Documentary Survey of American Indian History.* Bedford/St. Martin's.

Chiang-Waren, Xian. 2016. "Inside the Camp that's Fighting to Stop the Dakota Access Pipeline." *Grist.* Sept. 16. grist.org/justice/ inside-the-camp-thats-fighting-to-stop-the-dakota-access-pipeline.

Reprinted from *Rethinking Schools*, Spring 2017 (vol. 31, no. 3).

Standing Rock Sioux Tribal Member

You are one of thousands of Indians camped on the banks of the Cannonball River, on the edge of the Standing Rock Sioux Reservation in North Dakota. The Sioux Tribes have come together to oppose the Dakota Access Pipeline, a 1,200-mile pipeline owned by a Texas oil company named Energy Transfer Partners (ETP), which would snake across your treaty lands and through your ancestral burial grounds. The encampment on the Cannonball grows daily, as you are joined by hundreds of Native and non-Native allies.

You are part of a sovereign nation with legal standing to organize your own affairs and to control the lands allotted to your people by treaty, treaties your ancestors negotiated with the U.S. government. Although federal law requires the U.S. Army Corps of Engineers to consult with the Tribe about its sovereign interests, they approved permits for the project and construction began without meaningful consultation with you.

This permitting was accomplished by deceit. Remember, this is an almost 1,200-mile pipeline going through multiple water crossings and sacred sites. But ETP used Nationwide Permit 12. For permitting purposes, they chopped the pipeline into little pieces and did an environmental assessment on these. This is the lowest-level environmental review. Nationwide Permit 12 is used for a small-scale project, like a boat ramp or something like that. It's absolute madness. If ETP had to do a genuine Environmental Impact Statement, they'd never get this pipeline approved.

Your camp on the Missouri is surrounded by signs reading "Water Is Life." You and your allies call yourselves Water Protectors, because when the pipeline leaks or bursts, the impact will be devastating, poisoning your main source of drinking water. Although ETP says that the pipeline is safe, you know it is not. Since 1995, more than 2,000 significant accidents involving oil pipelines have occurred; from 2013 to 2015, there were an average of 121 accidents every year. Your people should not suffer the health and environmental costs due to the greed of the fossil fuel industry—and their government supporters.

This is not the first time that the Sioux Nation's lands and resources have been taken without regard to tribal interests. The Sioux peoples signed treaties in 1851 and 1868, but the government broke them before the ink was dry. The 1868 Treaty of Fort Laramie guaranteed the Tribes "undisturbed use and occupation" of land that included the Black Hills, a resource-rich region of western South Dakota. But in 1877, without the consent of "three-fourths of all adult male Indians" stipulated by the treaty, the government seized the Black Hills, along with the gold, timber, and minerals located there. The Wounded Knee Massacre in 1890 left more than 250 of your people dead at the hands of the U.S. military. Decades later, when the Army Corps of Engineers dammed the Missouri River in 1958, it took your riverfront forests, fruit orchards, and most of your fertile farmland to create Lake Oahe. Now the Corps wants to take your clean water and sacred places by approving this river crossing.

Your protest has been peaceful, yet you have been met by violence. The National Guard, local police, and private security officers hired by ETP brought their snarling dogs, automatic rifles, sound cannons, armored police trucks, bulldozers, tear gas, pepper spray, concussion grenades, rubber bullets, and water hoses (even in subfreezing temperatures) to use against your people.

But you are a resilient people who have survived unspeakable hardships in the past, and you will stay on this land until you achieve victory.

Standing Rock Role Play

Energy Transfer Partners

You represent Energy Transfer Partners (ETP), which has received permission from the U.S. Army Corps of Engineers to construct an oil pipeline. When built, the pipeline will stretch more than 1,100 miles from oil fields in North Dakota to a river port in Illinois. This pipeline is part of a major national network of pipelines, the largest in the world, with more than 2.4 million miles of pipe to safely and cleanly transfer oil and gas throughout the nation. The construction of a new pipeline would decrease the need for oil to be shipped by either truck or rail, reducing the risk of spill, accident, or waste, and increasing the efficiency by which oil can be accessed by consumers. According to your corporate statement, "Energy Transfer has long-standing commitments to the safety of people, the environment, and our property and assets. We do this because it makes good business sense, but more importantly, it is the right thing to do. These commitments are held as fundamental core values and are an integral part of us as a partnership and a corporate citizen."

Some may be concerned with the environmental impact of building a pipeline of this size and scope. You have worked tirelessly with the Army Corps of Engineers to ensure that the environmental impact of this project is minimized and conforms to all federal laws, including the Clean Water Act and the National Environmental Protection Act. The Army Corps of Engineers already has conducted a comprehensive environmental assessment before providing the permits necessary to build the pipeline, and that assessment and permitting process shows, without question, that the construction of this pipeline is legal and legitimate. By the way, this assessment came at considerable expense to your company.

ETP wants to protect the environment, not harm it. The transfer of fossil fuels through the nation is made significantly safer than when oil is moved by rail. One study showed that transfer of oil by pipe is 4.5 times safer than the transfer of oil by rail over the same distance. Recall some of the horrible train accidents that have occurred recently. In 2013, 47 people died when an oil train derailed in Quebec; and in 2016, 42,000 gallons of oil spilled near the Columbia River, accompanied by a massive fire, when 16 tanker cars derailed. Moreover, according to another study, less than 1 percent of all oil spills from pipelines results in any environmental damage whatsoever.

Of course, we would like to live in a world where we depend more on alternative energy sources. However, the fact remains that our country's consumption of and dependence on fossil fuels is increasing. By addressing this need in the safest way possible and reducing the risk of environmental calamity, ETP is promoting positive interstate commerce, providing new jobs, and reducing costs to consumers by helping to supply quality petroleum products at low prices. This pipeline must continue regardless of what a few law-breaking agitators say.

Standing Rock Role Play

Iowa Farmers

You are from a farming family in Iowa. Iowa produces massive amounts of corn and soybeans, most of which is sold to feed livestock, making your state one of the largest poultry, hog, dairy cow, and cattle producers in the United States. Iowa is our country's grocery store. Without this food, the U.S. diet would be seriously compromised. A bad or contaminated crop would mean major increases on the price of food throughout the economy. You cannot afford having your farmland disrupted by pipeline construction. Even worse, an oil spill would wreak havoc on you and other Iowan farmers, as well as on the entire food economy.

The Dakota Access Pipeline (DAPL) will cut across thousands of acres of Iowa farmland, intersecting many rivers, including the Mississippi, your main source of irrigation and drinking water. When Energy Transfer Partners (ETP) sought to build in Iowa, they filed applications to use eminent domain to secure access to agricultural land owned by farmers. Eminent domain is the power of the government to take private property and convert it to public use in return for fair-market compensation. But it is supposed to be used only for the public good. How does this private oil pipeline help the public? Several farmers filed a lawsuit, asking the court to suspend the eviction of farmers. Since when has it been legal for a private corporation to seize farmland in the name of eminent domain? ETP is not a government agency! They are a private corporation!

The judge dismissed the case. That was in May of 2016. The government immediately began valuing your farmland for seizure. As far as you're concerned, this is theft. ETP is getting to build a pipeline that will earn it billions of dollars, while your community loses its livelihood. The whole thing stinks of corporate greed and the federal government corrupted by the deep pockets of lobbyists representing oil billionaires.

ETP promised that construction wouldn't begin in Iowa until it had secured all necessary state and federal permits, pushing work on the project into 2017, which would interfere with spring planting. Not only that, but you worry that the construction of the pipeline on your land will adversely impact the soil, which takes thousands of years to develop. When bulldozers and trenchers cross farmland, the soil compacts, making it impossible for root systems to develop and creating problems for proper water drainage. Restoration after this kind of damage is very difficult, very expensive, and takes generations.

You are also concerned about places where the pipeline crosses rivers, where flooding and water corrosion may cause a dangerous leakage. You need a healthy water table to irrigate your crops. Oil-polluted water will mean irreparable damage to thousands of acres of crops.

So, now you are one of 200 people following the lead of the Standing Rock Sioux. You are in an encampment on the Mississippi outside of Sandusky, Iowa. This small group is growing by the week, and recently a delegation from Standing Rock visited you to show support.

Standing Rock Role Play

Our Children's Trust

In 2015, you and 20 other young people from across the United States sued the U.S. government in a land-mark climate change lawsuit, *Juliana, et al. v. United States, et al.* The case accused the government of will-fully ignoring the implications of irreversible climate change. You believe that by permitting, encouraging, and enabling the continued extraction, production, transport, and use of fossil fuels, your government has created a dangerous, destabilizing climate system for the country, and for young people in particular. Your generation will be saddled with the climate crises of the future and your leaders should be held accountable for taking action now. In causing climate change, you believe the U.S. government has violated your consti-tutional rights to life, liberty, and property.

While both the government and fossil fuel industry tried to have your case thrown out, you scored a huge victory on Nov. 10, 2016, when District Court Judge Ann Aiken for the District of Oregon, Eugene Division, issued an order that denied both the fossil fuel industry's and the federal government's motions to dismiss this case, officially giving you standing in court. This case is going to trial! While a long way from over, this case is an important tactic for climate activists. You believe that in order to address the climate crisis, we need all kinds of activism—lawsuits, protests, boycotts—waged by all kinds of people from around the world. The goal of these actions must be to get the world to end its dependence on fossil fuels and to embrace renewable energy. You have been thrilled by the #noDAPL protest movement—the movement led by the Standing Rock Sioux in North Dakota to stop the Dakota Access Pipeline.

The Dakota Access Pipeline project is exactly the kind of project your lawsuit cited as evidence of the U.S. government's dereliction of duty. The people of Standing Rock are absolutely right to say no to this 1,134-mile black snake that would carry toxic fracked oil from North Dakota across four states and under the Missouri River, just upstream from the Standing Rock Sioux Nation. Though Energy Transfer Partners—the company building DAPL—insists the pipeline is safe, you know the statistics: Since 2010, more than 3,300 incidents of crude oil and liquefied natural gas leaks or ruptures have occurred on U.S. pipelines. These inci-dents have killed 80 people, injured 389 more, and cost $2.8 billion in damages.

But the safety of the pipeline is not your biggest concern. Even if the pipeline were perfectly safe, what will happen when this oil gets to its destination? It will be burned. It will add to the unsustainable rise in greenhouse gases, which will continue to heat the planet.

It is urgent that this pipeline be stopped. We are breaking every record—hottest year on record, highest sea surface temperatures on record, highest greenhouse gases on record. The Arctic continues to lose sea ice, forcing walruses to shore and fish populations to seek cooler waters that cannot be found. Harmful algal blooms spread in the Pacific. Killer cyclones worldwide are well above average. Now is not the time for more fossil fuels. And yet, even with these clear signs of impending climate devastation all around us, the U.S. government is enabling the fossil fuel industry to build more pipelines, to ease the extraction and burning of even more oil.

While the members of the Standing Rock Tribe have historic, cultural, and spiritual ties to the land on which the pipeline is being built, you believe we all have a stake in the future of our planet and should be joining in the fight against fossil fuels everywhere. #noDAPL. #nomorepipelines.

Standing Rock Role Play

North America's Building Trades Unions

Your organization represents 14 building trades unions with more than 3 million members. It's the workers in your unions who are responsible for literally *building* this country. You built the bridges, the highways, the skyscrapers, the schools, the hospitals, people's homes—and, yes, the pipelines that transport the fuel to power this great country.

You know that there is controversy surrounding the construction of the Dakota Access Pipeline. You respect people's right to peacefully protest. But the country needs this pipeline to provide for our energy needs. And building this pipeline provides good, family-wage jobs. These are not fast-food jobs. These are not minimum wage jobs, where workers are forced sometimes to piece together two or even three jobs to make ends meet. The Dakota Access Pipeline is providing 4,500 excellent jobs—jobs with healthcare and other benefits. Jobs that pay as much as $37 an hour. Jobs that can allow workers to save money for their kids' college education—jobs that allow workers to put something away for retirement.

Some people say that these are "just temporary jobs," as if there is something wrong with that. But stop and think: All construction jobs are "temporary jobs." That's the point, to complete a project and then move on to another project. And think of all the people besides the pipeline workers who benefit from this work. Recently, you saw an article from a newspaper in Cherokee, Iowa—a town with about 5,000 people. Are people there demonstrating against the pipeline? No. They are cheering it. People in Cherokee are thrilled by all the business that the pipeline construction has brought. As one city official said: "When I drive in in the morning, I see all the construction rigs parked in hotel parking lots. Our hotels are full. I see a lot of people in lines at the grocery store that I've never seen before." Energy Transfer Partners estimates that, in Iowa alone, the pipeline will generate $33.1 million in state tax revenue and $2.1 million in local sales tax revenue.

The Dakota Access Pipeline is a huge and magnificent project that will stretch 1,172 miles, across four states, and carry as much as 570,000 barrels of crude oil every single day. But don't misunderstand. Your organization is not just about building fossil fuel infrastructure. You also support building renewable energy projects like solar and wind. And you support building nuclear, another source of energy that creates no climate-changing greenhouse gases.

Richard Trumka, president of the AFL-CIO, the largest labor federation in the United States, also supports building this pipeline. He says: "Pipelines are less costly, more reliable and less energy intensive than other forms of transporting fuels, and pipeline construction and maintenance provides quality jobs to tens of thousands of skilled workers." The Army Corps of Engineers has already said that the pipeline is safe, and you know that the skilled workers of North America's Building Trades Unions will make sure to keep it safe.

Standing Rock Role Play

Dakota Access Pipeline Role Play Questions

As you read your role, please underline important information about your position, beliefs, goals, and motivations. Then, answer the following questions.

1. Do you support the building of the Dakota Access Pipeline? Why or why not?

2. What are the three most compelling arguments or pieces of information that you want the president to consider when making his decision to proceed with or halt the construction of the pipeline?

3. How do you think the president should respond to the Standing Rock Sioux protesters (and other protesters) currently blocking the way of the pipeline's construction?

Meeting with Other Groups

Group name	What is this group's position on DAPL? Might you build an alliance? Or is this a group you will need to argue against?	What new information did you learn from this group about DAPL?

Tipu
Connections, Love, and Liberation

BY CURTIS ACOSTA

In the spring of 2012, only a few months after the banning of Tucson's Mexican American Studies (MAS) program by the state of Arizona, I decided that I would attempt to keep elements of our classes alive by establishing the Chicanx Literature, Art, and Social Studies (CLASS) course at the John Valenzuela Youth Center in South Tucson. I had been inspired by the historical precedent of Freedom Schools during the Civil Rights Movement and also the contemporary example of Freedom University in Georgia—a space where undocumented students could be offered college academic experiences since Georgia state law had barred them from attending the top public universities. CLASS met every Sunday throughout the academic school year of 2012–13 and fluctuated between nine and 12 students.

Tipu was the only student in CLASS who did not identify as Chicanx, Latinx, or Mexican American. She was 19 years old at the start of CLASS and a multi-ethnic student who identified as Pakistani-American to most people. However, she was also quick to assert that she was of Kashmiri descent when given the opportunity to discuss her ethnicity in more detail. She told me:

> Well, it's funny, cuz I grew up being told that I was Pakistani and Irish, but I don't really identify as that. I feel like after you've been called a sand n----- [edited at Tipu's request] or a terrorist, you can't really call yourself white anymore, so I don't. I don't know. Anyone that says differently is full of shit and has obviously never gone through that before. I mean—yeah. You know what I mean? You're brown and someone's like, "Where are you from? No, I mean where are you from?" I don't really think about myself as being a white person or someone who's half-white. I think about myself in terms of being light passing and having light-skin privilege.

Racism toward Tipu's Pakistani heritage by European Americans pushed her away from identifying as white. This was exacerbated by her experience coming of age as a woman of Kashmiri descent in post-9/11 America, which she described as intense and scary later in our interview. The anti-Muslim discourse by political figures such as President George W. Bush contributed to her feeling paranoia akin to a witch hunt, and she was often the subject of hostility when people mistook her for being Arab and not South Asian. However, she was aware that she may have also been spared further conflicts due to the fact that she considers herself "white passing" and believes that if her complexion were darker, racist and discriminatory actions could have been more prevalent.

Tipu was also frustrated at being perpetually "foreign" due to the normalization of whiteness in mainstream America. This process of "othering" increased her alienation from being embraced or seen as American and led her to not identifying as a person with European ancestry. She also felt that her South Asian identity was given inauthentic and stereotypical treatment in the classroom. She explained that these feelings were the motivation for a lesson that she taught in CLASS about Desi Womanism.

Tipu's participation in CLASS provided an opportunity to answer the question of what the academic and personal impact might be for non-Chicanx/Latinx students who participate in a Chicanx

Literature program grounded in Ethnic Studies and culturally sustaining pedagogy and curriculum.

Structure of CLASS

I intended for CLASS literature and writing assignments to reflect the diverse cultural experiences of my students; although a vast majority were of Chicanx descent, they were a diverse group beyond ethnicity, including their ages, interests, and identities. The literature in my classes had a firm Chicanx/Latinx foundation in multiple genres; however, I also believed it was important to include counter-narratives representing other forms of oppression in order to increase the possibility of students identifying with the narrative voices and characters in multiple ways. CLASS curriculum was built around Chicanisma (Mexican American Feminism) and LGBTQ literature, voices that have been largely absent or marginalized in the history of public education.

CLASS was a liberating space for youth, but it also had a clear, organized structure. Each session would include time for self-reflection through personal written reflections that were tied either to the text we were exploring, their organizing and activism outside of CLASS, or their own personal journeys. CLASS usually lasted two to three hours. If we were embarking upon a self-contained lesson for that day, we would begin reading together and then proceed to analyzing the text or media that was provided; when students had read for homework prior to our Sunday meetings, we would immediately engage in the analysis of the story through prompts or questions that the students would answer in small groups.

Most of our discussions were informal, and I often took the role of facilitator by asking critical questions to elicit student perspectives of the literature. However, as the year progressed, students became comfortable in taking responsibility to co-facilitate. During informal sharing, students presented casually from their tables without extensive preparation. With our more formal presentations and discussions, I required students to prepare by writing responses on large chart paper or by using a computer program that we could project on the wall so that their peers could see their answers. Sharing our analyses in this way allowed students to practice synthesizing different ideas that were generated by their peers, a skill that is particularly useful for organizing/activist work, as well as writing research.

As a summative assignment, students created a 90-minute lesson centered on any of the themes that we had explored in CLASS. The idea was for students to deepen the investigation and analysis of the topic while also providing their own unique lens as they guided their classmates through the class. Each student was asked to provide an objective for their lesson and an activity aligned to that objective. I also encouraged each student to use the technology we had at the youth center during their lesson to deepen the experience with the music and videos for their peers. Most facilitators used PowerPoint presentations along with Word documents, which helped the lesson facilitator and their classmates in organizing and focusing on the academic content of the lesson.

Tipu's CLASS project focused on contemporary Desi hip-hop artists. Her lesson, titled "Feminism Hip-Hop and the Desi Identity," focused upon the history of Womanism from the context of her Kashmiri heritage. After providing key definitions for the class, Tipu provided an overview of major historical events of women from South Asia. Tipu then transitioned to an analysis of hip-hop artist M.I.A. and Indian-American hip-hop artist Heems. Both songs emphasized South Asian cultural nuances and complexities in terms of racism, feminism, and the tensions found between Eastern and Western cultures.

M.I.A., a British hip-hop emcee of Tamil descent, uses her art to bridge the modern Western world with that of her ethnic heritage and the issues of the Tamil people in Sri Lanka. Thus, her experiences are quite similar to those that Tipu has experienced as a young Kashmiri woman growing up in the United States. Tipu told me:

> I feel like oftentimes when we're learning about these Eastern cultures or these different cultures, it's always a school project or something. I always see Desi women are Indigenous women in *National Geographic* or something like that. I never see them as rappers or shit like that. That's why—I don't know—bringing M.I.A. to a classroom is really important to me, because she just bends so many identities. I guess what I

want people to realize is that there's a difference between what a culture is and what a culture is perceived as through a Western gaze. I want to—I don't know—reclaim that.

"Cool. Would you say your culture is exoticized?" I asked.

"Yeah, definitely, all the time," she replied.

As can be seen in this example, Tipu also identifies with the term *Desi*, a word that represents a South Asian, pan-ethnic identity. In addition, her awareness that many of her prior academic experiences had been produced by teachers "through a Western gaze" illustrates the need for Ethnic Studies when compared to the normalized public school curriculum. To be clearer, Muslim communities, as well as communities of color, have faced an overwhelming amount of Eurocentric academic content in U.S. educational institutions. This has led to superficial and aesthetic attempts to diversify the dominant Eurocentric curriculum, often through the addition of stand-alone lessons or units that are not fully integrated into the course of study. Tipu's example illustrates the power of Ethnic Studies to liberate students of color from the "Western gaze."

Like her peers in CLASS, she felt comfortable enough to take academic and personal risks in areas where she had felt anxiety before in order to improve her confidence and scholarly skill set. She said:

> I kind of close up more in school. I wasn't as forthcoming as I am like in your classes and in these classes. I think I've been a lot more talkative because it's a group of people that I know really well and we're talking about material that I'm familiar with and that I really enjoy. I'm more vocal. I'm more likely to give insight, but at the same time I'm kinda hesitant because I don't wanna dominate discussions.

Tipu said she feels more comfortable in CLASS because she knew her peers so much better due to its structure, pedagogy, and the authentic caring produced through both the class culture and the Chicanx literature curriculum. This is a dramatic shift from the experiences she had in education up until then. Tipu began to enjoy reading feminist authors

and artists of color in CLASS. This development of her academic identity transformed her own attitudes and activity in class. Instead of closing herself up, she became comfortable and assured of her own value as a South Asian woman, scholar, and human being; she was now finding herself with the desire to fully engage in dialogues, as well as teach from her own Desi perspective.

Mesoamerican Indigenous Epistemologies and Pedagogies of Healing

Tipu's participation in CLASS reveals a radically different type of educational approach in both pedagogy and curriculum from the majority of her academic experiences. Pedagogically, CLASS was rooted in Mesoamerican Indigenous epistemologies that were focused upon rehumanizing the learning process and experiences for students. This powerful cultural knowledge provided the affirming framework that embraced the diversity and intersectionality of all of our students in CLASS. The Mayan concept of *In Lak Ech*, translated in English to "you are my other self," provided a pedagogical foundation of empathy and equality as essential elements for all interactions within CLASS. For example, it was critical from our very first gatherings that the content of the course be co-constructed and that my role would be one of facilitator of student learning. This included collective decision-making regarding what literature we read or what types of social justice themes and community issues we should study together. Dialogue and discourse between students was key in developing trust and confidence in one another to take risks and eventually lead classroom activities, projects, and social movements outside of the classroom space. The growth of students as leaders inside and outside of the classroom space was organic and not teacher-driven; it was In Lak Ech–driven. The class needed to be our space together and all of our voices needed to be present, respected, and valued.

The application of the *Nahui Ollin* (four movements), which lies at the center of the Mexica *Tonalmachiotl* or sun stone, was also an essential pedagogical framework for CLASS and MAS before it. In short, the Nahui Ollin represents the principles of *Tezcatlipoca* (self-reflection), *Quetzalcoatl* (precious and beautiful knowledge), *Huitzilopochtli* (the will to act), and *Xipe Totec* (transformation). Within the classroom setting, the Nahui Ollin was used to nurture and cultivate critical consciousness by asking students to reflect upon their own personal experience while simultaneously developing a critical lens to analyze curricular content. Once this process took place, we could continue to focus on the possibility of action in order to transform the societal situations that led to dehumanization.

By grounding our work together in Tezcatlipoca (self-reflection), we systematically reflected upon the many forms of privilege that gave some of us advantages not afforded to others, as well as the connections and complexities of our own histories as both the colonizer and colonized. These moments helped build a desire to create and institute change in our world.

The idea of finding our common humanity despite differences in gender, race, or sexual orientation allowed room for students such as Tipu to identify with the core concepts of CLASS despite the fact that she was not a Chicana/Latina herself. When I asked if any experience in these Ethnic Studies classes connected her to her own ethnic identity, she replied,

> Yeah, because even if it wasn't the same, there were cultural differences. I think that it raised questions for me about my identity and people in my community and where we stand with— well, it's the first time I realized that we probably—like our communities have the same issues with immigration and stuff like that sometimes. It made me realize that a lot of the struggles are similar in that way.

Tipu's words reflected Mesoamerican Indigenous principles that were of critical importance in creating a reflective and empathetic academic environment. The opportunity to practice Tezcatlipoca while she was a member of CLASS assisted the development of her own ethnic identity. Thus, through a thoughtful and sincere study of another ethnicity, Tipu found connections to her own ancestry. She also applied the Mesoamerican Indigenous principle of In Lak Ech in her own life when she detailed the connection to her Chicanx classmates due to the shared experiences with immigration and colonialism.

Instead of concentrating on differences between the cultures, Tipu experienced a classroom space that was more authentic to her life, along with the freedom to explore her own identity.

> It was sort of cool being around other people whose parents were immigrants. I appreciated that, because, honestly, I don't really think I have been around that a lot in past, in other classrooms—being in a room where I would say a large majority of the kids have parents who weren't born in America or maybe were but don't—aren't often considered American, typically American. It was—I don't know. It was really eye-opening for me. It made me think about—yeah, I don't know. It just raised all these different questions for me about my culture that I wouldn't have thought to ask if I hadn't taken those classes.

Another example of Tipu employing In Lak Ech as a way to find cross-ethnic solidarity was evident in the following example where she expressed ways in which her ethnic identity had cultivated her academic growth.

> It's been an asset in the way that it's inspired me to have a universal sort of knowledge of occupied people. I feel like I come from that background. As far as me—I don't know—to learn about social justice, I think. Even if I can't explain why something is wrong, I almost feel like I know when it's wrong. Yeah, I feel like maybe having a good moral compass is a really important part in education. It's—I guess it's probably—I guess my ethnic identity and my identity as someone who was raised as being Muslim made me really attracted to these sorts of struggles.

Tipu displayed a clear understanding of her own ethnic heritage and the historical relationship between the colonization of South Asia as compared to North America. By referring to Chicanxs as occupied people, Tipu demonstrated a sophisticated perspective of Indigenous history in the Southwest that is not commonly taught through traditional high school American history classes, including the complexity of being from a family of immigrants on stolen land. Prior to her Ethnic Studies experience, Tipu felt disengaged, angry, and isolated in public school. However, being exposed to an Ethnic Studies experience that was grounded in humanizing Mesoamerican Indigenous knowledge provided a more authentic space for her to recognize the value of her heritage and proved to be critical in nurturing her ethnic and academic identities. The focus of Mesoamerican Indigenous knowledge, a social justice emphasis in curriculum, and association to a common struggle engaged Tipu in her education regardless of the specific curriculum content being centered on the Chicanx/Latinx experience.

Agency and *la Futura*

As Tipu's academic, personal, and ethnic identities were being supported through CLASS, so was the development of her own agency and self-determination. In respect to how she believed education and activism would play a part in her future plans, Tipu voiced some strong feelings toward the type of community involvement she would prefer.

> I don't want to go my whole life educating people. That's not what I'm here for. I just want to like, exist and, you know, pretty much just be left alone. Like, I don't want to educate anybody about like why they shouldn't say *A-rab* or whatever. But at the same time I don't want to be reactionary. I want to build something. You know, that's why I want to focus on art. It's because I want to, like, create something. I don't always want to just be completely reactionary. But at the same time it's like when shit hits the fan, what are you going to do? Like, you do have to take action sometimes.

Tipu rejected the obligation to educate and help the cultural literacy of European Americans, a role many people of color are burdened with due to the normalization of "whiteness" in the United States. Her comment about being left alone is most likely directed at the dominant European American culture and the need to be liberated from the objectification and stereotypes she has endured.

Tipu appeared to be gravitating toward creation as action and the idea of building new structures as a form of her agency. Although it is clear that she respected the nature of direct action, she also articulated a desire to balance reaction and creation in her future activism. Even though she had expressed a desire to be left alone, she was also clear about valuing art and creation, as well as a respect for collaboration and collectivism. It was this broadening of her own definition of activism that revealed how Tipu viewed her own agency in directing her energies after CLASS.

The development of her own academic identity combined with the academic structure of CLASS provided the foundation for her own scholarly pursuits. This was not the case in her experiences with education before CLASS, and as a result, investigating the experience of Asian women became a primary focus for her. She said:

> It's funny, because I'm reading this book on racial and ethnic relations, and they have this section on Asian women and how they felt; they had to be like, even in these supposedly progressive movements, they were still hyper-sexualized. They had to be, you know, demure. And they were still, you know, submissive or whatever. And so, they—all the women—were, "Yeah, fuck that. We're going to start a completely, you know, we're going to start our own thing."

It is in this vision where Tipu's sense of self as a Kashmiri American intersected with her own agency toward social change. During CLASS, Tipu gained valuable time, experience, and support in the development of her own identity, while practicing the pedagogical principles and Mesoamerican Indigenous knowledge grounded in cultural and community responsiveness. CLASS was born out of necessity after the dismantling of MAS from public schools in Tucson. It was created to fill a gap of an academic, student-centered space that had once existed in our community. Tipu shared a vision for creating liberating spaces that are far from the "Western gaze" that has violated, exoticized, and sexualized Asian women in the past. She witnessed how such spaces can exist through CLASS and felt a sense of excitement and responsibility to ensure that such spaces exist.

Her future will be guided by the humanization that she has experienced through Ethnic Studies. Tipu was not simply appreciative of what she has experienced, nor did she engage with her education only as an individual consumer. Instead, she felt connection and empathy to people like herself—youth who have not been fortunate enough to find their own personal, ethnic, or academic identity. Although she understood that such efforts will be difficult, they are possible.

Conclusion

Tipu's story powerfully demonstrates the value of Ethnic Studies to those who actively resist humanizing education, since it directly tackles a couple of the most tired narratives used by Ethnic Studies detractors for generations. One such narrative is that Ethnic Studies classes are divisive and anti-American. My students and colleagues in the MAS program in Tucson were often attacked for creating anti-American spaces in our schools, which focused on teaching students of color that they were victims. This perspective fueled discourse that demonized Ethnic Studies as the remnants of segregation. In actuality, our spaces were built on the direct opposite, since we focused our instruction on Mesoamerican Indigenous epistemologies that emphasized our common humanity through the lens of Chicanx/Latinx literature and experiences. Grounding our classes in Mesoamerican Indigenous wisdom provided a framework for decolonization and anti-racist classroom practices that are core ethnic studies pedagogical tenets, as Tintiangco-Cubales, Kohli, Sacramento, Henning, Agarwal-Rangnath, and Sleeter describe it in "What Is Ethnic Studies Pedagogy?" (see p. 20) and as Cuauhtin emphasizes in the Ethnic Studies Framework (see p. 65). Ironically, by embracing knowledge from North America, we were condemned as foreign, dangerous, and anti-American.

A second narrative repeated by critics of Ethnic Studies has been the impracticality of designing courses of study for students of every ethnicity. In other words, their argument is that each student in an ethnically diverse school would need to have their own personal Ethnic Studies course, such as Bosnian Literature or Irish-American Studies. Beyond the ignorance exposed by these comments toward addressing the generational erasure of people of color, women, and LGBTQ voices from the traditional school curriculum is the understanding of pedagogy. Proponents of Ethnic Studies do not simply focus upon curriculum but also on the need for a dramatic shift in how we teach students of color. Historically, public schools have focused on a teacher-centered model without taking into account the cultural wealth, knowledge, and power of the students who are experiencing the lessons. Like the tenets of Ethnic Studies that offer a critique of the traditional Euro-centric curriculum through a decolonial and anti-racist lens, culturally sustaining pedagogy as developed by Django Paris places the students at the center of the educational process and shifts the responsibility of adapting and creating academic experiences that respond to the needs of the students. Culturally sustaining pedagogy is also explicit that our classrooms need to be spaces designed for students to acquire power in a country that is rapidly changing from monocultural and monolingual to multicultural and multilingual. When this is effectively accomplished, students within a culturally diverse classroom will benefit, even if their ethnic identity is not the sole focus of each particular lesson. Tipu's story is testimony to this claim.

When the critics of Ethnic Studies begin their rant about such classes being divisive and a new form of segregation, I will think of the amazing, multi-ethnic Kashmiri American woman who read literature that humanized and illustrated the power and beauty of many different American stories in her Chicanx Literature class, and I will smile. ✳

Teaching Freire's Levels of Consciousness
A Lesson Plan

BY JOSE GONZALEZ

This lesson focuses on providing students with a Freirean lens to "read the world." This critical lens will help the class move the analysis and dialogue of social, historical, and cultural inequality beyond the traditional scapegoats of blaming bad luck or chance (magical consciousness) or blaming oneself or one's culture (naive consciousness) to a more accurate analysis and systemic critique (critical consciousness). The Freirean levels of consciousness will help move the discussion to a more productive level and avoid the pitfalls of blaming the victim and name calling.

Content Objectives

- Students will be able to evaluate and explain how Freire's levels of consciousness can define the impact the dominant group's hegemony has upon the perceived roles and consciousness of Chican@s in a subordinated society.
- Utilizing Freire's critical consciousness framework, students will be able to recommend measures that can be used to create a more just society.
- Students will interpret Freire's levels of consciousness vocabulary words by completing the "four tables" exercise.

Language Objectives

LISTENING AND SPEAKING

- Delivery of Oral Communications: The student will express orally his or her own thinking and ideas.
- Standard English Conventions: The student will identify, describe, and apply conventions of Standard English in his or her communications.
- Comprehension of Oral Communications: The student will listen actively to the ideas of others in order to acquire new knowledge.

READING

- Vocabulary: The student will acquire English language vocabulary and use it in relevant contexts.
- Comprehending Text: The student will analyze text for expression, enjoyment, information, and understanding.

WRITING

- Writing Applications: The student will express in writing his or her own thinking and ideas.

Materials

- Copies of the worksheets tied to this lesson
- Blank sheets of paper

Activity 1: Anticipatory Set

Conscientization is the process in which the people are encouraged to analyze their reality, become more aware of their constraints in their lives, and take action to transform their situation. —Paulo Freire

Write Freire's quote on the overhead/chalkboard and have the class analyze it. Students are to write a paragraph on their interpretation and should be prepared to share their responses with the class. You may make copies of Worksheet 1 and share with the class the expectation of a one-paragraph essay. You will have to introduce the paragraph essay template and field clarification questions from the class. I inform my class that this is the template they are to follow whenever I ask the class to write a one-paragraph essay.

Activity 2: Pre-Level of Consciousness Exercise

According to Freire's model of critical pedagogy, students may move through different stages of consciousness. They can move from magical to naive to critical consciousness. According to Freire, transitioning from the magical stage to the naive stage and then to the critical consciousness stage corresponds with the literacy process of reading the world.

With students in groups of four, provide them with information about test scores in your school district broken down by race. They will analyze and discuss why there exists a discrepancy in academic achievement between people of color and their white counterparts.

- Place the students into four heterogeneous groups. Disseminate to each group copies of the test scores and make a transparency of the results to be simultaneously reviewed as a whole class via the overhead projector. Once you have viewed the results with the class, specifically have them ponder the following question:

    Why do students of color in our school district have lower scores on standardized tests than their white counterparts?

- Introduce the One-Paragraph Template (Worksheet 2) and ask the students to quietly reflect on the question and to write a quality one-paragraph response to this question.
- After the students have completed their one-paragraph response, have them share their response with their respective groups.
- Next, have them discuss why their responses are similar or different.
- Finally, after students analyze and share their responses in small groups, bring the discussion back to the whole class.
- Allow students to voluntarily share their responses with the class.
- Ask probing questions in order to provide a more enriching dialogue. Students might find it challenging to think of systemic reasons for these discrepancies. You might need to offer questions to prompt their thinking, such as "What do white middle-class students have that students of color and/or low-income students don't have?" Some possible answers might include better/more books, money for test-prep courses and enrichment activities, better access to computers, or parents who have a college education and can give them more help with their homework.
- Explain that many researchers have found that standardized tests are biased—the results are not accurate indications of the achievements of students of color and students who are immigrants to the United States. Discuss whether this might be a factor here.
- Share that Freire believed that part of really understanding something is wanting to change it for the better. Ask students what they think they could or should do about this issue.

Activity 3: Table Exercise on the Three Levels of Consciousness

- Introduce students to Freire's three levels of consciousness. Place the levels of consciousness on the chalkboard for the students to view. Go through the levels one at a time and explain the nature of each level and its relevance within particular perceptions. Encourage students to ask questions regarding the different levels.
- Once students have a clear understanding of the levels of consciousness, distribute copies of the levels (Worksheet 3) to each student.
- Students then create "four table" vocabulary charts. Using a half sheet of scrap paper, students are to create four even-sized boxes. The four tables should be constructed as follows:

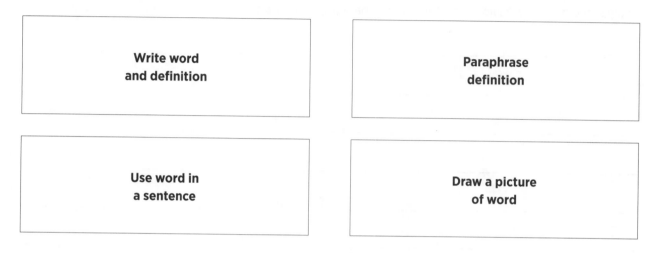

Write word and definition	Paraphrase definition
Use word in a sentence	Draw a picture of word

- The most important part of the four tables is the picture section. Encourage students to draw elaborate pictures rather than stick figures. It is through pictures that your students will create understanding and meaning. As the saying goes, "A picture is worth a thousand words."

Activity 4: Closure Activity

- Place Freire's quote on the overhead and ask the students to reflect on how the quote and the three levels of consciousness are connected. Have the students reflect and write their response in their journals. Students should be prepared to share their response with the class. Use this as the focus of a class discussion.

Worksheet 1: Freire's Levels of Consciousness

"Conscientization is the process in which the people are encouraged to analyze their reality, become more aware of their constraints in their lives, and take action to transform their situation." —**Paulo Freire**

CLASS ASSIGNMENT

Analyze the quote by Paulo Freire. Write a one-paragraph essay on your interpretation of the quote.

_____

_____

_____

_____

_____

_____

_____

_____

_____

_____

_____

_____

Worksheet 2: Freire's Levels of Consciousness

ONE-PARAGRAPH TEMPLATE

Below is a suggested five-step process for writing a one-paragraph essay. Please note that this is only a suggested approach and not a mandatory one.

Step 1: Start with a **topic sentence** or **thesis statement** in which you make a claim that you will "prove" by providing evidence in the form of three or more supporting sentences.

Step 2: Come up with three reasons that **support or back up** your thesis.

Step 3: Convert the reasons into sentences using the following transition words (or your own) for organization:

For example,	OR	*For instance,*
Also,		*Moreover,*
Furthermore,		*Finally,*

Example:
Poverty continues to prevail in America. For example, out of all developed countries throughout the world, the United States has the highest poverty rate. Seventy percent of Americans live from paycheck to paycheck. Also, many Americans are unable to develop a savings plan, thus contributing to their economic status. Furthermore, the minimum wage in our nation is too low to allow people to earn a livable wage.

Step 4: Summarize why the evidence you provided supports your claim, which will serve as your conclusion.

Example:
In conclusion, the United States' high poverty rate ranking and many Americans' inability to establish a savings plan and earn a livable wage are proof that poverty continues to thrive in the United States of America.

Step 5: Put it all together and produce your final copy.

Example:
Poverty continues to prevail in America. For example, out of all developed countries throughout the world, the United States has the highest poverty rate. Seventy percent of Americans live from paycheck to paycheck. Also, many Americans are unable to develop a savings plan, thus contributing to their economic status. Furthermore, the minimum wage in our nation is too low to allow people to earn a livable wage. In conclusion, the United States' high poverty rate ranking and many Americans' inability to establish a saving plan and earn a livable wage are proof that poverty continues to thrive in the United States of America.

Worksheet 3: Freire's Levels of Consciousness

MAGICAL
At the magical stage, students may blame inequality on luck, fate, or God.

Whatever causes the inequality seems to be out of students' control, so they may resign themselves to doing nothing about it.

NAIVE
At the naive stage, students may blame themselves, their culture, or their community for inequality.

Students may try to change themselves, assimilate to the white, middle-class, mainstream culture, or distance themselves from their community in response to experiencing inequality at the naive stage.

CRITICAL
At the critical stage, students look beyond fatalistic or cultural reasons for inequality to focus on structural, systemic explanations.

Students with a critical levels of consciousness look toward changing the system as a response to experiencing inequality.

Chicana/o–Mexicana/o Resistance and Affirmation in the Post–Treaty of Guadalupe Hidalgo Era

A Curriculum Unit Narrative

BY SEAN ARCE

Why was Juanita hanged? Described by the local news-paper as a "dark," aggressive, and independent Mexican woman who was an experienced miner and an avid gambler, for Juanita, these facts were too much for the white male colonizers who were coming into California to accept because she challenged their under-standing and expectations of gender and racial norms. She was the first person ordered by a judge to be exe-cuted by hanging in the state of California because she was [a] Mexicana who held these positions, a woman who exercised self-defense against sexual violence from white men, and was a mujer *who lived in a society that viewed Mexicanas as less than human. There is much that we can learn from this ugly episode in U.S. history. Unfortunately, much of this sentiment toward Chi-cana-Mexicana women remains with us today.*

—Valerie Castro, 2016–17 Chicanx-Latinx
Studies Student, Azusa High School

This excerpt, written by a former student as part of the unit on resistance that I teach, provides insight into how students become critically conscious as a result of the content that I provide them in my high school Chicanx-Latinx Studies classes. This nuanced student excerpt reflects the pedagogy implemented in my Chicanx-Latinx Studies class—that being the pedagogy of the *Nahui Ollin*—as evidenced in her critical reflection, obtain-ing and creation of knowledge, and the supporting evidence she used for her position on Chicana-Mexi-cana resistance to colonization.

The Nahui Ollin—a central pedagogical frame-work that was operationalized in parts of the for-mer Mexican American/Raza Studies (MARS) program in Tucson and is currently being imple-mented in numerous Ethnic Studies/Chicanx-Lat-inx Studies classes throughout California—is a holistic pedagogy that addresses the sociocultural, intellectual, and emotional needs of Chicanx-Lat-inx youth as well as other youth of color. Because of their experiences and position(s) as colonial subjects in the United States, Chicanx-Latinx and other racialized youth often bring various forms of trauma and/or *susto* with them into the class-room. The fundamental Mesoamerican principles, concepts, and systems of knowledge of the Nahui Ollin—namely *Tezcatlipoca*, critical self-reflec-tion; *Quetzalcoatl*, the obtaining and creation of knowledge and *consciencia* (consciousness); *Huitzilopochtli*, the *ganas* (desire) and/or will to act; and *Xipe Totec*, transformation—constitute the pedagogical framework that creates the con-ditions for these youths both inside and outside of the classroom to address their trauma and/or susto and ultimately work toward their rehuman-ization and transformation of their lived realities. Chicana scholar-activist Silvia Toscano refer-ences the Nahui Ollin in her *Urban Review* piece, "Teaching as a Healing Craft: Decolonizing the Classroom and Creating Spaces of Hopeful Resis-tance Through Chicano-Indigenous Pedagogical Praxis," testifying to the pedagogy of the former MARS program.

In this article, I will explain how I operationalize the pedagogy of the Nahui Ollin in the Chicanx-Latinx Studies curriculum unit "Chicana/o-Mexicana/o Resistance in the Post–Treaty of Guadalupe Hidalgo Era" to increase academic engagement and sociocultural and sociohistorical responsiveness and to facilitate processes that lead to rehumanization and social transformation for my students. In addition to highlighting the structure of this curriculum unit, I offer two pedagogical narratives that accompany Lessons 1 and 2, which provide insight into the Nahui Ollin approach for this curriculum unit, including how it directly impacts the students in our Chicanx-Latinx Studies class.

Chicana/o-Mexicana/o Resistance and Affirmation in the Post–Treaty of Guadalupe Hidalgo Era Unit

INTRODUCTION

In keeping with the tradition of resistance initiated by their Mexican Indigenous ancestors, Chicanas/os-Mexicanas/os in the newly conquered territories of the United States, immediately following the U.S. War on Mexico of 1846–1848, continued to resist the oppressive and colonizing forces of land theft and attempted eradication of their Mexican culture, families, and entire communities.

IMPLEMENTATION GUIDELINES

This unit is designed to be taught in grades 11 or 12 in a general Ethnic Studies, Chicanx-Latinx Studies, or U.S. history course. The lessons within this unit are intended to be used in a sequential fashion. The time required to cover this curriculum unit is at least two full weeks, or 10 instructional days.

TEACHER PRE-INSTRUCTIONAL INFORMATION

This unit should be taught after a thorough examination and study of the U.S. War on Mexico (1846–48) and the Treaty of Guadalupe Hidalgo, the treaty that officially brought an end to that war.

This curriculum unit concerning conflict, resistance, and resolution serves the purpose of dispelling the myth of the "sleeping giant," or the idea that the Chicanx-Latinx are a docile people, unaware of their political, social, and economic potential. Furthermore, this curriculum unit is intended to familiarize the student with important historical figures in Chi-

cana/o-Mexicana/o history who have resisted dominant society's hegemony in the years immediately following the Treaty of Guadalupe of 1848 and to make critical connections to the contemporaneous and vibrant resistance taking place within the Chicanx-Latinx community of today. The historical and contemporary critical analysis of this unit covers the dominant society's prevalent attitudes toward Chicanas/os-Mexicanas/os, specifically where and when this community has undergone processes of racialization and dehumanization. Equally important are the analytical and evaluative exercises in the unit, as they encourage the rehumanization, transformation, and liberation for both oppressed and oppressor groups.

UNIT CONCEPTS

- To analyze the impact that Euro-American hegemony had on Mexicanas/os in the post–Treaty of Guadalupe era in the U.S. Southwest, which led to counter-hegemonic responses.
- To define and articulate Chicana/o resistance and affirmation within the colonial context of the United States that Chicanas/os had and continue to experience in the post–Treaty of Guadalupe Hidalgo era.
- To define, analyze, and articulate the roots of conflict between whites and Chicanas/os-Mexicanas/os in the newly conquered territories.
- To examine the vital role that Chicana/o folklore has played in the articulation of the history of Chicana/o-Mexicana/o resistance and affirmation.
- To analyze and evaluate the different models of Chicana/o-Mexicana/o resistance and affirmation in the post–Treaty of Guadalupe Hidalgo era.
- To interpret and synthesize the various models of Chicana/o-Mexicana/o resistance and affirmation in order to understand their contemporary applications.

STANDARDS ALIGNMENT

The lessons within this curriculum unit are aligned to the 21st-century core curriculum for social studies and language arts as well as the California state standards for U.S. history and language arts.

REQUIRED RESOURCES
Publications

- Abu-Jamal, Mumia. 2001. *All Things Considered.* Seven Stories Press.
- Acuña, Rodolfo F. 2015. *Occupied America: A History of Chicanos*, 8th Edition. Pearson.
- Acuña, Rodolfo F. 2011. "Occupied America" in *The Latina/o Condition: A Critical Reader,* 2nd Edition (Richard F. Delgado and Jean Stefancic, eds.), 61–64. New York University Press.
- Burciaga, José Antonio. 1993. *Drink Cultura: Chicanismo.* Joshua Odell Editions.
- Enríquez, Evangelina, and Alfredo Mirandé. 1979. *La Chicana.* The University of Chicago Press.
- Freire, Paulo. 1970. *Pedagogy of the Oppressed.* Continuum.
- Garza, Humberto. 2001. *Joaquin Murrieta: A Quest for Justice.* Chusma House Publications.
- Mirandé, Alfredo. 1987. *Gringo Justice.* University of Notre Dame.
- Stavans, Ilan, and Lalo Alcaraz. 2000. *Latino USA: A Cartoon History.* Basic Books.
- Valenzuela, Angela. 1999. *Subtractive Schooling: U.S.-Mexican Youth and the Politics of Caring.* SUNY Press.
- Zinn, Howard. 1990. *Declarations of Independence: Cross-Examining American Ideology.* Harper Perennial.

Research Studies

Ruiz, Vicki. 1996. "From Out of the Shadows: Mexican Women in the United States." *OAH Magazine of History*, 11.1:33–35.

Solórzano, Daniel G., and Dolores Delgado Bernal. 2001. "Examining Transformative Resistance Through a Critical Race and LatCrit Theory Framework: Chicana and Chicano Students in an Urban Context." *Urban Education*, 34.3:308–42.

Multimedia Resources

The Ballad of Gregorio Cortez. Dir. Robert M. Young. 1982. American Playhouse. DVD.

Tiburcio Vasquez: The Lost Bandido Trailer. Dir. Charley Trujillo. 2009. Chusma House. YouTube video. Retrieved from youtube.com/watch?v=0stTol-AFok.

Lesson Summary

LESSON 1: CHICANA/O RESISTANCE AND AFFIRMATION VOCABULARY

- **Chicana/o Resistance and Affirmation Vocabulary List:** The students will individually read the key Chicana/o resistance and affirmation vocabulary list and definitions of words that will be found throughout the proceeding lessons in this unit. The vocabulary words are *hegemony, colonization, resistance, affirmation, accommodation, internalized oppression, white supremacy,* and *racism.*
- **Four Tables:** The students will complete a four tables sheet for each word from the Chicana/o Resistance and Affirmation Vocabulary list. The students are to draw a horizontal line and a vertical line across an entire sheet of paper that results in the creation of four boxes. The four tables sheet consists of the word itself in the first box, the definition of the word in the second box, the use of the word in a sentence in the third box, and a drawing of the picture of the word as interpreted by the student in the fourth box.
- **Four Tables Student Presentation:** The students will present their completion of the four tables exercise.

I explicitly frame this lesson with my students using the *Nahui Ollin* as pedagogy, specifically the concepts and principles of *Tezcatlipoca* (critical self-reflection) and *Quetzalcoatl* (obtaining and creation of knowledge, or *consciencia*). For example, I asked my students to critically reflect on themselves when using a vocabulary word from this lesson in a sentence. I prompted the students with "When you utilize any given vocabulary word in a sentence, make certain that you use it in a manner that directly relates to yourself and your experiences. Practice Tezcatlipoca—look in the mirror when making the word relative to yourself, your *familia*, and your community."

One student, Xochitl Bernal, responded by using internalized oppression in a sentence: "Mexicans who are employed by the U.S. Border Patrol show *internalized oppression* because they are hunting down undocumented people who could easily be a family member or relative." Xochitl exhibited the pedagogical principle of Tezcatlipoca that calls for critical examination of the realities of her own community.

When instructing students to draw a picture of their interpretation of the meaning of the word from the vocabulary list, I prompted them by clearly framing the pedagogical principle of Quetzalcoatl, encouraging them to "develop your consciencia—that consciousness and knowledge of the word that you will draw to demonstrate your understanding of that word."

Xochitl proceeded to draw a picture of a brown-skinned border patrol agent with a *nopal de enfrente*, a cactus protruding out of the forehead, which within a Mexican cultural context is a mockery of a person who denies their "Mexican-ness" or "Indian-ness."

LESSON 2: RACISM, COLONIZATION, AND THE CHICANA/O EXPERIENCE

- *Subtractive Schooling* **Excerpt:** The students will read aloud Christine Sleeter's foreword from Valenzuela's *Subtractive Schooling: U.S. Mexican Youth and the Politics of Caring* (1999, p. xvii–xviii).
- *Subtractive Schooling* **Critical Thinking Questions:** The students will answer critical thinking questions in groups of three or four and present their responses with the class.

This lesson was framed within the pedagogical principle of Tezcatlipoca—critical reflection of self, family, and community. After a reading of Sleeter's piece on the two stages of racism (economic and cultural), particularly on how it was used by whites against Mexicans in the United States to steal their land and legitimize that theft, students were engaged in a critical discussion of how this racism has had an impact on the Chicana/o experience, specifically regarding schooling. Part of the lesson asks a series of critical questions and prompts; the following prompt garnered the highest level of engagement with my students:

Consider the following quote by Sleeter and determine whether you believe this statement to be true relative to the Chicana/o experience. Make certain to support your position with evi-

dence in complete sentence responses. Be prepared to discuss your position with the class.

"Schools are the instrument of the maintenance of the colonial relationships in that they constitute an arm of the state through which belief systems and cultural relationships are taught."

I employed the pedagogical concept of Tezcatlipoca by directly asking my students to reflect on their experiences with schooling, their parents' experiences with schooling (if possible), and their grandparents' experiences with schooling (if possible). If non-Chicanx-Latinx students are in a class, they too can engage in this exercise, as Sleeter frames it in her chapter in *Everyday Anti-Racism: Getting Real About Race in Schools*, and can view it as a "window" or critical insight into the Chicanx-Latinx experience.

The responses and discussion to this question revealed a trauma for many of my students, as their school experiences (and their parents' and grandparents' if they had attended school in the United States) had been painful, given that they had experienced processes of deculturalization, "de-Mexicanization," and dehumanization. For many of my students, this was the first time that they had reflected upon and discussed their experiences with schooling, which allowed them to directly face their personal histories and begin the process of healing.

Relative to this healing process, student Marcos Martínez said, "This exercise was like a huge weight lifted off of my chest. I have never been given the chance to talk about my *familia*'s and my experiences in school where we have been treated as less than just because we are Mexicanos. After learning much of this history about Chicanos and other Raza in our class, I now know it is the schools who have the problem, and that problem is racism. We as Mexicanos are not the problem." My pedagogical framing for this lesson using Tezcatlipoca had proven to be what Silvia Toscano termed "teaching as a healing craft."

LESSON 3: THE INTERNAL COLONY

- **"Occupied America" Excerpt:** The student will individually read (silent sustained reading) the "Occupied America" chapter from Delgado &

Stefancic's (2011) *The Latina/o Condition: A Critical Reader* (p. 61–64).

- **Group Interpretations**: Groups of three or four students will be assigned sections of Acuña's "Occupied America" chapter. They will explore the meaning, application, and evaluation of their designated sections as provided in the Group Interpretations Template.
- **Student Presentations on Group Interpretations Template**: The assigned groups will present their template findings to the class.

LESSON 4: EURO-AMERICAN JUSTICE IN THE POST–TREATY OF GUADALUPE HIDALGO ERA

- **Activity 1—Examination of 19th-Century Euro-American Quotes**: The student will analyze and evaluate a series of 19th-century quotes about Mexicans from Euro-American historical figures.
- **Activity 2—Analogies Worksheet**: Students will complete an analogies worksheet to familiarize themselves with vocabulary from the PowerPoint on Alfredo Mirandé's theory of *Gringo Justice* (1987).

Directions: An analogy is a pair of words that correspond in some way or illustrate a relationship. They are often found on tests of one sort or another, primarily because they require a thorough command of vocabulary—the basic building blocks of language. Before you get started, there are a few things that you need to know. To begin, look at the following example:

easy : difficult :: simple : complicated

The symbol ":" stands for "is to," while the symbol "::" stands for "as." Thus, the above example would read "easy is to difficult as simple is to complicated." Can you see the relationship between each pair? The words *easy* and *difficult* are antonyms—they have opposite meanings—as are the words *simple* and *complicated*. In analogies, each pair should have the same relationship. In other words, if the first pair are antonyms, the second pair should be also. Likewise, if the first pair are synonyms (words with the same meaning), the second pair should be also. To begin, determine the relationship between the first pair of words in each of the analogies below. Place an "A" for antonym or "S" for synonym in the box to the left of each pair. Then, choosing from the word list from Mirandé's theory of *Gringo Justice*, find the antonym or synonym for each of the second pairs and write it in the box to the right. The first one is done for you.

A	submissive: rebellious :: harmless :	**pernicious**

- **Activity 3—Group Matrix**: Students will be assigned to groups of three or four to cover and present on the theoretical underpinnings and basic tenets of Mirandé's (1987) theory of *Gringo Justice*.

Directions: Each group will be assigned to complete a matrix on a given item from Mirandé's list. In this matrix, the student is required to cite the item, interpret its meaning, and determine its applicability to the contemporary experience of the Chicanx-Latinx. After all the groups have completed their matrices, select a student from each group to present their findings to the rest of the class.

- **Activity 4—PowerPoint Presentation**: The students will examine a series of slides from the PowerPoint presentation and evaluate its historical influence on Chicana/o-Mexicana/o people in the post–Treaty of Guadalupe Hidalgo era by answering a sequence of critical questions.

LESSON 5: BANDITS OR FREEDOM FIGHTERS?

- **Activity 1—Tiburcio Vasquez**: First, the teacher will choose students to read aloud "Tiburcio Vasquez: A Chicano Perspective" (p. 119–28) from José Antonio Burciaga's *Drink Cultura: Chicanismo*. Second, the students will screen a short seven-minute mini-documentary, *Tiburcio Vasquez: The Lost Bandido*. After the reading and screening, the students will write a two-page persuasive editorial on the life and times of Tiburcio Vasquez, taking the position for or against his actions.
- **Activity 2—Joaquin Murrieta**: The students will read from Humberto Garza's *Joaquin Murrieta: A Quest for Justice* (p. vii–ix) and "Social Banditry"

Sample Excerpts of Group Matrices

THEORETICAL UNDERPINNINGS OF THE PERSPECTIVE (Excerpt of matrix)

Citation	Interpretation of Mirandé's theoretical underpinning	Applicability to the contemporary Chicanx-Latinx experience
The image of Chicanos as criminals or bandits has persisted since the initial contact between Anglo settlers and Mexicans on the frontier.		
Theories that characterize Chicanos as criminal, delinquent, or violent are not benign but pernicious and must be actively resisted and rejected, even when they are ostensibly sympathetic, for they ultimately work to control Chicanos and maintain their subordinate status.		

BASIC TENETS OF THE PERSPECTIVE (Excerpt of matrix)

Citation	Interpretation of Mirandé's theoretical underpinning	Applicability to the contemporary Chicanx-Latinx experience
Conflict with law enforcement intensified during the 20th century. With growing barrioization, the police assumed an increasingly important role in maintaining Chicanos under control and enforcing the social and physical isolation of the barrio.		
Although Chicanos are essentially a landless people not integrated into the American "melting pot," barrios are a symbolic land base and an important sense of identity and pride.		

(p. 144–45) from Rodolfo Acuña's (2014) *Occupied America: A History of Chicanos* to themselves (silent sustained reading). After reading these selections, students in assigned groups and roles will perform a short *teatro* or engage in a debate centering on the following question: "Was Joaquin Murrieta a bandit or a hero?"

- **Activity 3—El Corrido de Joaquin Murrieta:** The students will listen to the song "El Corrido de Joaquin Murrieta," following along with the lyrics provided. After a discussion of this *corrido*, students will create their own corrido, rap, or poem identifying a historical figure who embodies resistance to oppression. The student will present/perform this corrido, rap, and/or poem to the class.

- **Activity 4—The Ballad of Gregorio Cortez:** The students will actively screen *The Ballad of Gregorio Cortez*, paying particular attention to issues of race, class, and gender that emerge from the film and taking notes. Student will also read to themselves (silent sustained reading) "The Ballad of Gregorio Cortez" (p. 75–76) from Rodolfo Acuña's (2014) *Occupied America: A History of Chicanos*. After the screening of the movie and the completion of the assigned selection, the teacher will assign a critical media analysis of the film in the form of a two- to three-page extended writing response.

LESSON 6: CHICANA/MEXICANA RESISTANCE

- **Activity 1—Juanita de Downieville:** The students will read the "Juanita de Downieville" piece from Mirandé's (1987) *Gringo Justice* and "The Mexican Prostitute" (p. 140) from Rodolfo Acuña's (2014) *Occupied America: A History of Chicanos* in groups and apply their understanding of Juanita de Downieville's experience by completing a first-person narrative.

- **Activity 2—"From Out of the Shadows" Reading:** Students will be assigned to read "From Out of the Shadows: Mexican Women in the United States" by Vicki Ruiz (1996). While reading this research article, the students will write notes that highlight each of Chicana/Mexicana historical figures who resisted racism and gender oppression.

- **Activity 3—Group Matrix:** After completing the group reading and group note documentation of "From Out of the Shadows," the students will complete in their assigned groups the Group Matrix. This exercise requires the group to fill in all sections of the matrix by completing the following sections: Who were the Chicanas/Mexicanas identified in this article and what were they resisting? What were the outcomes of Chicana/Mexicana resistance as specified in this article? The teacher will assign groups to present their findings with the class. ✳

Sample of Activities Within Lesson #5:
Bandits or Freedom Fighters?

Learning Objectives:

1) The student will read a historical accounts of Tiburcio Vasquez and determine whether his exploits were justified by writing a two-page persuasive editorial piece.
2) The student will read and listen to historical accounts of Joaquin Murrieta and appraise his status as a hero or bandit by enacting a short *teatro* or debate.
3) The student will listen to "El Corrido de Joaquin Murrieta" and apply its meaning by creating their own *corrido*, rap, or poem about a historical figure who enacted resistance against oppression.
4) The student will actively watch *The Ballad of Gregorio Cortez* and analyze and evaluate its meaning by completing an extended writing response.

Introduction:

- The student will apply prior knowledge to examine historical accounts of the Chicana/o experience in the post–Treaty of Guadalupe Hidalgo era. In addition, the student will be introduced to the importance of folklore as a historical resource in examining Chicana/o-Mexicana/o resistance and affirmation in the post–Treaty of Guadalupe Hidalgo era.

Anticipatory Set: Write the following quote on the board and choose a student to read it aloud for the class:

"Contrary to popular belief, conventional wisdom would have one believe that it is insane to resist this, the mightiest of empires. . . . But what history really shows is that today's empire is tomorrow's ashes, that nothing lasts forever, and that to not resist is to acquiesce in your own oppression. The greatest form of sanity that anyone can exercise is to resist that force that is trying to repress, oppress, and fight down the human spirit."
—Mumia Abu-Jamal

The teacher is to facilitate discussion among students on: 1) how this quote relates to the notion of resistance; 2) whether they agree or disagree with Abu-Jamal's assessment of resistance; and 3) why they agree or disagree with Abu-Jamal's assessment of resistance.

Lesson 5: Activity #1—The students are to read "Tiburcio Vasquez: A Chicano Perspective" (p. 119–28) from José Antonio Burciaga's *Drink Cultura: Chicanismo*. Also, students are to actively screen and take notes on *Tiburcio Vasquez: The Lost Bandido*. After reading the selection and screening the mini-documentary, the students are to write a two-page editorial on the life and times of Tiburcio Vasquez, taking the position for or against his actions.

Lesson 5: Activity #4—The students will actively watch *The Ballad of Gregorio Cortez* by taking notes on the themes of race, class, and gender that emerge from the film. In addition, students will read to themselves (silent sustained reading) "The Ballad of Gregorio Cortez" (p. 75–76) from Rodolfo Acuña's (2014) *Occupied America: A History of Chicanos*. After completing the screening of the film and the assigned reading, the teacher will assign a two- to three-page writing response that addresses the following:

1) Setting: time, place, and context.
2) Story: Describe plot, central events, main symbols, and dominant point of view.
3) Major Characters: Are the Chicana/o characters stereotyped or authentically portrayed? Explain.
4) Gender, Class, and Race: Does the film normalize, ignore, or challenge the oppression of Chicanas and Chicanos portrayed in the film?

The extended writing response must be at least two pages in length and double-space typed.

ADOLFO VALLE

ALL WE WANT IS FOR OUR STORIES TO BE TAUGHT

✳ ORGANIZING FOR AND SUSTAINING ETHNIC STUDIES

Moving Ethnic Studies from Theory to Practice
A Liberating Process

BY GUILLERMO ANTONIO GÓMEZ AND EDUARDO "KIKI" OCHOA

"Having a rifle range that teaches kids how to shoot for target practice at our high school with a zero-tolerance policy on weapons is a complete contradiction."
—Alex Velarde, student leader

In the fall of 2007, Lincoln High School had just reopened in Southeast San Diego. The campus was thriving, and excitement filled the air. Most students were in love with all their new classes except for one. First-year students were being placed in the Junior Reserve Officers' Training Corps (JROTC) program without their consent or their parents' approval. They were being forced to purchase an expensive uniform as part of the program or their academic grade in the course would suffer. However, the straw that broke the camel's back was the fact that students were being taught how to shoot guns on a school campus.

One of our students, Alex Velarde, who was taking our Ethnic Studies course that focused on self-love, community, self-advocacy, and activism, felt this contradiction was completely unacceptable. Alex asked us what he could do.

How does a course in Ethnic Studies build the foundation for organizing a student-led campaign to ban rifle ranges in all San Diego schools? As teacher-organizers we believe education must go beyond the four walls of our classroom. We must read the word and read the world in order to change it. Praxis, theory becoming action that establishes concrete change students can feel, is a critical element of our course. Fostering community organizing and social activism with our youth is a process whereby education plays a fundamental role. But becoming activists does not happen by accident; we are intentional with how we have designed our course.

Based on what we call the five-step liberation process, derived from Jeff Duncan-Andrade and Ernest Morrell's Definite Dozen (originally conceptualized by Summitt and Jenkins), we taught the students to organize themselves and others against the rifle range. The five-step liberation process consists of 1) identifying a problem; 2) analyzing what factors contribute to this problem; 3) coming up with a plan to confront this problem; 4) implementing the plan; and 5) evaluating the plan to determine whether the objectives were met or if it needed to go back to the drawing board. Our students took the lessons from the classroom and gave them life through organized struggle.

Creating Change Through Education and Organized Activism

Before Ethnic Studies becomes an actual practical reality for creating change, teachers have to realize that students can't move into learning the history of others before learning about themselves. And they can't learn about themselves if they don't trust the people around them. In order to critically understand social movements that alter the course of history and change their own conditions, they must truly understand who they are and what their ancestors have sacrificed. Developing a strong sense of identity and self-advocacy is vital to students' solidarity with their communities and other oppressed groups. In our teaching over the years, we have witnessed how the internalization of a critical social consciousness motivates youth to immerse themselves in community activism and their struggle for a better world.

Our Ethnic Studies course culminates in a unit

that guides students in what Paulo Freire refers to as "the liberation process." The primary goal of this end-of-course unit is to analyze current issues that impact our communities and propose solutions. Social activism becomes a lesson that engages students in learning the methods of creating social change in their lives. This unit becomes critical because it humanizes our youth by transforming their apathy into self-empowerment. There is a purpose for what we've studied, and students become determined change agents who put in the necessary work for organizing. This process alone, although not always successful, gives our youth the tools for liberation and self-advocacy. Students who have always wanted to create change but felt powerless now see themselves in a completely different light and are ready to take on the world.

Theory into Practice

The student-led campaign to end the rifle ranges encompassed a twofold strategy: an internal strategy to educate and organize the student body and an external organizational strategy to build with allies and reach out to the surrounding San Diego community. We saw the creation of Lincoln High MEChA

> **Students posed questions like "Why are we teaching students to shoot rifles if we have a zero-tolerance policy on weapons at school?" Students learned firsthand the time-consuming struggle of organizing others for a common purpose.**

and the African Revolutionary Student Organization (ARSO) internally, both of which became critical student-organizing vehicles in the emerging campaign. Students learned that a collective, organized front is a must in order to create the change we want. We also learned from our historical analysis of popular struggles such as the Chicano movement, Black Panther Party, and the East Coast Young Lords. Using a historical critical lens from readings, documentaries, and independent films like *Panther* and *Walkout*, students learned firsthand that organizing the masses would not be easy and that commitment was essential since there would most likely be bumps in the road. Classroom lessons required student research. Youth immersed themselves in literature that highlighted gun violence in our society, gun control, and school policies regarding weapons. Students began collecting student stories and testimonies about how gun violence in their communities affected them and criminalized their school and community.

Student leaders from MEChA and ARSO began educating the student body using the information they collected in their research. Students met continuously to build a platform of persuasive talking points. Students met with administration in order to project and demand their dissatisfaction with rifle ranges in public schools.

Students posed questions like "Why are we teaching students to shoot rifles if we have a zero-tolerance policy on weapons at school?" Students learned firsthand the time-consuming struggle of organizing others for a common purpose. Outside school hours, some students created unity with Mission Bay High School students and educators who were passionate about the same issue. Together they established the Education Not Arms Coalition (ENAC), which was composed of students, educators, parents, community members, grassroots organizations, and activists.

Numerous meetings took place; numbers grew, petitions were signed, and many board meetings were attended. Each time our youth participated in a board meeting, they felt disrespected by the lack of interest from district leadership. But their tenacity only grew, and they doubled down on their commitment. About 30 students attended the first board meeting. The number grew to about 100 at meetings that followed, which led to about 600 on the night the decision to eliminate the gun ranges was made. The students' two-year campaign culminated with the elimination of gun ranges throughout the entire San Diego Unified School District. It was a sight to see: theory into practice.

The Ban of Border Patrol on a School Campus

For the last 10 years, the teachings of our Ethnic Studies course have implemented a culture of resistance on campus; only through an organized front have students been able to change some of the oppressive practices on campus. For example, on a typical school day in the fall of 2016, a border patrol agent was invited by a criminal justice teacher to be a guest speaker in her class. An uncomfortable scenario unfolded that ignited a student-led campaign that eventually banned the border patrol from ever stepping foot on our campus.

The agent was invited to highlight the daily work of the border patrol. During his presentation, the agent referred to undocumented individuals as "illegal aliens." This language did not sit well with some of the students present in class who, having already taken our course, had regained their humanity by embracing every facet of who they are and letting the world know they would never again be oppressed. Furthermore, some of the students themselves were undocumented and others had been separated from their parents due to their documentation status.

The students approached us with this concern and asked how to address it. Our first response was for them to implement the liberation process taught in our Ethnic Studies classes. Students should identify why this was a problem, analyze why it was happening, and ultimately implement a plan to prevent this dehumanizing situation from happening again.

In conjunction with MEChA, the students met, discussed, and presented their analyses. The students argued the campus was supposed to be a safe environment for all students. They felt the words used were dehumanizing and criminalized their families and community. Another student expressed that having the border patrol on campus created anxiety and a sense of fear. Although the criminal justice teacher assured the students that the agent was not on campus to conduct any investigations or to determine whether students were documented or not, the students still felt unsafe and uncomfortable having just the mere presence of border patrol on a school campus. Relying on what they learned in our unit about Maslow's Hierarchy of Needs, the students were able to argue that an unsafe environment for students interrupts their learning and self-esteem. The next step was for students to present their arguments to the criminal justice teacher. When they did, the teacher unfortunately disagreed, saying the agents were not a threat to students' safety and that there were already plans to invite them back to a career fair on campus. Students proceeded to bring their arguments to the principal. The principal sided with the criminal justice teacher, didn't feel that the agents were a threat, and refused their request to ban the border patrol.

The students then had to reevaluate their plan. They decided to survey the student body about having the border patrol on campus. The results of the survey overwhelmingly showed that students did not feel comfortable with border patrol on campus. They created a presentation, educated the rest of the student body through the history department, and passed around a petition to ban border patrol agents from campus. This led to securing more than a thousand signatures within a week. A small percentage of students had no problem with the border patrol being on campus; they wanted to follow a career in law enforcement. But this small sector was drowned out by the large majority opposed to their presence.

The topic became controversial and the local media became involved. The principal quickly called a meeting with the students leading the campaign, district staff, and the criminal justice teacher. At the meeting, the students said they were being coerced into stopping the campaign. The students held their ground and refused to stop. Students then had to reflect and plan their next move. They contacted immigrant rights groups, university professors, psychologists, and other prominent community members to write letters to the principal in support of their campaign. The Ethnic Studies teachers also asked for a meeting with the principal and the criminal justice teacher to reason in support of the students. Eventually, after much community pressure, media reporting, meetings with school board members, and the students' ongoing campaign, the principal reluctantly decided to ban the border patrol from campus.

Seeing the lessons learned in our classes playing out in real-life circumstances, actions being implemented, and objectives being met was a humanizing experience for everyone involved. The teachers were inspired because the literature read, the discussions that took place, the organizing tools that were shared, and the education that was embraced in the Ethnic Studies classes came alive beyond the four walls of their classrooms.

Will Social Activism Endure?

Increasingly, more teachers and students in K–12 schools across the nation are engaging in an Ethnic Studies curriculum or some form of culturally responsive teaching practice. Ethnic Studies engages historically marginalized students by providing purpose, reaffirmation, and a sense of self-love that ignites empowerment and advocacy in an educa-

Will the district support a course that cannot be confined to a textbook? Will a class that puts theory into practice be allowed to survive?

tional system that often neglects their identities and their stories. By moving the theory into practice, education fulfills what it was set out to do: provide the tools for change and liberation.

Will the district support a course that cannot be confined to a textbook? Will our Ethnic Studies class experience the same fate our sisters and brothers faced in our neighboring state of Arizona? Thankfully, even after many years of litigation, a federal judge found that the banning of Ethnic Studies in Arizona violated the rights of Mexican American students (see p. 341). Will a class that puts theory into practice be allowed to survive? If the nation is truly about freedom, democracy, and justice, the answer is clear: YES! However, a historical analysis of power in America may conclude the opposite. We will continue this urgent work to build a better world for all here in San Diego.

Critical Consciousness Takes Time: An Overview of Our Yearlong Curriculum

Over the last 10 years, we have written, revised, enriched, and delivered a curriculum that has emphasized family, community, love, advocacy, human rights, agency, and systemic change through organized collective action. Here we share an outline that highlights the key curricular experiences that are generative and build into the final unit on Creating Change and Contemporary Issues.

UNIT 1
BUILDING COMMUNITY:
HUMANIZING FOR A LEARNING SANCTUARY

The goal of this unit is to establish a community of mutual respect and trust. Creating a healthy classroom community allows us to build a core set of values that guides our coursework and class discussions. Most of the students in urban schools who arrive at our classroom door have spent nine years buying into the system and have either assimilated into dominant mainstream culture in order to survive socially and academically or completely rejected the educational process, which they have learned to mistrust. Our central focus and objective, therefore, is to begin the healing process by humanizing our students to rid themselves of their fears, stereotypes, anger, and for many, self-hate.

To establish an environment of trust and solidarity, a loving community must be built in the classroom. A learning sanctuary has to be established before any other concepts, ideas, theories, and histories could be addressed.

The initial concepts we tackle are responsibility, respect, honesty, loyalty, work ethic, study habits, character building, belief, self-improvement, self-reflection, humility, problem-solving, and resilience through Jeff Duncan-Andrade and Ernest Morrell's "Definite Dozen" from *The Art of Critical Pedagogy*. To further solidify a culture of mutual love and respect, we recite Luis Valdez's Mayan-inspired "In Lak'ech." The daily reading of this short poem lays the foundation for each class session and is a reminder of our duty toward one another. Again, we reinforce community; we establish a family in the classroom in order to enact authentic dialogue of the sensitive subject matter of the course.

Another essential part of the course's opening unit is built upon Mehl-Madrona's concept of narrative medicine. Based on the ancient practice of healing circles by Native American, Asian, and African Indigenous communities, we come together and sit in a circle to discuss personal and academic issues. By participating in this ancient tradition, students build mutual respect, engage in dialogue, and learn that we all share similar fears, experiences, wants, dreams, and aspirations.

UNIT 2
MASLOW'S HIERARCHY OF NEEDS: WHAT EVERY HUMAN DESERVES

The goal of utilizing Maslow's framework is to define what every human being needs to live a full and productive life. Once a strong sense of community and trust has been established, we ask students to take an introspective look and analyze their current realities, critical literacy, current events, and popular media through a framework driven by Abraham Maslow's theory of basic human needs. When introducing this unit, we ask students to write what things are essential to living a productive life. Students first draft a personal list, then come together in groups to create one list, a process that involves lively discussions, rationalizations, and compromise. In most lists, family is salient. "Love/Belonging and Self-Esteem" is the stage in Maslow's framework that incites the most critical dialogue. Most of the students express that family is ultimately a human need they cannot live without. Exposing the value of family also highlights how the lack of some of the items in Maslow's stages results in conflicts in family relations. A culminating project for this unit is to create a family tree that includes at least 10 family members or people they perceive as part of their family.

UNIT 3
IDENTITY: RECLAIMING OURSELVES

The purpose of this unit is to examine and understand one's own identity and every facet that shapes our worldview and our lives. Once an in-depth analysis is in process and students uncover the cause of issues they face on a personal level, we take students into a deeper self-analysis to create consciousness about their identities. Students struggle to see how our identities are shaped by our experiences and society. Students realize the ways they are forced to sacrifice the beautiful cultures, languages, and abundant histories they bring with them as they enter their formal educational experience at the early age of 4 or 5. This type of marginalization is shared among all oppressed communities and it impacts our youth, preventing them from becoming fully human. We introduce students to the concept of nature vs. nurture. There are physical traits they cannot control since they are born with them, but there also are things they have more control over.

Students create an identity presentation that requires them to decorate a shoebox with personal traits that form their identity. These traits include their likes and dislikes, hobbies, words that describe them, individuals they admire, and goals for their future. They also have to place three symbols or objects into their boxes that represent three values they have. The items in their boxes usually include pictures of family members or personal items that are meaningful. The identity presentations allow for the students to not only present themselves and think deeply about what makes them who they are and the influences in their lives; it also affirms the value of their own identities. Some students have phobias of speaking in public and struggle, while others capitalize on the opportunity and disclose significant themes, such as family separation, death, violence, love, and family. By developing and reclaiming their identities, students empower themselves and thus move forward in uniting with others.

UNIT 4
ATTACKS ON OUR IDENTITY: I CONTROL MY STORY

The vision of this unit is to look at how everyday human interactions, systems, and society are impacted by assumptions and discrimination and to examine historical and contemporary acts of oppression. Once students have solidified who they are and where they come from, they embark on a deep analysis of historical and contemporary oppressive systems that attack and marginalize youth and their identities. Students learn about the different isms—such as racism, ageism, and sexism—and how they have been perpetuated in the past and today. Above all, they are exposed to decolonial pedagogy, which is unchartered territory for many since it's not addressed until the college years, if at all. The students' journeys in deconstructing our world and uncovering its limitations through a lens of colonialism are truly eye-opening. Uncovering hidden messages in popular media and methods of institutionalizing racism helps students understand how society misrepresents

The students' journeys in deconstructing our world and uncovering its limitations through a lens of colonialism are truly eye-opening. Uncovering hidden messages in popular media and methods of institutionalizing racism helps students understand how society misrepresents and/or harms people's identities.

and/or harms people's identities. Through activities that use primary and secondary documents, students analyze when identities are praised, diminished, or just marginalized. This unit can bring confusion and even anger for some of the students who have been or are being affected by past and present attacks on their identities. Engaging in these challenging activities brings out necessary conversations for students to realize that many of their peers have experienced institutionalized racism.

One of the highlights in this unit is the study of a historical immigration timeline from 1492 to the present. Images and descriptions of significant immigration policies or events are displayed in chronological order around the classroom. Students are asked to reflect on what policies or events impacted them the most and then to explain in their own words how identities have been falsely manipulated throughout history using critical Socratic seminars and

writing prompts. The culminating project for this unit is for students to interview a family member, friend, teacher, or neighbor who has immigrated or migrated to the United States. The purpose of this project is not only for students to value the identities of the diverse people who live in the United States but also to learn about the hardships that push people to leave their home countries and how hard life is for many immigrants. Through the art of storytelling, students realize the power they possess to control their narrative.

UNIT 5
HUMAN RIGHTS: RECOGNIZING INJUSTICE AND REHUMANIZING STUDENTS

The work of this unit is to analyze the Universal Declaration of Human Rights and make it a living document. Once students have a strong sense of their identities and can identify forms of oppression, it is important to give them the tools to advocate and defend their humanity. The 30 articles that make up the Universal Declaration of Human Rights (un.org/en/universal-declaration-human-rights) are used as a primary document to expose students to their rights as human beings.

Recently, with the elimination of DACA and other viable programs, immigrants continue to be under attack and have been the scapegoat victims to social ills. These attacks have increased under the Trump administration. Students experience mixed emotions and at times react angrily to the fact that our universal human rights grant us the freedom of movement within borders. Apparently, the intensity of Immigration and Customs Enforcement (ICE) operations and random stops based on racial profiling violate this right. Some of our students' family members have been deported due to their undocumented immigration status. The separation of families, especially children who are born citizens being separated from their parents, creates a cycle of anger, depression, and mistrust toward the system that is supposed to protect them. This unit of study is essential for students to recognize injustice and regain their humanity. The injustices in their hearts are reaffirmed and validated by a document recognized by nations throughout the world.

UNIT 6

SOCIAL MOVEMENTS AND HISTORICAL FIGURES: WE CAN MOVE SOCIETY

The aim of this unit is to educate ourselves about historical figures and social movements that have been absent from our schooling. Just when students feel disillusioned and powerless, this unit gives them a sense of hope and urgency. Often missing from our curriculum are historical figures and social movements that have defended and fought for human rights and have created change. For example, in our classrooms, you will encounter posters of figures like Che Guevara, Malcolm X, Assata Shakur, Yuri Kochiyama, and Emiliano Zapata. Not only do these images create interest, but they engender topics of discussion like "I've seen that guy on a T-shirt," "My teacher told me that Che was a cold-blooded murderer" and "Someone said that Malcolm X was violent." Misconceptions change once students are exposed to other people's histories and how these historical figures fought or continue to fight for a better world. Besides researching and teaching each other about these people, students also learn that none of these individuals created change on their own; they were part of bigger movements and organizations. We then introduce students to social movements led by organizations like the Black Panthers, the Chicano movement, and the farmworkers' struggle led by Filipino and Mexicano organizers. It then becomes apparent to students that social change can only be accomplished when one unites with others and becomes part of a collective, an organization for social change.

UNIT 7

CREATING CHANGE AND CONTEMPORARY ISSUES

As we mentioned earlier, the course culminates with a unit that guides students toward what we refer to as Freire's liberation process. The objective of this unit is to analyze current issues that impact our communities and our world, create solutions, and act as change agents. Social activism becomes a lesson, whether theoretical or practical, that engages students in learning the methods of creating social change within their communities. This unit becomes critical because it evaluates how determined students are to put in the necessary work for organizing. Most students have a desire to change their surroundings but are likely to struggle in the process. This unit exposes them to basic organizing tools. Those who fully commit become empowered leaders on our campus and throughout our local community. They excel academically for collective purposes as opposed to their own individual achievement.

There have been many successful actions in our school—elimination of the rifle range, rallies and marches against budget cuts to public education, the removal of an autocratic principal, the hiring of a democratic leader the district opposed, and a campaign to change the graduation requirements to reflect California university entrance requirements, among others. Students who have taken our course have led every single one of those struggles. We live in a world where youth feel disconnected to education. They feel powerless, that things can never change. Our Ethnic Studies classes challenge our youth to change that narrative. As Salvador Allende said, "To be a student and not a revolutionary is a complete contradiction." ✻

The Missing Pages of Our History

BY KAIYA LAGUARDIA-YONAMINE

"I will gladly say that the Portland Public Schools board has unanimously voted 'yes' on Ethnic Studies in the PPS high schools!" As soon as that beautiful statement filled our ears, the crowd broke into an earsplitting roar. All I could process over and over again was "We did it. We actually did it. We did it." Screams of joy, laughter, tears, and happiness filled the room as we raised and shook our makeshift last-minute signs, me holding my personal favorite featuring Batman saying, "Batman Supports Ethnic Studies!" with a thumbs-up. Pink and black swarmed my vision, the colors of our ALLY T-shirts creating a fist on the center of our chests.

After all our hard work, we did it.

But of course, we couldn't leave without a picture.

Herds of high school students, parents, and APANO (Asian Pacific American Network of Oregon) staff stampeded to the center, moms holding five different cameras in both hands to capture the moment with as many devices as possible. Someone shouted, "Fists up everyone! Say 'ALLY!'" and for the next wonderful minutes of hugs all I could see was a sea of smiles, grinning ear to ear and making my cheeks hurt, but I couldn't help it.

After the painfully anxious hours of waiting for the other announcements from the general public to finish, watching the excited faces of my parents in the audience, and finally being able to give my final part of my testimony, it was done. Ethnic Studies is now going to be implemented in all PPS high schools.

And it was all because of us.

I started with ALLY, or Asian Leaders for the Liberation of Youth, in the summer going into 8th grade two years ago. It was a summer camp that lasted a couple weeks, so I invited some really "down" friends to come with me. I was the youngest in the group. The camp was about social justice and the different forms of oppression in society, from everyday racism and microaggressions to imperialism to ageism. Different social justice organizations were brought in to talk with us on the subjects that they specialized in and what we could do to help. Then came the question: What do we do from here?

The mission of ALLY is to uplift the voices of Asian and Pacific Islander (API) youth within our community and make the change we want to see happen. A list started of areas where we wanted change, eventually leading to the bigger umbrella of education in the school system, specifically in Portland. Finally, the decision narrowed down to one thing: Ethnic Studies. I helped bring up the idea after watching an amazing film called *Precious Knowledge* and really wanted to do something like what they did in Arizona here in PPS. After researching whom to talk to on the PPS board and what benefits Ethnic Studies has and creating a timeline for the implementation that we would like to see, we launched a campaign called "The Missing Pages of Our History." From there, history was created.

For ALLY as a group, Ethnic Studies was important to us because we did not see our people and their history within the textbooks that we learn from in today's classrooms. We never learned how they fought back, the resistance and power that they had, even though they were a part of American history as well. Instead, if you opened a U.S. history book, it would most likely have a smiling Christopher Columbus sailing the ocean blue or the Founding Fathers proudly signing the Declaration of Independence. And *if* other people of color were represented, it would be things like the Vietnam War or the slightest mention of the bombing in the Marshalls; even then, APIs and other people of color have always been shown to be weak or have hopeless lives filled with violence and sadness. I'm sure that's what it's like in most other textbooks, and we did not want that to stay any longer.

Personally, as a 13-year-old Pacific Islander girl who at the time was itching to make her voice heard, Ethnic Studies was important to me because

I definitely did not feel like Pacific Islanders were represented in the classroom *whatsoever*. The only time I heard anything about my people was whenever the teacher suddenly felt like talking about climate change, which is heartbreaking to hear when you know your family and friends' families are on the other side of the world trying to stop the ocean from swallowing them up. There was no positivity, no pride or power, no talk about the climate warriors, the Paris Climate Agreement, or the rich cultures and traditions of the beautiful Pacific Islands. But on top of that, Ethnic Studies can also help build an empathy toward other people's cultures and identities and can build the growing respect for the other people in your life, because everyone's culture is beautiful and we should all be able to celebrate ourselves for who we are no matter where we are, classroom or not.

If I'm being completely honest, what worries and frustrates me the most about the passing of Ethnic Studies is actually how slow the Ethnic Studies committee is progressing. The curriculum building is going a lot slower than I would like for it to be, as we even created an oversight committee once the proposal was approved in order to make sure that the Ethnic Studies board is going along schedule. I just finished my first year of high school and would love to experience having Ethnic Studies by the time I graduate to see how much we have grown by making this all happen. ALLY has continued to go on to other issues that we see in our Portland community, but there are some people who have been there from the near start (like me) who are still trying to stay engaged in what is going on with the progress of Ethnic Studies.

I hope that, with the help and insight from our different communities of color in Portland, the progress will go along faster in order to give knowledge to younger generations of students who will eventually take this class. I hope that Ethnic Studies will soon become required for students in PPS, as it is in some school districts in California, since it's an addition to our U.S. history classes and should be treated that way; it is just as important if not more important to learn Ethnic Studies, especially at a time like right now where hate speech against other underrepresented or discriminated groups is becoming more accepted by the public, which should not ever be the case. But most of all, I hope Ethnic Studies becomes a major success and that our work will influence other school districts to spread it across the country.

To all the teachers reading this and wondering, "What does a 15-year-old girl know about teaching a whole new curriculum? Does she know how hard that is? What makes this so special anyway?" I need to remind you that yes, I am an *extremely* young woman of color; yes, I am still in school; and yes, I still have a *lot* of things to learn in my life, but one thing I do know is that the time to show awareness and appreciation toward other people in our history has *never* been more important than it is right now.

The time, the effort it takes, all of it is and will always be worth it.

I promise you that.

The thing is, the Japanese internment camps, the labor movement, the bombing of the Marshall Islands by the U.S. military, the Kingdom of Hawai'i and taking Queen Liliuokalani away, the Battle of Okinawa and occupation by American military bases, the climate warriors, and even activists recently blocking Shell ships passing under the St. Johns Bridge in Portland: These points in history should have already *been* in our education from the beginning. Ethnic Studies brings that, and the mentality that as people of color, we should not all be represented through slavery. We should not all be represented through wars.

Our faces should not just be shown in books sobbing with dying children and drowning houses at our feet, but with fists in the air, throwing our heads to the sky with chants, my Batman Ethnic Studies sign gleaming as we start and spread the movement across the nation. We should be shown inspiring other adults, students, everyone, to continue to appreciate and cherish the underrepresented beautiful identities that make up the United States of America today. We should be shown continuing our social justice movement, as ALLY, my family, and I continue the work we love to do, striving for a better tomorrow.

As I stand there, fist in the sky and hollering happy gibberish while bursting with joy, I know that we are getting somewhere. We did it: We passed Ethnic Studies—a stepping-stone for PPS and for youth around the United States.

Now it's time to keep going. ✳

The Emergence of the Ethnic Studies Now Coalition in Yangna (Los Angeles) and Beyond
Two, Three, Many Tucsons

BY GUADALUPE CARRASCO CARDONA AND R. TOLTEKA CUAUHTIN

Yangna is the area of land often called downtown Los Angeles—a community center millennia before Placita Olvera, City Hall, Staples Center, Los Angeles Unified School District headquarters, and a dense gathering of museums and skyscrapers sat upon its topography. The word "Yangna" originates in the language of the Tongva, one of the Indigenous nations of this land, who during colonization were enslaved to build the San Gabriel Mission and who reside and move forward here today as the Gabrielino-Tongva nation. We acknowledge Yangna in the title in recognition of them and to symbolize native consciousness in communities throughout the city, county, metropolitan area, and beyond. The voices of the Ethnic Studies Now Coalition (ESNC or ESN) as a whole, its many chapters, and its supporters are vast, multitudinous, and from many different communities, races, ethnicities, ancestries, nationalities, and cultures. This is the story of the coalition's emergence through the lenses of ESN in this region, primarily based on a series of interviews and personal experiences.

Students Rise and Continue to Make Their Voices Heard

On November 18, 2014, the Los Angeles Unified School District (LAUSD) school board was determining whether or not Board Resolution (023- 14/15) would be passed, making Ethnic Studies a high school requirement. Hundreds of youth, along with teachers, community members, and families, were present, both inside the boardroom to speak on the mic and outside rallying, with a large crowd wrapping around the building. From elementary through high school age, these students were there to support Ethnic Studies in Los Angeles. One student, a passionate 5th grader named Joseph Moreno, stepped up to the megaphone, rallying and inspiring the crowd with his heartfelt words. Now a middle school student, he reflects on his experience that day:

> I had been doing animal activist work, speaking for those who cannot speak for themselves and defending those who were defenseless. I then realized that my generation's exposure was being taken hostage by those who planned out our standards of learning. Those people who had no interest in diversity in one of the most diverse districts in the entire nation were trying to erase history and rewrite the next generation's thought and beliefs by teaching history through their lens. They never bothered to teach students about other cultures who helped shape who we are now as a nation. When my *tía* (aunt) told me about this movement in Ethnic Studies, I quickly thought this would be my opportunity to help my generation learn something they didn't know they were missing.
>
> When I found out that I was going to the Ethnic Studies rally, I was a little nervous due to the fact that it was my first social justice rally, but I also felt confident because I wanted people to hear what I had to say. During the rally I never imagined that so many people were into Ethnic Studies like me. . . . The energy during the rally was electrifying. You could feel how devoted the students were toward Ethnic Studies. And if we wouldn't have won that day, I knew that we would have kept on fighting until we won. Also during the rally, I could tell how surprised the high schoolers were to see an elementary student be active in the social justice community.

The resolution was approved by the LAUSD school board that day, and after this hxrstoric victory making Ethnic Studies a graduation requirement for all students in the second largest district in the country, youth involvement grew at the school level and in follow-up events, including the Ethnic Studies Now Youth Summit, held at Santee High School in South Los Angeles (South Yangna), and the Indigenous Peoples Day Youth Conference, organized by XOCHITL-LA and held at Los Angeles Mission College in the Northeast San Fernando Valley, or Pasinka in the language of the Tataviam, and with their blessing. (The Tataviam are another Indigenous nation here, also known as the Fernandeño after their enslavement to build the city's San Fernando Mission.) At these events, the students of Los Angeles reaffirmed that they believed in the transformative power of Ethnic Studies and the need to move the implementation of the resolution forward.

One student from our school, the Social Justice Humanitas Academy (part of the César E. Chávez Learning Academies in Pasinka [San Fernando]), shared an inspiring story at the ESN Youth Summit in South Yangna, almost a full year after she had taken our course:

> My Name is Ines. . . . Ethnic Studies is truly life changing. Last year, I had the opportunity to learn the other side of the story, the one that doesn't belong to the European ethnicity. The only thing I have to say about that class was that it truly shaped me to who I am today. Who would have guessed that a class that I was only taking for high school credits would still continue to impact my life one year later? That's exactly what my freshman geography class continues to do to me today and trust me, I know that it was just a geography class, but my teacher, Tolteka, always found a way to make us think outside the box, to really question our whole K–8 education because throughout those years, the only thing that I have learned in history classes was the European perspective of things, but what about my people?
>
> What about those natives who were slaughtered and tortured upon the arrival of Christopher Columbus and I know no one likes to speak about it but unfortunately it's the sad truth! I will be honest with you, before high school, I had no idea about the massacre that began in 1492 and although no one likes to call it a genocide, let's be real, that's what it was. I also believed I only came from European descent. That my ancestors were all Europeans because the textbooks never spoke about the Indigenous, the ones who were here before the Europeans, my people, and the fact that I couldn't name from the top of my head my ancestral tribe or my ancestral roots is evidence that colonization has really made its way through the minds of the people. You don't know how frustrating it is to walk around or to be asked where your family is from, and all you can do is name the state that your grandparents are from.
>
> I know I wasn't the only one. You can approach others asking them the same question and the only answer you will receive is silence. If there's anyone who has to break that silence, it's me, it's us! It's time to show these kids their true history, their roots because I was fortunate enough to attend a school and have a teacher who truly believed that students should know both sides and base their opinion from it, but there's others who still look like me at the beginning of freshman year, clueless to reality. History can't be changed but it can be prevented (from repeating) and if we can do anything to prevent it, best believe I'll put my all. Ethnic Studies for all!

Youth involvement has been present in districts throughout California, from Oakland where youth catalyzed the push for the Ethnic Studies resolution, to Sacramento, where local youth and a large group from Napa presented to the state Board of Education to advocate for Ethnic Studies. There, more than 50 ESN representatives stepped to the mic that day, sharing with state Board of Education members the power of Ethnic Studies in their lives and why it's needed across California. The youth voice is imperative in any movement that is strategizing in their name and to their benefit; youth must be a major force and voice of the coalition to bring Ethnic Studies to any district, just as they were in Yangna.

The Birth of Ethnic Studies Now Through Coalition Building

In 2014, community organizers and LAUSD educators Sean Abajian, Jose Lara, and Javier San Roman met with LAUSD school board member Bennett Kayser to garner support of Ethnic Studies. El Rancho Unified, where Lara also sits as a board member, had recently passed Ethnic Studies as a graduation requirement; to do the same in LAUSD, considering its size as the second largest school district in the country, would be more challenging. This meeting inspired the formation of the Ethnic Studies Now Coalition to help take the organizing of it all to the next level. In the spirit of audacity, San Roman came up with a riff on Che Guevara's "Message to the Tricontinental." He said that we needed to create "two, three, many Tucsons." It would take extensive coalition-building efforts to make the passing of the resolution possible, including grassroots organizing at the Los Angeles and statewide levels. The initial grassroots push of ESN included countless hours and donated dollars to ensure that the message got out and that wide support was garnered.

The youth voice is imperative in any movement that is strategizing in their name and to their benefit; youth must be a major force and voice of the coalition to bring Ethnic Studies to any district, just as they were in Yangna.

GRASSROOTS ORGANIZING

The ESN coalition building required intensive outreach to spread the word and get support from the community, elected officials, school board members, teacher union leadership, university professors, and key political players. The work at the grassroots level is what provided the foundation for all the movement's successes both locally and statewide. ESN developed mass-marketing tactics, such as memes and branding via social media, the Ethnic Studies Now website, and email blitzes. In order for ESN to garner support and build trust with the masses, it was consistently in communication with followers via the internet. ESN used an inside-out strategy where they coordinated grassroots movement with both board advocacy inside of the school district as well as the state level and beyond. The grassroots level was an imperative because it was vital for local voices to be heard and represented at all times; at the same time, deliberate efforts to gain positions of power on formal committees, school boards, and local and state unions ensured that the voices would make an impact across the state of California.

UNITED TEACHERS LOS ANGELES/UNION SUPPORT

In Los Angeles, Ethnic Studies Now used a suite of labor-organizing tactics such as collaborating with teachers at the state teacher union level and employing coalition-building efforts led by such education organizers as Cecily Myart-Cruz, vice president of United Teachers Los Angeles union (UTLA); Melina Abdullah of California State University, Los Angeles and Black Lives Matter Los Angeles; and Suzie Abajian of Occidental College; and with letters of the support by many, including Theresa Montaño, who would go on to advocate for Ethnic Studies at the state level as the vice president of the California Teachers Association (CTA) a few months after the LAUSD resolution was passed, the first Xicana/Latina ever in that role.

UTLA's support for Ethnic Studies came at a critical time when UTLA was working to establish itself as a "social justice union"—that is to say, a union whose focus goes beyond typical union issues of salaries and working conditions. Lara and Myart-Cruz pressed for racial justice in our schools for a long time and viewed Ethnic Studies as a means to decolonize the curriculum that has been "whitewashed" for decades. According to Lara, "UTLA should be at the front line in supporting Ethnic Studies in our schools. As a teacher union, we have a moral imperative to fight for a culturally relevant curriculum that relates to the lives of the students in Los Angeles, who are overwhelmingly Black and Brown." UTLA overwhelmingly passed a policy in support of Ethnic Studies because the message was clear that the union's role in ensuring educational justice was of utmost importance.

It was vital to collaborate with teachers at the state teacher union level. Lara, Myart-Cruz, Sean Abajian, Kelly Flores (LAUSD high school special education teacher and member of the Association of Raza Educators), and fellow union activist Ingrid Villeda (LAUSD elementary schoolteacher from South Central Los Angeles) spoke passionately about Ethnic Studies and pushed for the CTA to establish policy in support of the cause. The passionate speeches of Villeda and Flores helped sway the state union body to overwhelmingly support Ethnic Studies, as an official CTA position, with more than 300,000 members. This would prove vital later on when the Ethnic Studies Now Coalition successfully pushed for the passage of a statewide Ethnic Studies bill, which was propelled forward in collaboration with the then newly formed Sacramento chapter of ESN and the leadership of Margarita Berta-Ávila (who would go on to become president of the Capitol City Chapter of the California Faculty Association, the CTA affiliate union that represents all the professors at Cal State Universities), Dale Allender, Gregory Yee Mark, and many more advocates. Our local union, UTLA, working in collaboration with statewide CTA union membership had a direct impact on ensuring that Ethnic Studies would be written into statewide legislation. The power of the union leadership in the coalition-building efforts proved to be powerful beyond Yangna/Los Angeles.

Ethnic Studies Now Coalition: Today and the Next Era

Currently, many districts throughout California have passed resolutions to commit to making Ethnic Studies a high school graduation requirement or at the least to offer Ethnic Studies to students. These districts include El Rancho, Los Angeles, Montebello, Compton, San Francisco, Sacramento, Oakland, San Diego, Coachella, Centinela Valley, Santa Ana, Azusa, New Haven, and more, while ESN organizers in districts such as Ventura, Santa Barbara, Santa Maria, Napa, and Fresno are still moving forward and should have resolutions passed by the time

of this publication. In being proactive in resolution writing, and planning for what happens after the resolution is passed, it is important to consider several questions:

1. How will the district define and frame Ethnic Studies curriculum and pedagogy and will it be done critically or superficially?

2. Who will compose the district's Ethnic Studies steering committee/task force?

3. Who will lead/coordinate Ethnic Studies at the district level? Will it be an administrator or teacher position?

4. Who will teach Ethnic Studies? Who will prepare new Ethnic Studies teachers?

5. What kind of professional development will Ethnic Studies teachers need to go through?

6. How will Ethnic Studies be funded, to what extent, and for how long?

7. Where do we go from here as a coalition?

These are all critical questions to address when drafting a resolution. Here are ESN's preferred answers for each.

1. ESN does not advocate the usually superficial "group of the month" approach, instead preferring a critical and thematic approach grounded in Ethnic Studies theory and legacy: relating and responding to the demographic imperative of the students in the room and their hxrstorical legacies as human beings, weaving the core racialized groups' responsive content and experiences into the themes of the program/course, and using ancestral knowledge and pedagogy as a foundation for learning. Group-specific courses, especially centered around the four core racialized groups (see "The Ethnic Studies Framework," p. 65), may also be considered Ethnic Studies courses.

2. There is considerable talent available in many school districts with expertise among the practi-

tioners of Ethnic Studies, and they should be represented in any Ethnic Studies steering committees or task forces the district forms, as should experts from the local universities. If there isn't Ethnic Studies activism demanding this, and/or if it is not written into the resolution explicitly, some districts disproportionately stack their steering committees with administrators without Ethnic Studies background, and the program can quickly become a diluted, superficial version of Ethnic Studies.

Ethnic Studies students do not need teachers assigned to an Ethnic Studies course they know nothing about or worse, have no desire to learn more about (or even worse, are ideologically opposed to the purpose of Ethnic Studies).

3. For coordinating/leadership roles, some districts make the mistake of putting Ethnic Studies implementation solely in the hands of administrators who are not versed at all in Ethnic Studies or who do not take a sufficiently critical approach to it, marginalizing the teacher expertise in the process. This often works as a counter-tactic to thwart implementation and expansion, self-sabotaging Ethnic Studies programs before giving them a chance to achieve the results they are capable of. Teachers need to be involved in district-level Ethnic Studies leadership.

4. Who will teach Ethnic Studies throughout the state? This is one of the most critical questions and it is yet to be adequately resolved. Most teacher education and credentialing programs that enroll preservice teachers do not explicitly prepare Ethnic Studies teachers. Where will they learn about Ethnic Studies, its theory, content, and pedagogy? There are a few Ethnic Studies teacher prep programs in their nascent stages, such as those at California State University, Northridge; Sacramento State; and the University of California, Los Angeles' Ethnic Studies cohort in its Teacher Education Program. But many schools of education need similar programs throughout the United States to ensure Ethnic Studies educators are "qualified and prepared."

5. Any teacher—new, mid-career, or veteran—who is new to teaching Ethnic Studies should be required to go through professional development to learn more about the field and how to teach it. Ethnic Studies students do not need teachers assigned to an Ethnic Studies course they know nothing about or worse, have no desire to learn more about (or even worse, are ideologically opposed to the purpose of Ethnic Studies). Social justice educators of color who have a critical race consciousness may transition easiest and most effectively to teaching Ethnic Studies; however, there are also many excellent white-ally Ethnic Studies educators who teach the humanity and criticality of Ethnic Studies. Ideally, districts should pay teachers or award them salary points for completing Ethnic Studies professional development; several districts are currently doing so, both hosting local training sessions for their teachers (and compensating them accordingly) and encouraging their teachers to travel to Ethnic Studies workshops and conferences outside of their locale. Organizations affiliated with the Ethnic Studies Now Coalition have stepped up to offer teachers professional development as well as build the necessary capacity to help public school districts implement dedicated Ethnic Studies courses and integrate critical Ethnic Studies into core content curricula. One example is the Association of Raza Educators (ARE), an educational liberation organization whose leadership created an educational cooperative called Praxis to assist public school districts with Ethnic Studies implementation in Los Angeles and beyond. ARE also participates in professional development training from XOCHITL-LA, an organization (and which the authors of this piece are co-founding members of) which sprouted out of a visit to Xicanx Institute for Teaching and Organizing in Tucson. XOCHITL hosts conferences where teachers can earn salary points and where the MAS Tucson teacher leaders share their expertise with

California educators. Another organization, the People's Education Movement, also hosts curriculum fairs based in Ethnic Studies for the community. Additionally in this realm of work, there are college and university partnerships that ESN members and supporters participate in throughout the state, with professional development being held among experienced teachers, college professors, and community members. Further, there are union-backed professional development efforts, including CTA/Stanford Instructional Leadership Corps, which has an Ethnic Studies teacher team that provides professional development opportunities to teachers in LAUSD and beyond.

6. Without funding embedded and secured, Ethnic Studies implementation will stall. To the extent that is possible, funding sources (e.g., California's Local Control and Accountability Plans, or LCAPs), specific minimal amounts of funding, and minimum certain duration of time for that funding should be written into the resolution itself (as Sacramento did). In the case of Santa Maria Joint Union High School District, it was the parents on the LCAP committee who wrote a requirement for the development of an Ethnic Studies and Gender Committee, who would be charged with creating Ethnic Studies and gender courses into the LCAP itself. This in turn helps resolve other important points, including funding for professional development, locally responsive ES curricular development, and ES resources.

7. By continuing to leverage the knowledge base, connections, and community cultural wealth of the coalition, together we are stronger. Assembly bill 2016 being signed into law at the state level, encouraging all California high schools to offer Ethnic Studies, is a testament to this power. At the final stages of this book's production, new legislation—AB 2772, which would have made Ethnic Studies a high school requirement across California, was vetoed by Governor Brown. ESN will continue working toward all students having access to Ethnic Studies, a goal dreamed of more than 45 years ago by Third World Liberation Front coalition members and in Ethnic Studies movements throughout the state. National organizing on this front is the next level for the Ethnic Studies Now Coalition. How do we help our students, communities, each other, and Ethnic Studies move forward together, now and into the decades ahead?

To those who have helped us accomplish these hxrstoric moments with Ethnic Studies throughout the state and beyond, thank you, gracias, tlazokamati. As a community, we make it all possible together. We look forward to sharing more of our story with you, and better yet, listening to your stories, as together they all compose the fabric that is the Ethnic Studies Now Coalition. Let's continue to move forward with racial, educational, and social justice for this next era—the time is now. Where is your district and state at with Ethnic Studies? Let's help it all move forward, together. ❋

The Struggle for Ethnic Studies in the Golden State
Capitol City Organizers and Activists

BY RUBÉN A. GONZÁLEZ, MARIBEL ROSENDO-SERVÍN, AND DOMINIQUE A. WILLIAMS

Sacramento, the state capitol, has been a hub of resistance movements in California. Farmworkers marched 340 miles from Delano to Sacramento to demand better working conditions. The Black Panthers took up arms at the steps of the capitol to defend their right to resist police brutality. More recently, Hmong advocates introduced and lobbied for state policy to include their history in social sciences curriculum.

In these moments, as in all social movements, the people at the margins of society have always challenged the oppressive sociopolitical institutions of this country. Education is no different. In particular, educational institutions have always been political, as they reflect a country built and sustained through oppression.

Ethnic Studies Now–Sacramento (ESN–Sacramento) attempts to build on the work of those who have come before us and strives in a collective and collaborative manner to foster educational spaces rooted in resistance and liberation.

The Demand for Ethnic Studies: A Coalition in the Making

About a dozen people gathered in a living room. We sat on couches, chairs, and the floor. Everyone was present in response to an email inviting them to a meeting meant to "strategize how to make Ethnic Studies a graduation requirement in Sacramento City Unified School District (SCUSD) and the surrounding areas." The group was composed of Sacramento State University professors of education, high school teachers from different Sacramento-area school districts, undergraduate university students, and community members. Most participants were also members of various organizing/activist groups, such as the Association of Raza Educators (ARE), the Black Parallel School Board (BPSB), and Hmong Innovating Politics (HIP).

The gathering was noteworthy for various reasons, but a few stand out: the diverse racial/ethnic representation of everyone in the room, the balance in gender and age representation, and how individual organizations with long and successful track records of working with their respective communities were collaborating with one another for the first time.

Over two hours quickly dissipated on a cold Sunday morning in December 2014 as everyone shared their initial thoughts and ideas:

> "Some teachers are already teaching Ethnic Studies in the district."
> "Who are other people and community organizations we need to reach out to?"
> "Who has relationships with school board members?"
> "There is already momentum—Los Angeles just passed an Ethnic Studies resolution!"

The meeting ended and a number of items remained unresolved, but what was clear was our strong commitment to this important work. We agreed to meet again in two weeks. Little did we know that this was the beginning of Ethnic Studies Now–Sacramento, facilitated by our indefinite biweekly meetings and our impending transition from regional to statewide organizing and activism.

A Student-Led Movement

After our initial meeting, we planned to spend the rest of the 2014–15 school year building support from the community and other SCUSD stakeholders through networking and community meetings. We would approach the school board with an Ethnic Studies resolution the following school year.

This all changed when we discovered high school students had already been mobilizing for months in order to make Ethnic Studies a graduation requirement and that they planned to present to the SCUSD school board in May.

The Student Advisory Council (SAC)—an after-school, student-led activism and advocacy group composed of high school students throughout the district—identified the need for Ethnic Studies courses as part of a Youth Participatory Action Research (YPAR) project under the guidance of Mark Carnero, a district employee and SAC advisor. For their YPAR project, students analyzed more than 1,000 open-ended surveys that were completed by their peers throughout the district. Their goal was to identify "issues that affect youth in SCUSD that need to be changed." The demand for "identity-based class enrichment" was one of their major findings. Students conducted further research and as a group decided that Ethnic Studies courses would address this demand and benefit all students throughout the district.

We contacted Carnero after learning about what his students were doing, realizing both of our separate groups were essentially working toward the same goal. In an attempt to stay true and faithful to the belief that this work was about the students and not about us, we made a collective decision to work at the pace of the students and support them as needed.

Initially, Carnero hesitated to collaborate with us. He later elaborated, "We had been approached by other adults before to work with us whose intentions were not clear or genuine." SAC students were also wary of this collaboration. In a meeting with Carnero, they informed him that although they were "excited to know that there are allies outside of the district working on the initiative," they did not want to be "overtaken or used by adults."

Carnero's reservation dissipated after attending his first ESN–Sacramento meeting in February 2015. He felt better about our intentions after meeting the entire group and later conveyed that this change was rooted in feeling "empowered and having

a strong connection to the folks in the room." This paradigm shift led Carnero and Asami Saito, a SAC student representative, to become core members of ESN–Sacramento.

The first act of collaboration between students and adults was to organize and facilitate a community meeting at a local middle school in March 2015. This meeting, along with networking and contacting individuals engaged in critical work throughout the community, ultimately solidified the remaining core membership of ESN–Sacramento. Now Sacramento State University professors of Ethnic Studies from Asian American and Native American studies and a larger number of community members were part of the coalition.

Students analyzed more than 1,000 open-ended surveys that were completed by their peers throughout the district. Their goal was to identify "issues that affect youth in SCUSD that need to be changed." The demand for "identity-based class enrichment" was one of their major findings.

Upon reflection, Margarita Berta-Ávila, the chair of ESN–Sacramento, identified beginning to work with the students as a pivotal moment—truly the driving force behind implementing Ethnic Studies as a graduation requirement. She recalled: "The students really pushed us. We realized they were moving quickly and that we had to catch up to them and support them."

No History, No Self. Know History, Know Self.

On May 19, 2015, Asami and two fellow student advisory council members entered the school board meeting to a standing-room-only audience eager to hear them speak. In the months leading to this day, school board members had heard from various other voices about the need for Ethnic Studies courses, namely those of university professors, school administrators, teachers, students, and community members. Now the resolution was finally going to be presented, and Asami and her peers were the first set of presenters. The three students approached the podium, standing tall and with a strong sense of confidence. In unison, they declared, "I am what I am because of who we are!" Each student repeated the phrase in their native language—Spanish, Japanese, and Hmong.

The students set the tone, and the energy in the room was palpable. They provided an overview of the benefits of Ethnic Studies, citing scholarly research and their own quantitative and qualitative data to support their claims. Saito ended the presentation with "We are all important and significant, but we may not be taught that in our traditional classes . . . in order to know our history, we have to know ourselves."

A few school board members smiled and nodded, and one shared the need for the resolution. Yet it was when the school district superintendent spoke that the room erupted in applause. "I am going to ask the [school district] staff to immediately work on a plan to integrate Ethnic Studies into the existing graduation requirement." One month later, when the resolution was formally approved, the school board president announced, "This may be the most important resolution that I ever sign as president of this board."

Three high schools would pilot the course during the 2015–16 school year; by 2020 Ethnic Studies will be a graduation requirement and taught in all high schools throughout the district.

We were ecstatic! Yet we recognized that the real work lay ahead. In particular, our organizing and activism for an Ethnic Studies course requirement would soon transition us to the state capitol.

Grassroots Organizing at the Capitol

In 2015 Assembly member Luis Alejo introduced Assembly Bill (AB) 101. The bill originally attempted to create an Ethnic Studies Advisory Committee that would work toward implementing an Ethnic Studies

graduation requirement and statewide model curriculum. During the legislative process, the bill was amended to call only for the development of a model curriculum. The bill was eventually vetoed by Governor Jerry Brown, who stated, "Creating yet another advisory body [outside of the Instructional Quality Commission] specific to Ethnic Studies would be duplicative and undermine our current curriculum process."

Alejo introduced AB 2016 one year later, this time requiring the Instructional Quality Commission to develop an Ethnic Studies model curriculum. High schools throughout the state could then adopt it if they chose to do so.

The regional and statewide implications of this bill were discussed in an ESN–Sacramento meeting, and various questions were raised around AB 2016:

> "Who is going to create this curriculum?"
>
> "How do we ensure the integrity and inclusiveness of the curriculum?"
>
> "What if teachers already have their own curriculum? Would they be forced to use the model curriculum?"
>
> "Are people who even know about critical Ethnic Studies going to be involved in this process?"

The issue around curriculum integrity had already presented itself in a Sacramento-area school district, as an ESN–Sacramento member told the group:

> Our school is paying an Ethnic Studies consultant to support curriculum development. Their curriculum approach is problematic—it's focused on "awareness of contributions" and has that superficial "Hispanic Month, Black History Month, Women's Month" approach. This consultant said social justice was "not a necessary element to this curriculum." This Ethnic Studies curriculum would be watered down.

As AB 2016 was about to be introduced, ESN–Sacramento members realized its importance and decided to be involved actively in the legislative and lobbying processes.

Lobbying at the Capitol

In early April 2016, we agreed to formally support AB 2016 by lobbying the bill during the policy and fiscal committee processes. An ESN–Sacramento member with extensive experience at the capitol moved our work forward. She informed us that "We can testify in support of the bill during the Assembly and Senate Education Committees. In addition, public members can advocate for the bill's passage to staffers of senators and assembly members in order to emphasize the need for the bill."

Others in the room contributed ideas, such as "We need teachers, community members, district representatives, and students to attend and speak during press conferences" and "We need people to testify during hearings on the importance and power of Ethnic Studies courses." These ideas became our action plans, and we prepared for them accordingly during the subsequent weeks.

On April 19, 2016, about 80 high school students from the Sacramento City and San Juan Unified School Districts made their way to the state capitol. Students and teachers met assembly member Alejo's staff members, who directed them to the offices of assembly members they would lobby. Teacher members of ESN–Sacramento, who were currently teaching the pilot Ethnic Studies courses, organized and prepared their students to participate in the legislative process. Prior to this day, they had their students read and study the bill in class, and reminded students of their right to testify if they wished to do so.

As students lobbied the members of the Assembly Education Committee, they shared personal narratives:

> "I am taking an Ethnic Studies course this year and other students should take this class to learn about their history and other cultures."
>
> "This course motivated me to do well in school and want to go to college."
>
> "I like that Ethnic Studies is real."

This experience was important and empowering for students as they learned how to participate and advocate for an issue that mattered to them. One teacher shared, "Students were excited; many were able to experience, for the first time, participating in the political process."

A few months later, after the approval of both the policy and fiscal committees, AB 2016 was signed into law by Gov. Brown on September 13, 2016. This was tremendous!

An exciting and truly monumental moment also signaled the beginning of a much longer road related to statewide work.

Building on AB 2016

We soon began to see the short- and long-term effects of this policy:

> "Some people believe AB 2016 makes Ethnic Studies a graduation requirement."
>
> "People need an understanding of critical Ethnic Studies curriculum approaches."
>
> "There must be better communication and collaboration with other Ethnic Studies Now chapters in order to sustain this statewide policy work."

In response to these and other factors, we decided to plan a statewide Ethnic Studies summit co-sponsored by Ethnic Studies Now–Sacramento and the Association of Raza Educators. The event came to fruition on February 25, 2017, in Sacramento. Ethnic Studies Now members from across the state attended, serving as keynotes and workshop presenters. Summit participants also came from as far as Texas, Tennessee, and New York.

The summit served as a space for everyone engaged in this struggle. Presentation topics included curriculum development and writing, textbook publishing, resolution writing, and how to create Ethnic Studies Now chapters. In short, this was a space to share information, foster leadership, and increase statewide coordination among individuals and groups engaged in this work.

At the time of this statewide gathering, we were still actively involved in ensuring the implementation of the Ethnic Studies courses and graduation requirement in SCUSD.

Putting the District Resolution into Action

In June 2017, the now Dr. Carnero, who had recently begun to serve as the district lead for the Ethnic

Studies course implementation, stood in front of the SCUSD school board. It was almost two years to the day since the Ethnic Studies resolution had passed. He was there, along with administrators, teachers, students, and community members to bring attention to the work that had been completed thus far and to ensure continued support from the district in the future. He began:

> Tonight we acknowledge that the youth, our teachers, our community, and our school district are pushing forward the legacy of people of color who have struggled for generations to have their stories and histories recognized and included within the broader United States' narrative.

Carnero then provided data from students who completed the Ethnic Studies pilot courses, explaining, "[Students] raised their empathetic capacity for others . . . grew respect for classmates . . . developed ideas about their social responsibility in regards to race relations, and students began to build a critical perspective on history."

He subsequently transitioned to the expansion of Ethnic Studies courses throughout the district. The 2017–18 school year would have 24 teachers from nine schools teach the course to about 1,500 students, an increase from four teachers in three schools and about 325 students the previous year.

He concluded, "It is our hope that this course can create an environment where students have the ability to process, analyze, and transform the many institutions in our society that promote systemic racism and interpersonal conflict."

Next, Dale Allender, Sacramento State University professor of education, ESN–Sacramento member, and co-chair of our curriculum committee, discussed the continuous professional development for current and future Ethnic Studies teachers:

> On the professional development front, we're working with teachers to build relationships with each other and their students, to explore implicit bias, deepen their knowledge of ethnic cultures, and develop Ethnic Studies curriculum for their classes.

The paid professional development would include 60 hours during the summer for new and returning Ethnic Studies teachers. In addition, there would be professional development throughout the upcoming academic school year, as was the case during the initial pilot of the Ethnic Studies courses.

One pilot teacher, an ESN–Sacramento member, attested to the value of the professional development she had received during the school year:

> One of my favorite PDs [professional development sessions] was getting with members from Nomtipom Wintu, Maidu, Nevada City Rancheria, and Nisenan tribes. We sat down at a table and each gave us a history of their tribes and a breakdown of Indigenous practices that are ages old that they still practice today. And for the first time it opened my eyes to how real peoples' Indigenous roots are in 2017.

This "rich PD," as she called it, was the result of ESN–Sacramento playing a vital role in professional development, coupled with curriculum writing and creating an accompanying textbook and workbook—*Our Stories in Our Voices*—which were adopted by the district. Chapters in the first-ever high school Ethnic Studies textbook, edited by ESN–Sacramento members Dale Allender and Gregory Yee Mark, focused on the local experiences of historically oppressed and dispossessed groups.

Teachers were able to learn directly from the chapter contributors, as the authors were integrated into the professional development sessions. Teachers learned about the community, from the community. One teacher shared, "The impact on me was really real because it just gave me the lens to see, and respect, and appreciate cultures, and look at them critically." Another professed the empowerment of having "sat down with some of tribal chairs who wrote the chapter [my students] were reading."

Students then addressed the school board, eager to share the benefits of Ethnic Studies. One 9th-grade student who recently completed the pilot Ethnic Studies course informed the board members:

> It has opened my eyes to things I didn't realize about myself and others. The school district

needs to make this a requirement because it equips people with knowledge about social issues, which is beneficial to making society better in the future.

A community organizer/activist and ESN–Sacramento member then spoke:

One of the great challenges facing our nation is to recognize the racism that is at the root of much of the inequality and injustice that our society suffers in our political, economic, and educational systems. Ethnic Studies is both a recognition of, and a remedy for, this problem… . It can be a powerful tool in our struggle toward a just and equal society.

The value, importance, and need for Ethnic Studies courses was made clear to everyone in the room. Even so, speaker after speaker continuously implored the school board members to continue to support the work that still needed to be done in order to ensure Ethnic Studies is taught in every high school throughout the district.

Lessons Learned

Research by Nolan Cabrera and his colleagues, that of Thomas Dee and Emily Penner, and Christine Sleeter's synthesis of research demonstrate the academic and social benefits of Ethnic Studies courses for high school students. For many, this is not a revelation. It simply supports what people and communities have expressed for decades—students benefit from seeing themselves and their experiences reflected in the classroom curriculum. The recent activism and advocacy for Ethnic Studies at the high school level can also be viewed as an extension of the foundational work of the Third World Liberation Front 50 years ago, when the fight for Ethnic Studies courses began at San Francisco State University. This work is not new or easy, and it is part of a long legacy of resistance and liberation.

As more schools begin to offer Ethnic Studies courses, and as more school districts adopt Ethnic Studies resolutions, it is important to note that this is only the starting point of this work. Simply offering Ethnic Studies courses will not guarantee the aca-demic and social benefits found by the research, and a district resolution will not ensure that all schools implement these courses with integrity. Further, there is no formulaic approach to avoid the possible pitfalls at the school- and districtwide levels. With that said, we posit two ideas that have emerged as instrumental to our work: the need for partnerships at various institutional levels and the importance of integrating oneself into all aspects of the Ethnic Studies course creation and implementation.

As a group composed of educators, students, and community members, ESN–Sacramento was on "the outside looking in" at the district bureaucracy. It was imperative to have strategic connections at various institutional levels, primarily at the school site and district levels. As a result, the work of Carnero and teachers throughout the district was invaluable. They understood the dynamics of the district and allowed us to better understand how to navigate the various systemic processes. With them, we were able to have access to speak to school and district administrators as well as school board members and to be a constant presence that was taken seriously at school board meetings and behind closed doors. The accountability was now real, as school and district administrators, along with school board members, had to follow through with the verbiage related to "equity," "cultural relevance," and "whole-child development" that is often touted in SCUSD. The pressure and accountability was now not limited to ESN–Sacramento and other outside individuals and entities, but included individuals from within the school district.

Further, from the very beginning, we recognized that a strategically written resolution would ensure the implementation and longevity of critical Ethnic Studies courses aligned with an anti-colonial and anti-oppressive paradigm. We created and integrated into the resolution the Sacramento State Ethnic Studies Teaching Credentials Consortium, which became the professional development provider. As a result, we became a key part of the teacher training and curriculum writing, both as professors of education and Ethnic Studies providing the professional development and as teachers tasked with writing the curriculum and teaching the courses. Another strategic approach was to coordinate with Carnero which teachers in what schools would phase in the courses. In this manner, we ensured that teachers with the appropriate sociopolitical consciousness and pedagogical skill initiated this work. Those same teachers served as the first cohort of teachers who received the professional development, and subsequently served as the teacher-leaders for future Ethnic Studies teachers as additional schools began to offer the courses and as the professional development was grown to include the additional teachers.

By no means has this work been easy, nor have the various stakeholders at the school and district levels been unconditionally supportive. In fact, while the school district has proclaimed their support for this work publicly, their inactivity and hands-off approach in certain areas is what has led to our work being accomplished. The district did not write the resolution, so we had the freedom to write it and integrate ourselves into the teacher training as well as in the creation and implementation of the courses. There was no curriculum and no district curriculum writer in the area of social sciences, so we wrote the curriculum. We were informed that the course needed to have a textbook, so we wrote the textbook ourselves. The partnership with SCUSD has not been perfect, and more has been desired from different stakeholders and from the school district as a whole, but it has been functional. We all continue to move forward, and ultimately students have benefited.

Every school district and region will have its own set of challenges to overcome when attempting to implement Ethnic Studies courses and a graduation requirement. Although there is no formulaic approach to attain these goals, the ideas mentioned above have been paramount to what ESN–Sacramento has been able to accomplish.

The Road Ahead

A lot of work remains to be done. At the regional level we are seeking to create a pipeline of teachers with the disposition and skill to teach critical Ethnic Studies courses. One approach is via ESN–Sacramento members in the Teaching Credentials and Ethnic Studies departments at Sacramento State University, who are finalizing the Sacramento State Ethnic Studies Teaching Credentials Consortium. This entity would waive students with a degree in Ethnic Studies from taking the California Subject Examinations for Teachers (CSET) in the social sciences content area. At the statewide level, we will continue to work with other Ethnic Studies Now chapters in order to develop a statewide model curriculum in collaboration with the California Department of Education and also support the creation and passage of legislation requiring an Ethnic Studies high school graduation requirement throughout the state. The latter has involved working with various state legislators in crafting and lobbying possible resolutions.

We recognize that there are small victories in this work, yet this is ultimately a continued struggle. Ethnic Studies is not a panacea for the various forms of oppression that students endure in schools and in larger social settings. These courses in and of themselves will not guarantee a transformation in the lives of our students. Yet we believe that it is a starting point with the potential to not only transform the paradigm of young people into one that is more critical, humane, and just, but ultimately has the potential to transform our current and future institutions. It is not, and will not, be easy work. We are attempting to counter hundreds of years of oppression that permeate every facet of society. Yet we owe it to those around us and to those who have come before us to continue this long legacy of struggle and resilience. This struggle for a more liberated educational experience for students falls in line with the Iroquois sensibility, in which we believe that our actions have the potential to benefit individuals seven generations into the future, just as we have benefited from the work of our ancestors seven generations before us. ✳

Ethnic Studies in Providence Schools

BY KARLA E. VIGIL AND ZACK MEZERA

"I deserve an education that makes me feel powerful."
—Diane Gonzalez

On a cool January morning, more than 75 students, educators, and community members gathered outside of the offices of the Providence School Department with a simple refrain: *Our history matters.*

Suppressing the histories of people of color is an American tradition; oppressed minorities' and non-dominant groups' histories largely *have not mattered* in the American education system. But a recent and resurgent movement for Ethnic Studies—courses that focus on the role of race, ethnicity, and power in the history of the United States—has challenged this tradition and asserted that underrepresented peoples also deserve a place in our nation's classrooms. In places like Tucson, Los Angeles, and Austin, students and educators have demanded new curricula that relate to the lived experiences of students in the classroom. Providence Student Union's effort to expand Ethnic Studies courses in Providence, Rhode Island, represents one of the first attempts to win Ethnic Studies on the East Coast.

Taking Action in Providence

For more than seven years, the Providence Student Union (PSU) in Providence, Rhode Island, has been building student power to ensure that young people can improve their education and well-being. PSU unites students from across the city, trains and elevates student leaders, and wins powerful advocacy campaigns. The idea is simple but bold: What if students had a union in the same way that teachers or firefighters might? What impacts might that have on improving the school system?

So far, the results have been remarkable. In only a few years, PSU has already won major advocacy campaigns that have deeply impacted thousands of students. In 2010, a student walkout and adult ally-aided lawsuit kept a popular, student-centered block schedule at one high school. In 2014, PSU student organizers were the primary drivers behind a permanent ban on high-stakes testing in Rhode Island. In 2015, students marched inside of Providence City Hall for four days straight to secure approximately $1.6 million in funding annually for free student bus passes to school. These few victories, among others, had solidified PSU's reputation as a genuinely youth-led organization that focused on building grassroots student power to deliver tangible results for young people. PSU was uniquely positioned, then, to make a bold call for Ethnic Studies in Providence Schools.

A PSU campaign for Ethnic Studies was a long time in the making. For years, student leaders had discussed the deep disconnect they felt between their identities and the curriculum they were learning in school. PSU's workshops on issues like systems of oppression, stereotypes, and internalized racism had provided students with a vocabulary to help name the deficits in a curriculum they had long sensed was inadequate; namely, that it was distant from their lived experiences. Students were also frustrated by a lack of representation, both in the teaching force and in the curriculum. In Providence, 60 percent of the 24,000 students are Latinx and 91 percent are students of color, but 80 to 85 percent of the teachers are white. Their textbooks, too, failed to adequately reflect not only the district's diverse student body, but also Providence's centuries-long history as a site of interaction for numerous ethnic groups. On this point, PSU members brought home the district's primary history textbook and counted, page by page, the number of pages relating to people of color: The number of pages made up less than 10 percent of the book.

Some of the students' interest in Ethnic Studies was prompted by the national movement. Conversations at conferences like Free Minds, Free People helped open PSU members' eyes to the fact that things "didn't have to be the way they are." But it was a showing of *Precious Knowledge*—the documentary on the fight to save Tucson's Mexican American Studies (MAS)—in the PSU office that finally prompted PSU student leaders to act. "If students in Arizona are fighting for these courses, we can too," students declared. Inspired, students prepared a plan of action.

In early 2016, PSU launched its #OurHistoryMatters campaign to bring the courses to all high schools in the district. The campaign had three demands: First, PSU urged district administrators to create a full-credit course offered in all schools. Second, it demanded that the teachers for the Ethnic Studies courses be both trained to teach the courses and be representative of the students being taught. In other words, the Ethnic Studies teachers should be teachers of color who can relate to and teach the courses' content thoughtfully and purposefully. Third, the curriculum should be personalized, relevant to the ethnic groups in Providence, and highly engaging. Young people should be able come to class and find an exciting environment where they can analyze history from multiple angles and learn about their own families' backgrounds and stories.

PSU members lack traditional forms of political power—including voting and access to social and financial capital—so they instead used powerful narrative and a comprehensive communications strategy to sway district leadership. First, a petition aimed at the Providence school board was signed by almost 800 people. Members called and texted hundreds of students to announce the campaign. And in a freezing-cold early-morning rally outside of the central district office, almost 100 students and supporters gathered in solidarity with PSU leaders as they argued for curriculum and content that is relevant and compelling to Providence's diverse student population.

At the rally, one PSU leader, Diane Gonzalez, stressed the importance of learning about leaders who looked like her and shared her background:

> We should also be learning about more in the world than just the United States. I'm Guatemalan, and I have no idea about our history at all. It's like our schools think it's not important for me to learn about my family history. They make it seem like our countries are meaningless, like they have never had leaders.

Diane continued by sharing her main request: that schools should be empowering for students who look like her. She shared her experience watching *Precious Knowledge*, saying that the students in the film "were not only learning about history; they were learning about oppression and about how to be leaders in their communities. I [also] deserve an education that makes me feel powerful."

Another PSU leader, Licelot Caraballo, preempted a common argument made against the MAS program, namely that Ethnic Studies courses are inherently anti-American. "Learning about my Dominican roots doesn't make me less American," Licelot said. She also pointed out the dangers of teaching a sanitized version of American history, arguing that "the oppression of enslaved African Americans and Native Americans is disguised as 'cultural exchange.'"

Speakers from PSU were joined by youth leaders from other local organizations, including Youth in Action, Providence Youth Student Movement (PrYSM), and the Environmental Justice League of Rhode Island. Numerous local media outlets covered the campaign launch, which helped educate the public about Ethnic Studies and students' desires to be reflected in their curriculum. National coverage of PSU's rally in publications like *The Atlantic* also helped build pressure for the cause. And PSU's front-end advocacy work proved quite effective. The petition signatures and the high level of interest from Providence students and residents helped make it possible for school board members and district leadership to state their support. Providence Schools Superintendent Chris Maher even signed PSU's petition and showed up at the rally, tweeting: "The @pvdstudentunion is demanding equity in the curriculum of our @pvdschools. I agree."

Implementation

Providence Schools was very supportive of the goal to offer the full-credit course in all schools. Almost immediately, the district began holding regular meetings with students and community leaders.

Design of the Courses

Ethnic Studies pedagogy can be defined as teaching strategies and practices that help students from diverse racial, ethnic, and cultural backgrounds gain knowledge and master skills needed to function in a democratic society (Banks, 1995). In Providence, students—along with teachers, community leaders, administrators, and families—worked together to fight for a curriculum in high schools that reflected the identities of the students it served. After several community meetings, students and committee members designed four Ethnic Studies units: 1) Un-Learning Your History; 2) Community Histories; 3) Oppression & Power; and 4) Community Organizing/Social Justice. Throughout the year, students analyzed racism and it social impact, explored their identities, researched the history of the communities they lived in, and analyzed recent social justice campaigns and movements.

Over the course of the next six months, PSU members and district representatives collaborated in committees to develop a proposal for a full-year, credit-bearing Ethnic Studies course open to all Providence high school students with the aforementioned four units. During the 2016–17 school year, Ethnic Studies was piloted in four high schools with a focus on engaging students in personally relevant discussions, activities, and hands-on projects.

The district's director of teaching and instruction led biweekly meetings with teachers and community partners to reflect on lessons. It was also during this time that teachers were able to make changes to curriculum, share resources, and discuss challenges. In most classrooms, students were responsive to the content and were engaged with the learning activities. However, we realized that some students, specifically those who were English language learners, found it difficult to comprehend the content. The team questioned how to develop curricula that is accessible to all students from culturally and linguistically diverse backgrounds. Ultimately, we want to find out what types of support are needed so that teachers can deliver the content successfully.

Launch of the First Four Ethnic Studies Courses

James Banks defines Ethnic Studies as the "scientific and humanistic study of histories, cultures, and experiences of ethnic groups within the United States and other societies." Providence students have a variety of histories, cultures, and experiences that their learning environments have neglected to mirror for quite some time. These students needed to engage with their own histories and communities as soon as possible. In total, about 80 students from four high schools selected the Ethnic Studies course. Teachers who participated in the pilot program all volunteered and received the support from their school principals. For a year, teachers met biweekly to reflect on challenges, plan, and revise the curriculum. The meetings gave teachers opportunities to work as a team and decide on content that was culturally relevant.

Personalized learning allowed teachers to utilize culturally responsive practices that provided opportunities for students to think critically about power, oppression, and racism. Students were also empowered to use an equity framework that challenged dominant perspectives. This integration of critical pedagogy with personalized learning helped students understand how knowledge is created and influenced by cultural assumptions, perspectives, and biases.

These Ethnic Studies courses are also being used to leverage more diverse, relevant, and engaging teaching practices and curricula in other courses and subjects as well. Providence Schools is already pulling together teacher-leader teams from the social studies and literary arts departments to examine how "Ethnic Studies–style" improvements might be infused throughout the curriculum.

Moving Forward

The commitment to offer Ethnic Studies courses in Providence was easily won, but implementing the courses became a serious challenge. While Providence's Ethnic Studies courses have been a big success with students thus far, it's clear that there is a challenging road ahead. In fact, none of PSU's three initial demands have been addressed fully: Although the courses are for-credit, they do not yet exist in all Providence schools; the courses still are not taught by specially trained teachers of color; and the curriculum still needs significant work before it can be considered highly engaging for all students. These are massive challenges.

Supporting more teachers of color in Providence and across Rhode Island continues to be a significant hurdle. Underrepresentation is a challenge for schools across the state, and all stakeholders need to unite to build new incentives and challenge old practices, cultures, and systems that keep talented people of color from committing to and remaining in the teaching profession.

Selecting content and delivering instruction reflective of the broad, complex, and dynamic population of Providence students with global origins proved just as challenging. In part, the challenges reflected staffing issues in the district: While they had committed significant existing staff time to facilitate a curriculum-creation process, Providence Schools did not set aside funds for a specific lead on the project, which made progress on crafting a curriculum difficult.

Moreover, even with the community input, determining exactly what to cover in the course and how proves quite challenging. How can Providence build a reflective curriculum in a district where students and their families speak more than 30 different languages and come from more than 50 different countries? For some students in the pilot courses, they had only recently moved to America. In addition to the challenges inherent to teaching ELL students, these students could also have a difficult time relating to historical issues in Providence, Rhode Island, and/or the United States. One solution was to allow students the space to pursue their own research projects, but that also presented challenges. For example, students in the same classroom could be refugees on different sides of a geopolitical conflict. Under ideal conditions, these situations could prove to be powerful learning moments, but for overburdened teachers already juggling the many unique challenges of teaching a new Ethnic Studies course, these opportunities could easily turn into crises. One local journalist, Tom Hoffman of *Common Ground Rhode Island*, stated the problem well: "Successfully designing, implementing, and teaching an ambitious, critical, anti-colonial, yearlong Ethnic Studies course in Providence schools is by no means impossible, but make no mistake, it is one of the most profound and politically fraught challenges a teacher, and a school system, could take on."

Despite these difficulties, Providence is now entering the second year of the program, and the courses continue to be offered at multiple schools. One small Providence high school—only 375 students—has more than 70 students enrolled in an Ethnic Studies course in the fall 2017 semester. Meanwhile, the Providence Public School Department and Providence Student Union will continue to work to improve the course. The district this year is focused on ways to make the courses more personalized and relevant to student interests. PSU will continue to monitor the curriculum development, will advocate to expand the courses to all schools, and will press for more teachers of color who can speak to the course's content from personal experience.

Caraballo, one of the student leaders of the Ethnic Studies campaign, had even bigger plans for the courses:

> I think that one of the long-term goals or effects that adding on this course can hopefully have is a long-term change in all of our departments, including science, art, math, history, everything . . . not just only history. This is a small step that will lead to larger steps . . . to materials that aren't solely Eurocentric.

Youth organizing at Providence Student Union and elsewhere has shown again and again that when students unite, they can make powerful, long-term changes to their schools and communities. The continued expansion of Ethnic Studies courses will help ensure that these student leaders can receive an education that is as powerful as they themselves are. ✳

We Don't Want to Just Study the World, We Want to Change It

Ethnic Studies and the Development of Transformative Students and Educators

BY KYLE BECKHAM AND ARTNELSON CONCORDIA

Designing an Ethnic Studies (ES) course was personal for us. We were youth who struggled to find meaning (and success) in our own experiences with schooling. We wanted to create a course that would speak to our younger selves, to the students we were in high school. We also could not accept the academic trajectory of too many of our students and understood deeply the need for a dramatic shift in the way we (as a district) were teaching. In the summer of 2007, with the support of Allyson Tintiangco-Cubales, a professor of Ethnic Studies and Asian American Studies at San Francisco State University (SFSU), and Pete Hammer, a teacher working within central office, a group of teachers set out to design a course for incoming 9th graders that we felt better reflected the students in our classrooms.

Now with several years of reflected practice in hand, we believe we have valuable lessons toward achieving that end. It is our hope that by sharing these lessons, we can contribute to advancing the statewide and national efforts to build Ethnic Studies curriculum that equips all students with hard academic skills, critical consciousness, and a deep self-love and commitment to serving our communities as a part of our larger project to democratize education.

Part 1:
Ethnic Studies in the San Francisco United School District

"I have great respect for the past. If you don't know where you've come from, you don't know where you're going." —Maya Angelou

As the teachers who pushed to institutionalize Ethnic Studies in San Francisco public schools, we see ourselves as the inheritors of an important local tradition. The work we continue to engage in is tied directly to the struggles of late-1960s student organizers across the nation and world, but specifically at SFSU. They presciently saw the importance of moving beyond calls for inclusive curricular reform and into calls for the institutionalization of Ethnic Studies that resulted in the creation of the first and only college of Ethnic Studies in the United States. They realized that simply having more courses offered in existing departments that focused on the histories and experiences of communities of color would not create the necessary investment to ensure their continued viability in rough financial or political times. By creating the college—a bureaucratic structure that's seen as formally equal to any other college in the eyes of the institution—the larger university was forced to permanently reckon with the creation of scholarship focused primarily on communities of color and its dissemination to the students who attend the university. This deep embedding in the larger institutional structure worked to ensure the continued viability of Ethnic Studies. Today, the College of Ethnic Studies (CES) remains the only college of its kind. While Ethnic Studies departments and programs have been cut or eliminated at other institutions, the CES at SFSU remains a haven for important work focused on the histories and experiences of communities of color.

Much of the energy generated at SFSU quietly permeated the San Francisco Unified School District (SFUSD). Throughout the 1970s, calls for a more inclusive curricula grew in strength. During the 1980s, a more formal commitment to multiculturalism arose, eventually becoming the dominant curricular and pedagogical form espoused by most teachers and administrators in the district. Though this commitment was often verbalized, there was little formal curricula developed to spread it widely. Of course individual teachers, departments, and schools did important work to push back against more conservative and traditional approaches to teaching an increasingly diverse student body, but there were no efforts to formally institutionalize an approach that centered the histories and experiences of students of color.

During the 1990s, teachers familiar with and trained in Ethnic Studies began to enter the system and agitate for its inclusion and offering. It was added as an official elective, and a binder of curriculum developed that teachers who sought it out could access, but as the millennium approached and the pressures of standardized testing and curriculum increased, fewer and fewer schools formally offered the course—until none did. Individual teachers infused Ethnic Studies into their practices, but the district offered no formal support or acknowledgement of its importance or potential efficacy.

In 2005, Eric Mar, a school board commissioner and faculty member of the CES, introduced a resolution to explore the creation/revival of an Ethnic Studies program in SFUSD. The resolution passed unanimously and provided district resources for an initial group of teachers to spend the 2007–08 school year laying the foundation for a 9th-grade historically based Ethnic Studies course that would launch sometime thereafter (specifically funding for professional development and the support of a teacher on special assignment who would facilitate the work, along with a stipend for Tintiangco-Cubales to consult). By the summer's end, a skeletal curriculum existed and schools were asked to see if they would support a soft pilot, with professional development support offered to the teachers who would teach it. Three schools emerged, offering a total of five sections across them.

The first formal implementation of a rudimentary curriculum occurred in the 2008–09 school year, the same year we were hit by the Great Recession. Because of the financial cataclysm faced by the district, by the end of that year, only two schools remained committed to offering the course.

With one year of professional development funding left, the collective of teachers involved in developing, sustaining, and teaching Ethnic Studies decided to spend the coming year working on the course, as well as organizing to institutionalize Ethnic Studies as an integral and permanent part of the district. We prepared an application to make the course a University of California "G" elective (meaning it would count toward UC admissions requirements) and reached out to community organizations, teacher and administrator allies, and members of the school board. Regular organizing meetings alternated with bimonthly curriculum development meetings. Through the work of Tintiangco-Cubales, we secured a commitment from the dean of the CES to allow ES students to qualify for CSU concurrent-enrollment credits as well.

The collective drafted a detailed resolution and plan for implementing an Ethnic Studies pilot that would lay the foundation for a deep institutionalization of the program to present to the SFUSD School Board. The pilot would need to be opt-in and limited to five schools willing to commit to ongoing professional and curricular development. These schools also would need to agree to a site-based funding commitment of 20 percent of a teacher's salary each year over a five-year period, with district funding for teacher professional development, classroom supplies to support curriculum development, and most importantly, a 20 percent teacher salary per-site allocation paid from the district's budget as an institutional signal of longer-term financial commitment. We also vetted our plan by key members of the board, built alliances with community members who could and would show up when needed, and found support at specific school sites among teachers, students, family and community members, and administrators. The night of the board resolution's introduction, more than 200 people showed up. It passed unanimously.

With official district support, we began the process of redesigning the course while engaging in year-round intensive professional development. There was a significant skill gap between the core group of teachers—most of whom had been there since the course's inception—and some of the newer teachers who would be teaching at some of the pilot schools. The latter group consisted of several people who had no actual experience with Ethnic Studies content; their schools believed them to be teachers with potential and saw ES as a way to develop and maintain them on staff. This meant that a substantial program of pedagogical and curricular development needed to be engaged in so that quality across the pilot schools could be maintained. This showed the difficulty of doing ES well at scale.

As the pilot progressed, we faced several key challenges. First was the constant threat of having what little funding we had secured being cut. Every year we would meet with an administrator from central office who would tell us to prepare for the possibility of funding to be terminated and to consider moving from a continual development model of the course to one where the curriculum would be standardized, published, and offered more widely as a book or web resource. Second was the continual turnover of teachers at two of the five schools and the eventual early withdrawal of one of them from the pilot. That meant that new teachers had to be onboarded, many of whom were unfamiliar with the previous work and often ES more generally. Third was the marginal position that we had in the eyes of the central office. In fact, because of our willingness to organize in defense of the course, we were seen as hostile and adversarial by some people who had never met or spoken with us but nevertheless had influence over our funding/resources.

In spite of these challenges, the schools with stable teachers and programs thrived. Stanford University researchers Thomas Dee and Emily Penner performed a first-of-its-kind rigorous quantitative analysis of the formal student outcome data produced by the course, which made causal linkages between Ethnic Studies enrollment (when the course was used as an intervention) and positive student gains in attendance, overall GPA, credit accumulation, and measurable positive impact on student performance in mathematics and science.

We engaged in a new round of organizing and planning during the summer and fall of 2014 to prepare for next steps. In December 2014, the SFUSD school board resolution "Institutionalizing Ethnic Studies in SFUSD" passed unanimously. This resolution mandated that every high school in SFUSD offer at least one section of the course. Today, the ES collective has more than 20 teachers, permanent

district support, a full-time teacher on special assignment whose entire job is to facilitate the growth and stability of the program by supporting its teachers, and a commitment from the district to pay for 50 percent of the program costs at all of the school sites, in addition to providing resources to purchase texts and technological resources to each site.

Stanford University researchers performed a first-of-its-kind rigorous quantitative analysis of the formal student outcome produced by the course, which made causal linkages between Ethnic Studies enrollment and positive student gains in attendance, overall GPA, credit accumulation, and measurable positive impact on student performance in mathematics and science.

After the pilot's conclusion, we created a course overview that would anchor our 9th-grade class. Though we had well over five years of classroom experience at a handful of sites, we did not have a unifying document that would coalesce our districtwide campaign. Central to our professional development (PD) were the veteran teachers involved with the pilot program. Many were apprehensive about this next stage of our work and wanted to limit participation in the PD to the handful of pilot program teachers. However, with the guidance (and gentle prodding) of a key central office administrator, we opened up the process to any district employee interested in participating. We gathered more than 20 history and social studies teachers and engaged in the work of envisioning and creating a course overview that defined us. Our task had two critical aspects: 1) We needed something that would unify our work throughout the district to which we could hold our teachers accountable; 2) we also needed something that would allow for (and encourage) local sites to create curricula that responded to their particular conditions. What we came up with does exactly that. Our course overview delineates several "non-negotiables" of the class, specifically our values, defined key concepts, unit progression, enduring understandings, and essential questions. Any site offering Ethnic Studies (and receiving central office funding for it) will be teaching curriculum anchored to these key aspects of the course overview but will also be given the flexibility to shape it to meet the needs of their students.

Next we set out to create sample curriculum maps and corresponding unit plans for each of the six units of study (the lesson plan for Unit 1, Identity and Narrative, is included at the end of this chapter). We understood that if we were to be expanding districtwide, many teachers assigned to the course may not have a background in Ethnic Studies. These sample maps and plans were created to be available as a resource but were not mandated. To support individual teachers, particularly those who were new to Ethnic Studies, the "teacher on special assignment" (TSA) conducts regular site visits and leads the planning and development of regular and intensive PD (monthly after-school meetings, semester release days, and summer PD). The TSA continually assesses teacher needs and works to provide both material and technical support throughout the school year. Lastly, the TSA regularly reports to the director of the district humanities office and when called for, provides updates to the school board.

Heading into its third year, the journey to institutionalize Ethnic Studies has progressed significantly. The course is now offered in every high school in the district. Regular PD is facilitated by the district-supported TSA to dozens of teachers and support staff spanning grades 6–12. All PD design takes into consideration the need for deep theoretical study relevant to the field of Ethnic Studies: modeling/sharing of exemplary units and lessons, other practical needs (e.g., classroom design, effective use of technology, software, applications, activities development), building community of support and reciprocity, and re/distribution of scarce resources. On-site support is prioritized for new teachers and teachers new to Ethnic Studies. Within our teacher cohort, veteran educators play a key role in the creation and implementation of PD that is focused on both pedagogical and curricular development. They are, and have been, essential in the building and maintenance of a strong community and are of the utmost importance to the ES teacher collective.

Furthermore, many of our veteran teachers have leadership roles and significant influence in their particular school community, which lends itself to securing and maintaining support for Ethnic Studies at each site. This in turn strengthens the thrust of the work for this year. The TSA will support existing efforts (and help initiate others) of non–Ethnic Studies teachers throughout the district to infuse Ethnic Studies concepts and practice into their teaching as a means to transform the core curriculum. This is challenging work. But because of the school board vision, which itself is supported by the leadership within central office and executed through the TSA, the creativity and commitment of the dozens of classroom teachers can be harnessed to make it all happen.

Part 2:
Ethnic Studies, Our Evolution

"To paraphrase from this dead old white dude that many people hate, but nevertheless is quite relevant . . . without a deep grasp of critical and meaningful theory, we ain't ever gonna get the change we need."
—Anonymous

WHAT DOES IT MEAN TO INSTITUTIONALIZE ETHNIC STUDIES?

The lessons we offer come from our specific struggle to make Ethnic Studies a central part of the functioning of SFUSD.

ES, if it is to be truly transformative, must become part of the way in which a district thinks of itself and how it teaches content and works for/with students.

LESSON 1: Ethnic Studies is not and can never be "just another class."

There are myriad required courses that a high school student must pass through in order to graduate. The knee-jerk and seductive approach to making ES a reality for as many students as possible is to make it a requirement for graduation. The fastest way to neutralize the power of Ethnic Studies is to make it something that school communities have to do rather than something that they want to do. When schools are forced to teach ES, or teach it largely because it comes with funding that can be used to prevent teacher layoffs or soften the blow of other institutional and financial burdens, what ends up happening is that the teachers who teach it either do not see it as essential to the vision of the school at which they teach or to the full development of their students. We dealt with this issue firsthand as the initial core group of schools in the pilot had a teacher who was not qualified to teach the course, having had no experience with the content and concepts of the course specifically and ES more generally, little classroom experience, serious classroom management issues, and a liberal multiculturalist approach that favored inclusion more than transformation. This problem emerged because that specific school community's administration saw ES as important but also saw the funding tied to it as a way to support teachers, even those who were not right for the class.

Imposing Ethnic Studies on any community without that community wanting it or seeing it as essential toward the full development of their students undermines the noble intentions of those who want to mandate it. If Ethnic Studies ever becomes a course or program where teachers do not want to teach it or where teachers who do not care about it are warehoused, then it should not continue. The larger project is dependent on robust and sustainable school-by-school programs that can withstand external criticism from those who are politically opposed to what the course represents. If it is just another standardized class, just another requirement, or not demonstrably transformative for students, teachers, and whole communities, then it should be reconsidered.

LESSON 2: Ethnic Studies is for everyone.

ES seeks to access the inherent desire of children (all children) to learn and create knowledge. We need to move away from seeing the purpose of education as principally a means to "get a job" and toward a critical understanding of it as an essential tool for addressing the needs and aspirations of our students and their families. By effectively reframing our purpose, we are able to unlock our students' energy and enthusiasm to get academic development that prepares them to secure employment and educational opportunity as well as mobilize their critical participation in our democratic society.

Imposing Ethnic Studies on any community without that community wanting it or seeing it as essential toward the full development of their students undermines the noble intentions of those who want to mandate it.

It cannot be understated that commitment to humanity, critical analysis of systems and power, building deep and meaningful connections (to self, community, and society), and developing academic skills (reading, writing, research, speaking, listening, and working collectively) within our students are all central to our pedagogy. We want our students to be able to effectively and powerfully read, write, and critically think and engage in school. Just as importantly, we want our students to apply their skills and knowledge in the service of the creation and maintenance of a just society.

LESSON 3: Avoid the allure of hard standardization and don't be afraid to change.

Ethnic Studies is not fast food. It is slow, home-cooked sustenance. Given our diverse contexts, teachers must be empowered to use an ES framework that they can adapt. When we first embarked on the development of SFUSD's ES program, we took a content-coverage approach. This meant focusing on the experiences of slices of particular racial and ethnic groups. We quickly learned that coverage was more constraining than it was liberating. There is no way to effectively cover the diverse histories, experiences, and lives that come with our students; no matter how much we wanted, there was not enough time to include every group. Because of this reality, we shifted to a frameworks approach in which larger, interrelated concepts allowed teachers and their students to co-construct knowledge.

Our ES course is not narrow. It is a critical examination of the social construction of race and racism so that students can critically examine other social structures in their lives. ES is the beginning of a process of analytical development. At this point in our work, ES is one course in the district. But it is much more than that. In reality, it is an approach, a way of thinking, and a way of doing things. We want ES to be the glue that holds all classes together and not simply an elective. If it is framed as a "culturally relevant elective" it will be difficult to move it from the margins and into the center of what is taught, how it is taught, and why it is taught.

This approach also avoids the allure of inclusive multiculturalism. Simply covering a slice of a group's history does not mean that inclusion has actually taken place. It also avoids the "X American history week" approach, which inevitably reduces the complexity of group histories since the next week will simply be the listing out of the history of another group. For an introduction to ES, we came to see that helping students understand important concepts that they can apply in future ES classes—as well as their other classes—was more important than them having fact-based knowledge of specific historical events and actors.

LESSON 4: Central office administrators are essential to the long-term sustenance and expansion of Ethnic Studies.

Sustainable ES requires a level of interaction with systemic schooling that many of its proponents are loathe to interact with (or reject altogether). The central district administration is a significant yet easily overlooked or oft-adversarial aspect of the larger system, specifically the parts of the bureaucracy that control funding and support for curricular and pedagogical reforms. We learned that mid-level district administrators would be key to sustaining the pro-

fessional development that drove the direction of ES development. Mid-level central office administrators hold a great deal of institutional memory and are responsible for ensuring continuity when change happens above and below them. They can leverage institutional inertia—for better or worse—in ways that site administrators, teachers, and community members cannot. They also possess a view of the workings of the district that is much broader than a typical teacher or even site administrator. We came to see these things as assets, even as some in the central office were reluctant to fully support our work.

In addition, in the early days of the board mandate, there were central office administrators who threatened to remove the funding under the guise of fiscal hardship. They would commend us on the work we were doing, on the quality that they themselves had seen in the classrooms they had visited, but then argue that supporting our efforts into the far future was not feasible and that we needed to consider moving away from a model of ongoing, regular, reflexive, deep PD into a phase where the curriculum could be packaged and handed off to individual schools and teachers across the district. This position was not irrational or even mean-spirited, rather it reflected the ways in which most curricula are developed. In other words, these administrators still needed to be moved to see more clearly the linkages between the work we were doing behind the scenes and the outcomes in the classrooms.

There were others who saw more what we were accomplishing and the qualitative improvements that were taking place in the teachers' practices and the students' classroom experiences. When we wrote a second board resolution to move from a pilot phase into an expansion phase, these administrators advocated for the necessity of the PD in conversations with their own superiors and the board itself. They too see themselves as part of the entirety of the project, and as their commitment deepens, the chances of ES being scaled back or eliminated decline dramatically.

LESSON 5: Sustainable programs of Ethnic Studies must generate meaningful data and partner with the educational research community.

The daily grind of teaching coupled with ongoing program development are two forces that could cause teachers engaged in the work of making ES a reality overlook the importance of data collection and research. We were fortunate to have had the opportunity to collaborate with Tintiangco-Cubales and her graduate students throughout the development of ES in SFUSD. They kept the importance of capturing what we were doing in order to share it with others front and center. They also caused us to think of ways to be more systematic in our claims about the efficacy of the program and to make sure that we were engaged in research-informed practices in developing and implementing it.

This approach to data collection and research is essential given the broad misinformation and misunderstandings about what Ethnic Studies is in the United States. There are concerted efforts by conservatives and traditionalists to paint the course as not rigorous, academic, or useful. We believe the best way to neutralize this tendency is to gather as much qualitative and quantitative evidence as possible about the course's efficacy. The Stanford study made international headlines when its preliminary findings were released. The fact that the study was quantitatively focused lent an air of scientific validity to what was taking place that, sadly, a more qualitatively focused study would not. Finding researchers who are willing to use their quantitative skills in service of improving and/or sharing the power of ES must be a part of any long-term plan for its expansion.

However, this does not mean that we should focus exclusively on working with quantitatively focused researchers. As impressive as the results of the Stanford study are, they do not tell us how the results were achieved. To find this out, there must also be rigorous qualitative documentation of the methods used in the classroom by both teachers and students. The quantitative results came about because of specific curricular, pedagogical, and political commitments that teachers and students engaged in, but without asking those involved, the details of what was done and how people may be led to think that any ES program is good and that simply having "inclusive" or "relevant" curriculum is enough.

LESSON 6: Ethnic Studies teachers are made, not born.
Institutionalizing ES means finding committed teachers who are willing to engage in a program of

sustained development and have the desire to constantly improve their courses. Having a solid core of teachers who stick around for years has been key to what emerged in San Francisco. We worked for a substantial amount of time before we knew anything would be successfully institutionalized, and we continue to work on improving and expanding the course or series of courses into something more: a new approach to teaching. We have become better teachers because we have remained steadfast in our belief that together we can make one another better.

Through all of our work, we remain committed to the belief that anyone who honestly engages in developing themselves as a teacher of Ethnic Studies can become skilled at it. This does not mean that everyone will have journeys of identical lengths to achieve that skill, but that with proper support, discipline, and commitment, anyone can get there. This also means that teachers who believe themselves to be skilled at ES because of their positions as members of oppressed groups may have to confront the very real possibility that they do not have the level of skill that they think they have. Simply having a room full of enthusiastic teachers of color does not mean that anything special will happen if those teachers uncritically replicate pedagogies and approaches that are anathema to the potential of Ethnic Studies. Conversely, having a room of white teachers who are willing to honestly engage in the necessary work does not inherently limit what is possible. The common denominator is that successful, long-term teachers of ES are committed to pedagogical, ethical, and political self-critique, humility, revision, and collective solidarity toward achieving the goals of the larger project.

Part 3:
Infusing Ethnic Studies into the Core Curriculum, Intensive Professional Development, and Continual Teacher Support

"All that you touch you Change. All that you Change changes you. The only lasting truth is Change. God is Change." —Octavia Butler, *Parable of the Sower*

In addition to the efforts specific to the implementation of the 9th-grade course, SFUSD is beginning the work of infusing Ethnic Studies concepts and pedagogy into the K–12 history–social science core curriculum. With grades 6–12 as the starting point, and working with a cohort of 10 middle school teachers from several sites, we met regularly during the last school year with the purpose of transforming their history–social science teaching. Specifically, to use Ethnic Studies concepts as a means of organizing their particular courses' content in the hopes of more effectively reaching our students.

At its core, Ethnic Studies reconstructs a more robust historical narrative that centers the teaching and learning on the perspectives of historically marginalized communities, specifically communities of color. In one of our lessons, we use high-definition TV as an analogy for the importance of more perspectives. The greater the number of pixels, the greater clarity. We believe that the more points of view (pixels) our historical narratives incorporate, the closer we move to a richer and more truthful understanding of our collective past. As historians and critical educators, it is our responsibility to uncover and rediscover more stories. This process can only bring us more collective clarity of our past, with the hope that it may better inform our creation of our future. Drawing from the disciplines of history, sociology, critical race theory, cultural studies, anthropology, and political science, the Ethnic Studies course is a compelling way to examine race, ethnicity, nationality, and culture in the United States. Ethnic Studies equips students with a critical lens to see the world and their place in it by understanding systems and power at the root of American society. Students are supported to discover and use their own power for the benefit of not only themselves, but also that of their community and society at large.

Appendix

"We do not learn from experience . . . we learn from reflecting on experience." —John Dewey

UNIT 1: Identity and Narrative

Foundational to our teaching is the importance of uplifting individual experiences and facilitating deep and critical meaning-making of our lives. We guide students to make connections between their lives and the lives of those around them to the larger social, economic, and political forces at play that shape much of what they/we experience. We believe that in order to effect change, we must help our students develop knowledge (and love) of self, critical consciousness, and hard academic literacies.

In this unit (and in all units to follow) we begin with the lived experiences of our students as the launching pad for all learning. In brief, students reflect on their path to this point in their lives (our "Road of Life" assignment) and develop critical vocabulary anchored to their realities (specifically around their race, ethnicity, nationality, culture, and identity). We challenge them to make connections within themselves and between each other and to build community and develop academic skills (establishing and practicing norms, effective note-taking, narrative writing, speaking and listening, presentation), culminating in an autoethnographic essay.

Week 1: Welcome. We Are Ethnic Studies.

This week, we welcome our students into the Ethnic Studies community. Many, if not all, of our students will be wondering "What exactly is this class?" On the first day of school, students will read and reflect upon former students' answers to that question. During this week, students will reexamine the terms "history" and "narrative." Furthermore, students will explore the "Five Core Principles of Ethnic Studies," learn/review how to take notes, and be introduced to our yearlong working metaphor (the road of life) for our classroom learning experience. We are all on this journey together.

Week 2: The Road of Life. What Has Been Your Path to This Point in Your Journey?

Students were introduced to the "Road of Life" assignment last week. With the guide of several prompts, they will reflect upon their journey and identify key events from their path to this point. Students will then artistically construct a representation of their path and share with (and listen to) their peers' significant experiences they have "traveled" that help make them the people they currently are. While celebrating individual experiences, it is important to begin the process of highlighting commonalities and building unity/community based upon both the diversity *and* the similarities of the people that make up our classroom community.

Week 3: Toward a "High-Definition" Picture of Our Past: Like an HDTV with Missing Pixels, History Without Our Points of View Is Distorted

A telling of U.S. history that does not reflect us is no history at all. Furthermore, a telling of U.S. history about us, told without us, is no history at all. This week, students will be introduced to key terms related to Unit 1 concepts: Identity and Narrative. We will define the terms master narrative, diversity, point of view, and power. Students will explore how power plays an important role in the telling of any story—the recounting of past events, of history. We will examine how and why the teaching of Raza Studies/Mexican American Studies in Tucson Unified School District became a point of controversy, ultimately leading to its banning in the entire state. We will explore the complexities of the situation and the various perspectives both in support and in opposition to Ethnic Studies in Arizona.

Week 4: Race Matters and the Social Construction of Inequality

Race is a social construct. Though it is technically not "real" in a biological sense, the consequences of racism—the use of power by the dominant race to oppress other races—are real and enduring. This week, we begin our "deep dive" look into the origins of racial divide and its impact on ourselves, our families, our communities, and our society.

Though our focus throughout this course will be on a critical examination of how we experience race and ethnicity, we will explore its intersections with class, gender, and sexuality. People face discrimination because they embody a racial, gender, sexuality, class identity, and/or other identities that do not match the "norm." We will examine the intersections ("cross streets") of personal identity in discussing injustice.

In the spirit of this course's "cross-cutting values" (Love and Respect; Hope; Community Solidarity and Unity; Self-Determination and Critical Consciousness), we seek to guide our students' explorations of all the intersections of who they are so that they can come to know and love themselves. From self-love, they can move toward getting to know and appreciate people who are different from themselves. That self-love can, to some degree, inoculate them against the array of institutions that would have them believe that they are worth less than others are.

Week 5: Exploring Race, Ethnicity, Nationality, and Culture

Though often used interchangeably, these related terms are distinct and absolutely necessary for a complex and nuanced understanding of social relationships in the United States. Students are guided to explore how one's race (skin color and phenotype as determined by other people) is related to one's ethnicity (ancestral origin), sometimes nationality (one's citizenship), and sometimes their culture (ways of seeing and ways of being). We define these terms and examine how each of them shape our experiences.

Week 6: Autoethnography: A Critical Reflection on the Relationship Between My Path (Road of Life) and My Race, Ethnicity, Nationality, and Culture

For our summative assessment, students begin to critically explore their lived experiences as it pertains to their race, ethnicity, nationality, and/or culture. They write in a narrative form and are asked how these aspects of their identity have shaped them, their families, and their communities. Here, students come full circle back to their Road of Life, where they are guided to reexamine how these aspects of their identity may (or may not) have impacted the decisions, experiences, and outcomes of their journey up to this point. ✳

Ethnic Studies and Community-Engaged Scholarship in Texas

The Weaving of a Broader "We"

BY EMILIO ZAMORA AND ANGELA VALENZUELA

Euphoric may be too strong a term to describe how we felt in June 2016 when we met during the first statewide summit on Mexican American Studies in public schools. We were definitely optimistic. At the time, members of the K–12 Committee of Tejas Foco of the National Association for Chicana and Chicano Studies had built momentum in a campaign to develop new curriculum, host professional development workshops, and advocate for Mexican American Studies. The five-year effort had produced important results, including district-based instructional programs like Academia Cuauhtli from Austin, Texas. Collaborations between public school teachers and faculty from San Antonio colleges and the University of Texas at San Antonio have generated new Mexican American Studies curriculum and sponsored professional development meetings. Rio Grande Valley educators associated with the K–12 committee have established an electronic site with curricular road maps for stand-alone and dual-credit courses. The K–12 committee has also pursued important advocacy work at the Texas Legislature and with the State Board of Education (SBOE).

University educators were now gathering in San Antonio to establish a statewide system of coordination that could help us align local efforts into a consistent and sustainable enterprise across the state. Our greatest concern, however, was a recently proposed textbook, *Mexican American Heritage*, that depicted Mexican Americans in disparaging and contemptible ways and threatened to overshadow our discussion and undermine the purpose of the 2016 summit.

Some of the summit participants lamented that none of our own had prepared a textbook for SBOE adoption. Others claimed that the publisher of the proposed textbook was unfairly capitalizing on the growing interest in Mexican American Studies that we had helped build. The most moving complaint was that the publisher was proposing a steady diet of offensive, if not racist, views that portrayed Mexican Americans as lazy, ignorant, and a threat to U.S. culture and national unity. Related to this well-established complaint was the observation that the authors had no training or experience in Mexican American Studies and disregarded the vast literature that scholars had produced since the early 1970s. Bias, and perhaps a heavy dose of ignorance, explained their blindness to our voice.

We managed to hold the summit without much disruption because the general assembly voted to treat the book as a separate issue and the participants mostly abided by the decision. Soon after the meeting, the K–12 committee announced a "Reject the Text" campaign that ultimately garnered the necessary support to convince the SBOE to unanimously vote against adopting the book. On the one hand, it was unfortunate that we had to put aside much of the work of the K–12 committee to pursue a strategy that included reviewing the book, reporting our findings, and building support for our cause with press conferences, marches, and protests outside the SBOE offices and what turned out to be a highly successful publicity drive. On the other hand, the campaign created opportunities that we used to advance the cause for Mexican American Studies. We recruited more than 40 scholars who participated in a well-organized review of the book. Several leading organizations throughout the state lent us different kinds of support. Most of the members of the Mexican American Legislative Caucus and the Senate

Hispanic Caucus joined at least 200 other persons who testified against the book. The overall friendly backing of the media and our electronic communications were instrumental in encouraging the participation of hundreds of persons in our rallies—some of whom came in busloads from Houston and other areas. In the end, we assumed responsibility for our interest in a public issue and capitalized on the support that we secured to energize our efforts into what social movement theorists call "a social cause."

Engaging Public Spaces

The campaign to reject the racist textbook should remind everyone that reforming education should not be restricted to public school classrooms or workshops that prepare teachers to implement new curriculum or adopt promising pedagogical tools. We must also reach out beyond the bureaucratic limits of our schools and connect with others in broadening and sustaining transformative and generative work. We propose interorganizational linkages to generate broad-based exchanges of resources necessary for advancing Mexican American Studies and its larger field of Ethnic Studies in public schools, as well as in community centers, colleges, and universities. We acknowledge that teachers are particularly important participants in this broad and interdependent form of Ethnic Studies development because they can ground and guide reform initiatives with their authoritative vantage points and firsthand classroom experiences. That said, collaborative ties with community organizations and higher education institutions legitimate, and thusly generate, public support for the work of such institutions, preempting unfair and often debilitating criticism that school officials may direct at them. As advocates for Ethnic Studies outside of public schools, we believe that community-based initiatives like Academia Cuauhtli provide "institutional cover," as it were.

Our point of departure in this article is the educational reform work that our community organization, Nuestro Grupo, has advanced in Austin during the last seven years. We wish to create a record of accomplishments that can guide like-minded persons—especially teachers—to replicate parts or all of the network-based initiatives that produced positive results for us. We do not pretend to have all the answers for developing a critical and culturally relevant pedagogy in Ethnic Studies but believe that our experience can serve as a model for building networks of partnerships and cooperative relations that could benefit our public schools. Such networks help cast a wide net for resources such as skilled and experienced individuals in content areas; curriculum development and implementation; formal and sustaining understandings of collaboration between institutions and individuals; funding support; and energized communities of interest outside the public schools that can provide social grounding, moral support, and added meaning to our work.

Our network building began in 2010, during the public review of the state's standard curriculum, known as the Texas Essential Knowledge and Skills (TEKS). The hearing attracted an unprecedented number of people calling for expanding the curriculum to correct the problem of the underrepresentation and misrepresentation of minority groups and women, as well as the lack of curricular alignment between the public school curriculum and university-level courses and programs. Almost everyone who testified—including public school teachers, parents, students, community leaders, and college professors—expressed concern that conservative members of the SBOE would not agree to expand the curriculum. Well over 500 persons participated in an electronic signature campaign, a march and three rallies, and press conferences outside the SBOE hearings in support of our testimony. A smaller group of approximately 25 organizers participated in regularly attended conference calls and meetings to plan the testimonies, outreach activities, and press conferences. They also supported Zamora's (2012) fundamental claim that TEKS lagged far behind the extraordinary amount of knowledge on minorities and women that college researchers and instructors have been producing and teaching since the early 1970s.

The Broader "We"

The frustration with the SBOE and the outpouring of concern turned the many individual decisions to testify and protest into what journalist and author Naomi Klein calls weaving "a broader 'we,'" an intentional attempt to find common cause among the various social movements and to give it a unified political direction. We would add that participation in such public expressions of discontent do not always result in a "broader 'we,'" but that educators who insert themselves in these larger public sites of contestation can find opportunities to identify networks and develop partnerships in solidarity with others in support of Ethnic Studies. Of course, the availability of such persons varies depending on the place, and the configuration of the networks can differ. This does not necessarily mean that such circumscribed settings limit the effort, but that the combination of skills, motivations, and other benefits unique to a locale will define the parameters for action.

The inter-institutional partnership that emerged in Austin involved key institutions, including the Tejano Monument, Inc., the University of Texas, the Austin Independent School District (AISD), and the City of Austin's Emma S. Barrientos Mexican American Cultural Center (ESB-MACC). The collaboration produced the Tejano History Curriculum Project, a two-year curriculum development and implementation project on Mexican American history that capitalized on the essential service of three members of the University of Texas faculty: Emilio Zamora, professor of history; Cinthia Salinas, associate professor in the College of Education; and María Franquiz, professor in the College of Education.

Zamora, the project's principal investigator, prepared lesson plans and assisted Salinas in teaching two undergraduate classes on curriculum development on Mexican American history. Forty-five undergraduates prepared approximately 32 journey boxes that resembled shoeboxes and contained primary documents, secondary publications, visual materials, and short narrative histories on various topics in U.S. history that focused on the Mexican American historical and contemporary experience. Salinas and Franquiz also assisted in garnering support from the Dual Language Program at AISD and ¡Adelante!, an organization of well over 300 teachers, college professors, school administrators, independent educators, and students who were associated with bilingual programs in local districts. We selected six AISD teachers who were members of ¡Adelante! and had secured master's degrees from the University of Texas to use the instructional materials with approximately 100 4th-grade students from four schools. Franquiz supervised and evaluated the classroom work, including enrichment activities at the ESB-MACC.

The Tejano History Curriculum Project was especially important in demonstrating that educators can find a sufficient number of capable and interested persons in their localities to contribute to effective reform initiatives. We were especially fortunate to have received initial funding from the board of directors of Tejano Monument, Inc., an organization that led a 12-year statewide campaign to erect the largest monument structure on the grounds of the Texas Capitol and one of the most important sites of Mexican American historical memory and recovery in the state. Prior to the completion of the majestic statuary in 2012, Andrés Tijerina, a professor of history at Austin Community College and a member of the Tejano Monument Inc. board who had participated in the previously mentioned 2010 TEKS protest, convinced other board members to use the remaining funds from the completed monument to support the project. Board members also used their influence to convince the Walmart Foundation to provide additional funding for the project.

The Tejano History Curriculum Project exceeded its goals. The undergraduate students in the university's teacher preparation program developed valuable instructional and research capabilities, while the 4th-grade students advanced their own academic skills. Parents and University of Texas, AISD, and ESB-MACC educators demonstrated the value of proven, skills-based partnerships in expanding our educational enterprise. The partnership with the University of Texas at Austin, AISD, and the ESB-MACC also demonstrated that the experience could spawn additional collaborations. This became an attractive proposition especially because Zamora, Tijerina, Salinas, Franquiz, the participating teachers, and ¡Adelante! representatives maintained their working relations beyond the life of the Tejano History Curriculum Project. For instance, they continued sponsoring teacher preparation workshops among dual language teachers to encourage a wider use of the curriculum that had been developed.

An Even Broader "We"

A major turning point occurred on September 20, 2013, when the participants in the Tejano History Curriculum Project coalesced again around a new initiative by Angela Valenzuela, the director of the Texas Center for Education Policy at the University of Texas, who organized a public meeting at the ESB-MACC to discuss the issue of literacy among Latino youth in Austin schools. The convening featured Armando Rendón, a Mexican American Studies and children's book author, and Oralia Garza de Cortés, a retired librarian and community activist, and it attracted approximately 45 educators, community activists, librarians, authors, parents, and students. After listening to moving presentations on the lack of culturally and linguistically relevant instructional materials, the audience entered into a spirited discussion on the need for community advocates to continue preparing instructional materials and establishing educational programs on the historical and contemporary experiences of Mexican Americans. They also came to unanimous agreement that a community-based, Mexican American organization should assume control over whatever the group wished to pursue.

The gathering decided to build on the earlier experience of the Tejano History Curriculum Project with a permanent program that would promote classroom learning on Mexican Americans. Some of the participants later established Academia Cuauhtli (Cuauhtli Academy) as an AISD project and a new community organization called Nuestro Grupo. Academia Cuauhtli was inaugurated on January 17, 2015, as a cultural revitalization project and Saturday school for approximately 25 4th graders from three elementary schools in East Austin geographically proximate to the ESB-MACC.

Once again, we capitalized on ongoing community discourse and action and helped build an even "broader 'we,'" an accomplishment that most likely would not have occurred if we had not already been engaging the Latino community at the proverbial public square. Even more, we would not have benefited from the energy and resources that Latino communities typically generate when addressing vital yet neglected issues like the education of our youth. We formalized yet again our partnerships. This time,

however, AISD assumed a major portion of the cost, and dual-language district officials became more involved in selecting the teachers and finalizing new additions to our lesson plans. The ESB-MACC also played a critical role by hosting Academia Cuauhtli and Nuestro Grupo's regular weekly meetings.

Nuestro Grupo has become the major site for developing Spanish-English instructional materials; sponsoring professional development workshops for teachers in the project and in the district's dual-language program; and planning regularly scheduled breakfasts for the children, meetings with parents, school bus transportation, and field trips. The organization includes some of the participants from the Tejano History Curriculum Project, retired and active teachers, graduate and undergraduate students, college professors, community advocates, elders, and a rotating set of nine to 14 AISD teachers who alternate Saturdays in teaching at Academia Cuauhtli. In order to promote teacher professional development, we always pair expert with novice teachers. The number of participating teachers fluctuates from year to year, but the number never falls below nine. Teachers regularly share with us how essential Nuestro Grupo and Academia Cuauhtli have been in providing them opportunities to teach in a more independent and creative manner, generally free from the test-driven, limited curriculum in the schools.

A special feature of Academia Cuauhtli is its use of cultural ceremony known as *danza Mexica* (Aztec dancing). Our intent is to enrich the Indigenous portion of our instructional program with the history and culture of Indigenous Peoples from Mexico and the Texas-Mexico border region, including symbolic movement, cosmology, music, and song. The instructional program also gives a regional focus to our program with a lesson plan and field trips on Tejano history that focus on events like the Battle of the Alamo (1836), the Pecan Shelling Strike (1936–37), and the Tejano Monument (2012). We have also begun to include the parents into the program by offering them referral services as well as some instruction with the same lesson plans on Mexican American history and culture that we use in the classes with the children.

In fall 2017, Cuauhtli parents began to receive regular English as a second language instruction classes from Cameron Allen, who is a community-based teacher from one of our partnering schools where parents gather regularly after school to discuss social issues affecting them.

We have completed our fourth year of operation, with an addition of two more elementary schools, now totaling five. At least half of all the curriculum we have co-constructed is available to all AISD teachers in grades 3–7 and 11. This means that in addition to regularly teaching a group of students, we are having districtwide impacts. Moreover, through teacher professional development workshops, we have also prepared up to 100 teachers overall to teach the curriculum to date.

Academia Cuauhtli has also become a research and professional development site primarily for graduate and undergraduate students from three area universities interested in Ethnic Studies. Teachers from ¡Adelante! have proposed that Academia Cuauhtli expand its training facilities by making it a laboratory for best teaching practices. Although we have not yet decided to do this, Academia Cuauhtli may expand into this area in two or three years. As teachers come into their own, they also seek career ladders into administration, a development we are addressing by recruiting teachers for the graduate program in education at the University of Texas. One challenge that needs addressing is the underrepresentation of principals in our Austin-area schools who understand and support Ethnic Studies and bilingual or dual-language education.

AISD has also incorporated some of the members of Nuestro Grupo—including Valenzuela; Zamora; Martha Cotera, a community elder; and three graduate students, Anthony Martinez, Brenda Rubio, and Randy Bell, into important planning activities (Valenzuela, Zamora, and Rubio, 2015). Valenzuela, for instance, has offered critical technical assistance to AISD for the adoption of a social studies course on Ethnic Studies, while others have assisted in developing Ethnic Studies curriculum for high schools, in pilot testing, and in teaching the course in six high schools this fall. Once again, the lesson is that civic engagement begets opportunities for programmatic and professional development.

The cumulative and self-enriching process has also involved opportunities for educational reform-

ers from Austin to participate in related statewide efforts and to even lead, in part because of our location at the state's capital. This became evident during the 2016 Reject the Text campaign that convinced the SBOE to reject a proposed textbook as technically inadequate and even detrimental to the development of young minds with the use of racialized views, including the claim that Mexican-origin persons and other Latina/os are a cultural and political threat to national unity. Academia Cuauhtli members, especially Zamora, were instrumental in conducting a formal review of the book and in presenting the findings of a significant number of factual, interpretation, and omission errors as well as racially charged ideas to justify the rejection of the textbook.

Valenzuela has also advised members of the Texas Legislature in the preparation of a bill that would have encouraged public schools throughout the state to offer Ethnic Studies courses in the social studies and cultural arts curriculum. The Legislature did not approve the bill; however, Valenzuela assisted a member of the SBOE to propose a change to the foundation curriculum for the state of Texas: Subsequent to full board approval, rule making, and standards setting, this would be a high school Ethnic Studies literature course that districts could adopt by 2022. This is still in process.

Lastly, we have used our experience with Academia Cuauhtli to advise the K–12 Committee of the Tejas Foco in its statewide campaign to promote Ethnic Studies in the schools of Texas. In short, Academia Cuauhtli could not have been possible without our new and extended social platform that enriches and advances our efforts at reforming education in Austin, nor could we have reached out to sites of statewide struggle without our prior experiences in the policy arena.

The hope is that institutional partners beyond Austin can discover that public school students are not the only beneficiaries of Ethnic Studies curriculum. University students can add to their education with the use of firsthand opportunities to learn curriculum development, assessment, and the teaching of Ethnic Studies. Collaborations between public schools and colleges and universities can also lead to dual-credit courses and other forms of academic preparation that will improve the pathway experience for college-bound students and receiving programs like Ethnic and Women Studies in colleges and universities. Ethnic Studies courses that incorporate the heritage of the community in a constructive and collaborative manner can also encourage parents to participate in the education of their children in public schools. The participating institutions—public schools, community centers, colleges, and universities—can also bring attention to a genuine interest in serving the public and, in the process, gain political capital for their overall operations.

Recommendations

Drawing on Ethnic Studies models that offer focused, single-ethnic-group, comparative, or infusion approaches, we ground our perspective in the experiences of mostly faculty of color in Texas. Our major recommendation is that local efforts advance Ethnic Studies in a systematic and effective fashion in the classroom as well as in the public sphere. This means building partnerships involving local institutions—colleges, universities, school districts, and community-based organizations—that can provide the needed expertise to fashion district-sponsored instructional programs. We especially call on local groups to grant a community organization a central role in developing curriculum, hosting professional development workshops for teachers, and supervising the instructional and evaluative work.

The curriculum should be developed and implemented in one of three ways. One set of curricula could provide focused lesson plans on the historical and contemporary experiences on Mexican Americans, African Americans, Native Americans, or Asian Americans with attention placed on themes such as colonialism, indigeneity, race relations, racism, homophobia, racialization, class, gender, sexual orientation—and intersectionalities, generally. Other themes include imperialism, federal and state policies, assimilation, white privilege, institutionalized oppression, current events, income inequality, unsung heroes, identity, and empowerment. The second comparative approach would use the above themes as points of intersectionality to understand the shared and dissimilar experiences of racial and ethnic groups. The third approach would infuse information, perspectives, and subject matter from

the aforementioned curriculum into the foundation curriculum required by the state.

We also think that Ethnic Studies should incorporate the following overlapping concerns:

1. Promote democratic values and ideals like dignity, respect, reciprocity, equality, freedom, due process, and social justice to prepare children and youth to participate in the continuous forging of the nation.

2. Incorporate well-prepared, research-based curricular materials and use politically aware, authentic, critical, and compassionate caring as classroom practice to evaluate the work and continue to develop sound pedagogy and curriculum.

3. Integrate critical perspectives like critical race theory, critical theory, and feminist frameworks—especially Chicana feminist perspectives.

4. Promote bilingualism, biculturalism, multilingualism, and biliteracy for an increasingly complex global world and society—and view these as consistent with a social justice agenda where they are regarded not as problems to be solved but as inalienable rights to be celebrated, honored, and elaborated.

5. Challenge deficit perspectives and subtractive schooling and promote positive dispositions from an asset-based perspective among our youth toward communities, community involvement, and community-based research.

6. Encourage self-discovery and agency so that students can see and understand how many of their personal problems and difficulties can be collective and systemic in nature with origins in policies, policy agendas, interests, and institutional hierarchies and dynamics that limit voice, power, and presence in academia and beyond.

7. Nurture epistemic virtues like open-mindedness, humility, and intellectual curiosity.

8. Adopt the method and theory of oral history, as well as the practice of participatory action research to teach academic skills and instill students with a

responsibility to know, understand, and promote positive change in the world.

9. Foster the study of current mobilization efforts on behalf of Ethnic Studies, including ongoing work to recover historical knowledge and rehabilitate a memory of protest, resistance, resilience, and survival.

10. Promote generational and ancestral, roots-based consciousness, beginning with the incorporation of elders into current efforts and initiatives together with *abuela* and elder epistemologies or ways of knowing.

Conclusion

Our work in Austin is part of a legacy agenda as a progressive Mexican American Studies curriculum to extend our voice, presence, and power in the university and in the community at large. We do not only ideologically connect to our histories, stories, and identities, but we tap into our roots through our lived, breathing connection to our ancestors—those past and present—who have been the wellspring of our inspiration. This is not an abstract or romantic notion but rather a cause that communicates hard work with our collective commitment, shared understandings, hopes, and desires for not solely the coming generations but for a current, renewed sense of urgency for the deepening inequalities in society and for the planet itself.

As we envisage through our collective work what the future of education might be, our vision is grounded in Indigenous epistemologies and a commitment to everyone's right to theirs, as well as other ways of knowing and being in the world. Hence, the approach to Ethnic Studies that we espouse is not a new orthodoxy, but rather a call to emancipatory ways of knowing and being that are otherwise marginalized, derogated, and dismissed. To move in this direction, we must operationalize epistemology along the lines of what Medina (2013) purports in *The Epistemology of Resistance*. On the one hand, as social justice educators, we must interrogate epistemological vices like arrogance, laziness, and close-mindedness. On the other, we must uplift and nurture epistemological virtues that promote open-mindedness, curiosity, humility, and just ways

of knowing and being in the world. Everyone should want this.

In promoting a critical Ethnic Studies narrative, we seek to allay the concerns and fears of those who may construe our outlook as a coercive attempt to institutionalize identities that may be seen as alien and foreign if not altogether objectionable. Rather, we assert that histories, narratives, communities, and stories have been systematically appropriated, subjugated, stigmatized, and derogated, and that the current moment cries for active recognition and a recentering of who we are as cultural, economic, social, and political minorities and people of color, generally, with a more complete and fair rendering of all that we have to offer and contribute to a world gone askew. ✳

REFERENCES

Medina, José. 2013. *The Epistemology of Resistance: Gender and Racial Oppression, Epistemic Injustice, and the Social Imagination*. Oxford University Press.

Valenzuela, Angela (ed.). 2016. *Growing Critically Conscious Teachers: A Social Justice Curriculum for Educators of Latino/a Youth*. Teachers College Press.

Valenzuela, Angela, Emilio Zamora, and Brenda Rubio. 2015. "Academia Cuauhtli and the Eagle: Danza Mexica and the Epistemology of the Circle." *Voices in Urban Education* 41: 46–56.

Zamora, Emilio. 2012. "Moving the Liberal-Minority Coalition up the Educational Pipeline," in *Politics and the History Curriculum: The Struggle over Standards in Texas and the Nation* (Keith Erikson, ed.). Palgrave Macmillan.

For Us, by Us
Ethnic Studies as Self-Determination in Chicago

BY NOEMÍ CORTÉS, JENNIE GARCIA, STACEY GIBSON, DUA'A JOUDEH, LUPITA RAMIREZ, CECILY RELUCIO HENSLER, CINTHYA RODRIGUEZ, MARALIZ SALGADO, DAVID STOVALL, JOHNAÉ STRONG, JESSICA SUAREZ NIETO, AARON TALLEY, LISA VAUGHN, AND ASIF WILSON

My native tongue was destroyed by public schooling. I was pulled out of "regular" classes to correct this mistake of a language as seen through the eyes of my white teachers. This language gifted to me by my Arab immigrant parents. As the rope of our Arabic tongues withered away with each English vowel and consonant I learned, the embrace of home and connection also withered away. Something always felt missing; I just didn't realize it was my connection with my ancestors and Arabic. —Dua'a

This chapter narrates a collective effort of teacher educators, classroom teachers, preservice teachers, and community organizers to make space amid a moment of engineered chaos. We are a multiracial/ethnic—Black, Latina/o/x, Arab American, and Asian American—collective of educators and organizers, born out of struggle and striving toward educational self-determination. Our telling of this story is an attempt to make visible our pedagogies of survivance within the neoliberal restructuring of Chicago schools, yet another era within a larger historical tradition of U.S. schooling designed with our subordination and dehumanization in mind. For these reasons, our aim is not to offer prescriptive solutions to the problems of education, but instead to empower ourselves to center our forms of knowledge production and to contribute to the dialogue regarding spaces of insurgency and, in Harney and Moten's term in their book *The Undercommons*, fugitivity.

Our story takes place in Chicago, a hotbed for educational "reforms," including mayoral control, mass school closings, the proliferation of "no excuses" charter schools, attacks on teachers and the teacher union, and the defunding of public education. While changes have been touted as positive, in actuality they have resulted in further marginalization of working-class communities of Color. Our movement is contextualized in recognition of the social, political, geographic, and economic realities of Chicago and the erosion of its majority–youth-of-Color public education system, as a result of large-scale neoliberal education policy and urban restructuring over the last four decades.

As community struggles for Ethnic Studies erupted throughout the country in the 1960s, artists, activists, educators, parents, and students echoed these demands throughout the Chicagoland area. Freedom Day boycotts against Chicago Public Schools (1963), the Black student sit-in that led to the formation of African American Studies at Northwestern University (1968), and the founding of a Puerto Rican–centric high school in response to the high pushout rates that Puerto Rican students had been experiencing in Chicago public high schools (1972) are just three examples of a genealogy of Ethnic Studies in Chicago. Chicago's version of Ethnic Studies, therefore, stands in opposition to the city's structural violence against our communities.

In the present day, Chicago Public Schools has created African American Studies and Latin America/Latino Studies curricula. These efforts have been applauded, and Chicago Public Schools was named an Ethnic Studies "pioneer." This curriculum misses two fundamental assumptions of Ethnic Studies. First, our communities are critical and primary sites of knowledge production. Second, Ethnic Studies is rooted in community struggles. The institutionalized curriculum does not center community knowledge and remains disconnected from our current fights for public education. The embrace of Ethnic Studies by the schooling apparatus in Chicago is a warning that Ethnic Studies can be co-opted—in similar and different ways to the institutionalization of Ethnic Studies in higher education. Given this, we must remain vigilant about what it means to fight for Ethnic Studies in the face of severe austerity, school militarization, and state-sanctioned violence.

For these reasons, our present enactment of Ethnic Studies is guided by the histories of those impacted by violence and their struggles to free themselves from it and centers our need for radical healing and humanization. Our commitment is to invigorate an Ethnic Studies movement in Chicago as an intervention to the miseducation enacted upon us and our peoples within systems of K–12 and post-secondary schooling in the United States and abroad. Throughout our journey, we have questioned, debated, and come to the resolution that our version of Ethnic Studies is not the traditional, institutionalized version of including contributions of People of Color to the United States in school curriculum; being "product-oriented" in this way is not our focus. Instead, in our understanding of Ethnic Studies, our "products" are our courage and self-determination to become better versions of ourselves so we can return to our educating and organizing spaces reenergized to continue struggling against oppressive systems alongside our students and communities.

Our Origin Story

Our story originates in the "Ivory Tower": an elite university with a "social justice"–centered urban teacher education program. While racism in the program was pervasive, the breaking point came when a white preservice teacher introduced a "game" called *Puerto Rico*—a board game that exploits the history of Puerto Rico's colonization, Indigenous genocide, and the transatlantic slave trade—to the Black middle school youth under his charge. Faculty and students of Color responded by calling for the teacher education program to address and repair the harm, but our demands were met with defensiveness and hostility. White faculty and students claimed they felt "unsafe" in dialogues about racism. The university protected the white preservice teacher—who received his teaching degree—and named people of Color's actions as divisive and cause for disciplinary action. The demands of people of Color and white allies to address white racial hegemony were met with the eventual pushout of faculty of Color and a return to the status quo.

For us, the *Puerto Rico* incident symbolizes the dehumanization and disposability of people of Color that is instrumental to the colonial project. U.S. schools and U.S. teacher education, as sites of social reproduction, are central to this project. Our collective's shared perspective on teacher education is illustrated in this member's *testimonio*:

> The program was designed to educate upper-middle-class whites to teach Black and Brown children. Our curriculum, from the readings to the teachers represented in demonstration videos, reflected that reality. As a student of Color, I could feel that the curriculum was talking about me rather than to me. I found myself bored and disengaged in classes about race, gender, and sexuality, while my white classmates were having moments of cognitive dissonance or revelation. Undoubtedly, many of them had never been taught to think critically of their privilege or identity, so for students like me, where my identity has come under assault in so many contexts, the curriculum did not speak to me nor did it wish to. —Aaron

The *Puerto Rico* incident also represents a significant moment of resistance, where critical educators of Color dared to question the legitimacy of the racial and colonial project. As we sifted through the rubble of our exile from the Ivory Tower, the solidarity between teacher educators and preservice teachers of Color formed the basis for our new political project. For those of us who had been pushed out of teacher education, our collective was a needed space for us to come to terms with the loss of our livelihoods while naming the moral outrage and alienation we felt as a result of being pushed out of hostile institutions. We expanded the space to come together with other educators who shared similar ethical and political commitments.

Our "Theory of Action" and Praxis

I graduated with an obligation to fight for children like me: Latino and bilingual students going through the Chicago Public Schools. I felt empowered since I had graduated from one of the best teacher education programs in the country. Or so I thought. The program taught me how to teach in a monolingual classroom; nowhere in their two-year curriculum did they include bilingual education. So, here I was, this university graduate unfit to do the job for which I had a master's degree. My time and money were spent in vain because I was not ready to be a bilingual teacher. How was [my university] expecting me to successfully teach Latino children if I had not been equipped to do so? How was an unprepared bilingual teacher going to teach her students to combat racism if I could not even teach them literacy? —Jennie

From its inception, our collective has been exclusively for people of Color. We drew inspiration from the work of scholars of Color, including Rita Kohli and Allyson Tintiangco-Cubales. We developed our "Theory of Action"—a confluence of *restoration, professional learning*, and *racial justice* with our **self-determination** at the center. We understood from the onset that everything needed to be generative, not prescriptive; our "theory of action" was a starting point for our journeys toward decolonization. Together we have articulated our beliefs about what it means to self-determine. We are intentional about grounding our work in our ancestral roots. We are unlearning colonial practices—ways of being that are antithetical to our people—and are learning to trust our Indigenous blood memory. We uphold the values of peoples of Color above the Westernized ideologies of our oppressors. Through these practices of resistance and the articulation of counter-narratives, we transform our relationships to each other in meaningful ways.

In studying Ethnic Studies and other social movements, we have learned that the leadership, authority, and work of women has been erased from the narrative, and that the harm caused by male violence reproduces the toxic conditions that we are working to dismantle. During our monthly gatherings, we meet in caucus groups—a men's caucus and women's caucus. In caucus, we reclaim our bodies, minds, and spirits. In addition to these healing practices of reclamation, we reflect upon the ways in which male violence shows up in our daily lives and in our classrooms, cultivating a praxis to dismantle heteropatriarchy.

Because we represent an amalgamation of unique contributions and experiences, our praxis is reflective of our collective struggle to reclaim our humanity and places of learning. Our voices provide a glimpse into the diverse positions from which we emerge. Our *testimonios* include one in Spanish; we have intentionally not translated it because Ethnic Studies, as we understand it, is about naming and dismantling systems of dominance, including English hegemony, which has served a colonizing, deculturalizing, policing function throughout all of modernity.

Lupita and Maraliz: The Form and Function of Why We Do What We Do

Our collective engages intentional practices, rituals, and protocols that push our vision forward. We meet in different parts of the city each month to resist the hypersegregation of our city. To create a space that represents our origins, we adorn every gathering with the sculptures, fabrics, scents, texts, and art of our people/ancestors.

We begin our time together with a PIES/N check-in: Each person shares their current **P**hysical, **I**ntellectual, **E**motional, and **S**piritual state while disclosing a **N**eed they may have at the moment. This takes time and we are careful not to rush it, as authentic concern is often not afforded to us as people of Color in white spaces. We check in within our caucuses first and then share out with the whole group to encourage transparency and accountability. During whole group meetings, we build consensus on any initiatives or decisions. We build community through practices that speak to the soul of our work, such as creation of visual art, music and dance, and shared stillness and breath work.

It is through these practices that we find the strength to hold each other in tough times. We prioritize this "restorative" time, recognizing that the daily psychological and emotional violence we experience needs healing.

Noemí: Naming and Claiming Space

I spent the better part of 2014 fighting a racial battle that left me exhausted and embittered. It took almost a year for me to gain clarity on what I needed for my own healing. I approached a small group of sisters and asked: Could we create a collective just for us? And by "us," I literally meant *just us*: people of Color. I was tired of working with so-called anti-racist educators who, when push came to shove, only claimed it in name and not in action.

Turns out I was not the only person who had come to an impasse in my career. Although it seemed like a small ask, it became evident how important it was for us as women to create a space for each other. It is an important recognition for us to realize that we need each other in ways that we weren't aware until we finally said: I need you! I need your Indigenous power, strength, and courage, the type that sits in our veins, in our blood memory of the struggles that our ancestors have fought throughout the centuries.

I am always encouraged by the ways our collective holds each other, not just in our gatherings, but in the in-between times. In the phone calls we make to each other when we have hit yet another wall. In the moments when we see our sisters and brothers emotionally distraught and understand the need to check in, if only because we understand how deeply the pain is felt when the struggle is real. This collective matters to me not just because it provides me with a space to be among others who are like-minded and action-oriented. This collective matters because in the times when we are not together I still feel everyone's presence. Our stories offer not only a means for connecting with each other but as remembrances of our collective power in our individual battlefields.

Lupita: Self-Identification and Resistance

Overcoming racist, classist, ageist, ableist, and gendered expectations encourage students' *ganas* to succeed and rise above marginalization and isolation. Making our students feel that their culture and identity are represented throughout the curriculum allows them to contextualize and visualize their academic success in their daily interactions with us as educators.

Teachers in urban schools have the responsibility to become knowledgeable regarding the diversity of their students and acknowledge the external fac-

tors associated with their academic achievements. Examining my transformative resistance in education began with the acceptance of my name, Lupita (*loo-pee-tah*). It has always been difficult for monolinguals to pronounce my name, and hearing people mispronouncing names and seeing their visual frustration made me accept others' versions of my name. I wonder, how often do we unintentionally devalue students' names and have them accept our own versions of who they are? In the beginning of the school year, I have my students complete a "self-identity survey." The first question asks them to share the story of how their names were chosen and interview their family members about the history behind their family's last name. Our last names are a form of belonging. In Spanish cultures, the word *de* was added before the last name; for example, *Maria De Candia*. The "of" symbolizes that we belong to a family. I want my students to learn how they felt their sense of belonging. I feel that taking ownership and understanding the value and significance of our names helps my students identify with their cultures and resist conforming to the dominant culture.

Teachers learn with and from students. I believe that teachers and students both have to be learners of their own identities to be critical agents of liberation. For these reasons, connecting classroom work to the larger society is essential. If students have knowledge of self, they are more willing to continue with their choices for social change, despite the current political, sociocultural, and economic moment.

Jessica: Transformar, No Solo Resistir

Quisiera, empezar con una frase del Che, "Todos los días hay que luchar porque ese amor a la humanidad viviente se transforme en hechos concretos, en actos que sirvan de ejemplo, de movilización." Con esto en mente, como docente tengo la responsabilidad de enseñar en una manera donde analizamos críticamente la relación entre lo histórico, sociopolítico, y las experiencias que nuestro estudiantes enfrentan en sus vidas; para poder crear maneras de no solo resistir, pero transformar estas condiciones.

Este año tuve la oportunidad de enseñar una clase de justicia social a estudiantes de octavo grado. La misma está fundada en los siguientes principios: 1) participar y crear entendimiento de una manera anti-capitalista, anti-imperialista, y anti-neoliberal; 2) el amor, respeto, y dignidad al ser humano y la tierra, usando la práctica de In Lak Ech; 3) ser protagonistas en el proceso de la transformación de nuestra sociedad; y 4) proveer un análisis global sobre nuestra situación política local. Las primeras semanas nos enfocamos en crear una comunidad entre nosotros, tomando en cuenta la cultura, lenguaje, historia, y nuestro entendimiento político.

Nos enfocamos en espacios centrados en la justicia. El enfoque no es solo en lo local, sino en el aspecto global. Un componente de la clase es la reflexión y el cuestionamiento constante sobre lo que pasa alrededor de nuestro mundo. Reconocemos que nuestras acciones afectan a los que nos rodean directamente e indirectamente. Por lo tanto, nosotros usamos este conocimiento y reflexión para poder transformar al mundo.

Los padres forman parte importante de este proceso de aprendizaje. Con ellos creamos una comunidad donde junto a los alumnos y docentes estamos en constante comunicación y reflexión para construir una alternativa a los sistemas opresivos. En tono con esta visión, los estudiantes lideran este espacio alternativo.

Asif: Our Classrooms as Organizing Spaces

As members of this collective, we see our classrooms, out-of-school spaces, and communities as intentional organizing spaces. As a member of the men's caucus, I am reminded by bell hooks that "patriarchy is the single most life-threatening social disease assaulting the male body and spirit in our nation. Most men never think about patriarchy—what it means, how it is created and sustained." Our caucus is structured to do what hooks points out in her book *The Will to Change* that men often don't do—define patriarchy and understand its historical context in social movements led by people of Color while cultivating praxis to dismantle it. My *testimonio* provides insight into my struggles to make hooks' challenge a reality.

I am an administrator and teacher at a community college in Chicago. Ethnic Studies has created the space for me to think about the ways in which my work does or does not create space for students of Color to explore themselves, their histories, and their legacies. It has provided me with resources to bring back to my colleagues and my students. My teaching has changed—I am more intentional about using materials authored by queer womyn of Color, more conscious about cultivating an intersectional analysis that includes gender and race, and more attentive to the social and emotional needs of my students in recognition of the structural trauma they hold.

Dismantling patriarchy was something new for me. I am often able to use my analysis of race to steer clear of any attention toward gender, especially the ways in which I have privilege as a male in the world, even as a Black man. During our summer institute, the men's caucus conducted an activity where we had to write and share four things: our role in gender violence, our understanding of gender justice, our understanding of the connection between gender justice and social justice, and our commitments moving forward. This was the first time in my life where I was forced to confront and name the ways in which I understood privilege as a cis man and the first time I was forced to name what I was going to do about it.

Stacey: Female-Centered Black Liberation

Female-centered Black liberation. Imagine that. What are the tenets, the rituals, and the pledges? Imagine who would be the covert spook by the door and what doors would they have to sit by. Who would be deployed to build coalitions with womyn across and beyond educational, ethnic, economic, ability, skin tone, and status lines? Imagine this female-centered Black liberation providing open access to ancestral messaging and futurescapes, and imagine what it would mean to have the dedication and devotion of Black men who would uphold, amplify, practice, and teach female-centered Black liberation with ferocity, love, and commitment.

Just as I have been punished for *not* co-authoring tyrannical whiteness, I have also been dismissed and erased from Black spaces for not pledging to and practicing the female "roles" in upholding Black male patriarchy. If Audre Lorde says, "Your silence will not protect you," then I must reckon with the reality that the patriarchy will not protect anyone else either. The radical questioning led to my ongoing commitments to excavating this internalized patriarchy during my work with the Ethnic Studies cohort. The results of that radical questioning are that in this moment I am more used to hearing my voice ask my many selves questions like:

1. What is repressed, erased, and muted in order for me to be seen approvingly by Black cisgender men?

2. When womyn vilify and harm other womyn who refuse to uphold the patriarchy, how does that horizontal violence leech our divine feminine powers?

3. When rehearsed rhetoric joins practices of abandonment and ongoing silences, then what?

4. Since anger is loaded with information and seeks alternatives, how can this anger about being harmed by patriarchy serve me in a truth-seeking way?

This piece is directly underwritten by my experiences in the Ethnic Studies collective. The monthly meetings are a much-needed and deserved space to practice the unmooring of dated, worn, and dangerous ideologies. It is a way to reimagine and reconfigure feminine-centered liberatory methods. Here I practice the Womyn of Color (WOC) feminisms I had to learn on my own and through experience. Since so much depends on the feminine informing itself beyond the patriarchies, it is vital to claim the spaces to realign. All will benefit from such practices.

Our Vision for Our Future

We are learning that we cannot engage in this work through a singular lens. While shared struggles against white supremacy and racism brought us together, we know that there can be no racial justice without gender justice. Yet the work of dismantling heteropatriarchy leads inevitably to conflict and disharmony. We recognize that our growing pains are rooted in us not knowing what it looks and feels like to live with the intention of being truly free of heteropatriarchy in our hearts, minds, spirits, and bodies.

This lack of knowing has brought tension to the group, as we struggle to engage in transformative and accountable conversations and interactions across genders. For the men, battling years of comfort with heteropatriarchy, sexism, and male privilege makes for a difficult transition to a justice-centered approach, but one we must confront nonetheless. It

is by no means easy work, and it relies heavily upon action, reflection, and subsequent action that reflects our commitment to rectify previous missteps. There is no road map here, but this cannot serve as an excuse to capitulate to the continued oppression of women. As a practice of self-determination, our version of Ethnic Studies includes our commitment to grapple with the unknown.

For the women, we are unapologetically embracing our pursuit of healing from intergenerational trauma, resulting from state and interpersonal violence that shapes the lives of cis and trans women, girls, and femme-identified people of Color. We are unlearning the ways we have been socialized to devalue feminized forms of labor that are centered in caring. We are reclaiming queer feminist of Color values and practices of leadership that are grounded in relationally focused decision-making and guided by the ancestral wisdom we hold in our minds, hearts, spirits, and bodies.

Our collective is one of the few spaces in our lives—professional and personal—where this kind of intimate, accountable work is happening. There is a heaviness in the current moment of our freedom-making, and the road toward a new social imaginary is unpaved. We ground ourselves in the love we have for each other and our commitment to struggling against the ethics and practices of harm and disposability that our peoples have been subjected to for so many generations. We understand that our enactment of Ethnic Studies is site specific and may not be for everyone. However, we maintain that our version of Ethnic Studies is about seeding and cultivating the soil for our collective liberation. ✺

Victory for Mexican American Studies in Arizona

An Interview with Curtis Acosta

BY ARI BLOOMEKATZ

In 2010, state lawmakers in Arizona passed legislation that banned courses that "promote resentment toward a race or class of people." But the legislation was, in reality, specifically targeting a Mexican American Studies program that started decades ago after Black and Latino students filed a desegregation lawsuit.

While Tucson initially kept the Mexican American Studies program, the school board caved in 2012 and ended it after threats that they would lose a significant portion of their state funding.

Part of ending the program meant banning the Rethinking Schools book *Rethinking Columbus* from classrooms, along with Paulo Freire's *Pedagogy of the Oppressed*, Rodolfo Acuña's *Occupied America*, and Elizabeth Martínez's *500 Años del Pueblo Chicano/500 Years of Chicano History in Pictures*. In some instances, school authorities shocked students by confiscating the books during class.

After several legal challenges, a federal judge ruled in August 2017 that the state of Arizona violated the constitutional rights of students by eliminating the program and further went on to say that those who targeted it were motivated by racism and political opportunism.

Ari Bloomekatz talked with Curtis Acosta shortly after the ruling. Acosta taught for 20 years in Tucson with the Mexican American Studies program, was a plaintiff in some of the initial legal challenges to the ban, and was an integral part of the challenge that eventually prevailed. This interview has been edited for clarity and length.

ARI BLOOMEKATZ: Were you surprised by the verdict?

CURTIS ACOSTA: Shocked is better than surprised. At the end of closing arguments, Judge A. Wallace Tashima made it pretty clear—he said it was going to take him a couple weeks and it took him a little bit longer than that. And so we knew it could be any day, and I wasn't surprised when it finally came, but we were definitely shocked with the intensity and the care and the totality of the victory. Judge Tashima's legal analysis was just exhaustive in how he connected all of the actions, both in the production and construction of the law as being highly motivated by racial animus—to the application, to the enforcement. It was amazing, so that's the reason the word "shocked" comes to mind. Just an incredible moment in history and an incredible punctuation to a long journey.

BLOOMEKATZ: It's been a really long journey. How did you feel as your lawyer was telling you about the verdict?

ACOSTA: Absolutely shocked and in disbelief that it went our way so decisively. We knew we had the truth on our side; we knew what we went through. We knew who these people were who did this to us, and it's just after so many years of being told "You're crazy," and we have tinfoil hats, and down is up and up is down—it was just shocking to hear the clarity and the affirmation, the validity of our program, of my colleagues and me. Our integrity was restored through a 9th Circuit judge. This is the United States of America judicial system, it's pretty amazing to think that Mexican American students and the Mexican American community and ourselves as Mexican American teachers could find this form of justice. We always believed in it; you have to, otherwise you don't keep seeking justice and you quit, and obviously we never quit. So the reaction was one of just exhilaration and disbelief. The disbelief part because that validation was never coming from the state of Arizona, and it certainly wasn't coming from our school district who bent to the will of these racist actors. And it turned the tide of what was once a very beautiful community—a strong program that was leading the way for what we see now kind of catching fire throughout the nation—and so our humanity was restored to a large degree. I was just overwhelmed with excitement about the fact Judge Tashima saw what really happened and the evidence was overwhelming and he saw it clearly.

BLOOMEKATZ: What was it that really happened? What did Judge Tashima see? When you think of the evidence that he focused on, what do you think of?

ACOSTA: Well there are the obvious ones that started permeating the national consciousness—unfortunately posthumously after our program had been dismantled. Mr. Huppenthal's racist blog post kind of revealed the person beneath the veneer. He tried to project a sense of this great patriarchal protector of these poor Mexican American kids and he was trying to do right by them. But doing right by them in his mind was ripping away the greatest program in the history of our state for these youth? That's what I meant by down is up and up is down—that's the world we were living in.

And there was so much. The state has authority, and so they spoke with that authority and many people believed it without really knowing the intimate details of what was going on or knowing these people. So his blog posts revealed—and also I think *The Daily Show* was another high-water mark for getting into the consciousness of this type of ideology—this really harmful and almost a malicious mind-set toward youth of color and communities of color. They used a lot of war type of rhetoric toward us: Huppenthal called his fight against our program "the eternal battle of all time" and that he was "waging a war against collectivism in the spirit of individualism." They were doing this almost like the Crusades.

It was just really bizarre to live this, Ari, it's amazing, there's so much, but I think to answer your question there are small moments of the trial that stood out to me. I'd come home and vent to my wife, or to my dad and my stepmom, or to my friends, or over the phone to my mom, to my colleagues in Mexican American Studies; I just couldn't get over the fact that when I was being cross-examined they were making a big deal—I mean, "a big deal" is too colloquial. It was essential to their case to show that I was a damaging educator and a damaging educator who indoctrinated children into believing in a certain type of anti-American ideology.

So what stood out to me is this moment: I'm being cross-examined literally by the state of Arizona about my use of a speech by Ernesto "Che" Guevara, and the state's attorneys are coming at me pretty hard, [using a] kind of bully type of tone about why was I teaching this speech, even missing the basic parts of my job description. They would be like: "You're an English teacher, why are you teaching this?" And I'm like: "Well, I teach rhetoric. I'm trying to get the kids ready for college and rhetorical analysis is one of the hardest things to do." And so it was continual other-izing of us; everything I was doing to them was so strange. So during my cross-examination they came at it from that angle, that I'm not teaching appropriately because I'm teaching a speech and I'm an English teacher, so God knows what these people think we really do in our classrooms, because they have no idea what we're supposed to do. So that was one piece.

They would read part of Che's very passionate perspective on the world—duh, he's a Marxist—and [the attorney] would read these excerpts to me and ask me if I thought it was appropriate to be reading this with my students. I said, "Absolutely." I had colleagues who were of European American descent who taught European history and had pictures and posters of Marx and Engels on their wall, along with others, not just Marx and Engels, obviously, but other historical figures. They read the *Communist Manifesto*, they read Che Guevara or historical figures like that. As far as rhetoric, we read a whole diverse group of different voices to understand rhetorical traditions. But for us, since I'm a Chicano, since I'm Mexican American, there was this understanding that I couldn't possibly do that in a responsible, scholarly way.

Folks like Huppenthal and Horne see us as predatory; they see us as damaging; they see us as other; they see us as deficient, as in we can't be scholarly, we can't be academic. Judge Tashima saw through all that and he emphasized that this was evidence that their default setting wasn't "Oh, he's doing it for rhetorical purposes or historical purposes." Tashima said there's so many reasons why a teacher would choose to teach that, and they never asked that question, they just jumped right to indoctrination and right to the racial codes placed upon Mexican American individuals, the Mexican American community, and Mexican American scholars.

It's a real teacher kind of thing that I think the audience at *Rethinking Schools* could really connect to in many ways. The racial lens, the power lens, what we've been going through for years now, probably since Reagan came after teachers in "A Nation at Risk"; just this battle we've been having, an unfortunate battle, a needless battle, with politicians telling us what's best, how to best educate our children. And something we always laugh at amongst ourselves is how that's working out for us, we always ask that question and it hasn't been working out very well. But that was just one of those moments in Judge Tashima's legal analysis and his findings that I thought indicated to me that he was really on his game; he was really listening to the arguments put forward.

BLOOMEKATZ: They went to the ends of the earth to go after this program. Why do you think they were just so absolutely threatened by it?

ACOSTA: We need to look to history; we need to look in the mirror at who we are, what this country has been built on, both the good and the tragic. And I'll never forget—my good friend and our director of Mexican American Studies, Sean Arce—we were in a meeting like eight superintendents ago in Tucson Unified School District. He was talking to the superintendent, saying you have to understand that Arizona, from the inception of our state, has had negative and hostile sentiments toward Mexican Americans. Mexicans first, and now Mexican Americans. It's been with us for a long time, for over 100 years. So that's still in the bloodstream. We can't ignore the historical memory. It's definitely still with us.

I don't think just as a country, and I haven't for a long, long time now thought that we do a very good job reflecting on our own history. It's progress, progress, progress; usually it's progress not socially but more through technology or through industry, progress that's fueled by capitalism is what we concentrate on. Always looking forward and never looking back. And I think there's a lot of value in looking back at our ancestors and gathering strength from the generations before us so that we can make better and informed decisions.

And this comes from a literature teacher, so I'm sure all of my history and social studies colleagues, if they read this part, will be really excited. There's value in the creative too, obviously, building new worlds and building art, but I think a lot of this comes from an ahistorical account of our country, of this state, of this continent. And so when you start talking about sovereignty, you've got to ask questions about that. When somebody's so fired up about the sovereignty of the United States of America, you want to ask questions. Those of us,

> **"Folks like Huppenthal and Horne see us as predatory; they see us as damaging; they see us as other; they see us as deficient, as in we can't be scholarly, we can't be academic. Judge Tashima saw through all that."**

especially on the West Coast, we all studied 1776 as kids growing up—but I was a California kid. What was happening in 1776 in the Bay Area? Right? Or in Tucson? It's more nuanced, it's more human, it's more multilayered, and I think when we grow up with a singular narrative, we can't see each other, we can't humanize one another, because we really don't know each other—which is again, the power, ironically, of Ethnic Studies.

I used to say all the time, and I still do, that what these folks need is Ethnic Studies—the Hornes, the Huppenthals—they don't know who we are. Even a lot of folks who think they know don't know, and there has to be some deference to that and commitment. So if we want to be who we already are, which is a nation that's turning toward a multicultural, multilingual, pluralistic place—we're always going to have English as this dominant language, I don't think that's to be debated—but to stomp out other languages, to stomp out other cultures, that's a mindset that comes from a very dark part of the way this country was built, and I think we're evidence of how one can get caught up in that.

The tonic, the antidote to this, is to learn about one another and to enjoy that. It's something that our students and our classrooms were unabashed about: loving one another and learning about each other

"Our students know where the country's going much more than we do, and we need to tap into that, and all that stuff frightens these folks."

and creating space for that, too. Our students know where the country's going much more than we do, and we need to tap into that, and all that stuff frightens these folks.

Another part of Tom Horne's testimony that would be really valuable for *Rethinking Schools* readership is he was offended by how we talked about our pedagogy. I mean viscerally offended; I mean almost as if you were talking about his family, almost as if you were saying awful things to him personally. He is a person who doesn't believe in constructivist and co-constructive types of education. He was very firm: The teacher should teach; the students should listen. Very much this patriarchal, paternalistic, asymmetrical power relationship. He loves that. He thinks that's wonderful. That one teacher should be the fount of information. It's very much anti–Paulo

Freire and critical pedagogy. He thinks that's damaging to students, literally said that; thus he thought we were damaging.

BLOOMEKATZ: This decision came down on the same day President Trump was in Arizona talking about pardoning Arpaio. How do you think about these two things happening on the same day? And how do you think about this decision happening in context of the era of Trump?

ACOSTA: It's funny. It might have been intentional, and if not it was just a very interesting confluence of events. But I can't get enough out of the idea that the current president continues to come back to Arizona—sorry, to Phoenix, I'll be more specific—where our agitators came from, by the way, the actors that were found to be discriminatory and racially motivated against Mexican American students; they're all from up there. So he goes to Phoenix, he's come twice now when he's in crisis, to almost get his bearings straight. As a person who grew up in California who also loves Tucson, Arizona, it's really difficult for me to know that this is where he comes to recharge that battery.

BLOOMEKATZ: Another question I have is about that transformation. What are the next steps, and what does this mean for the Ethnic Studies movement nationally?

ACOSTA: That one's easier, the latter, so let's start there. The question I was answering before the decision was what happens if it doesn't go your way? And of course it would set this awful precedent for all the areas of the country that have blossomed and are embracing Ethnic Studies after our untimely demise and it would unfortunately give the detractors a road map for how to challenge this in court and legal precedent. Thank God that didn't happen; the nightmare scenario is gone. So instead: affirmation, validation, and precedent to anybody who tries to kick this stuff up. We're still waiting on Judge Tashima's remedies, so we're not going to be sure about how this affects Tucson or Arizona for probably a few more weeks until Judge Tashima says, "This is what I expect to happen; this is what needs to happen."

At the local level it's going to be very interesting to see how they either ignore this, and they'll try, I believe, they'll try to ignore this, some of the politicians, especially on our school board. Or they'll try to dig themselves out of this. But they have seven years of awful precedent, where our local school board never supported us, and so I'm really, really hopeful that we can get some leadership either at the board level but hopefully from the new superintendent and TUSD, and they can start anew and just say: Hey you know what, you all have blood on your hands, we're moving forward because this program was great, it's a part of our community, it's a part of our history, and we need to embrace that and move forward.

BLOOMEKATZ: Why is this program so important for young people?

ACOSTA: I love answering that question. There are many particular, small, nuanced ways that our program may have been unique, but I think just flat out, if you boil it down, the space was powerful because it was a space where the students felt not only safe, but a space where they could be brave, a space where they could grow into their own strength. And we did that by being very real with our students about our expectations, how much we loved them, and what love means in a classroom, and that we were working not only for them but for their grandparents and for those that came before them, and that they needed to work for our children and the young ones coming up, and that we had this understanding that we were in this beautiful space together to work to get better as human beings. ✳

Originally published on the *Rethinking Schools* blog on August 31, 2017.

Contributors

Curtis Acosta is a former Mexican American Studies teacher in Tucson, Arizona, founder of Acosta Educational Partnership, and assistant professor of language and culture in education at the University of Arizona South.

Joni Boyd Acuff, PhD, is an associate professor of arts administration, education and policy at the Ohio State University. Acuff's research attends to critical multicultural art education, critical race theory in art education, and culturally responsive teaching, pedagogy, and curriculum development.

Ruchi Agarwal-Rangnath is an assistant professor at the University of San Francisco and co-author of the recent book *Preparing to Teach for Social Studies for Social Justice: Becoming a Renegade*.

Sean Arce is a teacher and Ethnic Studies coordinator in the Santa Monica-Malibu Unified School District and also serves as an educational consultant with the Xicanx Institute for Teaching and Organizing (XITO).

Prior to making her home as a middle-level ELA teacher, **Katie Baydo-Reed** taught for six years in elementary schools. She lives in Olympia, Washington, with her family, two cats, and lots of books.

Kyle Beckham is a doctoral candidate in the program of Race, Inequality, and Language in Education (RILE) at Stanford University; before doctoral study he taught for a year in Oakland, California, and nine years in San Francisco public alternative schools.

Courtney C. Bentley is the dean of the College of Education at the University of Montevallo. She is also a professor in the Department of Teaching, Leadership, Technology.

Bill Bigelow is the curriculum editor of *Rethinking Schools* magazine and co-director of the Zinn Education Project. He has authored or co-edited numerous books, including *Rethinking Columbus*, *A People's Curriculum for the Earth*, *Rethinking Globalization*, and the first U.S. anti-apartheid teaching guide, *Strangers in Their Own Country*.

Ari Bloomekatz is the managing editor of Rethinking Schools. You can reach him at ari@rethinkingschools.org and can follow him, and Rethinking Schools, on Twitter @bloomekatz and @RethinkSchools.

Rose Borunda is a professor at California State University, Sacramento, where she teaches in Counselor Education and serves as core faculty in the Doctorate in Educational Leadership and Policy Studies program.

Tracy Lachica Buenavista is a professor in Asian American Studies and core faculty member in the Educational Leadership doctoral program at California State University, Northridge. She is also a co-principal investigator for the CSUN DREAM Center, one of the first undocumented student resource projects in the California State University system.

Julio Cammarota, PhD, is a professor of Teaching, Learning & Sociocultural Studies at the University of Arizona.

Guadalupe Carrasco Cardona is a high school English, social studies, and Ethnic Studies teacher who lives in East Los Ángeles. She holds leadership positions in the Association of Raza Educators, XOCHITL Los Ángeles, and Unión del Barrio.

Artnelson Concordia is the teacher on special assignment (TSA) tasked with coordinating the effort to establish Ethnic Studies teaching and learning in the San Francisco Unified School District (SFUSD). He is in his 19th year with SFUSD (15 years in the classroom).

Grace Cornell Gonzales has worked as a bilingual elementary school teacher in Oakland, San Francisco, and Guatemala City. She now lives in Seattle. She is a co-editor of *Rethinking Bilingual Education* and the submissions editor for *Rethinking Schools* magazine.

Noemí Cortés was a teacher educator and school district administrator who now teaches 7th- and 8th-grade social studies in a public elementary school in Chicago.

Jaime Cuello has been implementing his distinct style of teaching in the Guadalupe Union School District since 1993. He has lectured on diversity, opportunity, and equity for more than two decades.

Edward R. Curammeng, PhD, is an assistant professor of teacher education in the College of Education at California State University, Dominguez Hills. His research examines the relationship between Ethnic Studies and education in shaping the experiences of students and teachers of color. He is also a member of the People's Education Movement.

Roderick Daus-Magbual is the director of program development for the Pin@y Educational Partnerships (PEP), a Filipina/o American studies education leadership pipeline that has supported teachers and students over the past 17 years to become community-engaged scholars and advocates.

Arlene Sudaria Daus-Magbual, EdD, has worked with Pin@y Educational Partnerships since 2003 and is currently the interim assistant dean of students for Asian American & Pacific Islander Student Services at San Francisco State University.

Cati V. de los Ríos is an assistant professor in the School of Education at University of California, Davis.

John DeRose has been teaching social studies at the high school level since 1994 and currently works for the Whitefish Bay Schools as a teacher and facilitator of professional learning. He completed his PhD in Urban Education from UW–Milwaukee in 2010 and has taught both undergraduate and graduate level courses at UW–Milwaukee and Concordia University since 2009.

Maharaj "Raju" Desai has taught at a variety of public and private schools in California and Hawai'i for the past nine years. He is currently teaching in the Filipino program at the University of Hawai'i while also completing his PhD in curriculum and instruction.

Roxana Dueñas is a history and Ethnic Studies teacher at Roosevelt High School in Boyle Heights.

Anita Fernández is a scholar-activist at Prescott College and the director of the Xicanx Institute for Teaching and Organizing (XITO).

Tricia Gallagher-Geurtsen is a scholar-activist who teaches, researches, and writes about multicultural/multilingual education, postcolonial interpretations of education, and Ethnic Studies.

Jennie Garcia is a 5th-grade bilingual teacher at Cesar Chavez Multicultural Academic Center in Chicago.

Stacey A. Gibson is a Chicago-based parent, writer, and educator who provides trainings about the ways abstract power dynamics shape educational experiences.

Guillermo Gómez has taught in public schools for 21 years in multiple grade levels from 1st grade to college-level graduate courses. He is currently teaching Ethnic Studies at Lincoln High School in San Diego.

Jose Alberto Gonzalez works for the Tucson Unified Culturally Relevant Department as a CR American history and American government teacher. In addition, he is an educational consultant for the Xicanx Institute for Teaching and Organizing (XITO) collective.

Mictlani Gonzalez was a former Mexican American Studies educator in the Tucson Unified School District and is currently a program coordinator for the Department of Culturally Responsive Pedagogy and Instruction in the same district.

Rubén González teaches English and AVID at Florin High School in Sacramento, California. He is also a member of the Association of Raza Educators (ARE) and Ethnic Studies Now (ESN)–Sacramento.

Jon Greenberg is an award-winning public high school teacher in Seattle and a writer whose work has been featured in *Everyday Feminism*, NPR, *Teaching Tolerance*, and *Yes!* magazine.

Eric "Rico" Gutstein teaches mathematics education at the University of Illinois at Chicago. Rico taught middle/high school mathematics in Chicago public schools, authored *Reading and Writing the World with Mathematics* (2006), and co-edited *Rethinking Mathematics* (a 2013 *Rethinking Schools* publication). Rico is a founding member of Teachers for Social Justice (Chicago).

Sandra L. Guzman Foster, PhD, is assistant professor in the Graduate Studies Department in the Dreeben School of Education at the University of the Incarnate Word in San Antonio.

Deirdre Harris is an English teacher who facilitates student learning and empowerment by studying and dismantling issues impacting Black people via the literature in her African American literature class. She is in her 19th year with the Los Angeles Unified School District.

Nick Henning taught high school social studies in Los Angeles and is now an associate professor of secondary education at California State University, Fullerton.

Cecily Relucio Hensler is a Pinay educator committed to struggling for the radical healing, humanization, and self-determination of educators of color in Chicago.

Dua'a Joudeh is a 2nd-grade teacher at an Islamic school in Illinois. She works to foster students' bicultural identities and pursues social justice through her teaching of literacy and mathematics.

Rita Kohli is an assistant professor of teaching and teacher education at the University of California, Riverside. She is also the co-founder and co-director of the Institute for Teachers of Color Committed to Racial Justice (ITOC).

Alison Kysia is the project director of "Islamophobia: A People's History Teaching Guide" at Teaching for Change and the education outreach coordinator at the Institute for Middle East Studies at the George Washington University.

Kaiya Laguardia-Yonamine is a 16-year-old student activist at Roosevelt High School in Portland, Oregon. She is Pacific Islander and Afro-Cuban, the oldest of four, a second-degree black belt, and has been a vocal part of the Ethnic Studies movement since she was in middle school.

Stephen Leeper teaches the first Ethnic Studies core class at a middle school in San Francisco. He currently lives in the East Bay with his wife and his baby girl.

Jorge López teaches Ethnic Studies at Theodore Roosevelt Senior High School in Los Angeles. He is currently a PhD student at Claremont Graduate University in the School of Educational Studies in Teaching, Learning, and Culture.

Eduardo Lopez taught social studies at Theodore Roosevelt Senior High School in Los Angeles for 12 years. He is currently a doctoral student in the Urban Schooling division at the UCLA Graduate School of Education and Information Studies.

Zack Mezera is the executive director at the Providence Student Union.

Angie Morrill is the program director of Title VI Indian Education for Portland Public Schools in Oregon. She holds a PhD in Ethnic Studies from UC San Diego and writes and teaches about Native feminisms and futures. She is enrolled in the Klamath Tribes.

Peggy Morrison is a bilingual and multicultural educator based in San Francisco.

Jessica Suarez Nieto is a middle school teacher currently teaching in Chicago public schools. She teaches mathematics and social justice courses.

Eduardo "Kiki" Ochoa has taught in middle and high school for over 20 years. He is currently teaching AVID and AP U.S. Ourstories at Lincoln High School in San Diego. He is a teacher in the classroom and an organizer in his community.

Bob Peterson is an editor of Rethinking Schools and former president of the Milwaukee Teachers' Education Association. He taught 5th grade in Milwaukee Public Schools for 30 years. He is a founder of La Escuela Fratney, Wisconsin's first two-way bilingual school.

Michael Pezone holds a doctorate in curriculum and teaching. He recently retired after teaching for 25 years in New York City public high schools.

Lupita Ramirez has taught 4th, 5th, and 6th grade in the Chicago charter school system teaching dual language to diverse Spanish and non-native Spanish speakers for five years.

Aimee Riechel is one of the core participants of the San Francisco Unified School District Ethnic Studies Curriculum Collective. She has taught Ethnic Studies at Mission High School in San Francisco since 2008.

Cinthya Rodriguez is a community-based educator and immigration organizer from the Southwest Side of Chicago. She recently graduated from Northwestern University in Ethnic Studies.

Augustine Romero is the school improvement coordinator for the secondary schools in the Baboquivari School District on the Tohono O'odham reservation. Dr. Romero is an architect of the Mexican American/Raza Studies in Tucson Unified School District and cofounder of the Social Justice Education Project.

Maribel Rosendo-Servin is a secondary social justice educator of Ethnic Studies and English learner courses in the Sacramento area.

Jocyl Sacramento is a PhD candidate in the Graduate School of Education at the University of California, Berkeley. She currently lectures in the College of Ethnic Studies at San Francisco State University.

Maraliz Salgado is an intermediate and upper grade instructional coach/coordinator at Erie Elementary Charter School in Chicago's Humboldt Park community.

Alan Singer is a social studies educator and historian in the Department of Teaching, Learning and Technology at Hofstra University in New York. He is a former New York City high school teacher and regularly blogs on *Daily Kos* and other sites on educational and political issues.

Vera L. Stenhouse, PhD, is an independent researcher, educator, and evaluator with a focus on teacher education, teacher preparation, faculty development, diversity, multicultural education, and Indigenous education.

David Stovall, PhD, is professor of educational policy studies and African American studies at the University of Illinois at Chicago. His work sits at the intersection of race, place, and school.

Johnaé Strong is a mother, educator, and organizer. She advances issues of racial, economic, and education justice through her work with BYP100 and Grassroots Education Movement.

Aaron Talley is an activist, writer, and educator whose work focuses on the intersections between race and queerness. He currently teaches 8th- and 9th-grade English on Chicago's South Side.

Allyson Tintiangco-Cubales is a professor in the College of Ethnic Studies at San Francisco State University. She is also the founder and director of Community Responsive Teacher Development with Pin@y Educational Partnerships and the co-director of the Teaching Excellence Network.

Waahida Tolbert-Mbatha is the co-founder and head of school of Kgololo Academy, a primary school in South Africa that provides scholars from the Alexandra Township with access to a world-class education. Prior to founding Kgololo, Waahida worked as a middle school humanities teacher in the United States.

Carolina Valdez is an assistant professor at California State University, Fullerton in the Department of Elementary and Bilingual Education. She taught elementary school in Los Angeles Unified and is a founding member of the People's Education Movement.

Angela Valenzuela is a professor in the educational policy and planning program area within the Department of Educational Administration and in the Cultural Studies in Education Program within the Department of Curriculum and Instruction at the University of Texas at Austin. She is the author of the award-winning *Subtractive Schooling: U.S.-Mexican Youth and the Politics of Caring* and *Growing Critically Conscious Teachers: A Social Justice Curriculum for Educators of Latino/a Youth*.

Born and raised in Detroit, **Lisa Vaughn** moved to Chicago to attend college and grad school. She is currently a 5th-grade teacher at a Chicago public school.

Karla E. Vigil is the co-founder of EduLeaders of Color Rhode Island, an initiative focused on cultivating spaces for leaders of color invested in dismantling inequities in education, strengthening organizations led by people of color, and fostering community partnerships to create systematic change in education.

Renée Watson (reneewatson.net) is an author, performer, and educator. Her children's books have received several honors, including an NAACP Image Award nomination. She teaches poetry at DreamYard in New York City.

Dominique Williams is in her fourth year of teaching the social sciences in Sacramento. She is currently working with Ethnic Studies Now–Sacramento to expand Ethnic Studies in her district and in the state of California.

Asif Wilson is associate dean of instruction and an instructor in the Department of Social and Applied Sciences at Harold Washington College.

Ursula Wolfe-Rocca has taught high school U.S. history since 2000 and lives in Portland. She is an editor of *Rethinking Schools* magazine and is a curriculum writer/organizer with the Zinn Education Project.

Pang Hlub Xiong has taught kindergarten and 3rd grade in Wisconsin and Minnesota. She currently lives and teaches in the Twin Cities Metro, Minnesota.

K. Wayne Yang is co-convener of the Land Relationships Super Collective, co-founder of East Oakland Community High School, and associate professor of Ethnic Studies at the University of California San Diego.

Emilio Zamora is a professor of history at the University of Texas at Austin. He has written extensively on Mexican American and Texas history and has received eight book and article awards from professional organizations in history.

Index

Indigenous pedagogies, 235–38, 271–74, 296–97, 334
  Filipino, 22, 98–101
  See also barangay pedagogy; Nahui Ollin
Indigenous peoples, 69, 208–15
  acknowledging and learning about local, 69, 87, 102, 139
  near U.S.-Mexico border, 166
  See also Native Americans
In Lak Ech, 255, 271–73, 296, 339
Inside the Gender Jihad (Wadud), 115
Institute for Puerto Rican Policy Analysis and Advocacy, 10
Institute for Teachers of Color Committed to Racial Justice, 11, 65
Institute of American Cultures (IAC), 9
Institute of the Black World, 12
internalized oppression, 39, 102, 218–19, 238, 283
intersectionality, 5
  in Ethnic Studies, 17
  and identity, 38–47
  as poem prompt, 41
interviews for classwork, 107–112, 166–71.
    See also oral histories
Islam, 113–15
Islam in Black America (Curtis), 115
Islamophobia, 113–18, 269
Island of the Blue Dolphins (O'Dell), 89

J

Jackson, Andrew, 158
Jacobson, Matthew F., 126
James, Carl, 13
Japanese internment, 301, 192–96
  children's books about, 196
Japanese language schools, 9
Jaquette, Ozan, 15, 21
Jenks, Deneen, 196
Jiménez, Francisco, 61
Jocson, Korina, 22
Johnson, Richard, 86
John Valenzuela Youth Center (Tucson), 269
Joudeh, Dua'a, **335–40**, 349

K

Kababayan Program (Skyline College), 97
Kadohata, Cynthia, 196
kagandahang-loob, 98–99
Kailua High School (HI), 10
kalayaan, 98

Kamehameha Schools, 9
Kānaka Maoli, 209, 212
Kansas, 2
katarungan, 98
Katz, William Loren, 159, 172
Kayser, Bennett, 304
Kiang, Peter N., 24
"Kids 'n Room 36, The" (Cuello), 88–90
Kindred (Butler), 150
King Leopold's Ghost (Hochschild), 136
King, Martin Luther, Jr., 222–23, 225
Klein, Naomi, 329
Kochiyama, Yuri, 299
Kohli, Rita, **20–25**, 274, 337, 350
Korematsu, Fred, 195
Kozol, Jonathan, 55
Kuttner, Paul, 56
kuwento, 22
Kysia, Alison, **113–18**, 350

L

Ladson-Billings, Gloria, 26, 28, 31, 68
Laguardia-Yonamine, Kaiya, **300–301**, 350
Laguna, Albert, 57
Laínez, René Colato, 166
language
  English language learners, 88–90, 166–71
  Hmong language, 120–24
  Nahuatl language, 89–90, 236
  Spanish language, 2, 88–90
  usage in *Rethinking Ethnic Studies*, 2–3
  using cognates in class, 88–90
Lara, Jose, 55, 304–5
Larger Memory, A (Takaki), 125
La Santa Cecilia, 35–36
Law, Government, and Community Service Magnet High School (Queens), 205–7
Lawsin, Emily, 98
"Learning About the Unfairgrounds," (Baydo-Reed), 192–96
Lee, Tiffany, 26, 28, 31
Leeper, Stephen, **181–87**, 350
Leopold II, 136
lessons, sample outlines of
  "Bandits or Freedom Fighters?" (Arce), 288–89
  "Cherokee and Seminole Removal Role Play" (Bigelow), 157–65
  "Color Line, The" (Bigelow), 172–76
  "Freire's Levels of Consciousness" (Gonzalez), 275–77

"Trial of the Genocide of Native Californians Role Play" (Riechel), 140–47
letter writing, 229–33
Levine, Ellen, 95
Librotraficante, 14
Liliuokalani, 213
Lilo & Stitch (film), 209, 212–15
Lincoln High School (San Diego), 293
Lindaman, Dana, 188
Lipka, Jerry, 20
Lopez, Clemencia, 189
López, Eduardo, **229–34**, 350
López, Jorge, **229–34**, 350
Lopez, Larry, 51
Lorde, Audre, 339
Los Angeles/Los Angeles area
  community academies in, 13, 14
  Indigenous nations of, 302
  organizing for Ethnic Studies in, 302–7
  teaching Ethnic Studies in, 59–64, 153, 229–34
Los Angeles Unified School District, 5, 10, 11, 66, 69, 216
L'Ouverture, Toussaint, 135, 185
Love and Rockets (Hernandez and Hernandez), 212
Luke, Wing, 195

M

Mabalon, Dawn, 99
machismo. *See* patriarchy
Macroscales of Ethnic Studies, 2, 66–73, 75–79
  graphic organizer, 76
Maher, Chris, 316
Maidu, 102
Mar, Eric, 320
Marcus Garvey School (Los Angeles), 13
Marín, James R., 11
Mark, Gregory Yee, 86, 305, 312
MARS. *See* Mexican American Studies in Tucson Unified School District
Martin, Trayvon, 239, 240
Martinez, Anthony, 332
Martínez, Elizabeth, 341
Martínez, Marcos, 284
Martinez-Alire, Crystal, 84, 85, 86
Marx, Karl, 342
Marx, Ronald, 15, 21
MAS. *See* Mexican American Studies in Tucson Unified School District
Maslow's Hierarchy of Needs, 295, 297, 245, 246, 251

news/current events used in classroom, 239–43, 257–68

New York City, student activism in, 205–7

Nieto, Jessica Suarez, **335–40**, 338, 350

"Night, for Henry Dumas" (Girmay), 239–43

Nobles, Wade, 251

Noddings, Nel, 50

Noguchi, Rick, 196

North America's Building Trades Union, 259–68

Nuestro Grupo, 329, 331

O

Oakland (California), Ethnic Studies in, 166, 303

Oakland Unified School District, 11

Obama, Barack, 260

Occidental College, 304

Occupied America (Acuña, Rodolfo), 341

Ochoa, Eduardo "Kiki," **293–99**, 350

Ochoa, Gilda, 62

Ohlone, 69, 85, 208

Okoye-Johnson, Ogo, 15

Oliver, Melvin, 244, 251

Omatsu, Glenn, 60

One Day at a Time (TV show), 209, 212

Open Minds to Equality (Schniedewind and Davidson), 38, 40, 42

Oppression, Four I's of (Bell), 216–19

oral histories, 107–112, 168, 333–34

Oregon, 2. *See also* Portland, Oregon

organizing for Ethnic Studies
  in California, statewide, 308–314
  challenges of, 301, 318
  coalition building, 304, 307, 308–14, 320–22, 324–25, 329–33
  curriculum building, 296–99, 301, 317, 326–327
  and district administration, 313, 324
  implementing Ethnic Studies, 317–18, 319–322, 323
  lessons and suggestions, 319–27, 333–34
  lobbying for, 311
  in Los Angeles, 302–7
  media coverage of, 316
  media outreach, 304
  in Providence (Rhode Island), 315–18
  questions to ask, 305
  in San Francisco, 319–27
  and teacher unions, 304–5
  in Texas, 328–34

See also student organizing for Ethnic Studies

Ortiz, Beverly, 87

Our Children's Trust, 259–68

"Our Oral History Narrative Project" (Riechel), 107–112

Our Stories in Our Voices (Allender and Mark), 86, 312

Outsiders, The (Hinton), 209–10

Owens, Tom, 85

P

pakikibaka, 100–101

pakikipagkapwa, 100–101

pakikiramdam, 98–99

Palumbo-Liu, David, 224

Panther (film), 294

Paris, Django, 26, 28, 31, 274

Patneaude, David, 193–94

patriarchy, 41
  learning/unlearning machismo, 236–37
  men dismantling, 339

Patterson, Orlando, 214

Peach Springs School, 20

pedagogy
  barangay pedagogy, 96–101
  community responsive pedagogy, 23–25, 26, 34, 59–64
  critical culturally revitalizing and sustaining pedagogy, 26, 31
  Culturally Humanizing Pedagogy (CHP), 235–38
  culturally responsive pedagogy (CRP), 22–25, 26–32, 34, 75, 170, 236–38, 317
  culturally sustaining pedagogy, 26, 31
  decolonial pedagogy, 26, 33–37, 96–101, 229–33, 235–38
  defined, 24–25
  Ethnic Studies pedagogy, 20–25
  historically responsive pedagogy, 26
  Indigenous pedagogies, 96–101, 235–38, 271–74, 296–97, 334

Pedagogy of the Oppressed (Freire), 34, 49, 99, 100, 283, 341

Penner, Emily, 15, 21, 54, 313, 321, 325

People's Education Movement, 307

People's History of the United States, A (Zinn), 172–74

PEP. *See* Pin@y Educational Partnerships

Perdomo, Willie, 239–43

Perry, Ravi K., 57

Personal Matter, A (film), 195

Peterson, Bob, **133–37**, 350

Pezone, Michael, **205–7**, 206, 350

Philadelphia, 10

Philippine-American War. *See* War of Philippine Independence

photovoice, in classroom, 62–63

Pin@y Educational Partnerships (PEP), 10, 14, 20, 96–101
  and community responsive pedagogy, 23–24

Pipes, Eliana, 216

poetry in classroom, 36, 50, 229–33, 238, 239–43, 245, 287
  sample student poems, 43–45, 242–43, 254–56

police and border patrol
  immigration checkpoints, 61
  killing of Black men, 239–43
  students organizing against, 295–96

Pollard, Diane, 20–21

Pomona College, 62

Pomona High School (California), 59–64

Portland, Oregon, Ethnic Studies in, 11, 14, 300–301, 258

Portland Public Schools, 1, 69, 209, 300–301

Posadas project, 60–61

Post Traumatic Slave Syndrome (DeGruy), 150

Praxis (cooperative), 306

praxis, 49, 53
  turning theory into action, 100, 293–99, 337

Precious Knowledge (film), 300, 316

privilege
  of European Americans, 126
  in "Stars and Dots" activity, 181–87
  See also Four I's of Oppression; Matrix of Social Identity and Intersectional Power

Providence (RI), Ethnic Studies in, 1, 2, 11, 315–18

Providence School Department, 315–18

Providence Student Union (PSU), 315–18

Providence Youth Student Movement (PrYSM), 316

Puerto Rico (board game), 336

Purépecha, 209

Puyallup Fair (WA), 192–96

Q

Queens (New York), student activism in, 205–7

Queen Sugar (TV show), 209, 211–12

Quetzalcoatl, 236–38, 271, 281, 283–84
  defined, 236

Quran, 113

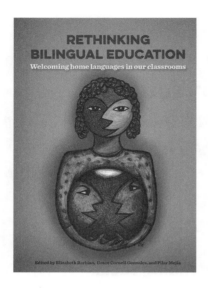

Rethinking Bilingual Education
Welcoming Home Languages in Our Classrooms

Edited by Elizabeth Barbian, Grace Cornell Gonzales, and Pilar Mejía

In this collection of articles, teachers bring students' home languages into their classrooms—from powerful bilingual social justice curriculum to strategies for honoring students' languages in schools that do not have bilingual programs. Bilingual educators and advocates share how they work to keep equity at the center and build solidarity between diverse communities. Teachers and students speak to the tragedy of language loss, but also about inspiring work to defend and expand bilingual programs.

2017 • Paperback • 343 pages • ISBN: 978-1-937730-73-4
Print: $24.95*

Teaching for Black Lives

Edited by Dyan Watson, Jesse Hagopian, Wayne Au

Teaching for Black Lives grows directly out of the movement for Black lives. We recognize that anti-Black racism constructs Black people, and Blackness generally, as not counting as human life. Throughout this book, we provide resources and demonstrate how teachers can connect curriculum to young people's lives and root their concerns and daily experiences in what is taught and how classrooms are set up. We also highlight the hope and beauty of student activism and collective action.

Paperback • 368 pages • 978-0-942961-04-1
Print: $29.95*

"This book is not just for teachers in the classroom, but also for those of us who care about making Black lives matter in the community. It should be required reading for all who care about the future of Black youth."
—**Opal Tometi,** #BlackLivesMatter, co-founder and executive director of the Black Alliance for Just Immigration

"Every teacher in America needs to pick up this book."
—**LINDA SARSOUR**, national co-chair of the Women's March and co-founder of MPower Change

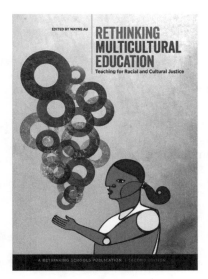

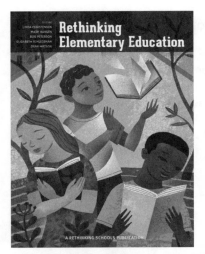

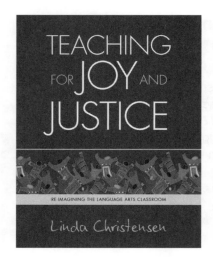

Teaching for Joy and Justice
Re-Imagining the Language Arts Classroom

By Linda Christensen

Demonstrates how to draw on students' lives and the world to teach poetry, essays, narratives, and critical literacy skills. Part autobiography, part curriculum guide, part critique of today's numbing standardized mandates, this book sings with hope—born of Christensen's more than 40 years as a classroom teacher, language arts specialist, and teacher educator.

Paperback • 287 pages • ISBN: 978-0-942961-43-0
Print: $19.95* | PDF: $14.95

Rhythm and Resistance
Teaching Poetry for Social Justice

Edited by Linda Christensen and Dyan Watson

Practical lessons about how to teach poetry to build community, understand literature and history, talk back to injustice, and construct stronger literacy skills across content areas—from elementary school to graduate school.

Paperback • 272 pages • ISBN: 978-0-942961-61-4
Print: $24.95*

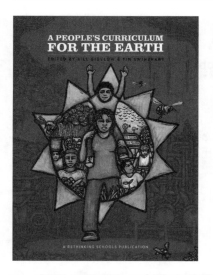

A People's Curriculum for the Earth
Teaching Climate Change and the Environmental Crisis

Edited by Bill Bigelow and Tim Swinehart

Engaging environmental teaching activities from *Rethinking Schools* magazine alongside classroom-friendly readings on climate change, energy, water, food, pollution—and the people who are working to make things better.

Paperback • 433 pages • ISBN: 978-0-942961-57-7
Print: $24.95*

THIRD

The New Teacher Book THIRD EDITION
Finding purpose, balance, and hope during your first years in the classroom

Edited by Linda Christensen, Stan Karp, Bob Peterson, and Moé Yonamine

Teaching is a lifelong challenge, but the first few years in the classroom are typically the hardest. This expanded third edition of *The New Teacher Book* grew out of Rethinking Schools workshops with early-career teachers. It offers practical guidance on how to flourish in schools and classrooms and connect in meaningful ways with students and families from all cultures and backgrounds. As education scholar Michelle Fine wrote, "This book is a timely and multi-voiced volume braiding critique and radical possibility. This may be the very text that young educators need to press beyond those trying first years, to teach fully and creatively, and to inspire freedom dreams in their classrooms."

Paperback • 352 pages • 978-0-942961-03-4
Print: $24.95

Rethinking Sexism, Gender, and Sexuality

Edited by Kim Cosier, Rachel L. S.Harper, Jeff Sapp, Jody Sokolower, and Melissa Bollow Tempel

There has never been a more important time for students to understand sexism, gender, and sexuality—or to make schools nurturing places for all of us. The thought-provoking articles and curriculum in this life-changing book will be invaluable to everyone who wants to address these issues in their classroom, school, home, and community.

Paperback • 400 pages • ISBN: 978-0-942961-59-1
Print: $24.95*

Rethinking Popular Culture and Media SECOND EDITION

Edited by Elizabeth Marshall and Özlem Sensoy

Beginning with the idea that the "popular" in the everyday lives of teachers and students is fundamentally political, this provocative collection of articles examines how and what popular toys, books, films, music, and other media "teach." The second edition includes revised articles, nine new articles, and an updated list of resources.

Paperback • 340 pages • ISBN: 978-0-942961-63-8
Print: $24.95*

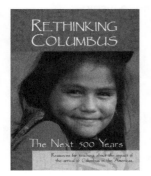

Rethinking Mathematics
Teaching Social Justice by the Numbers

Edited by Eric "Rico" Gutstein and Bob Peterson

Expanded and updated edition shows how to weave social justice issues throughout the mathematics curriculum, and how to integrate mathematics into other curricular areas.

Paperback • 300 pages • ISBN: 978-0-942961-55-3
Print: $24.95!*

Open Minds to Equality
A Sourcebook of Learning Activities to Affirm Diversity and Promote Equity

By Nancy Schniedewind and Ellen Davidson

Activities to help students understand and change inequalities based on race, gender, class, age, language, sexual orientation, physical/mental ability, and religion.

Paperback • 408 pages • ISBN: 978-0-942961-60-7
Print: $24.95*

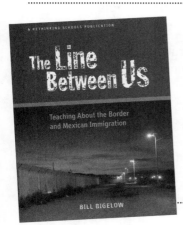

The Line Between Us
Teaching About the Border and Mexican Immigration

By Bill Bigelow

Using stories, historical narrative, role plays, poetry, and video, veteran teacher Bill Bigelow shows how he approaches immigration and border issues in his classroom.

Paperback • 160 pages • ISBN: 978-0-942961-31-7
Print: $16.95*

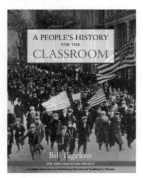

A People's History for the Classroom
By Bill Bigelow

This collection of exemplary teaching articles and lesson plans emphasizes the role of working people, women, people of color, and organized social movements in shaping U.S. history. Includes improvisations, role plays, imaginative writing, and critical reading activities.

Paperback • 120 pages • ISBN: 978-0-942961-39-3
Print: $12.95* | **PDF: $7.95**

Rethinking Our Classrooms, Volume 1
Teaching for Equity and Justice

Creative teaching ideas, compelling narratives, and hands-on examples of how teachers can promote values of community, justice, and equality—and build academic skills. *Second Edition.*

Paperback • 240 pages • ISBN: 978-0-942961-35-5

Print: $18.95* | PDF: $13.95

Rethinking Our Classrooms, Volume 2
Teaching for Equity and Justice

This companion volume to the first *Rethinking Our Classrooms* is packed with more great articles about teaching for social justice as well as curriculum ideas, lesson plans, and resources.

Paperback • 240 pages • ISBN: 978-0-942961-27-0

Print: $16.95* | PDF: $11.95

Pencils Down
Rethinking High-Stakes Testing and Accountability in Public Schools

Edited by Wayne Au and Melissa Bollow Tempel

Exposes the damage that standardized tests wreak on our education system, while offering visionary forms of assessment that are more authentic, fair, and accurate.

Paperback • 300 pages • ISBN: 978-0-942961-51-5

Print: $24.95* | PDF: $19.95

Teaching About the Wars

Edited by Jody Sokolower

Provides insightful articles and hands-on lessons to prompt students to think critically about U.S. military engagement in the Middle East.

Paperback • 132 pages • ISBN: 978-1-937730-47-5

Print: $12.95* | PDF: $7.95